W9-ACL-965

THE WORLD READERS
Series edited by Robin Kirk and Orin Starn

THE ALASKA NATIVE READER
Edited by Maria *Shaa Tláa* Williams

THE CZECH READER
Edited by Jan Bažant, Nina Bažantová, and Frances Starn

THE INDONESIA READER
Edited by Tineke Hellwig and Eric Tagliacozzo

THE RUSSIA READER
Edited by Adele Barker and Bruce Grant

THE SRI LANKA READER
Edited by John Clifford Holt

THE LATIN AMERICA READERS
Series edited by Robin Kirk and Orin Starn

THE ARGENTINA READER
Edited by Gabriela Nouzeilles and Graciela Montaldo

THE BRAZIL READER
Edited by Robert M. Levine and John J. Crocitti

THE COSTA RICA READER
Edited by Steven Palmer and Iván Molina

THE CUBA READER
Edited by Aviva Chomsky, Barry Carr, and Pamela Maria Smorkaloff

THE ECUADOR READER
Edited by Carlos de la Torre and Steve Striffler

THE MEXICO READER
Edited by Gilbert M. Joseph and Timothy J. Henderson

THE PERU READER, 2ND EDITION
Edited by Orin Starn, Iván Degregori, and Robin Kirk

Socialist rule 1970-1977

Capital comes from East Asias South Korea, Japan,
Taiwan, HongKong

p.157 Climb Mountain to foot of Adam to be absolved from
Sin

Pico de Adao

Tsunami 2004

Temple of the Tooth relic in Kandy (Dalada Maligava)

THE

SRI LANKA

READER

HISTORY, CULTURE, POLITICS

John Clifford Holt, ed.

DUKE UNIVERSITY PRESS   *Durham and London*   2011

© 2011 Duke University Press
All rights reserved
Printed in the United States of America on acid-free paper ∞
Typeset in Monotype Dante by BW&A Books, Inc.
Library of Congress Cataloging-in-Publication Data appear
on the last printed page of this book.

Dedicated to all Sri Lankans
who have died
as a consequence of political violence
and those who work for peace.

Contents

List of Illustrations

PLATES (BETWEEN PAGES 224–225)

Acknowledgments

This project proved to be far more challenging than I had originally envisioned, owing in part to the complexity and sensitivities of Sri Lanka's political and cultural history. In the end, decisions about what to include and what to exclude were not easy. (I included only about a third of the initial round of selections.) Then, after making many difficult decisions, I was frustrated by my inability to include a number of very pertinent extracts because some publishers, particularly those located in the United Kingdom, demanded truly exorbitant fees to publish even small fragments of previously published works. This eliminated some works by eminent Sri Lankan writers that one might reasonably expect to be included in a volume like this. Even so, the costs incurred in producing this volume were daunting. Subventions from Duke University Press and Bowdoin College helped to meet some of them.

Titles of works that are listed in the table of contents and not in the "Acknowledgment of Copyrights and Sources" section were written expressly for *The Sri Lanka Reader.*

It is not possible to list all of the various people who assisted my thinking in putting this volume together. Valerie Millholland, senior editor at Duke University Press, kept my spirits up with her unstinting encouragement and support. Sree Padma Holt listened patiently over many hours, days, and months as I tried out various ideas and strategies for putting the volume together. Jorge Flores and Dennis McGilvray were superb in their constructions of sections on the Portuguese and the Muslims—their assistance was much needed. Udaya P. Meddegama, a truly gifted linguist, undertook many original translations of sources from the Sinhala, including some that I was not able ultimately to include in the volume. C. R. de Silva made timely and substantive suggestions based on his broad and deep historical knowledge. Other helpful suggestions, for which I am grateful, came from Charles Hallisey and Philip Friedrich. Samuel Holt produced the general map of Sri Lanka, and Tilak Jayatilaka created several illustrations. Michael Glantz provided crucial technical support by scanning literally thousands of pages of texts under consideration. Rosemary Chunchi photocopied reams of material from books in the Intercollegiate Sri Lanka Education Program library in Kandy. ISLE's library of English works on Sri Lanka has become one of the best resources in the hill country for studying the history, politics, and culture of Sri Lanka. Without access to its resources, this volume would never have been produced.

Introduction

The island nation of Sri Lanka, the teardrop-shaped land mass located just off the southern tip of India, has been known by many different names throughout its long history. To Ptolemy and the Mediterranean world, it was the gem-bearing island known as Taprobane. In Mahayana Buddhist Sanskrit literature, such as the *Avalokitesvara-Guna-Karandavyuha Sutra*, it was known as Simhaladvipa ("the island of the Sinhalas"). For the Theravada Buddhist monks of the Mahavihara monastery in the Lankan capital of Anuradhapura who wrote and read the *Dipavamsa* and *Mahavamsa*, chronicles dating to the fourth and fifth century CE, it was Dhammadipa ("the island of the Buddhist teaching"). To Tamils throughout history, it has been known as Eelam. For the Sinhala people, it has always been Lanka. For the Arabs, the island was Serendib, from which in English we derive the term "serendipity." For the Portuguese, it was Ceilao. It was also known to the British colonial world as Ceylon, which remained its official name until the Sinhala-dominated government formally changed it to Sri Lanka in 1972. The island's changing name indicates that its geographical location has proven historically congenial to the intersection of many different cultures for over more than two and a half millennia.

Before I first visited this physically beautiful and topographically diverse country in the late 1970s, I imagined it as a manageable version of India, its giant neighbor to the north. I was deluded. Sri Lanka was far more complex socially and politically than I had imagined. Indeed, over many years of living in the country, I have been often overwhelmed by its labyrinthine character: layer upon layer of culture peels away to reveal another significant detail. Sri Lanka's history records numerous waves of immigrations emanating out of various regions of the South Asian subcontinent, and has been home to the formation of Sinhala Buddhist and Tamil Hindu civilizations, whose linguistic, religious, and cultural elements originated in India; in addition, it has seen the arrival and integration of Arab Muslim traders from the eighth century forward, and then the prolonged four and a half centuries of colonial interventions by the Christian Portuguese, Dutch, and British, from the sixteenth through the twentieth centuries. All these events have contributed to the complex evolution of Sri Lanka's society, one that clearly possesses a distinctive ethos of its own. Sri Lanka is not merely a "little India." Nor has it ever been, contrary to what many Westerners assume, a political part of India either. It is an island unto itself, but one that has been influenced from many directions throughout its long and varied history.

As a legacy to its complex social and political history, contemporary Sri Lankan society is marked by its variegated religious, linguistic, and so, disparate ethnic identities (Sinhala Buddhist, Sinhala and Tamil Christian, Tamil Hindu, and various Muslim communities). It is also divided by urban and rural, caste, and class distinctions. Despite its small size (approximately that of West Virginia), Sri Lanka remains an enormously complicated society. Unfortunately, an inability on the part of Sri Lanka's politicians to manage effectively the country's diversity, to capitalize on that diversity as a virtue, has contributed to postcolonial political convulsions that have wracked its public life for the past fifty years. Instead of celebrating Lanka's diversity, its politicians have sought to gain and retain power by appealing expediently to ethnic affinities. Sri Lanka is now a classic case of how the tyranny of a majority, one elected on a politics of exclusivity and ethnic chauvinism, has bred alienation and extremism in its minorities.

Since the early 1980s, Sri Lanka endured what amounted to a protracted civil war between its Sinhala majority and elements of its Tamil minority. While some observers have sought the roots of this conflict within the deep recesses of ancient or medieval history, the fundamental causes of the current conflict are more recent, causes that have more to do with competition for the relatively scarce economic resources in this comparatively poor South Asian nation (per capita income is roughly two thousand dollars per year). Secondarily, however, the causes of Sri Lanka's social and political conflict are also a byproduct of awakened modern and nationalistic ethnic identities fostered, ironically, by democratic enfranchisement that leads to a majoritarian rule.

Observers outside of Sri Lanka have often stressed religion as a key divider between Sri Lanka's communities. While Buddhism, Hinduism, Islam, and Christianity are definitely ethnic markers delineating Sri Lanka's various communities, religion has rarely been a primary motivation for discord. Rather, its significance more often surfaces within post hoc arguments that rationalize aggressive or defensive political and military strategies and tactics adopted by the majority. Until recently, Buddhism has been less of a motivation than a rationalization among the Sinhalese. The role of religion, however, is beginning to change. In 2004, a new Buddhist monastic political party was launched and gained nine seats in Sri Lanka's parliament as the result of its success in general elections. This monastic-based political movement equates the well-being of the religion as dependent upon the well-being of the country and vice versa. It represents the antithesis necessary for an inclusive umbrella formula demanded by a multiethnic population. At the moment, no dominant perspective that transcends the expediency of ethnic appeal stands on Sri Lanka's horizon pointing a new way forward. Neither Sinhala nor Tamil leaders have seemed poised for a constructive dialogue leading to a meaningful partnership in the future. As this book goes to press, the Sri Lankan government's forces have defeated the Liberation Tigers of Tamil Eelam (LTTE), but the island's future remains as clouded as ever. (I have provided a "political epilogue" at the conclusion of the book that discusses possible ramifications of the LTTE's defeat, but these items were added literally within days of the Tigers' debacle and have no benefit of hindsight whatsoever.)

When Sri Lanka gained independence from Britain in 1948, it was a relatively prosperous country and regarded as a "model colony" in some quarters. As the Allies' chief source of rubber during the Second World War, Sri Lanka had stockpiled considerable wealth and so its public financial situation was advantageous during its early years of independence. During those early years, much of the country's surplus was invested in its burgeoning free public education system and in its national health care system. Consequently, the country's literacy rate remains quite high and its life expectancy quite long (the highest and longest respectively in South Asia). As such, despite the ongoing civil conflict, Sri Lanka continues to enjoy the highest quality of life index in contemporary South Asia. Moreover, on the eve of independence, Sri Lanka did not experience the types of political and communal violence that India or Burma endured. Independence came peacefully to Ceylon. In the initial years of its independence, at least until the mid-1950s, a spirit of inclusion, if not political tolerance, seems to have characterized much of the public political life. Because of Sri Lanka's current circumstances of contestation, war, and poverty, it is difficult to imagine that a government delegation from another newly declared nearby independent state, Singapore, visited Ceylon in the early 1950s to see what it might learn about how to effectively manage ethnic diversity and how to allocate public spending responsibly. It is a national political tragedy that the country was not able to sustain the climate and conditions of its auspicious origins.

Some hold the view that long-simmering antagonisms between the Sinhalas and Tamils erupted only in the aftermath following British colonial control. This perspective is erroneous, though some British policies did certainly contribute to heightened acrimony between these communities.

Throughout twenty-five hundred years of history, numerous wars were fought between various sovereigns identified in modern histories as either Sinhala or Tamil, but nothing of the sort of demarcated national identities that now claim the loyalties of some within these respective communities seems to have existed during earlier epochs. For instance, it is clear that the Sinhala kings of the fifteenth- and sixteenth-century Kotte period, and the first of several Sinhala kings of the sixteenth- through nineteenth-century Kandyan period, were not only inclusive in their public rhetoric and in the cultural life of their courts, but that the last four kings of the nominally Sinhala Kandyan Kingdom were actually ethnic Tamils who ruled over a predominantly Sinhala but ethnically variegated population. One of these Tamil kings, Kirti Sri Rajasimha (r. 1751–82), was responsible for a veritable renaissance in traditional Sinhala Buddhist culture.

While it may be true that the chief causes of civil discord are comparatively recent, a consequence of the past several generations rather than past centuries of strife, how Sri Lanka's historical past is now being written in some quarters of the country (and within its diaspora populations) abets the contemporary experience of political stress between communities. The Sinhala-speaking majority of Sri Lanka constitutes some 75 percent of the current population; the Tamil community comprises roughly 18 percent; Muslims about 7 percent. Yet, in the postindependence democratic context, both the Sinhala and Tamil communities would seem to have suffered, at least from a social psychological point of view, from a type of a "minority complex." From a Sinhala perspective, the Sinhalese are a small but ancient people with a language spoken by only about twelve or thirteen million people (within the context of more than 1.3 billion people in the South Asian subcontinent), most of whom practice a religion (Theravada Buddhism) that became extinct in most parts of India by the thirteenth century CE. They understand themselves as proud survivors of history, having resisted the major religious, political, and cultural trajectories that earlier spread throughout the Indian subcontinent in the forms of a resurgent *bhakti* (devotional) Hinduism and a conquering Sunni Islam (Mughal India). From their point of view, a mostly rural agrarian population suffered relegation to a subservient status during its history of European colonialism, especially during British colonization (1796–1948 CE): a two-thousand-year-old line of kingship (which patronized the Buddhist religion) was disestablished; vast tracts of lands were alienated from traditional use and turned into tea, rubber, and coconut plantations benefiting European colonizers; Buddhism was first "betrayed" by the British (who had originally promised to protect it) and then further abused by Protestant Christian missionaries, while the language (Sinhala) was wholly neglected at the expense of English. Rightly or wrongly, there is a perception that the British had privileged the Tamil minority by affording them a disproportionate share of educational opportunities, such that the Tamils eventually came to dominate the colonial civil service and the professions of education, law, and medicine, as well as business. In the mid-1950s, the majority Sinhalese asserted their new democratically derived power on the basis of their demographic predominance by advocating a series of reforms aimed at elevating Buddhism and the Sinhala language to a special national status, while redressing perceived inequities in the educational and government bureaucratic systems through the establishment of quotas. They also launched ambitious colonization schemes, some in regions of the country that had been inhabited previously by Tamil-speaking people primarily.

From a point of view shared by many Tamil people, this Sinhala agenda amounted to a severe disenfranchisement of basic civil rights by depriving them of an unfettered use of their Tamil language, equal opportunity on the basis of merit to secure education at the tertiary levels, and discrimination by the Sinhala-dominated government in terms of economic opportunities. While resistance was periodic and took many forms, the first signs of sustained violent resistance by Tamil militant groups began to surface in the early 1970s and mushroomed spectacularly following the 1983 ethnic riots, a watershed in recent Sri Lankan history, when thousands of Tamils living in predominantly southern Sinhala regions of the island were systematically attacked and murdered, while their homes and businesses were looted and torched during a week of mayhem that has become known infamously as "Black July." Four sustained periods of civil war have followed (and countless numbers of violent or terrorist attacks from both sides have occurred), severely scarring ethnic relations, until a Norwegian-brokered cease-fire agreement was reached in February 2002, which remained largely intact until the summer of 2006. Since then, the Sri Lankan government has waged a military offensive against the Liberation Tigers of Tamil Eelam. At the time of this writing, the Tigers have been defeated as a conventional fighting force and their leadership has been decimated, but it is doubtful that any successful military campaign will assuage the grievances of the Tamil people and bring about a new era of countrywide solidarity. To the contrary, unless the Sinhala-dominated government takes immediate steps to address the legitimate grievances of its Tamil minority and allows the international community to assist it in rebuilding the lives of thousands of internally displaced people, it is possible that the current situation will only further exacerbate communal relations.

This thumbnail sketch (and there is much that is missing—including two armed, class-based, and Marxist-inspired rural Sinhala insurrections against Sri Lankan governments in 1971 and in 1988–89, and a related Indian military intervention from 1987 through 1990) is enough to indicate both the complexities and sensitivities that characterize Sri Lanka's recent political history. Within this context, how does one fairly represent "Sri Lanka" when identities, nationhood, and the trajectories of history itself are being so hotly contested? The Tamil side of history, ancient and recent, is further complicated by the problem of access. Unlike on the Sinhala side, there are few written sources to rely upon with regard to the history of Sri Lankan Tamil culture and society, especially before the colonial period. Moreover, in the contemporary period, the predominantly Tamil region of the north and northeast has been largely inaccessible to outside observers because it has been frequently under a state of siege. In such a condition, thoughtful reflection by inside observers on cultural productions has also been limited.

In putting together this volume, I have tried to counter the forces of fragmentation that, at present, are clearly ascendant on both sides of the ethnic divide. The principle of my method has been to find cultural materials and interpretive voices that are not only representative of what it has meant to "be Sri Lankan" (through many of the country's vicissitudes), but also to err on the side of inclusivity. Many of the sources I have included are, indeed, "classics": the kinds of entries that one should expect to find in a volume such as this. These include extracts from such venerable tracts as the fifth-century CE Pali Theravada Buddhist *Mahavamsa* and fifteenth-century Sinhala *sandesaya* (poetic) literature, as well as poignant observations made by more astute foreigners, including Chinese (Fa-Hien), Muslim (Ibn Batuta), Portuguese (Ribeiro), Dutch (Seeuwart), and British (Knox, Woolf, etc.) observers. But I have also endeavored to give voice to many writers and artists whose works have not received wide exposure to date or whose works have not yet been translated into English. Throughout, I have attempted to be fair and representative, though I am fully aware that the result is less than perfect.

The presentation of sources that follows is fundamentally historical. My overarching aim has been to allow cultural expressions of various types to articulate a sense of the social and political history of the island. Because the civil war or "ethnic conflict" looms so large in Sri Lanka's contemporary experience, I have selected a number of sources focused on the past that have some bearing on understanding aspects of the conflict in the present. Though I believe that the basic causes of the current conflict are comparatively recent, and that the postcolonial political convulsions that have wracked Sri Lanka's public life for the past fifty years are more the result of badly formulated government policies, the distinctive qualities of Sri Lanka's many communities are evident to the keen observer of the past. Whether or not future Sri Lankans celebrate these differences proudly, or whether these differences are used as a wedge to further divide one from the other, the differences are palpable indeed.

I

From Ancient to Early Modern

Sri Lanka is an ancient land by any comparative standard. Drip ledge caves, with hewn or carved inscriptions written in the archaic Brahmi script and located in what is now the country's North Central Province, indicate that by the third century BCE Buddhist laymen believed that they were earning merit for a better rebirth by providing Buddhist monks with a refuge to pursue their monastic vocations. Theravada Buddhist monastic chronicles assert that by about this time, royal power, with its chief seat in Anuradhapura —a settlement that was to become eventually a great cosmopolitan city supported by a system of sophisticated irrigation works—converted to Buddhism as a result of missionary efforts led by children of the great Indian emperor Asoka. These remarkable texts, the *Dipavamsa* (Chronicle of the Island) and earlier sections of the *Mahavamsa* (Great Chronicle), were written in the classical Prakrit language of Pali, purportedly by monastic incumbents of the Mahavihara fraternity of the Theravada school of Buddhism during the fourth and fifth centuries CE, when Anuradhapura was in full cultural bloom. Aside from archaeological information now coming to light, these texts, while largely sectarian in perspective, still remain our earliest interpretive windows into Sri Lanka's distant past.

Anuradhapura was the ritual and administrative center of the island's chief kings from the third century BCE until the destruction of its infrastructure by imperial Cola invaders from Thanjavur, south India, in the early eleventh century CE. For thirteen centuries, the city's society and culture flourished, supported by a robust economy made possible by the control and distribution of water. The most outstanding feature of Anuradhapura society was the symbiotic relationship between royalty and monastery. At the time of their construction by the Anuradhapura kings in the early centuries of the first millennium, the massive Ruvanvelisaya, Abhyagiriya, and Jetavana stupas (reliquary mounds) built within the city's Buddhist monastic complexes were the largest man-made structures in the world after the pyramids of Egypt. By means of generous royal support and the ethic of gift

Contemporary map of Sri Lanka

giving or merit making by the laity, the Buddhist monastic sangha thrived. The Chinese pilgrim Fa-Hien (whose writings are excerpted in this *Reader*) mentions some five thousand monks in residence at the Abhyagiriya monastery and three thousand in the Mahavihara monastery alone. Each of the three major monasteries developed extensive administrative systems that served as the central bureaucracies for the many far-flung village temples that constituted their *nikayas* (chapters or sects). In effect, the sangha became the central source of literary and artistic culture and, in many ways, the economic arbiter of capital wealth. In the later centuries of the first millennium, Anuradhapura continued to be a cosmopolitan city. For many Sri Lankan Buddhists the city represents the pristine purity of a Sinhala Theravada Buddhist past, but in fact the monasteries of Anuradhapura (especially the Abhyagiriya and Jetavana) were quite eclectic in nature. Inscriptions and sculptures reveal that the Mahayana and Vajrayana Buddhist traditions were also well represented. Indeed, twentieth-century archeological finds indicate that the Mahayana cult of Avalokitesvara was widespread throughout the island from the eighth through at least the tenth centuries.

The *Mahavamsa* contains an account of the political gyrations that eventually led to the invasion by the Cola empire based in Thanjavur (modern Tamilnadu), which seems to have resulted in the almost total demolition of Anuradhapura's civic and monastic infrastructure in the eleventh century. The Colas established their new power base on the island in Polonnaruva, about 80 miles to the southeast of Anuradhapura, ostensibly to better fend off any counterattacks from the Sinhalese, whose royalty had fled to the southeast quadrant of the island. The Colas maintained their position for many decades into the eleventh century, before the Sinhalas captured Polonnaruva and turned it into their own capital. The *Culavamsa* (the extension of the *Mahavamsa*) extols the great irrigation works (Parakramabahu *samudra*) and building achievements (especially the monastic complex Alahena Pirivena, said to have been attended by some ten thousand monks) of Parakramabahu I and other kings, including Nissamka Mala. When the *bhikkhusangha* was reconstituted in Polonnaruva, only Theravada monks (and none from the Mahayana tradition) were ordained and supported; no *bhikkunnishangha* (order of nuns) was reestablished at that time. This composition of monastic Buddhism is still in place today.

It is clear from archeological and sculptural remains that the Polonnaruva capital also sustained a Hindu Saivite presence after its capture by the Sinhalese. Even the *Culavamsa* account contains numerous references to Saivite practices in the royal court, probably owing to the fact that Sinhala Polonnaruva kings revived the practice of marrying queens from south

India. It is possible that the later blending of Hindu and Buddhist popular religion received its impetus from the social and political realities of the Polonnaruva courts at this time. But Polonnaruva was also the venue for the writing of the first Sinhala literary compositions, especially those by the celebrated writer Garulugomi, which took Buddhist subjects for their substance.

Polonnaruva was sacked by Magha, an invader from Kalinga (modern western Orissa) in the thirteenth century, a disaster so thorough in nature that the Sinhala kings abandoned their splendid capital and began to retreat in a southwesterly direction situating themselves in a series of backwater capitals. The invasion was followed by another several decades later, this one led by Chandrabhanu of Sri Vijaya (modern Malaysia and Sumatra) who purportedly sought possession of the Buddha's tooth relic and thereby the right to rule over Lanka. Indeed, the entire thirteenth through fifteenth centuries marks a period of great social turbulence and political instability throughout the island and with it, the increasing political enervation of Sinhala kings. At the same time, this was a period of unprecedented migration of peoples from various regions of south India, many of whom were originally mercenaries enlisted to fight in the ongoing conflicts. Their presence further abetted a Lankan cultural fermentation, the increased mixing of Hindu and Buddhist elements seen, for example, in the architecture and ritual practices of the Gadaladeniya and Lankatilaka temple complexes constructed during the Gampola (near Kandy) period of the fourteenth century. Also at this time, a powerful merchant family, the Alakesvaras, originally from Kerala, supervised the rule of the weakened Sinhala kings of the up-country from their own power base in Kotte (near modern Colombo). In the fourteenth century, an independent Tamil kingdom was established in Jaffna, ruled over by a king of the Aryacakravarti dynasty, in effect creating three competing political power centers. In the early fifteenth century, a coup orchestrated by the great Chinese admiral of the Ming dynasty, Cheng Ho, installed Parakramabahu VI on the Sinhala throne at Kotte; his long reign, beginning in 1412 and lasting fifty-five years, united the island under one rule for a twenty-year period—the only such time of unification between the Polonnaruva era and the disestablishment of Kandyan kingship by the British in 1815. The Kotte period under the rule of Parakramabahu VI was especially rich in the production of new genres of literature and the increasing influence of Hindu culture.

Buddhist Visions of a Primordial Past

Anonymous, comp. Mahanama Thera

Sri Lanka's renown in the Asian Buddhist world, especially in Southeast Asia, de-
rives from the fact that it was here that the Theravada Buddhist tradition, one of
the two main forms of the Buddhist religion in Asia, developed and thrived, from
the third century BCE forward. In the eleventh century CE, the Sinhala Theravada
lineage spread from Sri Lanka to Burma, and then from Burma to Buddhist king-
doms in northern Thailand (first to Chiang Mai's Lan Na Thai, then to Sukhothai,
and finally to Ayutthaya); from there, over the three following centuries, it spread to
Cambodia's Angkor, and Laos's Lang Xang in Luang Phrabang. Sri Lanka has been
regarded as the motherlode of Buddhism for these Southeast Asian religious cultures
ever since.

While it is relatively certain that the Buddha lived and taught in the fifth and
sixth centuries BCE in India's Ganges River Valley, and probably never left this re-
gion of northeast India during his lifetime, each of these Buddhist countries associ-
ates visits by the Buddha with the establishment of their higher civilizations. Here
is the account of the Buddha's first visit to the island of Lanka as it is preserved
in the fifth-century CE Theravada Buddhist monastic chronicle, the Mahavamsa,
compiled in Lanka's great capital city of Anuradhapura by the Theravada monk
Mahanama Thera; *it was written in Pali, the literary language of the Theravada*
tradition's sacred texts.

The Visit of the Tathagata (The One "Thus-Gone")

Having made obeisance to the Sambuddha the pure . . . , I will recite the
Mahavamsa, of varied content and lacking nothing. That [previous] (*Mahavamsa*) which was compiled by the ancient (sages) was here too long drawn
out and there too closely knit; and contained many repetitions. Attend now
to this [*Mahavamsa*] that is free from such faults, easy to understand and
remember, arousing serene joy and emotion and handed down (to us) by
tradition. . . .

On seeing the Sambuddha Dipamkara, in olden times, our Conqueror

The Buddha in his rebirth as a lion receives the prophecy of his eventual buddhahood from Dipamkara Buddha. Painting (approx. 14 × 21 in.), late eighteenth century, on the ceiling of the *buduge* (Buddha shrine room) at Degaldoruva Rajamahavihara. Photo by editor.

resolved to become a Buddha, that he might release the world from evil [*dukkha*, suffering]. When he offered homage to that Sambuddha and [to the remainder of the] . . . twenty-four Sambuddhas and having received from them the prophecy of his (future) buddhahood he, the great hero, when he had fulfilled all perfections and reached the highest enlightenment . . . , delivered the world from suffering.

At Uruvela, in the Magadha country, the great sage, sitting at the foot of the Bodhi tree, reached the supreme enlightenment on the full-moon day of the month Vesakha. Seven weeks he tarried there, mastering his senses, . . . [and] knew the high bliss of deliverance and . . . its felicity. Then he went to Baranasi and set rolling the wheel of the law; and while he dwelt there through the rain-months, he brought sixty (hearers) to arahantship [enlightenment]. When he had sent forth these bhikkhus [monks] to preach the dhamma [truth], and when he had converted the thirty companions of the company of Bhadda then did the Master dwell [in] Uruvela the winter through, for the sake of converting the thousand jatilas [ascetics] led by Kassapa, making them ripe (for deliverance).

Now since a great sacrifice by Kassapa of Uruvela was near at hand . . . , he . . . went to seek alms among the Northern Kurus; and when he had eaten

The two merchants (Tapusa and Mallika) and the four *lokapala* deities offer alms to the Buddha during the seventh week after his enlightenment. *Buduge* wall painting (approx. 9 × 13 in.), late eighteenth century, at Ridi Rajamahavihara. Photo by editor.

The Buddha preaching the *Dhammacakkapavattana* (Setting the dharma in motion) *Sutta* to his first five monk converts at Deer Park, Sarnath (India). *Buduge* wall painting (approx. 9 × 13 in.), late eighteenth century, at Ridi Rajamahavihara. Photo by editor.

The first five monastic converts become enlightened. Mural (approx. 45 × 64 in.), late eighteenth century, at Ridi Rajamahavihara. Photo by editor.

his meal at evening time near the lake Anotatta, the Conqueror, in the ninth month of his buddhahood . . . set forth for the isle of Lanka, to win Lanka for the sasana [religious tradition]. For Lanka was known to the Conqueror as a place where his dhamma should (thereafter) shine in glory; and (he knew that) from Lanka, filled with the yakkhas [demons], the yakkhas must (first) be driven forth.

And he knew also that in the midst of Lanka, on the fair riverbank, in the delightful Mahanaga garden . . . , the (customary) meeting-place for the yak-khas, there was a great gathering of (all) the yakkhas dwelling in the island. To this great gathering of the yakkhas went the Blessed One, and there, in the midst of that assembly, hovering in the air over their heads, at the place of the (future) Mahiyangana-thupa [reliquary], he struck terror to their hearts by rain, storm, darkness and so forth. The yakkhas, overwhelmed by fear, besought the fearless Vanquisher to release them from terrors, and the Vanquisher, destroyer of fear, spoke thus to the terrified yakkhas: "I will banish this your fear and your distress, O yakkhas, give . . . me . . . a place where I may sit down." The yakkhas answered, "We all, O Lord, give you even the whole of our island. Give us release from our fear." Then, when he had destroyed their terror, cold, and darkness, and had spread his rug of skin on the ground that they bestowed on him, the Conqueror, sitting there, made the rug to spread wide, while burning flame surrounded it. Daunted by the burning heat thereof and terrified, they stood around on the border. Then did the [Buddha] cause the pleasant Giridipa [island] to come here near to them, and when they had settled there, he made it return to its former place. Then did the [Buddha] fold his rug of skin; the devas [gods] assembled, and in their assembly, the Master preached them the dhamma. The conversion of many . . . took place, and countless were those who came . . . [to hold] the (three) refuges [Buddha, dhamma, and sangha] and the [ethical] precepts of duty.

The prince of [the] devas, Mahasumana of the Sumanakuta mountain [Sri Pada, or Adam's Peak], who had attained to the fruit of entering into the path of [dhamma], craved . . . something to worship. The Conqueror, the (giver of) good to living beings, he who had pure and blue-black locks . . . bestowed on him a handful of hairs. And he [Saman deva], receiving this in a splendid golden urn, when he had laid the hairs upon a heap of many colored gems, seven cubits round, piled up at the place where the Master had sat, covered them over with a thupa [reliquary] of sapphire and worshipped them.

When the Sambuddha had died, the thera [elder] named Sarabhu, disciple of the thera Sariputta, by his miraculous power received, even from the funeral pyre, the collar bone of the Conqueror and brought it . . . (to Lanka), and, with the bhikkhus all around him, he there laid it in that same cetiya

The multiple constructions of Mahiyangana's stupa. *Solosmasmasthana* (sixteen sacred places) wall painting (approx. 9 × 13 in.), late eighteenth century, at Ridi Rajamahavihara. Photo by editor.

Sri Pada (Adam's Peak) hallowed by the Buddha's visit. *Solosmasmasthana* wall painting (approx. 9 × 15 in.), mid-eighteenth century, at Gangarama Rajamahavihara. Photo by editor.

[reliquary], covered it over with the golden colored stones, and (then he), the worker of miracles, having made the thupa twelve cubits high, departed again. . . . The son of king Devanampiyatissa's brother, named Uddhaculabhaya, saw the wondrous cetiya and (again) covered it over and made it thirty cubits high. The king Dutthagamani, dwelling there while he made war upon the Damilas, built a mantle cetiya over it eighty cubits high. Thus was the Mahiyangana thupa completed. When he had thus made our island a fit dwelling place for men, the mighty ruler, valiant as are great heroes, departed for Uruvela.

What immediately follows in the Mahavamsa are detailed accounts of two more visits to Lanka by the Buddha: the first to the island of Nagadipa (modern-day Nainativu to the west of Jaffna), in which he settles a dispute between two Naga kings who are fighting over a gem throne; and the second, to Kelaniya (just north of modern Colombo), where he is feasted and preaches the dhamma. From Kelaniya, the Buddha proceeds to Sumanakuta (Sri Pada, or Adam's Peak), where he leaves his footprint; he goes on to hallow five more sacred places, including the future locales of Sri Mahabodhi and several stupas in Anuradhapura.

The Mahavamsa's *account of the civilizing of the island, however, was not complete without an explanation of the coming of kingship. Thus, another cycle of stories in early portions of the* Mahavamsa *recounts the origins of Sri Lankan kingship, and, in the minds of many, the origins of the Sinhala people as well, since these stories refer to the establishment of a line of political rule that remained unbroken, if at times severely challenged, until the British disestablished the last of the Kandyan kings in 1815. Vijaya, the protagonist of the mythic quest articulated below, is the legendary progenitor of the Sinhala people.*

The Coming of Vijaya

In the country of the Vangas . . . there lived once a king. . . . The daughter of the king of the Kalingas was that king's consort. By his spouse the king had a daughter; the soothsayers prophesied her union with the king of beasts. Very fair was she and very amorous and for shame the king and queen could not suffer her.

Alone she went forth from the house, desiring the joy of independent life; unrecognized she joined a caravan traveling to the Magadha country. In the Lala country a lion attacked the caravan in the forest, the other folk fled this way and that, but she fled along the way by which the lion had come.

When the lion had taken his prey and was leaving the spot he beheld her from afar, love (for her) laid hold on him, and he came towards her with waving tail and ears laid back. Seeing him she bethought of that prophecy of the soothsayers which she had heard, and without fear she caressed him stroking his limbs.

The lion, roused to the fiercest passion by her touch, took her upon his back and bore her with all speed to his cave, and there he was united with her, and from this union with him the princess in time bore twin children, a son and a daughter.

The son's hands and feet were formed like a lion's and therefore she named him Sihabahu, but the daughter (she named) Sihasivali. When he was sixteen years old the son questioned his mother on the doubt (that had arisen in him): "Why are you and our father so different, dear mother?" She told him all. Then he asked: "Why do we not go forth (from here)?" And she answered: "Your father has closed the cave up with a rock." Then he took that barrier before the great cave upon his shoulder and went (a distance of) fifty yojanas going and coming in one day.

Then (once), when the lion had gone forth in search of prey, (Sihabahu) took his mother on his right shoulder and his young sister on his left, and went away with great speed. They clothed themselves with branches of trees, and so came to a border village and there, even at that time, was a son of the princess's uncle, a commander in the army of the Vanga king, to whom was given the rule over the border country; and he was just then sitting under a banyan tree overseeing the work that was done.

When he saw them he asked them (who they were) and they said: "We are forest folk"; the commander bade (his people) give them clothing; and this turned into splendid (garments). He had food offered to them on leaves and by reason of their merit these were turned into dishes of gold. Then, amazed, the commander asked them, "Who are you?" The princess told him her family and clan. Then the commander took his uncle's daughter with him and went to the capital of the Vangas and married her.

When the lion, returning in haste to his cave, missed those three (persons), he was sorrowful, and grieving after his son he neither ate nor drank. Seeking for his children he went to the border village and every village where he came was deserted by the dwellers therein.

And the border folk came to the king and told him this: "A lion ravages thy country; ward off (this danger) O king!"

Since he found none who could ward off (this danger) he had a thousand (pieces of money) led about the city on an elephant's back and this proclamation made: "Let him who brings the lion receive these!" And in like manner the monarch (offered) two thousand and three thousand [gold pieces]. Twice did Sihabahu's mother restrain him. The third time without asking his mother's leave, Sihabahu took the three thousand gold pieces (as reward) for slaying his own father.

They presented the youth to the king, and the king spoke thus to him: "If you can take the lion I will give you at once the kingdom." And he went to the opening of the cave, and as soon as he saw from afar the lion who came forward, for love toward his son, he shot an arrow to slay him.

The arrow struck the lion's forehead but because of his tenderness (toward his son) it rebounded and fell on the earth at the youth's feet. And so it fell out three times, then did the king of beasts grow wrathful and the arrow sent at him struck him and pierced his body.

(Sihabahu) took the head of the lion with the mane and returned to his city. And just seven days had passed then since the death of the king of the Vangas. Since the king had no son the ministers, who rejoiced over his deed on hearing that he was the king's grandson and on recognizing his mother, met all together and said of one accord to the prince Sihabahu: "Be (our) king."

And he accepted the kingship but handed it over then to his mother's husband and he himself went with Sihasivali to the land of his birth. There he built a city, and they called it Sihapura, and in the forest stretching a hundred yojanas around he founded villages. In the kingdom of Lala, in that city did Sihabahu, ruler of men, hold sway when he had made Sihasivali his queen. As time passed on his consort bore twin sons sixteen times, the eldest was named Vijaya, the second Sumitta; together there were thirty-two sons. In time the king consecrated Vijaya as prince regent.

Vijaya was intent on evil conduct and his followers were even (like himself), and many intolerable deeds of violence were done by them. Angered by this the people told the matter to the king; the king, speaking persuasively to them, severely blamed his son. But all fell out again as before, the second and yet the third time; and the angered people said to the king: "Kill thy son."

Then did the king cause Vijaya and his followers, seven hundred men, to shave over half the head and put them on a ship and sent them forth upon the sea, and their wives and children also. The men, women, and children sent forth separately landed separately, each (company) upon an island, and they dwelt even there. The island where the children landed was called Nagadipa and the island where the women landed Mahiladipaka. But Vijaya, the valiant, landed in Lanka, in the region called Tambapanni on the day that the Tathagata lay down between the two twin-like sala-trees to pass into nibbana [nirvana]. [*It is at this point in the* Mahavamsa *compilation that the cycle of stories related to the Buddha and the cycles connected to Vijaya intersect.*]

The Consecrating of Vijaya

When the Guide of the World [the Buddha], having accomplished the salvation of the whole world and having reached the utmost stage of blissful rest, was lying on the bed of his nibbana, in the midst of the great assembly of gods, he, the great sage, the greatest of those who have speech, spoke to Sakka [Indra, king of the gods], who stood there near him: "Vijaya, son of king Sihabahu, [has] come to Lanka from the country of Lala, together with seven hundred followers. In Lanka, O lord of gods, will my religion be established, therefore carefully protect him with his followers and Lanka."

When the lord of gods heard the words of the Tathagata, he respectfully handed over the guardianship of Lanka to the god who is in color like the lotus [utpalavanna].

And no sooner had the god received the charge from Sakka than he came speedily to Lanka and sat down at the foot of a tree in the guise of a wandering ascetic. And the all the followers of Vijaya came to him and asked him: "What is this island, sir?" "The island of Lanka," he answered. "There are no men here, and here no dangers will arise." And when he had spoken so and sprinkled water on them from his water vessel, and had wound a thread about their hands he vanished through the air. And there appeared, in the form of a bitch, a yakkhini [demoness] who was an attendant (of Kuvanna).

One of Vijaya's men went after her, although he was forbidden by the prince (for he thought), "Only where there is a village are dogs to be found." Her mistress, a yakkhini named Kuvanna, sat there at the foot of a tree spinning, as a woman hermit might.

When the man saw the pond and the woman hermit sitting there, he bathed there and drank and taking young shoots of lotuses and water in lotus leaves he came forth again. And she said to him: "Stay! You are now my prey!" Then the man stood there as if fast bound. But because of the power of the magic thread she could not devour him, and though he was entreated by the yakkhini, the man would not yield up the thread. Then the yakkhini seized him, and hurled him into a chasm. And there in like manner she hurled all the seven hundred one by one after him.

And when they all did not return fear came on Vijaya; armed with the five weapons he set out, and when he beheld the beautiful pond, where he saw no footstep of any man coming forth, but saw that woman hermit there, he thought: "Surely my men have been seized by this woman." And he said to her, "Lady, have you not seen my men?" "What do you want with your people, prince?" she answered. "Drink and bathe."

Then it was clear to him: "This surely is a yakkhini, she knows my rank," and swiftly uttering his name, he came at her drawing his bow. He caught the yakkhini in the noose about the neck, and seizing her hair with his left hand he lifted his sword in the right and cried: "Slave! Give me back my men or I slay you!" Then, tormented with fear the yakkhini prayed him for her life. "Spare my life, sir, I will give you a kingdom and do you a woman's service and other services as you wish."

And that he might not be betrayed he made the yakkhini swear an oath, and so soon as the charge was laid on her, "Bring here my men with all due speed," and she brought them to that place. When he said, "These men are hungry," she showed them rice and other foods and goods of every kind that had been in the ships of those traders whom she had devoured.

Vijaya's men prepared the rice and the condiments, and when they had first set them before the prince they all ate of them.

When the yakkhini had taken the first portions of the meal that Vijaya handed to her, she was well pleased, and assuming the lovely form of a

sixteen-years-old maiden she approached the prince adorned with all the ornaments. At the foot of a tree she made a splendid bed, well covered around
with a tent, and adorned with a canopy. And seeing thus, the king's son,
looking forward to the time to come, took her to him as his spouse and lay
(with her) blissfully on the bed; and all his men encamped around the tent.

As the night went on he heard the sounds of music and singing, and asked
the yakkhini, who was lying near him: "What means this noise?" and the
yakkhini thought: "I will bestow kingship on my lord and all the yakkhas
must be slain for (else) the yakkhas will slay me, for it was through me that
men have taken up their dwelling in Lanka."

And she said to the prince: "Here there is a yakkha city called Sirisavat-
thu; the daughter of the chief of the yakkhas who dwells in the city of Lanka
has been brought here, and her mother too has come. And for the wedding
there is high festival, lasting seven days; therefore there is this noise, for a
great multitude is gathered together. Today you should destroy all of these
yakkhas, for afterward it will no longer be possible."

He replied: "How can I slay the yakkhas who are invisible?" "Wheresoever they may be," she said, "I will utter cries, and where you hear that
sound, strike! And by my magic power shall your weapon fall upon their
bodies."

Since he listened to her and did as she said he slew all the yakkhas, and
when he had fought victoriously he himself put on the garments of the
yakkha king and bestowed the other raiment on one and another of his
followers.

When he had spent some days at that spot he went to Tambapanni. There
Vijaya founded the city of Tambapanni and dwelt there, together with the
yakkhini, surrounded by his ministers.

When those who were commanded by Vijaya landed from their ship,
they sat down wearied, resting their hands upon the ground; since their
hands were reddened by touching the dust of the red earth that region and
also the island were named Tambapanni. But the king Sihabahu, since he
had slain the lion (was called) Sihala, and by reason of the ties between him
and them all those (followers of Vijaya) were also called Sihala.

Here and there did Vijaya's ministers found villages. Anuradhagama
was built by a man of that name near the Kadamba river; the chaplain Upatissa built Upatissagama on the bank of the Gambhira river, to the north of
Anuradhagama. Three other ministers built, each for himself, Ujjeni, Uru-
veli, and the city of Vijita.

When they had founded settlements in the land the ministers all came
together and spoke thus to the prince: "Sire, consent to be consecrated as

king." But, in spite of their demand, the prince refused the consecration, un-less a maiden of noble house were consecrated as queen (at the same time).

But the ministers, whose minds were eagerly bent upon the consecrating of their lord, and who, although the means were difficult, had overcome all anxious fears about the matter, sent people, entrusted with many precious gifts, jewels, pearls, and so forth, to the city of Madhura, in southern (India) to woo the daughter of the Pandu king for their lord, devoted (as they were) to their ruler; and they also (sent to woo) the daughters of others for the ministers and retainers.

When the messengers quickly came by ship to the city Madhura they laid the gifts and letter before the king. The king took counsel with his minis-ters, and since he was minded to send his daughter (to Lanka) he, having first received also the daughters of others for the ministers (of Vijaya), nigh upon a hundred maidens, proclaimed with beat of drum: "Those men here who are willing to let a daughter depart for Lanka shall provide their daughters with a double store of clothing and place them at the doors of their houses. By this sign shall we (know that we may) take them to ourselves."

When he had thus obtained many maidens and had given compensation to their families, he sent his daughter, bedecked with all her ornaments, and all that was needful for the journey, all the maidens whom he had fitted out, according to their rank, elephants withal and horses and wagons, worthy of a king, and craftsmen with a thousand families of the eighteen guilds, entrusted with a letter to the conqueror Vijaya. All this multitude of men disembarked at Mahatittha; for that very reason is that landing place known as Mahatittha [Great Port].

Vijaya had one son and one daughter by the yakkhini; when he now heard that the princess had arrived he said to the yakkhini: "Go now, dear one, leave the two children behind; men are ever in fear of superhuman beings."

But when she heard this she was seized with fear of the yakkhas; then he said (again) to the yakkhini: "Delay not! I will bestow on you an offering by (spending) a thousand (pieces of money)." When she had again and again besought him (in vain) she took her two children and departed for Lanka-pura, though fearing that evil should come of it.

She set the children down outside and went, herself, into that city. When the yakkhas in the city recognized the yakkhini, in their terror they took her for a spy and there was great stir among them; and one who was violent killed the yakkhini with a single blow of his fist.

But her uncle, on the mother's side, a yakkha, went forth from the city and when he saw the children he asked them: "Whose children are you?"

and hearing that they were Kuvanna's he said: "Here has your mother been slain, and they will slay you also if they see you: (therefore) flee swiftly!"

Fleeing with speed they went from thence to Sumanakuta. The brother, the elder of the two, when he grew up he took his sister, the younger, for his wife, and multiplying with sons and daughters, they dwelt, with the king's leave, there in Malaya. From these are sprung the Pulinda.

The envoys of the Pandu king delivered up to the prince Vijaya the gifts and the (maidens) with the king's daughter at their head. When Vijaya offered hospitality and bestowed honors on the envoys he bestowed the maidens, according to their rank, upon his ministers and retainers. According to custom the ministers in full assembly consecrated Vijaya king and appointed a great festival.

The king Vijaya consecrated the daughter of the Pandu king with solemn ceremony as his queen; he bestowed wealth on his ministers, and every year he sent to his wife's father a shell pearl worth twice a hundred thousand (pieces of money).

When he had forsaken his former evil way of life, Vijaya, the lord of men, ruling over Lanka in peace and righteousness reigned, as is known, in the city of Tambapanni, thirty-eight years.

While the story of Buddha's visits and the colonization of the island by the Sinhala progenitor Vijaya establish the beginnings of religious and political order on the island, a subsequent cycle of narratives recounts the coming to the island of the children of the great third-century BCE Indian emporer Asoka (Mahinda and Sanghamitta) to establish Theravada Buddhist monasticism. Monasticism dominated the social, political, and economic life of the island for the next thirteen hundred years. As the subsequent narratives relate, Sanghamitta, Asoka's daughter, brought with her a sapling of the bodhi tree (Sri Mahabodhi), under which the Buddha had attained enlightenment, and established the order of nuns. Sri Mahabodhi, "the tree of enlightenment," was planted in Anuradhapura and has been one of the most important sites of Buddhist pilgrimage throughout Sri Lanka's history. The city of Anuradhapura's sacred boundaries are then ploughed by King Devanampiya Tissa, who was converted to Buddhism by Asoka's missionary son, Mahinda.

Note

1. Words enclosed in parentheses are in the original; words in brackets have been added by the editor.

A Tamil Hindu Vijaya:

Yalpana Vaipava Malai

Anonymous

This remarkable text surfaced in the eighteenth century in Jaffna, when Dutch officials requested an indigenous account of the country's origins. In what follows, a creative reworking of the Vijaya cycle of myths reflects the predilections of the Tamil Hindu community: the account is set within the traditional Hindu time frames (yugas); the bridge to historical time is provided by allusions to the epic Ramayana; *when the progenitor Vijaya first comes to the island, he is accompanied by a brahmin priest from Kashi* (Benares). *Finding it difficult to populate the island, Vijaya travels to Siam and Burma to recruit Buddhists who eventually become the Sinhalese people. Vijaya is portrayed as a dedicated follower of Siva, responsible for the construction of many important Hindu temples. In this context, Buddhist traders are accused of fouling temple wells with fish bought from the low-caste Tamil fisher folk who are then, in turn, sent on to Batticaloa; and the Vanni, or the forest region between Jaffna and Anuradhapura, is said to have been settled by a tribe of migrants from India. In these ways, an imaginative alternative to ancient Sinhala migration stories articulates rival claims to primordial ownership or settlement of the island.*

It is related in the ithihasas [histories] and puranas [ancient stories] that the Rakshasas held Langka during the first three yugas of the world. Tradition adds that Vibhishana, who received the kingdom from Dasarata Rama, the conqueror of Ravana, continued to reign up to and during the early part of the present yuga, and that when Vibhishana was taken up to heaven, the Rakshasas quit Langka from fear of foreign subjugation.

About two thousand four hundred years ago, Singha-bahu a Kshattriya of Banga was king of Lada. His eldest son, Vijaya-kumara, a lawless youth, rendered himself extremely hateful to his countrymen, and was in consequence expelled from the kingdom. The exile wandered from place to place in search of an asylum, but he found none.

When at last he reached Kashi he was informed in a dream that Langka was assigned to him for a hermitage and that he should go thither and establish himself at Kathirai-malai in the centre of the country. He went accordingly, and took with him, besides his usual retinue, a priest of the name of Nilakanda acharya, a Brahman of Kashi. The Brahman was accompanied by his whole family, which consisted of his wife, Akilanda-valli-ammal, and his sons and daughters with their wives and husbands. The expedition safely reached its destination, and advancing into the heart of the country took up its residence at Kathirai-malai.

In those days Langka was a great wilderness, inhabited only by the Vedar and wild animals. There were no human beings in it. And Vijaya-raja (for raja, i.e., king he now undoubtedly was) made constant efforts to obtain colonists from the adjacent countries. From Kanya-kumari to the Himalaya mountains, all despised "the country of the Rakshasas," as they termed Langka in contempt. The baffled king turned his thoughts to the Buddhists of Magadha, who had been driven from their country by reason of their having embraced Buddhism. Some of them had already found permanent seats in the countries lying to the North of the Himalaya mountains; but others, who had traveled eastward and crossed the Brahmaputra, were as yet leading a wandering life in Siam and other parts of Burma. Vijaya-raja went to Siam, and successfully induced a number of those wanderers to follow him into the new kingdom. He placed them in various parts of the country, and gave them liberty to follow their own faith. In process of time these Buddhists came to be called Singhalese from the fact of their inhabiting Singhalam—"Singhalam" being another name for "Langka."

Vijaya-raja did not himself profess Buddhism, but he only tolerated it as a means of peopling the country. He was a staunch worshipper of Siva and began his reign by dedicating his city to that god and building four Siva-layams as a protection for the four quarters of his infant kingdom. In the East he erected Konesar-koyil at Thampala-kanam; in the West he re-built Thiruk-kethich-churan-koyil, which had long been then in ruins; in the South he raised Santhira-sekaran-koyil at Maththurai; and on the North he constructed Thiruth-thampa-tesuran-koyil. . . .

After the building of the temples, Vijaya-raja returned to Kathirai-malai making a circuit of the whole country. On reaching his capital he removed the seat of government to Thammansi: a change which was followed by another and a cruel one, for he drove away his wife with her two children, a son and a daughter, whom she had borne to him, and took another wife in the person of a woman from Pandi.

Vijaya-raja reigned but a few years after this. He left no issue and his minister took charge of the kingdom and preserved it for a year until the arrival of the late king's brother's son, Pandu-vasu, whom the minister had sent for from Lada. This Pandu-vasu was the founder of an illustrious dynasty which continued to reign over Langka for numerous generations. . . .

Panda-maha-raja who ruled Langka from Anuradhapura was at this time absent from his capital, having come to Manat-tidal (the sand-heap), a name by which this part of his kingdom was then known. The inhabitants of Koyil-kadavai seized the opportunity to complain to the king against certain Singhalese traders in that district, who supplied dried fish to foreign markets. The complaint was that they exposed fish to dry in holy places and polluted holy wells by drawing water from them and that, therefore, priests and devotees felt constrained to abandon the temples. Pandu inquired into the matter and punished the offenders according to justice. Finding that the Singhalese themselves did not know how to fish, but that they employed for the purpose labourers of the Mukkuva caste—a caste whose hereditary occupation fishing was—the king ordered every individual of the Mukkuva caste to quit the sacred neighbourhood. The Mukkuva chieftains, Usuman and Senthan, migrated with their followers to Batticaloa and settled in Panakai and Valaiyiravu. A few remained behind in Manat-tidal, but formed new settlements on the sea coast far removed from Kiri-matai. From this time no Mukkuvar have been found in Usuman-thurai, Senthan-kalam, or Allith-thundal.

While Pandu was thus engaged here, his queen at Anuradhapura received information of the doings of Kulakkoddan, and dispatched a small army with instructions to drive him out of the kingdom. When the army reached Thampala-kamam and witnessed the gigantic undertakings of the enemy, it trembled with fear, and approaching Kulakkoddan represented itself to have come to him on a pacific mission, having been sent by the court of Anuradhapura only to inquire if he needed any assistance. Kulakkoddan affected to believe the representation, received the soldiers with apparent kindness, entertained them sumptuously, and dismissed them with valuable presents and a friendly reply to their mistress. On their return to Anuradhapura they published such exaggerated accounts of the stranger's greatness and liberality, that no attempt was ever afterwards made to molest him. . . .

As soon as Kulakkoddan had completed the buildings, he prepared seven large tracts of land with fruitful groves and fertile fields, and dedicated their income for the use of the temple. He sent for Vanniyar from the coast of India, and placed them over those tracts, with strict orders to them to cultivate the lands for the benefit of the temple.

At first, the income of these lands was regularly delivered, and was amply sufficient for the expenses of the temple, the monasteries and the akkiraram; and these institutions, accordingly, flourished. On the death of Kulak-koddan (which took place in his native country after his return from Langka), the Vanniyar, who had rapidly increased in number, and had besides received an accession of fifty-nine new families from Pandi, became too numerous to be capable of attending to their lands peacefully without a king. They began to fight with one another for supremacy, and the cultivation of the lands was necessarily neglected. A host of ephemeral kings rose and disappeared in succession. The most distinguished of them was Santhira-vanniyan. He, too, fell in the internecine contest, but the survivors continued the fight till they were all exhausted. A peace was, at length, concluded, and seven chieftains were elected from among the Vanniyar to exercise sovereign power, each within his own territory. The descendants of these chieftains continued to exercise the like power, and the territories over which they ruled came to be called the Vannis, i.e., the territories of the Vanniyar.

The Saga of Dutugemunu

Devarakkhita Jayabahu Dharmakirti

The controversial epic of Dutugemunu (Pali: Dutthagamini), is perhaps the best-known narrative concerning the much-contested ancient Sri Lankan polity. The earliest version is found in the Mahavamsa *and purports to be an account of events that occurred in the late second century* BCE. *The story continues to resonate for many contemporary Sinhalas, who find the defeat or subjugation of the island's Tamils an important dimension, for some paradigmatic, of their social and political identities. In this sense (at least for Sinhalas of this persuasion), the story symbolizes the prototypical encounter between the Sinhala and Tamil peoples, with Dutugemunu—the arch-defender of Buddhism—defeating the Tamil king Elara and his armies to establish Sinhala hegemony for the sake of the religion's well-being. The extract below comes from the shorter, fourteenth-century version found in the* Saddharmalankaraya, *which was written in the Gampola period by the Buddhist monk Devarakkhita Jayabahu Dharmakirti.*

In a former birth, Dutugemunu, having witnessed how an elder monk had been appointed to the post of chief disciple on the right hand of the Buddha, made a vow: "May I also become a monk of great wisdom and virtue, and be appointed as chief disciple of a Buddha in the future." Then, he sojourned on through *samsara* [the conditioned rounds of rebirth] for millions of years, accruing merit, enjoying divine and human pleasures, and eventually was born within a Sri Lankan family. As a youth, he received ordination in the Sangha, and while living in a beautiful temple near Kela Rock in Ruhunu, he thought, "Birth as a human being is very rare, and now born during the tenure of a Buddha, I must earn merit diligently." With this resolve, he completed the training of novice, waiting upon senior monks by providing them with clean water, tooth picks, etc. Then, performing all the rites at the stupa and the Bodhi tree, he lived there as a genuine, devoted monk engaged in meritorious deeds. One day he noticed the steps leading to the upper terrace of the stupa had become dilapidated, so he placed a large stone underneath to make them stable. By doing such difficult work, his body was weakened and he fell ill. Other monks, inspired by his exemplary behaviour, carried him on a stretcher to the great monastery at Tissamaharama where they kept him in the temple named "Salvasa pirivena." There they nursed him.

At that time King Kavantissa and Queen Vihara kept themselves busy with the performance of meritorious deeds while they ruled in Ruhunu. One day, after providing the Sangha with alms in the morning at the Vihara, the king accompanied by the queen, while visiting monks in their chambers and worshipping them, offering medicine and other requisites to those who were sick, and giving them eight kinds of drink, betel leaves etc., arrived at the Salvasa Pirivena, met with the incumbent monk there and sat to one side after worshipping him. The monk preached a sermon to the king and the queen and instructed them to carry on with more merit-making actions in order to receive greater rewards in the next birth. Then Queen Vihara said, "Your Honour! I have no children. I am barren. So why should I wish for more luxury?"

Then the monk determined with his divine eye whether the queen was blessed with a child or not, and realizing that she was in a fortunate condition said, "Auspicious lady! Go in, talk to the sick novice monk lying in there." She did as instructed, worshipped the sick monk and questioned, "Venerable Sir, you look very sick. What is wrong? Where would you like to be reborn?" The monk answered, "Kind Lady! Heaven is wholesome. I wish to be born there."

"Sir, what is the use of being reborn in heaven? You'll enjoy your time there only as long as the merit you've earned here lasts. There's no better rebirth than as a king for accruing merit. Please be born in my womb." The monk could not agree to this as he believed that birth as a human being was repulsive. Then, in order to convince the young monk, the queen beautifully decorated the monk's temple, and so demonstrated her wealth and power. She arranged a comfortable bed strewn with flowers and covered it with fine cloth, fed the monk with rare, delicious food, and offered him fragrant flowers, scents, clothes, medicinal food and beverages, etc. She said, "Sir, I give all these fine things to you so that you may perform merit-making activities by using these as you please. This will show you that if you are born as a king, you will be able to perform any meritorious deed." Then the monk, realizing that there was truth in what the queen had said, agreed to be born as her son, abandoning the heavenly pleasures that were readily available to him.

Queen Vihara, knowing this, worshipped him happily and took leave to go back to the palace. As she was leaving by carriage with the king, the sick monk passed away and was conceived in the queen's womb. As soon as that happened, the carriage wheel sunk in the earth up to the hub on the queen's side. She felt as if her womb was filled with crystal. Guessing that the novice monk had died, she sent a man to verify and turned back to return to the temple. The queen had the monk's body cremated with all due rituals and offerings.

Then immediately after conception, a pregnancy craving was born in the queen's mind. What was that craving? Lying by the side of a hundred-cubit-long beehive to offer honey from it with her own hands to twelve thousand monks, and to consume honey; to drink the water used to wash the sword, which was used to cut off the head of the chief warrior of [the Tamil] King Elara; to wear garlands made with manel lilies picked from the King Elara's manel pond in Anuradhapura and to bathe with the water brought from the Tissaweva and to drink of the same water standing on the Tamil warrior's head. The queen thinking that it would be impossible to fulfil her craving, did not mention it with her husband or anyone else. Her body got weakened and emaciated day by day as her craving was not gratified. When the king questioned her as to the reason, she told him all about her desires. The king announced in the city by the king's crier, that who ever would tell him about a beehive one hundred cubits long, that person would be lavishly rewarded. Then by the power of good karma of the child, on the beach of the *"Golu-muhuda,"* there appeared a one hundred-cubit-long bee hive inside an old boat turned upside down. When this was reported to the king, he took the queen there in a procession, had a beautiful pavilion erected beside the old boat and arranged for Queen Vihara to satisfy her craving.

Then in order to fulfil the rest of the cravings, the king spoke to the warrior Velusumana, who promptly promised to go to Anuradhapura and bring what the queen desired. Velusumana, having his hair shaved leaving only a knot at the top, showing marks of whiplashes by the king on his body, wearing red clothes, departed for Anuradhapura. On his way, at check-points put up by Elara, he deceived the sentries, . . . until he reached Anuradhapura. There he met with King Elara and deceived him with a promise to serve him faithfully and to bring King Kavantissa as a prisoner. King Elara believed him, and appointed him as the chief of guards in his stables. While working there, Velusumana checked all the king's horses and selected a horse named Ranamaddava. Then he bought a large pot, filled it with water from the Tissaweva and hid it by the River Kolom; picked manel flowers from the royal pond, made a bundle and kept it also hidden with the pot of water. Then riding the horse Ranamaddava, [he] uttered his war cry, announcing his name and rode away challenging Elara's mighty warriors. King Elara summoned at once a warrior called Meldeva and sent him with one hundred men to catch Velusumana. Two of Elara's cleverest warriors chased Velusumana on their horses, but on the way, Velusumana, disturbing dust on the track so as to blur the vision, took cover behind a tree, holding his sword across the path of his pursuers. The trick worked and Velusumana decapitated both of the Tamil warriors, picked up the severed heads, tied them up together, and carried everything with the two horses back to Magama.

The King of Magama was very happy to see him and rewarded him generously and helped his queen to satisfy her cravings. Then the king summoned soothsayers, and questioned them about the implications of the pregnancy cravings of the queen. They made the following prediction: "Your Majesty, a very brave, virtuous and fortunate son will be born to you. He will certainly ward off the Tamil enemy and unite Sri Lanka becoming the sovereign king. He will rule the country living at Anuradhapura, serving the people like Emperor Dharmasoka."

One day King Kavantissa went to the Vihara, listened to dharma, treated the monks and meant twice to gift a cloth to the monks, but he was unable to as he had no spare cloth except for the two clothes he was wearing. While the king was sitting there disappointed, brooding over it, a crow sitting in a mango tree near by the palace, spoke to him: "Your Majesty, give whatever you wish to give, I'll, in return, bring you three messages: Your Majesty, Queen Vihara, has just given birth to a lucky son. A she elephant of the Uposatha clan came by air and left a baby elephant by Lake Titti; a mare of the Valahaka clan came by air and delivered a foal near Gonagama; sixty ships loaded with silk have arrived by the Golu Muhuda, and finally, near a hill named Uturu Vadaman, in an area of sixteen Kiri, gold-plants have emerged. And further, an elder monk named Mahanada of the Giridipa state, attained *parinibbana*." The king smiled when hearing the messages brought by the crow. The elder monk asked him the reason for smiling. When the king told him why, the monk also smiled remembering the meritorious deeds performed by the king in a former birth. Then the king had gold, silk, etc., brought to the palace, gave some part of it to the Sangha, brought the foal and named it Dighatuni and the baby elephant he named Kadol, after the name of the fisherman who reported its whereabouts.

At the naming ceremony of the little prince, the king consulted the monks and after treating them with food and lavish gifts wished for some miracle to happen. The king's wish was granted at once. Some *arahant* monks arrived by air, and one of them named Gotama touched the baby prince's hand, as the king had wished. Then the king invited them to name the prince. They named him Gamini Abhaya, combining parts of the name of the kingdom and a part of the father's name. Queen Vihara also gave birth to another son who was named Tissa. The king gave great alms on the festival days of feeding rice, ear-piercing and the hair-cutting of the two princes. When the two princes were about ten or twelve years old, the king, in order to test them, had five hundred monks invited into the palace, and at the end of the alms giving, putting some left-over rice in a gold plate and having seated the two brothers on either side of it, and making three portions of the rice, told his sons: "My dear sons, eat one of these portions promising not to do anything against our masters, the Sangha, and that you wouldn't consume anything without first offering a part of it to them." The two princes ate at once the first portion of the rice saying, "We won't do anything against the Sangha." "Now eat the last portion promising that you will not wage war against the Tamils." Having heard that, Prince Tissa dropped the lump of rice from his hand and ran away.

Prince Gamini also dropped the lump of rice as his brother did, retired into his bed chamber and lay curled up in his bed folding his arms and legs. Queen Vihara saw him lying like that and questioned him: "What is this Prince Gamini, isn't this bed large enough for you to sleep comfortably, stretching your hands and legs?" The prince replied, "What do you say, mother, across the river, there are Tamils and on this side there is the Golu Muhuda. How could I sleep comfortably with my arms and legs straightened?" King Kavantissa, being informed of this incident, understanding well the intentions of his sons, trained them in all the skills in warfare such as fighting with weapons, horse and elephant riding, etc. Prince Gamini grew up gradually to be a handsome young man of sixteen. King Kavantissa entrusted him with the forces together with the ten great warriors, viz., Nandimitra, Suranimila, Mahasona, Gothayimbara, Theraputtabhaya, Bharana, Velusumana, Khanjadeva, Phussadeva and Labhiyavasabha. Each one of them trained ten warriors and those ten trained a hundred warriors who in their turn trained one thousand. . . . Thus, including the ten chief warriors, there were eleven thousand one hundred and ten altogether. Then the king, having granted them land for a living, and considering them the same as his own sons, appointed Prince Gamini the Commander-in-Chief. He dispatched the younger son Tissa to Digamadulla to develop that area in agriculture for the welfare of the people. Prince Gamini, in the meantime, having inspected his troops, informed his father that it was the opportune time to go to war with the Tamils. But the king thought otherwise, "victory in a war is not certain," and due to love for his sons he said, "What is the use of fighting with Tamils? This side of the river is sufficient for us."

Prince Gamini was so keen to fight that he asked for a second time and a third time. When permission was declined, Gamini became angry with his father and sent him a woman's costume and ornaments with the words,

"My father is no man, let him give up wearing men's clothes and wear the woman's costume from now on." The king was furious by seeing what his son had sent him and ordered his men, "Seize the prince, handcuff him and bring him over to me; there's no other way to control him." But Prince Gamini, having heard the king's verdict fled immediately to Kotmale in the Malaya country and lived there in disguise. As he went away angrily even without telling his father, he came to be named "Dustha Gamini," "Gamini the Wicked." One day the king, at a religious festival, summoned the ten great warriors to him and made them promise in front of the Sangha that they would not take the side of any one of the two brothers should there be a conflict between them.

King Kavantissa died, having ruled the country for sixty-four years. Prince Tissa came to Magama hurriedly, had his father's body cremated with due honours, took the state emblems, the elephant Kadol and mother Vihara and returned immediately to Digamadulla for fear of his brother Gamini. Ministers in Magama sent a message to Prince Gamini with the news and requested him to return at once. Gamini left Kotmale forthwith, came to Buttala and stationed security guards there, and then he proceeded to Magama where he was crowned as king with the blessings of the ministers. Then he sent a message to his brother Tissa asking him to return his mother, the elephant Kadol and other insignia of the state.

But the younger prince did not obey, saying, "Now father is no more. I'll live here looking after our mother." Prince Gamini replied, "I am the senior son, so, caring for our mother is my duty." He sent this message thrice. Yet Prince Tissa did not comply. Then for the fourth time, Gamini sent a message with words of anger. "If you do not obey this time, I know how I shall bring mother and Kadol the tusker." As Prince Tissa did not honor that request either, Prince Gamini set off with an army consisting of foot soldiers, horses and elephants. Prince Tissa too, disregarding relationship or brotherhood, advanced riding Kadol. The two brothers engaged in war at the field of Suluguna. The ten great warriors, honouring the pledge given to King Kavantissa, remained neutral without taking sides. Prince Gamini was defeated in the battle as hundreds of his men fell. So he fled away on his mare Dighatuni in the company of a minister also named Tissa. Prince Tissa began to chase after with his men. But he was forced to stop with the sudden appearance of a rocky mountain, which had been conjured by the *arahant* monks. Tissa knew that it was the work of monks and went back to Digamadulla with his men. Prince Gamini, while running away in defeat, stopped by the Paspanduru stream, got off the mare, removed his armour and told the minister: "Friend, I am very hungry, have you brought something to eat?" "Sire, I have brought some rice in a gold plate, please eat it." So saying, he offered the rice to the prince. But the prince, wishing to share his meal with the Sangha, told the minister to call the monks. When the minister did so, an *arahant* monk named Gotama, a former acquaintance of Gamini, heard the call from the island of Puvangu. He dispatched one of his assistant monks, one Kutumbiya Tissa. He went there by air and remained in the sky near the prince. Gamini took the alms-bowl from the monk, put in it the share kept aside for alms and added his own share to it as well. Having seen that, the minister too offered his portion to the monk. The mare Dighatuni too, wishing to offer her share looked at the prince and indicated so by scratching the ground with her hooves. So, Prince Gamini put her share also in the alms-bowl.

Thera Kutumbiya Tissa returned to the island Puvangu and handed the alms-bowl to Thera Gotama. He consumed that food, sharing it with five hundred monks and collecting a lump of rice from each one, put them all in the alms-bowl and sent it back by air, wishing it to go where the prince was and to stay in the air at a distance easily reachable by him. Gamini took it, shared the rice with the minister and the mare, and placing his armour as a holder under the bowl, sent it back to the monk.

Gamini went back to Magama and prepared for war again. Having built up a large army he set off to Dighavapi. Prince Tissa also went forth with his army. As the fighting continued the two brothers advanced at each other. Gamini saw that hundreds of men on both sides were falling, and thinking of stopping such unnecessary loss of life, as he needed men for the more important war with the Tamils, sent a message to his brother: "Stop fighting and killing our own men. Come to me without any fear." Having received that message, Tissa was enraged and brandishing his spear, spurred the elephant he was riding at Gamini. "It is not with brotherly love that Tissa is coming." Thinking so, keeping his sword ready, waiting on his mare and dodging the spear thrown at him by Tissa, he went forward. Driving the mare fast around Tissa's elephant, making frightened soldiers to run away, Gamini spurred his mare to jump over the back of the elephant. In doing so the prince tapped on the back of Tissa's armour with the hilt of his sword. Thus Gamini won the battle that day.

Kadol was disappointed with Prince Tissa for allowing the mare to jump over its back. The elephant thought that it had suffered humiliation, and shaking his back so that Tissa could not sit on it, and letting Tissa cling on to a branch, the elephant went up to Gamini. Tissa descended from the tree and ran into a nearby *vihara*. Gamini gave chase commanding his men not to kill Tissa, but to take him alive. Tissa ran in, worshipped the chief monk and begged him to save his life. Further, unable to stay there standing in the middle of the room, he crept under the monk's bed. The latter spread a robe on the bed so as to cover the prince. Gamini came into the *vihara* and asked the monk where Tissa was hiding. The monk answered "Your Majesty, Tissa is not *in* the bed." Gamini understood that Tissa was *under* the bed, but thought that it was not proper to cross question the "family deity" [the monk], went out quickly and took guard at the gate having positioned soldiers around the temple.

The chief monk of the *vihara*, wishing to send out Tissa, put him on a bed, covered him with a robe and ordered four young monks to carry that bed out of the *vihara*. Gamini knew that it was Tissa who was being carried in that bed, and called out to him, "Tissa, travelling on the shoulders of our family deities is not becoming of you. It is not proper for me to seize you from them either. So remember this kind gesture of the venerable brethren in the future."

Having thus admonished Tissa, Gamini went back to Magama and had Queen Vihara brought from Digamadulla in a procession. Then a monk named Godhagatta Tissa at the request of Prince Tissa, took him to Magama disguised as an acolyte. He went to see the king, leaving Tissa at the foot of the stairs. King Gamini welcomed the monk and began serving them with food. The chief monk, refusing the food by covering his bowl with his palm, told the king, "Sir, I have come here with Prince Tissa."

"Venerable Sir," said the king, "where is that mischievous lad now?"

"He is waiting by the foot of the stairs," the monk replied.

Upon hearing that, Queen Vihara ran down weeping, embraced Tissa and took him upstairs to King Gamini. Then the king said, "Venerable Sir, why did you take the trouble to bring him here in the company of so many monks? You could have sent him to me with a seven-year-old novice monk." And furthermore, "If your reverence had given him this advice before, you could have saved the life of many men. Therefore in this conflict, Venerable Sir, you are to be blamed." Then the two brothers, embraced each other, wept remembering their father and, having washed and changed, came back to the presence of the monks and served them with food and beverages.

King Gamini decided that before starting war with Tamils, it was necessary to make the country self-sufficient in rice. So he sent Prince Tissa back to Digamadulla instructing him to develop agriculture there by growing rice. The king himself, remaining at Magama, had large extents of paddy fields cultivated in that area. Having thus making the country self-sufficient in rice, the king made his soldiers happy with payments of money and gifts. Then he armed his soldiers with every kind of weapon and armour, placed sacred relics on the royal spear, and advancing with the fourfold forces such as elephants, cavalry, carriages and foot soldiers, he first stopped at the Tissamaha Vihara to pay respects to monks. "Venerable Sir, I am going across the river Mahaveli in order to save the Buddha Sasana. Kindly assign monks to go with me, so that I can worship them making offerings on the way. The presence of the Sangha along the way would be for our welfare as well as our safety."

The monks too, as self-inflicted punishment for the [inadvertent] offence of not intervening to stop the war between the two brothers, detailed a group of five hundred monks to accompany the king. Then King Gamini, having the road from Magama cleared and mended, with the group of monks leading the way, and in the company of his mother Queen Vihara, eleven thousand one hundred and eleven warriors, flanked on either side by the multitudes of soldiers, set off for war with the Tamil king.

Hordes of men in the king's army filled the distance between Magama and Gutthala. Passing through many villages . . . the troops who were ready to engage in active combat extended for four *gavu* [leagues] from east to west and north to south. Observing that enormous army, the king thought, "In comparison with the mighty Tamil army, this army of mine is just a pittance. Nevertheless, if I am really devoted to the Buddha Sasana and if my genuine intention is to save and develop the tradition, let the gods help me." Having made this wish, the king spent the night there, and in the next morning he worshipped the relic and offered food to the five hundred monks. Then the king left that village with his army bearing weapons to the accompaniment of the sound of many kinds of drums, pipes, etc. The king led the way like Sakra, King of the Gods in splendor setting out to fight with the Asuras. When they arrived at Miyugunu, they fought with Chatra, the Tamil captain and his thirty thousand men, killed them all and threw the bodies into the river. Then the king had the stupa at Miyugunu renovated and enlarged to a height of eighty cubits.

From Miyugunu, King Dutugemunu advanced with his forces via Ambutuwa; he vanquished the Ambutu Tamil there in four months; from there he continued to Sat Bä Kotte, where he fought with the seven brothers and defeated them on the same day. From there he went to Aturamba and, having defeated the Tamil warrior Mahatunda with his soldiers, he then advanced through Denagama, Hālakala, Pälvatta, Vasittha, Gamini, Kumbha, Nandika, Khānuka, Tambunāgama and Damunnaru. In the fight at Damunnaru, the troops of the two parties, unable to identify the enemy in confusion, ended up killing their own men. So King Gamini declared the following truth: "I am not waging this war for the sake of enjoying the pleasures of kingship, but for the sake of saving Buddhism. By the power of this truth, may all the armour and arms of my men glitter, and may it not be so of the Tamils." As soon as the king made this declaration it happened as he wished. Having taken that fortress, Dutugemunu advanced to Vijithapura, taking over twenty-four enemy camps on the way.

At Vijithapura, before attacking that fortress, the king decided to test the strength of the ten warriors. He had a huge vessel placed on a heap of gold coins and filled it with sixteen pots of toddy. He then challenged the ten great warriors to drink up the toddy in one go. If anyone amongst them were capable, that one would own the gold. As most of the warriors kept quiet, the king challenged Suranimala. He drank up the toddy without leaving even a drop and distributed the gold to the people who had gathered to watch. Having tested him, the king thought of testing Nandimitra. For this purpose he made the elephant Kadol drunk with toddy thus making the beast mad and violent. The elephant went berserk, ran along the path destroying and attacking every one and everything on its way. When all others ran away in fear, Nandimitra clapped his hands and uttered his war cry. The royal elephant stopped and charged at the warrior, but the latter took hold of the beast's trunk and putting it over his shoulder, catching the two tusks, threw back the giant beast while squatting on its haunches. People were thrilled watching this fight between Nandimitra and the elephant and went away praising the strength of the warrior. The village where this fight took place came to be named as "Athupora" (elephant-fight).

After testing his chief warriors thus, Dutugemunu set off to attack Vijithapura. Tamils also came out to face the Sinhala army. In the ensuing battle Velusumana killed thousands of Tamil soldiers riding his horse near the eastern gate. The enemy soldiers then withdrew into the fort in fear of Velusumana and closed the gates. Then King Dutugemunu deployed the warriors to fight at the four gates with their men. Vijithapura was a strong fortification well protected with three moats and a massive wall eighteen cubits high. Fully armed soldiers guarded its gates with towers made of iron. Archers on the wall and those positioned in watch towers shot thousands of arrows at the attackers. At the same time, rocks and heated iron balls were shot by means of mechanical devices. Meanwhile Kadol was attacking the southern gate, trying to break in the iron door by piercing it with his tusks. The Tamils poured molten iron on his back from above. The elephant ran away in severe pain and jumped into the moat. Then Gothayimbara, the great warrior, bullied the beast saying, "Hey elephant, fighting is not easy as gulping pots of toddy. Get out of the water if you are smart. Break that gate."

The tusker Kadol, having heard those insulting words, trumpeted as loudly as the roll of thunder and lifting his trunk dashed out of the water. Veterinary doctors treated him and dressed the wounds. The king ascended his back, fed him delicacies and spoke to him with kind and cajoling words. Then he covered Kadol's back with several layers of leather armour and sent him back to break the gate. Kadol, roaring aloud, attacked the iron door and kicked it with his might. The large door and its frame broke, but the debris fell on the animal. Nandimitra saw this and dashed to save the beast; he flung the heavy debris aside with his shoulders. Kadol, on seeing it, forgot his previous displeasure with Nandimitra and offered to take him on its back to the fortress. But Nandimitra rejected the offer, saying, "Have I ever entered through a gate opened by another?" So saying, he attacked the wall with his bare shoulders by making a large opening. Once inside the fort, Velusumana, riding his horse as fast as a flash of lightning, killed the enemy. Kadol killed the Tamils by beating them with a carriage wheel. Nandimitra did so by using a cart wheel. Gothyimbara uprooted a coconut tree and beat the Tamils with it. Suranimala used his sword to kill the enemy. Mahasona took a palm tree for a weapon and Theraputtabhaya wielded an iron bar in the fight.

After destroying and taking the stronghold at Vijitapura, Dutugemunu continued seizing several more forts on the way and encamped at Kasagalu Galpakada. There, he constructed a reservoir and began enjoying water sports in the month of Poson. Having heard about this, King Elara of Anuradhapura summoned captains of his army and sought their advice. Then, his captains lead by Digajanthu, told the king not to worry, but to set off the next day to face Dutugemunu and his army. King Elara, making his men happy by giving them gold and other gifts, prepared for war and sent word to Dutugemunu, "Why do you tarry there having come to fight? Come for the battle tomorrow."

"You don't have to remind me, I am already on my way," Dutugemunu sent his reply. Then King Dutugemunu called his captains and consulted them, saying, "We have to face the mighty army of Elara tomorrow. This battle is not similar to the previous ones. What shall we do?"

The captains said, "Great king, not only Elara and his army, but even if the kings of India challenge us in war, still they won't be able to defeat us. Go to the battle field with no fear." So King Dutugemunu went forth the next day to face King Elara. The latter advanced on his elephant named Parvata followed by his mighty army.

Dutugemunu, for protection from Digajanthu, constructed thirty-two forts placing within them images of himself, made out of Kihiri wood, according to instructions given by his mother. He stayed inside a thirty-third

fortress. When the two rival forces were engaged in fierce battle, Digajanthu jumped up in the air and advanced somersaulting in search of Dutugemunu. He descended on the first fort cutting down the wooden image
within it. Thus, he flew from fort to fort cutting in half the images kept
in each one and finally reached the last. Warrior Suranimala saw him and
called out, brandishing his sword, "Hey, Tamil, come to me first!" Digajanthu heard this and deciding to kill Suranimala began descending upon him.
Suranimala saw him and waited, guarding his head with the shield. Digajanthu hit the shield with his sword but Suranimala let go of it at once. Digajanthu fell on the ground and Suranimala cut him in two without giving
him a chance to stand up. Phussadeva blew on his conch making a sound
similar to that of hundreds of thunder blasts. Tamil soldiers were driven
mad by that sound and ran away in fear. Elara, too, thought, "What fighting
is there left for me when Digajanthu has fallen?" He turned back with his
elephant at once and began to flee.

Water in a nearby lake got stirred and discoloured by the blood of the
thousands of heads that were cut off that day in the war. Therefore from
that day, that lake came to be known as Kalatha-wewa (the lake with stirred
water). Dutugemunu spoke thus: "Elara is my charge. No one else should
kill him." Having uttered these words he gave chase to Elara on Kadol and
caught up with him at the southern gate of Anuradhapura. The duel of the
two kings took place there.

This is how the two kings fought: King Elara threw his spear at Dutugemunu. Evading the spear, Dutugemunu spurred his elephant on and made it
stab Elara's elephant with its tusks. At the same time Dutugemunu stabbed
Elara with his spear, piercing his body. Elara fell on the spot with his elephant. Having thus vanquished enemy forces and uniting the entire country, followed by the fourfold force, King Dutugemunu entered the city of
Anuradhapura like Sakra, King of the Gods, in the company of his heavenly
retinue.

King Dutugemunu summoned people from around an area of four leagues
by beating drums, and conferring all due respects to Elara's body, having it
taken in a coffin made of gold, had it cremated. At the place Elara was cremated, enshrining his ashes Dutugemunu had a stupa constructed in the
name of the defeated king. Then he made the following declaration: "In the
future all the kings including me, should not pass this stupa riding elephants,
horses, carriages, palanquins, etc. They should not go beating drums either."
Then he had a stone inscription established with that decree.

Translated from Sinhala by Udaya P. Meddegama

Sirisamghabodhi and the Ideals of Buddhist Kingship

Anonymous, comp. *Mahanama Thera*

Today, Sri Lankan Buddhists may fondly recall many of their former kings—Devanampiya Tissa (third century BCE), for example, Dutugemunu (second century BCE), Parakramabahu I (twelfth century CE), or Kirti Sri Rajasimha (eighteenth century CE)—before they recall King Sirisamghabodhi, of the third century CE. A short account of Sirisamghabodhi appears in the Mahavamsa, *compiled by Mahanama Thera, and is reproduced below. Sirisamghabodhi, however, was so revered in earlier time for his ideals of moral purity and selfless sacrifice that every other king from the third to the sixteenth century CE included his name formally within his own. No other king in Sri Lankan history left such a legacy. Sirisamghabodhi symbolized the quintessential ideals of enlightened Buddhist kingship.*

The king, who was known by the name Sirisamghabodhi, reigned [only] two years in Anuradhapura, keeping the five [moral] precepts.

. . . When the king heard that the people of the island were come to want by reason of a drought he himself, his heart shaken with pity, lay down on the ground in the courtyard of the Great Thupa, forming the resolve: "Unless I be raised up by the water that the god shall rain down I will nevermore rise up from hence, even though I die here." As the ruler of the earth lay there thus the god poured down rain forthwith on the whole island of Lanka, reviving the wide earth. And even then he did not yet rise up because he was not swimming in the water. Then his counselors closed up the pipes by which the water flowed away. And as he now swam in the water the pious king rose up. By his compassion did he in this way avert the fear of a famine in the island.

At the news: "Rebels are risen here and there," the king had the rebels brought before him, but he released them again secretly; then did he send secretly for bodies of dead men, and causing terror to the people by burning of these he did away with the fear from rebels.

A yakkha [demon] known as Ratakkhi, who had come hither, made red the eyes of the people here and there. If the people did but see one another and did but speak of the redness of the eyes they died forthwith, and the yakkha devoured them without fear.

When the king heard of their distress he lay down with sorrowful heart alone in the chamber of fasting, keeping the eight *uposatha* [full moon day] vows, (and said): "Till I have seen the yakkha I will not rise up." By the (magic) power of his piety the yakkha came to him. To the king's question: "Who art thou?" he answered: "It is I, (the yakkha)." "Why dost thou devour my subjects? Swallow them not!" "Give up to me then only the people of one region," said the other. And being answered: "That is impossible," he came gradually (demanding ever less and less) to one (man) only. The (king) spoke: "No other can I give up to thee; take thou me and devour me." With the words: "That is impossible," the other prayed him (at last) to give him an offering in every village. "It is well," said the king, and over the whole island he decreed that offerings be brought to the entrance of the villages, and these he gave up to him. Thus by the great man [*mahasattva*], compassionate [*karuna*] to all beings, by the torch of the island was the fear pestilence brought to an end.

The king's treasurer, the minister Gothakabhaya, who had become a rebel, marched from the north against the capital. Taking his water strainer with him the king fled alone by the south gate, since he would not bring harm to others.

A man who came, bearing his food in a basket, along that road entreated the king again and again to eat of his food. When he, rich in compassion, had strained the water and had eaten, he spoke these words, to show kindness to the other: "I am the king Sirisamghabodhi; take thou my head and show it to Gothakabhaya, he will give thee much gold." This he would not do, and the king to render him service gave up the ghost even as he sat. And the other took the head and showed it to Gothakabhaya and he, in amazement of spirit, gave him gold and carried out the funeral rites of the king with due care.

Anuradhapura: Fifth-Century Observations by a Chinese Buddhist Monk

Fa-Hien

Fa-Hien, Hsuan Tsang, and I Tsing, three Chinese Buddhist monastic pilgrims who traveled extensively throughout South and Southeast Asia between the fifth and seventh centuries CE, left detailed accounts of their travels for posterity. Their observations remain key sources of information for the condition of Buddhist religious culture during these times. Fa-Hien's account of the practice of Buddhism in the royal capital at Anuradhapura during the fifth century is the only description beyond the Mahavamsa that dates to this general time period. It contains a number of illuminating observations about kingship, veneration of the dalada (tooth relic, that is, tooth of the Buddha), the Jatakas (birth stories of the Buddha's previous lives), the number of Buddhist monks in Anuradhapura and throughout Sri Lanka, cremation rites, and belief in the future Buddha Maitreya. His descriptions of life in Anuradhapura date to the time in which the city was reaching the apex of its cultural maturity.

Following the course of the Ganges, and descending eastwards for eighteen yojanas, he [Fa-Hien] found on the southern bank the great kingdom of Champa, with topes [monuments] reared at the places where the Buddha walked in meditation by his vihara [temple], and where he and the three Buddhas, his predecessors sat. There were monks residing at them all. Continuing his journey east for nearly fifty yojanas, he came to the country of Tamalipti, (the capital of which is) a seaport. In the country there are twenty-two monasteries, at all of which there are monks residing. The Law of Buddha is also flourishing in it. Here Fa-hien stayed two years, writing out his Sutras, and drawing pictures of images.

After this he embarked in a large merchant vessel, and went floating over the sea to the southwest. It was the beginning of winter, and the wind was favorable; and after fourteen days, sailing day and night, they came to the country of Singhala. . . .

The kingdom is on a large island, extending from east to west fifty yojanas, and from north to south thirty. Left and right from it there are as many as 100 small islands, distant from another ten, twenty, or even 200 le; but all subject to the large island. Most of them produce pearls and precious stones of various kinds; there is one which produces the pure and brilliant pearl. . . . The king employs men to watch and protect it [the pearl fishery], and requires three out of every 10 such pearls, which the collectors find.

The country originally had no human inhabitants, but was occupied only by spirits and nagas [a class of indigenous people], with which merchants of various countries carried on a trade. When the trafficking was taking place, the spirits did not show themselves. They simply set forth their precious commodities, with labels of price attached to them; while the merchants made their purchases according to the price; and took the things away.

Through the coming and going of the merchants (in this way), when they went away, the people of their (various) countries heard how pleasant the land was, and flocked to it in number till it became a great nation. The (climate) is temperate and attractive, without any difference of summer and winter. The vegetation is always luxuriant. Cultivation proceeds whenever men think fit: there are no fixed seasons for it.

When Buddha came to this country, wishing to transform the wicked nagas, by his supernatural power he planted one foot at the north of the royal city, and the other on top of a mountain, the two being fifteen yojanas apart. Over the footprint at the north of the city the king built a large tope, 400 cubits high, grandly adorned with gold and silver, and finished with a combination of all the precious substances. By the side of the tope he further built a monastery, called the Abhayagiri, where there are (now) five thousand monks. There is in it a hall of Buddha, adorned with carved and inlaid work of gold and silver, and rich in the seven precious substances, in which there is an image (of Buddha) in green jade, more than twenty cubits in height, glittering all over with those substances, and having an appearance of solemn dignity which words cannot express. In the palm of the right hand there is a priceless pearl. Several years had now elapsed since Fa-Hien left the land of Han; the men with whom he had been in intercourse had all been of regions strange to him; his eyes had not rested on an old and familiar hill or river, plant or tree: his fellow travelers, moreover, had been separated from him, some by death, and others flowing off in different directions; no face or shadow was now with him but his own, and a constant sadness was in his heart. Suddenly (one day), when by the side of this image of jade, he saw a merchant presenting as his offering a fan of white silk; and the tears of sorrow involuntarily filled his eyes and fell down.

A former king of the country had sent to Central India and got a slip of the patra [bodhi] tree which he planted by the side of the hall of Buddha, where a tree grew up to the height of about 200 cubits. As it bent on one side towards the southeast, the king, fearing it would fall, propped it with a post eight or nine spans round. The tree began to grow at the very heart of the prop, where it met (the trunk); (a shoot) pierced through the post, and went down the ground, where it entered and formed roots, that rose (to the surface) and were about four spans round. Although the post was split in the middle, the outer portions kept hold (of the shoot) and people did not remove them. Beneath the tree there has been built a vihara, in which there is an image (of Buddha) seated, which the monks and commonalty reverence and look up to without ever becoming wearied. In the city there has been reared also the vihara of the Buddha's tooth, on which, as well as on the other, the seven precious substances have been employed.

The king practices the Brahmanical purifications, and the sincerity of the faith and reverence of the population inside the city are also great. Since the establishment of government in the kingdom there has been no famine of scarcity, no revolution or disorder. In the treasuries of the monkish communities there are many precious stones, and the priceless manis [gems]. One of the kings (once) entered one of those treasuries, and when he looked round and saw the priceless pearls, his covetous greed was excited, and he wished to take them to himself by force. In three days, however, he came to himself, and immediately went and bowed his head to the ground in the midst of monks, to show his repentance of the evil thought. As a sequel to this, he informed the monks (of what had been in his mind) and desired to make a regulation that from that day forth the king should not be allowed to enter the treasury and see (what it contained), and that no bhikku [monk] should enter it till after he had been in orders for a period of full forty years.

In the city there are many Vaisya [merchant caste] elders and Sabean merchants, whose houses are stately and beautiful. The lanes and passages are kept in good order. At the heads of the four principal streets there have been built preaching halls, where, on the eighth, fourteenth, and fifteenth days of the month, they spread carpets, and set forth a pulpit, while the monks and commonalty from all quarters come together to hear the Law. The people say that in the kingdom there may be altogether sixty thousand monks, who get their food from their common stores. The king, besides, prepares elsewhere in the city a common supply of food for five or six thousand more. When they want, they take their great bowls, and go (to the place of distribution), and take as much as the vessels will hold, all returning with them full.

The tooth of Buddha is always brought forth in the middle of the third month. Ten days beforehand the king grandly caparisons a large elephant, on which he mounts a man who can speak distinctly, and is dressed in royal robes, to beat a large drum, and the following proclamation: "The Bodhisattva, during three Asankhyeya-kalpas [uncountable periods of time], manifested his activity, and did not spare his own life. He gave up kingdom, city, wife, and son; he plucked out his eyes and gave them to another; he cut off a piece of his flesh to ransom the life of a dove; he cut off his head and gave it as alms; he gave his body to feed a starving tigress; he grudged not his marrow and brains. In many such ways as these did he undergo pain for the sake of all living. And so it was, that, having become Buddha, he continued in the world for forty-five years, preaching his Law, teaching and transforming, so that those who had no rest found rest, and the unconverted were converted. When his connexion with the living was completed, he attained to *pari-nirvana* (and died). Since that event, for 1,497 years, the light of the world has gone out, and all living things have long contained sadness. Behold! Ten days after this, Buddha's tooth will be brought forth, and taken to the Abhayagiri-vihara. Let all and each, whether monks or laics, who wish to amass merit for themselves, make the roads smooth and in good condition, grandly adorn the lanes and by-ways, and provide abundant store of flowers and incense to be used as offerings to it."

When this proclamation is over, the king exhibits, so as to line both sides of the road, the five hundred different bodily forms in which the Bodhisattva has in the course of his history appeared: here as Sudana, there as Sama; now as the king of elephants, and then as a stag or a horse. All these figures are brightly colored and grandly executed, looking as if they were alive. After this the tooth of Buddha is brought forth, and is carried along in the middle of the road. Everywhere on the way offerings are presented to it, and thus it arrives at the hall of Buddha in the Abhayagiri-vihara. There the monks and laics are collected in crowds. They burn incense, light lamps, and perform all the prescribed services, day and night without ceasing, till ninety days have been completed, when (the tooth) is returned to the vihara within the city. On fast-days the door of that vihara is opened, and the forms of ceremonial reverence are observed according to the rules.

Forty le to the east of the Abhayagiri-vihara there is a hill, with a vihara on it, called the Chaitya, where there may be 2,000 monks. Among them there is a Sramana [recluse] of great virtue, named Dharma-gupta honored and looked up to by all the kingdom. He has lived for more than forty years in an apartment of stone, constantly showing such gentleness of heart, that he has brought snakes and rats to stop together in the same room, without doing one another any harm.

South of the city seven le there is a vihara, called the Maha-vihara, where 3,000 monks reside. There had been among them a Sramana, of such lofty virtue, and so holy and pure in his observance of the disciplinary rules, that the people all surmised that he was an arhat [one who has perfected the spiritual path]. When he drew near his end, the king came to examine into the point; and having assembled the monks according to rule, asked whether the bhikshu [monk] had attained to the full degree of Wisdom. They answered in the affirmative, saying that he was an arhat. The king accordingly, when he died, buried him after the fashion of an arhat, as the regular rites prescribed. Four or five le east from the vihara there was reared a great pile of firewood, which might be more than thirty cubits square, and the same in height. Near the top were laid sandal, aloe, and other kinds of fragrant wood.

On the four sides (of the pile) they made steps by which to ascend it. With clean white hair-cloth, almost like silk, they wrapped (the body) round and round. They made a large carriage-frame, in form like our funeral car, but without dragons and fishes.

At the time of cremation, the king and the people, in multitudes from all quarters, collected together, and presented flowers and incense. While they were following the car to the burial-ground, the king himself presented flowers and incense. When this was finished, the car was lifted on the pile, all over which oil of sweet basil was poured, and then a light was applied. While the fire was blazing, every one, with a reverent heart, pulled off his upper garment, and threw it, with his feather-fan and umbrella, from a distance into the midst of the flames, to assist the burning. When the cremation was over, they collected and preserved the bones, and proceeded to erect a tope. Fa-Hien had not arrived in time (to see the distinguished Sramana) alive, and only saw his burial.

At that time the king, who was a sincere believer in the Law of Buddha and wished to build a new vihara for the monks, first convoked a great assembly. After giving the monks a meal of rice, and presenting his offerings (on the occasion), he selected a pair of first-rate oxen, the horns of which were grandly decorated with gold, silver, and the precious substances. A golden plough had been provided, and the king himself turned up a furrow on the four sides of the ground within which the building was to be. He then endowed the community of the monks with the population, fields, and houses, writing the grant on plates of metal (to the effect) that from that time onwards, from generation to generation, no one should venture to annul or alter it.

In this country, Fa-Hien heard an Indian devotee, who was reciting a Sutra from the pulpit say: "Buddha's alms bowl was first in Vaisali, and now it is in Gandhara. After so many hundred years" (he gave, when Fa-Hien heard him, the exact number of years, but he has forgotten it), "it will go to Western Tukhara; after so many hundred years, to Khoten; after so many hundred years, to Kharachar; after so many hundred years, to the land of Han; after so many hundred years, it will come to Sinhala; and after so many hundred years, it will return to Central India. After that, it will ascend to the Tushita heaven; and when the Bodhisattva Maitreya sees it, he will say with a sigh, 'The alms bowl of Sakyamuni is come'; and with all the devas [deities] he will present to it flowers and incense for seven days. When these have expired, it will return to Jambudvipa, where it will be received by the king of the sea nagas [serpent people], and taken to his naga palace. When Maitreya shall be about to attain to perfect Wisdom (and become Buddha), it will again separate into four bowls, which will return to the top of mount Anna, whence they came. After Maitreya has become Buddha, the four deva kings will again think of the Buddha (with their bowls as they did in the case of the previous Buddha). The thousand Buddhas of this Bhadra-kalpa, indeed, will all use the same alms bowl; and when the bowl has disappeared, the Law of Buddha will go on gradually to be extinguished. After that extinction has taken place, the life of man will be shortened, till it is only a period of five years. During this period of a five years' life, rice, butter, and oil will all vanish away, and men will become exceedingly wicked. The grass and tree which they lay hold of will change into swords and clubs, with which they will hurt, cut, and kill one another. Those among them on whom there is blessing will withdraw from society among the hills; and when the wicked have exterminated one another, they will again come forth and say among themselves, "The men of former times enjoyed a great longevity; but through becoming exceedingly wicked, and doing all these lawless things, the length of our life has been shortened and reduced even to five years. Let us now unite together in the practice of what is good, cherishing a gentle and sympathizing heart, and carefully cultivating good faith and righteousness. When each one in this way practices that faith and righteousness, life will go on and doubled its length until it reaches 80,000 years. When Maitreya appears in the world, and begins to turn the wheel of his Law, he will in the first place save those among the disciples of the Law left by the Sakya who have quitted their families, and those who have accepted the three Refuges, undertaken the five Prohibitions and the eight Abstinences, and given offerings to the three Precious Ones; secondly and thirdly, he will save those between whom and conversion there is a connection transmitted from the past."

Editor's Note

1. Legge's extensive footnotes were deleted from this account in the interest of space.

Path of Purification

Bhadantacariya Buddhaghosa

Beyond the canonical literature of the Pali Tipitaka, regarded as the veritable words of the Buddha constituting his Dhamma, Bhadantacariya Buddhaghosa's Visuddhimagga *(The Path of Purification) is perhaps the most revered doctrinal text in all of Theravada Buddhist tradition. Buddhaghosa's purpose was to write a definitive commentary in great detail on the significance of sila (virtue),* samadhi *(meditative concentration or consciousness), and* panna *(wisdom or understanding), the three elemental principles that form the basis of the Buddha's Noble Eightfold Path culminating in the experience of nibbana (nirvana). The following extract is taken from the very beginning of the text, a section that focuses on sila.*

> "When a wise man, established well in Virtue [sila],
> Develops Consciousness [samadhi] and Understanding [panna],
> Then as a bhikkhu ardent and sagacious
> He succeeds in disentangling this tangle." (S.i,13) [*Samyutta Nikaya*]

This was said. But why was it said? While the Blessed One was living at Savatthi, it seems, a certain deity came to him in the night, and in order to do away with his doubts he asked this question:

> "The inner tangle and the outer tangle—
> This generation is entangled in a tangle.
> And so I ask Gotama this question:
> Who succeeds in disentangling this tangle?" (S.i,13)

. . . However, when questioned thus, the Blessed One, whose knowledge of all things is unimpeded, Deity of Deities, excellent Sakka [Ruler of the Gods], excelling Brahma, fearless in the possession of the four kinds of perfect confidence, Wielder of the Ten Powers, All-seer with unobstructed knowledge, uttered this stanza in reply to explain the meaning:

> "When a wise man, established well in Virtue,
> Develops Consciousness and Understanding,

Then as a bhikkhu ardent and sagacious
He succeeds in disentangling this tangle."

My task is now to set out the true sense,
Divided in virtue and the rest,
Of this same verse composed by the Great Sage.
There are here in the Victor's Dispensation
Seekers gone forth from home to homelessness,
And who although desiring purity
Have no right knowledge of the sure straight way
Comprising virtue and the other two,
Right hard to find, that leads to purity.
To them I shall expound the comforting Path
Of Purification, pure in expositions,
Relying on the teaching of the dwellers
In the Great Monastery [the Mahavihara in Anuradhapura]; let all those
Good men who do desire purity
Listen intently to my exposition.

Herein, *purification* should be understood as nibbana which, being devoid of all stains, is utterly pure. *The Path of Purification* is the path to that purification; it is the means of approach that is called the *path.* . . .

In some instances this path of purification is taught by insight alone, according as it is said:

"Formations are all impermanent:
When he sees thus with understanding
And turns away from what is ill,
That is the path of purity." (*Dhammapada* 277)

And in some instances by jhana [meditative consciousness] and understanding according as it is said:

"He is near unto nibbana
In whom are jhana and understanding." (*Dhammapada* 372)

And in some instances by deeds (kamma), etc., according as it is said:

By deeds, vision and righteousness,
By virtue, the sublimest life—

By these are mortals purified,
And not by lineage and wealth. (*Majjhima Nikaya* III, 262)

And in some instances by virtue, etc., according as it is said:

"He who is possessed of constant virtue,
Has understanding, and is concentrated,
Is strenuous and diligent as well,
Will cross the flood so difficult to cross." (*Samyutta Nikaya* I, 53)

A Hydraulic Civilization

Chandra Richard de Silva

None of the magnificent accomplishments that characterized the civilization that
unfolded at Anuradhapura and Polonnaruva for fifteen centuries—the construction
of massive stupas within sprawling monastic campuses housing thousands of Bud-
dhist monks, the robust literary and artistic culture, the impressive trade carried out
with far-flung centers of power including Rome in the West and China in the East—
would have been possible without the sophisticated engineering feats that led to the
control of water resources and therefore the ample production of food. Sri Lankan
kings were such masters at mobilizing labor to build reservoirs that politicians since
the country's independence in 1948 have all found it expedient to stress water man-
agement schemes as intrinsic to their domestic economic policies.

The economic base of the Anuradhapura kingdom was agriculture and the
major preoccupation of its people the cultivation of food crops. These included peas, beans and dry grains but the major crop and the staple food of
the Indo-Aryan immigrants was rice. . . . This region had considerable advantages for rice cultivation: extensive periods of sunshine, a high constant
temperature and large extents of flat or nearly flat land. The soils, though
not particularly fertile, could be sufficiently enriched with compost and animal droppings to produce good crops. As the forest was much less thick than
in the wetter regions it could be cleared with less labor. There was, however,
one major problem and that was water.

Although some varieties of hill paddy can be grown without supplement-
ing the water supply obtained from rain, the higher yielding varieties of
paddy all need to stand in water through much of their period of growth. In
a tropical climate with high evaporation this necessarily involves the supply
of extra water from a pond, stream or reservoir. Rainfall in the dry zone,
however, was seasonal, most rain falling between October and April. During the rest of the year ponds dried up and many rivers flowing through
the region became trickles of water. Thus, even the tapping of rivers could
ensure the cultivation of only one crop of rice per year. Indeed, even this

was not totally secure, for the dry zone was subject to significant annual variations in rainfall. Rains could be abundant in one season and fail in the next. The only way to alleviate disaster when the rains failed was to have a scheme [that] diverted water from a perennial river to the shrunken streams of the dry zone. Fortunately, there was one such river—the Mahaveli Ganga, the largest river in Lanka. The Mahaveli Ganga, with its headwaters fed by the rains in the wet zone, never ran dry, but the development of the skill and the technology to harness its resources took centuries to evolve.

The early efforts at irrigation were modest. Dams of earth built across streams and small rivers enabled the conservation of water in village "tanks." Water could thus be diverted from the reservoirs to the fields as needed. These tanks were built from very early times. Their earliest mention in the chronicles goes back to the third century B.C. and inscriptions datable to the second century B.C. also refer to them. Many of the early reservoirs appear to have been owned by individuals and they dotted the countryside in Rajarata [north central Sri Lanka] and Rohana [southern coastal Sri Lanka]. The large number of shallow river valleys into which the dry zone was divided appears to have dictated this pattern of small village reservoirs.

As we noted earlier, such a system was no insurance against the failure of rain, and the chronicles refer to occasional famines in the early period. With the development of political unity, the increase of resources at the command of the ruler at Anuradhapura and the strengthening of the Buddhist concept that the ruler was responsible for the welfare of his subjects, the stage was set by the first century A.D. for greater royal intervention in irrigation. The chronicles record Vasabha (A.D. 67–111) as the first major tank-building king. He is said to have constructed eleven reservoirs, at least six of which have been identified by modern historians. Although these tanks are not as large as the giant reservoirs of the later era, they were much larger than the village tanks of the early period, the largest of them having a circumference of over two miles.

As important as tank building was, the activity attributed to Vasabha [most famously was] . . . the building [of] twelve irrigation canals. Of these only one, the Alahara (or Alisara) canal, is mentioned by name in the chronicles but that alone was a great achievement. Vasabha's canal took water from the Amban Ganga, a tributary of the Mahaveli, to the Malvatu Oya basin. It was perhaps thirty miles long and though it could only have carried a small quantity of water in Vasabha's time, it marked an important development. The waters of a perennial stream had been harnessed to supplement the resources of the seasonal Malvatu Oya. The construction of the canal showed that the technical problems of constructing dams across large rivers and of levelling and contouring [land] had been mastered by the Sinhalese by the first century A.D.

The period [that] followed saw a considerable expansion in irrigation and cultivation. Inscriptions from the first to the third century name almost one hundred and fifty reservoirs and canals [that] are not referred to in the chronicles. Together with the expansion in the number of reservoirs came further technological development; the discovery of the valve pit or the equivalent of the sluice gate. The Sinhalese had already evolved the technique of building broad-based tank bunds to retain the water. The development of the valve pit enabled the construction of the giant reservoirs of later times with the confidence that the outflow of water could be regulated at will.

The next stage of development, the building of the first giant reservoirs—is associated with Mahasena (A.D. 274–301). Perhaps the best known of these was the Minneriya reservoir, a veritable ocean which covered 4,670 acres. The old Alahara canal was enlarged and diverted to direct water into the reservoir which irrigated a large surrounding area. Another reservoir, the Tissavaddhamanaka vapi or the Kavudulu vava, constructed by Mahasena was almost as large as Minneriya and was fed both by the Kavudulu Oya and by a canal from the Minneriya reservoir. The chronicles attribute the building of sixteen reservoirs and one great canal to Mahasena. . . .

The irrigation system as it had evolved in the Rajarata by the third century was supplemented by spurts of building activity in the reigns of a few able kings. Dhatusena (A.D. 455–473) for instance built the gigantic Kalavava by damming the Kala Oya. The embankment of this tank is said to have been over three miles long and surplus water from the reservoir was taken to the vicinity of Anuradhapura by means of the Jaya Ganga. The Jaya Ganga was a tribute to the skill and expertise of the Sinhalese canal-builders of old, for it was fifty-four miles long and the gradient in the first seventeen miles was just six inches to the mile. . . .

One hundred years later, Moggallana II (A.D. 531–551) supplemented the network by the construction of the Padaviya reservoir and the Naccaduva vava—two reservoirs of great size. A canal from the Naccaduva tank supplemented the water supply to the Nuwara vava, one of the tanks near Anuradhapura. A generation later the two kings Aggabodhi I (A.D. 571–604) and Aggabodhi II (A.D. 604–614) further extended the utilization of the waters of the Mahaveli. They built two immense reservoirs—the Kantalai and Giritale tanks. . . . A dam at Minipe diverted the waters of the Mahaveli through a canal to the Kantalai tank while another dam at Hattota on the Kaluganga, a tributary of the Mahaveli, redirected the waters of that river to the Alahara Canal.

Except for the reign of Sena II (A.D. 853–887) the construction of major irrigation works in the Anuradhapura period seems to have ceased after the reign of Aggabodhi II (A.D. 604–614). It is difficult to explain why no further major works were constructed for the next three and a half centuries as most of that period was one of peace. Perhaps the maintenance of existing tanks and canals was in itself a considerable task. Indeed, some indications of famine in the tenth century seem to indicate that parts of the irrigation network were not working as efficiently as they ought to have done or that they proved inadequate when the rains failed. It is clear, however, that the bulk of the tanks and canals constructed up to the seventh century continued to be in use for the next three centuries or so and that they provided the economic foundation of the Anuradhapura civilization.

The provision of water enabled the cultivation of two crops of rice instead of one and also the growing of other crops such as vegetables, pulses and beans. The growth of the irrigation network and the increasing role of the state in the construction of irrigation works increased the power and influence of the king. Royal revenues rose with the imposition of taxes on water and a complex bureaucracy of officials emerged to deal with the construction and maintenance of tanks and canals and the regulation of water supplies. On the other hand, the development of irrigation facilities did not lead to the growth of a centralized monarchy. Individuals as well as the state continued to own reservoirs and canals and despite the attention that the giant reservoirs attracted, most land continued to be cultivated from minor and village reservoirs built by individuals or communities. Indeed, ownership of reservoirs and canals formed an important factor in the economic dominance of the nobility in this period. What the great irrigation works achieved was to ensure greater productivity and greater protection against drought. They enabled the development of high population densities in some areas. The increased sophistication, however, implied increased vulnerability, for failure at one point due to defective maintenance or deliberate sabotage had disastrous consequences for the entire irrigation system.

Sigiri Graffiti

Anonymous

Sigiriya, a magnificent palace fortress situated on top of a spectacular six-hundred-foot-high rock located about forty miles south of Anuradhapura, was temporarily a royal capital during the reign of King Kassapa I (r. 478–96?). The bizarre story accounting for the reasons of its construction—one that figures in the parricide of the great king Dhatusena (r. 460–78); who had built the massive Kala Wewa reservoir, and fear of a brother's (Moggallana I) revenge—is detailed at length in the monastic Culavamsa [37:80–38:29]. One of the most notable features of the remains at Sigiriya is a series of paintings of female figures found in a cavernous pocket at a spot halfway up the western face of the rock, and accessible now only by ladder. (See fourth page of color plates between pages 224 and 225.)

These paintings are what survive of a much greater number that once adorned the face of the rock. Far below the paintings a pathway runs round the rock, leading through the claws of an immense brick-built lion to the summit. A stretch of this pathway is enclosed on its outer side by a wall coated with highly polished lime plaster. This wall, known as the "Mirror Wall," is covered with little etchings in ancient Sinhala script, a large number of which have now been deciphered and published in two large volumes (S. Paranavitana, Sigiri Graffiti [Oxford, 1956]). These poems, written at intervals during the four centuries or so following the reign of King Kassapa, are concerned mostly with the rock paintings depicting these heavenly maidens.

While the actual interpretation of many of these verses is still provisional, it is impossible to pass over these earliest recorded examples of Sinhala poetry, especially as they are so different from anything that followed them for a very long period of time.

17. We spoke
    But they did not answer.
    Those ladies of the mountain,
    They did not give us
    The twitch of an eye-lid.

19. She answers no one.
     For her king has died.
     So your eyes are jewels.
     They remain still.
     If they had stirred even a little.

51. Sweet girl,
     Standing on the mountain,
     Your teeth are like jewels,
     Lighting the lotus of your eyes.
     Talk to me gently of your heart.

65. Seeing these beauties with their golden skins,
     How can they set their hearts at rest?
     Though their faces smile,
     Their lips are silent.
     Is it for secret ends
     They linger on the mountain?

89. On their breasts are golden chains
     And still they beckon.
     Seeing these lovely ladies,
     I want no other life.

106. Dry as a flower
     That has fallen on a rock
     Are the hearts of those beauties
     Whose golden skins
     Have caught my mind.

124. The long-eyed women
     Are parted from their lover,
     Are grieving for the king.
     Their eyes are blue lotuses.
     The song sung to the painting.

126. The girl with the golden skin
     Enticed the mind and eyes.
     Her lovely breasts
     Caused me to recall
     Swans drunk with nectar.

216. Who is not happy when he sees
     Those rosy palms, rounded shoulders,
     Gold necklaces, copper-hued lips
     And long long eyes?

665. Seeing you posturing on the mountain
     My heart delighted when it saw
     That flowers were in your hand.

Translated from the ancient Sinhala by S. Paranavitana and W. G. Archer

Set in Stone

Mahinda IV and Anonymous

The long line of kings of Sri Lanka left, in inscriptions carved in stone and copper and gold plates, an extended historical record of their generous endowments and judgments. The first two inscriptions below come from the reign of Mahinda IV in the tenth century CE and tell us, in the first instance, much about how kings of Anuradhapura regarded their religious identities and chief responsibilities for the Buddhist monastic sangha. We also learn in detail about the nature and severity of laws and punishments for serious offences. The third inscription, which is not of royal origin, comes from Tiriyaya on the northeast coast. Only fragments have survived, but it remains a historically crucial inscription because it documents a Mahayana Buddhist community. In its conclusion, it refers to an ancient legend about how two merchants, the first laymen to encounter the Buddha following his enlightenment, enshrined a hair relic of the master at the local caitya (stupa) for veneration. The same myth has been retold in Afghanistan in relation to the relics of Bamiyan, and in Burma in relation to the relics of the Shwedagon Pagoda in Yangon.

Slab Inscription (No. 2) of Mahinda IV

[Lines 51–56] The regulations thus enacted should always be maintained with due regard by the descendants of our dynasty, the Ksatriya lords devoted to the Buddha, who [of yore] have received the assurance [made by] the omniscient Lord of Sages, the pinnacle of the Sakya race, that none but the Bodhisattas would become kings of prosperous Lanka; who are wont to wear the white scarf to serve and attend on the great community of monks on the very day they celebrate the coronation festival after attaining to the dignity of kingship, bestowed by the great community of monks for the purpose of defending "the bowl and the robe" of the Buddha.

[Lines 56–60] These regulations should also be observed by the great community of monks belonging to the line of teachers, the servants of the

Dharma, who do not transgress the Path of the Law, whose thoughts are bent upon the observation of the precepts and the elimination of passion, who preserve the Buddhist religion even though [in so doing] they sacrifice their life.

Vevalkatiya Slab Inscription of Mahinda IV

[Lines 1–6] Prosperity on the tenth day of the first half of the (lunar) month of *Undvap* (Nov.–Dec.) in the (ninth) year, after the canopy of dominion was raised by the great king Siri Sangbo Abhay, son of the great king Siri Sangbo, lord by lineal succession of the lords of the soil of the Island of Lanka, which has become [as it were] the chief queen unto the Ksatriya princes descended from the royal line of the Okkaka dynasty, the pinnacle of the very illustrious Ksatriya race.[1]

[Lines 6–14] Touching the *dasa-gam* from amongst the endowments to Demel-vehera [Tamil monastery] at Kibi-nilam in Amgam-kuliya in the Northern Quarter, each headman [of these villages], as well as those headmen and householders who have given security for Kibi-gam, shall ascertain [the facts], when in any spot within this [district] murder or robbery with violence has been committed. Thereafter they shall sit in session and inquire of the inhabitants of the *dasa-gam* [in regard to these crimes]. The proceedings [of the inquiry] having been so recorded that the same may be produced [thereafter], they shall have the murderer punished with death. Out of the property taken by thieves by violence, they shall have such things as have been [duly] identified, restored to the respective owners, and have [the thieves] hanged.

[Lines 14–18] If [offenders] are not detected, the inhabitants of the *dasa-gam* shall find them and have them punished within forty-five days. Should they not find them, then the *dasa-gam* shall be made to pay [a fine of] 125 *kalandas* [weight] of gold to the State.

[Lines 18–20] If [the case] be an aggravated assault and not murder, [a fine of) 50 *kalandas* [weight] of gold shall be exacted as [penalty for] damage to life. Should this not be feasible, *ge-dad* [retribution—*Ed.*] shall be exacted. If [however, the assailants] are not detected, the *dasa-gam* shall be made to pay [a fine of] 50 *kalandas* [weight] of gold to the State. . . .

[Lines 25–30] Those who have slaughtered buffaloes, oxen, and goats shall be punished with death. Should [the cattle] be stolen but not slaughtered, after due determination [thereof], each [offender] shall be branded under the armpit. If [the nature of the offence] be not determined, [the culprits] shall be beaten. The buffaloes, oxen, and goats which are brought from outside for sale, shall only be bought after due identification of them and on security being given.

[Lines 31–36] Those who have effaced brand-marks shall be made to stand on red-hot iron sandals. The inhabitants of these *dasa-gam* shall observe without transgression the privileges they enjoy on [occasions of] rejoicing and mourning that occur in their respective families. If there be a villager who has come from (outside?) the limits prescribed for these *dasa-gam*, [he] shall be [duly] identified, and after taking security, shall be allowed to remain [in the *dasa-gam*]. . . .

Tiriyay Rock Inscription

. . . by [those] who were having hearts of unceasing devotion, of pure virtue, who desired the merit of being the very first to give . . . [to] the Blessed One, the incomparable teacher, the ornament of Sakya kings, the Sugata . . . who had excellently obtained relics . . . in the presence of the companies of merchants who were skilful in navigating the sea, engaged in buying and selling and who [possessed] a display of goods laden in sailing vessels of divers sorts. Owing to the influence of merit, by a friendly *devata* [deity—Ed.] who was of their own [kin] . . . to come having crossed the ocean as performed by all the companies of merchants who were very tranquil, who possessed [various] virtues united together [in them], including the inhabitants of the city who had come [there], with unabated pleasure . . . that which is known in the world as the excellent Girikandika-caitya . . . where offerings have been made, which contains charming grounds of courtyards, which is frequently worshipped with devotion by multitudes of pious men, having worshipped that excellent Girikandika-caitya . . . the Great Sage, who is manifested . . . where dwells always the Bodhisattva, the teacher, known as Avalokitesvara, who is worthy to be honoured by gods and *kinnaras*, . . . the Blessed One . . . that Girikandika-caitya, I, too, . . . the Sage, too, of sweet speech, the burning poison of mental transgression . . . where the Blessed One, of very delicate body, attains indeed a corporeal splendor beautified by the brightness of golden ornaments, that excellent Girikandika-caitya, I, too, do worship Girikandi [ka-caitya], to which divine nymphs, [bearing] scented water in receptacles made of lotus leaves from the celestial river, and carrying, held in their hands, flowers, incense, jewel-lamps, and oblations, descend gracefully from the heavenly city, and perform, with delight, the worship, of the Blessed One . . . the king of gods, too, followed by numerous attendant gods, does obeisance at the excellent Girikandika, [sounding] very lovely celestial chanks, drums . . . and scattering heaps of fresh flowers produced in the celestial trees . . . worshipped daily, on the great rock . . . [at which are] hundreds of . . . , worthy to be honored, prepared by the lord of the Simhalas and [his] people . . . which causes freedom from affliction . . . I, too, worship the [relic] of the Buddha deposited in Girikandi which is adored by multitudes of noble ones . . . of the Blessed One, which dispels all darkness, . . . with mind bent on the shrine of the Girikandi-caitya . . . whatever merit has been caused, by that let the miseries of existence of the world be reduced . . . the Girikandi-caitya founded by the companies of merchants [named] Trapussaka and Vallika. All phenomena are transitory.[2]

Editor's Notes

1. The Vevalkatiya Slab inscription was first published in *Epigraphia Zeylonica* 1 (1912): 248–51; brackets and parentheses in original unless otherwise indicated.
2. Published in *Epigraphia Zeylanica* 4 (1943): 159–60.

Anuradhapura: A Photographic Essay

John Clifford Holt

Evidence of sophisticated civilization in Anuradhapura is found most clearly in its massive tank and irrigation infrastructure and also in its artistic and architectural legacy. Indeed, the sculptural works of the middle to late first millennium CE were never again rivaled in later periods of Sri Lankan history. While some of the styles were heavily influenced first by Amaravati and later by Pallava styles of sculpture from south India, much of Anuradhapura's symbolism remains unique. The enigmatic "Man and his horse" at Isurumuniya, for example, indicates that not all art was religious in substance.

Naga (serpent), symbol of water and therefore purity and fertility. Stone carving (approx. 4 ft.), circa eighth century, at the back end of the "Twin Ponds," Abhyagiriya Vihara (monastic complex), at Anuradhapura. Photo by editor.

Moonstone entry slab. Carving (approx. 5 × 8 ft.), circa eighth century, Abhyagiriya Vihara, Anuradhapura. Photo by editor.

Dvarapala "support" figure carved in one of the stairs above the moonstone entry slab. Stone carving (approx. 6 in.), circa eighth century, Abhyagiriya Vihara, Anuradhapura. Photo by editor.

Large, elaborate guard stone (such stones are typically placed at the base of stairs leading into important monastic buildings or shrines). Carving (approx. 6 ft.), circa eighth century, Abhyagiriya Vihara, Anuradhapura. Photo by editor.

(below) "Man and his horse." Image carved into a massive boulder above a royal pleasure pond that later became part of a monastic complex or *vihara* (approx. 3 × 3 ft.), circa eighth century, Isurumuniya, Anuradhapura. Photo by editor.

(above) Monastic bathing pond (approx. 300 yds. long), Abhayagiriya Vihara, Anuradhapura. Photo by editor.

(left) Ruvanvalisaya Stupa. First century BCE (restored twentieth century), Mahavihara, near the Sri Mahabodhi shrine, Anuradhapura. This is the first of the massive *caitya*s built in Anuradhapura during the first half of the first millennium CE. Photo by editor.

Avukuna Buddha (approx. 40 ft.). Amaravati style, eighth century, approx. fifty miles south-southwest of Anuradhapura near the massive Kala Wawa tank constructed by Dhatusena. Photo by editor.

"Modern Anuradhapura" by Tilak Jayatilaka. The tank to the right shows that the ancient city became a staging area for the Sri Lanka army in its war with the Tamil militants to the north. Drawn especially for *The Sri Lanka Reader*.

"Guarding Anuradhapura" by Tilak Jayatilaka. Drawn especially for *The Sri Lanka Reader*.

Tamil Identity in Ancient Sri Lanka

K. Indrapala

Little material evidence remains of a specifically Tamil presence in the northern regions of Sri Lanka before the thirteenth century. This material fact of the matter constitutes a difficult and perhaps intractable problem for Sri Lankan historians because the Tamils and their predecessors, the Nagas, are thought to have populated various regions of the country, especially in the north, for perhaps as long as the Sinhalas. In the following excerpts from his book, K. Indrapala, one of the leading Tamil historians of Sri Lanka, outlines the issues in play during the first millennium CE *that gave rise to a distinctive Sri Lankan Tamil identity by the ninth century. The page numbers from which each excerpt is taken appear in brackets at the end of the excerpt.*

The ethnic conflict in Sri Lanka has helped to publicise the name "Tamil" in many parts of the world in a manner that the Dravidian movement in Tamil Nadu could not achieve. But has that helped to define a Tamil? We hear of the Arab-Israeli conflict several times a week, but who is an Arab? In fact, the problem relates to almost every ethnic name. Such is the complexity of defining an ethnic group.

Ethnicity is a social attribute and not a physical one. A convenient definition of the ethnos, the ethnic group, accepted by historians and archaeologists, is quoted by the archaeologist Colin Renfrew: "a firm aggregate of people, historically established in a given territory, possessing in common relatively stable peculiarities of language and culture, and also recognizing their unity and difference from other similar formations (self-awareness) and expressing this in a self-appointed name (ethnonym)." Agreeing with this definition, Renfrew points out that this "allows us to note the following factors, all of them relevant to the notion of ethnicity: 1. shared territory or land, 2. common descent or 'blood,' 3. a common language, 4. community of customs or culture, 5. community of beliefs or religion, 6. self-awareness, self-identity, 7. a name (ethnonym) to express the identity of the group, 8. shared origin story (or myth) describing the origin and history of the group." This definition is useful in the study of the Sri Lankan situation.

Ethnic identities in the modern world are based on self-perception. This is the guiding principle in the identification of the different ethnic groups. There are, however, various indicators of ethnicity, although it is not always easy to use these to identify a person's ethnic group. Language, for instance, is one such indicator but it does not apply to every case. While the Sinhalese language is, without argument, an indicator of Sinhalese ethnicity, it is not possible to use the Tamil language in a similar manner as an indicator of Tamil ethnicity. The speakers of the Tamil language in Sri Lanka are not a single homogeneous ethnic community. Among the Tamil-speakers, there are three main groups, the Sri Lankan Tamils, the Tamils of Indian origin and the Sri Lankan Muslims, each perceiving itself as a separate ethnic group. Yet another small group, the Colombo Chetties, which considered itself as a part of the Sri Lankan Tamils until the last decades of the twentieth century, now wishes to be identified as a community distinct from the Sri Lankan Tamils. Not all speakers of the Tamil language consider themselves Tamils. The Muslims of Sri Lanka, the vast majority of whom speak Tamil as their mother tongue, do not consider themselves to be Tamils. And there are also some who do not speak Tamil but consider themselves Tamils. [2–3]

Evolution of major identities: a local development. The Sinhalese are an ethnic identity that evolved in Sri Lanka through the assimilation of various segmentary/tribal and ethnic communities that occupied the island at the beginning of the EIA [early Iron Age], about five or six centuries before the Common Era. Long distance trade brought traders who spoke Prakrit, the lingua franca of the South Asian region at that time. Shortly before the third century BCE, it is possible that Buddhist and Jaina monks, too, arrived in the island in the wake of trade. This would have strengthened the position of Prakrit as the language of the elite. Later, the adoption of Buddhism by the ruler at Anuradhapura and the people under his rule, the organization of a strong Buddhist church and the use of Prakrit as the written language of the elites helped to forge different communities together and to evolve a common language with elements from the local languages. The diversity of cultures in the island created the need for the use of Prakrit as the unifying language. As can be learned from the history of many other countries, such as Britain, language in this early period cannot be equated with an ethnic group. Those who argue in favour of "Indo-Aryans" settling in Sri Lanka assume that the Prakrit-speakers who came to the island were the people who introduced the Indo-Aryan languages to north India. It is often forgotten that in the subcontinent, too, Indo-Aryan languages spread through a process of language replacement among myriad cultural groups that were already settled there.

The Tamils of Sri Lanka evolved as a second ethnic group. Their evolution was parallel to that of the Sinhalese. The earliest inscriptions and the early Pali chronicles attest to the presence of the Tamils (Damedas/Damilas) in the EIA. The spread of cultural influences from the Tamil-speaking region of south India, possibly including the spread of the Tamil language, in the same period, is evidenced by archaeology. It would appear that Tamil-speaking traders formed the elite in northern Sri Lanka and their dominance began the process of replacing the local language or languages by Tamil. The proximity of northern Sri Lanka to Tamil Nadu and the frequent rise of dominant political entities there reinforced the local Tamil-speaking population in considerable numbers, thus working against the total assimilation of the Tamils into the majority Sinhalese group. The Tamils who lived in the southern parts of the island were assimilated into the Sinhalese population. This is a process that has continued until modern times. In the northwest, north and east, however, various ethnic groups, including the Telugus, Keralas, Kannadas, Sinhalese and, later, even some Malay (Javaka) elements, came under the dominant influence of Tamil-speakers and contributed to the evolution of a distinct Tamil community there. [30–31]

Emerging personalities. The period from about the beginning of the fourth century to about the end of the ninth century is a dark period as far as the northern and eastern regions (the present-day areas predominantly settled by Tamils) are concerned. The Pali and Sinhalese chronicles have no information of any significance about either the rulers or the people of these regions. While a few inscriptions have been found in the eastern region, so far no inscription of this period has come to light in the northern region, with the exception of an inscribed carnelian seal. Archaeological remains of this period, however, have been identified but no proper study of these artifacts has been undertaken. The references to this region in the south Indian Tamil literary sources are also few and far between.

Although the paucity of historical sources makes this a dark period, it is the most significant in the evolution of the separate Tamil ethnic group of ancient Sri Lanka. It is the phase in which various early historic communities in the northern third of the island came under the dominant influence of Tamil-speakers and the Saiva religion. Clearly, the two chief unifying factors in the evolution of a single Tamil ethnic identity were the Tamil language and the Saiva religion, which are seen as the distinctive features of the Sri Lankan Tamils at the beginning of the tenth century.

All the available evidence at the end of the third century points to the presence of various ethnic groups in the island. As seen earlier, from about 300 BCE, the people of the island, the descendants of the mesolithic inhabitants as well as others who had arrived later, were coming under the influence of very strong forces that were clearly leading to the emergence of a homogeneous group in the areas ruled by the Anuradhapura kings as well as in the southern parts of the island. In these areas, the Hela language and the Buddhist religion continued to be the chief unifying factors, although here too the Hela language appears to have been under notable pressure from Tamil. In the extreme north of the island a different process, culminating in the emergence of a Tamil-speaking group, was taking place at this time. The successive steps in this long process cannot be easily observed with the evidence that is available but the end result is clearly seen at the close of this period when the Tamil-speaking group is dominant in the northern parts of the island.

The evolution of the Tamil group during this period proceeded through the interaction of various peoples. Among them were the Nagas, one of the most mysterious peoples in the island. There were the Tamils whose dominating influence in spreading not only the Tamil language but also the Saiva religion is the most significant aspect of this evolution. There were also the Andhras or Telugus, whose influence in the Buddhism of the north and east is attested by archaeology. Possibly the Keralas, too, were there, if one is to go by the survival of Kerala laws and customs in the north and east. The Helas, who themselves were evolving as the dominant ethnic group of the south through the interaction of various groups, were also among those who contributed to the formation of the Tamil ethnic entity at this time.

A number of factors were responsible for the strengthening of the Tamil element in northern Sri Lanka in this period. These worked against the northward extension of the process of acculturation that went on in the areas under the direct control of Anuradhapura. These could be grouped under three main headings: political, economic and religious. Aspirants and claimants to the kingship at Anuradhapura, both Sri Lankan and south Indian, brought to the island armies recruited in the Tamil kingdoms on several occasions with consequences in many ways similar to those experienced in Britain in the fifth century when Germanic elements gained ascendancy in that country. The expansion of south Indian maritime trade under the Pallava rulers led to an increase in the activities of Tamil mercantile communities. This was accompanied by the arrival of skilled craftsmen from south India to create works of art and build monuments for the patrons of Mahayana Buddhism. There was also another important area of economic activity that seems to have attracted or provided the impetus for the arrival of unskilled and possibly skilled workers. This was the building of hydraulic works. And then there was the religious factor. Buddhist monks had always been coming to institutions in Sri Lanka from the Tamil kingdoms, just as monks from Sri Lanka went over to south India not only for religious purposes but also to escape from political and economic distresses. But after the fifth century, when Buddhism began to decline in the Tamil kingdoms and to face hostility, it is possible that not only monks but also lay Buddhists moved to Sri Lanka and found sanctuary there. [170–72]

The Nagas. About 300 CE, the area roughly covered by the Jaffna District, particularly the Jaffna peninsula, continued to be known as the land of the Nagas. The only epigraphic reference to the name Nagadipa (Nakadiva—the Island of the Nagas) is datable to the early centuries of this era. The Pali chronicles and commentaries of about the fifth century also refer to Nagadipa. One of these refers to a chiefdom in this region whose ruler was known as or had the title of Diparaja, King of the Island (connoting presumably "King of the Naga Island"). In the Tamil literature of about this time, there are references to a Nakanatu (Land of the Nagas), across the sea from south India, identifiable with Nagadipa. A city named Nakapuram (City of the Nagas) also finds mention as the seat of kings who had Sanskritised names. These references seem to relate to earlier traditions. In the second century, the Graeco-Roman traders had gathered information about Nagadipa and we find Claudius Ptolemy, in his celebrated *Geographia,* referring to Nagadiba as one of the thirteen major coastal towns in Taprobane (Sri Lanka). On the strength of all this literary and epigraphic evidence, the historicity of Nagadipa is beyond doubt. That Nagadipa referred to a region in the far north of the island and that it derived its name from a people called Naga who lived there are acceptable. As mentioned earlier, Siran Deraniyagala has speculated that "the term 'Nagas' refers to the protohistoric Early Iron Age peoples of Sri Lanka and that they displaced the earlier Mesolithic hunter-gatherers from the northern and western parts of the island from about 1000 BCE."

In the traditions preserved in the early Sri Lankan chronicles as well as in the early Tamil literary works the Nagas appear as a distinct group. The evidence of the Pali and Tamil literary sources indicates that the process of acculturation of the Nagas with the dominant groups of South Asia was well under way by the end of the third century. In the cultural milieu of the EHP [Early Historic Period], when personal names had special significance and were not adopted indiscriminately, the use of the name Naga along with personal names must have had some significance. A notable number of persons mentioned in the early Brahmi inscriptions of Sri Lanka bear the name Naga. Some of them are chiefs with the title raja. In the Pali chronicles, too, several persons including rulers of Anuradhapura have the name

Naga. At a time when Nagas were known to constitute a distinct group, persons outside the group or having no connection with that group could not have adopted that name without a reason. It would appear that in the EHP the Nagas had begun to lose their separate identity and to be affected by the process of acculturation that was going on in the island. In the kingdom of Anuradhapura and in the areas around it, the adoption of Prakrit, the acceptance of Buddhism and intermarriage may be included among the chief features of the process of acculturation involving several ethnic groups. The Naga connection is reflected in personal names.

A similar process took place in south India, too. The earliest Tamil poems, namely those in the Sangam anthology, provide the names of several persons with the name Naga. Many of them were Tamil poets. This would mean that the adoption of the Tamil language was helping the Nagas in the Tamil chiefdoms to be assimilated into the major ethnic group there. The survival of place-names such as Nagar-kovil and Naga-pattinam in Tamil Nadu indicates association with Nagas at an earlier date.

By the end of the ninth century, there is no evidence relating to the Nagas. Clearly by that time, or very probably long before that time, the Nagas were assimilated into the two major ethnic groups in the island. These two groups are now referred to as Hela and Demela in the inscriptions of the ninth century. The personal name Naga occurs in royal names until the sixth century. The bearers of this name are, without doubt, members of the Hela group. In the north, no record mentioning the Nagas has come to light. But in the Tamil literary sources of south India the personal name Naga occurs as the name of persons who belong to the Tamil group. The assimilation of the Nagas of Sri Lanka and south India into the main ethnic groups of the region was complete before the ninth century. One of the major developments in this period, therefore, was the transformation of the dominant Naga group of the northern region into a Tamil-speaking group.

What do we know about the Tamils in Sri Lanka in the six centuries between 300 and 900 CE? Although not much is known at present, the little that is available throws light on the process of transformation that went on in the northern parts of Sri Lanka culminating in the emergence of the Sri Lankan Tamil ethnic group in that region. In the first place, the interaction between south Indian and Sri Lankan communities that was seen in the protohistoric and early historic periods continued unabated in this period. It took place in the political, social, economic and cultural spheres. On the south Indian side, it involved not only the Tamils but also the Telugus, Kannadas and the Keralas. In the end, it resulted in the emergence of the two major groups, the Hela and the Demela of the ninth-century inscriptions. [172–74]

The Indigenous Veddhas

Robert Knox

While most discussions of precolonial Sri Lanka focus upon Buddhist culture, king-
ship, and the migrations of peoples out of the Indian subcontinent, Sri Lanka has
been inhabited by one or another community of Homo sapiens for many thousands
of years. There has been some discussion about "Balangoda Man," so called as a
result of paradigmatic archeological findings near the modern town of Balangoda
in the south central highlands, but little remains about the surviving aboriginal
Veddha community, a people of hunting and gathering culture living in shrinking
pockets of wilderness in the east-central regions of the island. People like the Ved-
dhas, if not the Veddhas per se, may have been inhabitants of Sri Lanka for many
centuries, even millennia, before the watershed events of the third century BCE that
eventuated in a Buddhist civilization. While some anthropological studies of the
Veddhas have been written during the twentieth century (see Seligman and Selig-
man, The Veddas, in the Suggestions for Further Reading), perhaps there remains
no better general and succinct depiction of the Veddhas and their way of life than the
one provided in the seventeenth century by the Englishman Robert Knox.

Of these Natives there be two sorts, wild and tame. I will begin with the
former. For as in these Woods there are Wild Beasts, so Wild Men also. The
Land of Bintan is all covered with mighty Woods, filled with abundance
of Deer. In this Land are many of these wild men; they call them Vaddahs,
dwelling near no other Inhabitants. They speak the Chingulayes [Sinhala]
Language. They kill Deer, and dry the Flesh over the fire, and the people of
the Countrey come and buy it of them. They never Till any ground for Corn
[rice], their Food being only Flesh. They are very expert with their Bows.
They have a little Ax, which they stick in by their sides, to cut honey out of
hollow Trees. Some few, which are near Inhabitants, have commerce with
other people. They have no Towns nor Houses, only live by the waters under a Tree, with some boughs cut and laid round about them, to give notice
when any wild Beasts come near, which they may hear by their rustling

and trampling upon them. Many of these habitations we saw when we fled through the Woods, but God be praised the Vaddahs were gone.

Some of the tamer sort of these men are in a kind of Subjection to the King. For if they can be found, tho it must be with a great search in the Woods, they will acknowledge his Officers, and will bring to them Elephants-Teeth, and Honey, and Wax and Deer's Flesh; but the others in lieu thereof do give them near as much, in Arrows, Cloth fearing lest they should otherwise appear no more. . . .

For portions with their Daughters in marriage they give hunting Dogs. They are reported to be courteous. Some of the Chingulays in discontent leave their houses and friends, and go and live among them, where they are civilly entertained. The tamer sort of them, as hath been said, will sometimes appear, and hold some kind of trade with the tame Inhabitants but the wilder called Ramba Vaddahs never shew themselves.

But to come to the civilized Inhabitants, whom I am chiefly to treat of. They are a people proper and very well favoured, beyond all people that I have seen in India, wearing a cloth about their Loyns, and a doublet after the English fashion, with little skirts buttoned at the wrists, and gathered at the shoulders like a shirt, on their heads a red Tunnis Cap, or if they have none, another Cap with flaps of the fashion of their Countrey . . . with a handsome short hanger by their side, and a knife sticking in their bosom on the right side.

They are very active and nimble in their Limbs; and very ingenious; for, except Iron-work, all other things they have need of, they make and do themselves; insomuch that they all build their own houses. They are crafty and treacherous, not to be trusted upon any protestations; for their manner of speaking is very smooth and courteous, insomuch that they who are unacquainted with their dispositions and manners, may be easily deceived by them. For they make no account nor conscience of lying, neither is it any shame or disgrace to them, if they be catched in telling lyes: it is so customary. They are very vigilant and wakeful, sufficed with very little sleep; very hardy both for diet and weather, very proud and self conceited. They take something after the Bramines, with whom they scruple not both to marry and eat. In both which otherwise they are exceeding shy and cautious. For there being many Ranks or Casts among them, they will not match with any Inferiour to themselves; nor eat meat dressed in any house, but in those only that are of as good a Cast or Race as themselves; and that which any one hath left, none but those that are near of kin will eat.

They are not very malicious one towards another; and their anger doth not last long; seldom or never any blood shed among them in their quarrels.

It is not customary to strike; and it is very rare that they give a blow so much as to their Slaves; who may very familiarly talk and discourse with their Masters. They are very near and covetous, and will pinch their own bellies for profit; very few spend-thrifts or bad husbands are to be met with here.

The Natures of the Inhabitants of the Mountains and Low-lands are very different. They of the Low-lands are kind, pitiful, helpful, honest and plain, compassionating Strangers, which we found by our own experience among them. They of the Uplands are ill-natured, false, unkind, though outwardly fair and seemingly courteous, and of more complaisant carriage, speech and better behaviour, than the Lowlanders.

Of all Vices they are least addicted to stealing, the which they do exceedingly hate and abhor; so that there are but few Robberies committed among them. They do much extol and commend Chastity, Temperance, and Truth in words and actions; and confess that it is out of weakness and infirmity, that they cannot practice the same, acknowledging that the contrary Vices are to be abhorred, being abomination both in the sight of God and Man. They do love and delight in those Men that are most Devout and Precise in their Matters. As for bearing Witness for Confirmation in any matters of doubt, a Christian's word will be believed and credited far beyond their own, because, they think, they make more Conscience of their words.

They are very superstitious in making Observations of any little Accidents, as Omens portending good to them or evil. Sneezing they reckon to import evil. So that if any chance to sneeze when he is going about his Business, he will stop, accounting he shall have ill success if he proceeds. And none may Sneeze, Cough, nor Spit in the King's Presence, either because of the ill boding of those actions, or the rudeness of them or both. There is a little Creature much like a Lizzard, which they look upon altogether as a prophet, whatsoever work or business they are going about; if he crys, they will cease for a space, reckoning that he tells them there is a bad Planet rule at that instant. They take great notice in a Morning at their first going out, who first appears in their sight: and if they see a White Man, or a big-bellied Woman, they hold it fortunate; and to see any decrepit or deformed People, as unfortunate.

When they travel together a great many of them, the Roads are so narrow, that but one can go abreast, and if there be Twenty of them, there is but one Argument or Matter discoursed of among them all from the first to the last. And so they go talking along all together, and every one carrieth his Provisions on his back for his whole Journey.

In short, in Carriage and Behaviour they are very grave and stately like unto the Portugals, in understanding quick and apprehensive, in design subtil and crafty, in discourse courteous but full of Flatteries, naturally inclined to temperance both in meat and drink, but not to Chastity, near and Provident in their Families, commending good Husbandry. In their dispositions not passionate, neither hard to be reconciled again when angry. In their Promises very unfaithful, approving lying in themselves, but misliking it in others; delighting in sloath, deferring labour till urgent necessity constrain them, neat in apparel, nice in eating; and not given to much sleep.

As for the Women, their Habit is a Wastcoat of white Callico covering their Bodies, wrought into flourishes with Blew and Red; their Cloath hanging longer or shorter below their Knees, according to their quality, a piece of Silk flung over their head: Jewels in their Ears, Ornaments about their Necks, and Arms, and Middles. They are in their gait and behaviour very high, stately in their carriage after the Portugal manner, of whom I think they have learned: yet they hold it no scorn to admit the meanest to come to speech of them. They are very thrifty, and it is a disgrace to them to be prodigal, and their Pride & Glory to be accounted near & saving. And to praise themselves they will sometimes say that scraps and parings will serve them; but that the best is for their Husbands. The Men are not jealous of their Wives, for the greatest Ladies in the Land will frequently talk and discourse with any Men they please, altho their Husbands be in presence. And altho they be so stately, they will lay their hand to such work as is necessary to be done in the House, notwithstanding they have Slaves and Servants enough to do it.

Tamilnadus in Rajarata

Charles Hoole

The fall of Polonnaruva following Magha's invasion in 1215 marked a major shift in the nature of political power for the north and north-central regions of the island known as the Rajarata (king's country). In the wide-ranging discussion that follows, Charles Hoole discusses how capital centers and regional political peripheries were linked by ritual tribute throughout the Anuradhapura and Polonnaruva periods, how the emergence of autonomous Tamil political power in Jaffna under the dynasty of the Aryacakravartis can be traced to the Maravar rulers of Ramnad (in the vicinity of Ramesvaram in Tamilnadu, directly across the Palk Strait from Mannar) and the Vellalar (land-owning caste), who dominated Jaffna society. The Aryacakravartis reached the apex of their power in the fourteenth century, before a series of losses: defeat at the hand of Alakeshvara's Sinhala forces in the late fourteenth century, further setbacks to Parakramabahu VI's Kotte forces in the fifteenth century, and complete subjugation by the Portuguese in the sixteenth. This effectively ended any claims to autonomous "Tamil rule."

The models of the pre-modern state developed by theorists such as Stein, Tambiah, and Geertz, help us to understand the historical material from Rajarata in terms of relatively loosely structured organizations built up on the bases of heterogeneity and on the ideal of the delegation of power from the centre. Burton Stein's work on South India exemplifies such an approach. Stein . . . argued that the pre-modern state in South India is best conceptualized in terms of segments or *nadus*:

> The parts of which the state is composed are seen as prior to the formal state: these segments are structurally as well as morally coherent units in themselves. Together, these parts or segments comprise a state in their recognition of a sacred ruler whose overlordship is of a moral sort and is expressed in an essentially ritual idiom.

> The chronicles [*Mahavamsa* and *Dipavamsa*] . . . provide lengthy descriptions of this style of sacred kingship, and not of a bureaucratic monar-

chy. . . . The Sinhalese king exercised symbolic overlordship in the regions beyond the capital province. This ritualistic form of hegemony is actualized when the lesser chieftains of those regions acknowledge the king at the centre as the upholder of the social order by virtue of the eminence that he acquires through a special relationship to the guardian deities of the island. The assumption of Sinhalese royal titles is the most common gesture of accepting overlordship. Emulating royal deeds such as gift-giving and tank-building, was regarded as the means by which the minor rulers could aspire for similar eminence.

Jaffna Peninsula or Yalapana kuda nadu: a secondary zone. It appears that the Jaffna peninsula was one such segment within the Rajarata state. The peninsula was known to the chroniclers as Naga dipa, over which Anuradhapura probably did at one time exercise ritual hegemony. By the beginning of the Christian era more than a trade relationship appears to have existed between the Naga inhabitants of the peninsula and the Sinhalese. Evidence shows that the Naga rulers adopted Sinhalese royal names. . . .

What was probably a somewhat ambiguous political relationship was however strengthened by common religious values. The Nagas and the Sinhalese . . . shared a common religious bond through their commitment to Buddhism. Archaeological surveys have shown that in the early Christian era there was a strong Buddhist presence in Jaffna. In its own refractive way the sixth-century chronicle, the *Mahavamsa*, also acknowledges this fact. In contrast to the Yakkhas, the Nagas are presented in the *Mahavamsa* as friends of the faith who accept the authority of the Buddha. There is, of course, no justification for believing the author's claim that the conversion of the Nagas occurred during one of the Buddha's three visits to the island. It is more likely to have happened much later and less dramatically through the influence of South Indian merchant communities.

As long as the centre remained strong, the local chieftains with their own power bases would be willing to lend various kinds of support to the Sinhalese overlords. From the time of the legendary Kuveni, the Veddha leaders have provided military support to the Sinhalese kings. In the middle ages, the Polonnaruva kings became dependent on South Indian mercenaries of the left-hand division—recruited for them by the powerful merchant communities resident in the port principalities. But such commitments were highly ambiguous, and involved a high degree of voluntarism where everyone's calculations of advantage had to be taken into account. Allegiances therefore could easily be switched to some rival overlord if conditions warranted. This is precisely what must have happened in the thirteenth century when the Sinhalese centre became very weak.

Well before the Cola invasions of the tenth and eleventh centuries, the Sinhalese kings had become entangled in the dynastic politics and military conflicts of southern India, as both plunderers and the plundered. Long-distance raids of plunder were becoming more frequent. Along with the building of monuments or of irrigation tanks, court-sponsored military expeditions were also seen as compensatory activities designed to strengthen the centre in weakly integrated political systems. Through the grisliest military deeds the warrior-king would earn fame and immortality, while the network of personal loyalties would be strengthened by the distribution of plunder. Rajaraja I [who conquered Anuradhapura], Magha [who destroyed Polonnaruva] and Parakramabahu I [during the halcyon period of Polonnaruva's history, late twelfth century] are examples of this newly emergent royal style.

Many modern historians have unfortunately followed the medieval court propagandists in exaggerating the effects of these raids of plunder. The medieval work *Culavamsa*, for instance, catalogues the Cola outrages in great detail, precisely because its compilers were the group most adversely affected by the plunder. As far as the Colas were concerned, the great *viharas* of Anuradhapura simply happened to be conspicuously prosperous and hence tempting as objects of plunder. At the same time, the Colas do not appear to have tried to disrupt the intricate irrigation system of Rajarata. The hydraulic civilization seems to have continued to flourish despite repeated invasions by South Indian kings and adventurers.

A great deal has been written about the destruction of the administrative machinery of the irrigation network by Magha of Kalinga, and the over-centralization of authority in the political system bequeathed to his successors by Parakramabahu I. These two developments are sometimes cited as the two principal causes of the "collapse" of the Rajarata civilization. On the other hand, if the central state thesis is rejected, . . . then the spread of malaria remains the most likely cause for the disintegration of Rajarata society. In the stagnant pools of water in the dry zone, anopheles mosquitoes found ideal breeding places when they were introduced to Sri Lanka, and they thereafter made large-scale occupation of the capital province virtually impossible—until the advent of DDT in this century helped rebuild the population in this area. As a result starting in the fourteenth century, the Sinhalese kings and their capitals seem to have retreated farther and farther into the hills of the wet zone in search of a new economic base on which to establish their authority.

While the Sinhalese capitals drifted southwards, peoples from the Malabar and Coromandel coasts, by now Hindus, continued to arrive in the

Rajarata region as peaceful immigrants, soldiers and traders. Coastal principalities centered in Batticaloa, Trincomalee, Jaffna and Mantota grew significantly in size and strength through colonization. Three Siva temples of antiquity, Tirukethisvaram at Mantota, Konesvaram at Trincomalee and Tirukovil near Batticaloa, enable us to make reasonable inferences regarding the growth of Saivism in these localities. The first two are mentioned in Tamil literature as famous Saiva centers which attracted pilgrims from South India.

The growth in population and the economic activity of the coastal principalities, made it more and more difficult for the sovereign, whose position was by now weak, to even control formally these domains. During the twelfth and thirteenth centuries when Cola power waned, a series of Pantyan warriors, notably one Kulasekhara (A.D. 1196–1215) had free rein over Rajarata. Under Maravarman Sundara Pantya I (A.D. 1216–1227) and Jatavarman Sundara Pantya II (A.D. 1227–1251), Pantyan power became supreme in South India. It is during these heroic days of Pantyan expansion that Sri Lankan chieftains from the modern Vanni and Jaffna regions appear to have thrown off their traditional political affiliation to the Sinhalese monarch and set off on an independent course of their own.

The allegiances of these rulers were switched primarily for defensive reasons, but also in a search for a new legitimacy. The rulers of Jaffna began in this period to style themselves as Arya Cakravartis, tracing their origins to Ramesvaram in the Pantyan kingdom. The founding of the Arya Cakravartin dynasty seems to have synchronized with an event recorded in the *Culavansa*, according to which, Aryacakravarti, the "Damila" general sent by the Pantyas, plundered and destroyed many political and religious centers in the island. The Tamil chronicle *Kailayamalai* identifies this Pantyan warrior as Cinkaiyariyan or Ceyaviran, the Tamil king who founded the Arya Cakravarti dynasty. Whatever the relationship between the two Aryacakravartis, . . . the invasion enhanced the prestige of the Jaffna kings. Certainly, for the Tamil chroniclers the link was crucial. . . . The royal motives of valor, destruction, plunder, and fame associated with the Tamil classic hero served to affirm the dynasty's prestigious origin and thus afforded it imperial legitimation.

On the other hand, modern Tamil historians have paid close attention to the study of lineage, in tracing the ancestry of the Jaffna kings to either Brahman or Ksatriya origins. In order to strengthen the Ksatriya claim the authors have shown ingenuity in establishing matrimonial links with families beyond South India, for example, Orissa, Gujarat or Bengal. None of these claims, however, are based on any reliable evidence. What the evidence does point to, with a great deal of certainty, is the dynasty's connections with Ramesvaram in the modern Ramnad district. This is borne out by the fact that the Aryacakravartis of Jaffna were also known by the epithet "Cetukavalan," and they also issued coins having the legend *cetu* in Tamil characters, thereby affirming their connections with the *cetupathis* of Ramnad.

The kings of Jaffna must have made their claim to the title "Cetukavalan," meaning "the guardian of *cetu*" on account of their descent from the *cetupatis* of Ramnad. The word *cetu* has several meanings: it may denote a causeway, a dike, or a landmark. Specifically, the island of Ramesvaram, as well as the reef connecting it to Mannar, are generally referred to as *cetu*. In the course of time several localities around Ramesvaram also came to be called *cetu*. Based on this evidence it may be inferred that the Aryacakravartis of Jaffna were closely affiliated to the Maravar rulers of Ramnad. . . .

In the middle ages, many of these Maravar families came to prominence through military exploits. Their eminence in the twelfth century is marked by the frequency with which they are mentioned in Cola inscriptions, the titles which they bore, and "the practice of including Cola royal titles." The adoption of royal names and titles by minor chiefs is one expression of ritual sovereignty. There were others who attained the status of Vellalars by imitating the modes of life appropriate to the peasantry. All the evidence shows that the Maravars—until the advent of the British—were not excluded by the *dharmic* society. On the contrary, some Maravar groups achieved eminence within this larger society.

During the period of Pantyan expansion, the Maravars who retained their predatory ways, would have found suitable employment as soldiers. For the Pantyan kings of a loosely integrated state, the predatory wars in Sri Lanka were vital to their more immediate purpose of winning the allegiance of the local chieftains. It was a long established practice that at the end of a successful expedition, the war leader would not keep the loot for himself, but would dispense it to his comrades and also make pious donations. For the warrior chieftains of the peripheral *nadus*, these military exploits were in addition, an opportunity to earn fame and royal titles. Inscriptions belonging to this period, in fact, mention that the title *Aryacakravarti* was a distinction earned in military service. There are also references to Aryacakravartis in Ramnad in the inscriptions of Maravarman Kulasekhara (1268–1310). At the same time we know that this dry plain was locally controlled by Maravar and Kallar chieftains. It is therefore highly probable that the Maravar rulers known as *cetupatis* would have both aspired to and attained this "high status in the Pantya kingdom." . . . It would then follow that the kings of

Jaffna known by the twin epithets *cetupati* and *aryacakravarti*, were the de-
scendents of the Maravar chieftains from Ramnad. . . .

A similar Vellalization process occurred in Sri Lanka. The Jaffna and
Mannar areas . . . [were] virtually extensions of the southern Coromandel
coast. On account of their geographical proximity these areas had been
exposed to South Indian colonization from pre-historic times. Around the
middle of the first millennium, the colonization of this region assumed a
new phase with the appearance of Vellalar and Brahman settlements along
the coast. Many Hindu temples, mostly of brick, were built in the Pallava
style. Among them, Tiruketisvaram and Konesvaram became sufficiently
prominent to draw the attention of two Brahman hymn-writers, Tirunana-
campantar and Cuntarar, who have sung of their glories. From this time on
the Hindu Vellalar influence grew steadily along the northern coast, primarily through peaceful immigration. By the year 1310, a date which marks
the decline of Pantya fortunes as Muslim power was extended to their part
of South India, the Vellalars had no doubt emerged as the dominant group
in the Jaffna peninsula.

The *Kailayamalai* and the *Vaiyapadal* are the earliest works on the colonization of Jaffna. They are written in poetic style, paying no attention to
chronological detail. Besides, the authors of these chronicles are mainly concerned with the deeds and achievements of the Aryacakravarti dynasty. The
pages of *Kailayamalai* are almost entirely devoted to the reign of Cinkaiyariyan, the founder of the dynasty. In outlining his reign in great detail, the
author, Mutturaca Kaviracar, also gives an account of the arrival of peasant
colonists from South India. They name chiefs, or Nattar, from the Coromandel coast, who had brought service castes with them to the peninsula.
The names indicate that most of these Nattar belonged to the Vellalar caste.
These chiefs and their large retinues are credited with the founding of many
of the well-known localities in the region, areas such as: Irupalai, Puloli,
Tirunelveli, Mayilitti, Tellippalai, Inuvil, Pachilappalli, Tolpuram, Koyila-
kanti, Velinadu, Netuntivu (Delft) and so on. The presence of a large number of high-status peasants with their menial laborers in Jaffna at the close
of the Polonnaruva period follows the classic pattern of colonization in the
Tamil plain of South India where too, Vellalars migrated from the core areas
to the periphery. The same pattern was also observed in the colonization of
Rajarata, a task accomplished by the [Sinhala] Goyigamas and their service
castes. Through the denser settlement of this region, Jaffna had, however,
emerged as the most South Indian region of Sri Lanka. It is this region that
created and preserved the most characteristic patterns of peasant domination. In fact, while in medieval South India the rise of Brahman secular

power through royal endowments sometimes obscured the ancient patterns based on the Brahman-peasant alliance, in Jaffna the older features of the ritual and social domination of the peasant settlers have been preserved. Here there are no *brahmadeyas*, or royal donations of Brahman villages. Secular power has thus remained in the hands of the Vellalars, whereas, the Brahmans, though relatively poor and powerless, are still accorded the highest rank, and are supported by the Vellalars.

Pathmanathan may be correct in his observation that this particular system of agrarian caste relations became fully established during the period of the Cola occupation of Rajarata:

> The social and cultural institutions of the Tamils settled in the island continued to be more or less the same as those found during the period of Cola rule and did not differ fundamentally from those of contemporary South India. They were vitalized by the streams of Indian cultural influences that flowed from South India as a result of the close contacts that existed between Sri Lanka and that region. The endogamous castes and the division of society as a whole into two broad categories called Valankai and Itankai—the two main characteristics of medieval Tamil society—were to be witnessed in the island during this period.[1]

These observations lead to the conclusion that Jaffna or Yalpana *kuda nadu* (Jaffna peninsula *nadu*) best preserves the features of intermediate *nadus* in South India. Economic and social powers were in the hands of the dominant Vellalar caste. The powerful brahmanical institutions associated with central *nadus* are not found in Jaffna. Vellalar domination of this region was achieved not through coercion in the Western sense, but by ritual design, which situated the Vellalars advantageously with respect to cosmic, divine, human and demonic powers. The result is a social order exemplified in the *varnasrama dharma*—rooted in religious beliefs profoundly accepted by everyone, including the subordinate castes.

The Vellalars were also ritually linked to the Aryacakravartis and through them to the Pantyan kings. It may well be true that the Maravar kings of Jaffna who maintained a martial tradition did deem themselves to be Ksatriyas [the royal and warrior caste]. But it needs to be emphasized that the Ksatriya model of domination has never found currency in the heartland of the South, the rice-growing plains. In Jaffna as in South India, the Maravars and Kallars were peripheral to the agrarian social formation.

Vanni nadu: a peripheral zone. Much of the land between Jaffna and Anuradhapura, commonly known as the Vanni, was on the other hand almost unaffected by the socio-economic forces operating in the peninsula. Cankam poetry identifies this type of region as *kurinci*, where people live by hunting and primitive cultivation. It is quite possible that the term *Vanni*, like *kurinci*, primarily referred to the nature of the tract. Among the many derivations assigned to this term, one is taken from Sanskrit or Pali *vana*, meaning "forest." Whether this derivation is correct or not, in Sri Lanka the word *Vanni* does denote forest tracts, and also refers to a distinct conception of social life peculiar to those tracts.

In the medieval Sinhalese and Tamil chronicles, the term *Vanni* or *Vanniyar* was used to refer to the chiefs of the Vanni areas. According to these sources, many chiefs in the North Central and Eastern Provinces claimed the title of Vanniyar around the thirteenth century, following a series of invasions by mercenary armies. It is also known that members of the Vanniyar caste, noted for their skill in archery, served in these mercenary armies and some of them were given land-grants as well as grandiose titles for their services when Magha seized Polonnaruva and the northern centres of Sinhalese power in A.D. 1215.

It is not difficult to understand why these soldiers chose to adopt these peripheral tracts as their new home. South Indian evidence shows that the Vanniyar were originally a "forest race" given to martial pursuits. The link between the name *Vanniyar* and their original habitat (Skt. *vanya*) appears strong in the North Arcot district bordering on the Telugu regions, where the Vanniyar still live and where the use of Sanskrit caste names is not uncommon. This would in part explain the soldiers' decision to settle in the forest tracts of Sri Lanka, because these areas enabled them to pursue the age-old occupation of hunting and *chena* [swidden] cultivation. That decision also helped them to escape from the debilitating effects of the caste system in their homelands. Since the fall of the Pallava dynasty these people had become gradually absorbed into the system as agricultural servants under the Vellalars. Joining a military expedition normally offered them only a temporary respite; since any such expedition consisted of no more than temporary assemblages of warrior-cum-service castes, belonging in this case to the right-hand division associated with the dominant peasantry.

Note

1. S. Pathmanathan, *The Kingdom of Jaffna* (Colombo: A. M. Rajendran, 1978), 83.

Promulgations of a Polonnaruva King
Parakramabahu I

About a century following the sacking of Anuradhapura by Tamil Cola forces, the Sinhalas took over the Cola capital that had been established to the east at Polonnaruva. Under King Parakramabahu I, the construction of the massive reservoir known as Parakrama Samudra (Sea of Parakrama) made possible a vibrant city that could be regarded in literary, artistic, and institutional fashions as an heir to Anuradhapura culture. At Polonnaruva's impressive Alahena Pirivena, which at its height may have been the residence of up to ten thousand Buddhist monks, the Buddhist sangha was reestablished and purified.

In the following lengthy and remarkable inscription from Polonnaruva, dating from the twelfth century CE, Parakramabahu I situates himself within Buddhist history as a great royal reformer along the lines of the great Indian emperor Asoka, who reigned in the third century BCE. Parakramabahu I takes credit for uniting the sangha into one chapter (as opposed to the three that had existed in Anuradhapura) and, to ensure its purity, delineates a series of expectations for the behavior of monks (bhikkhus) that reveal his profoundly conservative understanding of the Buddha's teaching, one that emphasizes social seclusion, asceticism, and meditation. Indeed, this image of Buddhism becomes normative for many in the Theravada tradition.

In fact, Polonnaruva was quite a cosmopolitan city at the time. An extensive Hindu community that followed brahmanical traditions was ensconced in Parakramabahu's royal court as a result of the practice of matrimonial alliances with houses of political power in south India. Moreover, many erstwhile Hindu mercenaries had been brought to Sri Lanka from India to serve competing military interests. As such, the twelfth and thirteenth centuries represent a high water mark for the emergence of Hindu and Buddhist religious cultures in Sri Lanka, both existing, at the time, in a kind of complementary relation. In the collection of the Polonnaruva Museum are sculptures of the Hindu deities Siva Natharaja, his spouse Parvati, and their son Ganesha, whose worship, along with the worship of Skanda or Murugan, dominated the religious culture of the Colas. These sculptures clearly derive from Thanjavur styles of Tamilnadu and reflect high degrees of artistic perfection. Later, the Buddhists would begin to absorb many Hindu elements at the popular levels of religious culture.

(left) Siva Nataraj. Bronze (approx. 7 ft.), twelfth century, Polonnaruva Museum. Photo by editor.

(below) Ganesha. Bronze (approx. 3 ft.), twelfth century, Polonnaruva Museum. Photo by editor.

Parvati. Bronze
(approx. 5 ft.), twelfth
century, Polonnaruva
Museum. Photo by
editor.

[Lines 1–4]¹ Our Buddha, having fulfilled the exercise of all the thirty pre-
eminent virtues over a period of four *asankhyas* [unlimited periods of time—
Ed.] and one hundred thousand cycles of years (*kalpas*), mounted on the dais
at [the foot] of the great Bodhi tree, which formed [as it were] the field of
battle with Mara, vanquished this [well-nigh] irresistible Mara together with
his host, and attained to the state of omniscience. Thereafter, for forty-five
years he manifested himself like a great rain-cloud over the four continents,
and so, with showers of nectar-like Dhamma, he assuaged [the torments of]
the living beings who were being burnt by the *klesa* [impurity—*Ed.*] fire of
many *kalpa* cycles old. . . . Having thus accomplished all the duties of a Buddha, he passed away into the . . . *nirvana* state in the grove of *sala* trees of the
Malla princes in the neighborhood of the city of Kusinara.

[Lines 4–9] At the expiration of 454 years [from this event], there reigned
the great King Valagam Abhä. Thereafter, for 1,254 years the Buddhist Fra-

ternity remained disintegrated, and the religion also continued its course of decadence. At this juncture, there came to the throne the mighty king of kings, Sri Sanghabodhi Parakramabahu, a scion of the lineage of Mahasam-mata, born of the Solar race and resplendent with the rays of [kingly] glory that diffused themselves through many a region [of the globe]. His Majesty was anointed with the unction of paramount dominion over the whole land of Lanka. And, whilst he was enjoying the delight of kingship with a display of abundant virtues, he witnessed sons of noble families of the Buddhist persuasion on the road to the *apaya* [hell], having succumbed to the evil effects of non-perception or ill-perception through ignorance or imperfect knowledge. Now, His Majesty reasoned thus: Seeing over and over again a blot such as this on the immaculate Buddhist religion, if a mighty emperor like myself were to remain indifferent, the Buddhist religion would perish, and many living beings will be destined to the apaya. Let me serve the Buddhist religion which should last five thousand years. So, with a heart animated by forethought and sympathy, [he argued further:] whose services should I enlist to restore the religion which has thus been ruined, so that I may make it endure for five thousand years?

[Lines 9–18] Then, noting the congregation of Buddhist monks resident in the Udumbaragiri monastery with Maha-Kasyapa Maha-sthavira as their chief—all of whom sparkled with the brilliancy of gems of virtues highest in the world, such as the body of moral piety which has been preserved, increased and cherished by the consolidation of various groups of good qualities that have no flaws or hiatuses; (His Majesty pondered that in days gone by) the great king Dharma Asoka, enlisting the services of Moggaliputta Tissa, the Great Elder of the Buddha Cycle acknowledged by the Buddha himself, crushed out the sinful *bhikkhus*, suppressed the heretics, purged the religion of its impurities and brought about the holding of the Third Rehearsal of the Dhamma. In like manner, His Majesty [Parakkama-Bahu] also enlisted the services of those (Udumbaragiri) bhikkhus and, removing from the Master's religion many hundreds of sinful monks, brought about a rapprochement of the three fraternities and a coalition of them into one single fraternity (*nikaya*)—a reconciliation which former kings, despite their great efforts, were not able to effect, even though there were at the time eminently holy personages endowed with aggregates of divers faculties such as the six psychic powers. At various spots in the Island of Lanka, His Majesty caused costly monasteries to be built, such as the Jetavana-maha-vihara. In these he provided lodgings for members of the Order over a thousand in number, and treated them to a constant flow of spiritual and material gifts.

Being desirous of enjoying the sensation of joyous thrills arising from seeing the priesthood, His Majesty, from time to time, had recourse to the observance of the *Uposatha sila* [eight moral] precepts. [On these occasions], he used to enter the monastery and go amongst the assembled priesthood. Then, moved by the sensation of thrills of joy emanating from the spectacle of the reverend monks, [he was wont to say:] in order that this union of the Buddhist priesthood, which I have effected with great effort, may last unbroken for five thousand years and also that future members of the Order may prosper, endowed with Virtues such as contentment and the like, devoting themselves diligently to the two tasks of scriptural study and contemplation, may the reverend Sirs preserve the religion by the administration of exhortations and instructions.

Having hearkened unto these [repeated] appeals made with manifestations of appropriate decorum, the Community of Theras, headed by the great Thera Maha Kassapa, formulated the [following] code of disciplinary injunctions without deviating from the customary formalities observed in the lineage of preceptors, and after due consultation of the Dhamma (doctrine) and the Vinaya (disciplinary regulations), in order that those of negligent conduct may not find an opening [for transgression].

[Lines 18–24] The head Theras of chapters of monks should not permit any negligence on the part of those among their respective co-resident *saddhiviharikas* and *antevasikas* who are eligible either to be vouchsafed the *nissaya* or to be released from it, but should set them to the task of studying the scriptures.

They should not be allowed to neglect the learning at least of the *Kudusikha* and the *Patimokkha* [from the Vinaya literature] and the three *Dasadhamma-sutta* and the *Anumina-sutta* from the *Suttanta* [Pitaka].

. . . Since it is stated that those engaged in the study of the scriptures should always cultivate concentration of thought in seclusion, they [namely the *saddhiviharikas*] all throughout the three divisions of the day, should mould their ways of deportment perfectly, and their character absolutely without blemish.

Engrossed in meditation on subjects such as the consciousness of the [impermanency of the] body and rehearsing [the prescribed texts] in two or three ways, they should day by day cultivate without interruption concentration of mind in seclusion.

Since it is stated one should set himself at first in the right, each one should establish for himself these (afore)said attributes of virtue and promote one's own welfare as well as that of others.

Those *antevasikas* and *saddhiviharikas* who are unable to master a great portion of the [prescribed] course of study, should [at least] be made to learn by heart [various other minor and uncomplicated texts]. They should thus be rendered capable of repeating correctly any portion of the text from beginning to end on being questioned every six months. They should be made always to remember the *dasa-dhamma* and cultivate the aforementioned concentration of thought in seclusion.

After they have finished committing to memory as much as they can [of the prescribed texts], they should be taught a subject of meditation conformable to the custom [in vogue] and be set to the task of contemplation thereon.

Thereafter, they should be made to spend the day in the manner related in the discourse on the fourfold circumspection. . . .

[Lines 25–30] No permission to enter the village at wrong times shall be given to any of these [monks and novices] on any business whatsoever, save on account of a journey for begging food in order to succour their unsupported parents who had given birth to them, likewise their consanguineous and widowed elder and younger sisters, as well as the co-followers of the religious life or, in case of illness, on account of a journey to procure medicine [for parents and sisters] or to beg for medicine and other requirements of the co-followers of the religious life, or [finally], on account of a journey to recite the *Paritta* at an appointed place.

As it is declared that if permission be given to those [bhikkhus] who have to go out [into the village] on duties due to sickness, those preceptors who grant such permission to those not versed [in the Buddhist regulations] shall be guilty of *dukhata* offence; so, no permission shall be given to unlearned (bhikkhus) unaccompanied. Permission, however, should be given [to them] on the responsibility of a learned bhikkhu who at least knows [the procedure of] the Uposatha and Pavarana services and is cognizant of what constitutes a fault and what not.

Should a bhikkhu who has come from one monastic community (wish to) take up his residence with another, no lodging ought to be given to him except after seeing either a letter [of recommendation] or a bhikkhu [emissary] from the Head Thera of the monastic establishment where he had (before) lived.

[Lines 30–35] The [Senior] Theras, the junior bhikkhus and those of the middle grade [in fact] every member of the Buddhist Order should seek sleep at midnight, engrossed in thoughts on the fourfold discriminations and (thereby) should give repose to the body.

They should rise at dawn and should pass the morning perambulating and immersed in meditation.

They should then rehearse a text which they had learnt.

They should, thereafter, don the yellow robe, covering themselves properly with it, and, after they have finished cleansing the teeth, and have attended to the duties specified in the *Khandaka*, such as those rules of conduct in respect of the *Dagabas* [reliquaries—*Ed.*], the Sacred Bodhi tree, the Temple terrace, the preceptors, the Theras, the sick and the lodging places, should, if need arise, enter the refectory, partake of the gruel and finish attending to the requirements of the refectory.

Then, with the exception of those (bhikkhus) who have pressing duties to perform, such as the consultation of books and documents, sewing (robes), dyeing, distribution of priestly requisites; all the rest, soon after they had partaken of the gruel, should pass the time deep in meditation.

After the midday meal too, they should be occupied in obligatory study and introspective meditation as already stated.

They should thus pass the time without consorting with lay or priestly society until the time arrives for [the performance of] obligatory duties.

[Lines 35–40] As it is declared, "Oh Bhikkhus! There are two things [one of] which should be observed by the assembled [monks, namely] religious conversation or noble silence," so, those [bhikkhus] also, who have congregated for [holding] a *Paritta* ceremony, should not dwell upon worldly talk or sinful thoughts, sensual and the like, which are outside [the sphere of] the two subjects, religious talk and meditation, unless indeed there exists a cause which precludes one from observing the correct deportment.

Moreover they should spend the first watch of the night in a manner void of emptiness, such as in preaching (the doctrine), reading (the scriptures), hearing or learning (the same) by heart, conversing on religious topics, and in the task of introspective meditation; and when the middle watch has come, they should seek sleep engrossed in discriminative thoughts.

The bhikkhu-wayfarers who arrive from some business which had to be transacted outside [monastery precincts] should take up their lodgings at an appropriate place, such as the hermits' hut, the image house and the like.

At all times, bhikkhus should refrain from uttering inappropriate words with any one either in anger or in fun. They should not hold conversation in secret either with the opposite sex, even though she be (one's own) mother, or with a youth, even though he be (one's own) younger brother.

They should not be angry with servants without [first] complaining to the elders [regarding the servants' misdeeds].

Articles whatsoever belonging to oneself should not be given away to another without the permission of the elders.

[Lines 40–45] If rain falls while the bhikkhus are on a journey, they should continue their natural walking gait, and arrive at a place where they will not get wet, provided that they do not carry in their hands any articles of equipment [robes, &c.] belonging to the elder monks, that are liable to be damaged by the wet. If there be such an equipment, they should indeed go in appropriate haste.

As it is stated . . . that is only proper, so, even if there be a just cause for laughter, the bhikkhus should only show their mirth with mouths closed and with no sound allowed to escape.

The disputes which are being settled in a monastery which one has entered, should not be made known outside, nor should one take upon himself the disputes of another monastery which are also being settled.

As it is stated a bhikkhu who does not give up even a little of the religious life ought not to exercise desire for material enjoyment, even in respect of things permissible to him [according to the Vinaya code], therefore bhikkhus should not be covetous even in respect of requisites allowed [by the Vinaya rules].

They should not talk whilst in the act either of worshipping the Dagabas, the Sacred Bodhi tree, or in the act of making offerings of frankincense, flowers, or of using the tooth-stick, or of slipping the begging-bowl into its case.

They should not converse with the laypersons of the village on matters touching the priestly requisites or on unorthodox subjects.

. . . Whatsoever person enters a congregation of bhikkhus and with no respect for them, stands or sits knocking against the senior bhikkhus or speaks standing [in close proximity to them] or swaying his arms to and fro or strokes the head of a boy [he commits a misdemeanour]. Therefore those [bhikkhus] who move amongst the members of the Buddhist Order, should not brush against them (the senior monks) either with their bodies or with their robes.

[Lines 46–51] If there be a matter which needs talking over with a senior bhikkhu, the junior should converse with him with a show of regard for him and with his body bent forward (respectfully). He should not stand too near or sway his arms.

He should never at any place put his arms round a boy's body and console him.

He should recite [and learn the scriptures] without disturbing those in the Hall of meditation.

As it is stated when admitting [persons] into the priesthood, admit them after examination, ordain them after examination, give them (your) protection after examination. For, when even one son of a respectable family receives admission into the priesthood and (subsequently) the *upasampada* ordination, he is instrumental in the establishment of even the whole Buddhist church. Therefore, admission into the Buddhist Order should be made after examination. Likewise the upasampada ordination as well as the nissaya protection ought to be conferred after examination. One should cultivate the *Dhutanga* ascetic practices as much as one can.

No ill shall be spoken [of any one] for unwillingly observing these aforesaid duties.

Whosoever conducts himself in disobedience to and in violation of the disciplinary injunctions which have thus been enacted, shall receive the punishment due to the offence committed and be warned.

When this has been done three times successively and the bhikkhu still continues his misbehaviour in the selfsame manner, he shall not be given nissaya protection, but, after letting him remain (in the monastery) a month, if his demeanour be not in accordance with the Vinaya precepts, he should be expelled, and no one should hold communion with him.

Likewise, if the Theras who are heads of chapters of monks should neglect their respective duties and [as a result] fail to bring their community of bhikkhus under discipline, they should receive the punishments determined by the Senior Theras.

Editor's Note

1. Brackets and parentheses in original except where indicated.

Buddhist Sculpture at Polonnaruva:

A Photographic Essay

John Clifford Holt

For more than two centuries, first under the Colas and then under the Sinhalas, Polonnaruva was an impressive royal capital, until it was sacked by the invader Magha, from Kalinga (modern Orissa in India), in the early thirteenth century CE. More compact than Anuradhapura, Polonnaruva was, nonetheless, the site of the maturing of much Sinhala literature and some of its greatest visual art. It was at Polonnaruva that Garulugomi wrote his celebrated classical Sinhala narratives about the Buddha and where the artists who painted the interior walls of the Tivanka image house reached the highest development of aesthetic sensibility in the history of Sri Lankan art. Moreover, the Vatadage dagaba (stupa) at the ritual center of Po-

Samadhi (meditating) Buddha image. Twelfth century, Gal Vihara, Polonnaruva. Photo by editor.

(above, left) Standing Buddha. Twelfth century, Gal Vihara, Polonnaruva. *(above, right)* King Parakramabahu I or the sage Pulasti. Twelfth century, Polonnaruva. Photos by editor.

lonnaruva and the Lankatilaka image house mark the culture's extraordinary archi-tectural accomplishment. The series of Buddha sculptures in meditation, standing, and parinibbana (reclining) poses, hewn at Gal Vihara during the reign of Parakra-mabahu I (r. 1153–86), are surely the most spectacular Buddha images remaining on the island today. Three images of Polonnaruvu sculpture are reproduced in this chapter. For images of the Vatadage, the Lantakila image house, and the Buddha in parinibbana pose, see among the color plates.

The Abdication of King Parakramabahu II

Mayurapada Buddhaputra

A number of Sinhala literary classics were composed in the early decades of the thirteenth century at Polonnaruva and subsequently during the long reign (1236–72) of Parakramabahu II at Dambadeniya. The Pujavaliya *is one of those. In the following passage from this work, we find an extraordinary list of important matters deemed central to a successful Sinhala Buddhist polity, matters that Parakramabahu II was unable to attend to himself, and comprising thus a litany of what was seemingly incumbent on Buddhist kingship of his era. Also quite noteworthy is how his eldest son and successor, Vijayabahu, is referred to is as a* bosat *(bodhisattva), signaling perhaps a legacy of Mahayana Buddhist ideals that historically infused Sinhala Buddhist kingship.*

Unremitting in his protection of his people and his religion, the great king, like the main gem in that necklace that was the royal dynasty, enjoyed his kingly power for many years. Then summoning his sons Vijayabahu, Bhuvanaikabahu, Tribhuvanamalla, Parakramabahu and Gajabahu, and his nephew Virabahu, making the sixth, he spoke to them as follows:

"My children, there are three kinds of sons in this world: *avajata, anujata* and *atijata*. Those who have lost the inheritance they received from their ancestors, on both sides, and who now live in poverty where their ancestors enjoyed prosperity—these are known as *avajata*. Those who maintain untouched what they have inherited from their ancestors and continue to live in the same way as their forbears are known as *anujata*, while those who increase the wealth they have inherited from their ancestors and enjoy greater prosperity than their ancestors are known as *atijata*, or the best sons.

"As for me, I inherited the one kingdom of Maya, that my father left me, and have now under my sway all three kingdoms. I have killed, or chased away from the country, all the Tamils that he was unable to subdue. I have brought all the great Vanni chiefs in assembly before me. I have taken to myself queens from India and received all kinds of treasure as tribute from them and thus made foreign kings your kinsmen. I seized crowns and priceless gems as tribute from the Chola and Pandyan kings and brought them back with me. I collected nine priceless royal treasures that are sufficient wealth to be enjoyed not only by you but also by my descendants to the seventh generation. I united sangha and state. My children, as a result of all these achievements I have become an *atijata* son to my parents. Do you also become *atijata* sons to me. In olden times there was a King called Sagara, who had sixty thousand sons, and these established sixty thousand cities, ruled independently but yet in amity. Ten other brothers divided India into ten districts and ruled. Do you too, in harmony with one another, divide Sri Lanka among yourselves and rule in peace. Do not give any opening to foreign invaders; and thus be *atijata* sons to me." After he had given them advice of this kind, he summoned the Great Brotherhood of monks and the citizens and asked them, "Among these my five sons and my nephew Virabahu, whom do you consider fittest to govern my kingdom?" The Great Brotherhood listened to his words and said: "Great King, these six have each got courage, energy, knowledge and strength. However your eldest son Vijayabahu, from the time he was viceroy, has been most devoted and faithful to the Three Gems, the Buddha, the Law and the Brotherhood. He has been full of compassion towards the old and infirm. He has always enquired daily after sick monks and given them the medicines they needed. He gave a lakh's worth of gold to the relations of the brotherhood, who had become poor and enslaved at the time when there was no king, and saved many hundreds of them. When he saw your officers collecting taxes from your subjects, he has also given them gold and not gone away until he had saved them from distress. Even robbers, who have committed treason against the royal household have approached him without fear and been pardoned. Indeed the Sinhalese Vanni chiefs who were afraid to come and see you, and had not been subdued, would see him, and through his mediation approach you. The wives of ministers exhort their husbands thus we hear: 'If you would save us all in the future, henceforward serve the Bosat Vijayabahu.' Little sucklings of two or three years, when asked fondly by their parents 'Son, whom will you serve?' will reply, 'We will serve the Bosat Vijayabahu.' Infants who have received loving blows from their parents, when they see Prince Vijayabahu will tell him how they have been punished and complain to him about their parents' harshness. Vijayabahu will listen to their complaints, summon their parents, and get them pardoned, and, after directing that they shall not be beaten, he will give them presents. Bosat Vijayabahu, acclaimed as king by the citizens by word of mouth, lives among us endowed with these virtues which delight the people. Sire, what is the use of asking us, when you know his good qualities? It is like looking up at the sky and asking where the sun is. He has both the strength and the merit to govern the whole of India, let alone the kingdom of Lanka. We need not wait for the future, for even today he is endowed with the power to be an *atijata* son to you." And with these and with similar utterances they praised his virtues, although their tongues were unequal to their task.

Then Parakramabahu the King, after he had heard the limitless virtues of his son, wept tears of joy, and summoned him to his side. He kissed him, comforted him, and made him sit on the same throne. He entrusted to his care the other five princes, the Tooth Relic, the Bowl Relic, the Great Brotherhood, the circle of ministers and the government of the whole island.

Because Parakramabahu had ruled from his own kingdom of Maya, and because the people of Lanka, who had become poor during the period when there was no king, were still suffering on account of the many wars they were engaged in, he had been unable to crown with a pinnacle the Ruvanvaelisaeya [stupa in Anuradhapura], which he had rebuilt; he had not been able to restore the prosperity of Polonnaruva, which had been the capital of the whole kingdom and which had been destroyed by the Tamils; he had not been able to bring back the Tooth Relic, which had been taken to Maya at the time when there was no king, and re-enshrine it in the capital; he had not been able to assemble the people and the Brotherhood at Dastota and hold an ordination, and he had not been able to go to the capital to complete his coronation ceremony. So he enumerated all the things which had yet to be done for the welfare of the people and of the Brotherhood, and said: "If you can, perform all these royal tasks, and thus be an *atijata* son to me to the best of your ability, even as I was to my father." Then he handed over the kingdom to Vijayabahu.

Dambadeni Asna

Anonymous

The Dambadeni Asna *belongs to a popular genre meant to appeal to imaginations delighting in rich images of wealth and prosperity. On the one hand, it is filled with wild exaggerations and, on the other, it is simple in its message: to report on the virtuous exploits of an accomplished king (Parakramabahu II) who has now defeated his Tamil enemies, amply supported the Buddhist monastic sangha, and paid due homage to the Dalada (tooth relic of the Buddha), which, by this time, had become the palladium of the Sinhala people. What the work also manages to reflect indirectly, amid its hyperbole, is an era of war and instability that followed the fall of Polonnaruva. Perhaps it is because the Sinhalas had so recently suffered a terrible loss at Polonnaruva that this new defeat of the Tamils at the hand of Parakramabahu and the glories of his newly established capital in the late thirteenth century are so wondrously extolled. Of the Sinhala kings who reigned afterward, none stands out as such an accomplished student [pandit] of literary culture as Parakramabahu II of Dambadeniya, who reestablished the capital of Buddhist kingship in the southwest quadrant of the island following the devastation of Polonnaruva by Magha, the invader from Kalinga in India. The Culavamsa is long and lavish in its descriptions of this learned king's activities on behalf of the sangha. Because of his own scholastic achievements, he is referred to as Pandit Parakramabahu.*

May all the faithful and wise people of Lanka including kings and chief ministers hear this message filling their minds with love and devotion.[1]

The city of Jambudroni, which fulfills the wishes of everybody, shining in glorious prosperity, entertaining the minds and eyes of men and women with song, dance and music of veenas and flutes, day and night, this city bedecked eternally like a city of gods, its gardens and groves full of lush mango, rose apple, ironwood, jak fruit, . . . jasmine . . . as well as sweet jak fruit, coconut, areca-nut, sugar cane and *sal* trees. . . . Furthermore that city was beautiful with groves and gardens that were full of many kinds of fragrant flowers. Thus the city of Jambudroni was as excellent as the Nandana Park of Sakra, the king of gods. The ruler of that city, King Kalinga Vijayabahu's son King Pandit Parakramabahu, was like a Bodhisatva engaged in fulfilling "perfections." In his young age, when he was being educated, he was taught subjects such as Grantha, Tamil, Sinhala, Niganthu, Grammar of Kaccayana, Magadhi, Sanskrit, Nisabana, Therabana, Vinaya, Sutra and Abhidharma Pitaka, Anguttara, Samyutta and Majjhima Nikayas, Dhatupatha, Chandas, Astrology, Shikhsa, Moksha, and Sirita or Biography. In addition to these subjects the Prince was trained in fencing, using the sword and shield, the twelve languages together with the skills in speaking in foreign languages, law, logic, known as the eighteen skills; he further . . . mastered the sixty-four arts and crafts. . . .

Then he went to the city of Dambadeni and in the year eighteen sixty-four in the Buddhist era [A.D. 1272], on the day of the festival of *Vap Mangul* [Ploughing Ceremony] he was consecrated as King Kalikala Sangita Sahitya Sarvagna Pandita Parakramabahu. While ruling the country righteously he had completed the building of a palace on the Dambadeniya rock by clearing the jungle, making uneven places even and constructing ramparts in stone. . . .

Further the king had constructed six large ponds with white washed walls around them, and a temple of twenty-two cubits in extent to house the Tooth Relic. On the four sides around the palace he had built storehouses of sixty-eight cubits in length and outside of that nine hundred and eighty chambers for the women of the harem, and further away from that, he had constructed around the city three ramparts of rock, clay and wood for the protection of the citadel. King Parakramabahu had built streets . . . establishing in each one judges, captains of force, dukes, viceroys, as well as twenty-five thousand soldiers who were paid by the royal treasury, and further, twelve thousand Tamil soldiers who were also paid by the royal treasury, nine hundred bowmen, nine hundred stone masons, nine hundred and seventy pottery makers, keepers for nine hundred and ninety elephants including the royal tusker named Airavana and keepers for eight hundred and ninety horses. Thus the king had all of them employed in their respective professions and duties.

Further the king had constructed seventy-five thousand quarters for the garbage collectors, and a similar number of wells to provide drinking water, and arranged for those people to occupy the houses built for them.

Presently the King of the Kalinga country declared, "My grandfather's country belongs to me," and came by ship to Sri Lanka with an army of twenty-four thousand soldiers, and landed at the port of Salavata.

That King of Kalinga advanced on the city of Dambadeniya capturing three encampments of King Parakramabahu on his way. The latter, having sent his forces to check the invader, silencing the sound of the war drums of the Tamils, killed the King of Kalinga. Then after some time, the King of Tamalingamu [Tamrat], having heard of that war, landed at the port of Tammanna, with forty thousand Tamil soldiers. King Parakramabahu, being informed of this, before setting off with his army to face the invader, offered alms to one thousand monks of the two chapters, made a magnificent offering to the Tooth Relic, then on the morning of a Thursday, after having had his morning meal, observed the religious precepts. . . . The king wore and was adorned with clothes and ornaments worked in gold, and took up a gemmed *solu* [mace] in hand. . . . Further he wore necklaces of many kinds: stone and pearl necklaces, pearl and jewel necklaces, jeweled chains with floral patterns, gold chains with carvings of figures, plain gold chains, round gold chains, chains with triangles, chains with squares, arm bands . . . and gold, silver and pearl chains for the waist. . . .

He selected whatever number of these clothes and ornaments and got ready. . . . Finally wearing the crown selected from crowns such as gold crown, lion crown, *siddha* [magical] crown, silver crown, jewel crown and the crown made of seven types of gem, bearing the royal sword in hand, mounting by a ladder made of gold the strong enclosure fixed on the back of the Tusker named Airavana, leading an army of nine hundred and eighty beautifully caparisoned elephants protected with armor, followed by eight hundred and eighty horses similarly prepared, the king set off from Dambadeniya in the company of a mighty army and encamped at a village called Annaruva.

Next day, in the morning, advancing with a multitude of soldiers to fight with the King of Tamalingamu [Tamrat] amidst the sound of the bells of hundreds of elephants and horses, being struck by the ear-flaps of those elephants, while their trunks got entangled as they walked in formation line by line, followed by the cavalry, as the riders spurred on their horses, accompanied by the din that rose from the clash of a thousand shields held in the hands of soldiers from countries such as Hemagiri, Nilagiri, Jaladhara, Gandhara, Mandhara, Sindura, Sirivatta, Kururattha. . . .

Bearers of shields, parasols, whisks, fans, lamps and flowers; barbers, removers of dirty clothes, astrologers, doctors . . . , store-keepers, chief tax-collectors, *bandaranayakas*, *kapuralas*, administrators of regions, heads of the treasury, supervisors of the elephants, head of the Mudliyars, attendants in the betel house, attendants in the confidential room, . . . and wrestlers-guards of the eight directions, . . . goldsmiths, carpenters, arrow-makers, pottery makers, weavers of winnowing baskets and mats, washer-men, barbers, performers of Bali rituals, performers of the Kali ritual, walked ahead followed by the king.

Further, a variety of drummers for the Tammata, Davul, Loho Davul, Jina Davul, tappu, talappu, large drums, metal drums, *pata* drums, one-sided drums, *pana* drums, *geta bera*, *pokuru* drums, *mihingu* drums, . . . and furthermore, musical instruments such as, horns, *virandam*, *kombu*, *darasak* . . . , flutes, reeds, . . . veena, . . . and also weapons of explosion such as *dum vedi*, *sara vedi* . . . and with the blast of all these kinds of explosions . . . causing all those who saw it to close their eyes in fear, deafening the ears of those who heard, making the enemy tremble; the king, bearing the "victory spear" in his hand, declared: "We shall save the religion of the Buddha by driving the enemy away!" Having made this declaration, full of the courage of royalty, and full of determination, amidst parasols of blue, red, and silver colors, parasols made with pearls . . . hoisted, sending ahead elephants protected by armor, followed by the cavalry, the king advanced in the battlefield amidst the scrape of thousands of bows of different kinds. . . .

. . . With the clanking that came from the collision of those weapons and that of the rain of arrows, without letting the rays of the sun fall on the ground, the king lead his troops in the battle killing twenty thousand Tamil soldiers on the spot.

King Pandit Parakramabahu riding the Tusker Airacana, saw the King of Tamalingama trying to flee on his horse, Dhanasekera, and called out to him, "King of Tamrat! It is not becoming of a king to run away in fear of another king. Come over here!" Having heard those words, that king stopped and turned back. Then King Parakramabahu stabbed him with his spear that went piercing through the enemy king's chest.

There, after he had the Tamil king's body cremated on that spot, issuing an order to spare the lives of the remaining enemy soldiers thus making his glory known in all the eighteen countries, he returned to the city of Dambadeniya. Then another king from the country of Java, invaded the island with an army of twelve thousand. King Parakramabahu vanquished that enemy as well, and gaining victory in twelve more wars, cleansing Sri Lanka of the fear of enemies, the king concentrated on the development of the Buddhasasana.

The king selected twenty-two monks from the forest-dwelling sect and twenty from the village-dwelling sect and . . . releasing them from the probationary period of training, and elevating them to the position of Mahathera and organizing a ritual of "higher ordination" twelve times, performed three hundred and sixty rituals of almsgiving to the Sangha.

Then the king arranged for almsgiving by the citizens at every household, further providing meals with the five-fold delicacies made with milk products such as, milk, curd and butter; offerings of the fivefold *"palavat"* such as camphor, *takul*, and listening to a sermon on the same night, giving alms to sixteenfold beggars such as the blind, deaf, dumb, lame, homeless, old and hunchback; giving alms to one hundred monks in the royal palace daily, observing the five precepts daily, observing the eight precepts on full moon days, making gifts of three hundred *kathina* robes annually, the king maintained these deeds without a break.

Further on the days of offering the eight requisites to all the monks in the three kingdoms of Lanka, he offered eighty *kathina* robes by completing on the same day the process of making the cloth, starting with the picking of cotton, beating, drying, spinning, and weaving it up to the sewing and dying of the robe.

King Pandit Parakramabahu continuously made offerings of light to the Tooth Relic at the Vijayasundararama Vihara day and night with lamps lit with ginger oil, cow-ghee, *urula* oil, camphor oil. . . .

Making offerings of one hundred thousand fragrant flowers, offering four baskets of alms with a variety of delicacies and sweets, then, in order to help many other people engage in meritorious deeds, . . . the king made a pathway decorated with flags, banners, coconut flowers, and flanked by *tambili*, *bodili*, *navasi*, *tal*, *kitul* and banana trees, as well as parasols, flags, whisks, torches, conches and shields, and making it bedecked beautifully, arranged for making offerings to the Tooth Relic for three months. Two hundred and fifty thousand villages in the Kingdom of Maya, four hundred and fifty thousand in the Kingdom of Pihiti and seven hundred ninety thousand villages in the kingdom of Ruhunu and further three hundred betel villages, five hundred *udii* villages, four hundred thousand *maha patunu* villages [market towns], five hundred mining villages, nine thousand Brahmin villages and seven hundred villages of Brahmin women—thus he established all these villages in the three kingdoms of the island.

Issuing orders to bring cow-ghee for one thousand lamps, one thousand flowers, fifty balls of milk-rice from each village, summoning from the three kingdoms professionals of dance, song and music, the king started the grand ritual of offerings with pomp and fanfare. . . .

Thereafter the king stated, "In the past, at the time of the kings who were fulfilling perfections to become Buddhas, the Tooth Relic had performed miracles, so what is the reason for not showing any miracles in my time?" Having made this statement, washing his hair with scented water, and having bathed, clad in white, wearing a pearl necklace, bearing the sword in hand, offering one hundred thousand lamps with *amu kapuru*, mustard oil, *urula* oil, and kneeling down before the Tooth Relic with deep respect, the king stayed there saying, "If the Tooth Relic does not perform any miracle today I'll cut off my neck with this sword!"

The Tooth Relic, at once emerging from the casket like a golden swan, rising to the sky, creating an image of the Buddha and a jeweled walkway, performed miracles for seven and a half hours.

Even the sun god, having seen that miracle, stopped his movement in the sky and uttered "sadhu, sadhu." Many were the people who attained to the fruit of "Stream-winner" that day.

Furthermore, in this island of Lanka wherein are found and well established the relics, images, *stupas* and the sacred Bodhi Tree along with the Buddha, Dhamma and Sangha, the Triple Gem, may all the kings who ascend the throne in this land protect Lanka so that it is like unto a storehouse of gems, that is the Triple Gem, without violating the law of the kings [*rajadharma*] and the law of the world, distancing themselves from the tenfold sin, engaged in the tenfold meritorious deeds, and striving for attaining the pleasures of heavens before finally gaining emancipation.

Translated by Udaya Meddegama

Note

1. A Sinhala version of this text may be found in K. Gnanawimala Thero, ed., *Kuveni Asna, Sihala Asna, Dambadeni Asna* (Colombo: M. D. Gunasena, 1960), 37–65.

Alakeshvara Yuddhaya

Anonymous

The Alakeshvara Yuddhaya (The wars of the Alakeshvaras) is a chronicle of politi-cal history that covers the period from the rise in power of the Alakeshvara merchant family, originally from Kerala, from the mid-fourteenth century until the coming of the Portuguese in the early sixteenth. It is quite clear that in the fourteenth century, this family had risen to such power that it eclipsed the Sinhala kingship in Gampola. It would soon establish itself on the throne down in the coastal regions of what is now Colombo. The excerpt below highlights the building of a new royal city in Jaya-vardhanapura (Kotte), the subsequent Alakeshvara defeat of the Jaffna Aryacakra-varti, and the establishment of island-wide rule under Parakramabahu VI of Kotte.

After the king of Lanka was taken prisoner by deception and taken away by those who came from Great China, there were no kings left here.[1] Therefore, the minister named Alakeshvara, who lived in the city of Raygam, arose to power. King Bhuvanekabahu, who was the king of the *udarata* [Upcountry] and lived in the city of Gampola, and the Aryacakravarti, the ruler of Jaffna, who lived in the port city of Jaffna [ruled over parts of Lanka].

Among those kings, the Aryacakravarti was foremost in terms of troops and wealth; he lived by having all kinds of revenue and tributes brought to him from the nine ports and kingdoms of Sri Lanka.[2] As he was living like that, Minister Alakeshvara one day thought, having observed his troops, "It is not fitting to live by paying taxes to another king when I have a great force as this." Having so contemplated, he thought of building a strong fortress and, while looking for a suitable location, found a site in Jayawar-dhanapura.[3] There he had a fort built with high ramparts, and within deep and large pools for the supply of water. Then he had constructed watch towers on strong foundations, a deep moat full of water, and collected and hoarded within it, rice, paddy, salt, coconuts, and other necessary provi-sions for surviving without having to bring anything from outside. Further he had deployed troops of soldiers armed with the five kinds of weapons, and chased away the officers of Aryacakravarti staying in various places for the purpose of collecting taxes.

King Aryacakravarti, having heard about this, was enraged like a cobra beaten with a stick. So he had brought in an army of thousands of soldiers from the Chola country and reinforcing it with his own forces, hoping to invade both the city of Gampola and the fortress at Jayawardhanapura on the same day, sent a section of his army by several ships and another by land. Those who went by sea in their thousands landed and encamped at Demata-goda, Gorakana, and some other places. Those who went by land encamped at Matale. King Bhuvanekabahu, having heard this, was so frightened that he fled to Raygamnuvara with his people, unable to stay in Gampola. Then the army of the Upcountry, hearing this thought, "We have no use for a king who has fled in fear." Thus the forces of the "five countries" coming to an agreement among themselves,[4] staying in camps during the night surrounding the enemy camp and breaking into it before sunrise, fought and killed many Tamils, and won a victory in that war.

Then Minister Alakeshvara, accompanied by his troops, riding an elephant, pounced upon the enemy forces vanquishing many Tamils. He had destroyed and crushed by elephants the ships anchored in the ports of Panadura and Colombo. Thus becoming victorious, the minister entered the city of Raygam. King Bhuvanekabahu of Gampola returned to his city of Gampola.

On Thursday the seventh day in the month of May in the year one thousand nine hundred and fifty eight in the Buddhist era,[5] at the astrological moment of Pusa, King Parakramabahu of Rukule, born to Queen Sunetra, wife of Jayamahalena, who was like a wish tree, and who was nephew of the Great King Parakramabahu, the son of Savulu Vijayabahu born in the Sri Tambana clan and the son of Prince Sumitra, a descendant of the Surya-vamsa also known as the Sri Vaivasta Manu.

This King Parakramabahu became the ruler of Sri Lanka with the support of the Great Elder monk Vidagama. Then, having lived like Sakra at the city of Raygam for three years, he moved to the city of Jayawardhana Kotte. There the king had built the Temple of the Tooth Relic, temples for the Mahasangha [monks] to reside, the royal palace, and streets and roads in the city developing it to look like a heavenly city, made it prosperous and lived there. Then conquering the rival parties through the fourfold stratagem [*upaya*] and having the threefold power [*shakti*] and the seven component parts, ruling the country by the fourfold wealth of charity and the tenfold *rajadharma*, making his subjects happy, being crowned annually, performing acts of great charity [*mahadana*] to the sixteenfold beggars that came from various countries and giving gifts of every kind of requisites to the Buddhist monks of Sri Lanka, the king lived there serving the world. He had married a princess of Keeravella, a descendant of the clan of Prince Anuradha who had come with the delegation that brought the Sri Mahabodhi to Anuradhapura, and brought up Prince Senanayaka Sapu and the junior prince of Ambulugala,[6] and he had a daughter by the name of Princess Lokanatha, also named Ulakudaya. While he was thus ruling the country extending up to the coast of the "four great oceans" happily, the forces of the king of Kannadi arriving by ship declared war. The king, coming to know about this, sent his mighty army there, vanquished them and became famous in all India.

Then this king sent a shipload of goods for trade, but a person called Rayan Malavaraya, at the port city of Adivira, seized that ship and ransacked it. The king being informed of the incident, sent forces by hundreds of ships, attacked that port, made seven villages in the country of Cholas including the Makulan Kottaya pay him taxes and tributes.

At that time the ruler of the Upcountry areas, called Jotiya Situ, stopped paying annual tributes to the king, abandoned sending men to serve at the court, and thus started a rebellion by bribing the forces of the five countries with positions and gifts. King Parakramabahu, having heard about this, sent a mighty army there and vanquished the rebels. He brought a few men from that king's clan to his city, summoned the princes of Gampola and Ambulugala and, entrusting them with the administration of the Upcountry, had due income and tributes brought from that region. Then, bringing peace to the regions of the eighteen Vanni, the king was living in excellent splendour. King Aryacakravarti of Jaffna, in the meantime, having built up a mighty force, was living there with no obedience or respect to King Parakramabahu. Being informed of that situation, deciding that it is not proper for two kings to rule Sri Lanka, he paid his army well and appointed Prince Sapu commander-in-chief of the army. The prince went forth and attacked some villages under the control of Jaffna and entered the city. Once again [Aryacakravarti] collected an army with reinforcements of Konnakkara Tamils, Panikkis, and Munnila Vanni, and sent them to fight. Having beaten the soldiers encamped at various places, followed by a mighty army, Prince Senanayaka Sapu, riding his blue horse, entered the city of Jaffna. Then a man called Yon Vadakkara, boasting "I'll cut both the king and the horse in two," challenged Prince Sapu. The prince, having ridden his horse up to to the challenger, attacking him with his spear so as to pierce through his body, and without letting Vadakkara's body fall on the ground, picked it with the tip of the spear and, holding the spear tightly under his armpit, carried it like a flag along the streets on his horse. Then he captured the soldiers of the Aryacakravati like someone catching deer in nets, and being honored with the title, Arya Vettiyarum Perumal, capturing brothers and sisters of King Aryacakravarti, taking valuables, weapons, elephants, and horses, returned to show them to King Parakramabahu. Having been honored by the king with positions and titles, Prince Sapu returned to Jaffna as its king.

When King Parakramabahu had ruled the country like God King Sakra for fifty years since his coronation, he passed away.

Thereafter, ministers and the army got together and made Prince Jayaveera the king by the name Parakramabahu, who was the son of Princess Ulakudaya, the daughter of King Parakramabahu. When this news reached Jaffna, Prince Senanayaka Sapu returned and, having entered the city of Kotte, killed King Parakramabahu and became king himself, assuming the name Bhuvanekabahu. When he was ruling at Kotte, the subking Kekulandala Siriwardhana in Pasyodun Korale, having spoken to people on the other side of the river Kalu up to the river Valave, started a riot called the Sinhala rebellion.

Then the king, having summoned his younger brother Prince Ambulugala, sent him with the army of the Four Korales together with many other men. He arrested the regional king and brought him to Kotte, and showed him to the king. The regional king pleaded guilty and said, "Please put me in prison for the offence I have committed." The king sent him to prison as requested; Prince Ambulugala went back to Ambulugala.

After several years, having released the "patiraja" subking from prison, King Bhuvanekabahu passed away after ruling the country for seven years.

Translated by Udaya Meddegama

Notes

1. That is, Kotte.
2. The regional kingdoms of Sri Lanka.
3. Jayawardhanapura, just southeast of modern-day Colombo.
4. The five divisions of the Upcountry.
5. The year 1958 of the Buddhist era is 1415 CE.
6. [Prince Senanayaka Sapu, or Prince Sapumal, was an ethnic Tamil who was an adopted son of Parakramabahu VI—*Ed.*]

The Observations of Ibn Battuta

Ibn Battuta

The inveterate Muslim traveler Ibn Battuta visited Sri Lanka in the middle of the fourteenth century. He provides a fascinating account of meeting the then Tamil ruler, the Aryacakravarti, who had by then made his base quite far south at Puttalam. Ibn Battuta won the favor of the Aryacarkravarti and successfully solicited his assistance for making a pilgrimage to Adam's Peak (Sri Pada). His account contains many details and asides: how the ruler in the gem-mining region of the island (near modern Ratnapura), most likely the wealthy merchant Alakeshvara, possessed a white elephant, a symbol of royal sovereignty; how the Chinese had previously visited Adam's Peak; how the city of Devinuvara was dominated by its great temple dedicated to Upulvan (later identified with Vishnu); and that the ruler of Colombo had five hundred Abyssinians under his command. Ibn Battuta's account also seems to reflect the fragmented condition of polity in Sri Lanka at this time, with none of the rulers he encounters in sole control of the island. Indeed, Parakramabahu VI, who ruled for fifty years in the middle of the fifteenth century, is the only ruler who unified the island politically from the time of the Polonnaruva kings in the early thirteenth century until 1815, when the British disestablished the Kandyan kingship.

The distance which separates the Maldives from the Coromandel Coast is three days' sail. We were for nine days under sail, and on the 13th we went on shore at the island of Ceylon. We perceived the mountain of Serendib raised in the air like a column of smoke. When we came near the island, the mariners said, "This port is not in the country of a Sultan in whose dominions the merchants can go in all safety; it is in the country of the Sultan Airy Chacarouaty [Aryacakravarti] who is one of the unjust and perverse. He has ships engaged in piracy on the high seas." Wherefore we feared to land at his port, but, the wind rising, we were in danger of being swamped, and I said to the Captain, "Put me ashore and I will get for you a safe-conduct from this Sultan." He did as I requested, and put me out on the beach. The idolaters advanced to meet us and said, "Who are you?" I apprized them that I was the brother-in-law and friend of the Sultan of Coromandel, that I was on my way to pay him a visit, and that what was on board the ship was destined for a present to that prince. The natives went to their Sovereign and communicated to him my reply. He sent for me, and I presented myself before him at the town of Batthetlah [Puttalam] which was his capital. It is a neat little place, surrounded by a wall and bastions of wood. All the neighbouring shore was covered with trunks of cinnamon trees, torn up by the torrents. This wood was collected on the beach, and formed as it were hillocks. The inhabitants of Coromandel and of Malabar take it away without payment, save only that in return for this favor they make a present to the Sultan of stuffs and such things. Between Coromandel and the island of Ceylon there is a distance of a day and a night. . . .

Of the Sultan of Ceylon. He is called Airy Chacarouaty, and he is a powerful King upon the sea. I saw in one day, while I was on the Coromandel Coast, a hundred of his ships, both small and great, which had just arrived. There were in the port eight ships belonging to the Sultan of the country and destined to make the voyage to Yemen. The sovereign gave orders to make preparations, and assembled people to guard his vessels. When the Sinhalese despaired of finding an opportunity of seizing them, they said, "We have only come to protect the vessels belonging to us which also must go to Yemen."

When I entered the presence of the idolater Sultan, he rose, and made me sit by his side, and spoke to me with the greatest good-will. "Let your comrades," said he, "land in all safety; and be my guests until they leave. There is an alliance between me and the Sultan of Coromandel." Then he gave orders to have me lodged, and I remained with him for three days, in great consideration, which increased every day. He understood the Persian tongue, and much did he relish all I told him of foreign Kings and countries. I entered his presence one day when he had by him a quantity of pearls, which had been brought from the fishery in his dominions. The servants of the prince were sorting the precious from those which were not so. He said to me, "Have you seen the pearl fishery in the countries whence you have come?" "Yes," I answered, "I have seen it in the island of Keis, and in that of Keck, which, belong to Ibn Assaoutimily." "I have heard of them," replied he; and then took up some pearls and added, "Are there at that island any pearls equal to these?" I said, "I have seen none so good." My answer pleased him, and he said, "They are yours: do not blush," added he, "and ask of me anything you desire." I replied, "I have no other desire, since I have arrived in this island, but to visit the illustrious Foot of Adam." The people of the country call the first man baba (father) and Eve, mama (mother). "That is easy enough," answered he. "We shall send some one to conduct you." "That is what I wish," said I, and then added, "The vessel in which I have come will go in safety to Malabar and on my return, you will send me in your ships." "By all means," said he.

When I reported this to the Captain of the ship, he said, "I will not go till you have returned, even though I should have to wait a year for you." I made known this answer to the Sultan, and he said, "The Captain shall be my guest until your return." He gave me a palanquin, which his slaves bore upon their backs, and sent with me four of those djoguis [yogis] who are accustomed to undertake the pilgrimage annually to the Foot; he added to the party three Brahmins, ten others of his friends, and fifteen men to carry the provisions. As for water, it is found in abundance on the route.

On the day of our departure, we encamped near a river, which we crossed in a ferry-boat formed of bamboos. Thence we took our way to Menar Mendely, a fine town, situated at the extremity of the Sultan's territory, the people of which treated us to an excellent repast. This consisted of young buffaloes, taken in chase in the neighbouring forest and brought in alive, rice, melted butter, fish, chickens and milk. We did not see in this town a single Musalman, except a native of Khorassan, who had remained on account of sickness, and who now accompanied us. We left for Bender Selaouat, a little town, and after quitting it we traversed some rough country, much of it under water. There were numbers of elephants there, which do no manner of harm to pilgrims, nor to strangers, and that is by the holy influence of Shaikh Abau Allah, son of Khalif, the first who opened this way to visiting the Foot. Up to that time the infidels prevented the Musalmans from accomplishing the pilgrimage, harried them, and would not eat or deal with them. But when the adventure . . . had happened to the Shaikh Abou Abd Allah, that is to say, the murder of all his companions by the elephants, his own preservation, and the manner in which the elephants carried him on its back, from that time on the idolaters have respected the Musalmans, have permitted them to enter their houses and to eat with them. They also place confidence in them, as regards their women and children. Even to this day they venerate in the highest degree the above-named Shaikh, and call him "the Great Shaikh."

Meanwhile we reached the town of Conacar, the residence of the principal Sovereign of the Island. It is built in a gully, between two mountains, near a great vale, called the vale of precious stones, because gems are found in it. Outside this town is seen the Mosque of the Shaikh Othman of Shiraz, surnamed Chaouch (the usher). The King and inhabitants of the place visit him, and treat him with high consideration. He used to serve as a guide for those who go to see the Foot. When he had his hand and foot cut off, his sons and slaves became guides in his stead. The cause of his being so mutilated was that he killed a cow. Now the law of the Hindus ordains that one who has killed a cow should be massacred in like wise, or enclosed in its skin and burnt. The Shaikh Othmin being respected by those people, they contented themselves with cutting off his hand and foot, and granted to him, as a present, the dues levied at a certain market.

Of the Sultan of Conacar. He is called by the name Conar, and possesses the white elephant. I have never seen in the world another white elephant. The King rides him on solemn occasions, and attaches to the forehead of this animal large jewels. It happened to this Monarch that the nobles of his empire rebelled against him, blinded him; and made his son King. As for him, he still lives in this town, deprived of his sight.

The admirable gems called *albahraman* (rubies or carbuncles) are only found at this town. Some of them are found in the vale and these are the most precious in the eyes of the natives: others are extracted from the earth. Gems are met with in all localities in the island of Ceylon. In this country the whole of the soil is private property. An individual buys a portion of it, and digs to find gems. He comes across stones white blanched: in the interior of these stones the gem is hidden. The owner sends it to the lapidaries, who scrape it until it is separated from the stones which conceal it. There are the red (rubies), the yellow (topazes), and the blue (sapphires) which they call neilem (nilem). It is a rule of the natives that precious stones whose value amounts to 100 fanams are reserved for the Sultan, who gives their price and takes them for himself. As for those of an inferior price, they remain the property of the finders. One hundred fanams are equivalent to six pieces of gold.

All the women in the island of Ceylon possess necklaces of precious stones of diverse colors: they wear them also at their hands and feet, in the form of bracelets and khalkhals (anklets). The concubines of the Sultan make a network of gems and wear it on their heads. I have seen on the forehead of the white elephant seven of these precious stones, each of which was larger than a hen's egg. I likewise saw in possession of Airy Chacarouaty a ruby dish, as large as the palm of the hand, containing oil of aloes. I expressed my astonishment at this dish, but the Sultan said, "We have objects of the same material larger than that."

We left Conacar, and halted at a cave called by the name Ostha Mahmoud Alloury. This person was one of the best of men: he had excavated this cave in the mountain side, near a little vale. Quitting this place, we encamped near the vale called Khaour bouzneh ("monkey vale"). Bouzneh designates the same as alkoroud (monkey) in Arabic.

Of the Monkeys. These animals are very numerous in the mountains; they are of a black colour, and have long tails. Those of the male sex have beards like men. The Shaikh Othman, his son and other persons, have related to me that the monkeys have a Chief whom they obey like a Sovereign. He binds round his head a wreath of the leaves of trees, and supports himself with a staff. Four monkeys, bearing staves, march on his right and left, and, when the chief is seated, they stand behind him. His wife and little ones come and sit before him every day. The other monkeys come and squat at some distance from him; then one of the four above mentioned gives them the word and they withdraw; after which, each brings a banana, or a lime, or some such fruit. The King of the monkeys, his little ones, and the four chief monkeys then eat. A certain djogui related to me that he had seen these four monkeys before their Chief, occupied in beating another monkey with a stick, after which they plucked his hair.

Trustworthy persons have reported to me that when one of these monkeys has got possession of a young girl, she is unable to escape his lust. An inhabitant of the island of Ceylon has told me that he had a monkey, and when one of his daughters entered the house, the animal followed her. She cried him off, but he did her violence. "We ran to her aid," continued the speaker, "and seeing the monkey embracing her, we killed him."

Then we took our departure for "the vale of bamboos," where Abou 'Abd Allah, son of Khalif, found two rubies, which he presented to the Sultan of the Island . . . ; then we marched to the place called "the house of the old woman," which is at the extreme limit of the inhabited region. We left that for the cave of Bald Thahir, who was a good man; and then for that of Sebic. This Sebic was one of the idolater Sovereigns, and has retired to this spot to occupy himself with the practices of devotion.

Of the Flying Leech. At this place we saw the flying leech, by the natives called zolou. It lives upon trees and herbs in the neighbourhood of water, and when a man approaches, it pounces upon him. Whatever be the part of the body upon which the leech falls, it draws therefrom much blood. The natives take care to have ready in that case a lime, the juice of which they express over the worm, and this detaches it from the body; they scrape the place with a wooden knife made for the purpose. It is said that a certain pilgrim was passing this neighbourhood, and that the leeches fastened upon him. He remained impassive, and did not squeeze lime juice upon them; and so all his blood was sucked and he died. The name of this man was Baba Khouzy, and there is there a cave which bears his name. From this place we took our way to "the seven caves," then to the hill of Iskandar (Alexander).[1] There is there a grotto called Alisfahany, a spring of water, and an uninhabited mansion, beneath which is the bay called "place of bathing of the contemplative." At the same place is seen "the orange cave" and "the cave of the Sultan." Near the latter is the gateway (derwazeh in Persian, bab in Arabic) of the mountain.

Of the Mountain of Serendib (Adam's Peak). It is one of the highest mountains in the world; we saw it from the open sea, when we were distant from it upwards of nine days' march. While we were making the ascent, we saw the clouds above us, hiding from view the lower parts of it. There are upon this mountain many trees of kinds which do not cast their leaves, flowers of diverse colours, and a red rose as large as the palm of the hand. It is alleged that on this rose is an inscription in which one may read the name of God Most High and that of his Prophet. On the mountain are two paths leading to the Foot of Adam. The one is known by the name of "the Father's path" and the other by that of "the Mother's path." By these terms are Adam and Eve designated. The Mother's route is an easy one, and by it the pilgrims return; but any one who took it for the ascent would be regarded as not having done the pilgrimage. The Father's path is rough and difficult of ascent. At the foot of the mountain, at the place of the gateway, is a grotto also bearing the name of Iskandar, and a spring of water.

The people of old have cut in the rock steps of a kind, by help of which you ascend; fixed into them are iron stanchions, to which are suspended chains, so that one making the ascent can hold onto them. These chains are ten in number, thus: two at the foot of the mountain at the place of the gateway; seven in contiguity after the two first; and the tenth, that "the chain of the profession of faith," so named because a person who has reached it and looks back at the foot of the mountain will be seized with hallucinations, and, for fear of falling, he will recite the words "I bear witness that there is no God but God, and that Muhammed is his prophet." When you have passed this chain, you will find a path badly kept. From the tenth chain to "the cave of Khidhr" is seven miles. This cave is situated at an open place, and it also bears the name of Khidhr. No one may catch these fish. Near the cave are two basins cut in the rock, one on each side of the path. In the grotto of Khidhr the pilgrims leave their belongings; thence they mount two miles further to the summit, where is the Foot.

Description of the Foot. The impression of the noble Foot, that of our father Adam, is observed in a black and lofty rock, in an open space. The Foot is sunk in the stone in such wise that its site is quite depressed; its length is eleven spans. The inhabitants of China came here formerly; they have cut out of the stone the mark of the great toe, and of that next to it, and have deposited this fragment in a temple of the town of Zeitoun (Tseu-thonng) whither men repair from the most distant provinces. In the rock whereon is the print of the foot, are cut nine holes, in which the idolater pilgrims place gold, precious stones and pearls. You may see the fakirs, arrived from the grotto of Khidhr seeking to get ahead of one another, and so to get what may be in these holes. In our case we found there only some little stones, and a little gold which we gave to our guide. It is customary for pilgrims to pass three days in the cave of Khidhr, and during this time to visit the Foot morning and evening: and so did we. When the three days had elapsed, we returned by way of the Mother's path, and encamped hard by the grotto of Cheith, who is the same as Cheith (Seth) son of Adam. We halted in succession near the bay of fish, the straggling villages of Cormolah, Djebercaouan, Dildineoueh and Atkalendjeh. It was in the last named place that the Shaikh Abou 'Abd Allah, son of Khalif passed the winter. All these villages and stations are on the mountain. Near the base, on the same path, is the derakht, "the walking tree," a tree of great age, not one of whose leaves falls. It is called by the name of machoah (walking) because a person looking at it from above the mountain considers it fixed a long distance of, and near the foot of the hill; while one who regards it from beneath, believes it to be in quite the opposite direction. I have seen at this place a band of djoguis, who did not leave the foot of the hill, waiting for the fall of the leaves of this tree. It is planted in a place where there is no possibility of getting at it. The idolaters retail some fictions concerning it; among them, this—whoever eats of its leaves recovers his youth, even should he be an old man. But that is false.

Under this mountain is a great vale where precious stones are found. Its waters appear to the eye extremely blue. From this we marched for two days as far as the town of Dinewer, a large one, built near the sea and inhabited by merchants. In a vast temple is seen an idol bearing the same name as the town. In this temple are upwards of a thousand Brahmins and djoguis, and about five hundred women, born of idolater fathers, who sing and dance every night before the statue. The town and its revenues are the private property of the idol; all who live in the temple and those who visit it are supported therefrom. The statue is of gold and of the size of a man. In place of eyes, it has two large rubies, and I was told that they shone by night like two lamps.

We took our departure for the town of Kay, a small one, six parasangs from Dinewer. A musalman there, called the Ship Captain Ibrahim, entertained us at his house. We then took the route for the town of Calenbou (Colombo) one of the largest and most beautiful in the island of Serendib. There dwells the Vizier, prince of the sea, who has there about 500 Abyssinians. Three days after leaving Calenbou, we arrived at Batthdlah [Puttalam], of which mention is made above. We visited the Sultan of whom I have spoken. I found the Captain Ibrahim awaiting me, and we left for the country of Malabar.

Editor's Note

1. This may be a reference to the Hindu god Skanda, son of Siva, sometimes associated in Sri Lanka with Alexander the Great. For Hindus—and Ibn Battuta notes their presence—the footprint on the top of the mountain is said to be Siva's.

Saelalihini Sandesaya
(The Starling's Message)

Sri Rahula

Given the sensuous nature of this 108-stanza poem abounding in Hindu and Vedic imagery, it may be surprising that it was written by perhaps the most eminent Buddhist monk of the era. Sri Rahula—the fifteenth-century "master of six languages" and intimate confidant of Parakramabahu VI's Kotte court, who founded an academy of higher learning that drew students from throughout much of the South Asian world—stands in stark contrast to the Buddhist monk described in Parakramabahu I's twelfth-century Polonnaruva inscription (see "Promulgations of a Polonnaruva King," earlier in part 1). Indeed, this poem, significant as an example of the genre of "messenger poems" introduced from India, reflects in its descriptions the degree to which the high culture of the royal court had become familiar with the details of Sanskrit Hindu literature. Thus, on the eve of the arrival of the Portuguese, the Sinhala kings seemed to have become quite eclectic in their ideology and inclusive in its content. If Sri Rahula's poetry is an indication, Sri Lanka's culture had begun to reflect the mosaic of its modern condition. The poem itself, regarded as a masterpiece of classical Sinhala literature, is essentially a request to a beautiful bird (Saelalihini) to make a pilgrimage to the shrine of the great deity Vibhisana (brother of the Ramayana antagonist Ravana and one of the four guardian deities of Lanka) in order to plead with the deity to bestow a male child on Ulukudaya Devi, the daughter of Parakramabahu VI, to be an heir to the throne and so continue the royal lineage of Kotte. Religious culture could not be more intimately linked to the history of politics than it is here.

Noble Saelalihini! Who charms with sweet speech in neatest [sounds]
Discreet as a minister in royal secrecies!
Live long with your kinsfolk!

As pollen of blown blossoms, golden those two shanks!
As a bud of the champak your beak of lovely light red!
As blue lotus petals, deep blue, your beautiful plumage!

So when you came through the air like a figure made of flowers,
Did not young *siddha*-wives lay you in long dark tresses?
Did not the bees who live in the lotus surround you?
Did wood nymphs not make of you an ear-ornament?

Dear friend, did you not suffer such annoyance by the way?
Where your love is joined, clinging it increases.
What need of other joys? Your sight alone suffices.

Like the moon without blemish brimming with tenderness,
Slenderness of the white water-lily, your bright form achieves.
Sweet-spoken as the chintamani that grants longed-for happiness
By seeing you we feel we have stored away good.

True friends, for good or ill alike,
Like frescoed figures never turn away.
Sweet friend of like virtue, fix your mind on my words.
Give ear to that which holds the future's gain.

5. Give this message to Vibhisana, that great King of Gods
In Kaelaniya city, full of all glories, as the city of devas:
His fame is spread forth as flowers full-blown on the World-Tree,
Whose roots are the naga world, Mahameru its trunk, its branches the
     regions.

As rain clouds give pleasure to pea-fowl as they go through the sky
So, friend, your appearance gives pleasure to me;
In a while I shall give you that message, its charm all intact.
Now listen to the landmarks of your journey from here.

Mark, noble friend, the great city Jayavaddana,
Where are rich men who love and pursue the Triple Gem:
Whose wealth puts the devas' city to shame
Whose name is well founded on triumphs that ever advance.

The stream called Diyavanna with its ripples and its wavelets
Seems a silk garment worn by the woman-city,
Worked with rows of red lotus, and figures of golden swans,
Its spreading cascades the long rippling waist folds.

The wall of this city has its broad gates like the buckles
Of the gem studded breast-band discarded with young days
By Lanka decked out and proud;
Samanala her hair-knot, the great sea her girdle!

10. With bells on trotting horses and clatter of hoof-beats;
    With flapping of yak-tail-decked ears of King-elephant;
    Din of varying music and blasts of triumphal conches;
    Like another sea's the incessant roar of the city!

    Tied with huge red yak-tails and innumerable bells
    That tinkle in breezes that waft from the gardens
    Scent of champak and sandal, gold pennants that flutter
    Stem the fires of the sun in the beautiful city.

    In rows of [storied] palaces, so strong and so lofty,
    The balconies, lovely with carvings of gods and sky dwellers,
    Are like mansions of gods who come down to behold
    This glorious city which keeps unending festival.

    With faces like moons, and slim waists to be clasped in a closed fist;
    With broad hips well turned like the wheel of a chariot;
    Swan-breasted, the city's women like creepers of gold
    Are not goddesses only in that they blink' their eyes.

    This flourishing city which stands in the principal region,
    Rich in much hidden treasure, where the thieving and base never come,
    Full of the generous and powerful, standing on ground free from
       affliction,
    Is finer far than the home of the Lord of the North.

15. When the star of Brahaspati rises shedding wide its light,
    And the moon ascends to the zenith from Asvin's house,
    It is right, my friend, that you go from this city,
    With heart full of joy, and mind fixed on your clan's guardian god.

    Mild scented breezes, pitchers brim-full, and sweet mango fruit;
    Full-blown white blossoms, maidens sweet-spoken, and golden urns;
    Waving white yak-tails, white parasols, lusty King-elephants;
    Look for these on your way, luckier than conjunction of stars.

    Bow down to the Sacred Tooth Relic that stands in its three-[storied]
       temple
    Spreading over the world rays white as the beams of the moon;
    That always gives full bliss of heaven, supreme bliss of Nirvana,
    Which has felt the great Dhamma stored in the mind of the Sage.

    Now leave this place: fly at once to the palace
    Where precious stones blaze from a pinnacle of gleaming gold.

From the eaves smooth festoons of pearls sway in the breezes
And great walls of moon-crystal stand in their ranks.

There, friend, feast your gaze on the great Lord Parakramabahu
Who is to the Sun's Race as the sun to the lotus-pond,
In whose bosom-home Lakshmi the goddess lies always;
Radiant, his beauty unblemished, like Ramba's lord.

20. Wearing all sixty-four kingly insignia, including the crown,
Like Vishnu incarnate, he graces the Lion-throne.
Bow low at his gracious feet and take leave of this king
Who comes down from Manu in unbroken line.

With mind set in intent to cross to the further shore
Fly, friend, from Kontagam's [?] ferry where dead lotus petals
Have fallen on the face of the waters, and lilies
That opened enfolded in moonbeams, stand all around.

Now perch in the beautiful Ishvara devale. Here
In fumes of camphor and aloes rows of banners wave.
Thunder of conch and mridanga, and clangor of bells fill the wide air,
And people, devoutly, sing Tamil hymns of praise.

When you hear the five instruments making morn music
Scatter sleep from your eyes, awake with the dawn
When the soft winds arise that bring cries of the lake-swallow
And waft powder of saffron from the harlot's full breasts.

When like a lantern on a palisade of gold, the sun
From Udagiri's crest fills the day with light,
Observe the forms of the ritual performed before Ishvara,
Cast off your sloth, through the blue sky take wing.

25. Dear friend, at that hour you will see to the East
Samanala rock imprinted with the Buddha's Holy Lotus Foot,
Which Saman the God-King adores in a train of heavenly maidens
With heaped blooms of mandar and parijat brilliantly hued.

To the south of the seat of our King there appears
Skanda's temple variously decked, as with cock-blazoned banners
That float from the tips of gem-crusted standards of gold
That gleam like the shafts of the sun.

Behold also the sea that shows then to the North,
With beaches that glisten with thanks, coral and pearl,

Whose huge ranks of waves skywards are hurled by the winds
As though yearning to embrace the river maiden of the sky.

Where sihingenda trees spread their shade on the wide sands
Rest here and there, for you are delicate. Then go on with joy
Asking the right direction of your journey
From parrots that carry gold ears of corn.

See Prince Sapumal, lord of the army, astride his black charger
With forces intact after capturing Jaffna.
His gem-crushed ornaments make his white parasol gleam.
He appears, it would seem, in the form of the Sun-God.

30. Fly on dipping down to the road that goes over the sandy white
    stretches
Strewn with pollen from flowers on the trees that stand by;
Where are flowering lakes on which the king-swan alights
And thickets of creepers of full flowering jasmine.

Behold at Kaikavala the warriors on guard,
With more than a thousand bows and spears and swords,
Firm to repel the onslaught of even Airavana.
Then fly swiftly away over thick flowering woods.

There look! The sweet forest nymphs play on couches of flowers
In creeper-hung arbors and thickets on sands
That shine pure as the light of the moon. Rest now
On a tender sal tree, that breathes coolness from all its young leaves.

Here now is Vallambalama; fly with joy by the pond
Whose banks are dark green with the jamala tree
Where maidens with beautiful flower-entwined hair-knots
That are scented with incense take their ease . . . fires quenched in cool
    waters.

Enter at noon the Sumutana forest
Where young bloods come and go and sport and make merry,
Their brows adorned with the smooth kasturi-tilaka,
And wreaths of red lotus bound round their heads.

35. Now flutter your wings and play on the pollen-thick crests of the
    flowers
Of na-trees and nim [?] trees, and domba and mora that make the road
    green.

Thrust your beak in and eat of the sweet ripened fruit;
Then in jambu trees rest, bird, and go on your way.

With nothing to hinder go to Gurulaketa [?]
Where wakened in sun's warmth, the lotus spreads over the lake.
Here jungle cocks make their wars by the roadside
And drunken cuckoo birds sing in the arbors' depths.

See, friend, and then go, the deep icy pool
Filled with lily and lotus, and red and white nymphaeae where many
     bees swarm.
Ringed with screw-pine in flower and flowering muruta,
A gold jewel it seems, ruby-set, of Lakshmi the forest.

Guruluketa fields stand ripe now for harvest. See them and go
Where free from malice the peasant girls play,
Bright bosoms spattered with pollen of red lotus
And blue water-lilies stuck in their ears.

A woman's necklace of coral, bright emeralds and pearls, seems
This ring of arecas with its nuts and flowers.
The woman is a village. The sight will seduce you. Indulge not in
     transports.
Glance at Velandagoda, stay but a while and go on your way.

40. Go, friend, through Veralana's broad rice fields,
Where the ears of the rat-kel now sag in their ripeness.
Cries of lapwing and wild fowl are heard here and there
Among blossoming champak, and hora, and screw-pine that stand all
     around.

Perch in a lovely domba tree, thick-leaved and full of flowers;
Among hill-minas ease your heart.
Enjoying scented airs, discard the weariness of flesh;
Then go, when it is afternoon, to Kit-siri-me temple.

There worship the stupa, massed glory it seems of the Wise One;
The Bo-tree, dark as luster of His eyes once fixed in salutation;
The image whose beauty fills the mind with rapture
As the moon that rests upon a bank of evening cloud.

On river banks made lovely with the shade of dark green branches
Of sal, sapu, kina and domba, raranga, na and midella,
Flowering ahala, palu, asoka, mi, mango and areca,
Plantain, sugarcane and cocopalm, and silk-cotton betel-entwined:

With kadupul blossoms adorning their dark hair;
And bright jewelled girdles swathed round their hips;
Their breasts assuaged with sandal-paste and pearls,
Casting dark beams from wide eyes this way and that:

45. The lovely naga maidens couch on the clean sands
    And sing of the Buddha sweet songs of praise,
    Their finger tips caressing the strings of jeweled vinas;
    Listen awhile by Kelani river and be refreshed.

Threading sapu and kohomba flowers prettily in their hair-knots;
On the tips of their breasts the shining domba buds are wound like
     strings of pearls;
Wearing pollen-scattering na flowers in semblance of ear studs,
After dallying all day with gay youths in gardens:

Their eyes the blue nymphaeae, white lilies their smiles,
Their lips the red water-lily, lotus-faced they seem;
When this crowd of young women, like gold vines swaying in the
     breeze,
Finish their games in the bright jeweled water,

The sun's disc seems a ripened fruit, dark red,
That nears the time of severance from its stalk, the Western Rock,
Of that vast tree the sky, lovely as sapphire, blue on blue,
Washed by the evening winds that play about its region-boughs.

Then with the sun the day will also fade,
As if to prove the rule that holds among all virtuous men
That when distress shall come the friendly patron
Who gave great help must never be cast off.

50. When in the West the evening clouds are seen, a ruby pavement
    With red silk spread by sea-dwelling God-King Varuna
    In all devotion upon the path his kinsman takes,
    The Sun-God of a thousand rays;

And the stars in array seem like flowers
Strewn on the glorious couch of the firmament, lovely and pure
By Night, filled with desire because her lord comes to her,
The moon that glistens with a soft effulgence;

Fly thence, see Maskeliya, where the lelu fish play
And leap in the water, making it bubble and foam,

As they reach and roll over each other to seize without fear
Food which the crowds of people have thrown.

Enter, O Saelalihini, the great city Kaelaniya,
Whose beauty from moment to moment is ever renewed.
Forests of bell-hung banners enclose its fine dwellings,
And glittering gems are set on its pinnacles' tips.

See, friend, in the great highway, the lovely colored lamps
Like the enchanting hoard of gems laid bare
When all the vast depths of the famed ocean's water became
A honey-drop in sage Agastya's lotus palm.

55. When to the East the moon appears transfigured by the evening clouds,
Washed, it seems, by Udagiri's ruby light, the river of the sky
Swollen by floods that drip from the lovely city's moonstone houses
Seems devoted to observing the virtues of a spouse.

Look, friend, women like gold creepers go, crescent browed, with dark
    clouds of hair;
Eyes, blue-lotus; lips, coral; teeth, white chanks; as bosses on elephant
    heads
Their bosoms, with Vishnu's bright hair mark; thighs, plantain trunks;
    laps wide as sand-plains;
Their calves, peacocks' necks; pearly-nailed, the young leaves their
    fingers.

When lady-night, charmed with such festal gaiety, pours
Silk stuffs so shimmering-bright from that chest of chank, the moon,
The gracious lady-city makes swift return, a girdle jewel-bright
Of rays from her casket of gleaming palaces, flung upon the sky.

Amorous husbands and wives, each with no thought but for the other
Wearing exquisite garlands of special fragrance,
Their bodies anointed with sandal-paste and saffron,
Lie in that city's moonlit balconies.

Go the length of the streets where are gardens adorned
With plantains lolling their flower heads, and ranuembilis [?] heavy
    with bunches.
Turn, friend, to the South, go and enter the Temple,
Mind set on the chant of the Buddha's Nine Virtues.

60. Go tell over all virtues world-famed of the Buddha. Dipping your wings
    To the ground, worship the Lord's great image in Lankatilaka,
    As though your eyes had seen Sakya-Muni himself,
    That heavenly bliss may be yours and bliss of Nirvana.

    Worship the holy lotus-feet of his lovely stone image
    Bright with the color of the very sea,
    Made by the Lord of Heaven to succor Lanka's creatures
    When, long ago, the ocean's great waters ran over land.

    In the five-[storied] mansion, where Maliyadeva the Great Monk
    Sat and expounded the Dhamma lest sixty theras be lost
    In the sea of Becoming, if you can see the gems' dazzling glitter,
    Look, friend, make obeisance and go.

    Worship the gleaming stupa in the circular relic-house
    That casts on all sides the color of moonbeams,
    Never losing its likeness of foam-spate that rose when Lord Vishnu
    Laying hold of Mandara churned up the sea long ago.

    Bow in the Western Hall before the image of the Lord recumbent.
    Unequalled his lovely, bright, golden form;
    Whose long eyes are blue lilies, whose red lips are coral,
    Whose charming countenance is gracious as the full moon.

65. Stand at the sixteen points and worship the mighty stupa
    Reared sixty cubits high where Sakya-Muni sat
    When, besought by King Miniak [?], he came through the heavens
    And preached the word among saints upon a jeweled throne.

    Please, then, to worship the image in the Naga image house
    Which shows to all men the Omniscient as he sat
    In shelter of Naga Muchalinda's hood, in the house of his coils,
    When in the sixth week rains streamed from all ten directions.

    See his perfect image in Samadhi posture
    As though the Lord Himself sat in calmest contemplation
    When with the nectar of his word He had saved the world from
       samsara,
    And, friend, worship, your mind's three states in accord.

    Worship the King of trees, that parasol of fine sapphire,
    Furnished with a staff of lustrous silver,
    Gift of the gods to our Lord in the Day of Enlightenment;
    Then take to thy soul the fruit of such devotion.

From the South gate whose pinnacle the moon grazes, hear without
flinching
The clash of a myriad instruments making devotional music.
Then, going down, after adoring the Trivanka images
That are made without blemish, and bright with the marks of good
fortune,

70. Worship, facing always, the Sivuru Dagoba,
Built where he stood, wrapped in three bright robes, the Unattached,
the Buddha,
When he bathed in cool water of Kaelani River, that seems
The stretched-out trunk of Samanala Rock, that mighty King-elephant.

Bow, charming one, to the image seated in the lovely hall,
Built in devotion by the worthy that place where stood
The seething pot of oil, into which, in frenzy of doubt,
King Kaelanitissa flung the innocent saint.

Storing in mind merit immeasurable drawn from such homage,
Taking it to make offering when you see him, the great god,
Useful friend, go then to his royal dwelling,
That is like Vijayot [?] Prasada, the home of Heaven's King.

Stand and gaze at the dancing-girls in the dance arena,
Whose hair knots are bound with scented confusion of flowers full-
blown,
Their pretty ears decked with shining gold leaves;
Their long, dark eyes painted with finely made salve.

Flickering lamp-flames they seem these dancers in array,
On whose broad hips hang the heavy waistfolds that ripple and flare,
Who shoot sidelong glances at their arms as they rise and they fall.
Transfigured their forms in the glare that beats from their jewels.

75. Drink in the charms of these women who dance,
Stamping feet of lotus to beaten-out rythms
To swing the girdles that are swathed round their lovely wide flanks,
And their anklets hung with bells that wake into sound.

Friend, give delight to mind, ear and eye! See the women
Like kinduru maidens who sing lovely songs
Contrived of the seven notes' flavors as though there were blended
Sweet sounds of the flute and the vina, the cuckoo-bird and the bee.

After such offering of music and dancing, fill your eyes
With the sight of Vibhisana, that great God-King,
Whose fame spreads through and flows over the world,
Who stands well-pleased in the midst of his house.

On his head who is World-Refuge and King of Gods appears
A crown of gold with gems and strings of pearls that gleams
As when above the summit of a darkling crag
Comes up the planet-glory of Rohini's car.

From darkest dark the storm-cloud grows pallid.
Has the lightning love-lorn, therefore, fled in distraction
To flash as the gold circlet on the brow of the God-King
Who wears the storm-cloud's hue changeless through time?

80. In this beautiful God-King's ears that seem like jeweled swings
Are lodged bright cylinders of heaviest gold that flash
Like twin golden mirrors of Lakshmi and Sarasvati
Who flourish continually in his face.

Two thick clouds lustrous-dark, the lines of the God-King's eyebrows
Thrust from the rock-flank of his brow, that give
Balm of cool water to the rice-fields of his adorers;
To the forest of his mighty enemies a sudden thunder-bolt.

The eyes of the lord like twin suns rising glower
To scatter at one stroke the darkness of enemy gods,
And even bring to flower the crowded lotus-thicket of his friends
Drying with one glance the dews of manifest danger.

The jeweled horn, that cannot rival the high, long, handsome nose
Of the God whose praises siddha goddesses sing forth
Grouped here and there in fine array, tires itself out, alt! [?] woe,
Shrilling in the service of kings and other gods.

At the corners of the God's red playful lips are gleaming tusks,
Dense rows of white swans on a pool of rich vermilion!
Two young bright moons, if such there be, that show
At each end of bank of lovely sunset cloud!

85. With light like flowering sprays, that springs from jeweled armbands,
And fingers long and fine, copper of tender leaves,
This God-King's drooping arms that grant what men desire
Outshine in glory the glittering boughs of Heaven's tree.

A sapphire plain where Lakshmi in unending love disports
The spreading shoulders of the King of Gods who bathes
In light from looks of manifest desire from goddess' eyes
Languorous and most soft, that deepens as with lac [?].

His handsome thighs like plantains trunks, massive and most sleek
Seem, from the light that beats from cat's-eyes studded in the belt
That binds the region of his fine broad hips,
In aspect as though splashed with water cool and bright.

Hue of pale copper, young asoka leaves seem shaken with affright
That the lotus is trodden by the soles of the Lord's feet
Which are lovely with that radiance delicate as lac [?]
Prisoned in glare of gems that tip the crowns of bowing gods.

Can one mouth end the tale of the beauty of this God-King,
Who like the sea has his charm, brilliant, pure, profound;
Alluring, yet inspiring all beholders with awe,
Endowed with the goddess Lakshmi, and with unblemished gems?

90. How is it that Heaven's Tree, Heaven's Cow, and Wishing Gem
Be held to him who grants the world's desires on mention only of his
    name?
Heard in learned talk only, the names of the heavenly healers!
But he casts out sorrow and disease, sin's fruit, as water from the lotus
    leaf.

Because he grants as soon as wished whatever heart desires
Of wisdom, glory, wealth and fame, great armies, victory, kingship,
Office and all success, long life and natural force,
This God-King in our time is recompense for good that men have
    done.

Bow three times at the lotus feet of this King of Gods
Ravana's brother who bent the three worlds to his sway;
Who scanned the three aspects of Time and became the loved friend of
    Rama;
Jeweled lamp of sage Pulasti's line, master of the three Vedas.

Wait then an opening on the God-King's pleasure.
Eschewing haste, mark well the sequence of your words.
Offer a paean of praises to the King of Gods,
Then, standing on one side, unfold the burden of your charge.

"Mount Meru in firmness and strength! Bright sun in great majesty!
In depth the famous sea! The blue sky in brilliance!
In serenity, great moon! In wisdom Instructor of Gods!
Live long, O Vibhisana! Great God of Kaelani city!

95. He who moves as a king-swan on royalty's full flowering waters;
Whose beauty ravishes, as of old, the God of Love;
Whose well-being is whole at all times, and never decreases;
Who shines with the jewels of majesty, heroism and power;

Who ever holds you in thought, who makes vast and desirable
 offerings,
The excellent minister, Nannuru Tunaya,
Bids me earnestly tell the wish of his heart.
Deign, O great God, to give care to his message awhile.

Who to the Latmeni [?] line of the Sun's Race is as the bright sun
That mounts to the clear zenith in autumn's season, whose great fame
Is as a string of pearls about the throats of a host of poets,
Whose glory is world-wide, who is Lakshmi's abode;

Who, learning the Buddha's Threefold Word, has put aside evil;
Who has crossed the ocean' of poesy, drama, and all warlike arts;
And, crushing the pride of fierce foes, showing knowledge of strategy
Brought all Lanka to the shelter of a single parasol;

Whose beauty is like fine salve laid on the eye of all men;
Who displays the glory of Indra come down among mortals;
Who in prowess is chief of the Princes of India;
Upon the daughter of him who is our Lord Parakrama-Bahu,

100. Upon her who is like Lakshmi, whose blessings grow great and
 flourish;
A Wishing Gem in lavishness to beggars who cry;
Who in wisdom is like Sarasvati manifested on earth;
Who is greeted with love as the new moon by all people;

Who has one thought for women friends in her own happiness,
And in kindness rains wealth on manservants and maids;
Who observes the chaste vow and all excellent rules,
And practices the Ten Virtues as with intellect born;

Who is well-versed in poetry's art and skilled in polite conversation
And has love over-flowing for the Word of the Lord of Sages;

Who never fails to observe pure ata-sil on the moon days;
On Ulukudaya Devi, the lovely, the famous;

Great God, who seems the one eye of the three worlds, whose lovely
  feet
Are wet with honey rain from scented wreaths on diadems of Gods,
Be pleased justly to bestow that jewel fair, a son well-favoured,
Blessed with long life and wealth, wisdom and fame.

Of old, with insight divine full of pity, the Lord Parakrama-Bahu,
By your grace, with joy, to the great Queen Ratnavali was given,
And became ruler of Lanka. What need
To publish your excellence, your great glory and power!

105. So grant to this princess of whom I speak, the jewel of a son,
To her who bows to the beautiful feet of that God,
Making offering of jasmine and water-lilies,
And your merit will increase with your fame and your glory."

PARTING WORDS
Fine friend, thus give this message to the King of Gods.
Walk round him with delight presenting your right side,
And worshipping with love. Then straightway appear
Before his Goddess Queen to sue in that same way.

That she may tell the God-King when he is alone at leisure,
Next to the God-Prince deliver your message;
To him who to his dynasty adds lustre
As the bright full moon that shines upon the milky sea.

As the sun at dawn unfolds the lotus-flower.
With abounding love all my intent unfold.
Go live, O Saelalihini, a hundred years with friends and kinsfolk,
Just as you may please with blessings attained.

The Colonial Encounter

The arrival of the first Portuguese ships in 1505 or 1506 inaugurated an encounter with Western political powers that continues to this day. From this date until 1948, Sri Lanka was a venue for European colonization strategies: first by the Portuguese (1505/6–1658), then the Dutch (1658–1796), and finally the British (1796–1948).

In introducing her readers to modern Sri Lanka, the historian Nira Wickramsinghe describes the general impact of European colonialism in the following way:

> The exceptional length—four hundred years—of the colonial impact on Ceylon, particularly in the coastal areas, radically modified social and economic structures of the island. Ceylon encountered modernity gradually and unevenly. In some respects, the colonial impact extroverted the economy, overturned the traditional streams of trade, and distorted links with India, while introducing into society new elements of heterogeneity: Christianity, the languages of the successive conquerors, new communities such as the Burghers and later Indian immigrant plantation workers. It also imposed unifying factors: modern modes of communication, a unified administrative system, a common language of domination, monetarisation of exchanges. However, the depth of the colonial imprint must not be overestimated: family structures, the caste system and Buddhism were maintained, especially in the center of the island where foreign domination was resisted for three centuries.[1]

The dominant direct legacy left behind by the Portuguese was Roman Catholicism, still practiced today by about 5 or 6 percent of the country's population, chiefly along the west coast of the island just north and south of Colombo. One can also readily see the Portuguese impact on Sri Lanka's diet (the introduction of bread and chilies, for instance), on music and dance (baila), and architecture (rounded roof tiles). Indirectly, the presence of Catholicism impacted the manner in which Buddhism is publicly articulated in the country as well. For example, the ubiquitous presence of Buddha images along public thoroughfares in the same manner as statues of Catholic saints in Sri Lanka, despite the fact that in traditional Sinhala Buddhist culture, Buddha images were only found within Buddhist viharas (monastic temples).

While the Portuguese were interested in spices and in monopolizing that trade, the succeeding Dutch and their single-minded interest in cinnamon was perhaps the first indication that eventually Sri Lanka would become the venue of a predominantly plantation economy. The economic efficiency of the Dutch and their deployment of Roman Dutch law, still an important fixture in Sri Lanka's legal code, remain important legacies, along with the Dutch Burgher community, which has contributed so much to the production of Sri Lankan English literature.

It is impossible to underestimate the impact of British rule on Sri Lanka. Not only is English its most powerful legacy, a language now spoken in some form by about a third of the island's population, but the country's educational, political, and transportation systems, not to mention its business community, owe their substance and structure to the British. As in India, much of Sri Lanka's modern infrastructure was established by the British. As the British were leaving Ceylon, they built and donated to the country the sprawling campus of the University of Ceylon in upcountry Peradeniya, near Kandy. This university, eventually named the University of Peradeniya, became the foundation for the education and training of generations of Sri Lankans following independence. The university system has spread from this auspicious origin to distant regions of the island.

Note

1. Nira Wickramasinghe, *Sri Lanka in the Modern Age* (Honolulu: University of Hawaii Press, 2006), 43.

Sri Lanka: National Identity and the Impact of Colonialism

K. M. de Silva

Colonialism is not simply a historical curiosity of the past in Sri Lanka. Rather, its legacy persists in a variety of ways that continue to impact contemporary political and economic trajectories. How the economic transformations and religious impacts of European colonial power under the Portuguese, Dutch, and British continue to influence postcolonial Sri Lanka is here described and analyzed by Sri Lanka's leading historian.

Introduction. We are just over 50 years from the end of the country's prolonged political subordination to a colonial power, the relationship of a colony to a metropolitan centre in Europe. In the case of Sri Lanka, colonial status goes back to the sixteenth century with the first of three successive layers of colonial rule under the Portuguese, followed by the Dutch and British respectively in the seventeenth and eighteenth centuries. There are very few former colonies of European and Western powers in South and Southeast Asia which have had such a lengthy colonial period under Western imperial rule as Sri Lanka. . . . In Sri Lanka the colonial experience has had a profound impact on its culture, its traditions and its development, and indeed on its national identity.

Economics and Development. As with religion, so with economics and development, Sri Lanka is currently grappling with its colonial inheritance. To the Portuguese and the Dutch, Sri Lanka was one of the fabled spice islands. The principal quest, at that stage, was for the cinnamon that grew wild in the forests of the southwest coast, and in the interior of the Kandyan kingdom. The cinnamon bushes and trees provided the branches that were peeled and gathered in bales for the state by a Sinhalese caste of cinnamon peelers. The colonial power, first the Portuguese and next the Dutch, had a monopoly of its external trade, one which gave them a massive profit. In the extraction of this profit the Dutch did far better than the Portuguese. For decades, Amsterdam was the centre of the international cinnamon trade. Indeed:

> Cinnamon was one article the price of which the Dutch were able to dictate. As sole suppliers both in Europe and in the east they were in a position to do so. This is reflected in the phenomenal increase in price both in Europe and in the east from the 1660s. . . . [The] cost price was next to nothing. . . . [1]

One other aspect of this trade needs special emphasis:

The country itself did not benefit at all from this enlarged export potential of one of its products. Cinnamon was not sold in the island's ports to any incoming trader and as such the country was deprived . . . of the use of a commodity of exchange of its imports. The profits of cinnamon did not appear even in the Dutch accounts of their Sri Lankan administration. The sales in Europe appeared as profits in the Netherlands chambers of the Dutch East India Company and the sales in the various ports counted as profits in those ports. It was a classic case of colonial exploitation of a cash crop without the country of origin seeing any of the benefits of its sales.[2]

During the last 30 years of their rule on the coasts of Sri Lanka, the Dutch introduced a new technique of harvesting the principal item of the colonial economy: the cinnamon bushes. Instead of extracting cinnamon from the forests they would plant cinnamon in chosen parts of the territories they controlled. The new technique of plantation agriculture was expected to ensure easier access to profits from this crop. But the profits began to decline.[3] The demand for Sri Lankan cinnamon dropped in the face of the high prices the Dutch expected, and the competition from cheaper producers, and cheaper substitutes.

Once the British replaced the Dutch as the colonial power in the island, they found cinnamon—the mainstay of the colonial economy's external trade since the beginning of Portuguese rule—to be in a state of rapid and irretrievable decline.[4] By the 1830s Sri Lanka began a new phase in its linkage to the world economy that had begun with the Portuguese intrusion, and had matured under the Dutch; it evolved into a plantation colony producing another commercial crop: coffee. The production of that crop spread with unprecedented rapidity and had amazing profitability. For the next 40 years or so, Sri Lanka emerged as one of the major producers of coffee,[5] indeed the most significant Asian producer of coffee for the British and European markets.[6]

Significant differences between the production of coffee and the production of cinnamon marked the beginning of processes of development and modernization that transformed the economy of the country. The production and sale of cinnamon were entirely controlled by the Dutch East India Company. The capital was theirs, the sales were theirs, and the profits were theirs. The local Sinhalese population, particularly the caste of cinnamon peelers, provided the virtually bonded labor. Had this system or something like it been continued under coffee the result would have seen the creation of what has been called a dual economy in the island, one in which the links between the modern plantation economy and the traditional economy would be minimal. What happened was substantially different under coffee. The capital was largely if not entirely British, much of the labor was immigrant Indian, and the product grew best in the interior of the country, in areas which had only recently come under colonial rule. This is to say that it grew best in areas away from the areas previously used for cinnamon production and the cinnamon trade. Coffee production transformed the economy of the country in a way that cinnamon never did. Quite apart from the scale of the operation, which was far greater than under cinnamon from the sixteenth to the early nineteenth century, and the linkage with migrant labor, the demands of coffee production required a network of roads linking the interior of the island with the coasts, thus marking the beginning of a modern transport system. Indeed every aspect of a modern economy in the island began with the coffee industry.

While the local population did not provide the labor on the plantations, they controlled the transport of coffee from the plantations to the coast. Until the railway was built in the late 1860s, transport of coffee was by bullock carts, all of them owned and operated by Sinhalese. The British planting houses tried very hard to establish a system of carts of their own, but every such effort failed.

Equally important was the fact that Sri Lankans—largely Sinhalese—established modern plantations of their own. They were few in number, but native producers of coffee were a phenomenon not seen in most British plantation colonies. More to the point: a third of the coffee lands were those the peasants themselves converted from their own holdings to the production of coffee for the market. It is doubtful whether the native population in any other plantation colony participated in the production of a commercial commodity of external trade on this scale.

Just when Sri Lanka's flourishing coffee industry had reached the peak of its prosperity in the later 1860s it was attacked by a leaf disease: *Hemileia vastatrix*. In less than a decade the coffee industry on the island collapsed. The speed and completeness of the process of destruction were virtually unprecedented for a commercial crop in any plantation colony. It is not known how and why it emerged in Sri Lanka at that time. Perhaps the virulence of the original outbreak would suggest that fungus could not have been endemic in the island before its first recorded appearance there. Some have attributed the major cause of the outbreak to the extent of monoculture in the planting districts. From Sri Lanka, the disease spread to other Asian producers in the last decades of the century, and severely affected coffee exports from Java and parts of India. As a result the supply of coffee to the world market shifted overwhelmingly to South America.

The principal beneficiaries of the Sri Lankan coffee industry were, of course, British investors and the planters. But it would be true to say that the people of Sri Lanka also benefited through the creation of economic opportunities that had not existed before, and by exposing Sri Lankans to the spirit of enterprise to a far greater extent than under the Portuguese and the Dutch. The rapid expansion of plantation agriculture in the mid-nineteenth century was the major catalyst of social change in Sri Lanka as it formed the basis upon which the economic development that arose in the period of British rule in the country came to have such a powerful influence in independent Sri Lanka. The large-scale production of coffee and the growth of services to support the needs of the plantations and their workers stimulated the development of the Kandyan highlands and the city of Colombo, and consolidated Sri Lanka's dependence on the cultivation and export of cash crops sensitive to fluctuations in the world economy. It was only in the last quarter of the twentieth century, with the rise of the garment industry, that there was any substantial success in lessening this dependence.

This radical change in the economy which came with coffee cultivation was itself a reflection of the strength of global capitalism, from which no country in the nineteenth century remained unaffected; a force which unified the world under the aegis of European domination. In Sri Lanka itself, one of the most significant consequences was in the old Kandyan kingdom where the highlands were profoundly transformed, socially and economically, under coffee production. Its incorporation to the world economy was accomplished within 30 years of the introduction of British rule. On the positive side, the commercialization of agriculture and the introduction of new economic opportunities offered new opportunities of economic advancement to the peasants in the Kandyan villages, but the flipside was the disruption of the traditional social relations in the Kandyan villages thus accentuating the inequality between the elite and the peasants. In addition, the growth of the plantations saw the migration of diverse peoples and cultures into the previously relatively homogeneous and isolated homeland of the Kandyan Sinhalese. Nevertheless the coffee industry served the historical purpose of facilitating the unification of Sri Lanka, by tying the former kingdom of Kandy to the maritime districts as a single social and economic entity far more effectively than any administrative or political decision of the colonial government.

While the Kandyan participation in commercial agriculture was greatly handicapped with the demise of coffee production, significant numbers of the Sinhalese from the lowlands continued their involvement with plantation agriculture. When the tea industry—the third wave of plantation production after cinnamon and coffee—developed and expanded, Sinhalese investments were already in place. Sinhalese capitalists were far more important in the rubber industry than in tea, and planting and production of coconut was almost a monopoly of Sinhalese plantation owners and smallholders. Unlike coffee, tea and rubber were introduced to the island by the colonial government and British entrepreneurs. By this time the share of the Sinhalese in the general commercial ("modern") sector of the economy was very significant, and one of the most notable features of this was the emergence of a considerable class of indigenous capitalists. (Apart from their role in the plantation economy Sinhalese played the predominant role in the mining and export of graphite.) The descendants of these capitalists eventually led the reform and nationalist movements.

The plantation sector of Sri Lanka's economy was relatively larger in comparison with the traditional sector than in most tropical colonies, and the interconnection between the two sectors was much stronger as well. Thus, Sri Lanka was not a typical tropical plantation colony with a dual economy: that would be to ignore the very significant role of Sri Lankan investors and smallholders in cash crop production, and their role in Sri Lanka's general economic development in the nineteenth and twentieth centuries.

At every stage segments of the indigenous population participated in plantation agriculture . . . indigenous planters—capitalists, smallholders, and peasants—played a much more prominent role in plantation agriculture than their counterparts in most other tropical colonies. . . .[7]

They also played a dynamic role in national politics. Sri Lanka was the first country in Asia to face the challenges of universal suffrage—introduced to the island as early as 1928. The first Sri Lanka general election under universal suffrage was held in 1931 only two years after the first such election in Britain. By the time Sri Lanka became independent in 1948 there had been three such general elections (in 1931, 1936 and in 1947). The election of 1956, the second after independence, confirmed the maturity of the system when the government in power was defeated at the polls—the first time the inheritors of power at independence in a former colony in Asia lost power to a rival party or coalition at a general election.

Colonialism and Religion. Sri Lanka provides one of the most striking illustrations of the truth of the contention that European imperialism was as much a religious as a political or economic or ideological problem. The religious phase of imperialism, which Sri Lanka confronted for the first time in the early sixteenth century, was one of those overpowering movements of historical forces whose impact and consequences last for centuries rather than decades. In their rigorous commitment to the Christianization of those parts of the country they came to control, the Portuguese, and to some extent the Dutch, reached out to attempt the transformation of the very heart of the culture and religious traditions in Sri Lanka. They significantly impacted literature, as well as the arts and architecture. Unfortunately, the study of the impact of Christianization on the culture and traditions of the country is one of the least researched aspects of Sri Lanka's history.

Naturally the colonial powers faced strong opposition to their policies. The resulting experience of conflict and resistance has had great historical consequences that have survived the expulsion of the Portuguese and the Dutch, in succession, and the departure of the British in ways that continue to play out in the public life of the country even today.

Christianity, Roman Catholic and Protestant, came to the island with the three Western colonial powers—Portugal, Holland and Great Britain—who had control over parts of the island (Portugal and Holland) or the whole of it (the British) from the mid-sixteenth century to the late 1940s. Roman Catholicism and Calvinism in particular, and Anglicanism (to a much lesser extent), enjoyed a special relationship with the ruling colonial power and with this the prestige and massive authority of the official religion of the day. Converts to the orthodox version of Christianity—especially under the Portuguese and the Dutch—were treated as a privileged group entitled to a range of special advantages. More important, severe restrictions, if not penalties, were imposed on the practice of the traditional religions—Buddhism primarily, but also Hinduism and Islam. These were severest under the Portuguese. The Dutch widened the scope of these restrictions to include Roman Catholicism as well, so that there was the bizarre spectacle of the battles of the Reformation and Counter-Reformation in Europe being fought in an Asian country.[8] Thus religious edifices and centers belonging to the Buddhists, Hindus and Muslims were destroyed by the Portuguese in the areas in the country which they came to control. The Dutch, for their part, were somewhat more restrained in this, but extended the principle by demolishing Roman Catholic and other religious churches and institutions constructed by the Portuguese. The result is that there are no Portuguese churches or public buildings in existence in Sri Lanka today despite the fact that Roman Catholics constitute 90 percent of the Christians in the island.[9] The oldest of the Roman Catholic churches surviving today were established in British times.

A crucially important feature of the colonial experience under the Portuguese and the Dutch was the conflict between Buddhism and the intrusive Western culture and civilization and the Christian religion. That intrusion and its inevitable tensions with the indigenous religions began in the middle of the sixteenth century, with Portuguese influence and later, Portuguese rule on the coasts. Portuguese colonialism was very much the child of the Counter-Reformation and if its emphasis on the principle of *cujus regio illius religio* perpetuated a central feature of the Sri Lankan political system—the link between state and religion which had originated as long ago as the third century BCE—the zealotry and harsh intolerance which characterized the imposition of Roman Catholicism on the coastal regions of Sri Lanka were something new and unfamiliar in a society and civilization which seldom confused the obligation to encourage adherence to the national religion with suppression of other faiths. Throughout the period of Portuguese and Dutch rule in the coastal areas of the island, the traditional religious tolerance of the Buddhists prevailed in the area controlled by the Sinhalese kings.[10] For example, the Sinhalese kingdom provided a haven for Roman Catholic priests to minister to their beleaguered flock in the coasts under Dutch rule.[11]

Conversions, whether forced or through conviction, increased the number of adherents of the official religion under Portuguese, and to a lesser extent, under Dutch rule. At the time of the conquest of the Dutch possessions in the island by the English in 1795/96, the majority of the citizens of these territories were assumed to be and were classified as Protestant Christians. With the more relaxed attitude of the English, the superficiality of conversions to the Dutch Reformed Church was amply demonstrated when the great majority of the people returned to the public practice of their traditional faiths. And once the legal restrictions on the Roman Catholics concerning the practice of their faith in public life were removed between 1806 and 1829, they emerged as the largest of the Christian groups in the island, a position they retained until the end of British rule, and still do today. Conversions to Roman Catholicism under the Portuguese thus stood the rigorous test of persecution under the Dutch and the disdain and indifference of the British.

If the colonial state under Portuguese rule in Sri Lanka, the *estado,* was a Roman Catholic one, the role of religion in the state system was no less significant under the Dutch, despite the fact that the maritime regions conquered by them from the Portuguese were administered by a commercial company, the voc [Vereenigde Oost-Indische Compagnie —Ed.] or the Dutch East India Company. The link between state and Christianity continued in the early years of British rule in the maritime regions of Sri Lanka, although the attitude to the Anglican church—theoretically the established church—was ambiguous at best. The religious issues the British inherited from the Dutch became relatively unimportant once the British gained control over the whole island between 1815 and 1818 with the cession of the Kandyan kingdom, the last of the independent Sinhalese kingdoms, and confronted a more complex set of issues.

The first of these was the attitude of the British rulers towards Buddhism and the adherence to the terms of the Kandyan Convention of March, 1815 and the requirement—under the Kandyan Convention—of state support for Buddhism. But the British attitude to Buddhism was ambiguous, and at best, a reluctant adherence to the terms of the convention. Yet, even this did not last very long. There was strong objection from missionary organizations to this undertaking given to the Kandyan chiefs in 1815. This pressure became so great, in London, and in Sri Lanka, that the provisions of the Kandyan Convention relating to the link between the state and Buddhism were severed in the 1840s. With that decision began the second set of issues.[12] The historical significance of this severance could scarcely be exaggerated. Quite apart from being a calculated repudiation of a guarantee given in the most unqualified terms at the cession of the Kandyan kingdom to the British in 1815, it also marked the severance of the traditional bond between the state and the national religion that had lasted almost without interruption from the earliest days of the ancient Sinhalese kingdom, which is to say, for over 2,000 years.[13] The resulting disestablishment of Buddhism was part of the common colonial heritage in Sri Lanka and Burma, when both countries— as colonies—shared the common feature of accommodating a seemingly durable and expanding Christianity. In Sri Lanka, Protestant missionaries operated throughout the island under British rule—their techniques of spreading the gospel were more subtle and less aggressive than those of the Dutch and the Portuguese and, in historical retrospect, much less successful for the purposes they were intended to serve.

The third set of issues in Sri Lanka related to Buddhism involves how the Sinhalese generally refused to acquiesce in the decision to sever the link between the colonial state and the "national" religion. Regular episodes of agitation by Buddhist activists for a reconsideration of this decision and the establishment of some sort of link between Buddhism and the state kept religious controversies alive throughout the nineteenth century. The British would not go back to the *status quo ante* 1840 in restoring the formal link between the state and Buddhism, but by the 1870s they saw advantages in an accommodation with Buddhists. In the course of doing so they devised arrangements, and made concessions, that in the long run constituted a formula providing what may be termed a special concern for, if not a special position, for Buddhism within the Sri Lanka polity.

As we shall see, Sri Lankan politicians have eagerly adopted and elaborated upon a similar formula, and even embodied it in the constitutions of 1972 and 1978 as a sort of compensation for the refusal to elevate Buddhism to the position of the state religion, when pressure for the restoration of the link between Buddhism and the state continued after Sri Lanka achieved independence in 1948. They were unaware of the British colonial origins of this formula.

The fact, however, was that the Roman Catholics and Protestants in Sri Lanka were never more than a tenth of the population during the period of British rule in the island and in the early years of independence, but that tenth of the population, a significant percentage of the island's elite, continued to exercise enormous political clout. Admittedly the proportion was not as high as in Kerala, and far below than that in the Philippines which became the only Christian—largely Roman Catholic—country in Asia. However, the Sri Lankan Christians, nine-tenths of whom were Roman Catholics, quite unlike their Indian counterparts in general, had much larger numbers of persons of wealth and elite status. They were and were seen to be a wealthy and socially prominent group. The distinctly privileged position of the Christian minority in the country's public life was one of the most divisive issues in Sri Lankan politics in the years before independence and for over two decades thereafter. Some of the ramifications of these contentions still have some significance in the country, as seen in the recent rise of a party of Buddhist *bhikkhus* in parliament, although they have been clearly overshadowed by the current conflict between the Sri Lankan state and a Tamil separatist movement.

Religion and Nationalism. As in many parts of Asia, the origins of modern nationalism in Sri Lanka may be traced back to programs of religious revivalism which were a reaction to Christian missionary enterprise.[14] This first phase in the emergence of nationalism in Sri Lanka would cover the last three decades of the nineteenth century. Incipient nationalism was primarily religious in outlook and content, asserting the need to protect and sustain Buddhist values and claiming that Buddhism was in danger.[15] The focus

was also on the traditional culture of the country which the new nationalists sought to resuscitate, and which they believed had been weakened, if
not damaged, through the propagation of Christianity and Christian values.
There was also the pervasive Anglicization of the Sinhalese elite. Among
the most notable critics of this Anglicization was the great Sri Lankan Orientalist, Ananda Coomaraswamy,[16] who urged the people of the country to
go back to the roots of their traditional culture.

The political overtones in this agitation became more pronounced in
the first two decades of the twentieth century.[17] On the whole, the Buddhist movement lacked an institutional apparatus which might have been
converted into a political organization. While politicization of Buddhist
agitation, or some aspects of it like the temperance movement of the early
twentieth century, seemed the logical and inevitable next step, once its appeal to the people became evident, it was a step not taken. Nevertheless,
attempts at a revival of the traditional culture became part of a maturing
nationalism.[18]

Old societies struggling to establish a new nationhood (of which Sri
Lanka is a good example) have seldom been able to put their long and complex history behind them. On the contrary, they are often so obsessed with
the past that they have allowed it to cloud the present and the future. D. S.
Senanayake, Sri Lanka's first post-colonial prime minister, was somewhat
of an exception to this; his policies on nation-building placed a premium on
securing political stability by a careful calibration of the competing interests
of the Sinhala-Buddhist majority and the island's ethnic and religious minorities. There was a vigorous discouragement of policies that would upset
the balance of political forces established to sustain the country's democratic
framework in the early years of the new nation's existence.

Yet the past soon caught up with the present and did so within a few years
of Senanayake's death (in 1952) and in so doing fashioned a future which,
in many ways, would have appalled him. Groups of activists among Sinhalese nationalists sought a redress of historical grievances, oblivious to the
threat that their insistence on this would pose to pragmatic compromises
that had formed the basis of the post-colonial polity in the early years of
independence. The restitution they sought could be summed up briefly as
a purposeful reduction, if not elimination, of the privileges enjoyed by the
Christians and less specifically a restoration of the link between the state
and Buddhism. Sri Lankan Christianity was too closely linked with colonialism to survive unscathed in the atmosphere of Buddhist religious fervor
that became evident in the mid and late 1950s.

The role of Christianity, and the Christian minority, in Sri Lanka's public life became the first of the contentious issues which set in motion a process of erosion of the political settlement devised by Senanayake at the transfer of power. The prominence of the Christian minority in Sri Lanka's public life had already been one of the most divisive issues in Sri Lanka's politics in the years before independence. For two decades thereafter it retained its salience in the politics of the country.

The debate on the nature of the post-colonial state between the advocates of a secular state and those who sought to underline the primacy of Buddhism and the Sinhalese was renewed in the mid-1950s just when it seemed as though Senanayake's pragmatic policies were working without much difficulty, despite the opposition they faced from some vocal Buddhist activists, lay and clerical, who were seeking to undermine the stability of the political system he had so skillfully put together. Soon those policies and that settlement were submerged under a nationalist tide.

Pressure for the restoration of the link between Buddhism and the state continued in the mid and late 1950s and thereafter, and, in response, Sri Lankan politicians hit upon something akin to the British formula referred to earlier in this chapter, without really knowing or, if they knew it, without acknowledging, that it was British in origin. This was embodied in the constitutions of 1972 and 1978 as a substitute for the elevation of Buddhism to the position of the state religion. Thus the formula of a special status for Buddhism first devised by British governors in the 1870s and 1880s proved to be a viable one in post-colonial Sri Lanka. In the context of the current ethnic conflict, it was a controversial one, with the Tamil separatists and other Tamil groups advocating the establishment of a secular state. In their tacit acceptance of this change in the 1960s the Roman Catholics were seeking a constructive accommodation with a political reality: the dominance of the Sinhala-Buddhists in the Sri Lanka polity. This the Protestants had done a generation earlier, with some reluctance at first but with greater conviction in the years before the transfer of power and thereafter.

Buddhist agitation against the privileged position of the Christian minority was generally peaceful, and with surprisingly few actual episodes of violence between Buddhists and Christians—in particular, the Buddhists and Roman Catholics. Nevertheless this rivalry was the most divisive factor in Sri Lanka's political life for 80 years or so, beginning in the last quarter of the nineteenth century. These religious rivalries—which divided the Sinhalese rather than the Sinhalese from the Tamils—had been at times so sharp that they gave every impression of remaining an abiding factor of division in Sri Lanka's political life. Many of these tensions had been linked to controversies over the role of missionaries in the education system. The state's role in education became increasingly more significant since the early 1940s until it became the principal one by the early 1960s. The Roman Catholic Church led the resistance to this process, but by the end of the 1960s the Roman Catholics had reconciled themselves to a more limited role of education and in Sri Lanka's public life. Yet they have ceased to be a contentious issue in politics since the early 1970s until there was a revival in the first decade of the twenty-first century.

Given Sri Lanka's post-independence record of regular episodes of ethnic violence, a search for the roots of this violence is an urgent calling for the political analyst. Religion, however, is not a prime factor in the conflict except to the degree that Buddhist sentiment strengthens Sinhalese ethnic identity. But one needs to look elsewhere for the prime causes of the conflict and to examine post-colonial policies of state-building and national integration, and for state policies on language, employment, and education.

Nationalism and the Economy. The contrast between the nationalist agitation in Sri Lanka and the more vigorous and vocal Indian counterpart could not have been greater. The principal feature of the reform movement in its first phase was the emphasis on constitutional reform as the major goal of political endeavor, and the establishment, in the course of time, of a Sri Lankan version of the British system of parliamentary government. This stood in sharp contrast to Indian nationalism under M. K. Gandhi. There was scant interest in broadening the bases of their political organizations, and was strong opposition to techniques of agitation that would bring the masses into politics. These attitudes were influential and powerful political forces in Sri Lanka throughout the first half of the twentieth century. Although the men in the reform movement contributed to the eventual transfer of power in Sri Lanka, many of them were not consciously motivated by a desire to shake off the bonds of colonial rule.

In contrast to the first two decades of the twentieth century, the 1920s were characterized by bolder initiatives. In retrospect, they marked the first phase in the transfer of power, when the British in Whitehall and in the colonial administration in the island began to contemplate the possibility—indeed the necessity—of sharing power on a formal basis with the representatives of the indigenous population.

One of the intractable problems was the economy and the problems related to the seemingly irrepressible dominance of the plantations and the question of food security, particularly the excessive reliance on imports of rice under British rule, a phenomenon that went back to the period of Dutch rule in the littoral. Earlier, the years from 1880 to 1914 had been a period of comparative prosperity for the tropical colonies, and the plantation sector of Sri Lanka's economy had shared in this. The dominance of the plantations in the national economy was seldom under much criticism. From the beginning of the twentieth century up to 1914, Sri Lanka's plantation sector had enjoyed a period of aggressive growth, its most notable feature being the rapid expansion of the rubber industry. Indigenous planters—largely Sinhalese—had a substantial interest in it from the inception. Tea and coconut held their own, although they were temporarily overshadowed by the rubber industry in the first two decades of the twentieth century in terms of the profits yielded on capital invested.

This comparative prosperity was followed by a long period of depression, from the beginning of the first world war to the outbreak of the second, the result of a decline in world trade in the wake of the first world war and then by the economic dislocation in Europe in the 1920s and the great depression of the 1930s. There was a decline in the rate of growth of the productive capacity of Sri Lanka's plantation economy, and the economy as a whole. Nevertheless, the dominance of the plantations in the national economy continued at independence and afterwards. Apart from this, the other striking feature of the economic system was the absence of an industrial sector of the economy independent of processing tea, rubber, and coconut for export, and the engineering and mechanical requirements of these processes. There had been since 1931, and especially since the outbreak of the second world war, some state-sponsored industrial ventures. None of them proved to be of much more than marginal significance and on the whole little progress has been made.

In the first decade after independence there was no great emphasis on far-reaching changes in the economic structure inherited from the British. This structure appeared to have taken firm root and modest changes and modifications were preferred to radical reforms. Indeed, the mood in 1948 as regards the economy, though subdued and earnest, was not unduly pessimistic. On the contrary, there were high hopes for economic growth.[19] The fact is that Sri Lanka, poor though it was, enjoyed a much higher standard of living than India, Pakistan or Burma, and the national finances seemed adequate to maintain the welfare measures to which the country had grown accustomed in the last years of British rule. Such a fact explains some of the complacency in this attitude. It was not yet evident that the burgeoning costs of these welfare measures could become an insufferable burden for a developing country and an economy whose principal feature was a dependence on the vagaries of the world market through its dependence on the plantations. Thus the economic legacy left behind by the British was more ambiguous than the political one.

Within a decade of independence, governments were taking a less benign view of the plantations than in the previous years. Important structural changes were attempted in the Sri Lanka economy in the period 1956–64 and, more purposefully, from 1970–77. From the left-wing sectors of the political spectrum came regular calls for nationalization of the plantations, but these were ignored and the prevailing system had survived virtually unchanged till the early 1970s. And then during the years 1970–77 the plantations—both locally-owned and foreign-owned—were nationalized in a period of social-ist rule. But that impulsive experiment neither succeeded in providing an adequate base for self-sustained growth of the economy by yielding a higher return to the new owners nor did it improve the technology of production. All it meant was that the overwhelming dominance of the plantations which characterized the island's economy at independence—since the late nine-teenth century, in fact—became far less pronounced and the plantations themselves less profitable than they had been under private ownership. Nor did the state-sponsored industrial ventures that were encouraged after in-dependence and especially in the 1960s and 1970s help provide the profits required for self-sustained growth to an economic system which diverged fundamentally from the plantation-dominated structure the country had inherited at independence.

Indeed the long-term problems of economic growth assumed greater ur-gency in the 1960s and 1970s with falling revenues from the plantations and the ossification of some policies of development pursued since independence or even earlier. The most prominent of these latter, the distribution of state-owned land to peasants—the state was the biggest landholder in the island in colonial Sri Lanka in the sense that it had very large tracts of undeveloped land—which had been pursued since the early 1930s as a matter of priority in economic and social policy alike, reached its natural limits.[20] After inde-pendence the size of the units of land has become smaller in the pursuit of equity. They have been reduced to the point where subsistence agriculture is the only real possibility, and with it a real danger of a perpetuation of the poverty from which this program was designed to save the peasants, and generally did. Yet one of the results of this policy has been very beneficial. Sri Lanka's dependence on imported rice, a feature of the period of colonial rule under the British, has been reduced if not eliminated, and the country has reached a very high level of food security. This achievement is one of the great success stories of the post-independence period, and the principal agent of progress has been the peasant cultivator.

Ironically, but perhaps understandably, the search for food security has been accompanied by a shift of attention from the plantations. This was partly because of the decline in profitability of the plantations due to a combination of several factors: the plantation stock—the tree crops as well as the machinery used in production—was old and generally needed renewal; second, it is the inevitable result of nationalization of the plantations and bureaucratization of management. Yields were lower than in most other plantation economies, and living standards of workers remain low despite all efforts made since 1977 to bring the wage structure and welfare facilities up to the level of the rest of the country.

If Sri Lanka's rubber industry, for instance, had the dynamism of its Thai counterpart,[21] or its tea industry that of its Kenyan competitors, the impact on the country's growth rate would be very significant and the workers in the plantations would have benefited enormously. Thus paradoxically one of the urgent items in the political agenda of the early twenty-first century is a regeneration of the plantations. Despite the mixed fortunes of its plantations Sri Lanka still retains its position as one of two major tea producers and exporters of the world, the other being India.

The real hope of the future lies in the industrialization of Sri Lanka, which has been proceeding apace over the last three decades, and which has accelerated since the late 1970s. The entry of foreign capital into Sri Lanka since the late 1970s has been very marked. Given the relative weakness of Sri Lanka's capitalist class, the need for foreign capital to regenerate its economy is greater than at any time since the 1830s and 1840s when British capital transformed the island's economy. The capital now comes principally from East Asia: South Korea, Japan, Hong Kong and Taiwan. The other point is the commercialization of its peasant agriculture through the encouragement of more systematic cultivation for the local and international markets or through crop diversification, and a shift from the emphasis on rice, since Sri Lanka now produces most of the rice required to feed its population. Sri Lanka is ideally located to produce fruits and vegetables for export (and on a more systematic basis for the local market) in areas close to the urban centers of the southwest quadrant of the country. Irrigated land which is currently used almost entirely for rice production could also be used for the production of high value crops which need much less water than rice. This would mean a lower priority for one of the main policy options pursued since the 1930s, the great emphasis on smallholder rice production. The political difficulties involved in making this change are very great, but the tangible evidence of improved living standards from crop diversification would make the change tolerable, at first, and acceptable later on. There are encouraging signs that this is happening already. Thus agriculture, whether it be in the plantations or the peasant sector, has much greater potential for

providing increased yields, higher incomes, and greater employment opportunities than it has been given credit for.

Notes

1. S. Arasaratnam, "Sri Lanka's Trade, Internal and External in the 17th and 18th Centuries," in *History of Sri Lanka*, ed. K. M. de Silva (Kandy: University of Peradeniya, 1995),
402.

2. Ibid.

3. K. M. de Silva, *A History of Sri Lanka* (London, 1981), 166–67.

4. Present-day studies of the history of the spice trade seldom discuss the cinnamon
trade in any great detail despite its importance in the early years of colonialism in South
Asia. See, for example, Charles Corn, *The Scents of Eden: A History of the Spice Trade* (New
York, 1999).

5. There is a substantial number of articles on various aspects of Sri Lanka's coffee industry, but no single monograph or book on the subject. Perhaps James L. A. Webb
Jr., *Tropical Pioneers: Human Agency and Ecological Change in the Highlands of Sri Lanka,
1800–1900* (Athens Ohio University Press, 2002), could be treated as a monograph on the
coffee industry.

6. Surveys of the international coffee trade have very little on coffee in nineteenth-
century Sri Lanka. A good example is Mark Pendergrast, *Uncommon Grounds: The History
of Coffee and How It Transformed Our World* (New York, 1999).

7. de Silva, *A History of Sri Lanka*, 292–93.

8. On these issues see K. M. de Silva, "Multi-Culturalism in Sri Lanka: Historical Legacy
and Contemporary Political Reality," *Ethnic Studies Report* 15, no. 1 (1997): 1–44. Also see
K. M. de Silva, *Religion, Nationalism and the State in Modern Sri Lanka*, University of South
Florida Monographs in Religion and Public Policy (Tampa, 1986).

9. Perhaps the only significant item of Portuguese times left is the chiselled Cross of
Christ and arms of Portugal discovered in 1875, and currently at Gordon Gardens ad-
joining the British governor's residence in Colombo. This is now part of the gardens of
President's House.

10. This is discussed in L. S. Dewaraja, *The Kandyan Kingdom of Ceylon, 1707–1782* (Co-
lombo, 1988). On religious tolerance in the Kandyan kingdom see the classic study of Sri
Lanka originally published in 1681 and reprinted several times thereafter: Robert Knox,
A Historical Relation of the Island Ceylon (Colombo, 1989), 219, 243.

11. Nihal Karunaratne, *Kandy: Past and Present* (Colombo, 1999), 43–50.

12. K. M. de Silva, *Social Policy and Missionary Organisations in Ceylon, 1840–55* (London,
1965), especially 64–137.

13. Ibid.

14. K. M. de Silva, "Religion and Nationalism in Nineteenth Century Sri Lanka: Christian Missionaries and Their Critics—A Review Article," *Ethnic Studies Report* 16, no. 1
(1998): 103–38. See also K. M. de Silva, "Buddhist Revivalism, Nationalism and Politics in
Sri Lanka," in *Fundamentalism Revivalists and Violence in South Asia*, ed. James W. Bjork-
man (Delhi, 1998), 107–58.

15. K. M. de Silva, "Nineteenth-Century Origins of Nationalism in Ceylon," in *History of Ceylon,* vol. 3, ed. K. M. de Silva (Colombo: University of Ceylon, 1973), 249–61.

16. Ananda Coomaraswamy, *Medieval Sinhalese Art* (London, 1908); see also Ananda Wickremeratne, *Buddhism and Ethnicity in Sri Lanka, A Historical Analysis* (Delhi, 1995).

17. This is discussed in K. M. de Silva, "Christian Missions in Sri Lanka, and Their Response to Nationalism," in *Senerat Paranavitana Commemoration Volume, Studies in South Asian Culture V,* ed. P. L. Prematilleke et al. (Amsterdam: Leiden Institute of South Asian Archaeology, University of Amsterdam), 221–33.

18. For discussion of some of these issues see de Silva, *A History of Sri Lanka,* 347–55.

19. For contemporary discussion of these issues, see Ivor Jennings, *The Economy of Ceylon* (Calcutta: Oxford University Press, 1948 and 1951); H. M. Oliver Jr., *Economic Opinion and Policy in Ceylon* (Durham: Duke University Press, 1957).

20. On this see G. H. Peiris, *Development and Change in Sri Lanka: Geographical Perspectives* (Delhi, 1996), 145–61.

21. From being an important rubber producer (around 9 percent of world production) at independence, Sri Lanka is now a peripheral producer (around 2 percent of world production). During the same period Thailand rose from being a peripheral producer to a successful challenger to Malaysia's position at the top of the table in international rubber production.

THE PORTUGUESE: AN INTRODUCTION

Jorge Flores

Sri Lanka occupied a prominent place in the political imagination of early modern Portugal. In August 1499, heavily influenced by the mythical aura that surrounded the island of Taprobane in medieval Europe, King Manuel I (r. 1495–1521) wrote for the first time about the wonders of Ceilão. The initial contact between Portugal and Ceylon occurred in 1506. It was not long before the Portuguese king decided to make Sri Lanka "the center of all the fortresses and things that we have there," since "it would be most agreeable and pleasant for us if you [D. Francisco de Almeida, the first Portuguese viceroy of India] and our fortress were in Taprobane, now called Ceylon and about which all the authors in the world have written and said so much, and which has been praised so highly for its wealth and other things."[1]

Instead, the port city of Goa on the southwest coast of India, became the capital of the Portuguese Estado da Índi. Yet, until the 1680s Sri Lanka played a key role in the Portuguese empire in Asia. The political elite, from the king and his courtiers to ordinary officers and ad hoc advisors, exchanged lengthy descriptions of Sri Lanka relevant to its economic potential, its strategic relevance, and its ever-evolving political situation. Catholic missionaries, from the Franciscans who arrived in the 1540s to convert the king of Kotte, to the Oratorians who settled in the late seventeenth century hoping to "win the soul" of the king of Kandy, wrote hundreds of letters, reports, and book on the "evils" of Buddhism and the "marvels" of conversion to the "true religion." Learned chroniclers, like João de Barros and his successor Diogo do Couto, wrote extensively on Sri Lanka using a vast array of sources that included (in the case of Couto) Sinhalese materials. Portuguese cartographers often portrayed Sri Lanka, and celebrated poets incorporated significant references to the island in their works.

Portuguese texts and illustrations represent a sizeable and crucial part

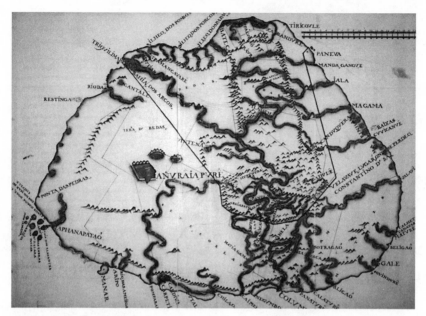

"The Island of Sri Lanka," 1638. Zaragoza, Biblioteca Universitaria, ms. 13, f. 42.

of the early modern European archive on Sri Lanka. The following pages present glimpses of that rich and diverse body of ethnographical knowledge about a "little known treasure," to borrow the words of the Luso-Malay cartographer Manuel Godinho de Erédia, writing in 1619.

Editor's Note

1. This introduction and the following six chapters, which focus on the Portuguese in Sri Lanka, were compiled and edited by Jorge Flores.

An Early Observer

Duarte Barbosa

Duarte Barbosa belongs to the first generation of sixteenth-century Portuguese who traveled to India. A fluent speaker of Malayalam, he lived most of his adult life in Kerala working as interpreter in the Portuguese settlements of the region. Around 1516, he completed his (untitled) book, an economic, political, and social geography of maritime Asia. In the sixteenth century the so-called Book of Duarte Barbosa became a European bestseller in manuscript form, and a considerable number of copies (some of them containing sizeable variations) are today housed in different libraries in the world. The Venetian Giovanni Battista Ramusio had access to one of these manuscripts and included it in the Italian translation of the first volume of his collection of travel narratives titled Delle Navigationi et Viaggi *(Venice, 1550). Barbosa never actually visited Sri Lanka, but by living in the port cities of the Malabar Coast, he was well acquainted with the island. The pages he dedicated to "Ceilam" in his book are among the earliest Portuguese testimonies.*

The people of this island are Heathen, yet in its seaports dwell many Moors in large towns, who are subject to the King of the land. The natives of this island, Moors as well as Heathen, are great merchants. They are stout and well-built, tawny almost white in hue, the larger part of them big-bellied; they are extreme luxurious and pay no attention to matters of weapons, nor do they possess them. All are merchants and given to good living. They go naked from the waist up, and below they are clad in silk and cotton garments; they wear small turbans on their heads; their ears are bored, and in them they wear much gold and precious stones in such quantity that their ears touch their shoulders; on their fingers they wear many rings set with the finest gems, and they gird themselves with golden belts set with stones. Their language is drawn partly from Malabar and partly from Coromandel. Many Malabar Moors come to settle in this island by reason of the great liberty which they there enjoy, and also because it is not only well furnished with all the comforts and delights of the world, but it is also a country with a very moderate climate, where men live in good health longer than in any other part of India, and very few become ill. Here grow many excellent fruits, the hillsides are covered with sweet and bitter oranges with three or four distinct flavors, and of some the rind is sweeter than the juice, and they are even larger than apples; lemons of a sweet bitterness, some large and some very small and sweet, also many other kinds of fruit not found in our lands, and the trees are continually laden with them throughout the year, so that flowers and fruits ripe and unripe are seen perpetually. There is also very great plenty of flesh of divers kinds from animals, and of fowls of the air, all delicate food, of fish of great store which are taken close to the island. Of rice there is but little, they bring most of it from Coromandel, and this is their principal diet. There is also great plenty of good honey and sugar which is brought from Bengal. Butter in abundance is found on the island.

In this island is found true and good cinnamon. It grows on the hillsides in bushes like bay trees. The King has it cut into fine branches and the bark is stripped and dried during certain months of the year. With his own hand he makes it over to those merchants who come to buy it, for no dweller in this country, save the King only, may gather it.

And in this island are reared many wild elephants which the King has caught and tamed. These he sells to the merchants of Coromandel, of Vijayanagar Malabar, the Deccan and Cambay, who come to seek them. And the manner in which they take them is this: they place a female elephant as a decoy on the hill where they graze, which is fastened by the foot to a tree with strong chains. Around it they dig three or four very deep pits covered with very fine branches spread over the ground as cunningly as they can. The wild elephants, seeing the female, fall into these pits where they keep them seven or eight days without food, and many men watch them night and day and speak to them as not to suffer them to sleep, until they become tame, and then feed them from their hands. When they are tame and broken-in they surround them very softly with thick chains, and in order to draw them forth from the pit they throw in so many branches that the elephant gradually rises until he can come out. They then tie him to a tree where they keep him several days more, men with fires always watching by night, coaxing him and speaking to him constantly, and giving him food in small quantities until they have him at their disposal. In this way they take both male and female, great and small. Sometimes two fall into one pit. These elephants are valuable merchandise worth much, and are greatly esteemed by the Kings of India, who keep them for war and labor. Some are very tame and have as much sense and understanding as men. The best and most thoroughly trained are worth a thousand or a thousand five hundred *cruzados*,[1] others four or five hundred according to their training, this in Malabar and Coromandel. In this island their price is small. No one save the King may take them, who pays those who catch them.

In this island also are found precious stones in plenty of various kinds, and so many lapidaries, who are skilled to such an extent, that if one should bring one of them a handful of earth in which precious stones were mixed he would say at once "These are rubies in this hand or sapphires in that." And in the same manner when they see the ruby or other stones they say "This must be kept for so many hours in the fire," and it will turn out very clear and good. The King sometimes ventures to place a ruby in a very fierce charcoal fire for the time the lapidary tells him; and if any ruby endures it without peril of destruction it remains much more perfect in color. When this King finds any precious stone he keeps it for himself and places it in his treasury. . . .

The King of Ceylon resides in a city called Colombo ("Calmucho"), which stands on a river with a good port whither sail every year ships from divers lands to take cargoes of cinnamon and elephants and bringing gold, silver, very fine Cambay cotton cloths and goods of many other kinds such as saffron, coral, quicksilver, cinnabar, yet is their greatest profit in gold and silver for they are worth more here than elsewhere. Likewise many ships come from Bengal and Coromandel, and some from Malacca to buy elephants, cinnamon and jewels. There are also four or five other ports in this island, populous towns, where great trade is carried on, which are under the rule of other lords, nephews of the King of Ceylon, to whom they owe allegiance; yet at times they rise up against him.

In the midst of this island there is a lofty range of mountains among which is a very high stony peak, on the summit whereof is a tank of water deep enough to swim in and a very great footprint of a man in a rock, well shaped. This the Moors say is the footprint of our father Adam, whom they call Adombaba, and from all the Moorish regions and realms they come thither on pilgrimage declaring that from that spot Adam ascended to Heaven. They travel in pilgrims' weeds girt about with great iron chains, and clad in the hides of leopards, lions and other wild beasts of the field, on their right arms they have great blisters caused by fire which they perpetually expose on the way that they may always bear open wounds with them, saying that they do so for the love of God and of Mafamede and of Adam. Many of them carry money secretly, and are very wealthy, intending therewith to purchase precious stones, which they do. Before they reach that lofty mount where is the footprint they call Adam's they pass through flooded lands and valleys and rivers, and must always go for five or six leagues up to their waists in water, and they all carry knives in their hands in order therewith to rid themselves of the leeches, which are so many that they would kill them if they did not so. When they reach the mountain they go up, but they cannot ascend the peak by reason of its steepness save by the ladders of very thick iron chains which are placed there with which it is surrounded. At the top they bathe in the water of that tank, and recite their prayers, and therewith they hold that they are saved and freed from all their sins.

Nigh to this island of Ceylon there is a shoal of about eight to ten fathoms between the island and the mainland where large quantities of seed pearls (*aljofre*), both large and small, and pearls can be found; the Moors and the gentiles of Kayalpatnam ("Cale"), which is a city of the King of Quilon, are allowed to fish two times each year. The oysters they find are smaller and smoother than those found in our country, and men with reeds in their noses retrieve them, and they travel from Kayalpatnam in small boats that they call *champanas*[2] during the season in which the King of Kayalpatnam permits them to fish; and so two or three hundred *champanas* arrive, each with ten to fifteen men and enough provisions to last them for the duration of their pearling expedition; and they all disembark on a small, uninhabited island and set up camp there, just as the tuna *almadravas* in the Algarves;[3] and so each boat fishes for itself, that is, the men break off two by two and they drop anchor where they wish and one of the men goes below with reeds for his nostrils and a stone at his feet and a sack made from cord at his neck and the other man stays above on the *champana*, with a rope in his hand, which is tied to the sack and the other stays under for the length of an hour grabbing oysters until he fills the sack. And so he lets go of the stone and heads toward the surface; so he flies upward on the rope and unloads the sack with the oysters, and now that this one has surfaced, the other goes below, and they fish for oysters in this way. And so they bring those oysters to shore and throw them on the ground and keep them there until they rot, and they wash them very thoroughly in metal or wooden barrels and remove their pearls. And if they find a big pearl it is for the King, who has scribes and officials who look after his money there, and the pearl is weighed so that the King can have his money and whatever is left they [the pearl fishermen] can take to their homes. The King of Ceylon loses this fishery because he lacks navigation, despite this wealth being in his domains, and the King of Quilon, which is on the mainland, comes here and takes it. . . .

Section Editor's Notes

1. Portuguese silver coin worth 360 *reis* (plural of *real*, the basic account unit in the Portuguese monetary system) at the time of Barbosa.
2. From the Malay *sampan*. Small boat used throughout maritime Asia, propelled with a scull and sometimes a sail.
3. Netting for catching tuna; fishing grounds for tuna in Southern Portugal and the Straits of Gibraltar region.

Visions from the Mid-Sixteenth Century:
The Economist, the Viceroy,
and the Missionary

António Pessoa, Dom Afonso de Noronha,

and Fr. Manuel de Morais

By the mid-sixteenth century, the Portuguese were already heavily involved in Sri Lanka and, consequently, texts and visual materials on the island became abundant and rich. Information exchanged in those years between Colombo, Goa (the capital of the Estado da Índia), and Lisbon about the island they called "Ceilão" often included detailed economic reports and careful assessments of political developments, as well as biased views on local religious life. The writings of António Pessoa, Dom Afonso de Noronha, and Manuel de Morais provide us with examples of such concerns and priorities. Pessoa, who served as Portuguese feitor in Kotte in the 1530s elaborated in his "Information on Matters Relating to Ceylon" (1548) on the multiple economic possibilities of the country. Dom Afonso de Noronha, viceroy of India from 1550 to 1554 and the first in that capacity to visit Sri Lanka, supplied King John III (r. 1521–57) in January 27, 1552, with details about the turbulent political situation of the island, centering on the assassination of King Bhuvaneka Bahu VII (r. 1521–51), and his own obsession with the seizure of the royal treasure of Kotte. Later that same year, the missionary Manuel de Morais wrote from Colombo to his brothers in the Jesuit College of Coimbra (Portugal) about the "false beliefs" and "spacious pagodas" he encountered in Sri Lanka.

António Pessoa

Your Lordship ordered me to give information regarding some of the things of Ceylon and of cinnamon and its price in order to deal with it as it pleases him. . . .

The cinnamon harvest begins in June, the time the blacks are made to go harvest it, which they do until the end of October and for part of November, until it has been gathered in the house; in these dealings there are always three Portuguese men, for without them it cannot be done, as they have to be very careful at harvesting.

If your Lordship wants us to harvest as much as possible, this can be done up to fifteen hundred *bahar*,[1] if great diligence is put into it. If that much is not needed, in March you can write to tell this to the *feitor*,[2] so that he harvests only the amount necessary, because, if more than necessary is harvested, the king is upset if it is not bought, and it seems he is right. This other way all [trouble] is prevented.

If there is war in Ceylon, I say that in no way can there be any cinnamon, even if there is a fortress there, because it is harvested by the native people and in many places throughout the whole island, so that when there is dissension in the land between one man and his brother, it cannot be so plentiful, except with much work on the part of the *feitor* and the Portuguese there, and more [work] when there is war.

In Ceylon as many masts and yards can be obtained as are wanted for galleons, galleys and ships, and all other things for which there is need, of *puna*[3] and *cherapuna*, which is the best type to be found.

In Ceylon I made in a year, fifteen hundred galley oars, and two *bastardas*,[4] and I believe they will cost about five hundred *xerafins*,[5] and these were made in the winter. If made in the summer and with moons cutting the wood, they would be better. It will be necessary, if they are made here, to send here someone who specializes in making oars in order to show the carpenters the way to work them and to cut them in the King's woods with his permission. . . .

In Ceylon, there is much fishing of chanks, pearls and coral, and each of great perfection, and there are on the land great mines of rubies and sapphires; the forests are rich in cinnamon and sweet orange trees, the fruit of which are the best in the universe, and there is around these forests great abundance of elephants, which are taken to all parts of India and are very valuable. In addition, Ceylon produces much cardamom of the very best kind, be it from Brazil or Portugal, and much eaglewood, but not as good as Malacca's. There is much pepper and, if one wanted to plant it, there would be as much of it as in Malabar. There is very fertile land and it would give great abundance of wheat and rice, and one of the reasons why it does not is that the people of the area have no property because it all belongs to the king. In addition there is in Ceylon a great abundance of very cheap meats, namely, cows, pigs, sheep, chickens, and many things of the woods, of hares, deer, and other animals, as well as great quantity of fish, especially swordfish, of which a great number is taken to India each year, because it is the best around, and also flounder, sardines, and many other kinds of fish. There is also in the land much pitch and much coconut oil, the cheapest in all India, which they load, and there is also another oil they make of wood and a great quantity of butter, and cottons from which one could make many clothes. The whole land is full of palm trees and areca-nut trees, from which is gathered every year a great quantity of coconuts and areca-nut that they ship to India and to the coast of Pegu and Martaban and, if one wanted to get coir rope from the coconuts, there would be as great an abundance of it, as there is in the Maldives. So there are many of the fruits of India and some grape vines from Portugal.

Dom Afonso de Noronha

The affairs of Ceylon seemed very important at the beginning and involved much labor for a large number of noblemen and knights who are serving Your Highness in these parts and who went there with me. It is therefore fitting that I should give you a full account in a special letter, and I am doing so in this letter.

When I came from Portugal and reached Ceylon, I found the country in a very restless and disturbed condition. The *Chingalas* (Sinhalas) were insolent towards the Portuguese, who had lost much of their prestige. . . .

The king of Kotte [Bhuvaneka Bahu VII, r. 1521–51] sent me a patent which he held from Your Highness, by which you ordained that his grandson, his daughter's son, should become king, though the kingdom did not belong to him by right. There I heard rumors regarding the king's treasure, though they now try to say that he exaggerated it to give himself importance. With regard to the succession and the treasure, I had left instructions for Gaspar de Azevedo[6] that, if by chance the king should die, he should seize the treasure and not recognize his grandson as king, and that everything should remain in that state till he sent me information. . . .

Mayadunne [king of Sitavaka, r. 1521–81] had already started a war against his brother, the king of Kotte, and had retaken several districts. . . . The king [of Kotte] then sent Vidiye Bandara ("Trivele Pandar"), his son-in law, to the frontier of his territories to prevent Mayadunne from entering into them, and to wage war against him. He himself, with the chief magistrate and the men who served on his guard, decided to go to Calane [Kelaniya], which is a *pagode*,[7] close to a river, a league or little more from Kotte, so as to support his son-in-law from there. They say that he was warned by some persons close to Mayadunne that Mayadunne had briefed some Portuguese to kill him. They say that this information reached the queen, his wife, who threw herself at his feet and pleaded with him not to go outside; but that the king had replied to her that for forty years he had trusted in the Portuguese and found them always so loyal, that he would rather die than harbor such a suspicion in his heart. These are words that cause much greater sorrow when we consider the kind of death he died.

They say that Gaspar de Azevedo also requested the king not to go. This is for me a far greater proof than what can be established by an enquiry. Nevertheless the king went, and with him went the chief magistrate and eighty Portuguese with their muskets. These all posted themselves on guard round the house which the king occupied. After the king had dined, he came to the veranda to see the Portuguese have their meal. From their post, they shot him with a musket and killed him.

Gaspar de Azevedo held no inquiry there regarding the matter. He only took the king and brought him back to the palace at Kotte. They say that when he arrived there the grandson [Dharmapala, r. 1551–97] told him that he would become a Christian, and give him the treasure, when it was found, and that he should be proclaimed king. Without considering these points, Gaspar de Azevedo set him up as king because of the document which he held from Your Highness, duly sealed with the leaden seal, in which Your Highness granted that he should be king on the death of his grandfather. . . .

As soon as I reached Ceylon I received a visit from the grandson of the dead king. He is styled emperor like his grandfather. He came together with his father, Vidiye Bandara. I told them how much I was grieved at the death of the king, and especially at the manner of it, and at the suspicion that there was regarding it, which I did not believe; and with reference to it I would do justice, as they would see, as soon as it was known who was guilty. . . .

The next day I went to the palace of the king and publicly asked them if they were aware that the kingdom of Ceylon belonged to Your Highness, that they held it from your hands; and if it was true that, without any request on my side, they had promised to give me the treasure of the late king in order to obtain that I placed on the throne the grandson of the king in the name of Your Highness, since it depended on your favor and decision the succession to the grandson; if it was true that I promised to win back the territories lost and that I had offered myself to go and destroy Sitavaka, and that I promised to supply a captain and soldiers to destroy Mayadunne. They replied that they were well aware of it. Of all this I caused a record to be taken down, mentioning that I had gone only to do justice for the death of the king.

Afterwards I told Vidiye Bandara, the king's father, that I knew that he and the lord chamberlain and Pandita[8] had divided among themselves what remained of the king's treasure. And that even if they had not promised it to Your Highness, the treasure belonged to his son who was a minor, and whose interests I was obliged to safeguard. . . . Afterwards the king, his grandmother and mother sent to request me that since the treasure belonged to them and their grandson, I should release Vidiye Bandara and the lord chamberlain, and should order that pressure should be brought to bear on the eunuchs of the king and on the clerks of the revenue, because they knew of the treasure which the king possessed and could give particulars of it. . . . For heathen kings entrust everything to their eunuchs and they usually do not reveal their treasure even to their heirs till they are about to die. The king's death was so sudden that he had no chance of mentioning it or of writing an *ola*[9] about it according to their custom. . . .

When this was decided upon, I went at once to the house where the king and his father were staying. The king kissed the Cross of the Order of Christ which I was wearing round my neck, and kissed also the bishop's hand. Then he gave orders to hand over the *pagode*. . . . Though my desire was that everything should be completed at once, yet the *pagode* was not in a condition to render it possible to say Mass there at once.

They remained there two days examining the precious objects and the other articles of the *pagode*, for there was much delay in separating those of gold from those which were of gilt copper and brass, of which there was a large quantity. Then the king and his father informed me that all the people of the city of Kotte and even from the rest of the country had fled, and that all or the majority of the captains had gone over to Mayadunne. This was true, for although my son Dom Fernando had taken the precaution to watch the city with all the noblemen and the men who went with me, it had not been possible to find means to prevent their going. And it was said that all this was due to the fact that the *pagode* was going to be turned into a church and that the king was becoming a Christian. The king begged me that, as soon as the gold was removed, I should restore the *pagode* to him, and that only after my return from Sitavaka the king would become a Christian and the *pagode* turned into a church, otherwise he would be left without any subjects. . . .

I assure Your Highness that this business of Ceylon has embarrassed me much more than I can explain.

Manuel de Morais

This island is 200 leagues from Goa. The main purpose for which I was sent to this island is the conversion of the king and also the welfare of the Portuguese of whom there are many here. These, being in the island and far from the governor, were in the habit of disobeying the law of God and man, committing many evils. . . .

In this country there are many false beliefs sown by the devil. To eradicate them there is need of much time and trouble. I shall mention those which I remember, for I do not know them all. There is a class of gentiles who do not kill any living creature, not even the most poisonous snakes, nor any insect or worm whatever. They do not eat anything that is killed whether it be meat or fish. They also do not eat bread, however hungry or needy they might be. Their usual food is made up of leaves of a certain creeper which climbs round other trees like ivy. These leaves are smeared with the same kind of lime which they use for whitewashing their houses. When they run short of lime, they scrape from the walls so that they smear it on the leaves which they want to eat. With these leaves they also eat a fruit which is like the nut of the cypress tree. This nut tastes like dry bread, and is equally hard, whether it is green or dried. They eat rice also; but, as I have already said, their main food is the leaves with the lime.

There is another class of people who do not kill any living creature, except those which they themselves need for their food, as rats and salamanders and lizards of the forests; for they do not eat beef of the flesh of other animals. There is another class of people who kill fish, and this is merely the caste they call Paravas.[10] These also do not kill any poisonous insect they may find in their house. And all these people, if they choose and are able to do so, kill men, and their doctrine does not forbid it. There is another class of people that eats fowls and wild boar and deer, but do not eat the flesh of cows since they believe that, after death, their souls enter into cows; thus they will never kill a cow or eat its flesh.

All these people adore idols of stone, bronze, and gold, and have spacious *pagodes*, which are their churches, where they perform their idolatrous worship with as much devotion as good Christians pray to the true God and offer the true sacrifice of the Mass. These unfortunate people have two different kinds of priests: the *jogues*,[11] and the *changatares*,[12] who are very zealous as friars are among us. They dress in yellow robes, and the dress is very different from the dress of other people. None of these priests wants to meet me. When they go by the road, they get out of the road if they can, till I have passed. I have already spoken with two of them, because they were not able to avoid me; but they did not want to tell me anything about their beliefs, nor answer any question. But when I have time, I want to meet a well known *changatar* who resides here, who never leaves his dwelling, whom all obey and whom they hold as a holy man. When they go out of their dwelling, they all carry a great fan which shelters them from the sun, and still more prevents them from seeing unseemly objects and from being seen. They live by the side of the *pagodes*, apart from other people, and their dwellings are secluded like our monasteries, and are ornamented with paintings like the *pagodes*.

Some of the *pagodes* are more magnificent than the most magnificent church of Lisbon, except that the buildings are not so spacious, but they are all ornamented in gold of all qualities. I entered a pagoda which impressed me more than the many buildings I have seen so far, for it seemed to me to be much richer and much more magnificent than the chapel of the archdeacon of Salamanca, and a more spacious building, since it is like the chapels of our churches! This is the richest building I have seen so far. And the altar of this shrine was round, like the altar of the church of the Conception of Lisbon. On that altar there are many statues of metal, all covered with much pure gold. It looked as if they had just been completed at that very moment. At each corner of that altar there were two statues of the size of two men, very well proportioned, made of metal overlaid with gold. The candlesticks, which were at the corners of the altar, were greater than those which are at Belém[13] in the main chapel, and like those great ones which come from Flanders; but for workmanship there are none superior. This is the way the devil even now tries to make himself equal to God, and find those who will serve and support him, while there are no persons to drive him away from the kingdom over which he rules tyrannically. It looks to me, brothers mine, that nobody has a greater obligation to wage war on him than we of our Society, for the friars and other priests do not have such possibilities and such obligation.

Section Editor's Notes

1. A measure of weight or dry volume, the exact value of which varied widely, roughly equivalent to 500 pounds.
2. "Factor," Crown trading agent.
3. Name of a tree whose wood was used to build masts.
4. Small sailing vessel.
5. From the Persian *ashrafi*. Silver coin worth 300 reis.
6. The Portuguese factor in Kotte.
7. Pagoda. Term commonly used by the Portuguese in Asia to denote a non-Christian temple (in this case, obviously a Buddhist temple).
8. The lord chamberlain (*camareiro-mor*) was Tammita Surya Bandara. Pandita, who visited Lisbon in 1542–43 as ambassador of Kotte, was Sri Radaraksa Pandita.
9. Palm-leaf manuscript.
10. From the Malayalam *paravar*.
11. Yogi. Hindu ascetic.
12. *Samghatthera*, or elder Buddhist *bhikkhu*.
13. The Jeromite Monastery of Belém, Lisbon, the construction of which began in 1501.

The Spin Doctors at Work:
The Island as "New Portugal"

Francisco Rodrigues Silveira and Jorge Pinto de Azevedo

The Portuguese took a clear interest in Sri Lanka as "territory" in the closing years of the sixteenth century. In fact, rather than pursue primarily commercial goals confined to a handful of strategic points on the coastline and engaging in intermittent co-operation with the local rulers, what the Portuguese intended to achieve in Sri Lanka was to colonize on the basis of effective control of the country. According to this continental approach, Kandy, the "Kingdom of the Mountains," became their main enemy, and there was frequent talk in Lisbon, Madrid, and Goa about the need to "eradicate" the "natural" kings of the island. It should come as no surprise that in addition to the idea of conquest there were also somewhat ambiguous plans to transfer the capital of the Estado da Índia to Sri Lanka. This idea was argued by the veteran soldier Francisco Rodrigues Silveira in 1599 in his Reformation of the Militia of the State of East India. *Almost half a century later, in 1646, Jorge Pinto de Azevedo underscored in his* Advice of Great Importance to the Majestic Crown of the King Our Lord Dom João the 4th *the need to conquer the island, alleging ten strong reasons to do so. For many opinion makers and political advisors, Ceylon was now the "El Dorado" of Portuguese Asia, the colony where one should invest material and human resources to create a sort of New Portugal.*

Francisco Rodrigues de Silveira

What we seek to say in this chapter is that even now . . . the great error first committed when the Portuguese arrived [in India], that is, that they did not follow the true path that would allow them to rule over it, and to acquire sufficient forces to defend it without people or another form of assistance from Portugal, may easily be amended; . . . and to this end it would have been necessary for them to rule over a fertile island, with abundant resources, where they would have had secure ports for them to house their armadas and on which they might found their empire.

No island would have been better suited to this purpose than Ceylon, because of the great fertility of the land, and for its wood and deposits of iron, steel, brass, sulfur, saltpeter, and everything else necessary for the construction of armadas, and with good ports to house them. It may be true that Sumatra seemed of greater importance, whether because of the richness and quantity of the things of great value produced there, or because of its proximity to many extremely rich neighboring islands and provinces. But that enterprise would have brought with it great inconveniences: firstly, this island is inhabited by Muslims, and as such it would not have been easy to conquer it or convert them to the Catholic faith, which should be our goal, both in order to serve God as well as to secure the support of the inhabitants in any military enterprises, for which they have to be Christians. Secondly, while [controlling] this island of Sumatra would allow us to master the trade and commerce of the southern sea, it would not be sufficient to control the northern sea, because of the great distance in-between, and because sailing in this direction is difficult and only possible in certain periods. One does not find these difficulties in the case of Ceylon, because it is populated by gentiles who would be much easier to convert than the Moors, and because it is situated midway between Malacca and Hormuz, which are the two poles around which revolves the entire machinery of trade and commerce in all the merchandise trafficked through the Eastern sea, and because the island seems to have been placed apart from the continent so as to govern over the commerce of these two seas, it being impossible to sail from north to south, nor from south to north, without all of the *naus*[1] and other vessels obeying it and recognizing its authority. . . .

With things thus established in Ceylon, and with a viceroy there given supreme authority, one could order that armadas be built, for which purpose masters could be sent from Portugal, and the natives could quickly begin imitating them so that in a short time the Portuguese could be relieved of the task. Men practiced in mining all metals could travel the island, and they could locate mines based on their experience and the information of the natives, and they could make them work in these mines so as to make them productive. In this way, with the Portuguese having taken control of this kingdom and taken the aforementioned measures, there is no doubt that aid from Portugal would soon be dispensable. This said, even if the help of men would be unnecessary, I would not argue the same for women, and a quantity of them should be sent every year to marry the Portuguese men, and in this way our nation would not discredit itself by degenerating here, by mixing with the *canarins*,[2] the vilest and lowest people to be found in India or in all of the world.

Jorge Pinto de Azevedo

God consented to grant us in a short time and for such good purposes the Kingdom of Ceylon, eighty leagues in diameter and two hundred thirty in circumference, which is the best land in all of this Indian archipelago . . . however we have failed to understand that this gift from the divine hand did not come by chance, but with the objective that it, becoming the head of the Portuguese state (and in this way of all Christendom [in Asia]), might serve as the base of and foundation for such a right and weighty task, and as an example for and boon to Christianity, for the change of government was not effected, nor were the resources dedicated to the achievement of this purpose. . . .

And in accordance with reason, which dictates the dedication of all that remains to Ceylon, the means of its conquest should be changed, because it is better to populate it slowly with life and with the multiplication of people than to conquer it many times at the cost of many lives (as has occurred until now) and to never possess it. Cities should be built in the interior, at intervals, so as to aid and support each other, and all the poor people who are dying of hunger elsewhere should be sent there, and wherever they are sent they should be given enough land to sustain them, because the forests there are not bad, as the land is fresh, and one knows that necessity and industry are sufficient to overcome any obstacle; and it is not reasonable that there are so few people in Colombo, with so much land as there is in Ceylon, which they cannot sustain or defend. . . .

And in this way, if one founds two cities every year with 300 settlers without payment, along with 200 soldiers from the garrisons (a thousand at minimum should come from Portugal alone, and in this way the armadas will be less needed), in a few short years there will be peoples and settlements against which the *chingalas* will not dare to rebel. . . . In addition, poor *topazes*[3] and *canarins* can be taken from all of our cities, and sent to the kingdom of Ceylon, and given lands with which to sustain themselves, and though they are not accustomed to labor, they will not be permitted to leave, and so necessity will oblige them to cultivate the land and the male children of these *topazes* and *canarins* will have to marry not with women of their caste, but only with the daughters of the *chingalas*, and the daughters with the sons, and in this way they will come to forget their caste, and they will live in the confusion of those we call *topazes*, who since they do not know their caste, live obediently without attempting to rebel. . . .

And so, My Lord, we arrive at the time in which we must recognize our errors, and the occasion that invites us to adopt this remedy as a better, less costly, and less difficult course; let the kingdom of Ceylon grow in this way, because in this way the hostile *chingalas* will be made subjects without the shedding of Portuguese blood, and further, unless extraordinary measures are taken to stop them, the Dutch will be able to master it [the kingdom of Ceylon]. . . . The opinions of the past [decision-makers] are not appropriate for the current times, My Lord, even if they made sense for their epoch. If they considered that it would be better for the viceroy to rule from Goa, this was because they were satisfied with the Indian coast they first discovered, on which they found clothes and pepper for Portugal, and on which they became prosperous, and accordingly made conversion a secondary priority, leaving this to those who would come after them; and as such their base was always on that Indian coast, and they likewise thought that the principal port of Ceylon should be on the corresponding coast, and as such Colombo is [the principal port] because it is easiest to defend it [from Goa] and bring cinnamon [from Colombo to Goa]. . . . Nor should Ceylon's lack of rice cause worry, because this is a frivolous concern when one considers and understands that where there is land, water and people there will be no lack of food. And when it is known that this [land] is very fresh because of the constant rains, and that it was always inhabited by more people than we will accumulate there over many years, and further, that of these people two parts were killed in the wars they fought with us, and will always fight with us . . . and as such there is much deserted land that can be given to the Portuguese. . . .

Let there be, My Lord, nothing that obscures [this plan] to secure Ceylon once and for all, because aside from losing the cinnamon that the ships bring to India, and which ennobles and enriches the Portuguese state, the loss of Ceylon will leave this state [the Estado da Índia] without a shield to defend itself; and a body without a shield is put in danger, and this is against reason and a sin, and it puts such a weighty project as conversion in danger, as is known; and such a noble, rich, and sought-after state as this one will certainly find in these means the right remedy, which in a few short years will entirely secure it.

Translated by Robert Newcomb

Translator's Notes

1. A large ship.
2. Plural of *canarim*, inhabitant of Kanara. However, the Portuguese used the term to designate, often in a derogatory manner (just as Silveira violently does in this text), the people of Goa (both Hindu and Christian).
3. Plural of *topaz*. Mestizo, people of Portuguese descent.

Kandy in the 1630s:

Through the Eyes of a Soldier-Poet and a Soldier-Ethnographer

Anonymous and Constantino de Sá de Miranda

In the 1630s the Portuguese suffered a major military disaster in their war against the kingdom of Kandy, when the captain-general of the island (Constantino de Sá de Noronha, b. 1586–d. 1630) died during his expedition to Uva in August 1630. The "downfall of Constantino" soon became the leitmotif of Portuguese writings on Sri Lanka, and the two texts considered in this section, unpublished in their epoch, were penned in such a context. The first work, Jornada do Reino de Huva *(1635), consists of a dialogue between two men: Cardenio, the veteran soldier of the Kandyan wars, who narrates to a newly arrived Portuguese soldier named Fabricio the death of Sá de Noronha and subsequent events up to 1634. The anonymous author of the text served under Sá de Noronha, took part in the 1630 attack on Uva, and was captured and kept prisoner in Kandy for three years, until he managed to escape. In his work, meant to glorify the late captain-general, the author hides himself behind Cardenio, one of Miguel de Cervantes's best-known characters. The author of this baroque dialogue was certainly a cultured person, a soldier-poet; in this excerpt he extolls the literary skills of the queen of Kandy, without neglecting her beauty. The second text (*Formas de todas as fortalezas de Ceilão*), written by a certain Constantino de Sá de Miranda (not to be confused with Constantino de Sá de Noronha) in 1638, represents a different genre. It was conceived as one of the four "Books on the cities and fortresses of the Estado da Índia" devoted to Sri Lanka, and it is known that Father Fernão de Queiroz made liberal use of Sá de Miranda's work to write a good many of the twenty-three chapters in book 1 of* Conquista Temporal e Espiritual de Ceilão *(1687). Constantino de Sá de Miranda was also a veteran of the Kandyan wars, but he was no poet. It would be more appropriate to present him as a "biased anthropologist," as his description of Adam's Peak, the city of Kandy, or the ruins of Anuradhapura demonstrates. What makes this codex, conserved in the University Library of Zaragoza (Spain), a unique example of Portuguese and European views of* *seventeenth-century Sri Lanka is the inclusion of illustrations of Adam's Peak and Buddha's Footprint, as well as two plans of the city of Kandy, one depicting the royal citadel.*

Anonymous

FABRICIO—What kind of features has the Queen?[1]

CARDENIO—Very good, for she is tolerably beautiful and pleasant. She has a squint, on account of which the left eye is always closed which gives her great grace.

FABRICIO—How old would she be?

CARDENIO—She says thirty.

FABRICIO—I wonder whether you know that no one ever admits age, folly and the *mal de França* [syphilis].

CARDENIO—At least in the matter of age we all lie, and whether this lady does so, does not appear, because she never bore children and leads such a good life that it is natural she should be well preserved. But to come to our account of her appearance; what struck me most in her was that while the others were adorned with jewels in honor of this entry, Her Highness had none, either because, as some say, she greatly regretted the death of Constantino de Sá, as that there had been some dealings between them and she had been resolved to leave the Court of her husband, not only because he had been the husband of her mother Dona Catarina, but also because he took her to wife by force, and had killed for the purpose of that marriage a certain Prince, a relative of hers, to whom she had been espoused for four years; to her there was so great satisfaction that even today there may be seen in her eyes signs of grief; though there had been between her and the King other [griefs] which made her take the satisfaction proper to a woman. Either because of these reasons or because she disdained the ornaments of this triumph, she was without any kind of gala attire, yet so comely and so modest that she attracted the eyes of all of us who were there, seeing that in the state in which we found ourselves, there was little to strike the eye. And to end this description of her, she writes verses with a genius so wonderful that I was in admiration, for which reason I was acceptable to her because she came to know that I wrote verses also, when we removed from Uva, she protected and favored me with a very liberal hand.

FABRICIO—Wait a while! The verses which this lady writes are in the language of Manicongo?

CARDENIO—In Portuguese. I saw some of them. Had they been in that other language which I do not understand, I could scarcely have admired them. . . .

FABRICIO—There is no competing with you. But my stomach cannot digest that a woman born in Kandy, who has never seen any other Portuguese except those taken in Balane and those taken in this rout, could write verses with wonderful purity when the culture and climate of Kandy is so different from Greece, Italy, and Spain.

CARDENIO—Father Friar Francisco Negrão, Religious of the Observance and Chronicler of the same order, was nine years in Kandy teaching her and the Princes Latin and Italian, and she was moreover a daughter of King Dom João[2] by Queen Dona Catarina, the former educated in the Kings[3] and the latter in Mannar, where one may suppose, they educated her in the best style.

Constantino de Sá de Miranda

Adam's Peak (Pico de Adão) is a mountain located fourteen leagues from Colombo, which can be seen from almost all of the island of Ceylon, as well as ten to fifteen leagues of the sea around it; in the two-and-a-half-league area around the mountain there are no settlements of people from the lands that are subject to Your Highness, and five or six of the King of Kandy's subjects, and two to four from Uva because of how cold it is there all year round.

All of the gentiles and Moors of India venerate the mountain in the highest, because of a footprint the Chingalas associate with one of the famous fables that they believe in their brutality and ignorance. What is certain is that Saint Thomas the Apostle put his foot there, and not Buddum as the Chingalas believe, saying that he put one foot there and the other on a mountain on the other shore near Tuticorin and urinated, creating the sea that today divides the island of Ceylon from that shore. These people take this ridiculous account to be infallible, and because they are little skilled in the arts of drawing and geometry they cannot represent this lie so as to give it the appearance of truth. The gentiles are in fact ignorant of all science, because they have imagined a foot with six palms, whereas no body can be larger than nine feet or fifty-four palms, and it is thus impossible to consider such a jump. And because of this mistake they commit another, which is to make the toes so small that the largest is only a little longer than a half palm, a measurement that in no way accords with the picture sculpted into a rock in the city of Kandy and which is so highly venerated, and was so roughly worked as one can see in the enclosed drawing, which is shrunk because there was no more drawing surface left.

The truth is that Buddum was a holy man, and if he was not Prince Josafat as Diogo do Couto argued in his seventh decade [section—*Ed.*] and in whose opinion the Buddha's life nearly conforms to the story of Josafat's life,[4] there is no doubt that he was a disciple of Moses, because the law he taught to the natives of this island is the same as that the Jews now keep, though the Chingalas observe it poorly, and have added to its principle beliefs rather sensual, brutish, and disordered elements as could only be held by men such as these, over whom the devil has such power; and as a result they know no other God than he, denying (with incredible brutality) the first cause. I went to this mountain twice, once to see it and once of necessity. One climbs it on a chain three fathoms in length, which serves as stairs for the pilgrims who journey there, and which is tied between two tanks, one of which is filled with six thousand cobras. At the summit there is a clearing one hundred fifty paces in length and one hundred ten in width, and near the middle there is a stone that rises nine palms from the ground, and has a length of twenty-two [palms], where they say the said footprint was, though now there is only a hole made oily and dirty because of the candles that the Jogues, who are the pilgrims I mentioned, put there, and they preside over that hole, and value the earth they take from there as a relic, as if this could be a relic. The Portuguese named the mountain Adam's Peak, though I cannot figure out why. The natives call it Deyorata, which means the land of God.

The city of Kandy is sixteen leagues from the city of Colombo, and is surrounded on all sides by very high mountains, and from one of these sides flows one of the four rivers that originates on Adam's Peak, flowing alongside a small hill on the top of which is the wall of the palace, which is more than a half-league around. The homes the King has there are many, and they are all very humble, and those in which he resides are less than ordinary. In this same place there is a *pagode* that is famous among the Chingalas, and in reality it is famous, though it is a melancholy place because unlike other *pagodes* it has two openings in the roof, and the light let in through them allows one to see seven demons placed on the altar, which these people take for gods and that have the snouts of pigs, dogs, or elephants—a horrifying and ignorant thing that is perfectly consonant with the ignorance of their followers. They call this *pagode* Daladasguey [Dalada Maligava], which means house of the tooth, and it has on its very altar, in seven gold boxes, a buffalo's tooth they are certain is that of Buddum, of which the devil has convinced them with ridiculous miracles. This tooth, if it really existed and if it wasn't fake like this one, was the one that the viceroy Dom Constantino de Bragança took in Jaffna, and that, ground into a powder, he threw into the bay at Goa after refusing to give it for four hundred thousand *pardaus*[5] to the King of Pegu [Burma], where they observe the same stupidities as in Ceylon, to where they say that the same tooth escaped the mortar in which they crushed it.

The King has a poorly designed garden in this same place, with many flowers and fruits from Spain, which Constantino de Sá hasn't destroyed neither the first nor the second time he torched that city, because the Queen, who writes very well, asked him not to do so in a letter in her own calligraphy.

In the courtyard of this same palace there is a wall which surrounds two *pagodes*, dark and poorly lit houses that, though people live there and though they are clean, even in their cleanliness contain all manner of filth, and one can finally see that they are houses of the devil.[6] Constantino de Sá blew apart nearly half the roof of one of these *pagodes*, and he did the same to two gigantic idols that, had he not done this, would have been impossible to destroy. People used to place slices of meat from cows, as well as cow heads and intestines, on the heads and laps of the idols next to the altar that were not damaged by the fire, and in this same pagoda they used to slit the throats of many [cows]. For this reason, they worked to restore the idols, and since the death of this nobleman [Constantino de Sá] until the present moment they have completed the demolition of the palace's *pagode*, and rebuilt it as it stands now. . . .

This city has two thousand five hundred neighbors [*vizinhos*],[7] and the reason for this small number is that only the captains, who are few, are obliged to have a home in the city. The majority of the population is composed of Moorish merchants and paravas from the other coast, who in this city have a famous street where they sell their merchandise, and though the captains have their homes here, they also make their homes in the lands over which they rule, and as the Sinhalese are a brutish people, and are inclined to live in the forest, their nature does not impel them to congregate, nor do they congregate in their own lands, because each one has crops to maintain him, and for this reason their homes are far away from each other and consequently all the kingdom is populated. The kingdom of Kandy is the most populous of all the kingdoms of Ceylon, because their present King is the best man and the best captain there has ever been on this island, and because the offenses they receive from the Portuguese compel them to consider foreign land as their homeland, thus leaving the land where they were born.

The city's name is Ingalegalnure, which means the city the Chingalas built in stone, as can be seen in the enclosed drawing. . . .

. . . In the county of Mangul Corla [Mangul Korale] there was the city of Anu Rajapuré [Anuradhapura], which means the city of ninety kings, of whose lives and deeds the Chingalas write monstrous lies, as they do of this city, such that one cannot confirm anything true about it. However, one cannot deny that certain great things were built in a barbarous style in the city in those times, because I saw two rows of columns whose number I counted at one thousand six hundred, and measuring one I found it to be fifteen palms in height, and according to the tradition of the Chingalas (which is where some truth can be found) it is said that they supported houses whose roofs were made of metal, and in which pilgrims and the poor rested, and though these people are somewhat charitable, they delight so much in lying that one cannot believe anything relating to them that one does not see for oneself.

Further, I counted something like a hundred pyramids in this place, which in truth are not [pyramids] because they are as high as they are in circumference, with the largest among them being fifty, seventy, ninety, a hundred fathoms. For a tiled structure this must have been laborious to build, and they have no other function than to guard relics in their center, whether of Buddum or of some other god of theirs.

In this place I also saw a reservoir, which they say is of twelve leagues. It must be so, because one loses sight of the wall around it, and there are two other reservoirs in this place, of four and two leagues respectively, which were used to irrigate the cultivated parts of that land, and which today preserve vestiges of their [former] grandeur.

Notes

1. The queen was Antanadassin, daughter of Vimaladharmasuriya (r. 1591–1604) and Dona Catarina (Kusumasanadevi). King Senarat (r. 1604–35), who was simultaneously her step-father and uncle, took her as queen after the death of Dona Catarina.
2. Before taking the throne of Kandy in 1591, King Vimaladharmasuriya was an ally of the Portuguese, as well as a Catholic convert under the name of Dom João de Áustria.
3. The *Colégio dos Reis Magos*, founded by the Franciscans in Goa in 1555.
4. In the fifth decade of *Asia* (book 6, chapter 2)—not in the seventh decade, as Sá de Miranda suggests—the Portuguese chronicler Diogo do Couto (1542–1616) identifies the Buddha with Josafat, thus echoing the well-known medieval legend of Barlaam and Josafat.
5. Silver coin worth 360 reis.
6. Natha Devale and Pattini Devale, both temples represented in Sá de Miranda's plan of the royal citadel of Kandy.
7. About ten thousand inhabitants.

The Final Dreamers

João Ribeiro and Fernão de Queiroz

In the latter half of the seventeenth century, after the Portuguese had been expelled from the island, Sri Lanka represented an unfulfilled dream. The systematic defeats of the Estado da Índia after 1665 confirmed the view of those who had grown used to imagining Portuguese Asia in terms of what might have been, had Ceilão been kept and treated as the "jewel of the crown." Some still dreamed of a return, and this is the premise of two crucial books written in the 1680s: Fatalidade Histórica da Ilha de Ceilão (Historical tragedy of the island of Ceylon) by Captain João Ribeiro (1685), and Conquista Temporal e Espiritual de Ceilão (Temporal and spiritual conquest of Ceylon) by the Jesuit missionary Fernão de Queiroz (1687). Ribeiro witnessed the Dutch victory in Sri Lanka, since he lived on the island from 1640 to 1658, when he was captured during the siege of Jaffna and later taken to Batavia as a prisoner. He would eventually return to Portugal, where he came to write Fatalidade in an effort to persuade the Crown to reinvest in Sri Lanka: "May God grant that in view of these examples there may arise on these ruins a structure more solid. Such was the purpose with which I undertook this little work." As for Queiroz, his voluminous work constitutes the most serious Portuguese and Jesuit attempt to produce a complete history of Sri Lanka on the Portuguese presence in the island. His goal coincided with Ribeiro's, as he states in the preamble addressed to the viceroy of India: "One of the greatest services which Your Excellency can render to the Divine and human Majesty is to persuade Portugal to recover India, and especially Ceylon, the only object for which I gathered this information, so that considering all this, the Portuguese might realise what they have lost and resolutely determine to seek a means for the recovery." Despite their colonial agendas, these two works (especially Conquista) pay close if biased attention to Sri Lankan history and society: in the following extracts, Ribeiro describes "The Habitation of the Bedas," and Queiroz writes about "what the Chingalas know of Mathematics."

João Ribeiro

It is not the less worthy of notice that though this country is an Island smaller than Borneo or St. Lourenço, countries which in view of their size and distance from the Continent are able to have a monstrosity of this nature (for we must note as we have already pointed out that the area of Ceylon is little more or less than that of our own kingdom), nonetheless it has for several centuries contained a race which for its customs and ways of life would appear to be some romantic tale; but all who have been in the Island have heard of it. From the lands of the Vani which belong to the kingdom of Jaffna, to those of Trincomalee, between the two rivers which divide one from the other, there are ten leagues of coast with a breadth of a little more than eight leagues; this district is thinly inhabited and covered with dense forest, and here there live a caste of people who are known as Bedas.[1] In color they are similar to us, and some are ruddy and good looking. Their language is not understood by the *Chingalas* nor by any other nation of India, and they can only communicate with one another. Similarly they do not show themselves to any people except those of their own race. They wear the skins of animals, for every kind which is the object of the chase is found in great abundance in their forests. Their arms are bows and arrows in the use of which they are very skilful; they have no fixed habitation or settlement and each family lives for six months only at some spot in the forest which it selects as suitable for cultivation; as soon as the crop is gathered in, it changes to another place to do the same.

The chief part of their food consists of the produce of the chase—wild boar, deer, elk; in no stew do they eat cooked meat but almost all of it is soaked in honey which is found in these woods in much abundance, and is produced by the bees which deposit in the hollows of the trees. To preserve the meat they cut down some trees of a large size, leaving a stump of a fathom in height; this they hollow out and fill the cavity with meat and honey, and cutting out plugs of the same trees they cover over this conserve which they will not touch for a whole year, while they live on the other meat which they had stocked.

When they are in want of arrows, axes, or any other implement of iron, they make models out of the leaves of trees to show the article which they require; with these they go at night, so as not to be perceived by anyone, to the nearest village, and hang the models on the door of the blacksmith's house, along with their payment for the work, which is half of a wild boar, or deer, or some similar article which they think is a little more or less than the blacksmith deserves. When he arises in the morning he knows by experience what is wanted, and he accordingly does the work; and three days later when he goes to sleep he leaves the article hung up in the same place; and often in the morning the smith will find there a quarter of meat, and so they are glad to perform this work for them.

The *Chingalas* offer an explanation of the origin of this race which appears to me incredible, but anything is possible. It is that many years ago there was in the Island a young King who was addicted to every kind of vice to which he paid no regard, nor had he any respect for either laws or ceremonies; and going beyond all bounds he ate every kind of animal which God created, not even sparing the cow—and this among these Gentiles is the greatest sin which a man can commit. When he had finished with the animals he bade them kill a child, which he ate as a stew. When his people and nobles heard of this fearful deed they arrested him with all who had helped him and in view of the horror of his act, they sentenced him to death as infamous: but as they were unwilling to die, they gave them permission to go where they would have no communication with any man. Those who accepted the offer concealed themselves in these woods, where they live in this fashion.

If this explanation of theirs is false, it is not badly conceived; for the majority of the histories of these Gentiles are fables and fictions which they have concocted. Our own criticism is that if this were as stated by them, in view of the length of time and the fact of their having no war with any nation, as they had taken with them all the women who followed the King, they should have multiplied in such fashion that at the least they would have densely populated that district; but as a matter of fact they are so few in number that they wander about . . . through the forests, and hardly hold any intercourse with each other except by accident.

I came across a young man from India, a mystic, who had chanced to get wrecked in that country in a boat; he had made his way to the shore by swimming and there he was found by these people who made him marry their queen, who was a widow. Here the poor fellow was compelled to remain for nine months, and he had such a good kingship of it that he set about discovering some escape; he turned the sandals which he wore so that the toes pointed to the heels, and started on the road. He thus effected his escape and came into our territory, where he gave us a good deal of information regarding these people. They have no idols, no religion and no ceremonies; their families wander about separately in the forest searching for food, and as a rule all of them give the queen provisions, each one on his day by turn—rice, millet, potatoes, meat, fresh and steeped in honey—sufficient to maintain six or seven people. Her palace is a straw hut in the forest; she sees no one except those who bring her food daily, and these do not entrust the food to anyone save to the queen herself, to whom they make a profound reverence which she only acknowledges with a nod. Her bed is made of straw, with a bear skin for a coverlet, and her clothes are also made of other skins. Their meat is soaked in honey and eaten, and it is very savoury; the fresh meat is wrapped in leaves and buried in a hole, over which they make a fire, and when this is burnt out the meat is found very tender and agreeable; they eat it without salt, which article they do not possess. They made a flour out of millet and rice and from this they cook cakes. He told us various other facts which it is not possible to relate.

Fernão de Queiroz

They call Mathematics *Mazastra*, and some think that they know no more of it than to compute some eclipses of the Sun and the Moon, and if they do it in the way which I find written, it is sheer superstition, witchcraft and league with the Devil; but it is certain that they have acquired better knowledge. The *Chingalas* divide the year into 12 Solar months, according to the statement of the document of Bento da Silva; but as he says immediately that they begin it with the new moon of March, and that the other months are reckoned and separated by the new moon, and that they are all of 30 days, of which they make four weeks, each week seven days and each day of 30 hours and the night of as many again, it is clearly seen how much they differ from the European computation; and that unless it does not go right, or else they neglect many days. I did not find the Era or Epoch they make use of. The days of the week, beginning with our Sunday, they name, *Iri, Sandu, Angarua, Bada, Braspatin, Segura, Senocera.* . . .

As there is in Ceylon some difference in the length of the days and nights, and as they reckon 30 hours of the day and 30 of the night, the hours cannot but be artificial in almost all the days of the year, and their clocks [cannot but be] Babylonian. They generally use the following. In a vessel of water, large and broad they place another of copper, smaller, with a fine opening in the middle through which the water of the larger vessel enters, and when full it falls to the bottom and then they say one *Pe* is over, which is an hour. They also divide the natural day into twenty-four parts, 12 of daytime and as many of night, and in the same manner unequal. . . .

Just as they divide the year into twelve months and 48 weeks, they also divide it into six seasons in place of the four into which we divide it in Europe, Spring, Summer, Autumn and Winter, giving each three months. They however following two of their authors, Videuiaga and Maluate give to each season two months dividing these seasons under the following names beginning from March; *Vasunta, Grisna, Varusacaen, Xara, Eumanta, Seyceyra.* . . .

They have a knowledge of the stars and their influences . . . and they had knowledge of this by way of the Romans at the time when they had dealings in Ceylon, and that among them there were three men distinguished in this science and they were Vidagama Ganê, Totaganua, and Maluate; but at the present day the masters of this science in the Island are the *beruayas*, a low people, and they say that the following was the occasion.

In the reign of the King Acab Rajerû, the second of that name, much given to Letters and a patron thereof, there was not in the neighboring realms a man of learning who did not pass over to Ceylon drawn by the rewards he gave them. Among them was one highly esteemed for Mathematics and Astrology called Vede Viaga, who puffed up and arrogant treated with contempt the *Chingalas* who did not think themselves inferior to him. One of the latter named Maluate, and in their opinion a great mathematician, to lower the conceit of the foreigner and the esteem of his art, in great secrecy taught it to the *Beruayas*, who being honored thereby never abandoned it, the Father teaching his children, and they are as versed in the computations of time as the *baneanes* in sums of arithmetic, that without any hesitation or opening a book they answer any question put to them about the changes of the weather, diseases, fury of the wind and rain, advantage of land, moderation of the summer, the coldness of winter, the composition and strength of the human body, physiognomy of the face and all else that pertains to such observations, and with such abuses they call them Magi and sorcerers, wherefore they are persecuted even by their kinsmen. Nor is it an easy thing for a pagan to distinguish natural science from what is the work of the Devil, especially in medicine, because both in Ceylon and in the rest of India they will not begin a treatment without first consulting the soothsayers, with whom the whole country is well supplied; and if in Europe dealing with the Devil is more peculiar to women, in India it is rather reserved to men, though there are many whom they call *panditos*, who understand the pulse well and are quite skilled in herbs. Finally the *Chingalas* explain the year like the Enigma of Cleobulus related by Diogenes Laertius, saying that he is a Father who has 12 sons, and each son 30 grand-daughters, half white and half black, that all of them are immortal but all die; meaning by the Father the year, by the sons the months, and by the grand-daughters the hours of the day and of the night. This is not the place to examine the truth of what is said, and those who heard them gave the information to us were not mathematicians, so we cannot fully rely on their information.

It is nevertheless true that they speak more sensibly than the Bragmanes of this Hindustan who teach intolerable nonsense on this subject. . . .

They divide time into four parts which they call *Nerutta cugao, Duabara cugao, Tirreda cugao, Caliyao*. The first three ages of the world, they say, are already past, and they were cycles of gold in duration and good fortune, as all experienced: that in the third age there lived a certain King, of whom we shall speak elsewhere, without children for 70,000 years, and after that period he had them. . . . And though so great was the duration of that life, that *Eugao*, or age of the world did not end in his days. Of the fourth age, *Caliyao*, which is still current, they say it is of iron, because of the many misfortunes and sufferings which men experienced in it, and because of the short duration of life. Of it they say that it began 404,048 years ago; and as they never change this reckoning in the course of years, it will always have the same antiquity, and we shall have a permanent time. It has still more to run, for all the past time is but an instant with respect to the future. Some think that when this age is over, the world will not persist longer; others, that when it is over, the cycles of gold which had passed will reappear.

And as this fable, well known among them, seemed but small to a certain Yogi, it is said in his book *Andaxarcarão*, or Chronicle of the world, that before these four ages, which suppose some knowledge of the image in Nabacodenosor's [dream], there were 14 others, and 18 in all, and to be excused from giving their names, it will be enough to state their duration. The first, they say, lasted 140 millions of years, the second 130; the third 120, the fourth 110, the fifth 100 millions, the sixth 90 millions, the seventh 80, the eighth 70, the ninth 60, the tenth 50, the eleventh 80, the eighth 70, the ninth 60, the tenth 50, the eleventh 40, the twelfth 30, the thirteenth 20, the fourteenth 10, the fifteenth 9 million and 600,000 years, the sixteenth 7 millions and 500,000 years, the seventeenth 5 million and 900,000 years, the eighteenth 4 million and 400,300 years, so that before the last four ages of the world it had already lasted 100,755 million and 706 years. In order to form an opinion of what they think of the visible world, [be it said] that they imagine that all stars are animated by a rational form, that they are married, have many children, though they are all gods. So much for the astrology of the Bramanes who cannot deny that the *Chingalas* speak more sensibly.[2]

Section Editor's Notes

1. Veddhas. Aboriginal inhabitants of Sri Lanka.
2. Original footnotes omitted.

The Catholics' Last Sigh:
Oratorian Missionaries in
Eighteenth-Century Kandy

M. da Costa Nunes

Catholic missionaries returned to Sri Lanka and settled there roughly three decades after the fall of Jaffna (1658). The Oratorians, who had been operating in Goa since 1682, produced reports of their mission on the island, which provide fascinating portraits of the successive kings of Kandy, from Vimaladharmasuriya II (r. 1687–1707) to Rajadhi Rajasinha (r. 1782–98) and pay special attention to their different religious policies. The missionaries, who were simultaneously participants and observers of a society that was experiencing tremendous pressures and transformations, found themselves in a privileged position to analyze a variety of political, social, and religious practices. Their letters constitute crucial testimony of the challenges faced by individuals and communities in between (and disputed by) different systems of belief, namely Buddhism, Catholicism, and Protestantism. The following excerpts are related to the reigns of Vimaladharmasuriya II and Narendrasinha (r. 1707–39) and include two pieces by Father José Vaz, who founded the Oratorian mission in 1687.

Father José Vaz (Kandy, September 10, 1697)

This king [Vimaladharmasuriya II], as he is much inclined toward the good and possesses reason, if he knew of the falsehood of his religion, and the truth of ours, could with God's favor convert, but there is no one here with the authority or knowledge, much less the spirit, who could do this. We, in addition to being unable to do this for being considered people of little importance, are prevented from conversing with him; for I have been in this city for nearly seven years and I have neither seen nor appeared before him. As he considers us poor, miserable creatures, he does not fail to remember and pity us, and he meets our needs. However, there is a law in his religion that adherents should not hear the things or read the books of other sects,

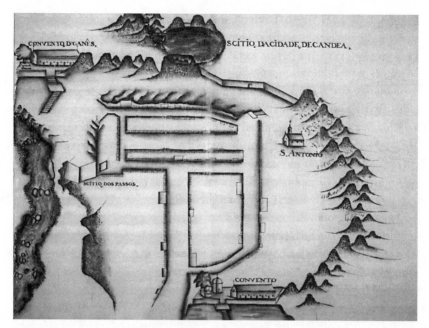

"The City of Kandy," 1638. Zaragoza, Biblioteca Universitaria, ms. 13, f. 39.

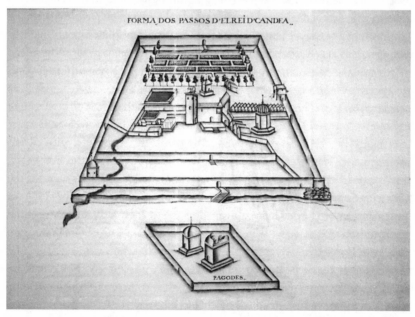

"The Royal Citadel of Kandy," 1638. Zaragoza, Biblioteca Universitaria, ms. 13, f. 40.

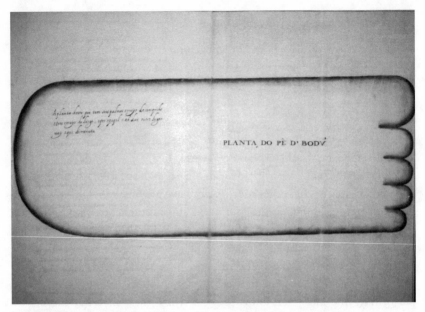

"Buddha's Footprint," 1638. Zaragoza, Biblioteca Universitaria, ms. 13, f. 36.

and because of this he never asks or hears of these things, and if he does by chance, it is out of courtesy and a passing thing, and not on purpose, with the intention of knowing their goodness and truth. Because he does not know, nor does he suspect, that his [religion] is false, and he has great (if false and vain) faith and hope in being among the chosen. As such he zealously works for the growth of his religion, and so that it would not be extinguished in this land with the death of all of its priests, and so that new ones might be ordained (there not being a bishop here), he with great dedication sent [men] to Arakan [Burma], and from there came thirty-three bishops, with two as their principal leaders. In receiving, sheltering, and honoring these, the king showed nearly the sum of his power and devotion, in his own way. Of the thirty-three, six died here, one of these being one of the leaders; the rest have left so as to embark on their return [journey] to their land, leaving behind one hundred twenty newly ordained *ganês*,[1] or priests, and of this first group they gave thirty-three the rank of bishop. . . .

Some thought, myself and other Christians included, and regretted that those who came from Arakan, either of their own will or induced by contrary teachings, would in speaking to the king say something against our Christianity, but they, by God's grace, praised it highly, saying that in their lands they also had our priests and churches, and that our holy law was true, though they did not believe theirs to be false.

Father José Vaz ([Kandy], May 28, 1699)

We do not know with certainty of what things they have accused us . . . but the principal accuser is one of his Imperial Majesty's favorites, who always acts in his service and has his house near our church. . . .

The *dissava*[2] is among those who joined the aforementioned accuser, and he was by order of the king obligated to watch us and feed us, seeing that if I went on a long voyage, and if during my absence his Imperial Majesty asked after me, he would be blamed. . . . Another is the *vedor da fazenda*.[3] He and others have said and say that because certain of the king's servants have become Christians, the other men do not have anyone to help them in sickness and with other necessities, nor in the superstitious ceremonies they do out of devotion, nor in bringing flowers or in doing other services at the *pagodes*. There are no women neither for their processions nor to perform the demon's other services, and all these men have excused themselves saying that they are Christians, and in this they do not obey. Some say that for not performing the aforementioned services, they [the converted Christians] should not be given what they need, and they have responded (according to one ignorant person) that the fathers would provide for them, and that even if made prisoners, they would when sick refuse to commit those superstitious acts that would not work because they are Catholic Christians. . . .

Then there are the caretakers of the *pagodes*, who complain that the aforementioned [former servants], in converting to Christianity, no longer make promises or bring offerings to the *pagodes*, and as such, they [the caretakers] have nothing to do. Others say, with the zealousness of their false religion, that the fathers' church has grown and that they have extended the Christian law over more people, and so if the fathers and the church remain, their [the caretakers'] law and the cult of the Buddha and the *pagodes* will be overshadowed.

Father Inácio de Almeida (Hanguranketa, February 20, 1713)

After going to Sitavaka in the king's [Narendrasinha] particular service and returning to court, the aforementioned king received me with demonstrable pleasure, as he was so pleased to conclude the business dealing, and from that day he has frequently sent his *apuamios*[4] to visit me and ask after my health.

The church the king allowed us to build in this city has been completed, and we celebrated the birth of the Child Jesus in it, with all the solemnity that is possible in these lands. Many people attended, including all the *apua-*

mios from the palace, and the king also wanted to come and see the church, but as it was heavily raining that night he did not come. During those same days he sent me a fine robe [*casula*] that had been at the palace ... along with ten panels depicting the ten Stations of the Cross, and his own silver lime holder [*chunambeiro*]. As such this was a very singular demonstration of affection, because normally he does not offer anything he wears and no one is supposed to own what he wears. For this reason, the king's action toward me made a great impression among his courtiers, and he also sent a large, curious candlestick. He received me so well and with much honor that day, and he did not wish to sit while speaking with me. He asked me to explain the captions of the panels he had given to me, and when I deciphered them for him he was very pleased, and in this way he shows much affection for our Holy Law. Let God convert him to it.

It happened that one night there was a debate at the palace concerning religion. Some Calvinists, and other sectarians in attendance gave their reasons, with each one defending his sect, but the king was gradually convinced by the defense of the Catholic religion, and at the end he concluded by saying that only the Catholic religion was true and that all the others were false, and everyone was shocked, and the next day the *adigar*[5] told Father Jácome Gonçalves of this.

One day an *andi*, a penitent for the gentiles, was walking down the street dressed in black; the king saw him out of the window and asked the *adigar* standing behind him what man this was, thinking that he was one of ours. The *adigar* responded and identified the man, and the king became irritated asking who had given him permission to dress like the priests. Consequently, the king ordered the same *adigar* to sharply reprimand [the man] and explain that if he appeared dressed in the same way again, he would be punished with all severity.

In January, some Christians who serve in the palace, whose names I do not mention, got into a big fight near the church, and an *apuamio* told the king of this. The king reprimanded three of them for their disobedience and for their lack of respect for me and for God's Church, and [warned that] if they dared to commit the same crime a second time, he would expel them from his service and from the city, and from that moment everyone has been very reluctant to be associated with us or with the things of the Church.

I say to Your Reverence in closing that the aforementioned king is much inclined toward us, and that various times and before many people he has given us praise that we do not deserve, and has said that in his kingdom no people can be found who are as loyal as we are.

Father Francisco Vaz (Goa, January 3, 1723)

The news of these new missionaries [António de Távora and Crisóstomo Fernandes] reached the king of Kandy and he then ordered them to come to his court. Father Jácome Gonçalves, the superior of the mission, took them there and presented them to the king, who received them with much pleasantness and courtesy, and he asked them of the various things they might need [from him], though the fathers pretended [that they did not need anything] so as not to have to remain at court, as they wanted to go to the missions. The king, having found out by other means that Father Crisóstomo Fernandes knew medicine, ordered him to remain as a guest in the home of one of his principal men, near the palace, because in this new city of Hangu-raketa ("Angirachitta"), where the king is at present, the fathers had neither a church nor a place to live, as they have in the old city of Kandy, which was always the seat of power of these kings. And it was necessary to concede to the king in order to satisfy him, because the presence of all [the missionaries] on the island and the stability of the mission depend on him, and moreover, because in this way the calumnious machinations with which the enemies of the faith are always assailing the priests and Christians will be more easily undone.

The king's esteem for the father [Crisóstomo Fernandes] increased during the time in which he enjoyed the father's talents, and on various occasions he tried to prove this by asking curious and strange questions on the natural virtues, on the qualities and manifestations of terrestrial things, and on the influence of the stars and the planets. Though the king is not an expert on these subjects, he is curious to inquire and know of them.

The father made a curious crèche out of wax to celebrate the birth of Our Lord, and when the king heard of it and saw it, he was so pleased that he did not cease to show this in his admiration and applause. This father became ill, and the king sent three doctors to cure him, asking after his health every day and sending him everything he needed from the palace, and seeing that he was not improving, he sent another doctor, his wisest and more favored, and he did not rest until he saw [the father] free [of his illness]. And when this father, having received the king's permission to visit the closest missions in order to improve them, stayed in the church of the city of Candia for a time, the king missed him, but he did not wish to openly order him to return, so using the greatest political skill, he sent him a *saguate*[6] of the best fruits of his land, and in this way obliged the father to [return and] give his thanks to him. At that time [the king] complained of his absence, sweetly threatening to never again give him permission to leave court, though he would give what was necessary to support the missions.

Something was robbed from the royal treasury, and being unable to find it through spells and witchcraft, some of the king's Christian noblemen told him of the power and talent of Saint Anthony in finding lost things. The king asked for an image of the Saint and very decently placed it in the armory, and wished to determine its power through tests of chance, and seeing that those tests conducted in his presence invariably pointed to those who are notorious thieves, he was so impressed by the power of the Saint and so venerated his image that out of devotion he did not dare to touch it, and would only do so after being encouraged by the Christians and after washing his hands with saffron and sandalwood powder. And taking the image from the armory, the king placed it in the royal treasury, building an altar and canopy with much decency and with candles and incense and with guards posted there to keep watch, and he ordered the father to bless that house, as the diabolic ceremonies of the gentiles had been performed in it previously. And repeating the same tests, now without the father being present, and applying them not only to the people of the palace, but also to those of his court, including the most prominent ones, and seeing that the tests always pointed to those who were known thieves, and not to others, nor to those to whom the gentiles' ceremonies had pointed as thieves, and who he now freed as innocent, he came to hold a better view of our holy law than of his own diabolical religion. And after this the king had a dream, and became afraid that he had angered the Saint, and he consulted the father, telling him of the tests of chance he had conducted, and the father, declaring to him that this was neither right nor permissible, sent the image of the Saint to the church so that it could be kept more decently there than in his palace.

Notes

1. From the Sinhala *ganinnanse*. Despite living in Buddhist temples, the ganinnanses were not ordained and did not observe the Vinaya monastic discipline.

2. Province or, in the present case, head of a province.

3. Treasury officer, in Portuguese. Controller of revenues.

4. *Appuhami*. Honorific. Son of a headman.

5. Chief officer of state under the kings of Kandy.

6. From the Persian *saughat*. Gift.

THE DUTCH: AN INTRODUCTION

The expulsion of the Portuguese from Sri Lanka came about because of a pact forged between King Rajasimha II of Kandy and the enterprising Dutch East India Company. The implacable hatred borne by Kandyan rulers for the Portuguese presence is seen as early as Sebald de Weert's testimony regarding the first king of Kandy, Vimaladharmasurya (see the next chapter in this section), some fifty years before the Portuguese were expelled and thirty-five years before a formal Kandyan-Dutch "deal." The political relationship between Kandy and the Dutch, however, was strained almost from the beginning. In exchange for expelling the Portuguese by means of their superior manpower and military resources, the Dutch wanted reimbursement for their efforts and a monopoly on cinnamon trade. After they evicted the Portuguese from Batticaloa and Trincomalee on the east coast in 1639 and handed these ports over to the Kandyans, the Dutch subsequently proceeded to take both Negombo and Galle on the west coast for themselves. They retained these strategic ports on the pretext that the king of Kandy had yet to reimburse them for their previous services in securing the east coast ports. These two west coast ports, not incidentally, were perfectly situated for the purpose of exporting cinnamon. It would be another twenty years (1658) before the Dutch finally expelled the Portuguese from their forts in Colombo and Jaffna.

For most of their history on the island, Dutch strategy was consistent: (1) to maintain tight political and social discipline over the coastal areas that they had captured from the Portuguese; (2) to accomplish this discipline not only through established military hegemony but also through the conversion of low-country inhabitants to the Protestant Christianity of the Dutch Reformed Church (see the excerpt from Philip Baldaeus's account later in this section); and (3) to keep the power of the Kandyan kingdom at bay, in a state of economic and political atrophy. Largely, they succeeded in preventing the Kandyans from interfering in their successful trading affairs (the Dutch East India Company, often referred to by its Dutch acronym voc, was the most successful commercial enterprise in the world for almost a century) and pauperizing the Kandyans by means of their shrewd and often unfair trade practices. Because the Dutch ensured that the Kandyan kingdom was eventually landlocked, they became the king's international "middlemen," posing in public as "His Majesty's Servants." In fact, they sought to control virtually all Kandyan intercourse with the outside world. Moreover, their message to the Kandyans, in the manner of the "Protestant ethic and the spirit of capitalism," was to champion the fact that spiritual and material well-being went hand in hand. The Dutch "predikants," by dangling the possibility of wealth as a lure for religious conversion—a practice allegedly pursued by Christian Protestant missionaries in contemporary Sri Lanka and much criticized—were thus harbingers of the acrimonious relations that developed between Christians and Buddhists in more recent times.

A Dutch Prelude

Sebald de Weert

As early as 1602, with the visit to Kandy of Boris von Spilgenberg, the idea of a Dutch alliance with the Kandyan kingdom against the Portuguese was advanced and discussed, though it was another fifty years, in 1658, before that alliance was forged and successful in its aim. The letter below was written from the town of Atchin by Sebald de Weert, to his superior Wybrand van Warwijck, who was staying near Bantam; it describes de Weert's visit to Kandy and his extensive discussions with King Vimaladharma Surya I about securing cinnamon and pepper in exchange for military assistance against the Portuguese. We also learn about this king's rise to power, significant in that he was the first legitimate king of the Kandyan dynasty. Unfortunately for de Weert, his life ended soon after this letter was written. He died at the hand of the Batticaloa chief who had originally welcomed him to the island, having entered into a dispute (alluded to below) and having insulted the chief.

Most honored, wise, very prudent sir. . . . The reasons that move us to go to Seylon I shall relate at length to your honor, together with what befell me there, [and] I beg your honor to take in good part my prolixity in writing, in order that your honor may the better have knowledge of the kingdom of Zeylon,[1] and receive favorably and approve of our effort.

After we had arrived with fair prosperity off the island of Zeylon at the altitude of about 7 degrees we went on shore at a place named Panem [Panama], where we learnt that Mattacalou [Batticaloa] where we wished to be lay about 10 or 12 miles higher, and that there had been there two large ships, the which by tokens they gave me of the captain as also of others I found to have been the general Spilbergen, the bearer of this, who had been up inland to Candy, where the great king resides, that he had also left there four men, and further that he had further laden for home, at which we were not a little rejoiced. In Mattacalou I heard the same; but as we were made to believe much regarding lading, and two clerks remaining on land saw no appearance thereof, we resolved to set sail again direct for Achin, and making ready therefor, there came the message from the king that we should not depart before we had sent a man or two to Candy to the great king, who could well lade us, that in the country there was plenty of pepper, wax and cinnamon, and all reasonably cheap; also a great quantity of precious stones; on hearing which, we changed our resolution, and arranged that two ships alone should depart, in order to advise those of Achin of our intention, and that, I remaining there should myself go to Candy, lying about 36 miles inland, and not be deceived by evil reports.

So I went ashore, taking with me some presents for the king, and as it was winter there, and was bad weather daily, our boat was thrown over by the breakers right from stern to stern, and I that could not swim right under it, but God be praised we suffered no harm except to our goods. (During all the time we lay there also we did not lose one man, though very seldom any boat or canoe went to land that was not upset or filled.) Coming on land we were well received, and immediately rode with six elephants to Mattacalou about a mile inland, where we were shown great honor by the king, and he begged much that I would be willing to send someone to Candy, [and] he would meanwhile cause to be collected all the pepper, wax and cinnamon that was possible to him, doubting not that within three months he would load us: but he is a cheat who has very little power, is tributary to the Portuguese, and obedient to the king of Candy more from constraint than good-will. His hope was, that through the daily bad weather our ship should come to be wrecked, whereby he would have got a booty, though he feigned himself otherwise.

Having waited quietly there one day, I sent on board again a part of the crew (because I had 15 men with me), and with six men set out on the journey upon elephants. On the way we had daily so much rain that we were fifteen days on the journey, often prevented by the rivers from pursuing the journey. On the road I found such friendly and obliging people that it is incredible: we were everywhere defrayed and well treated. On coming halfway, there met us seven men, who were sent by the king, as he had tidings that there were three ships on the coast, in order to learn what ships they were, who were very [glad] at seeing us, they brought letters from the Dutch that were in Candy, [and] begged that we would be pleased to write what people we were, because the king desired it much; whereupon they immediately sent back two men with the answer, other two forward to view my ship, and the rest remained with me. The king having received my letters was so delighted that he could not keep patience, longing so for my coming that he could not rest, he sent me every hour people with victuals, refreshments and every token of benevolence; he also sent his brother-in-law with 100 men with pipes and drums to receive and convey me. On coming near the city I was received with such magnificence and triumph that I know not if in our land one could do more after the manner of the country to his princely excellency. When we were two days' journey from the city he sent his own palankin in which I was carried.

On coming into the city, the people were all astir [with] the soldiers in order quite half a mile along the road through which I must pass; all the ordnance was fired, [and] they made such a noise of trumpet and such like instruments, that one could neither see nor hear. Thus I was conducted to my lodging; which was behung according to custom, whilst the king sent me word that I should rest a little and thereafter come and speak with him; but I had hardly the leisure in which I could eat something, [when he] summoned me immediately to him, [and] gave me no [time] to dress myself and make ready my presents. I was again conducted to the court with such playing, and number of people that we could hardly get unhindered along the street. My presents were carried uncovered before me, which were, a red cloth, two large mirrors, a handsome gilt musket, a beautiful gilt sword that I had taken with me for my own use, and further a lot of handsome glasses, but mostly broken on the way. . . . [There] stood all those of his council and captains on each side against the wall. In the middle hung the likeness of his princely excellency painted on a cloth full-size from life, presented to the king a little before by the general Spelbergen, and a handsome carpet spread in front of it, on which my presents were laid. At the side in a little recess stood the king leaning against the wall, having in front of him two children, son and daughter, rightful heirs to the country. Having come before him and greeted him in the manner of our country, with one knee on the ground, he having told me at once to rise and bidden me welcome through an interpreter deplored greatly the inconvenience that I had suffered on his behalf on such a far journey and in such weather. He asked me whence and why I came, to which I replied, I came from a country called by the Portuguese Frandes, which was several provinces confederated together and governed by the nobles of the country, whom we call "los estados," under the command of our prince whose likeness was hanging there. On saying which, there was great gladness among his lords, because I recognized the likeness of his princely excellency, since thereby he found the statement of the general Spelbergen, who had been there just four months before, to be true, and that we were from one country; because to that end was the likeness hung there. I said further to him that we were merchants (who had) come there to buy cinnamon, pepper, precious stones and other wares, and to sell ours, seeking the friendship of all kings and princes of the countries and islands of India, in order to be able to trade freely with their subjects, that we had for several years now had intercourse with Atchin, Bantam and the Moulucas, and were great friends of the kings, since we were enemies of the Portuguese, and that for over thirty years now we had warred with the king of Portugal, that we also had commission and command from our prince to assist and help all kings and princes that were expelled by the Portuguese. Whereupon immediately interrupting and breaking my recital, as he not only understands but also speaks Portuguese well, and has no need of interpreter except for honour's sake—he had me told that I had come at an opportune time, and that God had sent me there as to a king that more than any others was annoyed by the Portuguese, who contrary to right and reason wished to take away his country from him and drive him out, he begged accordingly that I would execute my commission and carry it into effect as early as possible. To which I replied that there was no doubt that God had brought me there, but it was not by chance, as one says, because I had come there by express command of our prince, who, having heard of the continuous wars that the kings of Ceylon (without knowing of Candy) had against the Portuguese, had sent me there to form alliance and friendship with, the king, [and] to promise him help and assistance; but that his majesty well knew that no princes or rulers gave anyone assistance to their own loss,— that we came from so far at great trouble and expense, that if in his country there was any probability of lading, help should not be wanting to him; that he should accordingly arrange to have pepper planted, and every year Dutch ships would come there; that he would now lade me, so that I might immediately sail home and return again with assistance. This he promised to do, on condition that I would wait there four months, because he must have the pepper brought from the mainland, seeing that there was very little pepper there, even though he should sell all his elephants therefor.

Upon this I took my leave in order to go to my lodging promising to come again to his majesty the next day when it pleased him to summon me. But when I thought to depart, the king called me back, and bade ask me how I was so bold that I durst hazard to come so far into his country, without knowing him or having advice from him and some hostages. To which I answered that many reasons had moved me thereto, but that the principal of them were the Portuguese. Being astonished at this, he asked, how that was possible, seeing that I had declared that they were our enemies, and that I also well knew that he was an enemy of the Portuguese, he did not know how he should understand that. Whereupon, I immediately replied that this was the very reason, which the Portuguese gave me, to embolden me to come so far into his country, without first advising him of my arrival. I omitted to ask permission, because I was confident that a king that was a real enemy of the Portuguese must necessarily be a friend of ours, likewise enemies of the same Portuguese, and that coming unexpectedly to such a king I should be all the more welcome; that I should also well avoid venturing such in other countries. At this there was great laughter, and the king asked me what were the other reasons that had moved me thus to come to him. Upon which I answered, in the first place, the honor, courtesy and good treatment that he had accorded to the general who had been there before me, who had come thence so freely; in the second place, that I should be ashamed not to dare venture what another had done before me, and lastly, the honor that the king of Mattacalou had shown me on arrival and the goodwill that I saw that the common people had towards us. Hereupon the king asked again if I trusted in the people so readily, seeing I had not spoken to the general himself. I answered, yes, as the words of many persons in different places agreed well, because it is not very possible that many persons in speaking do not contradict each other. . . .

With this the king well satisfied let me depart to my lodging, where were brought immediately so many pots with all kinds of whey, conserves, fruits and other confections, that I found the house far too small; also a majordomo with four male and three female slaves to serve us. When I was in the house, all the principal lords came to visit me and bid me welcome. [The king] also sent me immediately 50 larins . . . to spend.

Towards the evening the king again summoned me to him in order to speak with me alone. On coming up I found him walking about, having only three or four of his privy council with him; and when I offered to kiss his hands, he took me in his arms and squeezed me heartily, so that he made my ribs crack; (I had much rather have been embraced by a pretty maiden), meaning thereby to show how welcome I was to him. He at once asked me if I had no letter of credence from my prince, which having produced, he had it brought [to him] and a seal of his excellency's that the general Spelbergen had left with him, with the warning that whoever did not bring such a token was not of our people, with which having compared mine, and finding that they were both alike, he was greatly rejoiced, and at once promised me to make every exertion to lade my ships within four months; he was also sorry that I had sent away my two other ships, because he would have liked to lade them all together. Whereupon I made my excuse that we were destined to Atchin, where our general, with thirteen other ships was to come; that through fear that the latter should wait for us I sent two ships thitherward in order to advise him of my arrival, as I did not think that these would have been lading there for all our ships; that Atchin was our rendezvous, whence the ships were to be sent to various places; that if he could not help me earlier than within four months, it were better that I also went to Atchin, and come back in four months, or send another ship, the more so, in that it was winter and very risky to lie on the coast. To which he answered that I need not fear, that I could safely moor the ship, [as] he had anchors and cables enough for me. At this I began laughing, and when he asked me why I laughed, I answered that I saw well that his majesty did not know what ships we had, but imagined that we had champones or junks, that he was mistaken, because I should need to have for the lading of my ship at least 2,500 baeren of pepper; that I had on board 36 large cannon: which he would hardly believe, wherefore I begged that he would send one of his principal lords with me to view the same. At this the king being astonished immediately said that he had not imagined that my ship had been so big; that he did not wish to deceive me or to delay me to no purpose, that he did not know how to obtain any ladings for me, since the Portuguese had possession of his best land where the best cinnamon and pepper grew; that he could probably procure 1,000 quintals within three months, but for so much pepper he knew of no expedient, that he was no merchant but a soldier, who thought neither of the building of a house, nor of planting, nor anything else by which he should be able to make profit, but only how he should protect his country; that no ships had even been there, and consequently he had had no experience in trade, but that his country was as suitable for yielding plenty of pepper as any in India; if he were master of his country, he would cause great plenty of pepper to be planted. As regarded cinnamon it grew of itself in the woods, [and] cost him only the trouble of levying on each village to furnish a certain quantity, desiring no money also therefor. If we would afford him any assistance, he would promise to furnish us every year with 1,000 quintals and that for ever and aye; and if we [captured] the fort of Punta de Gaela [he would give us] 2,000 quintals, and [if] Columbo, all the cinnamon of the whole country. He would also bind himself and all his successors that they should not be able to sell a pound of cinnamon to anyone in the world, but deliver all to us, and whatever else we might further stipulate. That I should consider the matter, because here was to be honor for myself and profit for our country. That with great trouble we sought to build forts in other places that were near his country, against the will of the inhabitants, that he himself now called and begged us thereto. He promised all help: if we were on the coast, he would at once take the field with 20,000 men, desiring of us no more than to prevent by water that any victual came into Columbo from Goa: he could easily press the enemy on land. He would give the captured forts into our care (since his people were not fitted to take charge of forts), that from there we should be able to send our ships to all quarters, and always take our refuge in a king who should be our friend and ally. That we would be willing to seize this occasion, because if he were expelled through lack of assistance, such an opportunity would not offer in India in our lifetime, that we would therefore be pleased to hasten and take his affairs to heart, or otherwise he would have cause to complain at our arrival in his country, because the Portuguese would now attack him much harder than before, from fear that in time we might succor him; that the matter required haste; that the great trouble and expense that the Portuguese incurred in order to gain his country should serve us as a proof of the value of his country; that in the whole of India there was not so rich or so fruitful a country, nor one so well situated. That henceforth he wished to be called "Hermano en armas de sua ex timo Principe dorange," and other similar speeches in order to persuade me—who was only too greatly inclined thereto because of the great profits that our united masters would thereby be able to enjoy for so many years and the honor of our fatherland—to his help. To all of which foregoing reasons I answered him that such as he desired could with great difficulty be accomplished this voyage, that although we had many ships they were fitted out only for trade, and consequently not so provided with men that we should be able to put many men on land; that it was also uncertain if I should find the fleet still in Achin,—that it might have left before my arrival: that it were better that I should obtain my lading in haste, in order thus to sail home, and from there bring succor. To this he replied that his affairs did not admit of so long a delay; and that [as] I had come to-day, tomorrow I should rest, and the day after depart. And therewith he took a gold toothpick from his neck, set with small garnets, worth about 6 [pounds], and hung it round my neck and as it was dark, he let me go home, with the command to come to him as his guest the next day.

The third day he had me called to come and eat with him. Having come [there], as it was yet early, he chatted of various matters while walking about (because there it is not the custom to sit on the ground as in other countries: the kings when they speak to anyone, even of their own people, always stand, as also those that are near them). So I begged to see his children; and himself going in, he brought his daughter, about six years old, by the hand, with a gold cup full of wine made from the grapes that grow in his house, and presented [it] to me to drink. Having accepted the cup, I wished to kiss the young princess's hands, at which she being perplexed, since they are not wont to come near men, ran away crying out, and although her father called her several times, she would not come. Having drunk, I presented the cup back again, but he would not accept (it), saying that, seeing that his daughter had run away, I should take the cup with me; and as I refused this, he shut the door in my face. Shortly afterwards he came again with the young prince, about three years old, on his arm, who offered me his hand and bade me welcome; and when I had kissed his hands, the father requested that I would take him under my protection and be his guardian, and not suffer that he who was the rightful heir to the country (because he had won the mother with the sword) should be driven out of it: the which I promised him to do according to my small power, and to recommend him to my prince. Having heard this, the child drew from his side a little creese, with a silver sheath (if it was by order of his father I do not know), and presented it to me: at which I was so pleased that, having nothing else to give, I took from my side, with strap and all that belonged thereto, my swords, which with its accessories was worth over 20 pounds, and [which] I would not willingly have given to the father, even had he desired it of me, and presented it to the young prince; and although the father somewhat deprecated it, since I had no other for the road, he held it in such worth that it is incredible: he also promised that it should be the first weapon that the prince should use when grown up. After this he confided to me how he had won with the sword the mother (who was the daughter of the preceding king and rightful heiress to the country), defeating 800 Portuguese, among them the general with all the captains, and bore as a token of the victory the representations of the heads in the clasps of his anklets. Because when the Portuguese had cap-tured the city of Candy, and had defeated and expelled the King, who was the father of this daughter and a friend of the Portuguese, they brought the daughter, who had been brought up by them [and] baptized, as also the king, and was instructed in their faith, into Candy, with the intention to marry her (who was as yet only 12 years old) to a Portuguese nobleman. But Don Juan Doustria (so the king was called among the Portuguese, and so also he signs his letters—he was also so baptized, although afterwards he became a heathen again) having been summoned by the inhabitants of the country as a defender as being a brave captain, they so harassed the Portuguese that they had to leave Candy, and in their departure they slew them all and took the queen prisoner, whom he married against her inclination, as she did not wish to have him, because he was black and she was white, also because he being a Christian had more wives. But nevertheless the king proceeded therewith, and has now these two children by her.

Having chatted on these and other matters, it was time for eating, where-fore the king retired within to the queen, who had the desire to see us eat, standing behind the door, and we were very well treated after our manner at a small table. Having eaten, the king came again to me to chat, until my men had eaten, meanwhile he fasted until we had departed.

The next day, when I purposed to depart, it rained so hard that I had to remain. Meanwhile I went to view all the pagodes, which are made not without great art, among which some are five or six fathoms in height, proportioned symmetrically. I imagine that they are made according to the size of Adam, because the length and breadth exactly correspond with the footsteps of Adam, which I also saw and measured, they are 7½ spans long and broad, they are those whereof Jan Huygen writes, which the king caused to be brought from the mountain into the city.

The same evening I was again with the king, in order to take leave, who recommended his affairs to me in the strongest manner, and begged me that I would only make haste, [and] he would meanwhile (if the Portuguese left him in peace) make about 1,000 quintals of cinnamon, which if I came back with help I should have for nothing, or without help for money. He also presented to me in recompense for my presents 25 quintals of cinnamon and 16 quintals of pepper, and for my kitchen, so he said, five quintals of each though I got none or not much, because they were hindered from coming down by the great rain, and on getting aboard I could not wait for them.

On the return journey the king sent with me his highest captain (who is a Portuguese) with 50 or 60 men to convoy me and at the same time view my ship; and I was again treated and defrayed as before. He also sent me the first two days food from his house, with wine and some confections, so that I was astonished at his munificence.

This is what I could not forbear to write at length to your honor; hoping that it will not trouble your honor to peruse the same and consider somewhat over the matter. Were I to describe in particular all the magnificence and treatment of the reception and on the journey, I should be tired of writing. I place this alone before your honor, in order that you may be able to realize what kind of a king and what an island we could have devoted to us with little trouble and great profit,—a king powerful in troops, a brave soldier and much inclined towards us, who every day wishes for once to rule in his country over such people as ours, and even to send his son if he were old enough to his excellency in order there to learn good manners and the art of war, a king, I say, who now offers us even his country and means,—a country as fertile as any situated among all the East Indian [countries] that alone yields the cinnamon, which we can now bring into our hands alone, without, either Portuguese or Turk being able to obtain a pound thereof, except a little not very good from Nagapatam, and that for nothing, a country as well situated for a place of departure for our ships as any other could be from whence one would be able to direct the trade in East India, as the Portuguese [do] in Goa, to the detriment of the Portuguese, and none more convenient, since we have the king of the country and the people friendly to which also all ships that wish to come from Goa and that quarter to Santhorne, Bengaelen, Pegu, Malacka, Achin, must approach, in order to recognize the land, and so set a fixed course, namely, Punta de Galle, which we should have to capture, [and] thereabouts either build or cause to be built a fort, [and] garrison it ourselves, I do not know how we should be able to justify not having availed ourselves of such an opportunity, [and] I doubt, not also that if your honor were here in person you would no longer deliberate thereover, the more so, since now at this time we must not neglect anything anywhere, and even in five or six months shall find no pepper.

I greatly regret that we are so badly provided with men against such occurrences, because we shall have to leave there at least fifty men, the which makes my heart bleed, so long as we do not yet know where we shall get our lading. Consequently, in case your honor could spare from all your ships fifty men, selecting mostly from those that have first to sail for home, they would be very serviceable to us, the more so, if some among them were somewhat experienced in the art of war: if not, it will not be inexpedient that your honor by the first opportunity recommend this to our masters the directors, so that at least two hundred soldiers may be brought there; because it were better not to begin than to finish badly. We shall not fail to advise your honor by the first opportunity of the success of our enterprise so that you may act accordingly.

... This first April, 1603 on board ship before Atchijn.

Your honor's obedient servant, (Signed)

SEBALD DE WEERT,

Your honor's Vice-admiral.

Editor's Note

1. This is an exact transcription of the 1996 translation, and all inconsistencies in capitalization and spelling are as in the original.

Jaffna and Kandy through Eyes of a Dutch Reformed *Predikant*

Philip Baldaeus

Baldaeus published one of the earliest detailed European "ethnographic" accounts of the people of Sri Lanka, roughly contemporaneous with Robert Knox (an extract of whose reporting appears in the section on Kandyan culture). In the first section of Baldaeus's description extracted below, the Dutch Reformed minister describes the inhabitants of Jaffna, beginning with the upper-caste, landowning Vellalar and the priestly Brahmin communities and continuing in serial fashion down the caste hierarchy. In so doing, he also comments, among other things, about marriage customs and medical practices. In the second section, he briefly describes the Sinhalas of the Kandyan kingdom, mentioning their "friars" (Buddhist monks), processions (peraharas), images (the Kustarajagala image in Weligama), and, in general, their religious liberality.

It is time to say some thing of the inhabitants of *Jafnapatnam*. . . .

In *Ceylon* are diver Clans, or Families, as well as on the Coast of *Coromandel*. The Generation of the *Bellales* is the chiefest here since Christianity has been introduc'd, the *Brahmans* challenging the best rank among the Pagans.

The *Bellales* wear a kind of Garment from above the Navel, turning betwixt the Legs like a pair of Drawers. They also make use of *Seripous* (or Soles) tied to the bottom of their feet with Leather Straps, the upper part of the feet being bare, to prevent sweating. Upon the Belly they have a kind of Bag (call'd *Maddi*) being part of their Garment roll'd together, wherein they keep their *Areek* and *Betel*, and some Paper to make use of upon occasion. On the right side they carry a kind of Knife in a Sheath, and an Iron Pen pointed with Silver, as is likewise the Sheath, in which they keep a piece of Steel to sharpen their Knife upon. They make holes in their Ears from their Infancy, which being adorn'd with Golden Pendants, draw them down to their Shoulders. They live upon Husbandry, and are rich in Cattel, such as

Cows, Oxen for the Plow, Sheep, Goats, and Bufflers. Their Habitations are both convenient and neat, with pleasant Gardens, well planted with *Betel*, and furnish'd with excellent Springs, which furnish them (during the dry Summer Season) with Water for the watering of the Gardens. Their Harvest is in *January* and *February*; their Winter, or rainy Season being in *November* and *December*. In some places, *viz.* in the low marshy Grounds, they have Harvest twice a year: they thresh their Corn [rice] (after the manner of the *Israelites*) with Oxen, not muffled; these tread the Seed out of the Ears.

During the rainy Season it rains with such violence, that the Fields are overflown; and I remember that in my time a considerable part off the *Cortin* of the Castle was wash'd away by the Rains. This continues for two months, and it happens oftentimes, that for eight months after it rains not above three times, which is the reason that they are oblig'd even to water the Coco-Trees till they are six years old. If you dig about two feet deep you meet with rocky ground, so that if you will have a Spring you must cut them out of the Rocks with a vast Charge.

The before-mention'd *Bellales* make likewise Butter, but not after the same manner as we do in *Holland*. They take a kind of a Mill made like a Star at the bottom, this they roll betwixt both hands (as we do with our Chocolate) till the Butter comes. Some of our *Dutch* Women make also good Cheese, but it is not regarded among the inhabitants; but Butter is in great esteem among them as well as among the *Moors*, nay the Family of *Commety* use Butter like Drink. Milk turn'd to Curds (call'd by them *Tayr*) is also in great request with them, and used like a cooling Medicine in Fevers, and the Small-Pox, which are very frequent here.

Their Cattel they keep both day and night in the Field, tho towards night they drive them into a certain Enclosure: They are never hous'd in the Winter, but feed in the Grounds where the Corn first sprouts forth, and afterwards are fed with Hay till Harvest time. If the Cattel happen to break into a Neighbor's Field, the Owner is oblig'd to make good the Damage. The *Bellales*, are generally the richest of the Country; they don't marry except in their own Family, and commonly in the Spring; as the *Romans* did formerly in *May,* and the *Persians* in the Spring: if it happens to be a fruitful Year, they are more inclined to marry. They are very litigious, and will go to the Law for a Trifle, because they are constantly envious at one another.

The *Brahmans* living in *Jafnapatnam*, or any other part of the *Indies*, are for the most part men of great Morality, sober, clean, industrious, civil, obliging, and very moderate in both eating and drinking; they use no strong Liquors, wash or bathe twice a day, eat nothing that has had or may have Life, yet are as much addicted to Pleasure. Notwithstanding they are Christians, they carry still certain Beads, and . . . like those of *Cormandel*, never marry out of their Families, but frequently their Brothers and Sisters Children; tho else they are great Enemies to Incest, but excuse this near Alliance by the great Value they put upon their Generation, which they deduce from *Bramma*, and some Learned Men from *Abraham* and *Ketura*, whose Children, according to *Gen. 25 v. 6.* went into the Eastern Country.

Tho they bear the Name of Christians, and know how to discourse rationally of the Ten Commandments, and the other Points of the Christian Doctrine, they retain many of their Pagan Superstitions. If you tell them of the Christian Liberty in Victuals and Drinks, they reply, that they are not ignorant of it, but as the Essence of Christianity does not consist in eating and drinking, so they did not think themselves oblig'd to feed upon such things as are contrary to their Nature and Education, being from their Infancy used to much tenderer Food, which agrees best with their Constitution, and makes them generally live to a great Age.

They are not ignorant in the Course of the Stars, in calculating the Eclipses of the Sun and the Moon, know the *Seven Stars*. . . . They understand also the Names of the Planets, and chiefest of the fixed Stars, but this must be understood from the most Learned among them.

Tho we shall treat in particular hereafter of the Errors of the Pagans, yet can I not pass by here in silence, what I have observ'd my self concerning their Opinion of the *Creation of the World, its Age,* and *Transmigration of the Soul.* In the Year 1665, after I had catechiz'd the People after Sermon in the Church of *Paretiture,* happening to discourse concerning the *Creation* and *Age* of the World; some of the *Indians* affirm'd that they World had stood 4864 Years since the *Kaligam* or fourth Period. For they have four Periods, the first they called *Creitagam* the second *Treitagam,* the third *Dwaparugam,* and the fourth *Kaligam.* . . .

. . . In the preceding Chapter we told you concerning the Marriages of the *Bellales,* and how the *Brahmans* often marry their Brothers and Sisters Children. Among some of the Christians in *Ceylon* obtains a certain Custom to this day, to tye the *Tali* or Bracelet of the Bride about the Bridegroom's Neck, a thing introduced by the *Pagans,* and imitated by the Christians: for as *Rogerius* observes, the Inhabitants of the Coast of *Coromandel* look upon it as a Ceremony so necessary towards the Confirmation of the Marriage, that whenever the Husband dies, the *Tali* he wore about his Neck on his Marriage-Day is to be burnt with him.

As Maidens without a good Portion are a very bad Commodity here, hence it is that frequent Collections are made to help the poorer sort to Husbands. They are of Opinion, that a single Man is but half a Man; nay that those who neglect or lose any time in propagating their own Kind, are not far different from a Murderer and a Destroyer of Human Kind (according to the opinion of *Plato*, which was likewise encourag'd among the *Athenians* and the *Romans*) which is the reason they often marry their Daughters at 10 and 11 years of Age, and nothing is more frequent than to see them bring forth Children at 13 or 14.

After they have been three times proclaimed from the Pulpit, the Marriage Ceremony is perform'd by the Minister; the House where the Wedding is kept being generally adorn'd with a kind of Triumphal Arch raised without Door, made of Fig-tree Branches, Flowers, Pomegranates, and such like. The richer sort seldom fail to give a good Entertainment to their Friends, of Venison, Hares, Partridges, Fish, Fruits, Preserves, etc. and the Evening is spent in dancing, singing, and divers other Diversions. However strong Liquors are never made use on such Occasions, unless the *Hollanders* (who can't well be merry without them) bring some along with them. These Marriage-Diversions continue sometimes four or five days successively.

I remember that during my Residence here, sometimes Children of eight or nine Years of Age would have engaged in mutual Promises of Marriage, in mine and their Friends Presence; which I always opposed, fearing, not without reason, that they might repent their Bargain, before they came to a marriageable Age. For the rest they constantly observe this Custom, that the Female is younger than the Bridegroom; nay they seldom will chuse a Maid, that has already had her Monthly Times: this Custom is so strictly observed on the Coast of *Coromandel*, that if a *Brahman's* Daughter remains unmarried till that time, she must lay aside all hopes of it for the future. . . .

. . . The Tribe or Family of the *Chivias*, use formerly to attend the Service of the King of *Jafnapatnam*, but now do all sorts of Drudgery, as carrying of Water and Wood for the Dutch Inhabitants; they make use of them for Littermen, 10 or 12 of them being sometimes employed at a time, to carry a good bulky *Hollander*, 10, 20, nay 30 Leagues in a Litter. However, as they are descended from Courtiers, so they are too proud to carry any ordinary Person, who must be contented to be carried by the ordinary *Coelys* or Labourers, who live all over the Country, whereas *Chivias* inhabit in the District of the Church of *Chundecoult*.

Those of the Tribe of the *Parruas* do not live in such great Numbers in *Jafnapatnam*, as they do about *Tutecoryn*; they apply themselves to the Sea, and especially in diving for Sea-Horse Teeth and Pearls. They generally speak *Portuguese* and are an active sort of People.

The *Chittiis* live for the most part upon the Linen Manufacture and Traffick, the word *Chitty* signifying as much as a Merchant; they are a crafty

Generation. Each of these Tribes does not marry into any other, besides their own, nay commonly in the same Family. Besides which, each Handi-craftsman educates his Son to the same Trade he is of; thus a Weaver's Son follows the Weaving-Trade, as the Smith's Son does that of a Smith.

The Tribe of *Carreas* live upon Fishing, which they perform with mon-strous large Nets; they inhabit near the Sea-shore of *Jafnapatnam*, and the Banks of the *Salt-River*. Those of the Tribe of the *Mokkuas* are likewise Fish-ermen.

The *Nallouas* are generally Slaves to the *Bellales* and much blacker than the rest. Their Business is to gather the Liquor that flows out of the Coco-Trees, call'd *Suyri* and *Euwak* by the *Indians*, to dig the Ground, tend the Cattel, water the Trees, and such like Drudgeries, as in commonly done also by the *Coelys* or ordinary Labourers. They are a nasty Generation, you may smell them at a good distance, not unlike the *Hotteniots* on the Cape of *Good Hope*.

The *Parreas* are the most despicable of all, their Employment being to carry out Dung and such filthy things; they feed upon Rats and Mice.

It is observable, that the Tribes of the higher Rank look upon the infe-riour Ones with a great deal of Scorn, these being obliged to salute the oth-ers in the Streets with deep Reverence, and other Ceremonies to show their Submission. On the other hand, all the Men of what rank or Quality soever, exercise a great Authority over their Wives, whom they rarely honour so far as to eat with them, but commonly dine alone. None of all these Tribes eat Cows Flesh, which is the reason that no Cows are killed but by the *Dutch*, the Cow being look'd upon among the rest as a Sacred Creature, as it was formerly among the *Egyptians*, of which more hereafter.

Tho their Tribes are very numerous, yet do they relate to Some few Families, from whence they take their Original, like the Branches from the Stem of a Tree. The same was practiced among the ancient *Egyptians*, who distinguish'd their Nation into four Head Tribes, *viz.* the *Priests*, the *Soldiers*, the *Artisans* and *Handicraftsmen*, and the Sheep and Cowherds. Just as now-a-days some of the *European* Nations are distinguish'd into four Estates, *viz. Noblemen, Patricians* or *Gentlemen, Citizens*, and the Common People.

For the rest, the generality of the Inhabitants of the Kingdom of *Jafnapat-nam* are naturally ingenious, and have a strong Memory; they are very sober and moderate in their Diet, and (except the *Nallouas* and the *Parreas*) very clean in their Apparel, not quarrelsome, but very free with their Tongue.

Their general Vice is Fornication and Adultery, especially among the young Men, as the old Ones are much addicted to Superstitions, as to the choice of certain Days (whereof something was said before concerning *Raja Singa*), the Cries of Bird, and such like things used among the ancient *Ro-*

mans. Hence it is that the *Portugueses* in those Parts have a Proverb to this day, *I know not what unfortunate Sight* (Rosto Mosinho) *did not come in my way this day*.

Thus on the Coast of *Coromandel*, they look upon it as fortunate, if they see a certain red Bird, with a white Ring about his Neck. *John van Twist* in his Description of *Gusuratte*, tells us of the Natives there, that they look upon it as a good Sign, if they meet an Elephant or Camel loaden or unloaden, a Horse without a Burden, or a Cow or Buffler with Water on their Backs, for without a Load they were accounted unfortunate; a Ram or Dog with a piece of Meat in his Mouth, a Cat passing to the right hand of them: they also reckon it fortunate, if they meet any Body that carries Meat, Milk, and Butter, or if a Cock crosses their way. . . .

Besides the Artisans and Handicraftsmen, whereof there is great Plenty in *Jafnapatnam*, they have certain Persons who apply themselves to the Law; and in the high Court of Justice, composed of *Hollanders* and *Indians*, were set always (besides the *Modeliars*) a certain Person well versed in the Laws and Constitutions of his Native Country. They have also their Advocates, who make very long Speeches in their Pleadings.

Neither are they destitute of Physicians, such as they are; for so to speak Truth they are more than Empiricks, who practice according to certain Books and Traditions, transmitted to them by their Ancestors, and confirm'd to them by their own Experience. They know not what Anatomy is, and very little of the nature of purging Medicines, which are not often used in this hot Climate: However when a Purge is to be given (whether a Potion or Pills) the Composition is always made of fresh Herbs; and if it works too strong, they mix some poudered Pepper with Water, and apply it to the Navel in the nature of an Ointment. I can tell it by my own Experience, that it is a good Remedy against the Belly-ach and Looseness.

They have also good Store of Surgeons and Barbers, the last carry always a small Looking-glass along with them, their Rasors are thicker on the back than ours; they not only shave your Beard and Head but also pare your Hand and Toe Nails, and cleanse your Ears.

Weavers are here in abundance. These [looms] fit flat upon the Ground, their Feet being plac'd in a Hole dug for that purpose, whilst they are at work.

Callico-Printers or Painters are numberless here, who have a way of preparing their Colours, that they never go out by washing, tho those printed at *Jafnapatnam* are not near so good as those of the Coast of *Coromandel*, and especially those done at *Masulipatan*.

They are excellent Workmen in Ivory and Ebony Wood, as likewise in

Gold and Silver, and will come with their Tools (which are but few) to work in the Houses of the *Dutch*. They are exactly well versed in the essaying of Gold.

They are as well provided with Smiths, Carpenters and Bricklayers, as most Places in *Europe*, tho a Carpenter or Bricklayer gets not above five or six pence a day. . . .

. . . Having hitherto taken a view of those Places of *Ceylon* that are under the Jurisdiction of the *Dutch* company, we will now take a turn to *Candy*, the Imperial Residence, as the most proper place to be inform'd concerning the real Constitution of this Isle, and its Inhabitants.

The City of *Candy* is seated about 30 Leagues from the Sea-side and 9 from the *Vintane* up the River of *Trinquenemale*, about 21 Leagues by Land from *Matecalo*, and 9 from the Sea-shore, where the Emperor has his Docks for building and refitting his Ships and Gallies. The other Cities of *Ceylon* being not described in any Books, we must also pass in silence here. All over the Isle you see abundance of very splendid *Pagodes*. The Foundation of that of *Vintane* has no less than 130 foot in Circumference; it is of a great height, and gilt on the top; it is oval on the bottom, and arises into a four corner'd Point like a Pyramid. The *Great Pagode* betwixt *Gale* and *Matecalo* is also much celebrated, serving for a Light-house to Ships as well as that of *Trinquenemale*. In the large high *Pagode* before mention'd stands an Idol representing a Man with a naked Sword in his hand, lifting up his Arm, as if he were ready to strike. To this Idol the *Cingaleses* pay their Reverence, and offer their Sacrifices upon all Emergencies, or in that time of Sickness; for which reason they keep a Basket in every House, wherein they gather such Provisions as they are to sacrifice. They believe that the World will not have an end so long as that *Pagode* stands. Some worship an *Elephant's Head* of Wood or Stone, to obtain Wisdom. They adorn their Idols with Flowers. These Elephant Heads are plac'd sometimes on Trees in the High-ways, sometimes in little Brick Houses or Chappels. You see also frequently in the high Road certain heaps of Stones, Earth, or Dung, upon which each Passenger throws something as he passes by. Just by *Belligamme* I saw the Figure of a Man at least six Yards high, cut in a Rock about half a Yard deep, who us'd to be worship'd by the *Cingaleses*.

Near it is a high peak'd Mountain, accounted the highest in the *Indies*, call'd *Pico de Adam*, or *Adam's Peak*; because they are of opinion, that here stood formerly the Paradise, where *Adam* was created; they also tell you, that the Print of the Foot of *Adam* is to be seen to this day in the Rock, the Draught whereof is kept in the Imperial Court. Unto this Rock a vast number of People flock from far distant places, to see this Sacred Relick, tho the Mountain is of very difficult access, nay (if we may credit *Massaeus* the Jesuit) quite inaccessible, unless by means of certain Iron Chains and Iron Spikes fastened to the Rocks.

Some are of opinion that they reverence the Chamberlain of the Queen *Candace* in this place, who according to some Historians, but especially *Doro-thaeus* Bishop of *Tyrus* (a Man equally famous for his Learning and Sanctity under *Constantine* the Great) preach'd the Gospel in the *Happy Arabia*, *Eryth-raea* and *Taprobana*.

There are also divers Convents in *Ceylon*, and a great number of *Brahmans* and Priests, who are in great Veneration among the common People; they never eat any thing that has been living, or is capable of producing any living Substance, as Eggs, etc. Their Friers wear yellow Habits, with their Heads shaven all over, for which reasons they never appear in the Streets without Umbrellos, and Beads in their hands, muttering out certain Prayers as they go along. Their Convents have divers Galleries and Chappels, wherein are placed the Statutes of several Men and Women, who, as they say, have led holy Lives. These are adorn'd with Gold and Silver Apparel, and attended with burning Lamps and Wax-Candles day and night, plac'd upon Altars: The Candlesticks being supported by naked Boys artificially carved. The Friers have their certain hours for Prayers, which they perform in these Chappels.

They have also their publick Processions: The Head or Abbot of the Convent being mounted on a fine Elephant, sumptuously harnessed with an Umbrello over his Head, marches along the Street in great Pomp, Trumpets, and other such sort of Musick, making an odd kind of Harmony, accompany'd by a great number of Men, Women, and Children; the Maidens of Quality dance all along before the Elephant naked down to the middle, their Heads, Arms, and Ears adorn'd with Golden Bracelets and Jewels; the Garments which cover their under parts are of different Colours. They pay their daily Devotions to a certain Idol call'd *Sambaja*, by prostrating themselves upon the ground, and afterwards clasping their hands together over their Heads. But concerning the Religious Worship of the *Cingaleses* we shall have the occasion to say more in the following Treatise, which in effect differs very little from the *Malabars* and those of *Coromandel*, except that they are not altogether such Bigots, the Emperor of *Ceylon* allowing Liberty of Conscience to all Nations. The *Cingaleses* are not so stubborn, but that many of them have been without much difficulty converted to the *Roman* Faith, and since that to the Reformed Religion.

For the rest of the *Cingaleses* are naturally active and ingenious, and good Workmen in Gold, Silver, Ivory, Ebony, Iron Works, etc. Arms inlaid with Silver, eloquent, nimble, courageous, fit for Warlike Exploits, sober and watchful. They march one single Man after another, by reason of the many narrow Lanes in this Country; their Arms are a Half-Pike, their Drums are small, but make a great noise, which may be heard at three Leagues distance in the Mountains; they are best in the pursuit of a routed Enemy. Since they have conversed so much with the *Portugueses* and other *European* Nations, they are grown so cunning that they must not be too trusted, nor despised.

Incest is so common a Vice among them, that when Husbands have occasion to leave their Wives for some time, they recommend the Conjugal Duty to be perform'd by their own Brothers. I remember a certain Woman at *Gale*, who had Confidence enough to complain of the want of Duty in her Husband's Brother upon that account. The like happen'd in my time at *Jafnapatnam*, which had been likely to be punish'd with Death, had not at my Intercession, and in regard of the tender beginnings of Christianity, the same has been pass'd by for that time.

The *Cingaleses* are in Shape and Manners not unlike the *Malabars*, with long hanging Ears, but not so black. The Dress of the Men is a Vest call'd *Ropillo*, of Woolen or Linen Cloth; their under Garment is a piece of Linen wrapt about their middle, and drawn through both their Legs, like a pair of Breeches: On their Heads they wear a kind of red Caps, such as we call *Rock* Caps, which they look upon as a singular Ornament, and in their Ears Rings and precious Stones. The Hilts of their Swords or Scymeters are commonly of Silver, Ivory, or Gold, with flaming Blades.

The common People appear for the most part naked, having only a piece of Cloth wrapt round the middle to cover their Privy Parts. The Women go with their Breasts uncover'd, being generally well limb'd: instead of a Head-dress they have a way of tying their Hair together like a Cap. They wear Golden or Silver Necklaces about their Necks, and Rings on their Fingers and Toes.

The *Cingaleses* as well as the *Malabars* are much addicted to Idleness and Pleasures, and insist much upon their Pedigree. They marry as many Wives as they think fit, as well as the *Mahometans*, of which there live a considerable number in this Isle. They marry their Daughters at 10 or 11 years of Age, a Custom not to be rooted out among them, they being very fond of the Virginity of their Wives. They bury their Dead after the manner of the Pagans.

In their Houses they are excessive neat, use instead of Trenchards and Tablecloths the Leaves of Fig-trees; their Spoons are made of *Coco* Nutshells, and their drinking Vessels of Earth, with hollow Pipes, through which they pour (like the *Moors*) the Drink into the Mouth without touching their Lips; for as the *Cingaleses* and *Malabars* insist much upon their Noble Descent, so they will neither eat nor drink with those of an inferior Rank; nay many of them are so proud as not to eat with their own Wives.

The Price of Good Cinnamon

Sinnappah Arasaratnam

For the Dutch, procuring and selling cinnamon was their primary reason for being in Ceylon. The profits to be had were immense and so the means to extract them were especially calculated and strategic. For the better part of their colonial era, the Dutch presented themselves as middlemen, when in fact they limited trade in and out of Kandy. As long as the king did not interfere with Dutch profit-making, the Dutch left him alone while paying him a nominal tribute, though they continued to remind him of his mounting debt for the cost of their expulsion of the Portuguese. It was not until the 1760s, when Kirti Sri Rajasimha began to harass the Dutch in their coastal territories by currying the favor of Sinhalas who lived there, that the Dutch finally attacked and subordinated Kandy.

"The cinnamon of the island of Ceylon is the best and the finest and is at least three times dearer in the price." These words had been written by Linschoten about the time when the Dutch were developing an interest in venturing out to the East in order to find the spices for themselves in the places where they grew. The importance of Ceylon during the 16th and 17th Centuries, when the spice trade to the West was perhaps at its most prosperous peak, was, from the point of view of the European traders, derived almost solely from the fact that she was the prime cinnamon-producing country in the East. It had been the lure of cinnamon that had persuaded the Portuguese to attempt to found an Empire on the shores of this island and control those lands at least along the coast line where the cinnamon grew. When the Dutch came out East, in accordance with their policy of mastering the areas of spice production, their eyes too fell on Ceylon. Thus cinnamon was at the heart of the quarrel between the Dutch and the Portuguese, waged for over twenty years in Ceylon. . . .

Cinnamon grew wild in Ceylon over an extensive area along the sea coast, which was very fortunate for the European power. The cinnamon woods started from south of the Deduru Oya near Chilaw and extended southwards along a strip of territory, sometimes broad, sometimes narrow, up to about Matara. . . . These lands are broadly divisible into four districts—Negombo, Colombo, Kalutara, and Galle. The kind of cinnamon, that occurred in each district varied, and, broadly speaking, the quality deteriorated as one went more and more south. Thus the cinnamon around Negombo was the best and that in the Matara district the worst.

Cinnamon is a tree of stunted size that grows in wet soil. Its inner bark peeled from its trunk when dried in the sun rolls up and produces a fragrant smell and sharp taste and was used in a number of ways to spice food. The Sinhalese recognized ten different types of cinnamon, varying according to their shades of smell and taste. The Europeans, however, divided them into three categories—the fine, the medium and the coarse. There was also a fourth kind of cinnamon, generally found in Malabar which they called "wild cinnamon" or in Portuguese Canelle de Mato (*Cassia ligna*). This was held by them to be very inferior to the Ceylon cinnamon and was rated as of far less worth. Thus Ceylon produced the best cinnamon and in large quantities.

The Portuguese had succeeded in controlling the entire cinnamon-producing lands. Under them cinnamon had been a royal monopoly. But officials in Ceylon had amassed large profits for themselves by corrupt dealings in it. From time to time, the king had to issue strict edicts regularizing the delivery of cinnamon and cleansing it of corruption. When the Dutch took over from the Portuguese, they too made it a monopoly of the [Dutch East India] Company; their monopoly was much more rigorously administered and much more strictly observed.

Unlike the Portuguese, the Dutch, to begin with, did not control all the cinnamon lands. They did exercise direct jurisdiction over a substantial part of them, as much as was necessary to furnish their needs. But it was not only important to ship as much cinnamon as possible to Europe and India; it was even more important to see to it that other nations did not take any of it themselves. Thus the king had to be prevented from selling any of his cinnamon to any one else. The only means was to keep a strict watch on all the ports to see that none of the ships carried cinnamon out of the country. The Dutch based this right on the contract of 1638 with the Kandyan king.

This fear that the king would attempt to sell his cinnamon to other European powers was there all along and increased when relations with him worsened. The immediate power to be feared, soon after the expulsion of the Portuguese, was the English. They were very anxious to get cinnamon from Ceylon and this was one of the main factors which impelled them to seek to establish a factory on the East Coast of Ceylon with [the Kandyan king, r. 1635–87] Raja Sinha's assistance. These attempts came to nothing and with the outbreak of the second Anglo-Dutch war, these fears receded. The same fears are seen to rise again when the French tried to establish a foot-hold in Ceylon. The Dutch suspected that Raja Sinha had got his people to peel cinnamon in the West and transported it to the East to be given to the French, as an inducement to make them stay in Ceylon and fight the Dutch. That these fears were not unjustifiable is seen from the fact that when the Dutch occupied Batticaloa, they discovered a broken down warehouse in which they found small broken bits of cinnamon, a clear evidence that someone had taken cinnamon out of this port. This suspicion was further strengthened by the subsequent knowledge that there was cinnamon on the East coast as well.

The territorial expansion of 1665 brought them into some of the remaining cinnamon lands. One of the reasons why the [Dutch] authorities in Ceylon were reluctant to give up these lands to Raja Sinha, in deference to orders from Batavia, was the fact that cinnamon grew in them. The trees in the old lands had been peeled over and over again, while the new ones were fresh and unpeeled and therefore easier to harvest more cinnamon in a shorter time. The intense peeling for a long time had destroyed some of the cinnamon woods and they had to resort more and more to those in the interior. In fact, from 1679 onwards, they boldly ordered the peelers to go across the Maha Oya, which marked the Dutch limits into Pittigal Korale in the king's dominions. This Korale had very rich and abundant cinnamon forests. The change of heart on the part of the Ceylon officials towards Raja Sinha is partly explainable by the need to be allowed by him to peel cinnamon unhindered in his lands. . . .

Cinnamon was thus in the background to a great deal of Dutch policy in Ceylon. The defence of cinnamon lands was, therefore, crucial to Dutch strategy. When relations with Raja Sinha broke down in 1656, their aim was to be independent of him in the collection of cinnamon, and, if need be, to defend the lands and the cinnamon peelers while they were engaged in their work. Even before actual war against Raja Sinha had begun, a good portion of the army was posted to guard the peeling of cinnamon. This was essential because the king had once attacked and carried away several peelers to Kandy, thus striking at a very tender spot, because without peelers the Dutch could not get cinnamon. Thus before the peelers were sent out into the woods, the Dutch forces and lascarines would take up positions at strategic points to forestall any attack. Once war began, these precautions had to be strengthened.

When the debate over Dutch policy in Ceylon was being carried on, one of the points considered vital to the whole issue was whether Raja Sinha could obstruct the peeling of cinnamon or whether the Dutch could obtain it in spite of his opposition. Dutch officials in Ceylon were split on this question. It was vital to Dutch policy because if the Dutch were dependent on Raja Sinha for the cinnamon, then it was logical that they should pacify him at all cost and withdraw from his lands; if not, they could continue with the existing position and depend on their own strength. Some of the officials felt, and Governor Pyl agreed with them, that the cinnamon lands were too extensive to be protected by the army and that Raja Sinha's men could burn down the trees if they wanted. On the other hand, the Van Goenses, father and son, had been of the opinion that with a certain number of soldiers, they could keep out any intrusion from the hill country. The Dutch were not forced to choose between these viewpoints by the comparative peace and calm caused by the senile decay of Raja Sinha after 1681, when no serious threat was offered to the safety of the cinnamon lands. On the contrary, they found that they could venture deep into the king's lands and peel cinnamon.

The organization of the collection and delivery of cinnamon was a matter of great importance to the Dutch. There was, for this purpose, a separate department of cinnamon or "Mehabadde," directly under the governor. A captain was in charge of the department and he had under him the entire native community of cinnamon peelers known in Sinhalese as "chalias" [*salagama*]. The chalias were to be ruled according to the customs and usages of their country.

The customs and usages of the country were that the chalias were a distinct caste of people obliged to perform the labor of peeling cinnamon to the sovereign from whom they enjoyed certain lands that they could cultivate for their benefit. Tradition has it that they were originally a caste of weavers who had immigrated into Ceylon from South India. When the cinnamon trade grew in importance, the Sinhalese kings had ordered the peeling of cinnamon from them as their tenurial service. The Portuguese found this the position and utilized them in large numbers for their benefit. The Dutch could do likewise for they had stepped into Portuguese shoes as sovereign of the land and the services of the chalias were now obligatory to them.

With their flair for organization, the Dutch organized and regulated the working of this traditional system. The traditional hierarchical organization was not disturbed, but operated under the Dutch captain. Immediately below the captain were the Vidanes, whose authority was on a regional basis. There were four of them—each being in charge of the chalias in one of the four cinnamon-growing districts referred to above. Next to the Vidanes in rank were the Duraiyas, divided into two classes—Mahaduraiyas or Chief

Duraiyas and sub-Duraiyas. Each Duraiya was in charge of a certain number of chaliyas and he was responsible for the performance of the obliged labor by these men. Thus the native officials were a medium between the Dutch power and the peelers, through whom the aims and needs of Dutch policy were conveyed to the men.

Owing to the great importance of this work, it was also Dutch policy progressively to reduce their dependence on the native officials and deal directly with the men themselves. This is seen in their deliberate policy of reducing the number of Duraiyas. The beginning made in compiling an accurate list of the chalias with the villages they lived in, the lands they held, and the services due from them, also tended in the same direction. There was the suspicion that the Vidanes were using the services of the chalias for their private purposes and an accurate description would put the Dutch in a better position to prevent this. The general trend of Dutch policy was to get hold of as many of the chalias as possible for cinnamon peeling, for what was lacking now was a sufficient number of peelers to collect all the cinnamon needed by the Dutch. The Vidanes were not the only culprits in this connection. The Dutch officials too were seen to use the labor of chalias in their own interests.

When the proper time came for the peeling of cinnamon, the chalias were assembled from their villages under their heads and sent into the woods. With each batch of chalias, there was a company of lascarines and Dutch troops. The amount of cinnamon that each one had to deliver varied according to the individual's age. At the age of twelve, the chalia boy was obliged to peel cinnamon, and went on doing so till he was disabled by old age. An able-bodied chalia had to give 12 "roben" free of any charge. A robe weighed from 56 to 62 Dutch pounds. Besides this, he had to peel another "bhar" of about 600 pounds for which he was paid the nominal sum of 6 larines (72 Stuivers). Usually this latter sum was commuted for the poll tax that the chalia had to pay to the Government. Thus the Dutch got their cinnamon almost free of any cash expenditure. While working, however, the men had to be given rice, salt, fish and other eatables. The harvest took place twice every year, the major one from June to October and a small harvest in January and February.

Already under the Portuguese the chalias had begun to feel the strain of their work. They had petitioned to the Captain of Colombo to better their lot. It could be inferred, from the fact that under the Dutch they were made to peel 3 to 4 times as much as in Portuguese times, that their work must have been very oppressive. Furthermore, faced by a lack of chalias, the Dutch had rediscovered and reimposed services which the chalias had managed to escape by long abeyance. Instances of their running away from their lands to escape the obligation to serve are not infrequent. During the first five years or so the Dutch could peel about 400,000 to 450,000 pounds in all, for both the Indian trade and for export to Europe. But the Directors complained that the quota sent to Europe was insufficient and that they could do with more. The peeling was then stepped up to 500,000 pounds and then to 600,000. Finally they came to a stage when the chalias peeled almost 700,000 pounds and for this purpose had to leave their villages and stay in the woods for 8 months of the year.

Various expedients were adopted by the chalias to get rid of this ruinous burden. Some of them ran away from their villages to the king's lands. Some sold their children to people of higher castes so that these children might escape service. Some married or had illegitimate unions with women of other castes so that the offspring might escape the burden of their caste. None of these expedients was very effective. The Dutch passed laws that all children of chalias, whether legitimate or illegitimate, were obliged to serve in peeling cinnamon. They even enacted that all children of daughters of chalias, by whomsoever fathers, had also to serve as peelers—a law that went contrary to all social custom.

The policy of utilizing native institutions in the interests of Dutch policy thus proved particularly severe on the chalias. In view of the importance of cinnamon to the Dutch, the chalias were vital to their policy in the island. They were cynically referred to as the Company's children, for it may be said that they had to sweat blood in their effort to fulfill Dutch demands. Any misdemeanor was severely punished and the general picture conveyed by the evidence is that it was by striking terror in the hearts of the men that they hoped to hold them to their forced labor. Laurence Pyl, who seems to have had more concern for the plight of the Ceylonese subjects than most other Governors, first drew attention to the excessive demands on the peelers. This resulted in the Directors reducing their demands which in turn eased the burden on the men. The quantity demanded from them was reduced to 640,000 pounds and they were advised to peel this in one harvest so that they may be free during the next. The reply given by the men was significant in revealing their attitude of suspicion towards the Dutch. They preferred to peel this amount in two seasons because they feared that if they did it all in one season, the Dutch would impose further burdens on them in the next.

The cinnamon trade was very scrupulously controlled by the Company not only from foreigners but even from embezzlement by their own officials. No cinnamon was to be sold in Ceylon to any private traders, except under exceptional circumstances, such as the lack of cash to pay off merchants for goods they had brought. Such cases had to be carefully recorded and the amount, in any case, was insignificant. So that almost all the cinnamon harvested was sent in the Company's ships either to Batavia or to the Dutch factories in India. All the cinnamon that was to be sent to Europe was first sent to Batavia, in accordance with the practice of centralizing all trade in this place. This involved much wastage of freight and later on some attempt was made to ship cinnamon direct from Ceylon and pepper from Malabar.

About 400,000 to 500,000 pounds were sent to Europe annually. . . . The rest was used up in the Indian trade. This usually amounted to about 150,000 pounds. . . . The importance of the sales in these Indian regions was that they yielded the cash with which to conduct the country trade there. The cloth trade to Ceylon was partly financed by the sales of cinnamon and pepper in Surat and Persia.

The shipping of such large quantities of this spice produced a number of problems. There was the problem of how best to preserve the strength of the cinnamon during the long voyage to Europe. Much depended on proper packing. It was found that the cinnamon that lay in the packhouses of Batavia for a long time lost its strength owing to the intense heat. Those packed in sackcloth were also found to be weak and hence they were packed in leather skins. Once the cinnamon lost its spicy qualities, it lost all its value. It was found in Europe that such cinnamon would hardly fetch half the usual price. In some cases, the purchasers returned the product as being useless. All these matters worried the Directors greatly. In some cases, the loss of strength was due to the defects of the trees themselves and could not be checked. By and large only the cinnamon of the first grade was sent to Europe, the two lower grades being sold in the East. The amount sold in Europe was on an average about 350,000 pounds a year.

A significant feature of the cinnamon trade in Europe, after the Dutch expelled the Portuguese from Ceylon, was the steep rise in its price. This was a result of the Dutch monopoly of the Ceylon cinnamon. In the years when both the Dutch and the Portuguese were transporting cinnamon to Europe, it was about 48 Stuivers a pound. In June 1658 the Portuguese lost all their hold on Ceylon. From then on it was only the Dutch who took Ceylon cinnamon to Europe. In September 1658 the price had risen to 56 Stuivers. In the next sales in May 1659 it was 61 Stuivers and in April 1660 it had reached the staggering limit of 86 Stuivers per pound. Thereafter for some time the price remained stationary at about 70 Stuivers. The directors were wildly enthusiastic and referred to Ceylon as an invaluable jewel that must be carefully preserved. There are no figures of total sales available, but it is safe to assume from the above facts that the cinnamon from Ceylon fetched close upon one million Guilders per year. . . .

While prices in Europe were rocketing, in the East they were lagging behind because the same urgent demand was not present here as in Europe. In 1658 the price in the East varied from 15 to 8 Stuivers per pound, in accordance with the quality of the cinnamon. The Directors began to feel that, under these conditions, it might be profitable for other European nations to buy cinnamon from the Dutch Indian factories and transport it to Europe with considerable profit. With Dutch monopoly, prices in the East did tend to rise, but not as fast as those in Europe. Thus by the time the price in the East had risen to 20 Stuivers, in Europe cinnamon was selling at 61 Stuivers. The Directors, therefore, began to adopt a policy of regulating the price in India and fixing it at such a point as to make it unprofitable for others to bring it to Europe. When the price in Europe was 56 Stuivers, they ordered the Indian price to be fixed at 30 Stuivers. And when in 1660 it reached the peak figure of 86 Stuivers in Europe, they ordered that no cinnamon should be sold in the East at a price below 48 to 50 Stuivers per pound. . . . [F]rom 1665 onwards Dutch monopoly of cinnamon, both in the East and in Europe, was virtually an established fact.

An aspect of the Company's cinnamon trade was that all the accounts were kept in Holland. The officials in the East were not permitted to charge it up in the accounts. It was a strict order that all the cinnamon was to be sent absolutely free of any charge in the account books in Ceylon. They were allowed a small allowance to cover up the expense of peeling and packing, which amounted to about 2 Stuivers per pound. In Batavia, the cinnamon was valued at 6 Stuivers a pound and, in keeping with the legal fiction that the lands in Ceylon were to be held by the Dutch till Raja Sinha reimbursed them for expenses they had incurred in expelling the Portuguese, the amount was credited to the king's account. The 2 Stuivers per pound was, however, deducted from the 6 Stuivers. The balance thus credited to Raja Sinha's account was deducted from his alleged debt to the Company, a debt which went on increasing year by year and appeared in the accounts of the Company as one of its permanent assets.

Nor could the Government of Ceylon charge anything for the cinnamon sent to the Indian quarters. This too had to be exported free and the sum for which it was sold appeared in the accounts of the respective factories where it was sold as net profit. This meant that the Ceylon Government did not benefit a single stuiver from the cinnamon. This method was chiefly meant to ensure that the officials did not tamper with these accounts. From the point of view of the Company's overall accounts it did not make any difference. But it made the accounts of Ceylon unreal because, without taking into account its most profitable produce, it was always in arrears.

The Ceylon officials, particularly Van Goens, urged that some small charge be made in the account in respect of all cinnamon sent out of Ceylon so that it might help towards covering the expenses. He suggested charging 10 Stuivers a pound. When the accounts were closed in February 1661 there was a deficit of 65,234 Guilders which sum he took the liberty of writing off against the cinnamon that was sent that year. He was promptly reprimanded by the Batavian Government which ordered him never to burden the cinnamon with any fee except the small expense involved in peeling and packing it. This policy was continued throughout this period and even when the island was running heavy deficits, no charge was made.

. . . The monopoly of cinnamon and its harvest appear as established facts which nothing could or might change. This central fact was not in doubt. The steady supply of a certain quantity of cinnamon was assured. . . . In trying to secure the cinnamon, still more, in trying to export it as a free product without any charges on it, there had grown around it several other problems, not directly connected with it, yet fundamentally relevant to it. On the subject of cinnamon itself, one notices an uneventful period of collection and export in the manner followed by the Portuguese but with the customary efficiency and organization of the Dutch. The radical change over to an attempt to cultivate the cinnamon in plantations was to come only in the 18th Century.

How the Dutch Ruled

Ryckloff Van Goens

The term of each Dutch governor serving the Dutch East India Company (Vereenigde Oost-Indische Compagnie, or VOC) was usually a period of three years, though some stayed on longer for second terms. Each governor was responsible for instructing his successor in detailed fashion at the end of his appointment. Ryckloff Van Goens, one of the most powerful Dutch governors during the seventeenth and eighteenth centuries, was responsible for the final expulsion of the Portuguese, and served several terms as governor in the 1660s and 1670s before his son succeeded him in 1675, when Van Goens was promoted to governor general in Batavia. In the following extract from his memoirs, he writes about policies to be followed regarding the Muslims (who were the primary trading rivals to the Dutch), the Portuguese language (which should be banned from schools), marriage of Dutch military men to indigenous women, indigenous elites to be trusted in various degrees, and the importance of protecting the poor who harvest cinnamon.

The Moors come frequently to Galle with rice, oil, and butter, from Bengal, and this must be permitted to continue in some degree so long as they take away our elephants in exchange.

In order, however, to keep our money within the Island it will be necessary in due course to prohibit by public plakkaat its export without licence, but before doing so we must first await the wishes and orders of Their Excellencies, in order, as already stated, not to undertake unseasonably matters of such importance on our own responsibility. In the meantime, Your Excellency has seen in the letter dated the 12th of this month from Commandeur Roothaes that we should negotiate no goods for money but only for elephants and arecanuts, through which the money must then remain in the country.

It is also highly necessary for the welfare of the Colombo district that the entire jurisdiction of Colombo, particularly the city, should be kept free of Moorish residents, who since I was here last had considerably increased in number. They have now however been driven away again, and the Receiver (of the Port) or Sabandaer should adopt strict measures to see that the same vessels which bring the Moors from abroad should also leave with the identical people who arrive in them, and that they are not permitted to obtain domicile here; but the few tailors and others, 16 in number, who are provisionally allowed to remain here together with their families are shown in the list handed to Your Excellency, in order that they may be sent away should Your Excellency consider it necessary.

Your Excellency should also as a fixed principle for your government unceasingly proceed against and drive away from the country the Portuguese canaille, such as toepasses and similar folk. The names of those whom it is necessary that Your Excellency should send away are with the Captain of the Burghers, as regards this place, and with Commandeur Roothaes in respect of those at Galle. The chief reasons why it is imperative that they should be expelled are that they do nothing but continually pursue the native women who are married to Netherlanders in order to debauch them, live without toil, seduce the slaves to thieving, correspond with the papists on the opposite coast, and spy on all our activities; from all of which Your Excellency can appreciate the absolute necessity of expelling these scoundrels.

Hitherto, to our prejudice, timber and arrack were requisitioned from Batavia, although Ceylon could send fully 200 leggers of arrack a year to Batavia if there was need for it there. Timber too is available in such profusion in the forests that we need have no occasion to obtain it from anywhere else. What timber is at present in hand for constructing bridges over the rivers of Negombo, Colombo, and Paneture can be seen by Your Excellency in the lists with the Master Carpenter and the Dissava. All this timber could be felled almost without any cost and dragged to the river by elephants and then sent down by raft or punt, all according to the custom of the country, or, in extraordinary circumstances, by impressing people into the service, or by the ordinary slaves of Colombo and service tenants from the Pasdum Corle, which is full to excess of beautiful timber. It is difficult however to bring it down owing to the very hilly nature of the district, and my intention accordingly was to erect a sawmill worked by Moors and other service tenants in the heart of the forest at a place called Aglewatte so that the planks and beams could with little effort be brought to the river.

Since my last return from Malabar, I have ordered that all Moors coming from abroad should return in the same vessels, regarding the necessity of which Your Excellency and I are of the same opinion. This order should also be enforced at Galle in order that the Moors with their smooth talk (with which they are well equipped) may not displace our own people.

How rapacious some of our own people and nearly all of the Sinhalese are is partly known to Your Excellency, and Your Excellency also is well aware of the reason why the Dissava especially should be appointed from persons who are recognized as free from avarice and who cherish a love for justice and the rights of the humbler inhabitants howsoever poor and wretched they may be, above all those liable to perform service; for I could never regard them without being moved to the heart, seeing that they no less than we are God's creatures; and yet they are sometimes treated no better than brute beasts by the freeholders and some of our own people. Should these poor people's rights not be maintained by the Dissava, and, especially by your high authority, I fear that God would most seriously be offended with us.

To assist the Dissavas, there have been appointed over the Pasdum and Galle Cones each an Overseer, who is termed, according to the Sinhalese fashion, Captain of the Cork. Both these officers, as well as the Dissava, should be of good character and capacity and free from avarice.

Next to them follows the overseer of the cinnamon peelers (called in Sinhalese Captain of the Mahabade) in whose power it is at the same time to oppress those people greatly as already has been experienced. One can readily imagine how beholden our Company is to them, for it is really they who harvest the fruits of this country and must milk the cow for us.

I have already in our conversations discussed sufficiently with Your Excellency the mentality and disposition of the Sinhalese, so that it will be unnecessary to write about that at length. It has however always been my practice to keep near me some of the Sinhalese chiefs as it would otherwise be difficult to preserve the particular usages of the country among the inhabitants, and also to find out at the same time what was going on, exchanging them sometimes for others of whom the former are jealous. There would otherwise only be a very remote possibility of finding out everything that was happening and of which it was also important to be aware. It will be necessary for Your Excellency to keep Don Joan, Mudaliyar of Colombo, with you first for 5 or 6 months, as there is no one in the whole Island who is his equal in knowledge and experience. He is also sometimes a very good councillor in matters that are not adverse to his own interests or detrimental to the King's; and I have found by experience that the Sinhalese would never proffer any advice if they saw it was against the King's interests, while they would readily approve of anything (although to the King's prejudice) if they knew that it had already been decided upon; and in this respect experience will prove to Your Excellency that it is essential to be very careful that your intentions are not prematurely disclosed to them or to any of our people; for, in order to obtain a favour, they know very well how to creep into the confidence of those from whom they think they can discover anything in order to turn it to their own advantage. Next to Don Joan in knowledge are two clever fellows, the one called Moety Apohamy and the other Jacondouwa Apohamy. Both of them belong to the very highest families and are therefore greatly respected, but they are very jealous of each other and both in no lesser degree of Don Joan, upon whom they also look down as not being of such good family as themselves. Among those who have been most useful to us only in the war and have also continued faithful to us, I would mention Don Constantyn, Adigaer of Bentot, who, although his children and grandchildren had fled to the King, was faithful to us during the hottest part of the war in this Island and has also remained so, and as he is of high descent he must always be honoured above the Mudaliyar of Negombo. Louys and Manuel d'Andrado, of whom the Mudaliyar of Negombo and Louys d'Andrado are already known to Your Excellency. Manuel d'Andrado is lately returned from Jaffnapatanam, and although he has not acquitted himself to my entire satisfaction Your Excellency may very well employ him again on account of his knowledge of the Pasdum Corle, but he is prodigiously arrogant and extremely oppressive where the poor people are concerned.

. . . Much also depends on the choice of good sergeants and corporals, and it is most necessary that they should always be selected and appointed from the most sympathetic and thrifty of the men, and also as far as possible that they should all be Netherlanders or Germans, for these lesser officers (must) be regarded as the seed from which the higher officers should spring, for the military proverb says "A good corporal, a good sergeant, a good lieutenant or captain." The articles of war should be read at least three times a year at all watches in the presence of the Captain or Lieutenant, and the same should earnestly be recommended to the respective Commandeurs and Opperhoofds of this Government in order that Y. E. may always be assured regarding this matter.

Among the multitude of regulations which must be observed under this Government are those regarding the permitting of marriages of soldiers and others with native black women and mixties. The order . . . passed in Council is that, before permission is given, the Commissioners of Marriage Causes and the Predicants must certify that the desired spinster or widow is not contaminated by criminal conversation or immodest behaviour with other men, and also that they know their prayers well and can answer questions regarding the most important principles of our religion. How much now depends on good or bad marriages (from which countries and cities must take their rise) is shown by our daily experience, according to which

Governor Rykloff Van Goens, artist unknown. Oil on canvas, late 1660s. Permission by collection Rijksmuseum, Amsterdam.

soldiers who have good wives and are no drunkards prosper. These (God amend it!) are the fewest of them all; and we also see on the contrary that those who have unfaithful and whorish wives, or where the wives may be good if their husbands were not evil livers and drunkards (who unhappily are the majority), fare badly, grow homesick and dissatisfied, and through lack of energy can hardly perform their turn of sentry. Y. E. should see to it that enquiries are made regarding the good conduct of the men—as well as of the women, and that no marriage licenses are issued to evil livers and vagabonds, so that the good may be blessed of God and His wrath may not be provoked by the evil living of others.

Following the subject of marriages comes the most important and necessary duty of attending to the upbringing of the children, in order that they may as much as possible be educated in Dutch manners and in the Dutch language and at the same time be turned away from Portuguese and native habits. To achieve this there are necessary good schools and schoolmasters, which to our extreme regret are now fairly lacking not only in the outstations but even here in Colombo. In the Colombo orphan-school there are at present about 60 children under an exceedingly good master to whom I have given as an assistant the Crankbesoeker Christophorus Stevens in order that we may teach both the orphans and the children who do not belong to the orphanage. With this object another school should be opened in the orphanage. There are also two Dutch schools outside and one in the Fort (in addition to the orphan-school and the schools for natives), but they have only tolerably good masters who should be changed as opportunity offers. Both the masters first mentioned speak Latin and would therefore be competent to instruct the young- children of the officers, burghers and others as soon as Y. E. may consider this necessary or the parents of the children may feel disposed thereto. It has been decreed, yea verily in the whole of this Government, that no Portuguese should be taught in the schools or (even) spoken. Y. E. should rigidly maintain this order as a matter of the most vital importance not only in respect of the children of the Netherlanders but also of the natives, for so long as the Portuguese language is not wholly abolished from our people, the Portuguese priests and their following would have a great advantage over us, especially in this portion of India where the country round about our frontiers is still full of that people (who seek nothing but our destruction and ruin), so that all our activities are communicated (to the enemy) through means of that language, and much often discovered which it would have been more advantageous to have kept hid from them. According to a rough calculation I reckon that there are not less than 13 to 14 hundred children in Ceylon, Jaffnapatnam, Nagapatnam, Tutucoryn and Malabar, all by Dutch fathers.

The Buddha in *vitarka mudra* during the first week of contemplation after his enlightenment. Wall painting (approx. 30 × 24 in.), mid-eighteenth century, at Medavela Rajamahavihara. Photo by editor.

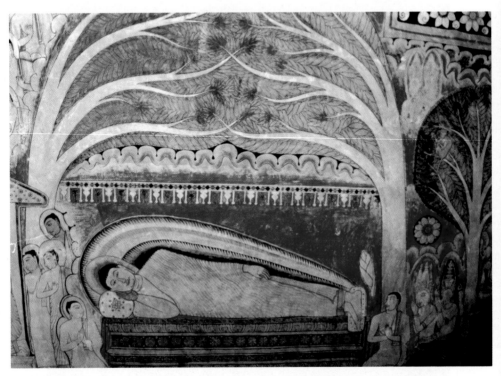

The Buddha in his moment of *parinibbana* (death and final enlightened attainment). Ceiling painting (approx. 50 × 80 in.), mid-eighteenth century, in the second cave at Dambulla. Photo by editor.

The establishment of Sri Mahabodhi (Bodhi Tree) at Anuradhapura. Painting (approx. 36 × 54 in.), mid-eighteenth century, in the second cave at Dambulla. Photo by editor.

The plowing of Anuradhapura's boundaries by King Devanampiya Tissa and the establishment of the order of monks by Emporer Asoka's monastic son, Mahinda. Painting (approx. 36 × 54 in.), mid-eighteenth century, in the second cave at Dambulla. Photo by editor.

Maidens, possibly *apsaras* (heavenly women). Wall paintings,
circa fifth century (restored 1960s), at Sigiri. Photos by editor.

Vatadage (a stupa-like building housing statues of the Buddha).
Twelfth century, at Polonnaruva. Photo by editor.

Parinibbana Buddha. Twelfth century, at Polonnaruva. Photo by editor.

Lankatilaka, the building housing the Buddha image.
Twelfth century, at Polonnaruva. Photo by editor.

Jaffna, artist unknown. Water color, early eighteenth century.
Permission by collection Rijksmuseum, Amsterdam.

Colombo harbor, by C. Steiger. Water color, circa 1710.
Permission by collection Rijksmuseum, Amsterdam.

Point de Galle harbor, by C. Steiger. Water color, circa 1710.
Permission by collection Rijksmuseum, Amsterdam.

Governor's House, Colombo, by C. Steiger. Water color, circa 1710.
Permission by collection Rijksmuseum, Amsterdam.

Dutch Policy towards Buddhism in Sri Lanka

K. W. Goonewardena

In the coastal regions of the island that came under Portuguese and Dutch control from the sixteenth through the eighteenth centuries, one will look in vain for evidence of material culture related to the Hinduism or Buddhism practiced at that time. In what follows, Karl Goonewardena compares the degrees of religious toleration that seem to have existed among the Dutch and Sinhalese in the seventeenth and eighteenth centuries.

" . . . And they hold that one can go to Heaven by many ways." To the Reverend Fr. Queyroz of the Society of Jesus writing in the latter part of the seventeenth century, this attitude of the Buddhists in Sri Lanka towards religion appeared to be as absurd and unacceptable as it had appeared to his fellow Portuguese who had ruled parts of the island for many decades in the latter part of the 16th century and the first half of the 17th. Likewise, the very first Dutchmen who visited the island around 1600 were astounded by the truly liberal attitude of the Sinhalese towards other religions. They noted that not only were the people prepared to hear contrary views regarding religion but even took criticism of Buddhism itself with equanimity.

The concept of religious "liberty" which the Sinhalese are thus found to hold at this time was a more developed entity than the religious "toleration," as between Catholics and Protestants, towards which contemporary Europeans were struggling. In this connection it is instructive to note Herbert Butterfield's observation made a decade or so ago that "in 1691, in his admonition to Protestants . . . , Bossuet still proudly described Catholicism as the least tolerant of all religions, and, as if to compete with this proud boast, the Walloon Synod of Leyden (an overwhelming majority of whose members were Huguenot refugees) firmly condemned religious toleration as a heresy."

With this background in mind, we are not surprised to find that the Portuguese set out to destroy Buddhism (and other indigenous religions in the island) and to induce the people to become Roman Catholics. On the one hand there was the destruction of Buddhist places of worship (in the course of armed incursions even in areas belonging to the King of Kandy), the killing or expulsion of monks and the prohibition of all Buddhist practices. On the other, were the reservation of all appointments to Christians, special rights and privileges to them in land ownership and inheritance, taxation etc., coupled with a system of religious schools, attendance at which was compulsory at least for all those who had become converts.

Portuguese religious policy provoked widespread opposition among the people under their subjection. The oppressed seem to have turned all the more towards the rulers of the independent Sinhalese kingdom of Kandy considering them to be the champions of their cause in this matter as in others. Moreover, whilst these people and the armies of Kandy, had not at first attacked the churches or the Catholic priests, they changed their attitude as the fanatic activities of the Portuguese continued unabated. That this change was a limited and temporary one meant to put a brake on Portuguese excesses, was clearly demonstrated when immediately after the Dutch captured Portuguese territory and began persecuting Roman Catholicism and the Portuguese, the erstwhile enemies were granted asylum in Kandyan territory along with freedom to practice and propagate their religion. Adherence to the idea of religious freedom had thus survived amongst the Sinhalese. This fact emerges equally clearly from the evidence of Robert Knox, an Englishman, who had spent the period between 1660–1679 in the Kandyan Kingdom as a prisoner who had been allowed to travel virtually untramelled through many parts of the kingdom. Said he:

> "As they [The Sinhalese] are not biggotted in their owne religion, they care not of what religion straingers that dwell amongst them are of, they doe believe there is a plurallity of Gods, and more than they know; therefor all nations have a free liberty to use and enjoy their own religion, with all or any manner of cerimonies thare to belonging, without the lest opposition or so much as rideculing."

Proceeding from an entirely different point of view from that indicated above, and with attitudes derived from the European environment mentioned by Butterfield and thus very much akin to those of the Portuguese, the Dutch embarked on a rather uncompromisingly hostile policy towards all non-Calvinist religions in Sri Lanka. The formal point of origin of that policy seems to have been the 1st Article on Religion in the Batavian Statutes of 1642, (almost all the provisions of which statute were made applicable to all Dutch possessions in the East). The 1st Article laid down that within Dutch territory:

> " . . . no other Divine Service or religion shall be practiced, much less taught or propagated, either secretly or publicly, except the Reformed Religion . . . and if any are found [contravening this order] . . . he shall, apart from forfeiting all his possessions, be imprisoned in (chains, banished from the country or corporally or capitally punished, according to exigencies of circumstances."

The Dutch attempted from the outset to act according to the provisions of this Article even at a time when they were explicitly holding the lands in the name of the King of Kandy. Governor Maetsuijcker could not help pointing out to Governor-General & Council at Batavia that it was a very difficult situation "to possess the lands in the King's name and forbid his own religion" in those lands as he himself had done with regard to the erection of a temple. His superiors' reply indicated both their determination to suppress Buddhism as well as the devious ways by which that was to be achieved under the circumstances. It also indicated their fervent belief that God would not bless their enterprise in the island if they suffered Buddhism out of diplomatic considerations. Thus they stated:

> "As far as our authority stretches, [therein] we shall not tolerate idolatry. But it must be averted with mildness and the most appropriate measures from that uncultivated folk, in just the manner you have done by preventing the erection of the temple . . . , for the Lord would not bless the Company's work nor its position in Ceylon, if, out of concern over (King) Rajasinhga's reactions, we were to suffer such abominations."

Before proceeding further with our discussion of Dutch policy towards Buddhism, it would be appropriate at this point to pause and note that Dutch hostility was also directed at other religions encountered in this Island. Islam was one such religion. Although alarmist sentiments were sometimes uttered by one or two administrators, the Dutch seem to have generally felt that not only was it virtually impossible to convert the Muslims to Christianity, but it was also not worth the effort because the numbers involved were so small. In so far as Dutch territory was concerned a few hundred Muslims were to be found in sectors of the coastal ports in the south-west. So, in general the policy towards Islam remained during the period under review more or less what was laid down on the 1st February 1646 by the Batavian authorities for Governor Maetsuijcker;

" . . . they shall be held in such restrictive bounds that their perfidious religion will not be spread among the inhabitants but only amongst the Moorish nation, and its descendants. . . . They must practice their religion under cover . . . in their private houses. . . . All contraventions must be punished in the most politic manner by disruption and other such means, as the situation of the time shall require."

Hinduism was another religion which they encountered in Sri Lanka. But here again there appear to have been only a relatively small number in Dutch territory in the south-west, the bulk of the Hindus being in the northern and eastern areas of the island. The Dutch authorities were opposed to Hinduism too, though not with the same zeal they showed in their opposition to Buddhism. The Dutch clergymen's reports to the Synods in the Netherlands and the records of the administrators, generally show that their continuous and overwhelming concern was with effacing Buddhism and not Hinduism or any other religion. In any case, our theme and the available time does not permit a discussion of Dutch policy towards Hinduism. It may, however, be generally assumed that in the south-west region of the island Hinduism encountered the same type of problem as Buddhism.

One other religion confronted the Dutch, namely Roman Catholicism. They had already been bitterly opposed to Roman Catholicism during their fight for independence from the Spanish Catholic power which had tried to brutally suppress Calvinism in the Netherlands up to the very beginning of the 17th century. So, when the Dutch set out to oust the Catholic Portuguese (whose king also happened to be the Spanish ruler) from Sri Lanka, religious antagonisms too gave an added motivation to the struggle. Moreover, even after 1658, when they had completely driven out the Portuguese from the Island, the fear of a Lusitanian come-back remained strong in their minds for many decades thereafter. This fear stemmed largely from the presence in the island of a large number of people who had become Roman Catholics under Portuguese rule. It was feared that many of these people could turn out to be a potential fifth column in the event of a Portuguese bid to re-establish their power.

The hostility to Roman Catholicism was, however, tempered by other considerations. The Dutch East India Company's servants soon discovered that the vast majority of the people under them in the economically most valuable part of the country, the south-west, adhered to Buddhism even though many had been nominally Roman Catholics up to the end of Portuguese rule. On religious grounds, Dutch hostility to Buddhism was far more intense than towards Roman Catholicism, however much they might

fulminate against the latter sometimes. To them, Buddhism was an idolatrous abomination; but despite certain very obnoxious aberrations, Roman
Catholicism was after all, some form of Christianity. Furthermore, throughout the century now under review, and well beyond it, very important political considerations made them antagonistic towards Buddhism. They all
the time feared that Buddhism would prove to be an extremely powerful
bond linking their Sinhalese subjects in loyalty to the King of Kandy. It was
in secret or open opposition to him that they had established a foot-hold and
begun to extend their power in the island, and they had found him to be a
very formidable opponent indeed.

This political factor, was, therefore, an important consideration behind
certain temporary concessions which they gave to the Roman Catholic
priests in areas under Dutch control even before the Portuguese power had
been completely driven out of the Island. Those concessions also give some
indication of how much more antagonistic they were towards Buddhism
than towards Roman Catholicism. Thus on the 31st July 1645 the Batavian
authorities wrote to their subordinates in the island as follows:

> "We think it to be better that Christianity should be maintained
> amongst the Sinhalese even in some sort of fashion by them [the Ro-
> man Catholic priests] than that they should again lapse into heathen-
> ism [Buddhism]. Meanwhile, affairs must be so directed that the in-
> habitants are gradually brought to our religion, whereby the political
> position will also be made secure."

In trying to bring the people over to Calvinism, however, the Dutch appear to have been reluctant, generally speaking, to antagonize them to the
point of rebellion or to provoke the Sinhalese ruler to intervention or retaliation. How far such restraint was exercised at any given time depended on
such factors as the character and inclinations of Dutch Governors and other
high officials and the Calvinist clergymen, as well as on the assessment of
the degree of opposition and of the relative strength or weakness of Dutch
power, both in Sri Lanka and abroad. But they tended not to compromise
on the fiat that once an individual became a Christian he had of necessity to
conform to certain rules and regulations. He had to marry as a Christian,
attend church, get his children baptized and sent to the church school, and
he could never change over to Buddhism (or any other religion) again. In
this they were undoubtedly following the Portuguese example; and like the
Portuguese they set up a church-school system by which compulsory religious instruction, baptism and marriage according to Christian rites as well
as records of all such activities could be maintained.

THE BRITISH: AN INTRODUCTION

In comparison to India, Ceylon was far more intensively colonized by the British, as witnessed by the dramatic physical transformation of land that occurred with the establishment of a plantation economy. Not only were the central highlands of the country transformed from forest to farm, but thousands of Tamil people were imported from south India to work the coffee and tea plantations that now dominated the interior countryside. Though British rule was largely uncontested and its introduction of Western modernity was imbibed quite thoroughly by a cultivated indigenous elite who were trained in English-speaking schools, two moments (in 1818 and 1848) witnessed serious movements of resistance aimed at reestablishing the Kandyan throne. Moreover, public Buddhist sentiments were reawakened from the 1860s onward, spearheaded first by Buddhist monks who had engaged English missionaries in the famous watershed public debates in Panadura about religious doctrine; then by the American colonel H. S. Olcott of the Buddhist Theosophical Society, who established more than two hundred vernacular schools; and, following Olcott, by the Anagarika Dharmapala and his Mahabodhi Society. These became the loci around which Sinhala nationalist sentiments were first articulated. Conflicts between religious communities surfaced in urban areas, first between Buddhists and Christians in Colombo and later quite seriously between Muslims and Buddhists in 1915—a riot that began in upcountry Gampola and that became so serious that the British, in severely repressing the situation, felt compelled to impose martial law for four years.

By the 1930s, the Donoughmore Constitution had granted universal suffrage to all (including women) who could prove residency on the island for five years. This basis of national citizenship subsumed all other conceptions of community based on language, religion, or lineage. A new modern democratic conception of identity had been introduced. But as a consequence, the question of immigration, specifically the status of the "Indian" or "plantation" Tamils, would continue to plague Ceylon's internal political life. Moreover, because much of Ceylon's external trade under the British was in the hands of non-Sinhalese (urban Chettiars, Moors, Sindhis, and so on, who were perceived as being in league with British imperialists), an anti-Indian sentiment or "antiminority" sentiment began to build among the Sinhalese. Within the Sinhala community, rivalries between emerging working- and middle-class educated Karava, Durava, Navandanna, and Vahumpura communities, on the one hand, and the traditionally dominant Govigama caste, on the other, surfaced in new and significant ways. Both of these types of social and political fragmentations were harbingers, of course, of late-twentieth-century social and political spasms: the former between Sinhalas and minority communities (especially the Tamils but also, at times, the Muslims) and the latter between the relatively poor people of the rural areas and the middle class of the urban. The extent to which the British practiced their trademark policy of "divide and rule" in these instances is a matter of historical debate. But there is no doubt that British recognition of indigenous categorical distinctions had the consequence of reifying them further and fostering a sense of identity at these important sublevels.

A British Description of Colombo, 1807

James Cordiner

The Reverend James Cordiner wrote very detailed descriptions of the natural and social worlds of Ceylon as they appeared to him in the opening years of British domination following the takeover from the Dutch and just before the fall of the Kandyan kingdom. In the following, he describes various neighborhoods of burgeoning Colombo, including the Fort, the Pettah, the cinnamon plantations that became Cinnamon Gardens, Slave Island, Grand Pass, Kelaniya, and so on, as well as the people who lived there (the Dutch, the Portuguese, the British, the Muslims, the Sinhalas). In addition to describing daily life in the city, Cordiner also writes about outrigger sail boats, wells, fans, and a variety of other items that were commonplace in those days.

Colombo, the seat of government, and capital of the British settlements in Ceylon, lies on the west side of the island 7° of north latitude, and 79° 48' of longitude east of Greenwich. Its fort is composed of seven bastions of different sizes, connected by intervening curtains, and defended by three hundred pieces of heavy cannon. It measures one mile and a quarter in circumference, and occupies a situation almost entirely insulated; the sea encompassing two-thirds of the works, and the other third being bounded by an extensive lake of fresh water. A communication is opened into the country on two sides by narrow necks of land, or causeways, running betwixt the sea and the lake, by the cutting of which the fortress would be converted into an island. From the nature of its position, and there being no rising ground which commands it, Colombo is a place of considerable strength, and, if well garrisoned, capable of making a vigorous resistance. It however surrendered, by capitulation, to the British arms on the 15th of February, 1796.

Four of the bastions look towards the sea: the three others face the lake, and command the causeways leading into the fort. The situation of it is cool, pleasant, and healthy: and in these respects it forms a more comfortable residence for a garrison than any other military station in India.

A projecting rock, on which two batteries are erected, affords shelter to a small semicircular bay on the north side of the fort. . . . Strictly speaking, there is no harbour at Colombo; for the little bay, which affords occasional shelter to small craft, does not deserve that name. The production of cinnamon is the only commercial advantage which belongs to the capital of the Ceylon coasts. . . .

The internal appearance of the fort is extremely beautiful, the streets being broad, straight, regularly planned, intersecting one another at right angles, and shaded on each side by double rows of trees. The houses are neatly built, fronted with verandas, or colonnades on pavements raised several feet from the ground, before which are plots of grass and flowers. . . .

While the verandas or piazzas, by their sloping roofs, exclude the glare of the sun from the houses through the day, they afford a comfortable apartment for enjoying the refreshing air of the evening. Some of these covered walks, by consent of the owners, communicate from one house to another; but in general they are divided by wooden balustrades. The partitions appear objectionable to a stranger, as they prevent walking on a smooth pavement, under a connected shade, through the whole town. But as the walk runs close to the houses, people passing and repassing would be an annoyance to the inhabitants: and few individuals choose to sacrifice their own private comfort to the public convenience.

The houses are built of stone, clay, and lime, and roofed with curved tiles. These are placed loosely on the rafters without any cement, but connected together with sufficient firmness by being laid double. . . . The roofs require to be frequently repaired: and, in order to render them water tight, the tiles are turned once a year. . . .

The houses, in general, have only one floor. There are a few, however, of two stories, which are much esteemed, and command charming prospects. The plan, according to which the houses are laid out, is almost uniform over the island. The pavement of the veranda is ascended by a flight of from six to twelve steps. A passage, which is sometimes large enough to form a comfortable sitting-room, runs through the middle of the house. On each side of this is one apartment, and behind these a hall as long as the house. . . . From the centre of this a portico or back veranda projects: and from each side of it, ranges of offices extend at right angles to the main building. These are terminated by a wall, and enclose an oblong court, which is paved with bricks, and contains a well of indifferent water. The two nearest rooms in the outhouses, that is, one on each side, are sometimes used as bed-chambers. The others afford a kitchen, cellars, pantries and stables. A back-door is generally attached to the end of the court: but many of the smaller houses are destitute of that convenience; and when the inhabitant of one of them keeps a horse, he enters at the same door with his master, passing through the vestibule and dining-room, on the way to his stable. This is far from being an uncommon sight, either at Colombo or any other of the towns in Ceylon. . . .

On the arrival of the English, all the houses had glass windows but many of these have been taken out, and Venetian blinds substituted in their place.

The long halls are the places where guests are entertained at dinner. Many of them afford sufficient accommodation for parties of from fifty to eighty persons. From the roof or ceiling is suspended a punka, for the purpose of ventilation when there is no natural breeze. It is an oblong frame of wood, covered with white muslin: and is hung by ropes along the centre of the room, the lower part of it being about six feet above the floor. The dining table is placed under it, so that the perpendicular frame, if lowered down, would bisect it lengthwise: and every person present partakes of its influence. . . . A stranger on his first arrival in the country, while sitting at table, and feeling the influence of this fan, naturally imagines that a refreshing breeze is entering at the open windows. This luxury was first introduced into Ceylon, in 1790, by Lieut. General Hay Macdowall, on his arrival from Calcutta, and is now adopted by all the English inhabitants. The Portuguese and Dutch bear the heat with greater patience; and having always been solicitous to exclude the natural winds from their houses, they are not inclined to create an artificial breeze. The rooms are lighted by glass lamps hung from the roof, and chandeliers fixed upon the walls. Owing to the open structure of the houses contrived for the admission of air, candles, and every description of lights, must be surrounded by glass cases, to prevent them from being blown out. . . .

The government-house, which fronts the sea on the north side of the fort, is a handsome building of two stories, with two wings of one floor. An arched portico, of a cubical form, open on all sides, and flat roofed, projects from the centre of the building, and leads into a large and lofty vestibule, on each side of which are two excellent rooms. These occupy the length and half the breadth of the principal building; parallel to them, a spacious hall extends about three hundred feet in length, from the one end of the house to the other. . . .

The government-house is only used on public occasions, as the roof is worn out and admits the rain. It is the place where the governor gives audience, holds levees, receives ambassadors, and confers honorary distinctions on the natives. It has been employed as the theatre of the most gay and festive amusements; and has also been devoted to the performance of the most serious and solemn duties. The spacious hall was often decorated as a ballroom, and served, at one time, both as a court of judicature and a church.

Eight hundred soldiers frequently attended divine service in it. Psalms and anthems were played and sung by the bands of his majesty's regiments, which still supply both vocal and instrumental music.

The church in the fort once had a roof, but owing to the effects of bad masonry it fell down before the English took the place, and has never since been rebuilt. Divine service was for some time performed within its naked walls, at half past six o'clock in the morning; but frequent showers of rain suggested the expedience of using the above-mentioned hall. The floor of the church is covered with gravestones, under which are vaults, or square compartments, used as places of interment by the principal Dutch families. The coffins are lowered down, and flat stones are laid across the mouth of the cave, but no earth is thrown in.

The funeral procession of the Dutch governor Van-Anglebeck paraded through the streets of Colombo, by torchlight, on the third of September, 1799. It was attended by a party of mourners in black gowns, all the European gentlemen of the settlement, and a crowd of natives. The body was deposited in the family vault, by the side of that of his wife, whose skeleton was seen through a glass in the cover of the coffin. No burial service was used on the occasion; but when the necessary duty was performed, a crier stood upon a tomb-stone, and proclaimed that nothing more remained to be done, and that the company might retire. Those gentlemen who felt inclined repaired to the house of the deceased, where a large party of ladies was assembled; and the rooms were soon crowded with a mixture of all nations, who spent the evening in drinking various liquors and smoking tobacco. This is the largest and best dwelling-house in the fort of Colombo, and is now occupied by Major-General Right Hon. Thomas Maitland, governor of the island. It is situated in the principal street, and composed of two regular stories. From the upper balcony on one side is an extensive view of the sea, the road, and shipping. On the other is a richer prospect, comprehending the lake, pettah, cinnamon plantations, and a wide range of the inland territories bounded by Adam's Peak, and many lesser mountains.

The hospital is a commodious building, and well aired; and the barracks are comfortable; but the prisons do not merit so favourable a description. . . .

Three gates open from the fort towards the sea. Three others communicate with the land; the delft or main gate, which leads to the pettah, the south gate, which opens on the road leading to Point de Galle, and a winding sally-port, which communicates, by causeways and bridges, with a rugged peninsula commonly called Slave-island. This peninsula divides the lake, and receives the above appellation from having formerly been occupied by slaves, who were employed in the service of the Dutch government. The English, on their arrival, made it a station for the Malay regiment. It contains a mud village, a bazar, or market stalls, an excellent parade, and two gentlemen's villas. . . .

A little elevated behind these houses stands a small-pox hospital, which is now about to be pulled down, the success of vaccine inoculation having superseded the necessity of that prior institution.

The rest of the peninsula is covered with a thick forest of cocoanut trees, which approach so near the fort that our government had it in contemplation to cut them down. This projecting piece of land extends, about two miles, to the most distant part of the winding lake, where it expands into the bosom of the cinnamon plantations, which stretch both to the right and left, and cover a circumference of upwards of twelve miles of the inland country.

The pettah, or outer town, is situated a few hundred yards to the eastward of the fort. Part of it encroaches upon the esplanade, and approaches too near to the outworks; but measures have been taken by the British government for removing the houses which come under this description. The town is neat, clean, regular, and larger than that within the fort. Five streets, each half a mile in length, run parallel to one another; and the same number intersect them at right angles. Verandas supported on lofty pillars shade the fronts of the houses, but they want the additional ornament of trees.

In one of the streets stands a large and commodious building of two stories, erected by the Dutch government as an asylum for male and female orphans. The boys were educated here until they attained a proper age for being bound apprentices to trades; the girls generally remained until they were married. Eight years ago, all the boys above eight years of age were removed from this seminary, and placed upon a separate establishment by direction of the governor, the honourable Frederic North, who did not approve of the children of both sexes being lodged in one house. These boys learned to read, write, and speak the English language; and soon acquire the manners and appearance of British children. They now perform the business of clerks in the various offices of the Ceylon government. . . .

Beyond the pettah many straggling streets extend, in various directions, several miles into the country. The fort is chiefly occupied by English inhabitants; the pettah by Dutch and Portuguese; and the suburbs, which are by far the most populous, by native Cingalese. Including all these, Colombo contains upwards of fifty thousand inhabitants. . . .

The houses inhabited by the natives are built on the same plan as those in the fort and pettah, but are considerably lower, and of smaller dimensions. Some of the walls are formed of a double row of stakes wattled together with canes, and having the interstices filled with clay; others are built of stone, and all the roofs are tiled. Most commonly there are one door and two windows in front; and a veranda extends along the whole length of the house. Within it, solid trenches of mason-work are raised close to the wall, on which the inhabitants are accustomed to recline. In the same shade women often perform the business of their simple cookery, placing an earthen pot upon two bricks, and lighting a fire of charcoal under it. Every morning they spread cow-dung mixed with water on the earthen floors and steps of the veranda, in the same manner as we lay on paint or whiting on a wall, but they use no other pencil than their hands. This practice is general over all India. It lays the dust, soon dries, and gives greater firmness to the floor than any other material which can easily be procured. In some places women are in the habit of spreading an ointment of the same nature over their face, neck, and arms.

The dwellings of the poorer classes, both on the coast and in the interior of the island, are larger, better constructed, and more comfortable than those of the indigent inhabitants of any other country within the tropics. . . .

On the borders of the lake of Colombo, on the south side of the fort, lies another burial-ground lately enclosed with palisades. It was rendered necessary for the garrison by the uncommon mortality which followed the campaign of 1803. Beyond it is a humble village formed by Bengal lascars, natives employed in the service of the artillery. The huts are made of sticks and cocoa-nut leaves, neatly built, laid out in parallel streets; and ornamented with rows of young trees, which give the hamlet an air of comfort. These lascars have taken Ceylonese helpmates, and their streets are animated with groups of healthy children, running about in the simplicity of perfect nakedness. About half a mile farther from the fort, on the same road, stands a Cingalese school-house, built of stone and tiled; adjoining to which is the burial-place of the parish of Colpitty, containing a great number of ancient tomb-stones.

On the opposite side of the lake, beyond the eastern esplanade, lies another simple hamlet, of a construction similar to the one above mentioned, likewise the residence of gun lascars, pioneers, and Malabar servants belonging to gentlemen of the garrison.

The inhabitants of both these little villages have chosen situations close to the water's edge, for the convenient performance of those ablutions so frequent and necessary in a warm climate.

Bathing in fresh water is a daily practice among the native inhabitants of Colombo, who frequent the lake and canals in large companies of men, women, and children, and immerse themselves indiscriminately. The women are covered with a sheet from the arm-pits downwards to the ankles; the men have a piece of muslin wrapped round their loins. They stand nearly up to the shoulders in the water, and dipping down a pitcher, lift it up with both hands, and pour the contents of it over the head. This operation they continue in quick succession for the space of half an hour, or longer if they feel inclined. One reason why the natives never bathe in the sea, is their natural timidity and dread of sharks; but, at the same time, they give the preference to fresh water as more conducive both to health and cleanliness. A great inducement to bathing arises from the pleasant sensations and grateful refreshment which it affords. The cold bath, in a warm climate, is nearly as great a luxury as the warm bath in a cold climate. . . .

The church of Wolfendal, where the Dutch inhabitants attend public worship, is situated on the summit of a gentle rising ground, in the midst of the suburbs, about a mile and a half from the fort. It was built for the use of the Cingalese and Malabar Christians, who still meet in it every Sunday, each congregation assembling at a different hour. It is a neat building, in the form of a cross, with a lofty dome in the centre; and it is furnished with an organ. All the public fasts and thanksgivings of the English settlement are kept in this church; but it lies at too great a distance to be constantly used by the garrison. When the troops set out at day-break, before they return from morning service the heat is so great as to be extremely uncomfortable: and were they to attend evening prayers they must march from the fort at four o'clock in the afternoon, when the sun is as oppressive as at any hour of the day.

About a mile farther off stands a Portuguese church, for the use of those natives who belong to the Romish communion.

The bazar, or market, formerly stood on the high road between the pettah and suburbs. It was merely a row of thatched sheds on each side: and such inconvenience arose from a busy crowd being continually collected in so public a situation. The people were exposed to danger from carriages and unruly horses; and the thoroughfare was by no means pleasant to persons whose business did not lead them to market. The bazar has therefore been removed to a declivity behind a late house of the governor called Hulfsdorff, on the borders of the canal, and entirely out of the way of common passengers. A regular set of stalls was erected there at the expence of government, and let to the natives. The sheds are ranged in parallel streets, and built of brick and mortar, with neat pillars and tiled roofs. In these, all the necessaries and many of the luxuries of life are daily exposed for sale from sunrise until late at night. But notwithstanding the superior comfort and convenience of this place, the Colombo merchants retired to it with considerable reluctance. They naturally thought that they had a better chance of vending their commodities in a more public situation. But an absolute prohibition of these articles being sold at any other part of the town removed this objection; and no person has any reason to complain of the change, unless the man who has to walk half a mile farther than he used to do to purchase a measure of rice or a fowl. This inconvenience is not felt by the inhabitants of the fort, for whom a small bazar is constructed in a field between the walls and the sea. A strict police, however, is necessary to enforce obedience to these salutary regulations, and to promote the public advantage. The removal of the market from its former situation has rendered the entrance into the pettah, which was before choked up and nauseous, now open and remarkably pleasant, presenting a fine prospect of the smooth lake on one hand, and the ocean on the other.

The water within the fort is brackish, and consequently not used for drinking. Good water must be brought from the distance of one mile and a half. In the Cingalese manner of transportation, two earthen pots are suspended from the opposite ends of an elastic piece of wood, and placed across one shoulder of a man. Women carry pitchers on their heads. Water for the use of the troops is conveyed in skins, or leathern bags, on the backs of bullocks. These are called puckawlies, and a certain number of them is attached to the quartermaster's establishment in every regiment. The water is drawn off through a spigot fixed at one corner of the hide, and thus served out along the lines in whatever quantity is required. It would not, however, be a difficult matter to introduce this necessary of life into the garrison by the superior means of leaden pipes. . . .

Few cultivated fields or open meadows are to be seen, the face of the country being chiefly covered with trees; some of which are planted by the natives for the sake of their fruits, and others have been growing in impenetrable forests from time immemorial. But the exuberance of vegetation and endless variety of foliage render the scenery superlatively rich and beautiful. The greater part of the grounds is entirely in a state of nature. Few attempts have been made either to cut down the brushwood, or to give the country the appearance of culture. Even when a road is formed, shrubs spring up upon it so rapidly that if it be neglected for the space of two months the traces of it can hardly be discerned. The province, however, is, beyond a doubt, capable of great improvement by industry, both in beauty and fertility.

Several pleasant rides, of from three to eight miles in extent, are formed by going out at one gate of the fort, traversing the intermediate country, and returning by the other. These afford morning and evening recreation to the ladies and gentlemen of the settlement. The coast stretching to the southward is flat, and several villas are erected along the east side of the road fronting the sea. They are cool and pleasant residences; and the communication between them and the fort is open and airy. The road was formerly a deep loose sand, but is now firm and solid, being laid for upwards of two miles with *cabooc*-stone, which is a mixture of sand and clay admirably adapted for that purpose. The ground to the north-east is more varied, being divided into a number of little mounts, on some of which country seats are built, forming still more delightful places of abode, commanding wider prospects, and a greater diversity of scenery. But in going from the fort to these houses, it is necessary to pass through the pettah, and a long narrow street of the native town, where vitiated and confined air renders part of the ride less agreeable. This road runs in many places close to the sea shore, and proceeds about four miles, when it is interrupted by the Calany ganga, at that place called the Mootwal river. Here is a ferry, and excellent boats with capacious decks, into which a one-horse carriage is often driven, and conveyed over without being unyoked. The river is not fordable; and a person who is riding merely for pleasure never crosses it. The road runs, for about a quarter of a mile, along the west bank of the river, through a grove of cocoa-nut trees, and then branches off into various walks, all of which lead through hills and dales to the town of Colombo. By continuing a winding excursion towards the south, one may prolong the ride to the length of twelve or fourteen miles, passing through the cinnamon plantations, and returning in the opposite direction to the fort. English villas are built to the northward, here and there, on each side of the road, but at a considerable distance from it, and so situated that they do not at all obstruct the views from one another. Those farther inland are placed on eminences, and those nearer the sea occupy the lower grounds.

Several other roads extend into the country, and take their rise chiefly from one point, at the termination of the pettah. One leads to the church of Wolfendal, where it opens into a square, at one corner of which stands a neat building with an arched portico, erected for the reception of the Candian ambassadors. From this, roads branch off both to the right and left; and others proceed forward farther inland. One road is directed to Hulfsdorff and the bazar: another leads to St. Sebastian's, and runs, four miles, in a southeast direction, to the village of Cotta: a third terminates at the grand pass. This is the name given to another ferry on the Calany ganga, about two miles farther up the river than the one formerly mentioned. A fine road runs from it a mile across the country, through a valley of paddee fields, and over two wooded hills, after which it joins the north road at right angles. This is one of the most frequented drives; and a ride, in that course, is called, in the phraseology of Colombo, "round the grand pass." All the roads, in their commencement from the pettah, are streets of a straggling village, having houses on each side extending to a considerable distance inland.

At the grand pass stands a country seat built by the late Dutch governor Van Anglebeck. Besides a row of offices and a handsome farm-yard, there are two houses of one floor each for the accommodation of the family. These lie parallel to one another, and it is necessary to pass through the first to get to the second, which is raised on an embankment of the river. The stream is seen gliding along from the windows, and is broad, deep, and rapid. The opposite banks are clothed with thick woods. The situation is pleasant, but low and flat; and the grounds about it are swampy, being employed in the cultivation of rice. In the morning they are covered with thick fogs, whence the place has been accounted unhealthy. . . .

From this part of the river a navigable canal is cut, extending to the lake of Colombo: from which another canal passes through the streets of the fort, and terminates at the sea-beach. It enters the walls through a low arched passage near the sally-port, and at different parts of it are flights of steps which lead up into the town. The top of the canal at the grand pass is constantly crowded with large flat-bottomed boats, which come down from Negumbo with dried fish and roes, shrimps, fire-wood, and other articles. These boats are covered with thatched roofs in the form of huts, and are often the only habitations occupied by the owners and their families. The shed of one of them contains two couches, which are put in for the accommodation of English gentlemen when they go to see the elephant hunts, or to enjoy other rural amusements. A draw-bridge is thrown over the above-mentioned part of the canal, and communicates with a retired and beautiful road, extending along the banks of the river in the direction of Hangwell. Three miles above the bridge stands the village of Kovilawatta, called by the Dutch Pannebakkery, on account of a brick-work, or manufacture of tiles, which is still carried on there.

At Pilligory, on the opposite side of the river, a little higher up than the house of the Dutch governor, the honourable Frederic North built a temporary bungaloe, of wooden pillars roofed with cocoa-nut leaves, where he occasionally gave grand entertainments, and gratified his guests with a pleasant variety of scene. The situation is a gentle eminence, perfectly dry, and completely rural, nothing being seen near it but the limpid stream, and its richly wooded and verdant banks. Excellent boats were always ready to carry over the party, and a band of music added gaiety to the other luxuries of the feast.

On many of the roads, particularly on those two, the one leading to the grand pass, and the other to Cotta, there are a great many commodious houses inhabited by Dutch and other European families. But they lie, generally, in low and confined situations, close to the road side, choked up with trees, and are by no means so pleasant to live in as those rural dwellings which command views of the sea and skirt the borders of the lake. Where there are no houses there are always large trees on each side of the road, except only in a few open spots, where there are cultivated fields. The cocoa-nut tree abounds most on the coasts, where but few other species are mingled with it. It predominates also in the more sheltered avenues, which are enriched with a beautiful intermixture of areka, jaggree, jack, breadfruit, jamboo, cotton, tamarind, and banyan trees. . . .

Some of the most striking scenes about Colombo are seen from the ramparts of the fort, round which there is an excellent walk. When looking to the south-east, the pettah lies on the left hand, the road to Point de Galle on the right; beyond each of them is the sea, and in the centre between them is spread the lake, encompassed with thick groves of cocoa-nut, jack, and other trees, amongst which appear delightful villas, the country residences of the governor, and other gentlemen of the settlement. Here, as well as in various other situations, Adam's Peak, and a chain of lesser mountains, form the back ground of many romantic prospects.

The view from the mouth of the Calany ganga is extremely beautiful. It exhibits an elegant winding of the river, which is separated from the sea by a long and narrow bar of sand, partly covered with grass; a small island, richly clothed with wood, divides the stream; and the opposite bank is lined with forests of cocoa-nut trees, but no mountainous scenery appears behind them. The Cingalese fishing boats, sailing in and out of the river, give a pleasing animation to the scene.

The construction of these boats is extremely curious as well as simple; and the velocity with which they move perhaps exceeds that of any other vessel. The principal part of the boat is a canoe, or hollowed tree, about fifteen feet long, and so narrow that a man has scarcely room to turn in it. It is three feet deep, contracted towards the top, but wider at the bottom. Along the edges of it one or two rows of boards are sewed or fastened with cords (for nails are never used), to raise it more above the surface of the water. In this state it might be launched into the sea, but it would be upset by a person simply stepping into it. To prevent this a log of wood, called an out-rigger, is placed parallel to the canoe on one side at the distance of six feet, and united to it by two sets of elastic poles bound together with ropes, and each bent in the form of an arch. The log of wood is shorter than the canoe, and sharp pointed at both ends, so as to cut through the water easily. The connecting poles are six or eight bamboos, or other pliant branches, of the thickness of a man's arm, bound into the form of one tree; and one set is fastened to each end of the log. On these the fishermen pass from the canoe to the out-rigger, and trim the vessel. It has one very large square sail, which is supported by two masts or poles angularly placed, the one perpendicular, resting in a plank laid across the canoe, the other swinging in a loop of rope tied round it. From the tops of each of these, ropes extend to the parallel log: and the masts and sail can be lowered down in an instant. One of these boats is commonly navigated by two persons, a man and a boy. The man steers the canoe with one foot, by means of a paddle fixed to it over one side of the stern, and, at the same time, fishes with both hands: the boy notices the sail, and throws water on it to make it hold wind the better. When three persons belong to the boat, one of them generally stands upon the out-rigger. These boats daily venture out ten or fifteen miles from the shore: and notwithstanding their apparently frail construction, an accident rarely occurs. Their filling with water does not distress them much, as the canoes cannot sink. The men are excellent swimmers; and as long as the out-riggers remain entire, they carry sail without either inconvenience or danger. But should any part of them give way, the hoisting of the sail is impracticable, and they must then paddle to the shore. Although the vessel is unwieldy in appearance, it is turned in any direction with the greatest ease. Its structure is such that it sails either by the bow or stern: and in tacking, nothing more is necessary than to swing the sail from the one side to the other. . . .

Colombo and the surrounding country have an enchanting appearance from a ship a few miles out at sea. Thick woods of cocoa-nut trees, on gentle rising grounds, extend on each side of the fort along the shore. Chains of lofty mountains rise behind them, a few only of which are discernible from the land. On a nearer approach the scenery becomes still more interesting. A wide semicircular bay expanding into the mouth of the Catany ganga has a grand and pleasing effect; and the prospect is enlivened by the villas of the English inhabitants placed in high and conspicuous situations. These delightful spots were unoccupied and overgrown with wood, when Colombo surrendered to the British arms. Many others equally desirable are still covered with impervious thickets, which, while they obstruct the view, proclaim the genial nature of the climate, and the excessive indolence of the native inhabitants. At the same time the soil is not esteemed favourable to the purposes of agriculture, being, as has been already mentioned, an accretion of sand and clay, in many places impregnated with iron. The Dutch inhabitants of Ceylon took particular pains to exclude the sea air from their houses; and placed them in sheltered valleys, in the midst of marshes, and often close to pools of stagnant water. It has been said that they even studied to promote unhealthiness as a security to their possessions; and in this object they have succeeded at Batavia, the capital of their Indian dominions. For the pestilential air, which is generated and encouraged there, has been the means of preventing the British arms from taking possession of the rich and valuable settlement.

Nothing about Colombo is more apt to excite admiration than the flourishing state of the vegetable world. So much beauty and variety are in few countries equalled, and no where excelled. The thick shade of majestic trees, the open prospects, the lively verdure, the flowering shrubs, and parasitic creepers unite their charms to render the morning rides delightful. To describe the variegated scenery, the different appearances of the trees, the ornamental shrubs, the perpetual summer, and never-ceasing spring, is a task which language cannot adequately perform. But the efforts of an able pencil, industriously employed, might be attended with better success; and the artist, who could do justice to the scenes, would be ravished with exquisite transport, whilst he exercised his art for the advantage of the public. . . .

No climate in the world is more salubrious than that of Colombo; and a person, who remains within doors while the sun is powerful, never wishes to experience one more temperate. During five years residence there I rarely heard of any person being sick, unless those whose illness was caught in the interior of the country. Before the commencement of hostilities with the king of Candy in 1803, a funeral was not a common occurrence at Colombo: and out of a thousand British soldiers, it often happened that one man was not lost in the space of two months. The air is, at all times, pure and healthy, and its temperature uncommonly uniform. Farenheit's thermometer usually fluctuates in the shade about the point of 80. It seldom ranges more than five degrees in a day, and only thirteen through the whole year, 86° being the highest, and 73° the lowest point, at which it has been seen in any season. The healthiness of this place may be ascribed to its dry and insulated situation, to the regular prevalence of the land and sea breezes, to its partaking of the salutary influence of both monsoons, and to the refreshing showers which fall every month in the year, cooling the air, and cherishing perpetual verdure. Three weeks of uninterrupted fair weather are rarely experienced; and a long continuance of rain is entirely unknown. Dirty streets or heavy roads are never to be seen. The soil is so dry that moisture is rapidly absorbed. When it rains at night, the following morning is always ushered in with sun-shine: when it rains in the morning, the evening never fails to be serene and pleasant. According to this order, rain falls, for some weeks, at one time, every morning about sun-rise, and at another time, every evening before sun-set. . . .

Colombo is, by far, the most eligible place of residence in the island. Besides the superiority of climate, it possesses an agreeable mixture of society, which cannot be enjoyed in the more confined circles of the other stations.

The Final Tragedy of the Kandyan Kingdom

John Davy

The physician John Davy was twenty-five years old when he arrived in Ceylon in 1815. He was one of the first Britons to travel within and observe the Kandyan kingdom immediately after its capitulation to the British in 1815. His description of social structures, methods of administration, ceremonies of the court, forms of religious worship, and so on, provides the most detailed British perspective since the account of Robert Knox a century and half before. In the following, Davy describes the turn of tragic and cruel events that led to the deposition of the last king of Kandy. No doubt, this description of the horrific events that unfolded in Kandy was also meant to legitimate the need for subsequent British control of the kingdom.

Between 1805 and 1815, the armistice, or mutual suspension of hostilities, in which the unfortunate war of 1803 terminated, experienced no serious interruption. During this period of mutual and gloomy forbearance on each side, little that is interesting occurred relative to Kandyan affairs except in the court of Kandy itself, where the worst passions of human nature were in horrible operation,—agitating the breast of a tyrant on one hand, and of conspirators on the other; and producing deeds quite diabolical, and, did not truth require the relation, too terrible to be described.

About 1806, Magasthene, second Adikar and Dissave of the Seven Korles, died. In his office he was succeeded by Eheylapola. The vacant Dissavony was divided between this chief and Molligodde Dissave, to the great offence and discontent of the people. Such a division, they said, "was contrary to custom; it was a grievance, as two Dissaves would require double the services and duties of one, and that they would resist it"; a rebellion in the Seven Korles was the consequence. On this occasion, Pilime Talawe assured the king, that were the district transferred to him and his nephew, Ratwatte Dissave, they would soon make the people submit to his orders. The experiment was made, the minister was as good as his word; for he immediately brought the people back to their duty. His success excited the king's suspicion and jealousy, and heightened the aversion he had some time begun to feel towards his old benefactor. The chief, nettled by the altered manner of the king, reminded him, who had placed him on the throne; and told him, he did not behave as he ought, nor listen to him and pay him that attention that he was wont to do. The monarch did not receive his reprimand patiently; he retorted—"He was not to be led by his chiefs, but they were to be directed by him." Farther, the minister expressed his disapprobation of the public works which the king was then engaged in, on the ground that they were vexatious to the people and oppressive. The works in question were several new roads; the lake of Kandy, which was made at this time; many new buildings, particularly the present Pattiripooa [the octagonal tower at the front of the Dalada Maligava].

These bickerings between the monarch and his minister created mutual hatred, which was soon coupled with mutual dread; the one imagining his life insecure from the machinations of the other. The king, who had little control over his passions, soon gave them vent. When the minister expressed a wish to unite his son to the natural grand-daughter of King Kirti [Sri], his majesty, taking it for granted that this was merely a step to the throne, assembled the chiefs, enumerated various grounds of complaint against the minister, charged him of mal-administration, and accused him of being the author of every thing cruel and unpopular that had been done during his reign; then suddenly relenting, he told the Adikar, that he forgave him all his offences, and as a proof he conferred new honors upon him. But this relenting and these new honors were merely delusive. Presently, having neglected some little trivial duty, the minister was summoned to appear before the king and chiefs assembled in the great square. His offences were recapitulated; he was deprived of all his offices, and sent to prison, from whence he was liberated in eight days, and permitted to go to his country residence, and lead a private life. The disgraced and irritated chief did not remain quiet at home. He soon hatched a plot to murder his ungrateful sovereign. He bribed the Malay Mohandiram and sixty of his Malays to attack the king on a certain day and assassinate him; and he prevailed on the headmen of Ooudeneura and Yattineura to raise the people of these districts in arms, about the same time. On the day and hour appointed, Ballinwattella-ralle finding the king awake, when it was expected he would have been asleep, begged the conspirators, whose spy he was, to wait a little. The two provinces just mentioned prematurely broke out in rebellion and marred the plot. The king instantly sent for Pilime Talawe, his nephew, and son; and had them secretly conveyed by night to different prisons, in the most difficult parts of the country. The Malay Mohandiram and his men fled to Colombo. The incipient rebellion was suppressed, and the ringleaders apprehended. Pilime Talawe and his nephew and son were sent for to undergo trial. The two former arrived together; and, in the presence of the king and chiefs, were confronted with the ringleaders, and were sentenced to death on their confession. They were immediately beheaded, and six petty chiefs were hanged and impaled around their bodies. The son, who was imprisoned farther off, was capitally condemned, at the same time; but not arriving till after the execution of his relations, and on a holiday, he was reprieved; and at the intercession of the chiefs his life was spared, but his lands confiscated. The execution of Pilime Talawe and the ruin of his family, the first act of retributive justice, took place in 1812.

Eheylapola succeeded Pilime Talawe as first Adikar. The king now became more suspicious and tyrannical than ever. Terrified by the past, apprehensive of future danger, and intent on his own security alone, without any regard to consequences, he ordered, that there should be no communication between the provinces which he considered tainted with the leaven of revolt, and the loyal ones of Hewahette, Doombera, Ouva, Kotmale and Walapane. Farther, he ordered, that no moormen, and that no priests, should remain in the latter provinces; and that all women, not born in these provinces, should also quit them, and return to their native districts. These orders were enforced in the same spirit in which they were issued. Wives were separated from their husbands, mothers from their children; the young bride and the aged parent,—all, indiscriminately, were torn from the bosom of their families, and driven from their homes; producing scenes of distress, and, feelings of anger and discontent, which might well shake the firmest loyalty. Intent on the same object, his personal security, the king made a great change in his household; he removed to distant situations all officers who belonged to the lately rebellious or suspected provinces, and would allow no one to be near his person, who was not a native of those he considered his loyal, as well as mountain districts and natural fortresses.

He had formed certain secret suspicions of the first Adikar, which the confessions of the conspirators in Pilime Talawe's plot had given rise to, and which, suppressed at the time, fermented inwardly, and produced cordial hatred of the minister. Having lost two sons and two daughters by his first queens, he married two more at the same time, and sisters. On the occasion of the nuptials, the king's ill-will towards the minister first showed itself; his present, though rich, was called mean, and unworthy of acceptance.

A crisis was now fast approaching. The people in general were disaffected; most of the chiefs were anxious for a change of government, either from hatred of the king, or as an easy way of getting rid of debts to his relations, of whom many chiefs had received large loans; the second Adikar's debt alone (Molligodde's) amounting to six thousand pagodas.

In this state of affairs, just after his marriage, the king sent the chiefs into their respective districts, to superintend the cultivation of the country, and the [collection] of the revenue. Eheylapola, in a discontented mood, hastened into his Dissavony (Saffragam), and presently began to act his part. Many circumstances, about the same time, gave rise to an open rupture between the king and his minister;—a village of Saffragam, belonging to one of the queens, refused to pay its dues, and illtreated her agent; the revenue derived from areka-nuts was not duly paid into the treasury; a charge was brought against the Adikar, by a Malabar merchant, of his having unjustly deprived him of a large sum of money, which the minister was required to disprove, or refund the amount; farther, he was ordered to return to Kandy, and bring with him the people of his district, who had neglected the payment of various dues to the king, particularly on the occasion of his marriage. The Adikar's answers were not those of a submissive subject, and widened the breach. A favorite, in his district, which is almost entirely cut off from the other Kandyan provinces by mountains inaccessible, excepting by two or three difficult passes, he began to think of opposition; he opened a correspondence with [the British in] Colombo, and made preparations for defence, with the concurrence of the people, who promised to risk their lives in his support. Intelligence of his measures soon reached the king, who instantly deprived him of all his offices, imprisoned his wife and children, appointed Molligodde first Adikar and Dissave of Saffragam, and ordered the invasion of the province by the new minister. Molligodde obeyed with alacrity; he entered Saffragam over the loftiest point of the island, and the most difficult pass—the summit of Adam's Peak. The hearts of the natives failed them on his approach; and he met with but little opposition. Eheylapola, with some of his adherents, fled to Colombo, and Molligodde returned to Kandy with a crowd of prisoners, forty-seven of whom were impaled. This happened in 1814. Now, one scene of horror and bloodshed rapidly follows another, till the tragedy is wound up, and retributive justice again appears on the stage. Pusilla, Dissave of Neurakalawea, had excited the king's displeasure, by a present that, through the ignorance of his brother, was offered in a disrespectful manner. The brother was imprisoned; the Dissave was soon suspected of correspondence with Eheylapola, and a letter from this chief, abusive of the king, having been found in the possession of one of his attendants. [A certain] Pusilla was considered guilty, his eyes were plucked out, his joints cut, and after this torture he was beheaded. The old offence of the Seven Korles was again ript open; all the headmen supposed to have been concerned in the rebellion in which Pilime Talawe was suppressed, were summoned to appear at Kandy. They were tried by a commission of three chiefs, of whom Molligodde, whose authority they had opposed, was one, and were condemned to death; after a severe flogging, about seventy were executed, all of them men of some consequence in their district. These transactions are horrible; but what remains to be related is worse. Hurried along by the flood of revenge, the tyrant, lost to every tender feeling, resolved to punish Eheylapola who had escaped, through his family, which remained in his power; he sentenced the chief's wife and children, and his brother and his wife, to death,—the brother and children to be beheaded, and the females to be drowned. In front of the queen's palace, and between the Nata and Maha Visnu Dewale, as if to shock and insult the gods as well as the sex, the wife of Eheylapola and his children were brought from prison, where they had been in charge of female jailors, and delivered over to the executioners. The lady with great resolution maintained her's and her children's innocence, and her lord's; at the same time submitting to the king's pleasure, and offering up her own and her offspring's lives, with the fervent hope that her husband would be benefited by the sacrifice. Having uttered these sentiments aloud, she desired her eldest boy to submit to his fate; the poor boy, who was eleven years old, clung to his mother, terrified and crying; her second son, nine years old, heroically stepped forward; he bid his brother not to be afraid,—he would show him the way to die! By one blow of a sword, the head of this noble child was severed from his body; streaming with blood and hardly inanimate, it was thrown into a rice mortar; the pestle was put into the mother's hands, and she was ordered to pound it, or be disgracefully tortured. To avoid the disgrace, the wretched woman did lift up the pestle and let it fall. One by one, the heads of all her children were cut off; and one by one, the poor mother—but the circumstance is too dreadful to be dwelt on. One of the children was a girl; and to wound a female is considered by the Singalese a most monstrous crime; another was an infant at the breast, and it was plucked from its mother's breast to be beheaded; when the head was severed from the body, the milk it had just drawn in ran out mingled with its blood. During this tragical scene, the crowd who had assembled to witness it wept and sobbed aloud, unable to suppress their feelings of grief and horror. Palihapane Dissave was so affected that he fainted, and was expelled from his office for showing such tender sensibility. During two days the whole of Kandy, with the exception of the tyrant's court, was as one house of mourning and lamentation; and so deep was the grief, that not a fire (it is said) was kindled, no food was dressed, and a general fast was held. After the execution of her children, the sufferings of the mother were speedily relieved. She, and her sister-in-law, and the wife and sister of Pusilla Dissave, were led to the little tank in the immediate neighbourhood of Kandy, called Bogambarawave and drowned. Such are the prominent features of this period of terror, which, even now, no Kandyan thinks of without dread, and few describe without weeping. Executions at this time were almost unceasing; the numbers put to death cannot be calculated; no one was perfectly secure,—not even a priest,—not even a chief priest; for Paranataley Anoonaika-Ounnansi, a man, in the estimation of the natives, of great learning and goodness, fell a victim to the tyrant's rage. . . .

Disgusted and terrified by the conduct of the king, the chiefs and people were ripe to revolt; and only waited the approach of a British force to throw off their allegiance.

Acquainted with what was going on in the Interior, it was impossible for our government to be unconcerned. His Excellency Lieutenant General (now General Sir Robert) Brownrigg prepared for hostilities, which seemed to be unavoidable. He had stationed a force near the frontier, in readiness to act at a moment's notice; and he had made arrangements for invading the Kandyan provinces should war break out.

Cause for declaring war soon offered. Several of our native merchants, who in the way of trade had gone into the Interior, were treated as spies, and sent back shockingly mutilated; and very soon after, a party of Kandyans passed the boundary and set fire to a village within our territory. The declaration of war against the Kandyan monarch immediately followed this act; it was made on the 10th of January, 1815. On the day following, our troops entered the Kandyan territory; they found the Three and Four Korles in a state of revolt, and they were soon joined by Molligodde, the first Adikar, and many of the principal chiefs. Almost without the least opposition, our divisions reached the capital; on the 14th of February our headquarters were established there; and on the 18th, the king was taken prisoner. Forsaken by his chiefs, he fled on our approach into the mountainous district of Doombera, accompanied only by a very few attendants. Driven by heavy rain from a mountain where he concealed himself during the day, he descended and took shelter in a solitary house in the neighbourhood of Meddahmahaneura, not aware that there was a force at hand lying in wait for him. The party was a zealous one, composed of natives of Saffragam, headed by a staunch adherent of Eheylapola; as soon as intimation was given of the king's hiding-place, the house was surrounded and the monarch seized. He was sent to Colombo, and from thence to Vellore, where he is still in confinement. He may be justly considered an example of the perfect tyrant; wrapped up in selfishness, possessed of ungovernable passions, destitute of religious feelings, destitute of moral principles, and without check, either human or divine.

A fortnight after his capture, on the second of March, in a convention held at Kandy, by his Excellency the Governor on one side, and the Kandyan chiefs on the other, the tyrant Sree Wikrime Rajah Singha was formally dethroned; the king of Great Britain was acknowledged sovereign of the whole island of Ceylon; the preservation of the old form of government of the Interior was guaranteed on our part, as well as the protection of the customs, laws, and religion of the people.

A board, composed of three civil servants, was soon established at Kandy, consisting of a resident, and of a commissioner of justice and of revenue; the first, the representative of the Governor; the other two, the presidents of their respective departments. The board, with the Adikars and the principal chiefs, formed the great court of justice, from whose sentence there was no appeal, except to the Governor. Besides the board, and a subordinate agent of government in Ouva, Saffragam, and the Three Korles, the civil authority of the country was exercised as before, by the native Dissaves and Ratemahatmeyas.

The military force which was kept in the Interior, was inconsiderable, seldom exceeding 1000 men, who were confined to a few stations where we had established military posts, altogether not exceeding eleven in number. The offices of first and second Adikar were filled by Molligodde, the former prime minister, and by a chief of the name of Kappawatte. Eheylapola, to whom the first appointment was offered, begged to decline it. There is reason to believe that he looked higher, and that he expected to have been made king. Be this as it may, he married again, and resided in Kandy; where he lived in considerable state, and was regarded by the natives as the great chief of the country.

Between March 1815 and October 1817, the Kandyan provinces remained quite tranquil. The terms of the convention were strictly adhered to by us; and the chiefs and people seemed contented under our mild and indulgent government. But these appearances were delusive. Having by our means got rid of a tyrant, having enjoyed a little rest, they seemed to have considered themselves sufficiently refreshed to try their strength, and attempt the expulsion of their benefactors.

Circumstances considered, such a desire, however ungrateful, was not unnatural on their parts. There was no sympathy between us and them; no one circumstance to draw or bring us together, and innumerable ones of a repulsive nature. The chiefs, though less controlled than under the king, and exercising more power in their districts than they ever before ventured to exert, were far from satisfied. Before, no one but the king was above them; now, they were inferior to every civilian in our service, to every officer in our army.

The Rebellion of 1818 and Consolidation of British Rule

Jonathan Forbes

Major Jonathan Forbes, a British civil servant who lived in Ceylon for many years following the disestablishment of Kandyan kingship, was as wedded to the British perspective as John Davy was. Forbes's thoroughly colonialist descriptions of the political events that followed the demise of the Kandyan kingdom, including the 1818 rebellion, emphasize the establishment of a new system of justice that had been put into place by the 1830s to succeed the former adjudicatory rule of the Kandyan chiefs.

Sri Wikrema Raja Singha was removed to Colombo, from thence to Madras, and finally to the Fort of Vellore, in which place he died of dropsy, 30th of January, 1832, aged fifty-two years; the last seventeen of these he passed in confinement. His features were handsome, his figure manly, and his general appearance dignified; but the qualities of his mind appear to have been a compound of the meanest with the most violent passions, without one redeeming virtue to weigh against selfishness, cruelty, and cowardice; he was equally destitute of any amiable quality which could excite compassion for his fate, even amongst those who served about his person, or had been advanced by his power. . . .

The Kandian leaders were left in possession of their former offices, and the people were governed according to their ancient laws; but the chiefs now felt that their influence had suffered by submitting to a regular and efficient Government, and that too a foreign one, which as yet they had not learned to respect, and from former examples hoped to overthrow. These were the first stimulants to a desire for change, and the over-conciliatory manner in which their headmen were treated by the highest British authorities, not only inspired them with a vain confidence in their own importance, but comparing this treatment with that of their late ruler, they came to the conclusion that so glaring a want of dignity could only proceed from conscious deficiency of power.

A rebellion was the consequence; it suddenly broke out in October, 1817, and soon after its commencement, the influential chiefs, with very few exceptions, were either in open rebellion, in confinement for favoring the rebels, or were only deterred by fear or policy from immediately joining a cause, to which they meant to adhere so soon as anticipated success should enable them to show their zeal, without incurring personal danger, or possible confiscation of property. Even Eheylapola, whose wife and family had been destroyed by the dethroned despot, and who had himself declined office, and only requested that he might be styled "The friend of the British Government," was arrested on well-grounded suspicion of his fidelity, and his brother-in-law, Kaepitapola, was the acknowledged leader of the rebels, and the undoubted instigator of their treason. He it was who had employed the pretender, who appeared as King, and was announced as Durra Sawmy, a member of the deposed royal family. The first open act of rebellion was the murder of a Moorman in the forest of Welasse, by order of this puppet of a King, the tool of those chiefs who were admitted into the secret. This act was soon followed by the death of Mr. Wilson, of the Ceylon civil service, who had proceeded to the spot with a small party of military, on receiving information of the murder, and some mysterious whisperings of intended treason; he fell by the arrows of the Veddahs, who had been summoned by the chiefs, and were assembled in considerable numbers, and on his death the party retired to Badulla.

The rebellion now spread rapidly; and in less than six months, most of those districts which had not already appeared in open insurrection, were secretly organized for revolt, and only awaited the fitting opportunity of joining the rebels. Luckily, the private animosity subsisting between Eheylapola and the first Adikar, Mollegodda, induced the latter to exert his influence in support of British supremacy, which he had good reason to identify with his own safety. By his influence in the district of the Four Corles, the people there were generally restrained from insurrection; a service of great importance at this period to the British interest, as through that province lay the principal defiles and mountain passes of the road, which led from Colombo to the Kandian capital.

A protracted warfare of small military posts established throughout the country, and detached parties in continual motion, pursuing an armed population in a mountainous and wooded country, was naturally productive of considerable loss to the British force; for, although few fell by the weapons of the Kandians, exposure and privations proved fatal to many. Driven from their villages, their cocoa-nut trees cut down, their property and crops destroyed, and, unable to till their land, the natives suffered severely from sickness and famine, besides those who fell by the fire of the British troops, or suffered execution for their treasonable actions. Dr. Davy, who had the best opportunities of ascertaining the loss of life occasioned by this rebellion, estimates that of the British at one thousand; and I believe he certainly is not over the amount, when he says that ten thousand natives were cut off by war or its consequences at this period.

After the rebellion had continued for nine months, no favorable impression had been made by the great exertions of our troops, who were nearly exhausted by incessant fatigue, and extreme privations in a tropical climate; it is even understood that arrangements were in contemplation for withdrawing the British force from the interior, when a sudden change occurred. This was principally caused by disunion amongst the leaders of the rebels, who were incapable of continued perseverance in any one object, or of sacrificing their petty jealousies and personal disputes, even to forward a cause in which they had periled their lives and hereditary properties,—things almost equally dear to a Kandian chief.

Madugalla, an influential headman of Dumbara, coming to an open rupture with Kaepitapola, detected, and openly exposed the impostor King, whom he placed in the stocks, and it was then ascertained beyond a doubt, that the pretender was a native of the village from which he took the name of Wilbawe, and that he had formerly been a Buddhist priest.

Wilbawe contrived to extricate himself . . . , and escaped to the remote province of Nuwara Kalawia; there he had the good fortune to remain unnoticed for fourteen years, although at one time he was compelled to assist a party who was searching for him near the deserted city of Annuradhapoora. The large reward that still remained offered for his apprehension, having stimulated the perseverance of a Buddhist priest (who was familiar with his features), he at last in his wanderings recognized the object of his search, and, having given information, Wilbawe was secured in 1829. When arrested, it was found that he had received a severe injury in the shoulder from a wild elephant, and that hard labor and anxiety had greatly changed his appearance, and given him a peculiarly melancholy cast of countenance; he had been a handsome man, and with features strongly resembling the Kandian royal family, of which native scandal said he was an illegitimate member. He was tried and convicted, but afterwards received a pardon by orders from Britain. After the detection of Wilbawe, our parties were uniformly successful, the insurgents gradually dispersed, their leaders fled, and the three of most influence, viz. Kaepitapola, Madugalla, and Pilame Talawe, were apprehended and brought to trial. Pilame Talawe, a weak and indolent man, was a son of the late first Adikar of the same name, but as free from the cruel propensities of his father as from his abilities and energy;—he was transported to Mauritius. Madugalla and Kaepitapola were beheaded . . . ; Eheylapola was not tried, nor were his lands confiscated; but he was banished to the Isle of France, along with several chiefs of inferior note. On the termination of hostilities and return to order, an entire change in the management of the Kandian provinces was accomplished. The paramount influence of the chiefs in the different districts was destroyed, by placing civilians, or British officers, in authority over them, to collect the revenue, and administer justice; while all the inferior headmen, instead of being appointed annually by the chief, received their situations direct from Government. This arrangement, not only gave increased security to the Government, but enabled the poor native suitor to obtain that justice which he had little chance of receiving under the former system, where money or influence might alike bias the judge, or direct the evidence.

We could not blame the chiefs if they had attempted to re-establish a native dynasty, which was hallowed in their eyes by its antiquity, and by conformity to the established religion; but, to call their exertions in this rebellion patriotism, would be to dignify it with a name of which their motives were unworthy. Self-interest, and to restore their own power over the mass of the people, whom they had so *long* oppressed, was their principal aim and final object; the restoration of a native monarchy was a secondary consideration, but a necessary step; the means by which they endeavored to accomplish their purpose were often cruel, and generally treacherous. It is true, the British had acquired the quiet possession of the Kandian country by a convention with the people, represented by their chiefs, and not by direct conquests; but this circumstance was more a point of honor, than a substantial difference to the people. Their history contained the records of many attempts to expel foreign invaders from the land, and hitherto, whether against Europeans or Asiatics, success had always sanctified these endeavors. This was a powerful incentive to the headmen, and must be considered as a proportionably strong excuse for their rebellion, by which they hoped to regain that position and precedence so much valued by Kandians, and which they perceived had passed from them to rest with Europeans. Many of them must also have felt that their indolent and intriguing dispositions were more suited to a despot's court, than to acquiring the habits of activity. . . .

After the rebellion was suppressed, no unnecessary punishments were inflicted; even to the rebel leaders, or their descendants, great consideration was shown, as soon as it could be done, without exciting the idea that our clemency was the offspring of timidity. Indeed, I cannot help thinking, that hundreds of British, and thousands of native lives might have been saved, if, at the commencement of the rebellion, a stern and severe example had been made of the persons and property of those who first committed acts of treason and murder, and had taken the field in arms against the British Government. It would have struck terror into all classes, and have been a sufficient excuse to the lower ranks for withdrawing to those homes which, in the event of their remaining absent, would be rendered desolate; for it was no affection for their leaders, or pretence at principle, that induced the multitude to rise in insurrection; they had no interest in the cause, and ventured their lives on no stronger temptation than ancient habits of blind obedience to the chiefs, or for fear of revenge in the event of their success.

The Moormen (as the Mohammedan inhabitants are called), who are numerous in several districts, attached themselves on every occasion, and zealously, to the British interest; and at the commencement of the rebellion, promises were made to them, by proclamation, with regard to their not again being put under Kandian (Cingalese) headmen, which I do not think were afterwards fairly and fully performed; for while compulsory labor existed, they were called out by, and performed duties under, Cingalese headmen; this never appeared to me either politic or just.

After the departure of Sir Robert Brownrigg, Sir Edward Barnes, who succeeded to the government, planned and superintended with unceasing vigilance the opening up of the Kandian provinces, by the formation of extensive carriage roads, and building substantial bridges. Under him, the country derived all the benefit that could be produced by unrecompensed compulsory labor, which was exacted according to the customs of that despotism, to the powers of which the British Government had succeeded. The untiring vigilance and personal activity which Sir Edward Barnes exerted in superintending public works, alone caused so vicious a system to be of public benefit; under any man of less energy, unrecompensed compulsory labor would have been an unmitigated curse, enforcing caste, depopulating the country, and producing no adequate results. Each subdivision of class or caste, was called out for service by its own headman, who, as he received no pay, depended for the amount of his perquisites and peculations on the number under him; it was, therefore, a motive paramount to all others in natives, self-interest, which insured the headman retaining all the members of his department in their original vocation and due subjection. Not only did this system maintain caste with the utmost strictness, but it retained and supported in full power over the people, those headmen whose interests could never be otherwise than opposed to a regular Government.

It must also be considered, that without injustice to individuals, regularity of system, backed by power to enforce all legal rights, enabled the British Government to exact much more, both of labor and revenue, than any native despot would have ventured to demand.

In 1831, Sir Robert Wilmot Horton arrived as Governor; and next year, in consequence of the report of His Majesty's Commissioners of inquiry, the Magna Charta of Ceylon, the order of the King in council abolishing all compulsory service, reached the island, and the native inhabitants passed in a day from a state more bitter than slavery to the most perfect freedom. In their former oppressed state, it is true, that justice was impartially administered to the rich and to the poor, in so far as the facts of the ease could be ascertained; yet the rich man was disgusted by impartial conduct in the judges, while the poor suitors did not benefit by it; for the rich litigant could bribe the influential native in office, and he could command the oaths of those who, placed and secured under his control, were not only liable to be overworked by his orders, but were even subject to punishment at his caprice.

A charter soon followed the abolition of forced labor, and the people, having already obtained freedom, now found easy access to substantial and speedy justice, whilst every situation was thrown open to their competition, and the acquirements and character of the individual, not the color of his skin, became the only tests of fitness for every office. Three gentlemen, natives of Ceylon, were introduced into the legislative council on terms of perfect equality with the other unofficial members, although it required some firmness on the part of Government to carry into effect this liberal provision of the supreme Government.

Of the new system for administering justice in Ceylon I shall attempt an outline, as it appears to me extremely simple, at the same time that it has proved most efficient. In the first place, a district judge, with three assessors, selected daily by lot, form the District Court, which exercises exclusive original jurisdiction within certain geographical limits. All civil cases whatever, arising within its bounds, must first be decided in that court; but every decision there pronounced may be appealed from, and revised before a judge of the Supreme Court, with three assessors, on half yearly circuit. . . .

In criminal cases the power of district courts was restricted, and persons accused of great crimes were committed for trial before the Supreme Court on circuits, where they were prosecuted by the King's advocate, and tried by a jury of thirteen intelligent persons of any class or color. In civil cases, where judgments were appealed against from a District Court, the appellant was prevented from benefitting by delay; and in criminal cases the judge, notwithstanding the appeal, might carry the sentence into effect on his own responsibility. Soon after the beneficial and important changes consequent upon the abolition of compulsory labor, and the introduction of the improved system of administering justice began to be felt.

The 1848 Rebellion

Governor Torrington

Next to the 1818 rebellion, the 1848 rebellion proved the most serious threat to British rule during their century and a half presence in Sri Lanka. In this remarkably revealing letter from George Byng, 7th Viscount Torrington, the then British governor of Ceylon, to Lord Grey, his superior in London, the perspective of the colonial gaze is perfectly reflected and a variety of important issues central to the political economy of the country in the first thirty years after the Kandyan kingdom was disestablished are clearly marked. By this time, Buddhist temple lands had been alienated from monastic control, European coffee planters had moved into the interior, roads had made the hill country accessible, and so on. The governor muses on how the British have failed to protect the religion of the Kandyans, how the Buddha's tooth relic retains enormous power in the eyes of the Kandyans, and that perhaps the British ought to think about a fresh treaty with a people who need enlightened British leadership for the future of their own well-being.

Private

Queen's House,
Colombo.
August 11 1848

My dear Lord Grey,

It shall be my endeavour to make my letter as short and precise as I possibly can of the important information I have to communicate. I have in the first instance to inform you that a Rebellion broke out in the Kandyan Provinces on the 28th of July, that a King was proclaimed, crowned at Dambool [Dambulla] and that with an armed force on that day he took possession of the small town of Matale 16 miles [north] from Kandy. Before I proceed any further in stating the steps I have taken, it will I am sure be satisfactory to you to know that at the date I am now writing the 11th of August the outbreak has been promptly and successfully subdued—and I hope by the latest accounts I shall be able to furnish you with by the 15th of this month, that order has been restored and the mass of the people returned to their usual avocation.

My letter shall be divided into three branches. Firstly the steps taken, secondly the cause of the Rebellion, thirdly the further policy to be followed. At eight o'clock on the morning of the 29th of July, I received an express from Mr. Buller, the Government Agent at Kandy, with the information above stated, that he had consultations with the authorities at Kandy and that Col. Drought, the Commander of the Garrison had marched a force of one hundred men of the 15th Regiment and 160 of the Ceylon Rifles at 8 o'clock in the evening of the 28th to Matale, little before daylight on the 29th—and, as it now for certain appears, from eight to ten thousand men arrived with guns and spears in the pass about 2 miles from Matale. Nothing could be better than the behaviour of the soldiers. The Malays were thrown in the jungle on both sides. The 15th [Regiment] advanced up the Pass and completely routed the rebels with the loss since ascertained to be 200 killed and wounded, besides a large number of prisoners. The first official report would make the loss much less, and the number of the rebels smaller—but Col. Drought by a letter received yesterday, states that the information since obtained leads to the undoubted accuracy of what I now inform you. We had only one man wounded—The King was nearly taken, his carriage, his cook and the Capt[ain] of his body-guard was secured.

Matale had been completely sacked—everything in the houses and bazaar stolen and many of the houses on the estates in the neighbourhood plundered, and buildings and machinery damaged—Sir Herbert Maddock who happened to be at Kandy at the time, writes me word the damage on his estate is quite equal to £2,000. On the 30th the rebels made an attack on Karnagalle [Kurunegala] a place of some importance about 26 miles from Kandy, at half past seven in the morning. Undoubtedly, out of the number there calculated at 4,000, a great portion were in the affair at Matale. Fortunately the Ass[istan]t Agent there had informed me that he thought something was going wrong tho[ugh] he could hardly tell what, and I had directed the Major General to send a detachment there, and Lt. Annesley with 25 Malays marched into the town within half an hour after the rebels had attacked, released all the prisoners in gaol and were endeavouring to break open the Cutchery. The rebels again in the first instance fired on the troops who returned it smartly and drove them out of place with the loss of 26 killed, besides wounded and prisoners—half an hour later all the money amounting to £1,300 and the stamps to £2,000 would have been lost.

Nothing [sic] can have behaved better than Lt. Annesley or with more prudence. When again attacked, he repulsed them without attempting to follow, which with his small force would have been madness. They again made their appearance for the third time but would [not] allow the men to get within fire of them. Since then we have every reason to believe the rebels have dispersed and tho[ugh] undoubtedly parties of armed men are taking advantage of the consternation of the peaceful inhabitants to plunder and rob, it is very improbable that any very large body of men will again concentrate to attack. But I regret to say that this rebellion has been of long standing as far as intention goes and that every chief, priest and headmen were aware of it and that they only were waiting for what might be considered an opportunity, and by the priests a fortunate moment, to commence. A mere accident caused the affair at Matale to take place—a drunken horse-keeper discovered the rebels in the jungles but the intention was to allow the troops to arrive at Matale unmolested, when, so it is stated, 20,000 armed rebels [who] were crowded in the jungle beside the road the whole way would have appeared and cut off the communications with Kandy. One of my reports says, "It is a thing never to be forgotten in the history of Ceylon, and it is not a bad guide for our conduct towards the Kandyans, that altho[ugh] there were thousands of insurgents concealed in the jungles all along the road near the pass and from there to Matale the greater portion were passed by Lillies' detachment unobserved—not a native in the country came to inform him or the Gov[ernmen]t Agent of the fact, and but for the Malabar horse-keeper the party would in all human probability have reached Matale without seeing an enemy, tho[ugh] seen by themselves all the way, and this detachment would have been effectively cut off from Kandy." More damnable treachery on the part of the Kandians could hardly be conceived. Betrayed by every one of our native public servants, is it such a wonder that our information was so slender? If they had succeeded in getting our troops safe to Matale another attack was to have been made on the other side so as to call off more troops from Kandy and having thus weakened the Garrison by every possible artifice. On Sunday the 30th at 11 o'clock whilst every-body, troops [and] all, were likely to be at Church, from the four roads immense bodies of armed men were to rush into the town and with such a force and at such a moment, it is impossible to overestimate the danger and misery which might have overtaken us. Either the town or the barrack might have been left to the tender mercies of the rebels, and if the king had got possession of the Tooth this outbreak (undoubtedly a religious one) would have flared with ten times more vigour. To you it must seem extraordinary, that such bodies of men should not have been observed—but a Kandian can steal through the jungles almost as well as an American Indian. A little rice and what they pick up is sufficient to supply their wants, and they will all disperse and reunite at a given point under priestly influence, and it would be difficult to observe it. Kandy is jungle all round the town.

Thus far I have stated what steps were taken before the receipt of any orders from myself. As it happened on the receipt of the intelligence, I was alone with the exception of the General—all my executives being down to Galle to meet Arthur Buller who was expected out, Mr. Bernard to meet MacCarthy, and the Queen's Advocate on circuit, tho[ugh] he fortunately came in about the middle of the day. I am happy however to be able to state that all the steps taken by me were fully approved of by the Ex[ecutive] Council which I called together at the earliest possible period. The first thing I did was to send over for Col[onel] Fraser who commanded in the last Kandian Rebellion, and whose knowledge of the Kandians and the country is undoubted. Having read the papers he unhesitatingly gave it his opinion that the outbreak was of the most serious nature and that unless decisive measures were immediately taken, it would speedily gain head; he further stated that he had always given his opinion to the authorities, that the Kandians would rebel if ever they could see any possible means or chance of succeeding. On the arrival of the General, and finding we two could make a Council, we formed one and put the Kandian District under Martial Law.

We also ordered 300 men to march from this immediately into the interior on different points to secure the road and pass between this and Kandy. Seaforth took a body of men down to Hambantotta [*sic*] who were to march from there to Badulla and reinforce that place—our weakest point, and he carried orders to Trincomalee for 2 companies of the 27th and one Company of Rifles to march to Dambool in the rear of the rebels. The map that I send home will show you the whole movement which it is a great comfort to feel was in every way right, and which on reflection we could not have altered. The number of troops at our disposal was under 3,000 and the necessity of keeping a strong force in Kandy and other places made it evident that the means at our disposal were insufficient and the General stated to me he could not answer for keeping open our communications, with the men at our disposal. I therefore called out the pensioners, placed the Pioneer Corps at the disposal of the general, amounting to 1,000 men, who were invaluable for carrying ammunition—and the *Lady Mary Wood* being at Galle, I secured her services and she steamed off that night to Madras with a dispatch to Pottinger stating how I was situated, and asking for 300 men to garrison Trincomalee and likewise requesting he would have other troops in readiness in case they should be required. The General at the same time wrote to Sir George Barclay. Nothing would have been more promptly executed. The 300 of the 25th Queen's Regiment were at Trincomalee on Thursday the 3 of August, thus enabling our own men to march immediately into the interior. Pottinger informed me he had troops also in readiness in case we should want more, and which I have every reason to hope will not be required. The Queen's Advocate when he arrived concurred in our views and immediately prepared the Proclamation which was printed immediately in English and Cingalese [sic], and was sent off by an express mail at 3 o'clock in charge of two officers, two soldiers and the Head of the Police. Not then knowing what had taken place at Matale we felt some anxiety about getting through the pass, however nothing impeded their progress, and when the Kandians opened their eyes on the morning, they found Martial Law proclaimed and posted all over the place. It is impossible to overestimate the value of this step; it took the people by surprise. There are plenty living who remember the year 1818 and the similar steps taken by Sir R. Brownrigg (th[ough] with eleven thousand men it took 13 months to subdue the country) they well knew the powers it gave, and a strong check was thus immediately given to what might otherwise have been an hourly increasing evil. In 1844 a rebellion similar to this was on the eve of breaking out, but an accidental circumstance discovered it to Major Kelson of the C[eylon] Rifles. The parties were tried but some of the principal leaders got off from insufficient evidence. One man was imprisoned for 14 years, a priest. Since this outbreak I have had him examined, and tho[ugh] he could know little—indeed nothing of what has been going on, his statements fully confirm all the information we have since obtained, and he reminded us of his remarkable words: "Remember there are four roads into Kandy." To Col. Drought of the 15th Regiment commanding in the Central Province the powers determined upon by the Government for the suppression the Rebellion has been entrusted. Most ably, firmly and vigorously, has he carried out his instructions. Property to a large amount has been sequestered amongst which is that of the H Chief [?], and one of those who had a key of the Tooth. Court martials have various prisoners—a sort of District King under the Pretender was taken in at Kurnagalla tried and shot, his body hung up as an example. The Captain of the body guard a notorious robber was tried and shot and another who fired from jungle on an escort. Many others have been sentenced to transportation. He [the Pretender] is still at large, but can hardly escape much longer. We are close also on the heel of his brother. In a former letter I mentioned that this pretender was moving about the country and we were endeavouring to secure him. He appeared from reports to have few followers, and government being completely betrayed by its servant prevented our obtaining information of the influence he had exerted; for years he had been moving about under various disguises. Thus far I have detailed to you the steps taken to restore order. Confidence is gradually increasing, tho[ugh] we are much tormented by bodies of armed men, who taking advantage of the state of affairs go about the country robbing and mal-treating the quiet and orderly inhabitants, and of course harassing and overworking the troops.

I must also state that it must be some time before it would be wise or prudent to reduce our force in the Kandian country—however successful we have been, we can place no reliance on them, their treachery to us is [of] the deepest dye. Now I come to a question of the greatest importance and important to myself as far as my reputation is concerned, and alike of the utmost consequence, that you yourself should be in full possession of every possible information that you may be in a position to decide on the important points that this Rebellion gives rise to. What is the cause of the Rebellion? That an attempt has been made here and will undoubtedly be made in England to prove that the financial policy I have thought it my duty to carry out, has created dissatisfaction in the minds of the people—produced hatred to the government and brought about a Rebellion, that this course will be pursued I have not the shadow of a doubt, any more than I am equally certain Mr. MacChristie will write the article in *The Daily News*. I am prepared to meet these statements with a direct negative. I am prepared to defend if necessary, every act of my government, not only by the (I may say) unanimous votes that were given in their favour, but by the approbation of those here who now find fault with them by the recommendations of various Committees of the Legislative Council since 1841 and by the recommendations of every able man who has written or interested himself in the affairs of Ceylon. I have no doubt that the measures passed by the government, if fairly and judiciously carried out, will lend greatly to the future, prosperity of this Colony. But whilst I state these opinions to you most broadly and distinctly, I cannot disguise from you the fact that Dr. Elliot of *The [Colombo] Observer Newspaper* ever since the news of the French Revolution reached us, has with the assistance of a few ruined men, bankrupts in fortune and questionable in character, laboured to infuse into the minds of the ignorant natives the most mistaken notions of the views and intentions of government. The policy of the French people has been held out to their ignorant minds, their political rights pointed out to them (not however that they understood what these rights were), they were told the government treated them as beasts of burden, and papers were circulated tho[ugh] unfortunately they cannot be brought home to the guilty parties, telling them to refuse to obey the law. You must understand that there is no folly that these unfortunate people may not be made to believe by ill-disposed persons. The views of Dr. Elliot and his friends in circulating all this inflammatory matter was with no intention of causing the Rebellion. They as well as the Government were ignorant of the deep and long considered plot of the Kandians to overturn the government. Their object was clear, the game they played was representative government to be gained by the people at their instigation and thus for the future the Colony would have been ruled by Dr. Elliot and a few half-caste proctors. But the priests and chiefs, sharp intelligent men, saw that all this inflammatory matter helped their cause, they encouraged it, added to it, and the meeting which took place mentioned in my last letter at Kandy was a sham got-up affair by the chiefs and the priests who took care to be absent, but stimulated the people previously with drink and thus created a noise and talk which would encourage a feeling of doubt amongst the people and add to the chances of the success of the Rebellion. In my dispatch I enclose a letter from Tennent to me, reporting his tour through the now disturbed district; his letter is worthy of your attention. The people complained not of the taxes, but even when explained to them rather rejoiced at them. The advantage to them was evident. The power of the chiefs, priests and headmen over them is great; the poor wretches were told to meet at particular places, were told they had a king and must obey him and they did so. The feeling against Dr. Elliot since the rebellion has been strong. Merchants, Planters and all have come forward with addresses of thanks for my prompt measures and offers of assistance. The amount of property that has been placed in fearful jeopardy by Dr. Elliot is immense; with the slightest success, in a few hours no coffee estate would have remained in the island, every shilling of British cap would have been swept away. Our coffee estates are a cause of deadly hatred to the Kandians—previous to their being planted, the Kandians turned their bullocks loose in them. War between the bullocks and the planters has long been a very serious grievance and difficult to deal with. The mass of the coffee planters, many of them the very worst class of Englishmen has very much tended to lower and degrade our caste and character in the eyes of the natives. The habits of the planters particularly with

the women has been most objectionable and in the eyes of a Kandian
a coffee planter is a term of reproach. Whilst coffee cultivation has
progressed with us, the Kandians have stood still, but their wealth has
increased prodigiously by the increased price of every article they have
to sell. Money in immense sums is buried for which they have no use,
and reports say that murder is generally committed over the treasure,
that the demon or spirit may protect it. Our roads, the only means by
which we can hold the country, are objectionable in the eyes of the
chiefs and priests. Our position has been safe and the time has fully arrived when means must be adopted not only for the proper government
of the country but for the security of life and property.

On the 26th of July an attempt was made at Borella about 4 miles
from this, by Dr. Elliot to get up a public meeting (nobody knew for
what exactly) a large mob arrived and immediately made an attack on
the Police and the Government Agent. A serious row seemed inevitable,
and an express was sent on to me for the troops which were on their
way in a few moments. I went out also myself and I am inclined to think
I was the means of stopping the disturbance—as the mob gave 3 cheers
for the Queen, 3 for myself and departed. Dr. Elliot brought the petition
pretended to have been got [up] by the people and signatured, tho[ugh]
the said petition and signatures were weeks old. It was in Cingalese, and
he pretended not to know exactly the contents. However he said he did
not sign it—if he had he would have been in a scrape as a treasonable
passage was the concluding paragraph.

If any doubt existed as to the people being well off, the fact that money
will not tempt them to work is in my mind very conclusive. I believe
any man could earn in one month's labour sufficient money not only
to pay every tax that could be thought of but nearly keep himself for a
year. They are rich and idle and live off lands probably stolen from the
Crown and spend their lives in drinking and every sort of excess. The
sum of money supposed to be subscribed to the Pretender is very great.
Men who pretended to complain of the taxation have subscribed £4 to
£5, a sum greater than they possibly could be called upon in their whole
lives to pay to the state. Neither must it be forgotten that supposing they
had succeeded in raising up the king, what were they to gain, or rather
what would they have returned to but a state of the most abject slavery
and oppression! But it is an undoubted fact that it is the sort of government they prefer. It is the only sort of authority which they understand.
The mildness of our government, and the excellence and justice of our
laws, is not only thrown away but it gives them a feeling of contempt

towards us. . . . I am now coming to the cause that has brought about the Rebellion, which has lost us the influence of the Chiefs and Priests, caused them to betray us and jeopardised our interests at stake—it is an evil which dates back from the first moment which idle British government violated the Treaty of 1815, in so far as they refused by warrant to appoint the head priests to some Buddhist temples. This I think was in the time of Stuart Mackenzie. A blow was then struck at Buddhism which each year has been more severely felt. Temples are without head priests; those who act cannot legally enforce their rights and are cheated of their dues. The temples . . . are falling to decay. This is felt equally by the chiefs who are a sort of lay priests. I cannot forget the words of one of their best men in addressing me. "What good have we gained by British rule if you violate your Treatises—not only cease to protect our Religion, but on the contrary endeavour to destroy it! I am a loyal subject of the Queen but we have been unfairly and unjustly used in this, a matter to us of the utmost importance!" They took over the Tooth from us with evident dislike; in our hands this prized treasure was safe, and possibly our custody of it increased its value in the eyes of the mass of the people. They cannot trust one another and there is the greatest danger of the Tooth being carried off. That it can be used as a means to cause an outbreak I have no doubt and tho[ugh] I dare not propose it I wish from the bottom of my heart the Tooth was safe in Buckingham Palace. Believe me, unless we have some moral control over the chiefs and priests and unless they have some advantage by supporting the government we shall always be liable to treason and Rebellion. They have great power over the people who will blindly obey their orders. The priest who crowned this King at Dambool is in custody. He states that the first question put to him by the King, was, are you for the Buddhist religion or for the government? When the priest said both, he got in a rage and said that was not possible.

That this outbreak would have come sometime or another I cannot doubt. Dr. Elliot (the [illegible] of Ceylon) in fomenting discord gave the [required] unity and brought matters to a crisis. The despatches which go by this mail I think truly and clearly prove that the disturbance at Borella had nothing to do with those at Kandy, that the former was an attempt to intimidate the government. The other was a deep and long concealed plot ready at any moment to burst. Now as to the future policy to be followed with the Kandians! They have been governed and are a savage treacherous and discontented people. First is to be done with our Headmen both paid and unpaid! All of them are implicated. It is easy to dismiss them but what are we to substitute in their place? This is the most serious question and I am going to Kandy on the 16th to consult what can be done. Their places are highly prized as they give power and influence. Those we retain must be moved to different parts of the country. The unpaid system is bad, the exemption of their lands from taxation as a remuneration is wrong. At first sight a percentage seems a fair plan on the sums collected. Then comes the settlement of the Buddhist question. Are the priests who raised the rebellion not to suffer, will it be right to exempt their lands now and increase their wealth and enable them to rebel again? They say we have violated the treaty of 1815. Equally so have they now. Why not do away with the treaty on both sides and start afresh! The Buddhist Religion is a harmless one. I doubt much if any real advance has been made to Christianity on the part of the natives. Even the sums spent by the Ceylon Government on edu- cational purposes has not produced the very best results, and therefore whether properly protecting their religion without at the same time encouraging it will not be our wisest plan! They are a helpless people and utterly unable to manage their own affairs. It is necessary to act for them or legislate for their temporal affairs and the law must give valid- ity to the Priests they nominate, or else a governor's warrant must be used as agreed on by the Treaty of 1815.

The government has been mild and gentle with them, and I fear much that in their ignorance they have judged it to be fear, base as they are. I do not desire to visit too harshly or severely on them the sins and mischief they have now committed, but I must say that in any instruc- tions you may give with regard to the Kandians, bear in mind that it can be only by firmness and determination they can be governed; the bending on our part or attempts at conciliation will be looked upon by them as fear and encourage them again to be troublesome. They have no causes of complaint except the inconvenience they experience and the expense they are put to by the complicated and lengthened pro- ceedings of our Law Courts and the question of cattle stealing and this difficulty is from its being almost impossible to decide on the evidence. A man charges another with stealing his bullocks, he replies by charg- ing him with having stolen them in the first place and an equal amount of evidence is brought on both sides. I am told 1,500 cases in one District could not be settled from the amount of false testimony on both sides. The people are rich and lightly taxed. I believe there is no spot on the earth where less poverty exists than in Ceylon. Out of the disturbance (if you concur with my views) I believe good will come. The Kandians have had a severe lesson. Hitherto they have always had a sort of idea that by a bold but treacherous act they could reconquer the country. That delusion must be vanished I should hope forever.

The blood that has been shed, the lands that have been sequestered and the fear that Martial Law has produced in their minds cannot but be advantageous to the government. What I would wish is that the lands taken may in the first instance be used to pay the heavy expenses this outbreak has brought on the Colony. . . .

That attempts will be made to cast blame on me I well know. You have the whole case before you, not a point is kept back, nothing is highly coloured with a view of casting other matter in the shade. I can rely with perfect confidence on any conclusion you may deem it your duty to arrive at. If you approve of what has passed and agree to steps I have taken a few words to that effect will support and comfort me—and if on the contrary, you consider blame attached to my conduct, I shall submit with patience to your reproof with the confident belief that it will be with as much regret that you write it, as it will be painful to me to receive it—I may say that all who have acted with me have cordially sanctioned my measures, and given me every support during the disturbance.

Believe me my dear Lord Grey,
Yours very sincerely and truly, Torrington.

P.S.: Sir Herbert Maddock whose opinion on all subjects must be valuable has at my request written you his opinions on all these points. I have studiously avoided any knowledge of the contents of the letter thinking it would be most valuable in your eyes, tho[ugh] I at the same time must say he, Sir Herbert, is not a man to write anything he does not fully concur in—I am glad to be able to state that every public servant too has shown the greatest zeal and activity. All the respectable merchants and planters have come forward with addresses of thanks for my prompt measures and offers of assistance. Col. Drought who commanded at Kandy highly merits your approbation and I wish you may consider it right to show him some mark of favour. Lt. Annesley who defended Kurunagalla deserves also praise. You must forgive this hurried letter for the press of business and the number of interruptions makes it almost impossible to collect my thoughts. I hope by the next mail to be able to place before you something of a plan by which government can hold a proper control and influence over the Kandian people. Tennent, Sir H. Maddock all say that this outbreak should be made use of by government for its own advantage, not unjustly, but simply to prevent a recurrence of these evils.

Leonard Woolf's Ceylon

Leonard Woolf

Better known in the West as the husband who published the writings of his wife, Virginia Woolf, Leonard Woolf remains something of an icon in Sri Lanka. His novel Village in the Jungle *was made into a very well-received film by the film-maker Lester James Peiris, and the book remained in print with Oxford University Press into the 1980s through their Madras house. Woolf's diaries reflect a man with a piercing intellect, a sensitive moral consciousness, and an abiding affection for the people of the countryside. Woolf spent six years altogether in Jaffna, Kandy, and Hambantota as an assistant government agent for the British government between 1905 and 1911. As can be seen from the following excerpts, Woolf's experiences in Ceylon led him to oppose the imperial colonial enterprise. The introduction to his diary and three of its daily entries are followed by Woolf's short story about caste consciousness in Jaffna.*

From the Introduction to Diaries in Ceylon, 1908–1911

I was nearly three years in Hambantota as Assistant Government Agent. I grew to be extremely fond of the place and of its peace. It was pure Sinhalese, no planters, no Europeans at all except a District Judge in Tangalla, two Irrigation Engineers, and an Assistant Superintendent of Police. It was entirely rural agricultural in the west, and a vast stretch of jungle with some sanctuary in the east. There were no real towns, no lorry, hardly any roads. I continually travelled about the place and got to know well almost every yard of it, and to an extent the way of life and the attitude to the life of its inhabitants. From early times, I think, the British Government of Ceylon very sensibly required their administrators in the provinces and districts to keep a diary of what they did. These accounts often provide an extraordinarily interesting historical evidence of Ceylon life and British rule. For instance, I remember reading the diaries in the Jaffna Kachcheri which went right up to the early years of the 19th century. The diaries, which I had for the three years in Hambantota and which are now being furnished, show the work which I did there and to some extent its impact upon me. The impact of my experiences during those years was powerful. I was fascinated and deeply moved by the lives of the villagers and their psychology, and also by the perpetual menace of nature, the beautiful and at the same time sinister and savage life of the jungle. . . .

When I left Hambantota and Ceylon on my first leave in 1911, I was in considerable doubt about my future. I had practically decided that much as I liked the Island, its people and a great deal of my work, I would not spend my life as an imperial Civil Servant. When I first came out I had very few political opinions and had given little or no thought to the problems of imperialism. But my seven years in the Service had made me more and more doubtful whether I liked the prospect of spending my whole life as an imperialist ruling non-Europeans. After six months in England, all my doubts had vanished and I sent in my resignation from the Ceylon Civil Service. The first thing which I did after that was to write *The Village in the Jungle*. The book itself and the diaries show how the idea of the book came out of my experiences as the Assistant Government Agent. I do not think that when I left Hambantota the idea of the book was consciously in my mind, but it must have been at the back of my mind, and by the time I had resigned I knew exactly what I wanted to write.

Excerpts from Diaries in Ceylon

NOVEMBER 17th [1908]
Drove into Hambantota.
Government has approved the recommendation about chenas [slash-and-burn farming]. Chenas are not to be completely disallowed to villagers finally settled and that certain portions shall be set apart for chenaing in villages which need it. I see from the Galle Kachcheri file which was sent to me for my information that the G.A. reports that I am continually writing in to say that the villagers must have chenas or they will starve. I have of course never made such a statement which would be quite untrue. No people in Ceylon starve except a few Tamil coolies who are driven off or leave estates in Sinhalese Districts. But it is true that there are not a few villages in this District in which if chenas are disallowed the villages will gradually die out not from starvation but by a slow process of extinction which will undoubtedly be accompanied by a considerable amount of distress. There are village tanks in these villages, and I am compelling the people to restore them, and the people are restoring them; but they very rarely get a supply

of water which makes cultivation possible. There are no gardens and no coconut trees and no wells or if there are wells, there is no water in them for 9 months out of 12. These villages do not lie on the main roads but anyone who rides 15 miles due north of Hambantota will see two or three of them surrounded not by a "sea of chena" but by scrub jungle a great deal of which has probably not been chenaed for ages. It does not appear to be facing facts to refuse these people chenas except in extreme and extraordinary circumstances because kurakkan heats the stomach. The facts to be faced are that the people will not leave their villages unless they are driven to the last extremity and that in 5 years out of six, nothing will grow except a chena crop. If chenas therefore are not allowed in 5 years out of 6 in such villages it means that there is considerable hardship.

MAY 12th.

Holiday.

At 5 p.m. I was just going out when a messenger arrived to say that there was a riot going on in the town. The Buddhist procession had, he said, been stopped by the Mohamedans when passing the mosque and a large number of persons were now fighting with sticks and stones. I went at once to the mosque but the fight was over. Eight men were more or less injured including Mr. Amerasingha, Gansathawa Clerk, who lives near and had tried to stop the row when it began and been hit by a stone in the face. The story at first told to me was that the Mohamedans attacked the Buddhist procession first with sticks. I was therefore not a little surprised to see 6 or 7 Mohamedans wounded and covered with blood and only one Sinhalese. I got hold of 3 or 4 non-residents who had been present and began Police Court proceedings at once. They were all Sinhalese and their evidence very soon showed that the row had started by the Buddhist procession tom-toming before they passed the mosque. Some Mohamedans tried to stop this and the Buddhists fell upon the Mohamedans, the latter being severely handled. The Mohamedans in the Bazaar hearing of this rushed to the spot in large numbers tearing up the fences to provide weapons. The Buddhists seeing they would be overwhelmed sought sanctuary in the police officer's house where they were soon surrounded by a crowd of angry Mohamedans.

This was, of course, not quite the story as told by the Sinhalese, but as they had had no time to prepare evidence, they very clearly gave it away. After recording sufficient evidence to make it clear, I adjourned.

APRIL 20th.

To Ranna via main channel, Alutgama and Hatagala.

A curious incident happened at Mini Etiliya tank: I was walking round the back of the tank under some trees, trying to get a shot at crocodiles after some teal. I had just passed a tree when I heard behind me a tremendous hissing. Turning round I saw under the tree a crocodile standing with her mouth wide open 6 feet from a friend who was with me. The crocodile was hissing like a hundred serpents and lashing its tail from side to side. My friend fired with No. 4 two shots straight into her and she turned to make off and I gave her two more as she passed me. I followed her into a swamp where I found her with a huge hole in her head. To make quite sure she was dead I prodded her with a stick and she turned round savagely on us. We dispatched her and went back to the tree where we found many broken egg shells: apparently the young crocodiles had only just hatched out and her attack on us was due to her maternal feelings.

The Two Brahmans

Yalpanam is a very large town in the north of Ceylon; but nobody who suddenly found himself in it would believe this. Only in two or three streets is there any bustle or stir of people. It is like a gigantic village that for centuries has slept and grown, and sleeps and grows, under a forest of coconut trees and fierce sun. All the streets are the same, dazzling dusty roads between high fences made of the dried leaves of the coconut palms. Behind the fences, and completely hidden by them, are the compounds; and in the compounds still more hidden under the palms and orange and lime trees are the huts and houses of the Tamils who live there.

The north of the town lies, as it has lain for centuries, sleeping by the side of the blue lagoon, and there is a hut standing now in a compound by the side of the lagoon, where it had stood for centuries. In this hut there lived a man called Chellaya who was by caste a Brahman, and in the compound next to Chellaya's lived another Brahman called Chittampalam, and in all the other 50 or 60 compounds around them lived other Brahmans. They belonged to the highest of all castes in Yalpanam; and they could not eat food with or touch or marry into any other caste, nor could they carry earth on their heads or work at any trade, without being defiled or losing caste. Therefore all the Brahmans live together in this quarter of the town, so that they may not be defiled but may marry of their sons and daughters to daughters and sons of other Brahmans. Chellaya and Chittampalam and all the Brahmans knew that they and their fathers and their fathers' fathers had lived in the same way by the side of the blue lagoon under the palm trees for many thousands of years. They did no work, for there was no need to work. The dhobi or washer caste man, who washed the clothes of Brahmans and of no other caste, washed their white cloths and in return was given rice and allowed to be present at weddings and funerals. And there was the barber caste man who shaved the Brahmans and no other caste. And half a mile from their compounds were their Brahman rice fields in which Chellaya and each of the other Brahmans had shares; some shares had descended to them from their fathers and their grandfathers and great-grandfathers and so on from the first Brahmans, and other shares had been brought to them as dowry with their wives. These fields were sown twice a year, and the work of cultivation was done by Mukkuwa caste men. This is a custom, that Mukkuwa caste men cultivate the rice fields of Brahmans, and it had been a custom for many thousands of years.

Chellaya was forty-five and Chittampalam was forty-two, and they had lived, as all Brahmans lived, in the houses in which they had been born. There can be no doubt that quite suddenly one of the gods, or rather devils, laid a spell upon these two compounds. And this is how it happened.

Chellaya had married, when he was 14, a plump Brahman girl of 12 who had borne him three sons and two daughters. He had married off both his daughters without giving very large dowries and his sons had all married girls who had brought them large dowries. No man ought to have been happier, though his wife was too talkative and had a sharp tongue. And for 45 years Chellaya lived happily the life which all good Brahmans should live. Every morning he ate his rice cakes and took his bath at the well in his compound and went to the temple of Siva. There he talked until midday to his wife's brother and his daughter's husband's father about Nallatampi, their neighbour, who was on bad terms with them, about the price of rice, and about a piece of land which he had been thinking of buying for the last five years. After the midday meal of rice and curry, cooked by his wife, he dozed through the afternoon; and then, when the sun began to lose its power, he went down to the shore of the blue lagoon and sat there until nightfall.

This was Chellaya's passion, to sit by the side of the still, shining, blue waters and look over them at the far-off islands which flickered and quivered in the mirage of heat. The wind, dying down at evening, just murmured in the palms behind him. The heat lay like something tangible and soothing upon the earth. And Chellaya waited eagerly for the hour when the fishermen come out with their cast-nets and wade out into the shallow water after the fish. How eagerly he waited all day for that moment; even in the temple when talking about Nallatampi, whom he hated, the vision of those unruffled waters would continually rise up before him, and of the lean men lifting their feet so gently first one and then the other, in order not to make a splash or a ripple, and bending forward with the nets in their hands ready to cast. And then the joy of the capture, the great leaping twisting silver fish in the net at last. He began to hate his compound and his fat wife and the interminable talk in the temple, and those long dreary evenings when he stood under his umbrella at the side of his rice field and watched the Mukkuwas ploughing or sowing or reaping.

As Chellaya grew older he became more and more convinced that the only pleasure in life was to be a fisher and to catch fish. This troubled him not a little, for the fisher caste is a low caste and no Brahman had ever caught a fish. It would be utter pollution. . . . One day however when he went down to sit in his accustomed place by the side of the lagoon, he found a fisherman sitting on the sand there mending his net.

"Fisher," said Chellaya, "could one who has never had a net in his hand and was no longer young learn how to cast it?"

Chellaya was a small round fat man, but he had spoken with great dignity. The fisher knew at once that he was a Brahman and salaamed, touching the ground with his forehead.

"Lord," he said, "the boy learns to cast the net when he is still at his mother's breast."

"O foolish dog of a fisher," said Chellaya pretending to be very angry, "can you not understand? Suppose one who was not a fisher and was well on in years wished to fish—for a vow or even for play—could such a one learn to cast the net?"

The old fisherman screwed up his wrinkled face and looked up at Chellaya doubtfully.

"Lord," he said, "I cannot tell. For how could such a thing be? Such things are learnt when one is young, as one learns to walk."

Chellaya looked out over the old man's head to the lagoon. Another fisherman was stealing along in the water ready for the cast. Ah, swish out flew the net. No, nothing—yes, O joy, a gleam of silver in the meshes. Chellaya made up his mind suddenly.

"Now, look here, fellow,—tell me this: could you teach me to cast a net?"

The old man covered his mouth with his hand, for it is not seemly that a fisher should smile in the presence of a Brahman.

"The lord is laughing at me," he said respectfully.

"I am not laughing, fellow. I have made a vow to Muniyappa that if he would take away the curse which he laid upon my son's child I would cast a net nightly in the lagoon. Now my son's child is well. Therefore if you will take me tomorrow night to a spot where no one will see us and bring me a net and teach me to cast it, I will give you five measures of rice. And if you speak a word of this to anyone, I will call down upon your head and your child's head ten thousand curses of Muniyappa."

It is dangerous to risk being cursed by a Brahman, so the fisherman agreed and next evening took Chellaya to a bay in the lagoon and showed him how to cast the net. For an hour Chellaya waded about in the shallow water experiencing a dreadful pleasure. Every moment he glanced over his shoulder to the land to make sure that nobody was in sight; every moment came the pang that he was the first Brahman to pollute his caste by fishing; and every moment came the keen joy of hope that this time the net would swish out and fall in a gentle circle upon a silver fish.

Chellaya caught nothing that night, but he had gone too far to turn back. He gave the fisherman two rupees for the net, and hid it under a rock, and every night he went away to the solitary creek, made a little pile of his white Brahman clothes on the sand, and stepped into the shallow water with his net. There he fished until the sun sank. And sometimes now he caught fish which very reluctantly he had to throw back into the water, for he was afraid to carry them back to his wife.

Very soon a strange rumour began to spread in the town that the Brahman Chellaya had polluted his caste by fishing. At first people would not believe it; such a thing could not happen, for it had never happened before. But at last so many people told the story,—and one man had seen Chellaya carrying a net and another had seen him wading in the lagoon—that everyone began to believe it, the lower castes with great pleasure and the Brahmans with great shame and anger.

Hardly had people begun to believe this rumour than an almost stranger thing began to be talked of. The Brahman Chittampalam, who was Chellaya's neighbour, had polluted his caste, it was said, by carrying earth on his head. And this rumour also was true and it happened in this way.

Chittampalam was a taciturn man and a miser. If his thin scraggy wife used three chillies, where she might have done with two for the curry, he beat her soundly. About the time that Chellaya began to fish in secret, the water in Chittampalam's well began to grow brackish. It became necessary to dig a new well in the compound, but to dig a well means paying a lower caste man to do the work; for the earth that is taken out has to be carried away on the head, and it is pollution for a Brahman to carry earth on his head. So Chittampalam sat in his compound thinking for many days how to avoid paying a man to dig a new well; and meanwhile the taste of the water from the old well became more and more unpleasant. At last it became impossible even for Chittampalam's wife to drink the water; there was only one way out of it; a new well must be dug and he could not bring himself to pay for the digging; he must dig the well himself. So every night for a week Chittampalam went down to the darkest corner of his compound and dug a well and carried earth on his head and thereby polluted his caste.

The other Brahmans were enraged with Chellaya and Chittampalam and, after abusing them and calling them pariahs, they cast them out for ever from the Brahman caste and refused to eat or drink with them or to talk to them; and they took an oath that their children's children should never marry with the grandsons and granddaughters of Chellaya and Chittampalam. But if people of other castes talked to them of the matter, they denied all knowledge of it and swore that no Brahman had ever caught fish or carried earth on his head. Chittampalam was not much concerned at the anger of the Brahmans, for he had saved the hire of a well-digger and he had never taken pleasure in the conversation of other Brahmans and, besides, he shortly after died.

Chellaya, being a small fat man and of a more pleasant and therefore more sensitive nature, felt his sin and the disapproval of his friends deeply. For some days he gave up his fishing, but they were weary days to him and he gained nothing, for the Brahmans still refused to talk to him. All day long in the temple and in his compound he sat and thought of his evenings when he waded in the blue waters of the lagoon, and of the little islands resting like plumes of smoke or feathers upon the sky, and of the line of pink flamingoes like thin posts at regular intervals set to mark a channel, and of the silver gleam of darting fish. In the evening, when he knew the fishermen were taking out their nets, his longing became intolerable; he dared not go down to the lagoon for he knew that his desire would master him. So for five nights he sat in his compound, and, as the saying is, his fat went off in desire. On the sixth night he could stand it no longer; once more he polluted his caste by catching fish.

After this Chellaya no longer tried to struggle against himself but continued to fish until at the age of fifty he died. Then, as time went on, the people who had known Chellaya and Chittampalam died too, and the story of how each had polluted his caste began to be forgotten. Only it was known in Yalpanam that no Brahman could marry into those two families, because there was something wrong with their caste. Some said that Chellaya had carried earth on his head and that Chittampalam had caught fish; in any case the descendants of Chellaya and Chittampalam had to go to distant villages to find Brahman wives and husbands for their sons and daughters.

Chellaya's hut and Chittampalam's hut still stand where they stood under the coconut trees by the side of the lagoon, and in one lives Chellaya, the great-great-great-grandson of Chellaya who caught fish, and in the other Chittampalam the great-great-great-grandson of Chittampalam who carried earth on his head. Chittampalam has a very beautiful daughter and Chellaya has one son unmarried. Now this son saw Chittampalam's daughter by accident through the fence of the compound, and he went to his father and said:

"They say that our neighbour's daughter will have a big dowry; should we not make a proposal of marriage?"

The father had often thought of marrying his son to Chittampalam's daughter, not because he had seen her through the compound fence but because he had reason to believe that her dowry would be large. But he had never mentioned it to his wife or to his son, because he knew that it was said that an ancestor of Chittampalam had once dug a well and carried earth on his head. Now, however, that his son himself suggested the marriage, approved of the idea, and, as the custom is, he told his wife to go to Chittampalam's house and look at the girl. So his wife went alone to Chittampalam's house for the visit preparatory to a marriage, and she came back and reported that she was beautiful and fit for even her son to marry.

Chittampalam had himself often thought of proposing to Chellaya that Chellaya's son should marry his daughter, but he had been ashamed to do this because he knew that Chellaya's ancestor had caught fish and thereby polluted his caste. Otherwise the match was desirable, for he would be saved from all the trouble of finding a husband for her in some distant village. However, if Chellaya himself proposed it, he made up his mind not to put any difficulties in the way. The next time that the two met, Chellaya made the proposal and Chittampalam accepted it and then they went back to Chellaya's compound to discuss the question of dowry. As is usual in such cases the father of the girl wants the dowry to be small and the father of the boy wants it to be large, and all sorts of reasons are given on both sides why it should be small or large, and the argument begins to grow warm. The argument became so warm that at last Chittampalam lost his temper and said:

"One thousand rupees! Is that what you want? Why, a fisher should take the girl with no dowry at all!"

"Fisher!" shouted Chellaya. "Who would marry into the pariah caste, that defiles itself by digging wells and carrying earth on its head? You had better give two thousand rupees to a pariah to take your daughter out of your house."

"Fisher! Low caste dog!" shouted Chittampalam. "Pariah!" screamed Chellaya.

Chittampalam rushed from the compound and for many days the two Brahmans refused to talk a word to one another. At last Chellaya's son, who had again seen the daughter of Chittampalam through the fence of the compound, talked to his father and then to Chittampalam, and the quarrel was healed and they began to discuss again the question of dowry. But the old words rankled and they were still sore, as soon as the discussion began to grow warm it ended once more by their calling each other "Fisher" and "Pariah." The same thing has happened now several times, and Chittampalam is beginning to think of going to distant villages to find a husband for his daughter. Chellaya's son is very unhappy; he goes down every evening and sits by the waters of the blue lagoon on the very spot where his great-great-great-grandfather Chellaya used to sit and watch the fishermen cast their nets.

The Establishment of the Tea Industry in Ceylon

L. A. Wickremeratne

In contemporary Sri Lanka, tea not only dominates the landscape of the central highland mountain massif but remains a major industry, earning for the country the largest amount of hard currency in an economy that remains largely, except for the garment industry and gems, one of agricultural exports. During the 1970s, the industry was almost completely nationalized by Mrs. Bandaranaike's socialist-oriented government. In what follows, the historian L. A. Wickremeratne, relying on primary sources dating to the second half of the nineteenth century, details the collapse of the coffee industry and the establishment of tea by European planters. He focuses especially upon the consequences for the Sinhala peasant of this transformation of land.

I.

"The 'tea mania' has now fairly set in and many estates have extensive tea nurseries and some are planting tea under coffee and cinchona trees.[1] Oh! ye gods of agriculture, how in the name of commonsense do you expect all these products to thrive in the same six feet of soil?"

An anonymous Haputale planter's lament made in 1885 merely reflected the confusion which prevailed throughout the planting districts in Ceylon following the rather dramatic collapse of the coffee industry.

Contemporary documents clearly show that part at any rate of the confusion had been engendered by an unwillingness to accept the inevitability that the coffee industry was really on its last legs. Instead, in the late 1870's when the coffee leaf disease had spread its ravages far and wide and could no longer be shrugged off as a passing misfortune, G. H. K. Thwaites, whose views were widely sought after, expressed the view that imported varieties of coffee seeds—firstly the Liberian . . . and subsequently a lesser known West Indian variety—could arrest the disease. Although the newer varieties, which were incidentally distributed free to planters and peasants, seemed to stand up better to the disease, ultimately they too succumbed. Consequently by 1880 Thwaites too had abandoned all illusions regarding the condition of the coffee industry.

Interestingly, Henry Trimen, who succeeded Thwaites as the Director of the Royal Botanical Gardens, was in turn hopeful. Although he conceded that the leaf disease had not diminished notably, Trimen expressed satisfaction that coffee planters were overcoming a prejudice they had against experimenting with the Coffea Liberica variety. Moreover, Trimen urged planters to resort to—if their means permitted them to do so—"high cultivation and liberal manuring." He suggested that the government should obtain the services of a trained entomologist and complained that "no combined effort" had hitherto been made to prevent the spread of the disease "on the lines indicated by its known nature."

The expert view of the matter was shared by some at any rate of the run of the mill European coffee planters in Ceylon. "Coffee is still king in Ceylon. Who says coffee in Ceylon is rapidly going downhill past recovery?" asked an irate planter who . . . had produced unprecedented quantities of coffee. Another planter . . . reported that he had got "splendid coffee crops" despite the leaf disease and added that this was merely "proof of what can be done by careful cultivation."

Such robust hopes notwithstanding, the more general picture that emerges from the evidence was that the collapse of the coffee industry had gravely embarrassed the majority of European planters. Many planters were financially ruined and were constrained to leave Ceylon and start planting ventures in other countries. . . .

Individual coffee planters who opted to stay behind in Ceylon, came to terms with the crisis in a variety of ways. . . . Inspired by hopes of obtaining reasonably quick cash returns, the European planters took to the cultivation of certain products which had hitherto been confined largely to the Sinhalese peasants. . . . As if to make a virtue out of plain necessity, European planters were exhorted to grow a variety of crops and not make the "mistake" of depending on a single staple. . . .

There are . . . frequent references to pepper, nutmegs and cardamoms. The European planter was no doubt encouraged by the fact that these products together with cinnamon and citronella oil were after all traditionally profitable exports.

Particular mention may in this context be made of the beginnings of the cocoa industry. . . .

In some ways however cocoa was not ideally suited to match the problems of a transitional period. . . . Between the time of planting and the gathering of the nut for processing there was minimally a period of four years. The individual planter on the other hand who was struggling with his debts was looking out for crops which required a short growth period, promised quick returns, and above all, required a negligible outlay of capital. Moreover there was considerable confusion about the technical know how involved in cocoa cultivation. . . .

On the other hand this fact in itself proved to be a blessing in disguise. For it was now demonstrated that cocoa could be grown with sundry crops without entailing the complete clearing of the land, or the uprooting of the coffee trees which still gave the planter a small return. No doubt the practice of interplanting cocoa with rubber, which became a widespread and accepted method in later times long after rubber had become a fully fledged and independent industry, owed its origins to these early experiments.

The interests of the European planters were not however confined to cocoa and their success with regard to a number of crops helped somewhat to dispel the prevailing gloom. A typical example was the planter who had successfully grown coffee as well as cocoa and pepper on his estates in Kandy and who declared in the *Tropical Agriculturalist* that the time was opportune for new capitalists to come to Ceylon to take in hand the "new products" for which the subsoil in the old coffee districts was "still good." More revealingly, a detailed report on "Planting Prospects in Ceylon," published in the *Tropical Agriculturalist* in 1882 described the preoccupation with "new products" as the silver lining in a crisis atmosphere. The review compared the Ceylon coffee planter with the potato-cultivating Irish as well as with the wheat farmer in Australia who had all "made the grand mistake of placing their sole dependence on one product." . . .

Gradually, however, circumstances—not least the international price changes which made their cultivation vastly more economically remunerative—induced the European planters in Ceylon to confine their efforts to the specific spheres—cinchona and tea.

Although there was little economic inducement because the coffee industry was in a flourishing condition, cinchona, like tea, had been experimentally grown from the beginnings of the 1860's. By 1863, the indefatigable Thwaites was certain that in terms of climate and soil the hill districts of Ceylon—especially those elevations which were considered too high for coffee—were ideally suited for the cultivation of cinchona. Indeed by 1865 largely due to the energies of Thwaites thousands of cinchona plants had been distributed among the European planters and there was every indication that the demand for these plants would increase. . . .

The widespread popularity of cinchona, especially during the transitional era, would hardly require emphasis. To begin with, climatically cinchona could be grown in the very areas where coffee had flourished, which meant that the erstwhile coffee planter could replace the moribund coffee plants with cinchona, and at the same time continue to get what income he could from the still unaffected coffee trees. Secondly, comparatively fewer demands were made on the planters' knowledge and resources both during the period of its growth as well as during the process of refining the cinchona bark for export. Thirdly, there was the prospect of a limited outlay of capital and quick returns. Above all the over-all prospects were made all the more attractive by the dramatic increases in the price of cinchona. . . .

Despite the fact that as subsequent developments clearly showed, tea cultivation was comparatively more sophisticated than either coffee or cinchona, interestingly its rapid spread during this period was partly due to its appeal as a transitional crop.

To begin with there was the widespread belief that tea could be grown with coffee. Climatically the coffee lands, which were invariably situated at higher elevations, were basically suited for tea cultivation. More germane to cost considerations was the fact that abandoned coffee lands, or lands on which coffee was being indifferently grown, saved the planter the expense of clearing the jungle and gave him an income from the existing shrubs. Moreover such lands were invariably well roaded and drained and possessed buildings—and in some instances machinery too—which could be used for the requirements of tea.

Although statistical evidence on the point is wanting, it would appear that the interplanting of coffee with tea was fairly widespread. . . . [But] no planter could afford to dispense with any income he might get from coffee shrubs during this period in which the tea plant was not as yet in bearing. . . .

Contemporary estimates of tea production were in fact largely conceived from this standpoint. It would appear too that the role of the *Tropical Agriculturalist* was as much to impress the individual planter that tea cultivation could be taken in hand with comparatively limited resources, as to act as a medium disseminating information on various aspects of planting. The message had a wide topical appeal because the pattern of individual proprietorship—a characteristic investment feature of the coffee era—survived in the first decade of tea production in Ceylon.

But as the knowledge of tea cultivation increased and the methods of production became more sophisticated, it became evident that the possibilities of limiting the outlay of capital and of minimising running costs were not as simple as they had seemed at first. For example, technically there were serious limits to interplanting tea with other products, notably with coffee and cinchona. Experience showed that when the tea plant came into its own it required ample light and air as well as room for the roots to spread, and that in consequence after about the eighteenth month of its growth the adjacent coffee plants had necessarily to be eradicated. Similarly the growing tea plant had also to part company with the cinchona, whose large cabbage-shaped leaves provided too much shade and moisture to the tea plant, although many planters were understandably reluctant to uproot the high-yielding and thriving cinchona.

The difficulties of the individual tea planter who was constrained to rely solely on his resources were rather more dramatically highlighted with regard to the use of machinery, which of course enormously enhanced costs. It must be borne in mind that during this early period, tea was manufactured by machinery as well as by hand. The distinction was well recognised particularly in estimates of costs and had provoked considerable discussion in planting circles about the relative merits of the two methods of tea manufacture.

The fact was that as a result of the expansion of the tea industry in India firms had sprung up in Britain which were specialising in the manufacture of machinery for the different stages of tea production. Indian example inevitably influenced European planters in Ceylon and in the larger tea estates— Windsor Forest, Strathellie, Rakwana and Inibulpitiya—the manufacture of tea was being handled largely by means of imported machinery. Firms like Messrs. John Walter and Company, Mackwood and Company and Brown Rae and Company in Hatton, were the local agents for British firms such as the Sirocco Works in Belfast, A. Shanks and Son, London, and Marshall, Son and Company in Gainsborough.

However in terms of capital costs of machinery, the small run of the mill European planter could not afford machinery. For example, James Irvine, a tea planter in Lunugala complained that the "excessive" cost of Jackson's standard tea-producing machinery "placed them beyond the reach of the great body of planters." The fact that some form of power was necessary to drive the machinery added to the difficulties. The *Tropical Agriculturalist* observed that it was "impossible in these hard times to expect each tea planter from 40 to 100 acres under cultivation to provide rolling, drying and sifting machinery for himself in an adequate tea house." The journal made the interesting suggestion that "District Tea Factories" should be established to serve several estates in a given area, and reported that in many instances individual planters were dispatching their leaves to the larger factories.

Gradually however the individual tea planter began to realise that he could not altogether ignore the use of machinery. Especially in terms of costs it was more profitable to produce tea by means of machinery rather than by hand. It was estimated that as much as 5 cents per pound could be saved by using machinery and that the ratio of saving was likely to be greater with increases in the quantity of tea. There were also certain limitations implied in hand manufacture. For example, a single cooly, however efficient he was, could not roll more than 40 pounds of tea leaf. Secondly, whether uniform quality could be maintained in manufacturing tea by hand was uncertain. Often neither was possible, and consequently among different individually owned European tea estates there was a striking degree of variability in the manufacture of tea, notwithstanding a certain broad uniformity with regard to the size of the estate and the inputs of capital and labour.

In other words, in more ways than one, the tea industry was demanding a greater input of capital which the individual European planter was hard put to meet. It was plainly a situation which challenged him and ensured that his initial eclipse by tea companies—whose emergence was an outstanding feature in the history of the tea industry in Ceylon in the period 1895–1900 would be merely a matter of time.

II.

Meanwhile the Sinhalese peasants who lived in the plantation districts were themselves constrained to come to terms with the emergence of the tea industry. Their response was made evident in three rather distinct spheres: (a) cultivation of tea by Sinhalese; (b) the question of labour on European-owned estates; and (c) land sales.

When Thwaites discussed the desirability of beginning tea cultivation and prophesied that before long the hills of Ceylon would be covered with tea, he did not have in mind merely the European planter. Thwaites declared that tea cultivation was as much suited to the Sinhalese peasant.

The belief which lingered on in the 1870's, especially among the provincial agents of government, was typical of a characteristically transitional period when there was no small confusion about what actually was involved in tea cultivation and little knowledge with regard to scale and costs. In 1882 for example R. W. Ievers, who was the Assistant Government Agent in Kegalle, was persuading Sinhalese peasants to take to tea cultivation. "The shrub," he wrote, would "grow as easily as Lantana and would soon take the place of the now almost dead coffee on which the villager relied for money and taxes and clothes." Ievers had decided to make each headman in his district grow a small plot of tea, and was determined to advise them with regard to "the proper course of preparation of the leaf." If the peasants could not do so, at least, the leaves which they produced could always be sold to a neighbouring tea estate. In general Ievers took heart at the "keenness" of the Sinhalese to take to tea cultivation. His successor, Hubert Wace, was anxious to obtain technical advice from the government regarding tea cultivation for the benefit of the peasants amongst whom he hoped to distribute tea seeds. . . .

In spite of the enthusiasm of the individual Government Agents, to some extent the government frowned on the policy encouraging peasants to take to tea cultivation. . . .

However native interest in tea cultivation was significantly diffused and was not necessarily dependent on the idiosyncracies of the Government Agents. The fact was that there was an increasing demand for the green leaf which more and more Sinhalese peasants were growing. The demand was principally caused by increases of a rather remarkable nature in the London market for Indian and Ceylon teas at the expense of imports from the hitherto traditional source of supply—China. Consequently from the beginning of the 1880's when there was an upward trend in tea prices till about 1897 it was profitable for European tea planters to produce as much tea as possible. They usually bought green leaf from peasants, especially when the green leaf could be had for 5 to 6 cents per pound, which was well below the production costs of the average European tea planter, who had of course to cope with greater cost commitments. . . .

Nonetheless the precise extent of Sinhalese holdings in tea especially vis-à-vis the conventional European estates, must remain conjectural. As for the Central Province, the evidence suggests that native holdings were found least in the Uva District. Holdings in Uda Hewaheta were also reported to be "trifling." By contrast, in spite of its proverbial backwardness and lethargy of its peasants, the Walapana District could boast of 317 acres of peasant tea lands by 1890. More noteworthy was the Kotmale area in which peasant tea holdings had by this date aggregated 664 acres.

Meanwhile in the Southern Province as a whole native preoccupation with tea cultivation was notably more diffused. The *Tropical Agriculturalist* reported that in the Galle and Matara districts the Sinhalese were beginning to cultivate tea extensively in small plots on lands adjoining the European estates. It was suggested that the Sinhalese peasants did so in order to compel the neighbouring European owners to "buy them out by and by." In 1892 E. Elliott, who was the Government Agent in the province, remarked that tea planting was becoming popular with the Sinhalese, whose plots were particularly numerous in the Wellaboda and Talpe *pattuwa*s. More revealing were the remarks of his successor Ievers, who in 1893 attributed the extension of the tea acreages in the Galle and Matara districts primarily to the efforts of the Sinhalese who were "opening up small gardens all over the District." He added that the Sinhalese who were keen on buying crown lands preferred to cultivate such lands with tea rather than with coconut because tea cultivation was comparatively more profitable. . . .

It may be added that in general as in the Central Province, in Matara and Galle too, the pattern of Sinhalese tea cultivation was typically one of small peasant holdings. More genuinely entrepreneurial Sinhalese efforts in tea, even remotely on a par with the European estates, were significantly few and far between. . . .

The prevailing context in a sense held the clue to the situation. . . . Changes in the techniques of tea production demanded an increasingly heavy outlay of capital. Secondly, as far as the entrepreneurial-minded Ceylonese was concerned, tea was as yet a hypothetical investment. It was not a "safe investment" as it seemed to Ceylonese in the 1920's, when Sinhalese-owned tea estates were a feature of the tea industry in the Kelani Valley and in the Kalutara District. Thirdly, in the period 1880–1900 there were other spheres of economic activity which attracted the Ceylonese with his comparatively modest capital resources.

Indeed even the peasant's interest in tea seems to have waxed and waned in relation to price changes among other products, whose cultivation was in certain circumstances as economically attractive. For example in certain districts in the Central Province, Sinhalese peasants showed great interest in the cultivation of cardamoms. In Kotmale a peasant was able to sell a pound of cardamoms for about 65 cents. In fact in this area, as against a native tea acreage of 664, there were 932 acres of cardamoms. Similarly the cultivation of coconuts, which could be sold for anything above 6 cents a nut, was reported to have been a popular peasant preoccupation in Hanguranketa. It was also reported that Sinhalese peasants in the Nuwara Eliya District were taking in hand the cultivation of "English Vegetables." According to an Assistant Government Agent, vegetable growing was, in fact, "the chief local industry" among villagers there. In Matale the cultivation of cocoa was popular.

Meanwhile there was towards the end of the nineteenth century, a notable revival of peasant interest in cinnamon and citronella cultivation, in the Southern Province. . . .

Moreover in the Southern Province plumbago mining too militated against an exclusive preoccupation with tea cultivation. It attracted both the run of the mill peasant as well as the Sinhalese entrepreneur. In fact the demand for land which was believed to contain plumbago was an important factor in pushing up crown land sales in the Galle District. . . . The amplitude of plumbago deposits and the comparative ease with which these deposits could be obtained—lying as they were near the surface—without the use of costly mechanical contrivances, made plumbago mining an attractive occupation.

The establishment of tea estates moreover gave opportunities of employment to Sinhalese peasants in the plantation districts. These opportunities were availed of to a greater extent than has been generally assumed.

A variety of factors induced the peasants to seek employment on tea estates. Typically the average peasant who depended solely on rice cultivation looked to estates as a means of earning additional income. In his report on the Central Province, R. W. Moir remarked in 1890 that the existence of estates and the tradition of "prompt" payment . . . to labourers, was a great boon to villagers whenever the latter were faced with crop failures of one sort or another. In less exceptional circumstances too, because rice cultivation was geared to subsistence levels of production, the peasant's capacity to gratify a greater amplitude of economic wants depended on income which he could earn from other sources. . . .

The benefits were however not entirely one-sided. During this period many European planters were confronted with the difficulty of finding labour for work on estates. The theme recurs in successive issues of the *Tropical Agriculturalist*, which in 1882 expressed fears that the lack of adequate labour would impede the expansion of the tea industry in Ceylon. In fact it was claimed that already labour resources were barely sufficient for existing requirements.

It was evident that the problem of a scarce labour supply had been caused principally by two factors. To begin with, there had been a considerable exodus of South Indians who had been originally attracted to Ceylon by steady wages as well as by the fringe benefits which the planter provided for them. The exodus was in turn caused by the coffee crisis, when many estates were compelled to make do with fewer labourers in an effort to reduce running expenses. Secondly, it became apparent that in striking contrast to the coffee industry, basically more labour was necessary both for the cultivation and manufacture of tea. It was estimated that whereas one cooly for each acre had been enough to collect "the biggest crop" of coffee, three or four coolies were necessary to pluck an acre of tea which yielded 600 pounds. More conservative contemporary estimates put the labour requirement at "three-quarters of a cooly" per acre of coffee as against two coolies for each acre of tea. On the factory floor too the input of labour was greater in tea manufacture. Moreover one need hardly add that the difficulties of those tea planters who could not afford machinery but were constrained to resort to hand manufacture of tea were rendered all the more intolerable, in a context of scarce labour.

Theoretically, a possible solution was to induce South Indian labour to "speedily find their way back to Ceylon," if need be in greater numbers. Their influx however depended on the fortunes of the tea industry. In other words tea had to convince all and sundry that it had come to stay, that it was capable of supporting a constant wage rate, and was not merely a transitory phenomenon. Alternatively greater incentives than had hitherto been made available had to be provided to the potential immigrant labourer. . . .

To the European tea planter in Ceylon, however, the employment of Sinhalese labour seemed to be a simpler and less costly solution to the problem. Many at any rate were hopeful. It was said that Sinhalese women and children were "specially" fitted to be tea pluckers. Some tea planters expressed the view that since the Sinhalese were reputed to be partial to the system of payment by contract, both weeding as well as plucking could be done by this means. Others felt certain that the Sinhalese could be "easily taught to pluck properly."

In fact too, an increasing number of tea planters were able to vouch for the satisfactory manner in which Sinhalese labourers worked on tea estates. The *Tropical Agriculturalist* observed specifically with reference to the Kalutara District that European tea planters were not only pleased with Sinhalese labour but even thought that the Sinhalese were superior to the Tamil immigrant labourer. It was said that plucking in particular has a sphere in which Sinhalese women and children actually excelled.

Meanwhile with regard to the question of wages the use of Sinhalese labour was presumably an advantage than otherwise. If one may attempt to reconstruct the picture with regard to wages it will be seen that in the absence of a statutorily defined wage rate, in different parts of the island, the rates paid for daily hire varied in relation to the demand for labour. Moreover there was also no hard and fast rule about the mode of payment, and sometimes labour was remunerated in kind. Even in the plantation areas proper, where more than elsewhere there was a formal tradition of wages, it would appear that the wage rate as well as the manner of payment varied. A lot seems to have been left to the judgement of the individual planter. . . .

The fact was that the intrusion of Sinhalese labour did not materially alter existing wage rates in the plantation areas. One may visualise two possibilities. Firstly, that the scarcity of labour was so great as to cause an unprecedented rise in wages, a circumstance which encouraged Sinhalese in increasing numbers to come over from neighbouring villages to the estates. Secondly, that the influx of Sinhalese labour was numerically so great that even after allowances had been made for a considerable reduction in the number of Indian immigrant labour on estates, there was over-all a surfeit of labour resources, which caused a fall in wages. Neither situation did in fact materialise.

There was, however, an impression among the European planters that it was possible to obtain Sinhalese labour at comparatively cheaper rates. They believed that on account of the failure of coffee, and one may add, the limitations of paddy production, the Sinhalese villager was more than ever dependent on European enterprise. There was, in other words, a certain competition among the villagers themselves to get employment in neighbouring estates which gave the European planter a supply of labour and possibly placed him in a bargaining position with regard to payment of wages. Indeed a European tea planter in Dolosbage reported that he could rely on as many as 1,000 Sinhalese turning up for work on his estate. Another European planter in Hunnasgiriya, who would have been happy to obtain Sinhalese labour at the "usual rate" of 33 cents per day was gratified to discover that he could find an ample supply even at 30 cents. E. Elliott too observed in his administration report for the Southern Province in 1886, that Sinhalese labour could be got for "much lower rates" and added that the European planter who employed Sinhalese labour was invariably spared the necessity of providing lines, making advances and the "other drawbacks" attending the securing of coast labour.

Meanwhile when economic pressures drove the villager to the European estates, cultural factors which might have ordinarily militated against estate work became much less important. Among the European planters the general impression was that there was little difficulty in obtaining Sinhalese labour provided that the planter concerned realised that he was dealing with a people "who had their own bits of land," and who were reputedly sensitive about the treatment they received at the hands of the European employer. One had to be mindful too of the predilections of the Sinhalese labourer. For example, tea planters came to recognise the fondness of the Sinhalese for getting ready cash. It was observed that the Sinhalese were unlike the Tamils in that they did not like "long accounts or to have their money kept against advances in rice." . . .

Nevertheless in taking tea-planting districts as a whole it was evident that the employment of Sinhalese labour varied in different parts. The phenomenon, which attracted considerable attention on account of its very novelty, was more evident in the Low Country tea-producing districts of Kalutara, Galle, and Matara, than in the strictly Kandyan areas. In the Kalutara District in particular it was said that tea planters were virtually dependent on Sinhalese labour. . . .

By contrast, in the Kandyan areas, although the employment of Sinhalese labour on estates was becoming "more and more common," there was a certain antipathy to the idea of working for wages often at considerable distances from home, and having to do so cheek by jowl with Indian immigrant labourers. The prevailing prejudice was well put by a Sinhalese Headman who declared that Sinhalese who worked on tea estates had in popular estimation become "like Tamils." In fact the *Tropical Agriculturalist* claimed that on account of this antipathy, the European planter in the Low Country had a distinct advantage over his counterpart in the Kandyan areas.

The evidence also suggests that to some extent even in the Kalutara District, social factors determined Sinhalese attitudes to work on estates. In some estates although Indian labour had been employed to do the main portion of the work, it was only low-caste Sinhalese women who had been readily found to undertake weeding. In a particular estate the phenomenon of a number of Sinhalese women working under the supervision of the wife of an Indian *kangani* was attributed to the fact that the latter had "won the favour of the villagers." It was in general reported that Sinhalese of the "better castes" confined their participation in estate work to road cutting and draining and evinced great interest in lining, holding and pegging, leaving the more routine tasks of plucking and weeding to others.

Finally as far as the Sinhalese villager was concerned there were also the possibilities of selling land to European planters, who in view of favourable market conditions were clearly anxious to expand the cultivation of tea.

In the immediate aftermath of the collapse of the coffee industry however there was little demand for land. Both cinchona and tea cultivation, which were becoming increasingly popular, were grown on the existing coffee lands rather than on new lands. Consequently in the period 1880–1886, the sale of crown lands, which had been a lucrative source of government revenue, became comparatively unimportant. In the Central Province as a whole, although in 1877 as many as 13,711 acres of land had been sold, in subsequent years the acreage was progressively reduced, until by 1883 the government was able to dispose of only about 3,400 acres, . . .

By 1885 a more favourable trend was made evident on account of the revival of European enterprise "especially in the Central Province." Specifically the demand for land was stimulated principally by increases in the cultivation of tea, although in Dumbara and in the Matale District in particular the growing enthusiasm for cocoa cultivation was a significant factor. . . .

Similarly in the Kalutara District and in the Southern Province, although the expansion of the tea industry was the principal factor in pushing up land sales, the demand for land for purposes of plumbago mining, the extension of cinnamon cultivation—and to a lesser extent—sugar cultivation were important contributing factors. Indeed by 1892 there were in the Galle District alone 3,346 acres cultivated with cinnamon.

Notwithstanding these developments, the sale of crown lands was not as great as it had been during the heyday of the coffee industry. For one thing in the central highlands forest land was "rarely obtainable" partly because it was the policy of the Government to prevent the indiscriminate sale of crown lands. Indeed over the years official policy concerning crown land sales had been almost imperceptibly hardening. In 1873 Sir Joseph Hooker had urged the government of Ceylon to reserve forests which were situated at high elevations in the Central Province. In addition, in 1883, a special report on forest administration in Ceylon had expressed scepticism about the considerations which had hitherto determined the disposal of crown lands. The report, which was the work of F. D. A. Vincent, an Indian civil servant, pointed out that crown lands had been simply sold to the highest bidder irrespective of considerations of climate and the need to conserve timber resources. It was said that for a slight and "temporary augmentation" of revenue, the forests of the crown had been rapidly destroyed.

The note of warning did not pass unheeded particularly in the quarter of the provincial agents of government. For example in 1885, the Assistant Government Agent in the Nuwara Eliya District reported that applications for crown land above 5,000 feet in the Ramboda area had all been turned down, although there was a striking dearth in the demand for crown lands in the district as a whole. Meanwhile in the Western Province, where successive Assistant Government Agents had themselves urged a policy of restraint in the disposal of crown lands, in 1890, the Government Agent went so far as to urge that crown lands in the entire province should not be put for sale until the government had consulted the experts and made up its mind about possible forest reserves.

The policy however ran counter to the belief of the European tea planters that tea grew better on higher elevations and on clayey rather than on micaceous soil—the latter being a characteristic of soils in the low country—as well as on land which had not been impoverished by haphazard peasant cultivation. Moreover as matters stood they saw little real hope of obtaining large and contiguous tracts of land which were unencumbered by pockets of native holdings. In short the European tea planter felt that land which conformed to these criteria was likely to be found in the higher elevations rather than in the low country districts.

The clamant demand for more land was heard everywhere. A European tea planter in Ceylon complained in the *Indigo and Tea Planters' Gazette* that the Ceylon Government was trifling with prospective British investors. He added that it was difficult to see how tea cultivation could be expanded in Ceylon if extensions depended solely on the acquisition of crown lands. . . .

Apart from the tightening of official policies, the inability of the Survey Department to deal with even those lands which could be safely offered for sale, was a source of unhappiness both to the provincial agents as well as to the European planters. As far as the latter were concerned government surveys ensured that the lands in question would be free from claims which sometimes natives preferred. . . .

Above all the Government Agents were concerned with the alienation of village lands by peasants to Europeans. Indeed when difficulties of one sort or another prevented Europeans from obtaining as much land as they would have liked from government, they turned to native land owners. There was every indication that the sale of native lands to Europeans was taking place to a very considerable extent. With regard to the Matale District, Burrows affirmed that he could mention "at least a dozen estates . . . entirely made up of the purchase of land in small blocks from the natives." His successor G. S. Saxton reported that land sales of this sort had occurred "frequently" in 1896, . . . in the Matale District. . . .

Matale was merely typical of what was happening elsewhere. Herbert White for example reported that in the Uva Province native land sales to Europeans were "far too prevalent." Meanwhile it was reported that in the Kegalle District alone well over 10,000 acres of peasant land had been sold to Europeans. In the Central Province as a whole Allanson Bailey remarked in 1896 that although "exact figures" were not available, "large extents of land had been purchased from natives by planters for the cultivation of tea."

To some extent official objections to the indiscriminate sale of native lands to Europeans for tea cultivation were based on legal considerations. The fact was that more often than not the lands which peasants sold to Europeans were *chena* lands or the so-called "high lands" in and around villages which peasants often encroached on for purposes of cultivating dry grains. Such encroachments had been made possible because, although the government was opposed to *chena* cultivation, individual Government Agents often permitted a certain amount of *chena* cultivation on the ground that its rigid suppression would react harshly on the economic well-being of the peasant. . . .

When land transactions between Europeans and peasants were taking place extensively, the government contended that the occupation of *chena* lands by peasants did not give the latter the right to sell such lands to third parties. On the other hand, the peasants were accustomed to lay claim to legal rights on the grounds of cultivation for a number of years as well as on the basis of taxes paid to government on the produce of *chena* lands. . . .

Secondly, it often happened that when land was being jointly held by a number of peasants, one or more shareholders would sell the land to a European planter without the knowledge of the other shareholders. Not infrequently the European purchases of such lands were challenged by the other shareholders. As H. L. Moysey, who was the Assistant Government Agent in Sabaragamuwa observed, even at the best of times shareholders were rarely able to agree among themselves about individual lots. In a subsequent report Moysey declared that dishonest native middlemen have been as much responsible for the situation as was the European who showed "great readiness to pick up land cheap."

Thirdly, the demand for land inspired the activities of land speculators who exploited both the peasants as well as the prospective European buyer. The speculators were usually either Moormen or Low Country Sinhalese. As a rule they turned their attention to land which had doubtful title and re-sold the lands at high prices. . . .

Closely intertwined with the legal arguments were the social considerations which were pregnant in the situation. The Government Agents feared that the Sinhalese peasants who were only too ready to part with lands to European planters for the sake of obtaining cash resources would be reduced ultimately to the position of a class that had lost all real contact with the land. . . .

According to Herbert Wace, in the Southern Province village lands had been sold with great frequency irrespective of whether such lands included houses and fields. Le Mesurier, who as an Assistant Government Agent was noted for his sympathy to the village peasant, observed that the benefits which tea plantations had conferred on the peasants "in the way of opening up land, distributing money and giving employment were more than offset by the enormous evil of a floating and unsettled population" which was the inevitable concomitant of peasant land sales.

On the other hand there were the provincial agents like Allanson Bailey who believed that although the sale of peasant lands to Europeans was happening all the time, the selling of houses as fields was quite exceptional. It was also reported that in the Sabaragamuwa District although villagers were "unable to resist the temptation of a little ready money," they were careful to exclude the gardens and fields on which they depended for their livelihood. . . .

For his part S. M. Burrows, who had evidently made a detailed study of peasant land sales, did not minimise their possible social consequences. His almost philosophical musings on the subject clearly transcended the boundaries of the Matale District, of which he had been Assistant Government Agent.

"Where are all the Natives gone to? What effect has the sale of their land upon their mode of life? What have they done with the purchase money? . . . Does work on estates more than compensate for loss of products from *chenas* and gardens sold? What is the moral and physical result of this change also on the people?"

Interestingly Burrows himself ventured no answers to his questions pleading the absence of "careful statistics." Sadly the deficiency has remained uncorrected. Nonetheless even the woefully threadbare statistical knowledge which the modern researcher is able to muster buttresses the view that the emergence of European-owned tea estates was a powerful catalyst which affected traditional peasant society in the plantation districts. As a contemporary observer noted, the peasant sector had witnessed "a quiet revolution."

Note

1. The bark of this tree is used for making quinine, the medicine used to combat malaria.

KANDYAN CULTURE IN THE COLONIAL ERA:

AN INTRODUCTION

The last of the Sri Lankan indigenous dynasties, the kings of Kandy, ruled from their upcountry capital (Mahanuwara—"great city") from the last decade of the sixteenth century until 1815. They always shared political dominion over the island with a colonial power. Though they at times entered into collusion or agreement with the Portuguese and the Dutch (and the island's Sinhala chiefs did so, fatally, with the British as well), perhaps their greatest ally in preserving independence was the topography of the kingdom, dominated as it is by almost impenetrable mountainous terrain. Though the Portuguese invaded and destroyed most of Kandy on four occasions, and the Dutch burned the capital down in the 1760s, no colonial power, until the British in 1815, were able to sustain control of the capital town and its outlying regions. Because of the kingdom's remote location and its inhospitable landscape, which inhibited most means of conveyance, one of the first emphases of British rule in the early nineteenth century was to build roads from all four cardinal directions into the kingdom's capital city to make it more accessible.

Copious amounts of late medieval literature and the performance of traditional ritual remain extant today as witness to the rich cultural life that obtained during these centuries of political insecurity. Buddhism and the worship of deities, some of Hindu origin, remained at the center of ritual observance and native conceptions of power, along with festivals marking the New Year in April and the annual *perahara* processions in July and August. Painting, dance, and drama were copiously supported by the royal Kandyan court, as were the *devalayas* (deity shrines) and *viharas* (Buddhist monastic temples) by means of generous land endowments and the declaration of *rajakariya* ("royal prescription") services for their upkeep.

On the whole, the highland Kandyan kingdom's economy was quite limited in trade (to precious stones and elephants) by the colonial Portuguese and Dutch, and was otherwise largely subsistence in nature. Society was hierarchically maintained according to caste status. But unlike the traditional hierarchical *varna* or caste system of India, and apart from the Ksatrya status claimed by its kings, the Sinhala Govigama rice-growing caste was regarded as the highest social group and probably comprised more than one-half of the population. The limited population of other castes, compared to their great strength in numbers in the lowland regions under colonial control, is a witness to the relative homogeneity of village-based Kandyan society. Political rule split between Kandy and the lowland colonized regions ensured the eventual development of a split Ceylonese society. The legacy of this bifurcation, though it is breaking down somewhat after independence, is still seen in the fact that, for many in Sri Lanka, traditional Kandyan culture—as articulated through its music, dance, drama, and ritual—is understood as the country's indigenous national culture.

The chronological thread of the *Reader* must back up several centuries in time to account for developments in the noncolonial portions of the island from the sixteenth to the nineteenth century. Indeed, this section could be read as a continuation of part I, insofar as many of the cultural assumptions in play during the eras covered in part I continued among the Kandyans.

Vimaladharmasurya:
The First Kandyan King

Anonymous

A very different view of the first king of Kandy from the one offered previously by the Dutchman Sebald de Weert is found in the monastic chronicle Culavamsa. *Here, Vimaladharmasurya is praised for securing the Dalada (the Buddha's tooth relic) and for reestablishing the Buddhist monastic sangha* (community) *by sending for monks from Burma so that enough ordained Theravada monks could be present to perform the monastic ordination rite according to Vinaya (disciplinary code) regulations. It was precisely these two acts on behalf of the sangha that constituted Vimaladharmasurya's legitimation as a Buddhist king and established the religious basis of the Kandyan dynasty. This last of the Sri Lankan dynasties prevailed in the hill country of the island for some 223 years until 1815, when the kingdom collapsed under internal dissension between the king and his primary circle of chiefs, abetted by external pressure from the British, who had succeeded the Dutch in occupying the lowland coastal regions in 1796.*

In the days of this King a scion of the Sun Dynasty in Gangasiripura had betaken himself to the harbour of Kolamba. As he did not receive permission to remain there, he went to the province of Gova. After he had dwelt here a long time, he slew a mighty and famous chieftain by name Gajabahu. After the victory he received distinctions of many kinds, and because in his prudence he understood the favorable moment, returned to Lanka. The mighty one brought the troops of the five districts of the highland country over to his side and after the death of (Rajasiha) the slayer of his father, when the year two thousand, one hundred and thirty-five from the nirvana of the Master had arrived, he (the prince), full of faith, mighty by reason of his merit, became a king under the name of Vimaladhammasuriya, highly famed, in the town of Sirivaddhana [Kandy].

He surrounded the whole of the vast city with a massive wall on the heights of which he had placed at intervals eighteen tower structures. Then to ward off the foe, he posted sentries, freed the whole kingdom of Lanka from all oppression and after he had raised a princess of equal birth to the rank of first *mahesi* and had received his consecration as King, this famous (prince) who in his faith desired meritorious works, set about furthering the laity and the Order. The Ruler of men reflected where the tooth of the Enlightened One could be, and when he heard it was in the Labujagama-vihara, he rejoiced greatly. He had the Tooth Relic which had been brought to Labujagama in the province of Saparagamu fetched (thence) and in order to venerate it day by day in his own fair town and to dedicate a ritual to it, the wise (prince) had a two-storeyed, superb relic temple erected on an exquisitely beautiful piece of ground in the neighbourhood of the royal palace. Here he placed the tooth and in lasting devotion brought offerings to it.

As there were no bhikkhus in the island of Lanka on whom the ceremony [*upasampada*] of admission to the Order had been performed, the King sent officials to the country of Rakkhanga [Burma], invited Nandicakka and other bhikkhus, had them brought to the island of Lanka, made them take up their abode in the noble city of Sirivaddhana and cared for them in reverent manner. Then in the Mahavalukaganga, at the landing place called Ganthamba, within a boundary drawn in the water, he had a fine building erected and thither in the year two thousand, one hundred and forty after the nirvana of the Victor, he led the bhikkhus, had the ceremony of admission to the Order performed in this great bhikkhu community on many of the sons of good family and thus protected the Order of the Enlightened One. And he also made many sons of good birth submit themselves to the ceremony of renunciation of the world and provided them also abundantly with the four articles of use, and after he had in this and many other ways, striving after good, performed many meritorious works, he cleared himself a pathway to heaven. Later the selfsame wise King made his younger brother who had gone through the ceremony of renunciation of the world and (as member) was in the Order of the Buddha, leave the Order, entrusted him with the burden of the government and then passed away in accordance with his deeds.

In this wise the Monarch equipped with kingly power, after performing many meritorious works, adorning the Order of the Victor, made manifest a blameless sovereign power. And yet such a discerning man whose highest good was religion, fell under the power of Mara [the personification of death]: when one has once realized the permanent condition of misery and of all other (suffering), one must find his joy in unwearied striving.

Concerning Their Religions . . .

Robert Knox

Robert Knox, a young Englishman who lived in and around Kandy for almost twenty years, was held hostage by the Kandyan king Rajasinha II in the 1660s and 1670s. His famous account of his capture by the king's men after he was shipwrecked off the east coast of the island near Trincomalee, his further account of imprisonment and gradual adjustment to life among the seventeenth-century upcountry Sinhalas, and then of his dramatic escape through Anuradhapura to Dutch-controlled Mannar, are supplemented by his thorough depiction of Kandyan social customs of those times. Knox's account later formed the inspiration for Daniel Defoe's classic, Robinson Crusoe.*

  In Knox's description of religious practices in Kandy, there are few references to the Buddha and to the religious practices of Buddhist monks. Perhaps monasticism was somewhat moribund in his time. In what follows, Knox is his usually candid self in describing, in general, religious and household life among the Kandyans. Also included here is his description of Kandyan houses, hospitality, and social appearances.*

Concerning their Religious Doctrines, Opinions and Pratices. There are few or none zealous in their worship, or have any great matter of esteem for their Gods. And they seldom busie themselves in the matters of their Religion, until they come to be sick or very aged. They debar none that will come to see the Ceremonies of their worship; and if a stranger should dislike their way, reprove or mock at them for their Ignorance and Folly, they would acknowledge the same, and laugh at the superstitions of their own Devotion, but withall tell you that they are constrained to do what they do, to keep themselves safe from the malice and mischiefs that the evil spirits would otherwise do them, with which, they say, their Country swarm.

  Sometimes in their Sickness they go to the House of their Gods with an Offering, with which they present him, intreating his favour and aid to restore them to health. Upon the recovery whereof they promise him not to fail but to give unto His Majesty (for so they entitle him) far greater Gifts or

Rewards, and what they are, they do particularly mention; it may be, Land, a Slave, Cattle, Money, Cloth, etc. and so they will discourse, argue and expostulate with him as if he were there present in Person before them. If after this, he fails on his part, and cannot restore them to their health, then the fore-promised things are to remain where they were: and instead of which perhaps he gets a Curse saying, He doth but cheat and deceive them.

It is a usual saying, and very frequent among them (if . . . their fortune, be bad) What can God do against it: Nay, I have often heard them say, Give him no Sacrifice, but shit in his Mouth, what a God is He? So slight an estimation have they of their Idol-Gods; and the King far less esteems them. For he doth not in the least give any countenance either to the Worshipper, or to the manner of worship. And God's name be magnified, that hath not suffered him to disturb or molest the Christians in the least in their Religion, or ever attempt to force them to comply with the Countreys Idolatry. But on the contrary, both Kin and People do generally like the Christian Religion better than their own: and respect and honour the Christians as Christians; and do believe there is a greater God than they adore. And in all probability they would be very easily drawn to the Christian or any other Religion: as will appear by this story following. . . .

[A certain noble] carried all what he had plundered out of the Pagoda with him to Columba, and stole one of the King's Elephants to carry it upon. Where being arrived, he declares himself to be Son of the King of Mautoly; who was elder Brother to this King that now is, and for fear of whom he fled to Columba; being at that time when the Portugals had it; who sent him to Goa, where he died. . . .

This being noised abroad that he was a Prince, made the People flock faster to him than before. Which changed both his heart and behaviour from a Priest to a King. Insomuch that the Dutch began to be in doubt what this might grow to. Who to prevent the worst, set a watch over him: which he not liking of, took the advantage of the night, and fled with all his Followers and Attendance up to the King again, and came to the same place where he lay before.

No sooner had the King notice of his arrival, but immediately he dispatched five of his greatest Commanders with their Soldiers to catch him, and to bring him up to him. Which they did, laying both him and all his followers in Chains. The King commanded to keep him in a certain Pagoda of the Chingulayes, until the matter were examined, the People in general much lamenting him, tho not able to help. The chief of their Church-men, viz. their Gonni-nancies, were all commanded to make their Personal appearance at Court. Which all thought was to see the Prince or Priest should have a legal Trial. But in the mean time, the King commanded to cut him in four quarters, and hang them in places, which he appointed. Which was done.

Nevertheless the Vulgar People to this day do honour and adore the name & memorial of the nameless God. With which if he could have been content, and not have gone about to usurp the Crown, the King so little regarding Religion, he might have lived to dye a natural death.

These people do firmly believe a resurrection of the body, and the Immortality of Souls, and a future State. Upon which account they will worship their Ancestors. They do believe that those they call Gods are the spirits of men that formerly have lived upon the earth. They hold that in the other world, those that are good men tho they be poor and mean in this world, yet there they shall become high and eminent; and that wicked men shall be turned into beasts. There is a Spider among them, that breeds an Egg, which she carries under her belly, 'tis as wide as a groat, and bigger then the body of the Spider. This egg is full of young Spiders that breed there: it hangs under her belly wheresoever she goes: and as their young ones grow to bigness they eat up the old one. Now the Chingulayes say, that disobedient children shall become Spiders in the other world, and their young ones shall eat them up.

They hold that every mans good or bad Fortune was predetermined by God, before he was born, according to an usual Proverb they have, Ollua cottaula tiana, It is written in the head.

They reckon the chief poynts of goodness to consist in giving to the Priests, in making Pudgiahs, sacrifices to their Gods, in forbearing shedding the blood of any creature: which to do they call Pau boi, a great sin: and in abstaining from eating any flesh at all, because they would not have any hand, or any thing to do in killing any living thing. They reckon Herbs and Plants more innocent food. It is religion also to sweep under the Bogaha or God-Tree, and keep it clean. It is accounted religion to be just and sober and chast and true, and to be endowed with other vertues, as we do account it.

They give to the poor out of a Principle of Charity which they extend to forraigners, as well as to their own Country-men. But of every measure of rice they boyl in their houses or their families they will take out an handful, as much as they can gripe, and put into a bag, and keep it by it self, which they call Mitta-haul. And this they give and distribute to such poor as they please, or as come to their doors.

Nor are they charitable only to the poor of their own Nation, but as I said to others: and particularly to the Moorish beggars, who are Mahometans by religion. These have a Temple in Cande. A certain former king gave this

Temple this Priviledg, that every Free-holder should contribute a Ponnam to it. And these Moors go to every house in the land to receive it. And if the house be shut, they have power to break it open, and to take out of goods to the value of it. They come very confidently when they beg, and they say they come to fulfill the charity. And the people do liberally relieve them for charity sake.

There is only one County in the Land, viz. Dolusbaug, that pays not the aforesaid duty to the Moors Temple. And the reason is, that when they came first thither to demand it, the Inhabitants beat them away. For which act they are free from the payment of that Ponnam, and have also another priviledg granted them for the same. That they pay no Marral, or Harriots, to the King as other Countreys do.

These Moors Pilgrims have many pieces of Land given them by well disposed persons out of charity, where they build houses and live. And this land becomes theirs from generation to generation for ever.

They lay Flowers, out of religion, before their Images every morning and evening, for which Images they build little Chappels in their yards as we said before. They carry beads in their hands on strings, and say so many prayers as they go. Which custom in all probability they borrowed of the Portugueze. They love a man that makes conscience of his ways. Which makes them respect Christians more than any others, because they think they are just and will not lye. And thus we have finished our discourse of their Religion.

Concerning their Houses, Diet, Housewiferie, Salutation, Apparel. Having already treated of their Religion, we now come to their secular concerns. And first we will lead you into their houses, and show you how they live.

Their Houses are small, low, thatched Cottages, built with sticks, daubed with clay, the walls made very smooth. For they are not permitted to build their houses above one story high, neither may they cover with tiles, nor whiten their walls with lime, but there is a Clay which is as white, and that they use sometimes. They employ no Carpenters, or house-builders, unless some few noble-men, but each one buildeth his own dwelling. In building whereof there is not so much as a nail used; but instead of them every thing which might be nailed, is tyed with rattans and other strings, which grow in the woods in abundance; whence the builder hath his Timber for cutting. The Country being warm, many of them will not take pains to clay their walls, but make them of boughs and leaves of Trees. The poorest sort have not above one room in their houses, few above two, unless they be great men. Neither doth the King allow them to build better.

They are not nice nor curious in their houses. They have no Chimneys in them, but make their fires in one corner, so that the roof is all blacked with the smoke.

The great people have handsome and commodious houses. They have commonly two buildings one opposite to the other, joined together on each side with a wall, which makes a square Courtyard in the middle. Round about against the walls of their houses are banks of clay to sit on; which they often daub over with soft Cow-dung, to keep them smooth and clean. Their Slaves and Servants dwell round about without in other houses with their wives and children.

Their Furniture is but small. A few earthen pots which hang up in slings made of Canes in their houses, having no shelves, one or two brass Basons to eat in, a stool or two without backs. For none but the King may sit upon a stool with a back. There are also some baskets to put corn in, some mats to spread upon the ground to sleep on: which is the bedding both for themselves and friends when they come to their houses. Also some Ebony pestles about four foot long to beat rice out of the husk and a wooden Morter to beat it in afterwards to make it white, a Hirimony or a Grater to grate their Coker-nuts with, a flat stone upon which they grind their Pepper and Turmeric. With another stone which they hold in their hands at the same time, they have also in their houses Axes, Bills, Houghs, Atches, Chissels, and other Tools for their use. Tables they have none but sit and eat on the ground.

And now we are mentioning eating, let us take a view of this people at their meals. Their Dyet and ordinary fare, is but very mean, as to our account. If they have but Rice and Salt in their house, they reckon they want for nothing. For with a few green Leaves and the juice of a Lemmon with Pepper and Salt, they will make a hearty meal. Beef here may not be eaten; it is abominable: Flesh and Fish is somewhat scarce. And that little of it they have, they had rather sell to get money to keep, than eat it themselves: neither is there any but outlandish men, that will buy any of them. It is they indeed do eat the fat and best of the Land. Nor is it counted any shame or disgrace to be a niggard and sparing in dyet; but rather a Credit even to the greatest of them, that they can fare hard and suffer hunger, which they say, Soldiers ought to be able to endure.

The great ones have always five or six sorts of food at one meal, and of them not above one or two at most of Flesh or Fish, and of them more pottage than meat, after the Portugal fashion. The rest is only what groweth out of the ground. The main substance with which they fill their bellies is Rice, the other things are but to give it a relish.

If these people were not discouraged from rearing and nourishing of Cattle and Poultry, provisions might be far more plentiful. For here are many Jackalls, which catch their Hens; and some Tigres, that destroy their Cattle: but the greatest of all is the King; whose endeavour is to keep them poor and in want. For from them that have Hens his Officers take them for the Kings use giving little or nothing for them; the like they do by Hogs, Goats none are suffered to keep, besides the King, except strangers.

In dressing of their victuals they are not to be discommended: for generally they are cleanly and very handy about the same. And after one is used to that kind of fare, as they dress it, it is very savoury and good. They sit upon a mat on the ground, and eat. But he, whom they do honour and respect, sits on a stool and his victuals on another before him.

Their common drink is only water: and if they drink Rack, it is before they eat, that it may have the more operation upon their bodies. When they drink they touch not the Pot with their mouths, but hold it at a distance, and pour it in. They eat their Rice out of China dishes, or Brass Basons, and they that have not them, on leaves. The Carrees, or other sorts of Food which they eat with their Rice, is kept in the Pans it is dressed in, and their wives serve them with it, when they call for it. For it is their duties to wait and serve their Husbands while they eat, and when they have done, then to take and eat that which they have left upon their Trenchers. During their eating they neither use nor delight to talk to one another.

They always wash their hands and mouths both before and after they have eaten; but for others to pour the water on their hands is looked upon as an affront. For so they do to them, whom they account not worthy to handle their Water pott. But when they wash, with one hand they pour it themselves upon the other. They are very cleanly both in their bodies and heads, which they do very often wash, and also when they have been at stool they make use of water.

But to give you a little of their Cookery. If People be in the room talking together, the woman being ready to put the Rice into the Pot, bids them all be silent till she has put it in, and then they may procede with their discourse. For if they should talk while the Rice is putting in, it would not swell.

At the time of the year that there is most plenty of Lemmons, they take them and squeeze the juyce into an earthen pot, and set over the fire, and boil it so it becomes thick and black like Tar. This they set by for their use, and it will keep as long as they please. A very small quantity of it will suffice for sawce. They call it Annego. . . .

They lay the Rice on the ground, and then beat it, one blow with one hand, and then tossing the Pestle into the other, to strike with that. And at the same time they keep stroke with their feet (as if they were dancing) to keep up the Corn together in one heap. This being done, they beat it again on a wooden Morter to whiten it, as was said before. This work tho it be very hard, belongeth only to the women: as also to fetch both wood and water. The wood they bring upon their heads, the water in an earthen Pot, placing it upon their hip. To the women also belongs a small bill to cut Herbs, Pumkins which she is to dress. Which bill she lays upon the ground, the edge upwards, and sets her self upon the Staff or handle to hold it fast, and what she meaneth to cut, she lays it upon the edge, and shoveth it on it. . . .

When one comes to anothers house, being set down the Entertainment is, green Leaves, they call Bullat, which they eat raw with Lime and Betelnut, and Tobacco. And being set a while, the man of the house will ask the Stranger what he comes for, which if he does not suddenly, the Stranger will take exceptions at it, as thinking he is not welcome to him. Neither do they ever go one to visit the other, unless it be for their own ends, either to beg or borrow.

And if Kindred that are very nearly related come together, they have no loving or private conference one with the other, but sit like strangers very solid and grave. And if they stay above one night, which is the common custom, then they do help and assist the man of the house in any work or service he hath to do.

When any friends go to anothers house to visit, they never go empty handed, but carry provisions and sweet meats with them to their friend. And then he makes them a Feast according to his ability, but they never eat of those things which themselves brought. But there is but little feasting among them unless at a Wedding.

When they meet one another, their manner of Salutation or obeisance is, to hold forth their hands, the Palms upwards, and bow their Bodies: but the superior to the inferior holds forth but one hand, and if the other be much beneath him, he only nods his head. The women salute by holding up both their hands edgways to their Foreheads. The general complement one to another at first meeting is to say Ay; it signifies how do you: and the other answers, Hundoi, that is, well.

The Habit of the men when they appear abroad is after this sort. The Nobles wear Doublets of white or blew Callico, and about their middle a cloth, a white one next their skin, and a blew one or of some other colour or painted, over the white: a blew or red shash girt about their loyns, and a Knife with a carved handle wrought or inlaid with Silver sticking in their bosom; and a compleat short Hanger carved and inlaid with Brass and Silver by their sides, the Scabbard most part covered with Silver, bravely ingraven; a painted cane and sometimes a Tuck in it in their hands, and a boy always bare-headed with long hair hanging down his back waiting upon him, ever holding a small bag in his hand, which is instead of a Pocket, wherein is Betel-leaves and nuts. Which they constantly keep chewing in their mouths, with Lime kept in a Silver Box rarely engraven, which commonly they hold in their hands, in shape like a Silver Watch.

The great ones also generally, and spruce young men do wear their hair long hanging down behind: but when they do any work or travail hard, it annoying them, they tie it up behind. Heretofore generally they bored holes in their ears, and hung weights in them to make them grow long, like the Malabars, but this King not boring his, that fashion is almost left off. The men for ornament do wear Brass, Copper, Silver Rings on their Fingers, and some of the greatest Gold. But none may wear any Silk.

But the women in their Apparel do far surpass the men, neither are they so curious in clothing themselves as in making their wives fine. The mens Pride consists in their Attendance, having men bearing Arms before and behind them.

In their houses the women regard not much what dress they go in, but so put on their cloths as is most convenient for them to do their work. But when they go abroad, and make themselves fine, they wear a short Frock with sleeves to cover their bodies of fine white Calico wrought with blew and red Thread in flowers and branches: on their Arms Silver Bracelets, and their fingers and toes full of Silver Rings about their necks, Necklaces of Beads or Silver, curiously wrought and engraven, guilded with Gold, hanging down so low as their breasts. In their ears hang ornaments made of Silver set with Stones, neatly engraven and guilded. Their ears they bore when they are young, and roll up Coker-nut leaves and put into the holes to stretch them out, by which means they grow so wide that they stand like round Circles on each side of their faces, which they account a great ornament, but in my Judgment a great deformity, they being well featured women.

Their other ornaments and Apparel show very comely on them. Their Hair they oyl, with Coker-nut oyl, to make it smooth, and comb it all behind. Their hair grows not longer than their wasts, but because it is a great ornament to have a great bunch of hair, they have a lock of other hair fastened in a Plate of engraved Silver and guilded, to tie up with their own, in a knot hanging down half their Backs. Their hands are bare, but they carry a scarf of striped or branched Silk or such as they can get, casting it carelessly on their head and shoulders. About their Wasts they have one or two Silver girdles made with Wire and Silver Plate handsomely engraven, hanging down on each side, one crossing the other behind. And as they walk they chew Betel. But notwithstanding all their bravery neither man nor woman wears shoes or stockings, that being a Royal dress, and only for the King himself.

It is in general a common custom with all sorts of People, to borrow Apparel or Jewels to wear when they go abroad, which being so customary is no shame nor disgrace to them, neither do they go about to conceal it. For among their friends or strangers where they go, they will be talking saying, This I borrowed of such a one, and this of another body.

Poetry and Proclamations in the Kandyan Kingdom

Anonymous and Kirti Sri Rajasimha

During the long colonial period, literature and the arts developed and thrived in the upcountry Kandyan kingdom, reaching a peak during the reigns of Kirti Sri Rajasimha and (r. 1751–82) and Rajadhi Rajasimha (r. 1782–98). Poetry was written celebrating the "careers" and exploits of the gods, including deities who rose in fame as the result of Tamil migrations into the upcountry (as evident in The Ballad of Pitiye Devi *below), or as the result of resistance to Portuguese rule (as in the case of Devata Bandara, also known as Daedimunda, in the* Galakaeppu Sahalla *below). Sannasas, royal proclamations inscribed in stone or on gold or copper plates dedicating land and human resources to temples and shrines, were composed by kings, such as Kirti Sri Rajasimha (below) to endow the well-being of the religious culture. In the mid- to late eighteenth century, Buddhist temples were rehabilitated during a period of cultural revival led by the Tamil-speaking kings of the Nayakkar dynasty, the last to rule as kings of Sri Lanka.*

Galakaeppu Sahalla

(BREAKING THE STONE)

Anonymous

1. Great seer Siddhartha,
    The Dhamma he expounded to the world,
    The Sangha—to these three gems
    I bow my head in reverence.

2. When ten earth-loads of Mara's retinue
    Congregated to declare war,
    The gods all fled on sight
    Taking refuge beyond Mt. Meru.

3. [The Buddha,] his back against the Bodhi Tree,
   Sitting on the Diamond Throne, declared:
   "Even if Mara comes for war
   I shall not move before I am enlightened."

4. On that day, Vasavarti Mara
   Gathered together his battalions of death
   And tried to prevent Buddhahood's realization
   Surrounding the Buddha with his forces.

5. Abandoning the Buddha,
   The gods departed;
   But a strong-willed [Daedi] deity came forward
   And declared he was ready to fight:

6. "Without any weapon in hand
   And only a golden walking cane,
   I shall attack and sever them
   In combat," he told the Sage.

7. Having provided the ten-fold gift
   By creating persons of the ten perfections [*paramitas*],
   The Buddha declared, "Wait, O Mara!
   I shall show you how to fight!"

8. In surveying the six heavens
   The world of *nagas*, and the three worlds,
   There is none comparable to you
   Who received the epithet "Munda Daedi."

9. Venerating the Buddha and setting forth,
   He saw Lord Vesamuni.
   Entrusted with the command over all *Yaksas*,
   He went to see Upulvan Deviyo.

10. Having surveyed the surroundings,
    He descended to the Maya country.
    There it was commanded
    That a city be constructed for Devata Surindu.

11. A child was conceived in Somavati's womb.
    After nine and a half months,
    The mother died and was reduced to ashes
    As her house was set to flame.

12. The child of that burnt woman
    Came out of her womb as a prince.
    In the morning the king and his ministers
    saw him besmeared with ash.

13. In the middle of the ocean, rejoicing reigned
    Amidst the constant light of torches.
    In the guise of a sandalwood log
    Wafted by the waves, he came ashore,

14. Assuming the form of a divine image,
    Two persons went mad
    Near the city of Maya.
    A mountain stream appeared.

15. Having performed the *asala* festival,
    He ordered the various realms of his kingdom.
    By charity and benevolence,
    He protected his kingdom for twenty-five years.

16. Then that king of the gods,
    Being fond of Udarata [the upcountry],
    According to ancient custom,
    Took a shine to the Satara Korale.

17. (Daedimunda) went to Kirungandeniya
    To survey the environs
    And took the road
    That led to the Golden Stone Cave.

18. He made the milk from the cows of the royal herd
    Turn into blood!
    The wise royal ministers
    Declared it as the work of his magical power.

19. The king who had dreamt this
    Cleared an area of trees and stumps
    Where the golden walking cane had been planted.
    There he erected a three-storey palace of pure gold.

20. He built Alutnuwara with
    Its inner shrine of sandalwood,
    A dancing chamber at its center
    And thirty-six halls.

21. "In the descending path to the compound,
    There is a boulder obstructing.
    We cannot break it!"
    The plaint was made to Devata Surindu.

22. Advised by his ministers, the king examined the situation
    Finding the difficulty of creating a flat ground.
    So he declared: "I shall manifest my power by employing the *yaksas*
    To smash this rock to make the ground flat for the compound.

23. "Make *kavun* [oil cakes] and *kiri bath* [milk rice].
    Do not make these in small pieces.
    Offer these to the *yaksas* so they will not tire.
    May the *yaksas* blast this rock tonight!"

24. Bedecked in sandalwood paste and smeared in cow-dung,
    Covered with coconut flowers and tender coconut leaves,
    Attended by coquettish and charming women,
    That place was filled with *kiri bath*.

25. *Yaksas* from Bengal, Gauda, Malla countries,
    Yaksas from Kongani, Java, and Andhra countries,
    Yaksas from Kannadiga, Kaudi, and Kaberi countries,
    All *yaksas* were summoned to Sri Lanka.

26. "*Yaksas*, eat whatever you desire.
    Take spears, swords and iron cudgels.
    Take whatever weapons you please
    And smash this stone into tiny pieces."

27. As a strike of thunder in the sky,
    As the earth rumbles in an earthquake,
    As the ground shakes when guns burst,
    They blasted that rock as if playing hand ball.

28. Their languages varied according to their countries.
    The Tamil *Yaksas* shouted loudly.
    In anger some attacked each other.
    The *Yaksas* from the Sinhala country made little noise.

29. Some break the stone just by chanting.
    Some show their strength in fighting each other.
    Some stay away after being beaten.
    Some shoulder the rocks and roll them down.

30. So they broke the stone to make the ground flat.
    They filled the streams and canals in equal measure.
    They fixed stones for a breakwater in the tank.
    This they informed (to Daedimunda) and worshipped at his feet.

31. "If we are allowed to stay in this country
    We shall perform all work asked of us by this king.
    It is verily difficult to meet this god."
    Saying so, they fell down at his feet.

32. These women full of charm are like golden images.
    They chatter in a lovely manner like the golden parrots.
    They tie their long hair bedecked with flowers and eschew wigs.
    "Oh, how can we leave these lovely women behind?"

33. "O *Yaksas*, you are ignorant of (our) Sinhala charms.
    (Our) *mantras* will bind and imprison you.
    (Our) *mantras* will punish you severely. You will stand on *yantrai*,
    Be confined to a smoke-filled chamber, and sprayed by nasal unguents.

34. Do not sicken the women you encounter.
    (Leave us) without grief. Get away!
    Like a lake empties when the dam is burst,
    Each of you get back to your respective countries!

35. With the blasting of the rock being a display of great power,
    Group after group of people from towns and villages came
    To see (Daedimunda)
    And to worship him intimately.

36. They clean their teeth, wash their heads and bathe (their bodies).
    They wear clean clothes with pleats a-plenty.
    They offer betel, coconut, rice and gifts,
    Worship him and happily leave.

37. They bring their women possessed by *Yaksas*,
    Women with intense burning pain in their loins.
    (Women) dance vigorously in the (*devalaya*) compound.
    "We must leave!" the *Yaksas* plead.

38. (*Yaksas*) are tied to trees, beaten and broken by canings.
    (*Yaksas*) are made to stand in the sun with stones on their heads.
    "Take a vow, go and do not lie!"
    "We shall go now not looking back on this country!"

39. All around the compound, silk-cotton poles were erected.
    The *Devol Yaksas* were summoned from this (Sinhala) country,
    Raised to silk-cotton poles and tethered.
    "Leave! Out with your curses!" It is decreed.

40. What punishments were meted to *Pilli* and *Suniyam Yaksas*!
    They were summoned in groups and beaten mercilessly.
    Faces paled, they groveled for mercy at (Daedimunda's) feet.
    "*Pilli Yaksas!* Leave or face further torment!"

41. *Yaksas!* Don't you know the teachings of Gautama Buddha?
    Yaksas! Don't you know the commands of Lord Vesamuni?
    Yaksas! Don't you know that *Yaksas* are afraid of the gods?
    Yaksas! Don't reckon with the power of Daedimunda! Leave now!

42. *Davul, tammaettan, pataha,* and *morahu* drums are beaten.
    Dancer here and there wearing masks perform.
    Is anyone in the world superior in making war?
    Behold Daedimunda's display of martial arts!

43. (Daedimunda) takes his bejeweled cane in hand.
    I take flowers, lamps, and gifts in a golden plate and offer them.
    Clothes, canopies, and curtains are hung for a week.
    There is no one on earth who compares to Devata Bandara
       of Aluthnuvara!

44. It is Devata Bandara, commander of the *Yaksas*,
    Who I worship and recite poetry pleasing to his ear.
    Proclaim his divine virtues so the three worlds may hear.
    See him and all diseases will be quelled forever.

45. An elephant came to the *devalaya* compound and gave a mighty thrust
       at the *kitul* tree.
    By a single right-handed blow to the body (the elephant's)
    Back was broken, (the elephant) paralyzed and crawled to its death.
    In these three worlds, there is no one tougher than you who dwells
       where the stone was broken.

46. Some of you *Yaksas!* You go into the country, spread disease and beget
       ritual offerings.
    Do not be rash! Accept ritual offerings and cure disease and affliction.
    He is like the king of the cobras in exacting vengeance, poisonous to
       all, know this!
    He is like the lord of the clouds, O *Yaksas*, remember this too.

47. In breaking the rock, your arrival in Satara Korale was revealed.
    Go[ne] forth from [to?] all quarters, from[to?] all countries one after
        the other.
    The Gods of the Four Quarters, with their divine eyes, have seen
        (these) great courageous deeds.
    From then, the Sun and Moon flags of Satara Korale were raised and
        the people began to dance in joy.

48. The Portuguese who came here surrounded Sunuvela and
        Aluthnuvara.
    Challenging the god with abusive words, they tried to rob (our)
        treasures here.
    The *Yaksas* were summoned and the Portuguese chased beyond the
        river at night.
    Only then did Devata Bandara's suzerainty over the *Yaksas* become
        renowned.

Translated by P. B. Meegaskumbura

The Ballad of Pitiye Devi

Anonymous

He goes to Dumbara,
Sees the glade of Dumbara;
He shoots Rama's arrows
And drives Natha Deviyo across [the river].

Protecting people
He comes in the golden chariot;
Having obtained the boon of gods,
Pitiye Devi arrives.

On account of the great king of Soli [Chola],
He was born of the womb of Princess Haliyapuli.
In this ceremony of seeking protection,
We offer betel to the Soli [Chola] prince.

In a customary manner a bed is made of Sal, Sapu and Na.
At the news of his arrival, two yak tail fans are placed on both sides.
A bed covered with soft divine clothes is prepared;
May it please the Soli king to come quickly to this altar of flowers.

On hearing the woman's tale of the "Bull with a Broken Horn,"
King Gajaba, the ruler at Beligala,
Considered the Soli king with his contemptuous gaze;
Here is betel for the prince of Soli.

Into the royal family of Sinha of the Soli city
A great prince was born indeed;
He was a lord of war games
And was flanked by skilled followers.

The Soli prince ascended his chariot;
His skin shined like a red banana plant;
There, the disaster fell upon him, according to his past deeds.
Let us worship the Soli prince with pleased minds.

The cow laments in her motherly grief;
The shaking bell resounds plaintively;
A search for the doer of the injustice is made;
Then the afflicted prince comes forward.

For the cruelty meted out to the calf,
A cruel curse fell upon the prince accordingly.
The moment death fell upon him, a curse fell upon the city.
He, born as a yaksa, displayed his powers.

Gifts and offerings he received;
He punished and destroyed the enemies who speak the [Tamil?] language
Pondering over a suitable country all the while.
And he sailed away in a ship.

With mind well pleased, the prince set forth
Surrounded by Vadiga Tamil priests;
A flag was raised on the ship
Depicting Pitiye Devi riding a horse.

Wondrous is the way the ship was built;
Wondrous are the followers on both sides;
Wondrous is the flag on the ship and
Wondrous is the Soli king on the ship!

He sailed passing the Blood Sea.
He sailed passing the Pearl Sea.
He sailed passing the Milk Sea
And forthwith reached the land of Sinhala.

Verily you have come from the Soli country.
Verily you have no regard for the low country.
Verily you are the demolisher of the World Mountain by the wind's power.
Verily you have come to Pata Bulatgama.

You have passed by the low country.
You have passed by Batticaloa and Vellassa.
With compassion you have come to Sinhale [upcountry Lanka].
You have come looking for the hill of Uda Dumbara.

Like the cluster of stars in the sky,
An immense crowd has come from afar.
Ill feelings towards sword-bearers wearing turbans [Chola soldiers?]
You were compassionate and happy upon seeing Dumbara.

That comely prince stayed there,
A sportive boy in his youth,
His tresses were tied with a festoon of flowers,
That prince, Pitiye Devi, has thus arrived.

When on his way to Yaggahapitiye,
The agitated yakkhas began to tremble.
There he slew deer and chased away Natha Devi
Across the river to that side.

He cleared the land to settle at Udugoda,
Surveyed the feasibility of living in the jungle.
He built a three-tiered mansion with proper proportions
And went to live in Mahaletenne.

The picture of Gautama Buddha was painted.
Who else to make all beings cross over from samsara?
The picture of the god on horse-back under a parasol was painted.
Pitiye Devi is like a curative medicine.

Like a vatadage, a stone wall was built on top of the rock
And a picture was drawn by a master craftsman
In the three-tiered building open to the sky.
Lo and behold, the Soli king is like the sun and the moon.

The glade of Dumbara is called Pitiye.
Those who venture there are surprised to see him.
There Pitiye Devi sports day and night
And rests on the upper floor of the mansion.

Dambarawa is a magnificent field.
Bimbarawa is a magnificent field.
Of royal blood and destined to be the Buddha,
Pitiye Devi is like a swan.

The prince of Soli came to this city
And looked for a suitable field at Giragama.
There at Giragama with mind well pleased
Pitiye Devi remained on horse-back.

At Amunugama, Pilavala and Gurudeniya,
The high queens did not realize his powers.
My verses are now disconnected;
[To these places] Pitiye Devi visited.

He quells strife and remains unperturbed.
Often he goes along the river
Like a quick stream across the jungle.
Lo and behold, the gait of him!

Of our lord, well composed, who evokes delight,
The walk along the river is fine indeed.
Listen to my poems recited quietly.
The two elegant hands [of the Vadiga prince] are worthy of a kingdom.

Fully dressed and accompanied by a retinue,
Wearing flowers and buds about his tresses—
The flowers and buds of victory—
Behold the elegance of his arrival.

When he, this symbol of comeliness, arrived at Haragama,
The people, pleading for protection
Thronged at his feet.
Thus came the heroic Pitiye Devi.

Having encircled the city with the retinue of yaksas,
He appeared in a dream to the king
And declared that the city is beyond protection.
Thus the Soli king showed his powers [to the king].

He then proclaimed: "Make an enclosure at Gonawatte,
Collect deer and sambhur into the enclosure
And provide me with the flesh of deer and sambhur."
Thus did the Soli king display his power.

Seven amunus of rice were set aside,
A sword of silver was also made.
Sixty-seven king coconuts were also made ready.
With these offerings, the channel of Gurudeniya was cut.

Musical horns were blown at Rajavela,
From there a direct route was made to Gurudeniya.
Water on this course flowed right over the rock.
That blow of the sword will be remembered forever.

He then wore choice clothes and ornaments
And paraded with yak tail fans and parasols decked with pearls
To the music of five instruments and the trumpet.
His power is well established and understood by all.

Supplying water to a traditional field,
Where for a long time there was no channel.
Some used to graze animals there;
Behold how the channel was made at Gurudeniya.

Splinter after splinter was removed
And the rock became thinner and thinner.
Behold the mighty task done at Gurudeniya!
Rice sewn ripened like pears and [shined like] gems.

Pitiye Devi, lord of this world,
Stood on the rock with his holy feet
Like a flower does not crush its petals;
There is a devale for him on the rock at Gurudeniya.

Translated by P. B. Meegaskumbura

Urulewatte Sannasa

Kirti Sri Rajasimha

When His Majesty King Kirti Sri Raja Simha, the descendent of King Manu of the illustrious royal family of Maha Sammata, was reigning in Kandy the prosperous city, he inquired as to the state of religion in Lanka, and he was told that there were no ordained Buddhist monks, but only novices (*samaneras*); on this His Majesty said, "While I am reigning it is a pity to see the religion decline"; accordingly he set his mind on patronizing the tradition [*sasana*], assisted by the sub-king Rajadhi Raja Simha; he sent an embassy to Siam with presents worth one *lakh* [100,000] of coins, and invited monks from Siam, such as Upatissa and others, who came bringing with them *bana* [preaching] books. Then thousands of respectable men were robed, taught *pitakas* ["baskets" of Scriptures]; hundreds of them were daily fed; and hundreds of offerings of necessaries were made yearly; hundreds of ruined *viharas* [temples] were repaired in different places, including the Relic Temple, offerings of gardens, fields, and flower gardens were made to Anuradhapura, Samantakutaya, Mahiyangana vehera, the Dalada Maligawa, and other *viharas*. Thus it is laid down as a rule that if anyone were to take forcible possession of temple properties given by him or by any others, he shall be born and re-born a worm in a heap of cowdung for 60,000 years, and any one who takes a stick of firewood, a blade of grass, a fruit, or a flower out of temple lands shall be born a *pretaya* [hungry ghost] with a body fifty to six *yodun* long and belly in proportion, to pass his time with a chain of sighs, eyes full of tears, heart full of sorrow, without obtaining even refuse as food, and without being able to slake his thirst even if the current of the Ganges and Jumna were to pass through his throat, as such a current would evaporate from the heat of his body as the current of the ocean is evaporated by the heat of hell fire. On the contrary he who defends the temple rights or improves them will never be born in the four cardinal hells, but in celestial worlds, and enjoy bliss in heaven and earth. It is further said that out of the two, the donor enjoys bliss in heaven and to the defender attains Nirvana. So virtuous men, may you act up to these and attain Nirvana.

An Open Letter to the Kandyan Chiefs

Ananda Coomaraswamy

Ananda Coomaraswamy, whose father was Sri Lankan Tamil and mother a European, completed his Ph.D. dissertation and published it as Medieval Sinhalese Art *in 1907. In 1905, while researching that dissertation in Kandy, he wrote the appeal that is published below. He went on to serve as the curator for Asian art at the Boston Museum of Fine Arts for some thirty-five years, during which time he wrote numerous books for the Western public explaining the subtleties of Hindu and Buddhist religious cultures. In his famous letter to the Kandyan chiefs reprinted below, he laments the condition of so many Kandyan buildings and their frescoes, urging the Kandyan aristocracy to take it upon themselves to rescue the remains of their culture before modernity and time completely obliterated it. Coomaraswamy's sentiments correspond to a rising awareness of a vanishing indigenous culture during the final half-century of colonial rule. One of the major implications of the disestablishment of Kandyan kingship was that the artistic community, like the monastic community, lost its primary patrons in the king and his royal court.*

Sirs,

There is a subject which has for a long time greatly occupied me, and which appears to me of the greatest importance, and I therefore hope that you will pardon me for addressing this letter to you as a body; a letter setting forth some ideas on the Preservation of Ancient Buildings in Ceylon.

It is mainly to buildings of the seventeenth and eighteenth centuries (the Kandyan Period) that I refer; the much older buildings of Anuradhapura and Polonnaruwa are not at present, of course, in much danger of neglect or injudicious restoration. There are three kinds of buildings that must be specially mentioned, perhaps I should say four; these are viharas, devales, private houses and ambalams.

In the Kandyan districts the Sinhalese or Sinhalese-Hindu style of architecture prevailed until the end of the eighteenth century, during which not a few of the best of the surviving buildings were erected. At the end of that period a radical change set in, a change only comparable with that which took place in England and throughout Europe at the time of the Renaissance when the beauty and restraint of Gothic architecture yielded to an unrestrained and classical style which one may like or dislike as one pleases, but which spelt the doom of Gothic architecture, a doom rendered irrevocable by the steadily progressing industrial revolution which has since taken place. At the present time there is no architectural style in Europe, but buildings are put up of all sorts, from mechanical reproductions of Gothic churches, to the last jerry-built villa of the suburbs. The fundamental change, whose architectural expression I have just referred to, has taken place in Ceylon in one hundred, instead of the four hundred years it occupied in Europe; and it is therefore the easier here both to realise the former life of men in simpler times, and to measure the greatness of the change, of the very existence of which so many of us are nevertheless quite unconscious.

So then, there was a Kandyan style of architecture which flourished till the end of the eighteenth century; this Kandyan style having many obvious Hindu features but yet with a character all its own. Architecture needs for its complete expression, the reasonable intelligent co-operation of all the arts; and in the days I speak of it did not lack this, amongst the Kandyans; the stonemason and carpenter, the blacksmith and silversmith, the painter and potter, even the weaver combined to produce buildings of a lovely and harmonious character, part as it were of the very soil they grew from, and perfectly harmonious in style from the finials, the roofs to the inlaid keyplates on the doors, and from the carved Moonstones. . . .

Well, during the last two years, I have given my spare time to studying old Kandyan work in architecture and all the crafts that flourished in those times that seem now so far away. I have seen old buildings and new; and in the minor arts it has not been once or twice only that I have attempted to get made for myself some one or other of the wares that were once produced so easily and so well, and of which a little of the wreckage survives in a few museums and private collections; and it has been again and again borne in upon me as the result of bitter experience both in the remotest villages and in Kandy itself, that the character of steady competency which once distinguished the Kandyan artist-craftsman has gone forever; a change such as the industrial revolution has brought about almost all over the world.

Still more evident is the change when one passes from the personal efforts referred to, to the consideration of modern Kandyan buildings, and still more to that of the repairs and alterations which have been made in ancient buildings in modern times. In this latter sort of work the level of incompetency attained is nothing short of appalling; and the sad part of it is, that while the wholly new buildings do no permanent harm, the ill-done and often quite needless redecoration of old work destroys what is at once a work of art such as can be no longer produced, and at the same time effaces what is often a valuable historical document.

In repainting viharas nowadays the chief errors lie in the bad colours used; ill-judged attempts at the introduction of perspective; careless and ignorant, nay often irreverent work, and the introduction of unsuitable objects; I say bad colours because the old way of making colours has been given up, and with it all restraint in the use of colour, so that where a few colours only were once used (mainly red, yellow, black, white and a greyish green), the painting now displays all the colours of the rainbow; and at the same time the beautifully conventionalised and restful traditional style is abandoned in favour of a weak and ineffective realism, so that the inside of a vihara whose walls were once covered with worthy and decorative paintings are now as much like an ill-drawn Christmas card as anything.

No wall painting can satisfy that has not beauty of colour and restfulness of form, and these are no longer given. In the old days the pictured wall was a wall still, and not a window; nay a book rather, where, if you would, you might read the stories of the gods and heroes and whose characters, whether you read them or not, delighted you always with the beauty of their form and colour. Moreover, the expression of these great things being so well understood and so limited, it was not above the powers of execution of numbers of average workmen, and there was no danger of the holy and elevating subjects being treated absurdly or stupidly, so as to "wound the feelings of serious men" (William Morris, speaking of Egyptian decorative art). Instead of this, the most unsuitable objects are often seen in new paintings, such as pictures of street lamps, clocks and what not of that sort, and in one of the worst cases (at Ganegoda Vihara) a picture of a clerk at his table with topee and pipe beside him.

It is not at all unlikely, that under the new Ordinance larger funds will be available for the upkeep of Dewalas and Viharas than are now devoted to these purposes; if that is so, the danger of injury by injudicious redecoration and rebuilding will be not a little increased. I beg you to use your great influence in this matter and to see that these funds are devoted rather to the protection than to the unnecessary redecoration of these buildings. A little care and thought only are required to preserve what are sometimes priceless historical documents, and almost always works of art, such as cannot in the nature of things be produced under modern conditions.

Let me take one instance as an example, that of Degaldoruwa. I see with alarm that this vihara is specially mentioned in the petition as being in a dilapidated state, and urgently in need of repair. I know this vihara pretty well as I have lately spent 15 or 20 hours in copying part of the frescoes there. Let me recall to your minds the pictured stories on the walls, right and left of the inner door. Immediately on the left is the Vessantara Jataka, pictured in the worthiest and most beautiful manner imaginable. The wall is divided horizontally in panels wherein the story is set forth in order, the chief scenes being specially indicated by a few words of Sinhalese beneath. One of the grandest is that of King Wessantara riding on his elephant with all the insignia of state. The elephant is drawn with the greatest skill, the slow movement of the lifted feet and the swinging bells give just the right idea of dignified slow progress; immediately afterwards the elephant is seen again but King Wessantara has climbed down and is walking in front, with one hand pouring water into the hands of the Brahmans from Kalinga, betokening the gift of the elephant, and with his other arm round the elephant's trunk; the elephant has stopped the while, and the swinging bells are still. The gorgeous trappings of the elephant, the king's and the attendants' dresses and the royal insignia are drawn with very great care and just like the early illuminated manuscripts of Europe are invaluable records of past manners and customs. Two other scenes I must refer to; the first is the scene at the well, where Jujaka's wife Amittatapa is scoffed at by the other women fetching water; this scene is a fine piece of drawing; beside the well are two coconut trees, the conventional decorative treatment of which is quite perfect.

In yet another scene we are shown Madridewi and the two children walking, and next thereto, falling down and worshipping the late King Wessantara, now a hermit monk. The drawing of the trees, (chiefly nuga trees) is most lovely; and we have also a broad river flowing by, filled with fishes, and a lotus tank with six hamsas swimming in it and two others marching solemnly along the road from the river to the tank.

On the right side of the door is shown Sutasoma Jataka; tracings of part relating to King Baranas, who, as you know became for a time a cannibal, lie before me now. The picture of the king's cook preparing food in the royal kitchen is a valuable historical record; the man is seated on a combined vegetable slicer and coconut scraper and is slicing up a human arm for the king's repast. On one of the posts of the kitchen is hung a pingo, with a gaboniya hanging from each end, covering the chatties in which the king's provisions had been brought that morning. Further on we see King Baranas in the jungle, seated beneath a nuga tree with a great thorn in his foot; and he vows to offer a hundred king's sons to the Ruk-deviyo who appears in the branches above if he will cure him. He recovers and thinks the deviyo has cured him, and in another scene is shown hanging the king's sons to the deviyo's tree, as he had vowed. Ultimately of course all these are released and the wounds in their hands healed by rubbing with the bark of the tree, and King Baranas is converted by the preaching of Lord Buddha, in his then incarnation, and he is restored to his kingdom; most of which is faithfully depicted.

All these pictures are drawn in a perfectly flat decorative style; the only colours used are red, black, yellow, white and greenish-grey. These colours, as you know, were made by the artists themselves. The wall appears to glow with colour, though it is now some hundred and twenty years since the work was done. There are two other jatakas on the left and right of those already told of; these are not in quite such a good state of preservation, owing to leakage between the outer roof, and the overhanging rock, leakage which could easily have been avoided by a little care and attention. Inside the rock chamber are also very fine pictures of the life of Lord Buddha; some part of the painting inside too was never completed, as if the artist had left but yesterday. Well, you will see that here are a series of paintings of great artistic and historical value; and if they are once destroyed or injured by complete or even partial repainting, nothing can replace them.

Is it not worthwhile to preserve even one memorial of the steady competency of by-gone Kandyan artists? These are the best paintings I have yet seen in Ceylon, but there are many other good ones, that is, so far as they have survived the danger of repainting—work often entrusted not even to traditional Kandyan craftsmen, but allowed to be done by men from the towns or the low country, who have picked up a smattering of perspective and lost their traditional instinct for flat and dignified decorative treatment of mural decoration. Even if the painter be a Kandyan, who sees to it that he uses the right colours in the right way? The repainting of the Dalada Maligawa, now in progress, reveals the greatest possible neglect in this respect. For instead of the traditional home-made colours with their quiet richness, are used cheap paints bought in the boutiques, and these (especially the new fangled green and blue) put on with little or no care and taste. It is just the same everywhere; for example the good old painting of the Potgulkanda Vihara near Ratnapura, was being quite spoilt when I last saw it.

So far I have spoken chiefly of paintings, but all that I have said is equally true of every branch of architecture; the building is either altogether neglected; or repaired and restored in such a way as to make it a veritable eyesore; if the roof is not actually mended with corrugated iron as sometimes happens, it is at least usual for the old flat tiles to be thrown away, and new semi-cylindrical ones or even Mangalore tiles to be substituted; no one dreams of getting new flat tiles made, an easy enough thing one would think; but it would mean just a little more trouble, and no one cares enough about the matter for that.

But let us turn for a moment from the effects of injudicious restoration to those of neglect. The ruinous state of many ancient buildings, not only of devales, which have indeed suffered most in this respect, but even of viharas and those the most beautiful and important, is a crying shame. The beautiful Poya Maluwa at Kandy is fast spoiling for want of a few tiles and a little care to the woodwork to keep off the white ants; what were once great massive adze-hewn beams are eaten through and through, and scarcely hold together. . . . In fact, this specially lovely building could scarcely be in a worse state; it may fall to pieces any day. Every day and in every district, some such memorial of your national ideals and your national art is rotting before your eyes, and you do nothing to save it.

The delicate stonework, too, is plastered over with whitewash; but thank heaven, that is not a permanent injury, but one that can be amended any day. But once more as to the structural repairs (and they ought to be taken in hand at once), it is worse than useless to try and get such a building as this repaired by contract; the work must be done under the constant supervision of some one in full sympathy with, and with full knowledge of, Kandyan architecture. We should rest satisfied with nothing less than the protection and preservation of all good work remaining protection alike from ruin at the hands of would-be friends, and destruction at the hands of evident foes such as damp and ants.

Speaking generally the ancient temples have fallen into a state of disrepair, and some of them are partly in ruins and a considerable number of the valuable gifts and ornaments have been stolen away. The rev-

enues of temple lands have been misappropriated by trustees, members·
of the District Committees and others. Some examples are given in the
Dambulla Vihara; the historical architectural façade at the entrance has
been allowed to fall into a state of disrepair. Some parts of the interior
are in a dangerously dilapidated state. Most of the valuable works of art,
being gifts made by the Kings of old to the priests of the temples, have
been stolen. . . .

It may be argued that the devales are not connected with Buddhism,
and so are of less consequence. But it is not now on religious ground
that I appeal to you on behalf of ancient buildings, although so far as
the viharas are concerned, a good deal might be said on that score; it is
for the buildings as works of art, which once destroyed, can never be
replaced, and on account of their value as historical documents, that I
appeal for their preservation. If you suffer these monuments of the Sinhalese architectural style to perish—and some of the buildings I have
referred to are almost past hope—remember that no power on earth
can replace them, that you can no longer build as men built then; you
can no more do that, than we in Europe, by any expenditure of money
and pains whatsoever, can raise up a Gothic building, no not even a
barn, such as simple unlettered men could build six hundred years ago.

It is heart-rending for so many buildings and frescoes to be ruined by
mere neglect of the simplest and often quite inexpensive precautions;
all that was needed being a few tiles and a few repairs here and there,
a beam protected from white ants and so forth. I thought, when I was
working lately at Degaldoruwa, of Robert Browning's "indignant vindi-
cation of the early mediaeval painters"; here are some of his words.—

"Wherever a fresco peels and drops,
Wherever an outline weakens and wanes
Till the latest life in the painting stops,
Stands one whom each painter pulse-tick pains.
One wishful each scrap should clutch its brick,
Each tinge not wholly escape the plaster,
A lion who dies of an ass's kick,
The wronged great soul of an ancient master."

I hoped too that the artist was glad to see there one to whom the remembrance of his good work will be a lasting pleasure and who thinks
of him and his fellows as still surely living, still real men and capable of
receiving love whom "I love no less than the great men, poets and painters and such like, who are on earth now."

I have said no word of the other sorts of buildings I meant to speak of, viz., private houses and ambalams. Of the latter I know but few really fine and ancient examples; of these, one is at Mangalagama near Kegalla; this ambalam was rebuilt so late as the middle of the last century from the materials of an earlier one, and is, even so, a very fine specimen of Kandyan architecture, especially as regards the timbering of the roof and the beautiful gates or drooping lotus capitals, so different from the careless modern copies that are sometimes seen, as for example in the new ambalam at Ratnapura, which is indeed built in a real Kandyan style, but much degraded in the details of its wood-work. Of private houses, walawwas and smaller houses of the old sort, with their beautiful massive doors, and stout adze-cut timbers, fewer and fewer survive each year; even if their owners feel their old homes unsuited to their present needs, may not a few of these be preserved to tell their children's children how men lived and wrought in the old days before progress and commerce changed the very face of the earth?

Things have gone the same way in Europe; sadly indeed as our English mediaeval buildings have suffered from neglect, and even intentional spoliation, they have suffered even more in the last century at the hands of the decorator and restorer. The ruin caused by the Puritans was light in the comparison to the wreckage that has been occasioned by churchwardens and ignorant persons in modern times. For once more I do assure you that the day of steady competency on the part of the Kandyan craftsman, though but a hundred years behind us, is no less far off and out of reach than are the traditional art and skill of the European craftsmen of five hundred years ago.

It is, then, in the words of the manifesto of the English Society for the Preservation of Ancient Buildings founded by William Morris in 1877, "for all these buildings that we plead, and call upon those who have to deal with them, to put protection in the place of restoration, to stave off decay by daily care, to prop a perilous wall or mend a leaky roof by such means as are obviously meant for support or covering and show no pretence of other at and otherwise to resist all tempering with either the fabric or the ornament of the building as it stands; . . . in fine, to treat your ancient buildings as monuments of a bygone art, created by bygone manners, that modern art cannot meddle with without destroying."

COLONIAL POSTSCRIPT: THE OTHER EDEN

Richard de Zoysa

An outspoken opponent of the Sri Lankan government in the 1980s and a trenchant critic of Sri Lanka's colonial rulers of the past, Richard De Zoysa is represented here with a poem that constitutes a powerful indictment. De Zoysa was murdered by unknown parties, as were so many others, during the presidency of Ranasinghe Premadasa (1989–93), when the country was threatened by insurrection. De Zoysa, however, did not come from the alienated rural masses but rather from Colombo's educated elite.

Fat white man
sitting with elbows on the batik cloth (the table rotting underneath)
nibbling like dowager at potted shrimps imperial dominance
    emphasised with fork in languid hand.

White slug
burrowing the fertile Orient soil, and boring me with needle eye
    behind steel rim,
tales of (erotic)
                conquest.
Boring me to the quick, piercing my soul!

A street away, my lover waits for me
the lamp burns low, tomorrow needs refilling. O, Christ died not so
    hard on Calvary
for love of Man, nor went he forth so willing as I do now.

The Romans on their thighs
wore sword and dagger, and they crucified spreadeagled nations,
    naked to the skies and pierced with spears, but no, not in
the side.
Here, in the centre of my aching earth
I hold the pain, the rotting maggot seed

of the white carrion.
Clenched in my fist (O, clenched to fight the fight)
The Mater Dolorosa—
Mother of Dollars
at least tomorrow's
lamp will burn bright.

III

Emerging Identities

The emerging identities that now constitute the mosaic of contemporary Sri Lankan society are the byproduct of a long and complicated history. They continue to evolve. Despite the protestations of some modern politicians, religious figures, and nationalist historians, none of these emergent identities is timeless or primordial, nor are the relations obtaining between them. They are, as most philosophically sophisticated Buddhists and Hindus would have it, *conditioned* by time and circumstance, a byproduct of the process of inevitable change.

Perhaps it is the great strength or tenacity of each of these emergent identities in the contemporary period that represents the greatest challenge to Sri Lanka's future as a united country. For deep emotional loyalties to its constituent communities at times seem to eclipse affinities for the country's constituted whole. Many now elderly Sri Lankans, who attained social consciousness in the 1950s or 1960s, or even in the early 1970s, can be heard to say that in their time of growing up they were rarely aware of much, if any, ethnic differences among their cohort. Certainly, they aver, ethnic difference did not seriously inform their political visions or sensitivities. While that may be white-washing the past somewhat, a dose of wistful "reverse anachronism" as it were, it does indicate how the ethos of the current situation characterized by strained ethnic consciousness contrasts with the experience of the past, real or imagined, in the minds of many. In frustration, some are tempted to ask: Is it presently the case that the vision of the whole of the country is now largely construed by some as simply a matter of insisting on the privileging of one of its parts? That entitled Christians of the 1960s, for example, argued for English as the official language because they regarded it as their birthright as Sri Lankans? Or, that Sinhalas have argued for Buddhism as a national religion of special status for the country as a whole? Can they argue that Sri Lanka is actually a *Buddhist* country? Or, that Tamils have argued that they required their own recognized homeland where other ethnic groups may not live as well? Or, that they require their own independent separate state apart from the rest of the country?

The current situation in the country would seem to beg the central question: whither *Sri Lankan* identity per se? Is there any collective identity of the "international" sort possible within the context of such powerfully centrifugal emergent identities such as the Sinhala, Tamil, and Muslim? How does a multiethnic society like Sri Lanka's develop a condition in which it is secure enough to celebrate its diversity rather than championing one community's rights at the expense of another's? In the immediate aftermath of the tsunami's devastation in 2004, a palpable expression of unity in the face of adversity surfaced, though all too briefly. That unity dissipated within weeks as political interests on both sides of the ethnic divide sought the spoils of international disaster aid. While the moment of unity was momentary indeed, its brief fruition did indicate that unity is, indeed, a possibility, and perhaps ultimately a matter of will.

Is the answer to Sri Lanka's fissuring condition to be found in the various models of federalism represented by India? Canada? Switzerland? Or is devolution of power at the center of a unified state, rather than at the periphery, a preferable solution? Or are there any structural political answers possible in a time when memory is still raw from wanton acts of violence that have killed so many innocent Sri Lankans, Sinhala, Tamil, Muslim, and Christian? What is necessary for a process of healing to occur in which people can learn to transcend the deep wounds they have suffered during the past generation of violence?

In identifying the various factors constitutive of each community's emergent identity, one can also begin to identify certain possibilities for rapprochement. That each community in Sri Lanka seems quite innocent of the other's culture and history, and consequently its emerging identity, is clear to any sensitive external observer who has had the opportunity to talk and meet extensively with Sri Lanka's people from across the spectrum. It does seem that religion, as the double-edged sword that it has always been historically, contains within its various teachings the possibility of inspiring concord as much as discord. It is certainly the case that both Buddhist and Hindu traditions, perhaps even much more so than the Muslim and Christian, have not insisted on exclusive claims to truth and power, but have historically, at times and to the contrary, understood the veritable truism that philosophical meaning can be derived from multiple methods and multiple perspectives. Can that philosophical perspective be converted into social, economic, and political realities? Rather than simply functioning as an ethnic marker of identity, can religion foster an attitude of compassion for suffering, or an ethic of dignity of labor regardless of class or caste? The challenges for Sri Lanka are real, require courage, the transcendence of expediency, and genuine good will.

In the third part of *The Sri Lanka Reader*, we shall trace the development of Sinhala Buddhist, Tamil Hindu, Muslim, and to a lesser extent, Christian identities as these came to fruition in the latter years of British colonialism and following independence. The fourth part of the *Reader* will focus on specific moments of political import.

BUDDHIST IDENTITIES: AN INTRODUCTION

"Theravada" means "the way of the elders," and Theravada Buddhists in Sri Lanka are often proud to construe the name of their religion to mean "original Buddhism." For many Sinhala Buddhists in Sri Lanka, Theravada represents the unaltered teachings (dhamma) of the Buddha that have been preserved throughout history by his order of monks (sangha). Ostensibly, Theravada is, indeed, a conservative religious tradition. But pious protestations notwithstanding, the Buddhists of Sri Lanka, like any other religious community, are conditioned by history. Therefore, their understandings of Buddhist tradition have varied depending upon time and circumstance. No doubt, the nature and speed of those changes in understandings have accelerated during the past century and a half with the advent and impact of modernity, nationalism, capitalism, universal suffrage, and democracy. In the section that follows, examples of how Buddhists have adapted and transformed their religion in response to these social realities are presented. Collectively, these examples reflect the dictum that changes in the social order, or changes in the political economy, will necessarily be reflected in changes in the emerging religious culture.

Old Diary Leaves

Henry Steele Olcott

*Henry Steele Olcott, a retired and decorated United States Army colonel who had
fought for the Union in the American Civil War, came to South Asia as a student of
Madam Blavatsky's Theosophical Society. The purpose of his visit to Ceylon was
to establish the Buddhist Theosophical Society. His direct impact was enormous,
following as he did on the famous Christian/Buddhist debates in Panadura that
had signaled the resurgence of Buddhism on the island. He regularly attracted huge
crowds, in part due to the novelty of an educated white man espousing Buddhist
philosophy. Olcott channeled that momentum on his tours into the establishment
of a series of Buddhist schools patterned on the curricula of the elite Christian missionary schools. He also orchestrated a reorganization of public Buddhist ritual,
including the celebration of the monthly full moon* poya *days, especially Vesak (the
full moon day in May celebrating the Buddha's birth, enlightenment, and* parinibbana). *It would not be wrong to attribute to Olcott's influence a good deal of the
public ritual and symbolic articulation of Buddhism that has dominated Buddhist
discourse in the late nineteenth and twentieth centuries. Indeed, the puritanical elements of what later scholars have referred to as "Protestant Buddhism" are clearly
seen in the passage that follows. Olcott's most influential Sinhala follower was the
Anagarika Dharmapala, who went on to establish the Mahabodhi Society and can
be seen, perhaps, as the forerunner of the militant forms of politically inclined Buddhism that appeared in the mid-twentieth century and after.*

"Second Series [1878–1883]."

Before dawn on the 17th we were off Galle light, . . . anchored about 500
yards from shore. The monsoon burst, and there was tremendous wind and
rain, but the view was so lovely that we stopped on deck to enjoy it. A beautiful day; a verdant promontory to the north, against which the surf dashed
and in foamy jets ran high up against the rocky shore; a long, curved sandy
beach bordered with tile-roofed bungalows almost hidden in an ocean of
green palms; the old fort, custom house, lighthouse, jetty, and coaling sheds

to the south, and to the east the tossing sea with a line of rocks and reefs walling it out from the harbor. Far away inland rose Adam's Peak and his sister mountains.

After breakfast, in a lull of the storm, we embarked in a large boat decorated with plantain trees and lines of bright-colored flowers, on which were the leading Buddhists of the place. We passed through a lane of fishing boats decked out with gaudy cloths and streamers, their prows pointing inward. On the jetty and along the beach a huge crowd awaited us and rent the air with the united shout of "Sadhoo! Sadhoo!" A white cloth was spread for us from the jetty steps to the road where carriages were ready, and a thousand flags were frantically waved in welcome. The multitude hemmed in our carriages, and the procession set out for our appointed residence, the house of Mrs. Wijeratne, the wealthy widow of a late P. and O. contractor. The roads were blocked with people the whole distance, and our progress was very slow. At the house three Chief Priests received and blessed us at the threshold, reciting appropriate Pali verses. Then we had a levee and innumerable introductions; the common people crowding every approach, filling every door and gazing through every window. This went on all day, to our great annoyance, for we could not get a breath of fresh air, but it was all so strong a proof of friendliness that we put up with it as best we could. Our hostess and her son, the Deputy Coroner of Galle, lavished every hospitality upon us, loading the table with delicacies and delicious fruits, such as we had never seen equalled, and dressing it in the charming Sinhalese manner, with flowers and pretty leaves; and the walls were beautified with them in artistic devices. Every now and then a new procession of yellow-robed monks, arranged in order of seniority of ordination and each carrying his palm-leaf fan, came to visit and bless us. It was an intoxicating experience altogether, a splendid augury of our future relations with the nation.

As it had been arranged that I should give a public lecture on Theosophy on the 22nd, I made desperate efforts to think over my subject and prepare some notes. For I was then quite inexperienced in this business and was afraid to trust myself to extemporaneous discourse. But I might as well have tried to compose an aria in a machine shop where fifty blacksmiths were hammering on anvils, fifty turning lathes were whirling, and fifty people were gathered about to criticize my personal appearance, my pen, and my handwriting! Our house was a Babel, our rooms occupied by a friendly mob from morning till night. I would have done far better to have just gone to the platform without preparation, and trusted to the inspiration of the moment, as I soon learned to do. I think my first lecture in Ceylon is worth a paragraph. It was delivered in a large room in the Military Barracks, imperfectly lighted, and packed to suffocation. A temporary platform had been erected at one end and a figured canopy suspended over it. Besides our delegation there were upon it Sumangala, Maha Thero, the chief priest Bulatgama, chief priest Dhammalankara, of the Amarapoora Sect, who had come twenty-eight miles to meet us, and a number more. The whole European colony (forty-five persons) were present, and, inside and outside, a mob of some 2,000 Sinhalese. I was not at all satisfied with my discourse, because, owing to the interruptions above noted, my notes were fragmentary, and the light was so bad that I could not read them. However, I managed to get through somehow, although a good deal surprised that not even the special passages elicited applause—from the unsympathetic Europeans that was to have been expected, but from the Buddhist! As soon as a passage could be cleared our party passed out, H.P.B. and I arm-in-arm and holding each other tight so as not be separated by the jostling crowd. "Was it a very bad speech?" I asked her. "No, rather good," she said. "Then," I continued, "why was there no applause; why did they receive it in such a dead silence? It must have been very bad." "What? What? What are you saying?" broke in a voice from the Sinhalese gentleman who had hold of H.P.B.'s other arm. "Who said it was a bad speech?" "Why, we never heard so good a one in Ceylon before!" "But that can't be," I replied; "there was not a hand-clap, nor a cry of satisfaction." "Well, I should just have liked to hear one; we would have put knife into the fellow who dared interrupt you!" He then explained that the custom was to never interrupt a religious speaker, but to listen in respectful silence and, after leaving, to think over what he had said. And he very proudly pointed out the high compliment that had been paid me in the packed audience hearing me without making a sound. I could not see it in that light, and still think my lecture was so bad as to be not worth applauding; unless, perhaps, the Galle public had by common consent agreed to obey the injunction of Thomson!

"Come then, expressive silence, muse his praise."

"CHAPTER XI. THE POPULAR ENTHUSIASM."
This was the Prologue to such a drama of excitement as we had not dreamt we should ever pass through. In a land of flowers and ideal tropical vege-tation, under smiling skies, along roads shaded by clustering palm trees and made gay with miles upon miles of small arches of ribbon-like fringes of tender leaves, and surrounded by a glad nation, whose joy would have led them into the extravagance of actually worshipping us, if permitted, we passed from triumph to triumph, daily stimulated by the magnetism of popular love. The people could not do enough for us, nothing seemed to

them good enough for us; we were the first white champions of their religion, speaking of its excellence and its blessed comfort from the platform, in the face of the Missionaries, its enemies and slanderers. It was that which thrilled their nerves and filled their affectionate hearts to bursting. I may seem to use strong language, but in reality it falls far short of the facts. If anybody seeks for proof, let him go through the lovely Island now, after fifteen years, and ask what they have to say about this tour of the two Founders and their party.

Almost the entire Buddhist population of Galle massed together to see us leave town, and rent the air with friendly shouts. Our first stage was to Dodanduwa, five miles, the seat of the grand Vihara and pansala of our friend Piyaratana Tissa Terunnanese, a monk of erudition, energy, and high character. At every favorable point along the road crowds had gathered to look at us, we were invited to stop and refresh ourselves with cocoanuts, milk, tea and cakes, and at several points, so large was the concourse, I had to get out of the carriage and make addresses. At Dodanduwa we were greeted with such a downpour of monsoon rain as had not been seen in years. During a lull we were conducted to an immense shed that Piyaratana had had erected, and I gave the expected address to 2,000 people. After that we visited his temple, which we found scrupulously tidy and well kept—an unusual circumstance in the Island. We saw a huge standing image of the Buddha, more than a century old. We passed the night in a bungalow provided for us by Mr. Weerisooriya and friends.

On again the next morning, in the two stage-coaches supplied by our friends, the Galle fishermen. I had to make four speeches this day—the first from the steps of the coach, before starting; the second from the steps of the bungalow at Ambalangoda; the third at Piyagale, where we breakfasted at 3 P.M. [!] and were so besieged that we could scarcely breathe; the fourth at the temple at Piyagale, where an audience of 3,000 to 4,000 had collected. We were taken there in a fine rain, in procession, with banners, and tom-toms making a hideous racket; each beater trying to outvie the others and working the crowd up into a sort of frenzy of jubilation. The temple is situated on top of a steep, rocky hill, up which we were helped or, rather, dragged; giving poor H.P.B. agony with her lame leg, which had never fully recovered from the blow she got on board [ship] in the storm, when she was pitched against the corner of the dining table. The drizzling rain blurred my glasses so that I could not properly see where I was walking and, to make things worse, my pince-nez dropped from my nose and smashed on the rock over which I was passing; thus leaving me, with my myopia, in an uncomfortable plight. The gathered monks presented us an address through their Maha

Terunnanse, to which, of course, I replied at some length. Continuing on, we at last reached Kalutara at 9 P.M., but our troubles were not yet ended, as there was another bevy of monks to encounter, another address to listen to, and briefly answer, and then, after a needed meal, to bed, worn out. We were amused by an incident which happened en route, after dark. A man came rushing out of a wayside house with a bright light in his hand, stopped our coaches, and excitedly asked for each of us in turn. We thought he had something of importance to communicate, . . . perhaps even to warn us against a plot of the Christian party to do us injury. But he said nothing except to repeat each of our names with a sigh of satisfaction, and then turned away. Our interpreter called after him to know what it was all about. "Oh, nothing," he said, "I only wanted to look at them."

There was no time for lying abed on this tour, so the next morning we were up at dawn when the birds began to greet each other in the palm groves, and we men had a surf bath. Under very disadvantageous circumstances, truly, with a sharp coral bottom to stand upon that was like standing on a floor covered with inverted carpet tacks, the certainty of sharks, and the presence of a critical audience, watching us as though they were a class in . . . calisthenics! Still it was a bath, and that means much in the Tropics. We made a charming acquaintance today—a graduate of Christ College, Cambridge; one of the most intellectual and polished men we have met in Asia. Mr. Arunachalam is a nephew of the late Sir M. Coomaraswamy, the well-known Orientalist, and at the time of our visit was Police Magistrate of Kalutara. His eldest brother is the Hon. P. Ramanathan, who is a warm friend of mine, and the official representative in the Legislative Council of the Tamil community. We breakfasted at Mr. Arunachalam's house, and his courtesy drew out H.P.B.'s most charming traits, so that the visit was in every way a pleasant episode. As a dessert, or rather *pousse*-cafe, my colleague abused the Missionaries in her best style.

The same afternoon we had a taste of the other style of official, the Government Agent—a most satrapy grade of public servant—having forbidden the use of any public building, even the verandah or steps of the schoolhouse, for my lecture. The poor creature acted as though he supposed the Buddhists could be overawed into deserting their religion, or into believing Christianity a more lovable one, by excluding them from the buildings that had been erected with their tax-money and that would be lent to any preacher against Buddhism. But the fields and the sky were left us, the one for lecture-hall, the other for roof, and the meeting was held in a cocoanut grove. Some bright cloths, laid over cords stretched between trees, made our canopy and sounding-board and a chair placed on a big table my rostrum. The audience numbered two or three thousand. It may be imagined that the occasion was improved to point out the malicious spirit which actuated the Christian party, and their dread of the Sinhalese being made to see the merits of Buddhism.

Our gravity was sorely tried the next morning. Wimbridge, Panachand, Ferozshah, and I were made to mount a sort of bedizened triumphal car and, under an escort of a company in comical uniform, carrying wooden guns and sticks, their dark brown faces whitened with flour or chalk (to give them a quasi-European complexion), and with much music and many banners, were taken to the village of Wehra, three miles off, for a reception ceremony. I spoke to a large audience, in a very fine preaching-house (Dharmasala), with two rows of white columns, stained glass windows, hanging lustres, and a large preaching pulpit. In the Oriental fashion, I sat while speaking. After that we went to pay our respects to Waskaduwe Subhuti, Terunnanse, a monk better known among Western Orientalists than any other save Sumangala, who, of course, is the representative and embodiment of Pali scholarship. After lunch at Mr. Arunachalam's, we visited another famous priest, Potuwila Indajoti, Terunnanse, who enjoys a great renown as a Vederale, or native Physician. He is sent for from all the Buddhist parts of the Island, and has made numberless cures. We found his conversation very interesting, his views as to the survival of the ego in Nirvana being those of his late Guru, the Polhawatti priest and opposed to those of the Sumangala school. He applied for admission to our membership and was accepted.

At that time the railway ended at Kalutara, and we here took train for our next station, Panadure (pronounced vulgarly Pantura), the locality where Megittuwatte debated against the Missionaries the respective merits of Buddhism and Christianity; and got the better of them, it is said. We were lodged in a new pansala adjoining a Vihara, which had just been erected by a picturesque-looking old man, named Andris Perera, at his own cost. He was tall, thin, dark, had a spacious forehead, wore his hair brushed back and twisted into a long switch, which was put up like a woman's hair, with an immense and costly tortoise-shell comb; and a circular comb—a Sinhalese fashion—arched over his fine head. He wore the country dhoti and a single-breasted, last-century coat of blue cloth, with long skirts, turnover cuffs, twenty large gold buttons down one side of the front and as many loops and lacings of gold lace opposite them, and the same ornamentation on the collar and cuffs. A gold-laced scarlet baldric, passed over one shoulder and under the opposite arm, supported a short sword with a gold scabbard; a huge gold medallion plaque, as large as a dessert plate, was suspended diagonally in the contrary direction by a golden chain; a heavy and richly embossed gold girdle was buckled about him. His feet were bare and he wore leather sandals! The figure was so striking, so unlike any other we saw, that I noted the above details in my Diary. He had advanced some little distance from the house to receive us, and behind him stood his six tall, striking-looking sons and three handsome daughters. The group struck us as being very picturesque. I bethought me of Torquil of the Oak and his stalwart sons, though I cannot say that I thought the Sinhalese family would have withstood the Gow Chrom as well as the champions of the Clan Quehele. Without delay, the old "Mudaliyar" (the title of a Headman's office) led the way to a large permanent preaching-shed, and I addressed some 4,000 people. The Missionaries had been doing what little they could since our landing to try and weaken our influence with the Buddhists, so I paid my compliments to them and their questionable policy. This produced a sequel which will be mentioned later on. In truth, these Protestant Missionaries are a pestilent lot. With the Catholics we have never had a hard word. . . .

"CHAPTER XXI. CREATING A SINHALESE BUDDHIST FUND."
If anyone fancies that the influence which our Society enjoys in the East has been gained without hard work he should look through the pages of this Diary. Day after day, week after week, and month after month are to be seen the records of journeys taken in all sorts of conveyances, from the railway carriage to the ramshackle little hackney, jutka and ekka, drawn by a single pony or bullock; to the common country cart, with its huge wheels, its bottom of bamboo poles, sometimes but thinly covered with straw, and its pair of high-humped Indian oxen straining at their yoke—a thick pole laid across their tired necks and tied to them by coir ropes; to roughly built boats covered with arches of dried palm-leaves, but with neither bench nor cushion; to elephants carrying us in their howdahs, or, more frequently, on great pads, which are simply mattresses belted around them by giant girths. Journeyings by clear days are recorded here, and days of pouring tropical rains; nights of moonlight, of starlight, and heavy showers; nights, sometimes, when sleep is broken by the earsplitting sounds of the jungle insect world, the horrid yelp of the jackal pack, the distant noise of wild elephants pushing through the cane groves, the ceaseless shouts of the driver to his lagging bullocks, and his country songs, mostly in falsetto, and usually discordant, to keep himself awake. Then the mosquitoes swarming about you in the cart, with their exasperating drone, menacing slow torture and white lumps swelling on the skin. Then the arrivals at villages in the dawn; the people all clustered along the road to meet you; the curiosity that must be gratified; the bath under difficulties; the early breakfast of coffee and

appas—a thickish sort of rice cakes—with fruit; the visit to the monastery; the discussions of plans and prospects with the Buddhist monks; the lecture in the open air, or, if there be one, the preaching pavilion, with a great crowd of interested, brown skinned people, watching you and hanging on your interpreter's lips. Then came the spreading of the printed subscription-sheets on a table, the registering of names, the sales of Buddhistic tracts and catechisms; the afternoon meal, cooked by your servant between some stones, under a palm tree; perhaps a second lecture for the benefit of newly-arrived visitors from neighboring villages; the goodbyes, the god-speeds of rattling tom-toms and squeaky gourd-pipes, the waving of flags and palm fronds, the cries of Sadhu! Sadhu! and the resumption of the journey in the creaking cart. So on and so on, day after day, I went all over the Western Province on this business, rousing popular interest in the education of their children under the auspices of their own religion, circulating literature and raising funds for the prosecution of the work. So great was my discomfort that at last I set my Yankee ingenuity to work, and had built for me a two-wheeled travelling cart on springs, which could give ample sleeping accommodation for four people; had lockers projecting from the sides, for holding table-furniture, tinned provisions, a small library, and my bathing kit; two large ones under the floor for baggage, sacks of vegetables and curry-stuffs; a tight canvas roof on hoop-iron ribs, a chest in front for tools and spare ropes, hooks underneath for water-bucket, cattle-trough, etc., a secure shelf over the axle for the driver's cooking-pots, and rings behind for attaching a led bullock. After we got that, our troubles were at an end, and I lived in that conveyance for weeks at a stretch. It weighed less than a country cart, and was as comfortable as need be. By a simple change of longitudinal seat-planks inside, I could, at will, have a writing room, dining room, sleeping room, or an omnibus-like arrangement, with two cushioned seats running fore and aft, to accommodate eight sitters. It was as much a novelty to the simple country folk as the *Buddhist Catechism*, and priests and laity used to flock around to see its mechanical wonders. After the lapse of fifteen years the cart is still in serviceable condition, and has been used by Dhammapala, Leadbeater, Powell, Banbery, and various other workers in Ceylon. I have travelled many miles in the best Indian bullock-coaches, but not one compares for comfort and convenience with this. It would be a kindly act for someone to build it for the public, for it is equally useful for any part of the world where there are roads for a two-wheeled conveyance and stout oxen to draw it. If I have permitted myself to say so much about it, it is only that my readers might fancy themselves along with me in my pioneering educational mission among the good Sinhalese, and realize how some of our time has been spent in Asia.

The ordinary steam-passenger sees little of the loveliness of Ceylon, although that little is calculated to whet his desire to see more. The drives about Colombo, the exquisite railway trip by the seashore to Mount Lavinia, and the climb by rail to Kandy and Nuwera Eliya are experiences never to be forgotten; but I have seen the Island thoroughly, have visited almost every little village in the Maritime Provinces at all times of the year, and I can endorse every word of praise that Professor Ernest Haeckel has written about it as fully deserved. And I saw the people as they are, at their best; full of smiles, and love, and hospitable impulse, and have been welcomed with triumphal arches, and flying flags, and wild Eastern music, and processions, and shouts of joy. Ah! Lovely Lanka, Gem of the Summer Sea, how doth thy sweet image rise before me as I write the story of my experiences among thy dusky children, of my success in warming their hearts to revere their incomparable religion and its holiest Founder. Happy the karma which brought me to thy shores!

One of the most delightful of my trips of 1881 was that to the hill-district of Ratnapura (City of Gems), the country where the famed precious stones of Ceylon are dug, and where the lordly elephant rules the forest. The scenery is charming, the verdure that clothes the landscape is of that brilliant tint peculiar to the Tropics in the rainy season. The encircling hills are blue and misty in the clouds which float about their crests. As I strolled down the road that passes through the town I met a string of tamed elephants with their mahouts, and stopped them to pay them some agreeable civilities. I fed them with cocoanuts bought at a neighboring stall, and patted their trunks and spoke friendly to them after the fashion of the wise. It was interesting to see how they got at the contents of the hard-shelled fruit. Holding them in a curve of their trunks, they smashed them against a stone or laid them on the ground and stepped on them just hard enough to break the shells. One cracked his against a stone, let the juice run into his proboscis, and then poured it into his mouth. A large beast is worth Rs. 1,000—say, rather more than £55 in our now degraded rupees. Feudalism still holds its own in the hill tracts of Ceylon, having hardly yet been extirpated with the change of Government from native to British rule.

I lectured first at the Dewali, a temple dedicated to one of the Indian "patron deities" of Ceylon. Iddamalgodde Basnayaki Nilami, a noble of the old regime, is the incumbent of this temple, and derives from it a considerable income. These Dewalis, or Hindu shrines, one sees in many places actually adjoining the Buddhist Viharas and within the same compound (enclosure). They are an excrescence on pure Buddhism, left by the Tamil sovereigns of former days, and, for the most part, are handsomely endowed with fields and forests.

A *perehera*, or elephant procession, was a fine sight. Imagine fifteen or twenty of these huge beasts marching along, all decorated with rich trappings; tinsel covered carts; Buddhist priests in yellow robes, borne along in portable shrines, trying to look meek but really swelling with pride; devil dancers (*kappakaduwe*) in fantastic costumes, and wearing huge, hideous masks, and harlequins following after; the three *Nilamis*, or noble headmen, in carriages, and the rear brought up by a long procession of men carrying food in baskets slung to *pingoes*, flexible poles of elastic wood, such as are commonly employed for carrying burthens; the whole scene lit up by torches innumerable, of dried cocoanut fronds, which burn with a bright glare that turns every dusky figure into a charming artist-model.

After breakfast the next morning we "went gemming," that is, to dig a little in a piece of ground that one Mr. Solomon Fernando had given me for what I could get out of it for the Fund. For the first and only time in my life I realized the gaming excitement of mining. The chances were even whether I should get nothing or turn over a sapphire worth £1,000. I handled the spade first myself, but the climate soon warned me to turn over the search to the hardy coolies who stood waiting. We dug a half hour, and got imperfect cat's eyes by washing the dirt. I took them away in high glee, fancying in my ignorance that the whole sum we needed for the Fund might perhaps be taken from this pit. Alas! when I had the gems appraised in Colombo, I found there was not a single stone of any commercial value in the lot. I never got anything at all from the pit, which was not the generous Mr. Fernando's fault. But I am wrong; I did get something later from him—a good *loupe*, or magnifying-glass, which he had cut for me from a pure rock crystal taken from my pit.

At 4 o'clock that day I spoke at the preaching-shed in the town and got Rs. 500 subscribed. But most of it is still unpaid; subscribing, for show, and paying, for conscience' sake, being two quite different affairs, as we found by sad experience in India as well as in Ceylon. Stupid people to believe in the law of Karma, and then break such voluntary contracts as these! They remind me of the Sinhalese folklore story of the dull-witted fellow who engaged a blacksmith to make him a knife, and cheated him by giving him soft iron instead of good metal!

A local Branch of the Society resulted from my visit to this town. Another lecture followed on the next day, and the five most important *Nilamis* and *Retemahatmeyas*—chief officials—were admitted into the membership of the Society. A Baptist missionary, attended by a grinning black catechist, came to my lodgings for an intellectual wrestle with me upon the respective merits of Buddhism and Christianity. They retired sadder, if not wiser men, and made no converts that time. At 11 P.M. our party embarked in a paddy boat, a platform laid over two canoes, to descend the river to Kalutara, where we were to take train. The Captain proved a cheat and a traitor, for, although our bargain was for the exclusive occupancy of the boat, he let come aboard about twenty-five men, despite our remonstrances. Finding argument useless, I bade our friends remove our luggage, and, collaring the fellow, took him before a police magistrate, who was close at hand. Leaving him in custody we engaged another boat and pushed off at once. We learnt afterwards from an acquaintance who was on a third boat, that, tying up by the bank at a village down the river, he overheard the men on our first boat talking near him about the failure of their plot to rob me of the money I had collected at Ratnapura, and, if necessary, despatch me! It seems that these villains were notoriously bad characters from the Pettah of Colombo.

We spent the next day delightfully on the river, admiring the green banks, the luxuriant foliage, the bright-plumed birds, and the mountain chain with its ever shifting tints. Our meals, cooked on board in the most primitive style, consisted of curry and rice, and were eaten off leaf plates, with our fingers, in Eastern fashion. The night was lovely as Paradise, with first a blaze of stars and then the fairy moonlight, creating about us a dream landscape and silver paved stream. The jungle noises were most novel to me, a stranger, and so was a huge crawling animal we saw moving at the water's edge, which I took to be an alligator, but which proved to be a huge lizard, seemingly six feet long. We shot the rapids at one place, and enjoyed the excitement of watching to see if our frail craft should go to pieces and leave us floundering in the water. But our Captain proved a splendid helmsman, and his son, a handsome, well-shaped lad of 13 years, stuck to his bow oar with cool courage, and we soon passed down to the calm water below. This boy was wonder to me. He ate nothing but curry and rice, and had not got his growth, yet he plied the oar throughout the trip of fifty-seven miles, for twenty-two hours at a stretch, save occasional short reliefs, and was as fresh at the end as at the start. I thought it would be hard to find a Western youth who could equal that feat of endurance.

We had no cots or bunks to comfort us, but sat all day and slept all night on mats laid on the bamboo deck, after a bone-crushing fashion which I prefer to leave to the reader's imagination rather than dwell too long upon details. I will only say that a night passed without a mattress, on a tiled roof, is luxury in comparison with it. We reached Kalutara before cockcrow the next morning, took train, and got back to Colombo, for early breakfast, tired enough. . . .

The cocoanut palm has been the theme of hundreds of poets, for it is one of the most beautiful objects of the vegetable kingdom. But to see it as we saw it on the night of 23rd March, at Ooloombalana, on the estate of Messrs. Pedalis de Silva and R. A. Mirando, was to take into the memory a picture that could never fade. The stars shone silvery in the azure sky, and in the extensive cocoanut grove many bonfires had been built to protect the fruit from the depredations of thieves. The effect of these lights upon the enamelled surfaces of the huge fronds was marvellously artistic. Their lower surfaces were brought out into high relief, and standing at the foot of a tree and looking upward, one could see the great circle of star-studded sky that was opened out by the outspringing foot-stalks, while, as the wind shook the fronds, their spiky points would wave up and down and bend sidewise and back again, so that the hard, smooth, emerald-hued upper surfaces would glint and sparkle in the yellow glare of the fires. It was one of the most entrancing pictures I ever saw in my life. Our pitched cart with its white tent top, the white oxen, our camp-fire, and our group of persons, were vividly lighted up, and I could not but fancy what an exquisite painting Salvator Rosa would have made of the quiet scene.

We entered the village of Madampe with a great procession that had come to meet us, and made noise enough with their barbaric tom-toms and horns to frighten away all the *pisachas* [demons] within the circuit of five miles. Of course, our public lecture was attended by a huge crowd, who displayed much enthusiasm. Leadbeater, who is now working in America, will doubtless be entertained by these notes of our associated tourings. I doubt, however, his recalling with pleasure the trip from Madampe to Mahavena, in a country cart without springs, over a fearfully rough road, on which we got, as Horace Greeley did over a Kansas railroad, more exercise to the mile than was good for the soul. Every bone in our bodies was shaken up so as to make us painfully conscious of its anatomical position, while, as for poor Leadbeater, he suffered agony with his weak back. However, we came out of the experience alive, and that was something.

At one village, which I shall not name, we found the Buddhists [to be] killers of animals for food and drinkers and vendors of arrack—a pretty mess indeed—quite after the Indian Christian model. Well, it may be safely said that I walked into them in my discourse citing the Silas to show what a real Buddhist should be, and pointing to what they were. The very headman whose hospitality was offered us was an arrack-renter, and fish-catching and selling was the order of the day. In defining Nirvana and the Path towards it, I gave them one and all to understand, on the authority of Lord Buddha Himself, that if they imagined that they could get to Nirvana with a jug of arrack in one hand and a string of fish in the other, they were mightily mistaken; they had better go over to the Christians at once if they believed that, for fishing and arrack-drinking put a man quite outside the pale of Buddhism!

On 7th April we closed the tour and started back for Colombo, but in the night our driver, having fallen asleep, dropped from his seat, and the bulls drew the heavy cart over his foot, so my servant "Bob," who was up to any emergency, took his place and brought us at 3 A.M. to the house of our good friend Hendrik Aracchi, where we stopped until 9 o'clock the next morning and then proceeded on towards home. We got to the Headquarters at 3 P.M., and I went at once to my desk to deal with arrears of work. . . .

"Sixth Series (1896–1898)."

While I was at Colombo the author and lecturer, Dr. Peebles, arrived there on one of his round-the-world tours, and as we were old acquaintances, I put him in the way of seeing some things which would not normally come under the notice of globetrotters. Among other incidents was a visit to an interior village, named Walpolla, in the jungle back of the village of Rambakkana, where it had been arranged that I should lecture to delegates from several villages of very low caste people, something like the Indian Pariahs. Although there is no caste in Buddhism, yet, all the same, the Indian dynasties who have ruled Ceylon have left behind them marked social distinctions, and in the hill country the Kandyan aristocracy have treated the laboring classes with as much harshness and injustice as though they had been their slaves. The people in the district to which I was going had been taught next to nothing about Buddhism, and since they were made by the aristocrats to feel themselves the vilest of the vile, they fell a natural prey to proselytizing agents of the Salvation Army, who told them that if they would drop this accursed Buddhism and come into Christianity, they would be free men and could look anybody in the face. It was to open their eyes to the truth that I was asked to go to this obscure hamlet in the heart of the forest.

Accordingly I left Colombo on the sixteenth of April, in the early morning, with my old colleague and friend, C. P. Goonewardene, as interpreter, a Buddhist priest to hold the service, and an indefatigable Bob Appu, my old servant, for Rakwana; Dr. Peebles, coming from Kandy, met us there and went on with us. The poor people had sent as transport one big elephant, one half-grown one, and an ox-cart, without springs and apparently constructed with a view to pulverizing the bones of unfortunate travellers. As Dr. Peebles had never had an elephant ride except as a boy at the circus, he gleefully accepted my benevolent offer to let him ride the big beast; without howdah or pad, be it said. Although experience had prepared me for the terrors of the ox cart, I preferred to face them rather than the risk of being swept off the big elephant's back by a bough of some one of the many trees of the forest that we would have to pass under. This however, I did not mention to Dr. Peebles, for I thought that it might do him good if his pride should have a fall. He having mounted by a short ladder to the back of the kneeling elephant, and been nearly flung off when the beast rose to its feet, we entered the forest. Dr. Peebles had on, I remember, white trousers, and although his legs were long they were not long enough to bestraddle the elephant's broad back; so, perforce, they stuck out straight athwartship, and I was nearly convulsed with laughter to see him clutching at the back of the guide who sat in front of him, and trying to balance himself so as to adjust himself to the elephant's stride. As to myself, there was not a bone in my body that did not feel as if it had been passed through a threshing-machine. When we reached our destination it was as much as Dr. Peebles could do to get down to *terra firma*, and then his white "continuations," after serving as a clean towel to wipe the elephant's dusty back, were more like a crash roller that was hung all day in a machine-shop for the use of the men, than anything else that I can recall. As for his body he said that he felt as if "there would have been two of him if we had gone much farther"! A large audience had assembled to hear my lecture, which I gave after the Buddhist priest with us had given the *Pancha Sila* (the Five Precepts). It was a beautiful landscape that spread out before us, one of broad stretches of emerald green fields, majestic forests, and encircling hills. I placed my back towards the wall of the monastic building that stood there and the people sat cross-legged on the ground in many hundreds. Of course the theme of my discourse was an indignant protest against the treatment which these hard-working peasants have received from the Kandyan higher classes on account of caste. I gave them to understand as distinctly as possible that, not only was Buddhism free of caste distinctions but that the Lord Buddha, himself, had denounced it as an unnatural and unwarrantable social injustice. I quoted to them things that he had said in various sermons, or sutras, among others, those known as the *Vasala* and *Brahmajala*, wherein he says that it is not birth that makes a man a Brahman or a Pariah, but the actions of the person. "By deeds," says he in the Vasala Sutra, "one becomes an out caste, by deeds one becomes a Brahman." I illustrated the principle also by telling them the story of Prackriti, a girl of the Matanja, or Pariah, or *Chandala* caste, from whom Ananda, the great disciple of the Buddha, took water at a roadside well. Passing along in the heat of the day and feeling thirsty, he asked the girl to give him water to drink. She said that she dare not do it because she was of such a low caste that he, a high-caste man, would become contaminated by taking water from her hands. But Ananda replied: "I asked not for caste but for water, my sister"; and the Matanja girl's heart was glad and she gave him to drink. The Buddha blest her for it. I told them, moreover, that in that very sermon, the *Vasala Sutra*, the Buddha told the Brahmana Aggikabharadvaja, who had sought to insult him by calling him an outcaste, that a certain *chandala* of the Sopaka caste had become a Buddhist monk and attained to such a glorious renown as was very difficult to obtain, and many Kshattriyas and Brahmanas had rendered their personal services to him; whereas there were many Brahmanas born in the highest families who are continually caught in sinful deeds and are to be blamed in this world, while in the coming (world) hell (awaits them); birth does not save them from hell nor from blame. I then called up the acknowledged headman of the outcastes and, through the interpreter, asked him to bring me a drink of water. I took it, held it up before the people, and said: "I drink this water as a Buddhist who protests against the falsehoods that have been spread among you about our religion."

There were no more conversions made by the Salvation Army in *that* village, and I never saw an audience in Ceylon hang more attentively upon the lips of a public speaker than they did upon those of the Buddhist priest who had come with me and who preached to them after I had done. At their request he stopped with them some days and held religious services day and night.

The Western Invasion and the Decline of Buddhism

Anagarika Dharmapala

*The anti-Christian rhetoric found in Olcott is greatly intensified in Dharmapala.
It is not difficult to see that this anti-Christian sentiment was as politically motivated as it was religiously intolerant in nature. One might say that what Olcott had
begun to tap, in terms of instilling a pride in being Buddhist in the modern context,
Dharmapala parlayed to the next level, to one of grievance and sometimes vitriolic protest. Indeed, Dharmapala conjured up a vision of the past still retained by
many Buddhist nationalists in Sri Lanka today, one in which what had once been
a glorious civilization had been tainted by the Tamil Nayakkar kings of Kandy and
ruined by the Portuguese, Dutch, and British interlopers. Dharmapala's telescoped
view of history holds that the "Aryan Sinhala race" was politically independent for
almost 2,400 years before its subjugation and consequent "hybridity." According to
Dharmapala, the task at hand was not only to rehabilitate the Buddhist community
to its former state of righteousness but also to achieve a political autonomy for the
Sinhalese. The religiopolitical stance that Dharmapala took in the late nineteenth
and early twentieth centuries was a harbinger of the hard-line Sinhala Buddhist
politics that emerged after 1956. He is near to attaining a kind of sainthood in some
sections of the contemporary Sinhala Buddhist community.*

The Sinhalese people for the first time came face to face with a Western
race four hundred years ago; and their ancient glory, so closely associated
with Buddhism, began to decline simultaneously with the appearance of the
invaders. Thenceforth, for nearly three hundred years, Ceylon became the
hunting-ground of the Portuguese and Dutch, and both these powers carried out vandalistic work. They destroyed the ancient Buddhist monuments,
and forced a Semitic religion down the throats of the Sinhalese. The Mahavansa chronicler (chap. 95) writes: "These men were called Parangis [for-
eigners] and were all of them wicked unbelievers, cruel and hard of heart.
And they entered into fruitful provinces and laid waste fields and gardens,

and burned houses and villages, and ravished women of rank, and sorely troubled the Sinhalese in this manner. They broke into towns and temples and image-houses, and destroyed Bodhi-trees and images of Buddha, and such-like sacred things."

Narendra Singha, who died in 1734 after Christ, was the last of the Sinhalese line of kings.[1] Thenceforward the country passed into the hands of the Tamil princes who came from Southern India. In consequence of these foreign invasions and conquests, the Sinhalese of the maritime provinces became alienated, and a new race of Sinhalese, with foreign traditions, customs, laws, and religion, came into existence. The weakening process was consummated by the surrender of the Kandyan territory to the British in 1815. The "law of change," acknowledged as inevitable as the Buddhist doctrine, was thus verified; and the "brave and lion-hearted Sinhalese," who had enjoyed the spirit of independence for fully 2,359 years, ceased to exist as an individualised race.

The British have built roads, extended railways, and generally introduced the blessings of their materialistic civilisation into the land; and with this inception of the modern era the Aryan Sinhalese has lost his true identity and become a hybrid. Practices which were an abomination to the ancient noble Sinhalese have today become tolerated under the influence of Semitic sociology. The Buddhists complain that opium, alcohol, arrack, bhang, ganja, and other poisons are distributed in the villages by men holding licences, without regard to the degenerating effects they produce in the human organism. In the days of the Sinhalese kings and under the Buddhist rule no liquor was sold, no animals were slaughtered; land was not sold. The people held the land in common, there being no landlords except the "Rajabhogis," who received certain grants of property for having rendered special service to the country and king. Now the Sinhalese, once the lord of the soil, is but a stranger in his land. It is sold to him—his own land—and his future is indeed dark.

The Present Position. The present spiritual condition of the Buddhist population in Ceylon is causing anxiety to the orthodox followers of Buddha. There is very little inclination shown by either the clericals or the laity to observe strictly the precepts of the "Noble Eightfold Path." As regards materialistic development, however, the Buddhist community in the island has, since 1869, been showing its ability to march with the times. Printing presses, newspapers, and journals devoted to the religion have been established, and colleges for teaching Pali, Sanskrit, classical Sinhalese, Ayurvedic medicine, astrological mathematics, and kindred subjects have been founded. The Vidyodaya College at Colombo was founded in 1873.

The present generation of Buddhists in the maritime provinces of the island are showing remarkable activity in opening elementary schools for children. Several English colleges and about 400 Buddhist vernacular schools under Buddhist management have been established, while about 7,900 Bhikkus (monks) are keeping up the ancient traditions, and new temples are being built in various parts of the island. Ancient historic dagobas (monuments) in the ruined sacred city of Anuradhapura, in the North Central Province of Ceylon, and in Magama, in the hill country, another of the ancient capitals of Lanka (Ceylon), are being restored by Buddhist contributions. Pilgrims from Japan, China, Cambodia, Burma, Siam, Tibet and even from distant Siberia, still visit Ceylon in large numbers to worship at the ancient shrines, to adore the Sacred Tooth of Buddha at Kandy, and to ascend the sacred mountain of Samana-Kuta (Adam's Peak), a conspicuous elevation of 7,353 ft. in the south-central portion, whereon Buddha left his footprint.

But in spite of the activity of the leaders of the 1,700,000 Sinhalese Buddhists to conserve their ancient religion, the flower of the land, the rising generation of Sinhalese youth, has come under the influence of Christian propagandists. Supported in their efforts by the 120 millions of Christians in England and America, the Christian missionaries are striving to uproot this "noble and aesthetic religion of righteousness."

An Appeal for Official Countenance. But it is in the power of the British Government, which now rules the land with absolute sway, to protect the Sinhalese race from further losing its ancient religion by following the ennobling instructions laid down by the Tathagata. Let the Buddhists be given a form of local self-government according to the ancient traditions, based on the beneficent teachings of their Saviour. By nature the Sinhalese Buddhists "are polite, kind to their children, and fond of learning." Let the noble British nation, so eager to do good, prevent the sale of opium, arrack, and other intoxicating drugs to the Buddhists. Let industrial and technical schools be started in populous towns and villages. Let the methods adopted in the ancient days by the good kings of old, like Gamini, Buddhadasa, Parakrama Bahu, and other rulers, be repeated. Let the Mahavansa be a guide, and let the learned elderly Maha Theros (high priests) of the different parts of the island be asked to advise the Government as to the best means to be adopted for promoting the material and moral welfare of the Sinhalese Buddhists. That both the British and the Buddhists may thus thrive side by side in Ceylon is the sincere wish and prayer of the Anagarika Dharmapala.

Buddhist Studies in Ceylon. In Ceylon the home of Pali scholarship and Pali Buddhism of the Great Elders of the Arhat School, at the present day we have to sorrowfully witness the gradual decline of the spirit of self-abnegation that is so much needed in a research scholar. In the days of Buddhist sovereigns, scholars were held in high admiration and their wants were supplied by order of the King. For 2,100 years the patrons of the Holy Wisdom Church were the Kings of Ceylon. Buddhism was the National State Religion, and scholars were never lacking in the fragrant isle. Since the British advent there had been a gradual driving in the thin end of the wedge to make the National Church lose its high authority. In 1815 by the King of England's proclamation, it was declared that the Religion of the Buddha in Ceylon will be held inviolable; but by a process of vulgar diplomacy by England's Secretary of State for the Colonies the contents of the proclamation have been misinterpreted, and the high position of the Buddhist Church that should be maintained uninterrupted is more visible. The British Colonial administrators of Ceylon belonged to the category of political adventurers that filled high offices in Ireland in the 18th century. Since 1815 there had been only one Englishman who gave his spare moments to understand the language of the powerful ecclesiastical organization of Ceylon. Since 1834 British scholarship in Ceylon is dead. Shiploads of British adventurers have landed in Ceylon since 1815, and after a hundred years we see only an army of revenue Collectors, Civil Servants of the Subjunta type, adventurous planters who are full of the spirit of the 17th century British slave dealers and pirates of the Sir William Drake species, diplomatic bureaucrats of the Clive species, whose ideal is exploitation and their object to reduce the Sinhalese Buddhists by illegitimate means to a state of penury and serfdom. The Temple Land Commissioners in 1854 alienated nearly 100,000 acres of land that belonged to the Buddhist Church and made it British property; in 1860 the Educational Commissioners deprived the self-sacrificing Elders of the Buddhist Church of their tutorial office as guardians of the youth of Ceylon and by diplomatic cunning prevented the growth of the spirit of individuality in the child by making it penal to attend the temple schools. Since 1870 the economic disintegration of the Sinhalese race is visible on every side—in the destruction of home industries, in trade, in scholarship, in agriculture and in morals.

The annual allowance voted by the local Colonial Legislature for the diffusion of Oriental learning among 2½ millions of Sinhalese, would you believe it, only amounts to 1,000 rupees or £66 pounds sterling. This is how the Colonial adventurers help the dissemination of native learning in the island noted for its historic associations based on antiquarian Culture. Vernacular Schools of the island are so many "black holes" where the brains of the Sinhalese children are scooped out and when they leave the school only one in ten thousand has the vitality to survive the moral disintegration. The adventurous Colonial has one ideal—filthy lucre. Collect revenues by all means; increase the salaries of the white Civil servants; see that the surplus revenue of the island is annually remitted to England; and as for the welfare of the permanent population, whose ancestors bequeathed the island to the British in expectation of a higher moral administration, all that is done is to make them "hewers of wood and drawers of water." The religion of the Buddha prohibits drinking of intoxicating liquor, and the sale and manufacture thereof; and liquor was for 2,358 years taboo; but the British by their Excise Policy have flooded the once peaceful island with the filth of poisonous alcohol.

The civilization that Buddhism introduced into the island was ethical, economic, and altruistic. The stupendous reservoirs of water for irrigation millions of acres of rice fields that are visible in various parts of the island are permanent symbols of the economic development of a once virile race, whose altruistic nature was made manifest in the building of majestic temples to worship the Supreme Lord of Compassion, where they assembled in the spirit of universal love and communalism to foster the ideal of a democratic brotherhood cherishing the desire that all should meet in the distant future under the canopy of the Dharma, when the next Buddha appears in India, ages hence. To understand the spirit of the holy teachings of the Tathagata one should study the Pali Dharma. How is one to have faith in the wisdom of Buddha as the Supreme Master? We are asked to study at least one of the five Nikayas in completeness. Two Volumes of the Digha Nikaya have been published, we have now an epitomised translation of the Majjhima Nikaya, and now we are presented with three out of the ten Nipatas of the Anguttara Nikaya. In the Anguttara we have a kind of History of Indian affairs. The Buddha was a Promulgator of the Ethics of conduct, a Prince of Story tellers, and the supreme Master of Psychology.

The Anguttara belongs to the Sutta Pitaka, which is the history of the philosophy of folklore of ancient India. When one has finished the perusal of the five Nikayas of the Sutta Pitaka, he may congratulate himself on having a knowledge of the primitive history of the ancient Aryan race. To the historian of the Aryan race a knowledge of the five Nikayas is essential. Thousands of scholars are to be found in Europe, they study the history of the degenerate tribe of Israel and then they begin to spin cobwebs trying to catch into their nets, the undeveloped minds of the ignorant. How much better would it be if they would study the life and teachings of the great Conqueror who spent forty-five years of His perfect manhood in the moral regeneration of the greater part of advanced Humanity. He is the true scholar who interprets the life history of the Tathagata. The life of the Nazarene Jew was not of cosmic usefulness. To the philosophic thinker there is not an idea in the teachings of Jesus that may be called philosophic. His parables about the mustard seed, the sower, the wheat and tares are absurd. There is no ethical code that may be called complete outside Buddhism. The Buddha had half of a continent and thousands of philosophic thinkers as His congregation, whom He daily taught from the 35th years to the 80th year of His age. Jesus had eleven disciples, men of low intelligence, and his congregation was the riff-raff of Galilee—the backwash of the barren portion of Asia. The life of Jesus was an absolute failure. He was a victim of megalomania and at times suffered from paranoia. His ethical subjects were all outside the Jewish community. His followers were men of low morality. Peter may be styled the "bed rock" liar. He was a sneaking coward who denied his own teacher at a crisis. How sublime are the virile, vigorous manly ethics of the Tathagata. The English-knowing student of religious thought has now the means of knowing the virile utterances of the Lion of the Sakyas, thanks to Mudaliyar Gooneratna. Gifted with all that a wealthy householder needs, Mudaliyar Gooneratna has left a rich legacy to posterity not only in Ceylon, but throughout the world. "Rupam Jirati nama gottam na jirati," the atomic body disintegrates; not so the name—the latter has a kind of psychical hereditary transmission, in the work that one has done after mature thinking. The thinking man alone lives; and Buddhism is for those who dare ascend high into the realms of thought. The translation of the Anguttara Nikaya is carefully done. Certain psychological technicalities may be translated differently. . . . To the English-knowing student of hygienic psychology Mudaliyar Gooneratna's translation of the Anguttara Nipata is a necessity. It requires careful study. To the readers of the Maha Bodhi Journal we cordially recommend the book.

Editor's Note

1. Narendra Sinha died in 1739. Moreover, since his paternal grandmother and his mother were of Tamil lineage from south India, it is difficult to accept Dharmapala's Sinhala nationalist claim that Narendra Sinha was the last of the ethnic Sinhala kings.

Ape Gama (Our Village)

Martin Wickramasinghe

In comparison to the militancy espoused by the Anagarika Dharmapala, we have the approach articulated in the first half of the twentieth century by Martin Wickra-masinghe, a prolific novelist and anthropologist, who sought not so much to reform or to purify his rural village Buddhist culture as to preserve it. While Dharmapala represented a politically oriented urban militancy for the middle and upper classes, Wickramasinghe cherished the traditional ritual ways and mythic perspective of the rural Sinhala village. His understanding of Buddhism was not focused upon an austere asceticism, or upon a moral and doctrinal purity, but rather on how it nourished the cultural life of the village and how the temple formed the centerpiece of social life. In many of his writings, Wickramasinghe laments how the wisdom of the village, its eclectic and tolerant philosophical approach to life, has lost ground to the jaded and contentious world of urbanity. The two extracts that follow attempt to capture something of that image of a bygone simple and yet profound cultural life in rural Sinhala villages.

A Religious Festival[1]

Religious festivals which centred round the chanting of Buddhist texts (which are considered a protection against evil influences) in a special pavilion constructed for the occasion gave the villagers a means of satisfying their taste for amusement as well as of paying homage to the Buddha. The village community found entertainment not in secular festivities which were very rare, but in religious festivals; since there were no carnivals or fairs as such, these were the occasions which gave the villagers an opportunity to enjoy themselves. It is because of this that in Eastern countries, music and the allied arts often come into being with religion and are nourished by it. Men's desire for amusement must be satisfied as well as their religious piety. The religious festivals held at our village temples once catered to both these needs; but due to a few clamorous and educated busy bodies they have now turned into dull gatherings for the purpose of austere worship and

"Martin Wickramasinghe" by Bevis Bawa, Oil on canvas, 1950s.
Sapumal Foundation, Colombo.

contemplation which only appeal to hermits. It was this change that led to
the gradual dwindling of villagers in the temples on poya days.

The seven-tiered ceremonial pavilion set within the huge cadjan shed reminded the villagers not only of the seven-tiered palaces of ancient days, but
of paradise itself. Each tier of the pavilion save that in which the monks sat,
revolved continuously. It was not only we who were amazed and delighted
by this. In a period when modern mechanical devices were unknown even

adults found this revolving pavilion a marvel. The pavilion which the *Gutilla Kavya* describes:

> "It is painted to please each eye that sees,
> And tinkling lightly with each light breeze,
> Decked with pearls and small bells hang the gilded nets
> Between them unfurled shimmer gold bannerettes"

must have been very similar in its construction to the pavilions erected for religious festivals when we were children.

Placed in the space which surrounded this pavilion, and at various points in the shed were objects that excited the curiosity of young and old alike. A snake preserved in spirits is probably so common an object now that it cannot arouse the faintest interest in a villager. But in those days adults as well as children found it as fascinating as though it had been something exceptionally rare and wondrous. There is such a profusion of Japanese toys these days that not even a peasant would find a mechanical doll that could cry and move its limbs anything wonderful. But it was not rare to see a jostling crowd striving to see a huge doll of this type displayed on a curtained table after depositing two or three cents in the charity box. There was not a child nor an adult at the pinkama who could behold without amazement the doll dressed like the earth-goddess rising up from her subterranean dwelling to the accompaniment of an explosive sound, the pot of abundance poised on her head. The figures of bulls and lions moulded and painted by the potters of Kelaniya are now common enough in the villages; they were rare treasures then, which engendered wonder and delight at the festival.

The lowest storey of the pavilion had four doors at which stood ivory tusks supported on intricately-carved ebony stands. Perhaps it was not only budding poets to whom that ivory in its polished smoothness might recall the rounded cheek of an innocent village girl. The sight of the monks who had been brought in procession to chant the texts washing their feet in the stream of water that gushed from the mouth of the lion constructed at the entrance of the pavilion provided us with instruction as well as entertainment. If two or three of us got together at home and endeavoured to construct water works of this type by fitting tubes of bamboo or pawpaw stalks together, it was because we had profited by this demonstration.

It is the inclination of village adults to probe and question things which constitute the pursuit of pleasure, but it was diametrically opposed to ours. We who prized every aspect of this pursuit never worried ourselves with the question whether it was right or wrong, good or bad, sinful or meretricious.

It never occurred to us to wonder whether the monks who chanted pirith lived up to the ascetic ideals imposed on them by the rules of their order, or if it was wrong to enjoy ourselves by viewing curios at a place where we gathered for the specific purpose of receiving religious instruction. It was because of this that the monks in their silk robes impressed us so much. The little girls with their pretty faces glowing with happiness, the silk robed priests with their look of happiness and tranquility, inspired us with a loving reverence. We regarded the monk whose voice was most melodious as he chanted pirith as hero. Even now I cannot trace the reason why the pirith pavilion decorated with flowers and leafy sprays of tinsel should have reminded us of Paradise. Perhaps the impression gained from fairy tales that we had heard when we were small may have given us reason to find a similarity between the pavilion and the palaces of the gods.

The glittering many hued tinsel balls which dangled over the centre table, from the canopies hung over the pirith pavilion and from the cords slung under the canopies of the hall made us think of fairyland. That children should be enchanted by these glittering balls which caught the poet's fancy reveals a relationship between the poet and the child. Had children the verbal skill to express the joy they experience through seeing beautiful things, they would triumph over poets by virtue of their spontaneity.

Among the things which fascinated us at the festival were the booths on either side of the way. Were I to omit an account of them, this description of the festival would be as incomplete as a wedding feast which lacked curds and treacle to round it off. Though the booths were similar being all constructed of cadjan, the contents they displayed were varied enough to attract both children and adults. The only places which interested us were those which sold toys, sweets, and sugar-cane. We would not shift from the sugar-cane till the adult with us had bought some canes and handed them to the servant who was brought to take care of us.

I do not believe that any sweets in the booth attracted the children so much as the small sugar elephants and cocks which stood there on a show table. I now realize what clever salesmen those Tamils were when I recall the sugar elephants, cocks and the like which they made to capture the fancy of children. The children prized them not so much for any flavour they possessed, but because of their shapes. Some small children would not take the tiniest bite off the sugar cocks which they had bought until the sugar began to melt. Such was the delight they gave that the children were reluctant to bite off as much as a tiny fragment from the cockscomb. Like poets who protected things of beauty, or a mother nursing her child they protected the candy figure. However, there were those who bit into the head of candy without mercy. Whether these revealed traces of what might develop into villainous disposition later, I cannot say.

In those days when Japanese toys were rare a mechanical horse, dog, or man which moved its head or limbs, or a somersaulting doll were luxuries beyond the purse of the boutique keepers and the villagers. A doll which danced or somersaulted when it was wound up would be seen among the curios displayed for sale in the booths. Village children amused themselves with a tin whistle or a paper squeaker that gave out a shrill sound and lengthened when it was blown, or coiled up on itself as the air receded. Now even a village child can look forward to receiving a car or engine which runs when it is wound up among his New Year gifts. Yet it seems to me that the child of yesterday had more fun than the child of today.

The Jungle Hunters

Our village was a narrow strip of land lying between a lake and the sea. Apart from the many thickets with dense foliage there was a forested sand-dune which particularly attracted us. Though there were no giant trees bigger than cashews, mango and wild berries, the luxuriant clumps of bushes and shrubs which flourished there gave shelter to squirrels, snakes, shrews, mongooses and many varieties of birds. It was rarely that we could pick a ripe guava fruit, for barely had the fruit verged on maturity before a child plucked it. Nevertheless sometimes a green fruit indistinguishable from the leaves by its colour would escape the eyes of the children to mature and ripen, hidden among its leaves. When we found such a fruit, reddish yellow in colour, ours was the happiness of the gem-miner who discovers a large ruby. If you avoided the cactus clumps with their thorns as long as awls, and passed cautiously through the thorny eraminiya branches and entered the little wood, you would find a thicket that stretched tunnel-wise for about a quarter mile.

Cactus thorns inspired us with a terror reserved for cobras, vipers and other venomous snakes. This fear did not spring from the natural sharpness of the thorns, but had been instilled by adults. Thy told us that the mere prick of a cactus thorn meant instantaneous death. This reveals the fact that even the Sinhalese peasant is a deft poet—with an innate talent for romantic exaggeration.

The thicket had come into being by clasping, one after another the top of shrubs. It recalled the habit of the she-monkey who hides her offspring in her bosom. The creepers interwove themselves over the bushes as if to shelter them and made the thicket resemble the hood of a covered wagon. Babblers cheep cheeped incessantly as they hopped from twig to twig, without a moment's pause, dancing crest in accord with dancing body. There were Orioles with flashy wings like scraps of yellow cloth splashed with black, and crested birds with cropped heads crying "shirr-birri" in noisy couples. Little parrots and birds whose bills resembled hornbills frequented the grove. The murmur of the bees which haunted it when the creepers were in bloom gave us no pleasure, but the butterflies, brilliant with colours that might have shamed the rainbow fascinated us as they sucked the nectar with quivering wings. Were it not for us, certain of whose habits recalled the Veddahs of bygone days, a thicket where ripe fruit and worms were abundant might have been a bird sanctuary.

The "bovitia" fruit's hard rind bursts when it is ripe, letting the delicious black pulp emerge like a kurukkan pittu. Some varieties of birds relished this pulp [and] so did the boys. Because it leaves a dark stain on the lip and tongue when eaten, children called it the "mouth-blackener." We never ate fruits which ant or birds had nibbled at and left, for fear that a snake had nibbled it. Though the belief that "snakes too were pious, inoffensive vegetarians" was not one we had originated but imparted to us by adults, we came to accept it as indubitably true. It is hardly necessary to say that had [a] hundred scholarly zoologists maintained for the space of [a] year that snakes were no harmless vegetarians but in fact entirely carnivorous in their habits, we would not have relinquished that certitude. Ripe half-eaten fruits were often to be seen on the "bovitia" shrubs, and we did not doubt that it was a cobra who had left them thus. That was why it never struck us that ants or little birds were responsible for this, and not snakes.

When we were children, our elders related endless tales about serpents to us. Each of these might have been suspected to be myths woven by the snake worshippers of ancient times. These myths related the nobility, the thaumaturgy and the vindictiveness of these serpents. In old age, the serpent sheds his segments, retaining only his head and the two segments adjoining it. Employing the little wings that sprout from these, the kobo-serpent (dove-serpent) flies in quest of the Himalayan rose-apple tree. Like those who become hermits when they grow old, the kobo-serpents who journey to the rose-apple tree spend their declining years as vegetarians!

Marvelous tales, such as this about serpents which I learned as a child, derive from the imaginative creativity which inspired myth making in ancient man as in little children. The peasants, and we, who enjoyed listening to such tales as children, were more fortunate than those erudite men who rack and torment their brains by always seeking for causes and origins.

Within the thicket, it was dark even in daytime, despite the trickle of sunlight which filtered through the interlacing boughs and lighted up the ground which was covered with dry leaves. To enter it and lie in ambush like Veddahs with their bows to shoot birds was the most wonderful sport we could discover then. To shoot at the birds, we used bamboo guns.

A bamboo gun could be seen in the hand of every village child in the season when the *aepala* shrubs bore fruit. In that season it was impossible to find a child who was not letting off the small bullet-like hard fruits with an explosive sound. We made our pistols from a section of bamboo, with segments lopped off at both ends. The aperture at the distal end had to be a fraction narrower than that at the proximal. It is then that the hard fruit makes a loud noise and gains velocity. Children came to me to consult me on making an effective bamboo pistol. I advised them or sometimes made bamboo pistols for them without prizing my specialized knowledge so highly as to be niggardly in sharing it. I had yet to learn that a display of reluctance in imparting knowledge is one way to gain the regard of others, and I later realized that sincerity and modesty are not conducive to social success. Even so, because I cannot shed a childhood habit, I still cannot profit by that realization.

Some wise men state that one of the aims of education is to prepare us for living or pursuing a career. If so, we should infuse every child who is now being taught in school, with a dose of the art of bluffing. "Many a man, being sensible that modesty is extremely prejudicial to him in making his fortune, has resolved to be impudent, and to put a bold face upon the matter; but it is observable, that such people have seldom succeeded in the attempt, but have been obliged to relapse into their primitive modesty. Nothing carries a man through the world like a true genuine natural impudence." This advice I had gained from an essay on "Impudence and Modesty" by the Scottish philosopher David Hume, which I had read as a boy. Even now, qualities such as arrogance do not remain in my mind, any more than water can cling to the surface of a lotus leaf.

To push the *aepala* fruit into the opening of the bamboo tube and shoot it out, we used a rounded length of areca-nut wood fastened to a handle of bamboo. This was the "ram-rod" of the gun. When one nut was pushed to the bottom of the tube and another was then driven against it forcefully, the nut which had first been wedged in would issue, not merely with an explosive sound, but actually emitting smoke like a shotgun pellet; the other nut would then be lodged in the bottom of the bamboo tube.

With this bamboo gun, it was occasionally possible to shoot down a tiny bird, but unless it was then captured, it could fly off again after a little while.

As it was not as dangerous to birds as the catapult, the adults showed no opposition to the bamboo gun.

Sometimes a small child, donning a garland of leaves and a fine set of demon-teeth made of seashells to cover his own, would take bow in hand and become a Veddah. This was then a game for us, yet there are some lessons in modern school books which declare that this is a commemoration, unconscious though it be, of man's early ancestry.

Editor's Note

1. The original notes to "A Religious Festival" have been omitted in this reprinting.

Ten-Precept Mothers in the Buddhist Revival of Sri Lanka

Justine Semmens

The bhikkhunisangha, *the order of Buddhist nuns, disappeared from Sri Lanka with the Cola invasions from south India in the eleventh century, or perhaps even earlier, in the waning years of the Anuradhapura civilization. It was not reestablished at Polonnaruva under Parakramabahu I in the twelfth century. The reappearance of female Buddhist mendicants wearing the saffron robe was a very significant element in the revival of Buddhism during the late nineteenth and early twentieth centuries. In this essay, Justine Semmens sets forth the view that a resurgence of Buddhism among women in the twentieth century, as seen in the* dasa sil matas *(ten-precept-holding mothers) movement, does not necessarily have its roots in either Western "custodial Orientalism" (read Olcott) or in so-called Protestant Buddhism (read the Anagarika Dharmapala), but rather within the reassertion of lay practices within Sinhala Buddhist religious culture itself. As such, she argues against much prevailing scholarship that the Buddhist revival in the modern period owes much, if not most, of its impetus to Western or Westernized sources.*

The *dasa sil matas* (Ten-Precept Mothers) have been linked in modern scholarship to two concomitant forces called "Orientalism" and "Protestant Buddhism." Orientalism is a construction by the West about the imagined East marked by a judgment that Oriental culture has been long in decline. As long as the East was in a state of extended decay, it was incumbent upon the Orientalist, as sympathizer, to speak for the Orient because the Orient, in all its docility, femininity, and submission, was incapable of speaking for itself.[1] Some scholarship has focused on the Western impetus to "save" or "resurrect" Buddhism in late nineteenth-century Sri Lanka through various endeavours, which we might term *custodial Orientalism*. This resulted in the outpouring of a Sinhala Buddhist revival based on the appropriation of a Christianized ethic.[2] According to this scholarship, these two forces contributed to a "revival" of Buddhism in the closing century of British rule in Sri Lanka. These common assumptions must be challenged in order to account for and explore indigenous agency more effectively.

The scholastic efforts of custodial Orientalists focused not only on speaking *for* the Orient, but also provoked a fascination with the study of Oriental history and religion. Buddhism was punctuated into three periods usually classified as "primitive," the "classical period," and "decline." The period of decline, emblematic of the modern era, was "marked by decay and impotence," resulting in the feminization and subordination of Oriental culture, which aided Western justification of European colonialism and cultural hegemony.[3] Female custodial Orientalists advocated "social reform and found a liberating message for women in the early texts and highlighted their 'feminist' content." They categorized modern Buddhism as emergent from a long decline and adopted custodial attitudes toward Buddhists, especially women.[4] Many custodial Orientalists, aiming to improve Buddhism through its classical reintroduction to South Asia, organized themselves into two spheres orbiting the Pali Text Society (PTS) and the Buddhist Theosophical Society (BTS).[5] Self-identified feminists were attracted to both groups. The first part of this essay will examine the construction of Buddhism in the Western imagination, paying particular attention to the work of female custodial Orientalists and investigating dasa sil matas through this milieu. The second part will look more specifically at Catherine de Alwis, known later as Sudharmacari, and how through her lay renunciation, rather than responding to custodial Orientalist sympathies, she was a part of longstanding continuum of indigenous protest and traditional feminine religious expression.

Female Orientalists have constructed a mythic connection between classical Buddhist monasticism and dasa sil mata lay renunciation. According to the *Mahavamsa* and *Dipavamsa*, Sanghamitta founded the lineage of the bhikkhunisangha in the third century BCE.[6] For custodial Orientalists interested in resurrecting the former glories of Buddhism, Sanghamitta represented the classical age (the height of Buddhist endeavour). But between the eleventh and thirteenth centuries, the number of Sri Lankan bhikkhunis waned to the point of extinction.[7] Similar crises among other Theravada bhikkhuni communities prevented the lineage from being restored.[8] Partly because of the custodial bias, the dasa sil matas of the turn of the twentieth century are often associated with the extinct bhikkhuni and compared favourably to them, rather than understanding the matas as having evolved from existing indigenous practices of household or itinerant renunciation, which likely serves as a more accurate comparison.[9]

There is a correlation between the proto-feminist rise of the "new woman" and the rising popularity in these circles in the study of the Orient. The feminist study of the Orient was sometimes associated with antiestablishment emancipation from church, state, and patriarchy that bred a "universalism" or "sisterhood" of women that extended to a feeling of custodial responsibilities for women of the East that was accompanied by nostalgia for primitive egalitarianism.[10] Beginning substantively as an academic fascination in Britain in the first part of the nineteenth century, emancipative scholarship, which often included at least a passing interest in the Orient, spread to the United States by mid-century.[11] Women were looking for a primordial hinterland of equality and equanimity and sought it in the primitive and classical East.[12] Some of these women developed a fascination with Buddhism, noting a distinction between the imagined equanimity and emancipative spirit of "primitive" Buddhism that contrasted sharply against the decline perceived by many people in the West. Women Orientalist scholars and theosophists alike pursued this search for the "new" East of "old."[13]

Buddhist women's religious experience, then, was subordinated to this classical ideal, prompting Western women to construct an arcane model of Buddhist practice as an expression of their own desire for emancipation. This fit very nicely with the Orientalist understanding of Eastern decline that contrasted Western ascendancy.[14] Caroline Rhys Davids, cofounder of the PTS, codified this association of the "new woman" with the primitive East in a translation of the *Therigatha* that she called *Psalms of the Sisters*. The *Therigatha* is a collection of songs by the female disciples of the Buddha. Rhys Davids identified with the women portrayed in the *Therigatha*, saying of one ancient disciple that her audience was "stirred to enthusiasm by this *new woman's* eloquence."[15] Rhys Davids recognized that *Therigatha* translates loosely as *Verses of the Elder Women*, yet she adopted *Psalms of the Sisters* as her title.[16] The term "sisters" is infused with a double meaning, referring first, to Rhys Davids's contention that all the women represented in the *Therigatha* were Buddhist nuns, and second, to Rhys Davids's belief that she represented the "sisterhood of womankind."[17] Having published the translation of the *Therigatha* in 1909, Rhys Davids also demonstrated a belief among European women that bhikkhunis provided the most legitimate form of primitive Buddhist religious expression.

Emerging under the influence of the PTS and Caroline Rhys Davids was I. B. Horner, who published the first monograph written by a woman about Buddhist women.[18] Publishing *Women under Primitive Buddhism* in 1930, Horner argued that women had joined the bhikkhuni sangha to escape the drudgery and degradation of womanhood.[19] In her preface to Horner's book, Rhys Davids refers to *Psalms of the Sisters*, commenting that women's lives were spiritually unfulfilling and sapping to the mind and body and that by joining the bhikkhuni sangha, the nun, "expanded side by side with men, as religieuse, and the Anthology [of the *Therigatha*] in which some of this self-articulation is collected, is a treasure unique perhaps in literature."[20] On the one hand, this speaks to Rhys Davids's association of the women of the *Therigatha* with her own cause. On the other, it demonstrates a conviction that Buddhist society without a bhikkhuni sangha limited women to drudgery and degradation, ignoring lay renunciation as an appropriate avenue for feminine religious expression that unconsciously promoted the notion of Buddhism's modern decline.[21]

Most Victorian accounts of Buddhism make no mention of bhikkhunis or dasa sil matas, though there is much focus on the "classical" renunciation of Sanghamitta.[22] If these accounts focussed almost entirely on the "primitive" and "classical" stages of Buddhist development (especially on Sanghamitta), then it is natural that the focus of Western women's attention on women in Buddhism would entail their contributions to primitive and classical monasticism. This concentration on the monastic ideal limited their legitimation of historical feminine spirituality to convent life. It should come as no surprise, given this channeled understanding, that in the twilight of the nineteenth century the first white woman to convert to Buddhism and pursue renunciation would enter a convent and rename herself Sanghamitta.

Countess Miranda de Souza Carnavarro, briefly known as Sanghamitta, was an American theosophist and wealthy socialite who converted to Buddhism in 1897 under the discipleship of the Anagarika Dharmapala. Under Dharmapala's tutelage, she sponsored and opened the first Sri Lankan dasa sil mata hermitage, called the Sanghamitta Upasikaramaya and girl's school in 1898, becoming the self-titled "mother superior" of the order.[23] According to the Countess, there was a serious need to reestablish the order of nuns in Sri Lanka as Buddhist women had lapsed from their faith.[24] The Countess had clearly appropriated the notion that Buddhist women's spirituality was most legitimately directed toward monasticism. While the Countess hoped to restore Buddhism through her lineage of nuns, Dharmapala wanted to "save her" from her superstition and confusion.[25] Dharmapala was not interested in reviving the bhikkhunisangha because there was no method of reviving a lineage that had been extinct for nearly a thousand years. Instead, he opted to apply the Ten Training Precepts often taken by lay renunciants, rendering the Countess a dasa sil mata, or "ten-precept-holding mother," and not a bhikkhuni. The distinction between these two lifestyles is significant. The bhikkhuni is officially in the monastic sangha, follows the ten precepts, an additional 311 monastic rules of the ordained, and wears yellow robes sewn together from separate pieces of cloth (*kada kapala*), as stipulated in *Vinaya* regulation.[26] The dasa sil mata remains a member of the laity, follows either the ten householder training precepts or the Ten Training Precepts, and wears a cloth of white or later, white with another color, that is sewn from a single bolt of fabric.[27] The most significant change that Dharmapala applied was in placing the Countess and her sisters in an *upasikara-maya*, or lay hermitage.[28] While Dharmapala was interested in reviving Buddhist practice by institutionalizing the dasa sil matas into an order of lay sisters, the Countess believed that she and her sisters were legitimate bhikkhunis based on "the code of the ancient ordained nun."[29] Misunderstanding Dharmapala's application of the ten precepts, she believed they were all she required to become an ordained nun. In 1899 the sisters dispersed and the hermitage closed its doors only a few months after the Countess had finally accepted the rules for her order.[30]

In 1907, a second hermitage was opened under the leadership of a dasa sil mata of Sinhalese descent. Sister Sudharmacari Upasika Maniyanvahanse, or Sudharmacari, was born in 1849 as Catherine de Alwis to a prominent Anglican-Sinhalese family.[31] She was educated in English and also read Pali.[32] Her widowed father died in 1874 when she was only twenty-five. In the month following her father's death, while she was still technically an Anglican, she invited some Buddhist monks to her family's home in order to offer *dana* to them. The chief monk would not accept the dana until someone in the household took the Five Precepts. She did this, effectively converting to Buddhism. Soon afterward she joined a group of Burmese renunciants, led by Sein Don, the former queen of Burma, on pilgrimage to the Temple of the Tooth. She accompanied them back to Burma where she took the Ten Householder Precepts.[33] She had returned to Kandy by 1905, took the Ten Training Precepts, and opened the doors of Lady Blake Hermitage in 1907.[34] Sudharmacari's benefactor, Lady Edith Blake, described her and her sisters in 1907 as "lay sisters and professed nuns." They all had shaved heads and bare feet and were "clad alike in a white robe over which one of pale salmon colour was folded over the left shoulder."[35]

Though unlike the Countess, Blake recognized that the dasa sil matas under Sudharmacari's care were not fully ordained, she still compared them favourably to bhikkhunis, either choosing to underemphasize or not notice the relationship between lay renunciation and the dasa sil matas at Lady Blake's. In a short article on the subject from 1914, Blake provided a brief history of Buddhist nuns leading up to the present community at Lady Blake's, referring first to Mahaprajapati (the first female renunciant)[36] and Sanghamitta. She links the "nuns" under Sudharmacari's authority with the extinct order of nuns, adding that "in due course of time either the eight regulations [given from Buddha to Mahaprajapati] were deemed too weighty, or religious zeal amongst Buddhist women must have grown faint," adding that while "priestesses are no longer to be found" in Sri Lanka, Siam and Burma, "*Upasikas* (which may be translated Deaconesses) are still an institution in Burmah and Sri Lanka, and are generally known as Buddhist nuns."[37] Blake translates *upasika* as deaconess, but *upasika* refers more accurately to a devoted "lay woman."[38]

Blake's misinformed use of the term *upasika* is significant. The robe represents one of the most potent symbols of Buddhist renunciation. The yellow saffron robe signifies the ascetic attire reserved exclusively for members of the Sangha.[39] Canonical literature alludes to renunciant householders (*gihi*) and celibate renunciant householders (*brahmacari*) dressing in white. While most of these female lay devotees, or upasikas, observed the five moral precepts (*pañcasila*), many also likely observed more.[40] Remember that Sudharmacari and her sisters wore "a white robe over which one of pale salmon colour was folded over the left shoulder," together with bare feet and a shaven head, which is reminiscent of the white dress of the traditional upasika on ritual occasions.[41] At the turn of the century, controversies erupted over the colour of robe that *upasakas* (male laymen) ought to have worn. Some campaigned for the adoption of the yellow robe while others argued for a continuity of traditional white dress, a practice maintained in other Theravadan countries such as Burma.[42] Sudharmacari made a choice to remain dressed in a core of white, signalling an appeal to such a continuity of ascetic dress. Additionally, she received her training as a dasa sil mata from a group of Burmese upasikas who also wore white as a primary colour. Sudharmacari distinguished herself from the bhikkhuni, choosing to dress according to a more traditional lay mode.

This raises an important question about the continuity of Buddhist practice in Sri Lanka. Despite efforts on the part of the British government to undermine the Sangha, Buddhists continued to resist and challenge missionary activity throughout the era of British colonial activity.[43] For many, Christianity was accepted only nominally, using it as a political and legal means to an end, suggesting that a Buddhist undercurrent remained under the surface during the colonial period.[44]

With the official disestablishment of Buddhism comes the assertion that English-educated Sinhalese needed external motivation for reform. Accordingly, it has been pointed out that they had no access to Pali texts until the concerted translation effort of the Pali Text Society started to make English texts available after 1881, and that the Buddhist Theosophical Society, coming to the island in 1880, was formatively indispensable in the fomentation of a Buddhist reformation later spear-headed by the Anagarika Dharmapala.[45]

While the PTS and the BTS certainly did have an impact, there was still a cogent interest in Buddhism and its maintenance before these groups became interested in Sri Lanka.[46] Protests against British missionary efforts in Sri Lanka go back as early as 1818, only one generation after the British takeover of the island's coastal regions in 1796.[47] Mohottavitte Gunananda instigated one such protest in 1862 with the launch of the Society for the Propagation of Buddhism, in direct conflict with the Society for the Propagation of the Gospel, founded in 1840.[48] Dodanduve Piyaratana founded the first nonmonastic Buddhist school in Sri Lanka in 1869, when Dharmapala was only five years old.[49] While the Buddhist schools, which increased slowly in number from 1869 to 1880, had difficulty competing with Christian mission schools, they still demonstrate a cogent effort on the part of Sinhalese to maintain Buddhism before custodial efforts were focused on the island.[50] Perhaps then, Sudharmacari, in choosing ten-precept renunciation, was responding to a continuum of Buddhistic practice and indigenous protest.

Bishop Reginald Stephen Copleston, in his 1891 observation of the "devotee of dasasil," commented that "a considerable number of women, generally old, are to be seen around the temples, especially in Kandy, or on the way to Adam's Peak," usually carrying "bowls as if for begging, and their shaven heads and dirty white dresses give them a pathetic appearance, and one . . . would naturally suppose them to be nuns," but are "only '*upasikas.*'"[51] William Knighton's *History of Ceylon* (1845) also mentions pilgrims at Adam's Peak in 1845, well before the revival. Unfortunately he refrains from offering any physical description of the people he encountered.[52] Copleston's remarks, in particular, suggest that in 1891, there was an observable dasa sil mata type of presence in Sri Lanka. Copleston's observations are concomitant with the institutionalization of periodic lay renunciation that occurred between 1885 and 1915. Periodic lay renunciation, known as "taking *sil*," involved the donning of white clothes and was likely standardized through the institutionalization of the monthly Poya festival.[53] Continuous lay renunciation involving the addition of the shaving of the head, such as that observed by Copleston and practiced by Sudharmacari and her sisters, may have developed from or alongside periodic lay renunciation such as that described above.[54]

While lay renunciation was institutionalized during this period, it belongs to a longer continuum of Buddhist practice.[55] The idea of the upasika appears in Pali literature, demonstrating that non-bhikkhuni devotees existed during the period of authorship of the texts. The Pali *pitakas* make reference to laypeople "taking precepts,"[56] which may indicate a corollary practice to some forms of lay renunciation observed in the nineteenth century. Not all the women of the *Therigatha* were bhikkhunis at their attainment of arhathood. Sukka, for example, became a lay devotee, which might point to an initial renunciation as a *dasasil* upasika or an *atasil* (eight-precept holder).[57] Bhadda's narrative begins with a physical description that is very reminiscent of the dasasil upasikas described by Copleston. The narrative comments that "with hair cut off, wearing dust, formerly I wandered having only one robe."[58] There is extracanonical evidence that women took an active part in public formulae of Buddhistic expression that did not necessarily involve formal monasticism. The Kandyan kingdom witnessed a limited feminine presence within the temple context. Around 1767, shortly following the Dutch invasion of Kandy, there is a reference to two women fulfilling the role of *kariyakarana-rala* (lay superintendent) of the Temple of the Tooth.[59] Moreover, women performed similar functions in minor *devalayas* to the goddess Pattini.[60] Edith Blake, in describing the duties of Sudharmacari's dasa sil matas, mentions that the sisters "assist in the charge of the Malagawa (the Temple of the Tooth relic), daily resort to the temple, sweep out the sacred precincts, decorate the shrines with flowers and tapers," suggesting a certain historical continuity between devoted lay women's traditional functions and Sudharmacari's sisters.[61] In the late seventeenth century, at a period of monastic decline, a group of laymen surfaced. These men were known as *ganinnanses* and took the Ten Precepts, often changed their names without receiving full ordination, did not necessarily reside in a monastery, but sometimes wore yellow, which was distinguished from the yellow monastic robe.[62] In 1899 there were reports of one or more women ascetics dressed in yellow who reputedly wandered Sri Lanka preaching and collecting alms.[63] Additionally, in March of 1907, four months before Lady Blake Hermitage opened, an anonymous young woman was ordained in a Burmese order of dasa sil matas at the Borella Burmese Avasaya.[64] This suggests that Sudharmacari was not only one woman belonging to a larger movement, but that her hermitage was not the first on the island. It also points, alongside the Burmese provenance of Sudharmacari's own vocation, to a long-standing tradition of exchange between Burma and Sri Lanka that predates European contact. Cultural and religious exchange between the two countries has existed for well over a millennium, beginning perhaps with the exportation of the first sangha lineages from Sri Lanka to Burma. Similar exchanges are documented for 1070, 1476, 1803, and 1863 respectively.[65] Finally, Sudharmacari's teacher, Sein Don, urged her not to admit women under the age of forty, suggesting that renunciant women in Burma were generally older.[66] Sudharmacari was fifty-eight years old when Lady Blake's opened its doors and, in the very beginning, took in mostly old and destitute women.[67] This is consistent with Copleston's observation that dasasil upasikas were generally older, and may speak to an older tradition observed in both Burma and Sri Lanka. Today most dasa sil matas wear yellow. Some, especially old women, dress in white and stay at home as householder renunciants. Other Buddhist renunciants "live singly or in pairs in caves, or in cells in their children's back gardens," not completely unlike the homeless women described above.[68] All of this speaks to an older tradition that predates the rise of Sudharmacari's dasa sil matas.

In addition to belonging to a longer continuum of protest and renunciative practice, it seems likely that Sudharmacari's decision to embrace Buddhism had little to do with the work of custodial Orientalism. The death of her father when she was twenty-five years old in 1874 left her "deeply distressed and disgusted with the nature of *samsara*."[69] Sudharmacari, then technically an Anglican, may have had a secret affinity for Buddhism.[70] Her interest in Buddhism became a public pursuit in the weeks following her father's death when she took the Five Precepts, signaling her official conversion, in order that bhikkhus might accept dana on her father's behalf.[71] This account places her conversion one full year prior to the formation of the BTS, six years before the BTS came to Sri Lanka, and seven years before the formation of the PTS. Thus, her interest in Buddhism and perhaps even her decision to undertake a renunciative vocation was rooted more in indigenous protest and practice and less in the well-meaning program of custodial Orientalism.

To conclude, while there are certainly observable impressions left by custodial Orientalism on Sinhalese society—such as the Pali Text Society and the Buddhist Theosophical Society—indigenous undercurrents were also at work that speak to a longer continuum of religious expression. Such undercurrents challenge traditional notions of the Buddhist revival and the emergence of Protestant Buddhism. These undercurrents helped to shape the motives behind Catherine de Alwis's decision to embrace Buddhism and accept a vocation to dasa sil mata renunciation. Western input as a source for Buddhist revival has relied on impressions left by custodial Orientalists who saw it as their prerogative and province to reform Buddhism in Sri Lanka. Their feeling of obligation was informed by colonial notions of Western ascendancy that contrasted to Eastern decline. It was further nuanced by women Orientalists who proposed that Buddhism boasted a primitive egalitarianism for which they yearned and with which they identified. The result was an overemphasis in the primitive and classical models of feminine religious expression that underemphasized other traditional and extant models.

Notes

1. Edward Said, *Orientalism* (New York: Pantheon, 1978), 322–25; the idea of the Orient itself demonstrated an essentializing tendency among many European and American thinkers that fails to recognize the plurality of Asian cultures. See also Philip C. Almond, *The British Discovery of Buddhism* (Cambridge: Cambridge University Press, 1988), 33–42.

2. See John Clifford Holt, "Protestant Buddhism?," *Religious Studies Review* 17, no. 4 (October 1991): 307–12, for a redaction of the term "Protestant Buddhism" since 1970. The effectiveness of the term "Protestant Buddhism" was first challenged by Holt in "Protestant Buddhism?"

3. Kumari Jayawardena, *The White Woman's Other Burden: Western Women and South Asia During British Colonial Rule* (New York: Routledge, 1995), 158.

4. Richard Gombrich, *Precept and Practice: Traditional Buddhism in the Rural Highlands of Sri Lanka* (Oxford: Clarendon Press, 1971), 54. Theosophy maintains that all religious traditions hold a valid spiritual kernel at their centre.

5. George Bond, *The Buddhist Revival in Sri Lanka: Religious Tradition, Reinterpretation, and Response* (Columbia: University of South Carolina Press, 1988).

6. Tessa Bartholomeusz, *Women under the Bo Tree* (Cambridge: Cambridge University Press, 1994), xviii; and Edith Blake, "A Buddhist Nun," *The Buddhist Review* 7, no. 6 (1915): 51.

7. Bartholomeusz, *Women under the Bo Tree*, 15.

8. Bartholomeusz, ibid., notes that the order collapsed by the eleventh century, while Lowell Bloss, "The Female Renunciants of Sri Lanka: The Dasasilamattawa," in Paul Williams, ed., *Buddhism: Critical Concepts in Religious Studies*, vol. 7, *Buddhism in South and Southeast Asia* (London: Routledge, 2005), 2, suggests this took place during the twelfth or thirteenth century.

9. This is suggested by Bartholomeusz, *Women under the Bo Tree*; Bloss, "The Female Renunciants of Sri Lanka"; Nirmala S. Salgado, "Religious Identities of Buddhist Nuns: Training Precepts, Renunciation Attire, and Nomenclature in Theravada Buddhism," *Journal of the American Academy of Religion* 72 (December 2004); Kitisri Malalgoda, *Buddhism in Sinhalese Society, 1750–1900* (Berkeley: University of California Press, 1976); and Bond, *The Buddhist Revival in Sri Lanka*.

10. Jayawardena, *The White Woman's Other Burden*, 9–11.

11. Ibid., 110–13.

12. Ibid., 3.

13. Ibid.

14. Donald Lopez, "Introduction," in Lopez, ed., *Curators of the Buddha* (Chicago: University of California Press, 1995), 6, commenting on Charles Hallisley's thesis, also published in *Curators of the Buddha* as "Roads Taken and Roads Not Taken," 31–61.

15. C. A. F. Rhys Davids, *Psalms of the Sisters*, xxxvi, quoted in Jayawardena, *The White Woman's Other Burden*, 160. My emphasis.

16. Rhys Davids, "Psalms of the Sisters (1909)," in *Poems of Early Buddhist Nuns* (Oxford: PTS, 1997), 5.

17. Jayawardena, *The White Woman's Other Burden*, 159–61.

18. Ibid., 161; and Kathryn Blackstone, "Standing outside the Gates: A Study of Women's Ordination in the Pali Vinaya," Ph.D. dissertation, McMaster University, 1995, 116–17.

19. Rhys Davids, "Preface," in I. B. Horner, *Women under Primitive Buddhism: Laywomen and Almswomen* (Delhi: Motilal Banarsidass, 1975; reprint of original published in London, 1930), xiii.

20. Ibid., xiii.

21. See Seemanthini Niranjani, *Gender and Pace: Femininity, Sexualization and the Female Body* (New Delhi: Sage, 2001), 25, for her suggestion that "assumptions of a universal (male) oppression and a universal sisterhood have been called into question by contemporary studies highlighting the differences—of race, nation, caste and class—amongst women themselves."

22. Bartholomeusz, *Women under the Bo Tree*, 26–28.

23. Ibid., 47–48.

24. Ibid., 54.

25. Ibid.

26. Ibid., 74–75, and Salgado, "Religious Identities of Buddhist Nuns," 944.

27. Salgado, "Religious Identities of Buddhist Nuns," 936 and 942–45.

28. Bartholomeusz, *Women under the Bo Tree*, 54–79.

29. Ibid., 74.

30. Ibid., 75.

31. Bloss, "The Female Renunciants of Sri Lanka," 2.

32. Blake, "A Buddhist Nun," 52–53.

33. Salgado, "Religious Identities of Buddhist Nuns," 944, and Blake, "A Buddhist Nun," 52.

34. Bloss, "The Female Renunciants of Sri Lanka," 2–3, Salgado, "Religious Identities of Buddhist Nuns," 944, and Bartholomeusz, *Women under the Bo Tree*, 92–95. See Senarat Wijayasundara, "Restoring the Order of Nuns in the Theravada Tradition," in Bhikkhuni Karma Lekshe Tsomo, ed., *Buddhist Women across Cultures: Realizations* (Albany: State University of New York Press, 1999), 79–90, esp. 80.

35. Edith Blake, "The Sacred Bo Tree," *The Nineteenth Century and After* 76 (September 1914): 671.

36. Kate Blackstone, "Damming the Dhamma: Problems with Bhikkhunis in the Pali Vinaya," *Journal of Buddhist Ethics* 6 (1999): 293–94.

37. Blake, "A Buddhist Nun," 51. The emphasis and parenthetical gloss are Blake's.

38. Ibid., and Salgado, "Religious Identities of Buddhist Nuns," 946.

39. Salgado, "Religious Identities of Buddhist Nuns," 943.

40. Ibid.

41. Blake, "The Sacred Bo Tree," 671.

42. See Bartholomeusz, *Women under the Bo Tree*, 34–35, and 39.

43. Kitisri Malalgoda, *Buddhism in Sinhalese Society, 1750–1900* (Berkeley: University of California Press, 1976), 191–232.

44. Ibid., 206–8.

45. Richard Gombrich and Gananath Obeyesekere, *Buddhism Transformed: Religious Change in Sri Lanka* (Princeton: Princeton University Press), 210; and H. L Seneviratne, *The Work of Kings* (Chicago: University of Chicago Press, 1999), 27.

46. Holt, "Protestant Buddhism?," 310, and Gombrich, *Precept and Practice*, 32, who talks about a revival in the eleventh century.

47. Malalgoda, *Buddhism in Sinhalese Society*, 213.

48. Ibid., 220.

49. Ibid., 234.

50. Ibid., 235.

51. Reginald Stephen Copleston, *Primitive Buddhism in Magadha and in Sri Lanka*, 2nd ed. (1892; London: Longmans, Green, 1908), 279.

52. William Knighton, *The History of Ceylon* (London: Longman, Brown, Green and Longmans, 1845).

53. Benjamin Schonthal, email correspondence, December 9, 2006.

54. The suggestion that these practices may have been related was first presented to me by John C. Holt. For a brief description of modern poya festivals, see A. G. S. Kariyawasam, *Buddhist Ceremonies and Rituals of Sri Lanka* (Kandy: Buddhist Publication Society, 1995), 25–31.

55. Bloss, "The Female Renunciants of Sri Lanka," 2.

56. Schonthal, correspondence.

57. Arvind Sharma, "How and Why Did the Women in Ancient India Become Buddhist Nuns?," *Sociological Analysis* 38, no. 3 (1977): 230 and 242.

58. "Bhadda," in K. R. Norman, "Elders' Verses II," in K. R. Norman, ed., *Poems of Early Buddhist Nuns* (Oxford: PTS, 1997), 165–228, at 182.

59. Kapila Pathirana Vimaladharma, *Women in the Kandyan Kingdom of the Seventeenth-Century Sri Lanka* (Kandy: Varuna, 2003), 126–27.

60. Ibid., 127.

61. Blake, "A Buddhist Nun," 51.

62. Malalgoda, *Buddhism in Sinhalese Society*, 57–58, and Bartholomeusz, *Women under the Bo Tree*, 40–41. Malalgoda remarks that the ganinnanses quickly began to disregard the formalities of lay renunciation, often keeping their families and wives near them, gaining little or no knowledge of "canonical" monastic sources.

63. Bartholomeusz, *Women under the Bo Tree*, 36–38.

64. Ibid., 102.

65. Ibid., 25 and 91, n. 2; and Gombrich, *Precept and Practice*, 32.

66. Bloss, "The Female Renunciants of Sri Lanka," 4.

67. Ibid. It was only later that she began taking in younger women. This also correlates to a later change in the order that fully incorporated the bhikkhuni ideal into convent dasa sil mata practice that is not immediately evident in 1907. See Bartholomeusz, *Women under the Bo Tree*, 99–108.

68. Gombrich and Obeyesekere, 275.

69. Bartholomeusz, *Women under the Bo Tree*, 93.

70. Ibid., 206–7

71. Bloss, "The Female Renunciants of Sri Lanka," 2.

Sarvodaya in a Buddhist Society

A. T. Ariyaratne

The best-known and most successful Buddhist nongovernment organization in Sri Lanka is Sarvodaya (Uplifting of all), founded by the charismatic A. T. Ariyaratne in the late 1950s as a way to apply Buddhist philosophy pragmatically to improve social, economic, and political conditions for the nation's rural poor. The movement is clearly inspired by Gandhi. Sarvodaya's programs are found in literally hundreds of villages throughout the Sinhala regions of the island, though it also attempted to operate programs in predominantly Tamil regions of the country in times when the civil war did not prevent them from doing so. Sarvodaya's success and Ariyaratne's popularity have sometimes drawn a jealous eye among politicians whose own programs have not been as successful or as popular among the people. In the extract that follows, Ariyaratne expounds on his philosophy, which consists primarily of a practical reinterpretation of basic Buddhist moral principles.

This essay is based on the Sri Lankan experience of the Sarvodaya Shramadana Movement. Therefore, whenever I refer to Sarvodaya what I mean is a Movement that was started in Sri Lanka in the mid-1950s to bring about a non-violent, but radical change in our society beginning with the poorest and the most neglected villages of Sri Lanka. Today it has taken an organizational form as a body incorporated by an Act of Parliament with a membership and an elected Executive Council. The Movement has its own fulltime professional staff and a body of voluntary workers helping in the development of over 2,000 villages in the country. It has its own Development Educational Institutes, Village Re-awakening Centres, Co-operative Economic Enterprises and other institutionalized bodies like any other organization committed to social change and development. By a Buddhist society I do not mean society composed exclusively of Buddhists. What I mean is a community of people whatever be the religion they profess now, who have been influenced by values and traditions of centuries of Buddhist practices.

The word "Sarvodaya" was first popularised by Mahatma Gandhi in India. It is said that Sarvodaya is the sanskritized word that Mahatmaji used to translate Ruskin's expression of "unto this last." Later to mean the concept of the well-being of all, he used the word "Sarvodaya," "Sarva" meaning all and "Udaya" meaning awakening. At the core of the Buddhist teachings is the idea of respect for all lives—the first precept that a Buddhist is expected to follow. In a world where man exploits man, in certain instances most brutally, how can one justify the concept of well-being of all as different from the Hegelian concept of the greater good of the greater number? Advocacy of the idea of Sarvodaya or the well-being of all necessarily follows that the Sarvodaya Movement has to accept Metta—Loving-Kindness—which is the opposite of violence. So non-violence becomes a cardinal principle of Sarvodaya. Does this mean that Sarvodaya accepts in principle unjust structural arrangements in the present-day world which keep the vast majority of people in want and misery? When Lord Buddha rejected Tanha and showed it as the root cause of all suffering it was clear that he rejected the promotion of acquisitive instinct in man but [instead] encouraged Dana—Sharing and Beneficence—a means to realize egolessness and supreme happiness. Non-violence could be utilized as a very effective weapon more than violence to bring about lasting structural changes without demeaning the dignity and worth of the human being. What Sarvodaya is attempting to do is to apply the Buddhist principles in development action including an effort to eradicate social, economic and political evils and injustices that plague our societies.

Sarvodaya believes that mind is the supreme Dhamma. If the motivating force in the mind is Metta or respect for all lives then a human being who accepts this principle has to necessarily translate this thought into concrete compassionate action called "Karuna." We are helping a landless cultivator to liberate himself from the bondage imposed on him by unscrupulous landowners not because we hate the landowner but because we love or respect the life of the poor landless cultivator. We are fighting the misdeeds of the doer, in this case the landowner, and not the doer himself. There is no trace of ill will towards him. It is a struggle against an unjust system. Only when lovingkindness and compassionate action are practised in this manner can we get a positive emotional and intellectual reaction in the form of an immediate joy of service. This altruistic joy we have named "Mudita." If an individual's action can sustain this quality of fighting the evil deeds and not the evil doers then only it can result in a more permanent development of a characteristic in one's personality which we have named "Upekkha" or equanimity. There is a thought, there is an action, there is an immediate reaction and finally there is a positive and more permanent character formation in the individual in such a process of thought and action. The Satara Brahma

Viharana or the four sublime abodes of the Buddha's teachings are practised in Sarvodaya programmes in this manner. We believe that Buddhist teaching devoid of this revolutionary meaning and application is incapable of facing the realities of the modern materialistic society. On the one hand we are strongly spiritual and on the other hand we are strongly revolutionary. We are not prepared to concede revolutionary monopoly only to those who base all their social actions on organised hatred. We have based our revolutionary approach on lovingkindness and the organisation of compassionate action. It is impossible to build up just and righteous societies without a high level of spirituality even under most trying and exploitative situations. The Bo-dhisatva had been fighting despots using even violence but without hatred towards the adversary. When King Dutugemunu fought King Elara the way he treated the fallen enemy shows that even in war one can fight without hatred towards the enemy. Progressive movements of modern times have mostly failed to bring in this magnanimity towards their opponents in their struggles for social justice. This is because their ideology did not embrace the totality of existence and did not pay heed to the fact that every human being has the potential to attain supreme enlightenment.

In the Sarvodaya Movement "Satara Sangraha Vastu" or the four cardinal principles of social conduct taught in Buddhism form the basis for its village development programmes. The land, wealth, knowledge skills, resources have to be shared by all and not utilised for one's well-being only. Enlightened public opinion has to be created so that any right of private ownership of property is permissible [only in] so far as it may be allowed by society for its own welfare. Wealth, energy, education should not be used for selfish satisfactions or in disregard to societal interests. The quality of Dana—Sharing or Beneficence—could be practised beginning with sharing one's time, thought and energy for community service programmes—Shramadana. Secondly, Priya Vachana or pleasant language is practised. Third all mental, verbal and physical activities should take a constructive form consummating in individual and social good. This is Arthacharya. Equality in association or Samanatmatha should be practised not only in a quantitative way only but also in harmony with quality. All the Sarvodaya programmes are organized in such a way that these four social principles are practised by its workers.

There are nearly 100 places in Sri Lanka called Sarvodaya Development Education Institutes and Gramodaya Centres where Buddhist philosophy has once again been brought into community actions. For example, all the social teachings of the Buddha such as the virtues embodied in Sapta Apari-haniya Dharma (seven factors of non-degeneration), teachings of Maha Mangala Suttra and Parabhava Suttra, the socio-economic principles embodied in Vyaggha Pajja Suttra etc., practised to a greater or lesser extent according to our diligence in these cooperative community ventures where members live under one roof like those of one large family.

The Sarvodaya Movement is not dogmatic in its approach. The freedom of the individual within his cultural milieu is respected at all times as long as it does not come into conflict with Buddhist values. The sanctity of all life is always foremost in our thoughts and actions. Caste discrimination, for example, is not upheld by the Movement. On the other hand every effort is made to fight this social evil. Division of community life on considerations of politics or religions is not approved by the Movement. In all Sarvodaya Centres in the true spirit of Buddhism all religions are given an equal place and their adherents are provided with time and facilities to practise their own religions.

In the industrialized world the basic material needs of most people who live in those countries have been satisfied. But the psychological and intellectual needs are hardly satisfied in their rush for creation of more and more material wants. In the poor countries of the world neither the material needs nor the intellectual needs have been satisfied for their vast majorities of people. Religions, customs and traditions have kept them satisfied at a psychological but at a sub-human level. Under these present realities of the world the Sarvodaya Movement besides its other activities, is attempting to give a more pragmatic development philosophy to the Sri Lankan society as well as other societies in the world.

Development should be man-centered. The changes that are brought about in the socio-economic and political environment should be such that they contribute to the fullest development of the personality of the individuals living in that society. There should be a spirituo-cultural and socio-economic content in all development processes. Development should start from the grass-roots from the village up. People should fully participate in planning for development and in the implementation of such plans. The technological knowledge prevailing at the people's level and the available local resources should be used initially. Progressively and appropriately it could be upgraded with advanced knowledge. National development plans should be based, not partially but totally on this broad-based people's participation. It should first strive to satisfy the basic needs of the people and not artificially created wants that are a blind imitation from materialistic cultures.

These are some of the ideas that the Sarvodaya Movement is trying to put across. . . . The ideal of Sri Lanka being a "Dharma Dveepa" (Land of Righteousness) . . . is always foremost in the minds of Sarvodaya workers.

Politically Engaged Militant Monks

Walpola Rahula

Since the latter part of the nineteenth century, Buddhist monks have become in-creasingly involved in the political life of Sri Lanka. In the document that follows, the "Declaration of the Vidyalankara Pirivena," composed by Walpola Rahula and passed unanimously on February 13, 1946, monks from the leading monastic educa-tional institution in Colombo declare that as conditions in society have changed, so should the role of the Buddhist monk. They argue that insofar as the sustenance of the Buddhist religion is dependent upon a healthy Sinhala nation, so it is in the interest of monks to assist in securing the well-being of that nation. This declaration has functioned as a type of charter for many politically inspired Buddhist monks from the time it was ratified through the early years of the twenty-first century.

The Buddha permitted *bhikkhus* to change minor rules of the *Vinaya* if they so desire. Nevertheless, there is no historical evidence to show that the *bhik-khus* of the Theravada school have on any occasion actually changed the rules of the *Vinaya*. Likewise, we do not say that even now they should be changed.

But it has to be admitted that the political, economic, and social condi-tions of today are different from those of the time of the Buddha, and that consequently the life of *bhikkhus* today is also different from that of the *bhik-khus* at that time.

In those days the ideal of monks generally was to realize *nirvana* in their very lifetime. In later times their ideal was to exert themselves to the best of their ability in activities beneficial to themselves and others with a view to realizing *nirvana* in a future life.

It is clearly seen that as a result of this very change, a great many other changes not known in the earlier days took place in the life of *bhikkhus* in later times.

The extent to which the life of monks today has undergone change can be clearly gauged when we take into consideration the prevailing conditions of life in temples, monasteries, and *pirivenas*, the teaching and learning of

Sinhala, Sanskrit and such other subjects, the present system of examinations, the editing and writing of books and journals, conferring and accepting *nayakaships* [head monk positions] and such other titles, participation in various societies and being elected as officers in them. It has to be accepted, therefore, that, although the rules of the *Vinaya* have remained unaltered, the life of monks has undergone change and that this change is inevitable.

We believe that politics today embraces all fields of human activity directed towards the public weal. No one will dispute that the work for the promotion of the religion is the duty of the *bhikkhu*. It is clear that the welfare of the religion depends on the welfare of the people who profess that religion. History bears evidence to the fact that whenever the Sinhala nation—which was essentially a Buddhist nation—was prosperous, Buddhism also flourished. We, therefore, declare that it is nothing but fitting for *bhikkhus* to identify themselves with activities conducive to the welfare of our people—whether these activities be labeled politics or not—as long as they do not constitute an impediment to the religious life of a *bhikkhu*.

We cannot forget that from the earliest days the Sinhala monks, while leading the lives of *bhikkhus*, were in the forefront of movements for the progress of their nation, their country, and their religion.

Even today *bhikkhus* by being engaged actively in education, rural reconstruction, anti-crime campaigns, relief work, temperance work, social work and such other activities, are taking part in politics, whether they are aware of it or not. We do not believe that it is wrong for *bhikkhus* to participate in these activities.

We believe that it is incumbent on the *bhikkhu* not only to further the efforts directed towards the welfare of the country, but also to oppose such measures as are detrimental to the common good. For example, if any effort is made to obstruct the system of free education, the great boon which has been recently conferred on our people, it is the paramount duty of the *bhikkhu* not only to oppose all such efforts but also to endeavor to make it a permanent blessing.

In ancient days, according to the records of history, the welfare of the nation and the welfare of the religion were regarded as synonymous terms by the laity as well as by the Sangha. The divorce of religion from the nation was an idea introduced into the minds of the Sinhalese by invaders from the West, who belonged to an alien faith. It was a convenient instrument of astute policy to enable them to keep the people in subjugation in order to rule the country as they pleased.

It was in their own interests, and not for the welfare of the people, that these foreign invaders attempted to create a gulf between the *bhikkhus* and the laity—a policy which they implemented with diplomatic cunning. We should not follow their example, and should not attempt to withdraw *bhikkhus* from society. Such conduct would assuredly be a deplorable act of injustice, committed against our nation, our country, and our religion.

Therefore, we publicly state that both our *bhikkhus* and our Buddhist leaders should avoid the pitfall of acting hastily, without deliberation and foresight, and should beware of doing a great disservice to our nation and to our religion.

Politics of the Jathika Hela Urumaya: Buddhism and Ethnicity

Mahinda Deegalle

The so-called ethnic conflict between the island's Sinhala Buddhists and Tamils and the rural-based insurrections launched by the Marxist-inspired Janatha Vimukthi Peramuna (People's Liberation Front, or JVP) against the Sri Lankan government have dominated domestic politics in Sri Lanka since the 1970s. Within these contexts, the legacy of S. W. R. D. Bandaranaike (prime minister of Sri Lanka from 1956 until his assassination in 1959), which emphasized the importance of Buddhism on the Sinhala side of Sri Lankan politics, has not abated but instead only increased. Consequently, every major Sinhala political party has its public monastic supporters who provide cover for this important political expediency. In 2004, however, a body of monks inspired by the memory of an especially nationalistic Buddhist monk, the Venerable Gangodawila Soma, declared themselves an autonomous political party and managed in the general elections to gain nine seats in Sri Lanka's parliament. No other event has better illustrated the manner in which Buddhism and politics are thoroughly wedded in contemporary Sri Lanka. In the following essay, Mahinda Deegalle, a Buddhist monk and academician, describes the series of events that have led to the founding and success of the Jathika Hela Urumaya (National Heritage Party, or JHU).

Until the twentieth century, Buddhist monks were [usually] passive agents in the political history of Sri Lanka. In the middle of the twentieth century, however, monastic involvement in politics took a remarkable turn. With Walpola Rahula's (1907–1997) advocacy of politics for Buddhist monks in *The Heritage of the Bhikkhu* . . . , a new political Buddhist tradition emerged in Sri Lanka encouraging and justifying political activism. . . . Since the publication of *The Heritage of the Bhikkhu*, the degree of *bhikkhu* involvement in Sri Lankan politics has gradually increased. . . .

When social and political conditions weakened the economy of the country, partly as a result of the severe disruption and destruction [from] two decades of ethnic turmoil (beginning from the 1983 ethnic riots), the monastic involvement in extremist, nationalist politics gave birth to radical innovations. . . .

This [essay] examines in detail the most recent radical development that occurred in Sri Lankan Theravada monasticism in the year 2004: the historic event of nine Buddhist monks becoming professional politicians in the Sri Lankan Parliament. By any standard, 2004 is the watershed in the entire history of the Theravada Buddhist monastic world in South and Southeast Asia. For the first time, a newly formed Buddhist monk political party identified as the JHU (National Sinhala Heritage Party) fielded over 200 Buddhist monk candidates for the parliamentary election held on 2 April 2004 to elect 225 Members of Parliament. . . .

Sri Lankan Buddhist monks' active involvement in politics began in the mid-twentieth century . . . in particular, with the young Buddhist monks who closely associated themselves with the left-wing Janatha Vimukthi Peramuna (JVP) [during the 1971 insurrection]. . . .

Another significant turning point in monks' involvement in [the] ethno-politics [of] Sri Lanka occurred in December 2001. In 1992, Venerable Baddegama Samitha, incumbent of Dutugamunu Vihara, Baddegama, stood in the village council elections and became an elected member of the Southern Provincial Council. In the parliamentary elections held in December 2001, Venerable Samitha stood successfully for Galle District and became the first Buddhist monk elected for the Sri Lankan Parliament. He contested the election under the People's Alliance ticket, although he had been a monk member of the Lanka Samasamaja Party [LSSP], a left-wing political party. . . .

In comparison with other Buddhist monks who have been involved in politics, Samitha stands out because of [his] genuine political views combined with a humanistic vision of the Buddha's teachings. In the contemporary politically and ethnically turbulent context, with regard to the peace negotiations that the Sri Lankan government undertook in the early part of 2002 with the Liberation Tigers of Tamil Eelam (LTTE), who had been waging a dangerous and destructive war for an independent Tamil state for Tamils over two decades, Samitha took a very positive stand as a Buddhist monk and a genuine politician. . . . In the 2004 elections . . . Samitha again reiterated the importance of peace for Sri Lanka and the significant contribution that religious traditions can make . . . [to that effect].

Samitha's election campaign for Parliament in 2001 and his success in winning the election generated a renewed debate on whether Samitha should go to Parliament or should give up his parliamentary seat because it is not the traditional custom in Sri Lanka that Buddhist monks become professional politicians. Although there was significant ideological opposition, Samitha stuck to his principles and took the oath in Parliament. Unfortunately, partly due to the ethnic sentiments raised by JVP politics in southern Sri Lanka, he lost his electorate in the April 2004 election.

Within the past six decades, several Buddhist monks contested elections before the JHU fielded over 200 monk candidates for the election in February 2004. However, the JHU's election campaign stands out from previous election campaigns since it fielded the entire party with Buddhist monk candidates and it is exclusively a monk-led political party. . . .

In the election on 2 April 2004, the JHU won nine parliamentary seats: three from Colombo District, two from Gampaha District, one from Kalutara District, one from Kandy District, and two from the national list. Altogether it polled 552,724 votes, 5.97% of the total polled in the election.

In the wake of the general election, as a new, unregistered political party, the JHU sought the legal validation of the Sihala Urumaya (SU) as a political party registered in Sri Lanka in order to contest the April 2004 election. To that effect, the JHU signed a memorandum of understanding with the SU (Sinhala Heritage Party, f. 2000) so that only the monks of the JHU would contest the election as opposed to the lay leadership of the SU. This political connection between the two groups, less transparent to the public, created considerable debate and speculation among both the Buddhist laity and the voting public in Sri Lanka. Because of these unclear political links, it is extremely important to understand and distinguish the foundational ideologies of both the SU and the JHU. . . .

As a political party eager to assert its power in Sri Lanka, the limitations of the SU are clearly visible. . . . Its objective is to seek "political power for the Sinhalese" and to "rebuild the unique Sinhala civilization." This objective may be valuable for the Sinhalese but how does it stand in the context of ethnic and religious minorities who form an important segment of the Sri Lankan population? Because of the SU's preoccupation on the "Sinhalese" nation and "Sinhala civilization," the media often accuses the SU of extremism and nationalism. . . .

The SU sees a threat to the very existence of the Sinhala nation posed by Tamil separatism and opportunistic Sinhala politicians. The JHU also shares this vision. . . . In addition, the JHU, like the SU, makes severe criticisms of Sinhala politicians and allegations of corruption. The SU maintains that the politicians are "prepared to barter the sovereignty of the nation for the sake of power." Similar accusations are also found in the JHU election campaign posters. The criticism of contemporary politics and Sinhala politicians remains at the centre of the political rhetoric of the JHU as well as of the SU.

The members of the su and the jhu come from a cross-section of the Sinhala population who are unhappy with the present political procedures in Sri Lanka. They see that, as a majority, Sinhala people are in a disadvantageous political condition. . . .

The following objectives make clear the nationalist aspirations of the su:

(i) To safeguard the independence and sovereignty of the nation, and territorial integrity of the country.

(ii) To safeguard the unitary form of the National Constitution.

(iii) To uphold Sinhala, the national language, as the only official language and the Sinhala culture as the national culture while respecting the other non-Sinhala cultures.

(iv) To uphold, protect and propagate Buddhism, the official religion, and to respect the principle of religious freedom for non-Buddhists.

(v) To protect and develop the national economy, focusing mainly on the advancement of the Sinhalese and Sri Lankan people in general.

(vi) To protect the rich environment and bio-diversity in Sri Lanka and traditional eco-friendly knowledge systems and technology.

(vii) To uphold the sovereignty of the people and social justice by practicing a democratic system of governance.

(viii) To establish ethnic cooperation and harmony in order to create a strong united Sri Lankan people based on human rights and the national rights of the Sinhalese.

To meet the cultural, social and religious needs of contemporary Sri Lanka, the su presents itself as more than a "political party but a national movement as well." It maintains that while seeking political power for the Sinhalese, it also has to rebuild "the unique Sinhala civilization" in Sri Lanka "independent of the political process."

The su had identified two key ideas that it should use for its growth as a political power in Sri Lanka: (i) to build Sri Lanka by following the 10 virtuous deeds of the righteous king (*dasaraja dharma*) as found in the Pali canon,[1] and (ii) to celebrate the secrets of the past glory of the "unique" Sinhala civilization that flourished in Anuradhapura from the third century BCE to the tenth century CE. The jhu also shares these two key ideas with the su.

The socio-religious context that led to the new political awareness and birth of the jhu is the controversial and untimely death of the popular Buddhist preacher, Venerable Gangodawila Soma (1948–2003). . . . The jhu has effectively exploited Soma's death for its own advantage by using rumors surrounding his death. The untimely death of Venerable Soma, who has been characterized by the newspapers as "the embodiment of Buddhist morality and paragon of virtue" and "the champion of Sinhala-Buddhist cause," . . . raised conspiracy theories and, most importantly, triggered a new awareness [about] the state of Buddhism in Sri Lanka, which the JHU employed in its election campaign. Many of [this] nationalist persuasion consider Soma's death a sacrifice to the nation and hold the opinion that there [was] a conspiracy to take his life since Soma himself had invoked alleged conspiracy theories over his own death in his last speech in Kandy. . . . Anti-Christian sentiments, which have grown over the years on the issue of unethical conversions, were evoked at the site of Soma's funeral.

Let me now introduce briefly Soma's life in order to show how he earned public sympathy over the years. Soma was often presented to the public as "the most outstanding and controversial religious leader" because of his "outspokenness and straightforwardness" in issues related to the Sinhalese and Buddhists. Like the JHU, Sri Lankan newspapers characterize Soma as "[q]uite identical" to the early twentieth-century Buddhist reformer, Anagarika Dharmapala (1864–1933), "who inspired and aroused Sri Lankan Buddhists from apathy and led them towards socio-cultural awareness."

Soma was born in Gangodavila, a suburb of Colombo, in 1948. At the adult age of 26 years, in 1974 he received novice ordination and began monastic training at the Bhikkhu Training Centre, Maharagama, under the guidance of two prominent Buddhist monks—Venerable Madihe Pannasiha (1913–2003) and Venerable Ampitiye Rahula. Even before his ordination, Soma had close links with Siri Vajiragnana Dharma Yathanaya and functioned as a "lay preacher" and student leader. In 1976, Soma received the higher ordination. In 1986, he visited Australia for three months. In his second visit in 1989, Soma established the Melbourne Sri Lankan Buddhist Vihara. In 1993, he founded the Buddhist Vihara [in] Victoria and served as chief incumbent until his death on 12 December 2003. After seven years of *dhammaduta* activities in Australia, Soma returned to Sri Lanka in 1996 in order to help the people of the country.

Soma's strength lay in his preaching. As a popular preacher, he was able to reach a wider young audience. He was respected widely for his "soothing and informative sermons," which reached "the hearts and minds of not only the Buddhists but the non-Buddhists as well" (Scott 2003). Soma's popular sermons and television discussions drew the attention of young and old, Buddhists and non-Buddhists, since they discussed problems faced by ordinary people in day-to-day life. Soma had two very popular television programmes: *Anduren Eliyata* ("From Darkness to Light") and *Nana Pahana* ("Lamp of Wisdom"). In these public discussions, he expressed his ideas about the issues relating to Buddhism and culture of Sri Lanka openly. . . .

His engagement in several national debates on the issues dealing with the rights of Sinhala people made him more popular among the public. Due to his heavy criticism of politicians and their "unrighteous" activities, it is widely believed that he was shut out from certain television stations.

After Soma's death, the JHU systematically invoked him for its own advantage. The JHU's national campaign to win the parliamentary election for establishing a righteous state [was] presented as a continuation of Soma's unfinished work:

> Ven. Soma Thera will continue to remain a guiding star as long as the much-cherished Buddhist civilization in the country survives . . . The aching void left by his sudden departure is unbridgeable and will continue to be felt by millions of Sri Lankans . . . What his departure reminds us is the fact that time is ripe for Sri Lankan Buddhists to re-evaluate and re-think of our collective stand on national and religious issues of our motherland. You can be a part of his campaign by strongly supporting the Jathika Hela Urumaya. This will be the greatest respect you can bestow on this outstanding monk. (Hewapathirane 2004)

The link between Venerable Soma and the SU, the prototype of the JHU, was firmly established towards the end of 2002. As *The Sunday Times* (Wijetunge 2002) reported, Soma and his Jana Vijaya Foundation joined the SU to "unite the Sinhala nationalist movement in order to defeat the elements bent on separating the country."

In the wake of the April 2004 election, the JHU produced [a] song presented [below] in honor of Soma. The song alludes to the fact that the three leading JHU election candidates—Kolonnave Sumangala, Uduwe Dhammaloka and Ellavala Medhananda—are following [in] the footsteps of Venerable Soma. They are requested to lead the Sinhala public in this time of crisis in order to protect Buddhism from outside threats. It aptly illustrates the frustrations of the majority Buddhists at Soma's death and raises religious concerns that they have in relation to potential threats to the survival of Buddhism in Sri Lanka.

A recent commentator who wants to support the JHU identifies Soma as being a part of a Buddhist social reform movement (Hewapathirane 2004). As a socio-cultural reformer, Soma was explicit in his criticism leveled at corrupt politicians. He believed that national and religious issues are interwoven within the body politic of the country. Soma believed it was the bound duty of the state to provide protection for Buddhism, as enshrined in the constitution. He [advocated] a state ruled in accordance with Buddhist principles of righteous living as the key for Sri Lanka's development, as also insisted upon by the JHU. . . .

THE JHU SONG FOR SOMA

Venerable Sir, Buddha's teaching
that you preached became an animosity.
Sacrificing your life,
you made the entire country cry.
Our Saddharma is, indeed,
the most supreme teaching in the world.
Because of those teachings, in the future,
wrong beliefs will disappear.
The heart of those who cannot bear it is cruel.
Indeed, the bullet is aimed at the Buddha's *dhamma*.
Venerable Srı Sumangala with
Venerable Uduve, Venerable Ellavala with the
Mahasangha, come forward.
May you save our *sasana*!
The supreme teaching in the world is
what the Buddha preached.
In the past, the Buddha visited and
left his footprint and
our sacred Tooth Relic and the relic Caskets.
We offer seven lotuses, prostrate and beg.
The country lost him, Venerable Soma!
Please be reborn here again and again.

Monks in the JHU election platform. Establishing a Buddhist state in Sri Lanka is the main objective of the monks of the JHU. In their political agenda, the highest priority is given to the [establishment of] a Buddhist state. Devout Sinhala Buddhists are also keen to see this happen since they are fed up with the moral decadence and chaos that has emerged in contemporary Sri Lanka.

On the whole, five reasons can be identified as motivating factors that led the Buddhist monks of the JHU to contest the general election held in April 2004: (1) the perception of Venerable Soma's untimely death as a systematic conspiracy to weaken Buddhist reformation and renewal, (2) increasing accusations of intensified "unethical" Christian conversions of poor Buddhists and Hindus, (3) continuing fears of the LTTE's Eelam in the context of recent peace negotiations, (4) the unstable political situation in which the two main political parties—UNP and SLFP—are in a power-struggle in the midst of resolving the current ethnic problem, and (5) the political ambitions of some JHU monks.

Traditionally, the majority of Theravada Buddhist monks have stayed away from politics. Monks of the JHU entering into Sri Lankan parliamentary politics is problematic both from cultural and religious perspectives. Due to the controversial nature of the issue and debates over [the] monks' actions, the JHU monks themselves have tried to explain the current political and social circumstances that led them to take such an unconventional decision. They consider their entry into active politics as the last resort, a decision taken with much reluctance. Before handing over the nominations for [the] April 2004 elections, Venerable Athuraliye Rathana, media spokesman of the JHU, remarked: "the Sangha has entered the arena of politics to ensure the protection of Buddhist heritage and values which had been undermined for centuries" (*Daily Mirror* 2004). Why did Buddhist monks decide to contest the parliamentary elections? Their answer lies in the following justifications.

The first justification [was] concerned with possible political disadvantages that the Sinhala Buddhist majority [would] face as a result of the current peace negotiations with the LTTE initiated by Norway facilitators. . . .

The second justification [was] related to the current tense environment created by unethical conversions initiated by non-denominational, evangelical, Protestant Christian groups. Various Buddhist groups, including the monks who formed the JHU, have demanded that the Sri Lankan government pass a bill in Parliament to ban unethical conversions carried out among poor Buddhists and Hindus. One member of the JHU, Venerable Omalpe Sobhita, fasted in front of the Ministry of Buddhasasana, demanding action on this issue. . . . The JHU believes that both major Sinhala-dominated political parties are not willing to ban unethical religious conversions. . . . These two main factors seem to have motivated monks to enter into politics. . . .

The Dharmarajya *concept of the JHU.* To attract an audience, the JHU has introduced more fashionable religious terms for its political rhetoric. One of them is the *pratipatti pujava*, which literally means "an offering of principles." The Sinhala term *pujava* is, strictly speaking, liturgical in its connotations and exclusively used in religious contexts rather than in the political platform. However, the JHU has employed it self-consciously . . . in order to introduce its political manifesto in religious terms connoting their ambition of establishing a *dharmarajya* in Sri Lanka.

The election manifesto of the JHU is rather unique because of its interesting religious content and the way it was introduced to the Sri Lankan public by invoking religious sentiments. Unlike other political parties, the JHU offered its political manifesto (*pratipatti pujava*) to the Tooth Relic of Gotama Buddha in Kandy. On 2 March 2004,[2] the JHU monks and lay supporters marched to the Tooth Relic Temple, Kandy, from Kelaniya Temple in the midst of thousands of Buddhist monks and lay people. . . . The JHU launched its political manifesto in the hope of restoring the weakening status of Buddhism in Sri Lanka. . . .

The JHU manifesto includes 12 points as principles for constructing a righteous State. . . .

(i) The first principle stresses that Sri Lanka should be ruled according to Buddhist principles as it was in the past, and the protection of the Buddhasasana should be the foremost duty of any government. The state is, however, identified in the manifesto as a "Sinhala state." The state also should safeguard the rights of other religions to practice their own religious traditions. Showing the urgency of addressing the religious concerns of the majority and achieving political ambitions of the JHU, the very first principle of the manifesto mentions the issue of unethical conversions. It asserts that "all unethical conversions are illegal." This is an indication that the JHU will take legislative action on "unethical conversions" once its members are elected to the Parliament.

(ii) The second article stresses that Sri Lanka is a Buddhist unitary state that cannot be divided. National safety is an essential condition. At times when there are threats to national security, without political interference, the police and the three armed forces should be given powers to act according to the constitution to safeguard national interests and the country.

(iii) Emphasizing the JHU's stand as the National Sinhala Heritage Party, the manifesto states that national heritage of a country belongs to the ethnic group who made the country into a habitable civilization. The hereditary rights of the Sinhalese should be granted while protecting the rights of other communities who inhabit the island.

(iv) The rulers of Sri Lanka should adopt the *dharmarajya* concept of Emperor Asoka, which was influenced by Buddhist philosophy, and should work for the welfare of all ethnic groups. Their exemplary attitude should reflect Dharmasoka's idea of "all citizens are my children."

(v) The Government should control and monitor all the activities and monetary transactions of the non-government organizations that are in operation in Sri Lanka. This is an indication of a religious concern that the JHU has raised with accusations [regarding] evangelical Christians, . . .

(vi) Following the *grama rajya* concept that Sri Lanka inherited, a decentralized administration should be adopted. This is the Buddhist option that the JHU plans to adopt instead of devolution proposals that successive Sri Lankan governments plan to implement to resolve the ethnic conflict. . . . The JHU sees the devolution of power as a solution to continuing ethnic problems in Sri Lanka from a negative perspective. They maintain that the notion of devolution of power is an imported concept imposed upon them. . . . Their negative attitude to devolution of power is based on two factors: their fear that it will lead to the creation of a separate state for Tamils and that it will lead to the creation of fanatical religious beliefs and conflicts within Sri Lanka. Instead of the devolution of power, the JHU prefers a "decentralization" within a unitary Buddhist state. They believe that effective "decentralization" to village level communes will solve many of the issues related to defence, administration, education, health, trade, agriculture, water, and transport.

(vii) Development should centre on the natural habitat, animals, and humanity . . . [and] based on the principle that by developing the individual human being, [the] country should be developed—the creation of a just, national economy based upon Buddhist economic philosophy and empowering local farmers and entrepreneurs.

(viii) An education system that fits into the Sri Lankan cultural context . . . that meets the needs of the modern world should be introduced. A society in which the lay–monastic, male–female, employer–employee, child–parent, teacher–student, ruler–ruled . . . are mutually bound by duty should be introduced. A righteous society, in which the five precepts are observed, should be built on the basis of Buddhism.

(ix) In the past, Sri Lanka was the land of *dhamma*, which spread Buddhism around the world. Therefore, international relationships should be established with sister Buddhist countries. . . . While maintaining close relationships with neighbouring countries, we should consider that Sri Lanka is an independent state.

(x) A Buddhist council should be held to reinforce Sinhala *bhikkhu* lineage, and the recommendations of 1957 and 2002 Buddhist Commission Reports should be appropriately adopted.

(xi) Female moral rights, which are destroyed by commercialization, should be safeguarded. Nobility and dignity of motherhood should be restored.

(xii) Independent, free and ethical principles should be adopted for mass media.

These 12 points demonstrate the guiding principles of the JHU as a Buddhist political party in Sri Lanka. In engaging in politics and in presenting this 12-point manifesto, the key visible political motive of the monks of the JHU is their desire to create a "Buddhist voice" within the Sri Lankan Parliament so that Buddhist and Sinhala interests can be secured and guaranteed within the legislature. Increasingly, they perceive that power-hungry Sinhala lay-politicians have betrayed the Sinhala and Buddhist rights of the majority population of the country.

Election victory, chaos, and the JHU in Parliament. The JHU monks have so far faced several controversies. . . . The act of nominating over 200 monks to contest a parliamentary election was controversial in itself. The JHU's act of using monks to contest the election has been criticized both in Sri Lanka and abroad. . . .

The election success of the JHU . . . was a shock for many who perceived their significance very lightly since none of the candidates were highly versa-tile politicians. In the election held on 2 April 2004, the UPFA—a combination of the SLFP and the JVP—won 105 seats out of 225. The UNP . . . secured only 82 seats. The Tamil National Alliance, backed by the LTTE, won 22 seats. The JHU and the Sri Lanka Muslim Congress (SLMC) had nine seats and five seats, respectively.

As the newest political party, the JHU had a significant success in the elec-tion; although its candidates were novices to parliamentary politics, they were able to convince a considerable section of the urban population in Co-lombo District, Gampaha District and Kalutara District of their national and religious causes. The success of both the JHU and the JVP in the 2004 election suggests that "national unity" has become an important concern for the ma-jority Sinhala population.

The chaos generated in selecting the speaker at the 13th Parliament ses-sion on 22 April 2004 [also] shows the significance of the JHU monks in deter-mining political processes in Sri Lanka. While the JHU cast the critical two votes . . . in electing the former Minister of Justice, Mr W. J. M. Lokubandara of the UNP (Opposition), as the new speaker, the monks of the JHU also faced abuse within Parliament from the UPFA Government benches, and outside Parliament by unidentified persons often associated with the JVP. When the JHU Member of Parliament, Venerable Athuraliye Rathana, began to speak in Parliament congratulating the elected speaker, he was disturbed by the Government peers, particularly JVP MPs, making noises, calling [the monks] names as supporters of "separatists, terrorists and Eelamists," and throwing books. . . . Outside Parliament, an array of offensive posters was posted on walls and billboards criticizing the JHU monks for casting votes against [the] people's verdict. This post-election chaos made front-page headline news in the local media. . . .

On 28 May 2004, the JHU MP Venerable Omalpe Sobhita published in the Gazette a bill entitled Prohibition of Forcible Conversion of Religion Act as a Private Member's Bill. The Sri Lankan Government also drafted a bill for the approval of the Cabinet. These two events are meant to fulfil a demand that Sinhala Buddhists made over the past few years with regard to "unethical conversions" carried out by evangelical Christians in the poor Buddhist and Hindu communities. These bills on "unethical" conversions bring [into focus] another phase of religious tensions present in the ethno-religious politics in Sri Lanka. As the youngest and the first monk-led political party, the JHU has already created a significant discourse on its policies and how it will adapt its policies in implementing them in the Parliament and outside it. It has already upset the newly elected ruling party, the UPFA, and continues to be an influential factor in Sri Lankan politics.

References

Daily Mirror. 2004. 19 February. Also in *Spotlight on Sri Lanka,* 8, no. 25, 20 February 2004, at http://xi.pair.com/isweb3/spot/c0825.html.

Deegalle, M. 2005. *Popularizing Buddhism.* Albany: State University of New York Press.

Hewapathirane, Daya. 2004. "The Buddhist Social Reform Movement of Ven. Soma." At http://shamika.50g.com/paramithaperahara/articles/27march2004.html.

Rahula, W. 1974. *The Heritage of the Bhikkhu: A Short History of the Bhikkhu in the Educational, Cultural, Social, and Political Life.* New York: Grove Press.

Scott, Andrew. 2003. "Soma Thera—Dedicated Buddhist and Nationalist." *Daily News,* 25 December. At http://www.dailynews.lk/2003/12/25/fea02.html.

Sobhita, O. 2004. "Prohibition of Forcible Conversion of Religion (Private Member's Bill)," *Gazette of The Democratic Socialist Republic of Sri Lanka,* Part II (supplement issued 31 May 2004).

Wijetunge, Pujitha. 2002. "Soma Thera Joins SU," *Sunday Times,* 3 December 2002. At http://www.dailymirror.lk/2002/12/03/News/7.html.

Notes

1. The *Jataka* (III. 274) enumerates the 10 royal virtues: (i) charity, (ii) morality, (iii) liberality, (iv) honesty, (v) mildness, (vi) religious practice, (vii) non-anger, (viii) non-violence, (ix) patience, and (x) non-offensiveness. Buddhists in South and Southeast Asia often allude to these 10 virtues since they are important aspects of Buddhist social and political philosophy.

2. The selection of both the date (2 March) and place (Kandy) are quite significant in historic terms. The date 2 March symbolizes an important historic event: the day that Sri Lanka lost her independence to the British under the Kandyan Convention signed on 2 March 1815. Another event that happened on that day in Kandy is still in the ears of the Sinhala nationalists: on that day in Kandy, when the British raised the Union Jack [flag of Great Britain] before signing the memorandum, the monk Kudapola protested against it and was shot dead.

A Buddha Now and Then:

Images of a Sri Lankan Culture Hero

John Clifford Holt

In 1977, the newly elected United National Party (UNP) led by President J. R. Jayewar-dene launched a new avowedly capitalistic "open economy" with a pro-Western dip-lomatic tilt. Several large-scale development schemes were put into place, including the massive Mahaweli development scheme, which included the building by Britain, Sweden, Germany, and Canada of several large reservoirs and irrigation projects, and also the establishment of free trade zones and a spectacular growth in the na-tion's tourist industry. The consequence of the "open economy" was rapid social change, particularly in the Sinhala regions of the country. The following essay is a reflection on how social change impacts religious culture, particularly how this change registered at the most important ritual and pilgrimage site for Sinhala Bud-dhists: the Dalada Maligava (Temple of the Tooth Relic) in Kandy. Also included are observations on how social change among the Sinhala Buddhists receives approval by being associated with the Buddha.

"Perception is the fore-runner of all mental formations."
   —*Dhammapada* 1: 1

I first came to Sri Lanka some thirty years ago, in 1979, a day after the cele-brations for Vesak (the full moon day in May on which are celebrated the Buddha's birth, enlightenment, and final attainment of nirvana). At the time, in spite of years of studying Buddhism in texts, I was almost com-pletely innocent of the manner in which the Buddha is understood cultur-ally by various types of Buddhists in Sri Lanka. As ridiculous as it seems to me now, I don't think I was even very aware that Vesak was one of the most important holidays celebrated in this country every year. Thirty years back, my knowledge of the Buddha was decidedly more philosophical in character, almost exclusively derived from scholarly books about religious ideas. The Buddha, in my own mind, was one of the great religious teachers of humankind who had tried to show a way out of the unsatisfactory nature and calamities of the human condition. But religious festivities like Vesak and other important modes of popular ritual expression were not what I had studied before I first came to Sri Lanka. Had I known about the importance of Vesak back then, I certainly would have made an effort to get here in time to see the colorful panoply of lanterns, "electric Buddhas," and popular poster art depicting various *Jataka* stories and to listen to the sonorous melodies of young, white-clad women singing *bhakti gee* (devotional songs). Experiencing Vesak close-up on my first visit to the island would have made for a fantastic introduction to the Buddhist people of this country and would have accelerated my understanding of how the Buddha has been understood within the Sinhala Buddhist culture of Sri Lanka. But I was late for Vesak, and as such, my learning curve with regard to the social and cultural significance of the Buddha was probably a little bit slower than it could have been as a result.

Because of my "late" arrival, my initial impressions of Sri Lanka were based on my first visual encounters with the lifeless, vacant streets I saw in the Colombo Fort that first day after Vesak: a few casual workers were taking apart the structure of a *pandal* that had been so brilliantly illuminated only the day before and small clusters of people were peering through the windows of department stores catching glimpses of the newest import from the West: the television. I remember thinking that Colombo was really a very drab city, the Fort being a former and thoroughly colonial place whose best times had probably passed by so many decades before. In retrospect, my initial impression couldn't have been more erroneous. The following day, when the holiday hangover was over and people had returned to work, Colombo turned out to be a thriving and teeming bustle of activity. I was overwhelmed by the beehive of work going on in the Pettah and by the intensive varieties of business being transacted in the Fort. I made a quick deduction based upon my first observations from the day before: the taking apart of the pandal and the fascination with television were somewhat paradigmatic of a pattern I suspected was then afoot—tradition (pandal) was waning and change (TV) was arising in modern Sri Lanka.

Recently, a movement by some Sri Lankan government officials to have Vesak recognized globally as an international holiday has been introduced—a very interesting idea that would lend greater visibility to the profound impact that the Buddha has made not only upon the Buddhistic cultures of Asia, but to world history in general. I can only wish now that Vesak and its significance had caught my attention earlier. What I didn't really understand when I made my first deduction about tradition and change in Sri Lanka was that although change may seem ubiquitous and inevitable, there is a staying power of traditional ways of apprehending life in general, and that this staying power is represented by the Buddha. That is, change and tradition stand in a reflexive relationship to one another.

From my formal studies in religion as an undergraduate and then as a graduate student, my perception of the Buddha had been conditioned first by my encounter with him in the relatively sanitized text books on "world religions" that I had read while attending college in Minnesota, books that reduced the distinctive philosophical orientations and rich varieties of religious cultures of Asia to an abstract and almost faceless common denominator. Later in my studies, I had been further influenced by impressions that had been formed as the result of studying Pali Text Society translations, especially the Buddhist monastic code of regulations (*Vinayapitaka* [*Book of Discipline*]) and the principal *nikayas* (didactic portions of the *Suttapitaka*) some years later while studying at the University of Chicago. For me, as I read and reflected on these texts, first in English and later in Pali, the Buddha seemed to cut the figure of a strict (and sometimes, in the case of articulating monastic disciplinary rules in the *Vinaya*, a rather downright intolerant) pragmatic disciplinarian of monks, on the one hand, and also that of a profound philosopher/teacher dispensing the advice of prosaic wisdom to would-be converts, on the other. I wouldn't go so far to say that my image of the Buddha was that of a "Victorian gentleman," to borrow a phrase from an American colleague who I think has aptly commented on how some nineteenth- and twentieth-century British scholars, like T. W. Rhys Davids and I. B. Horner, had portrayed the Buddha. But I would say that I probably had been carrying around an image in my head that was something of a cross between Plato, Solomon, and Confucius. At the time I was blissfully unaware that my view of the Buddha, whatever it was exactly, was nothing more than a narrow scholarly rendering.

When I recall my rather culturally and historically innocent understanding of the Buddha at that time, I think it was also concomitantly the result of my own lack of awareness regarding the manner in which my Protestant Christian (Lutheran to be precise) upbringing had affected my general understanding of religion, as well as my rather uncritical imbibement of the manner in which other earlier American and European scholars of a Protestant inclination had bequeathed a legacy of understanding the Buddha in the West. So, my perception of the Buddha was not only that of stern and wise Confucian Plato speaking the truth about human suffering and its transcendence (through the vernacular of the late-nineteenth-century "queen's English" of the Pali Text Society's translations), but also a perception of a religious genius (yet in Protestant or Germanic/Puritan style) who had eschewed all mediated forms of religious pursuit (thought, rituals, symbols, and myths, as well as other types of cultural media, which combine to create the rich tapestries of social and historical religious expression). In my perception, the Buddha was among the greatest of human teachers, but surely not a god. I thought the Buddha had been above or beyond all of the usual religious paraphernalia, a rather otherworldly-oriented figure of lofty philosophical maxims, whose sole purpose in life had been to point out an arduous spiritual path to the ineffable experience of *nibbana*. While I remain convinced, some thirty years later, that the ultimate significance of the teachings of the Buddha are soteriological in nature, my perception of the Buddha is no longer that of a Confucian Plato, although I do continue to see some affinities with many of Confucius's moral maxims. My education leading to a transformed understanding of the Buddha continues today, but it really began in earnest two days after my 1979 arrival in Colombo when I first entered the Dalada Maligava (Temple of the Tooth Relic) in Kandy.

In 1979, the Dalada Maligava remained a genuine place of pilgrimage. During the four days I spent at the temple photographing rituals, recording their sounds, and doing my best to see what kinds of religious experiences were facilitated by the formal orchestration of ritual activities in the temple, I met very few Western tourists, and I myself remained relatively unscathed by tourist hawkers. I absorbed as much as I could, from the early 4.30 A.M. *pujas* to the last ritual at night. I recorded the various drumming cadences, tagged along with various types of worshippers watching their every move, and pestered temple officials about what was done when and why. I came away from that initial visit with an understanding of how Buddhism, especially with regard to the rituals, symbols, and myths associated with the Dalada Maligava, formed a type of civil religion among the Sinhalese. The Buddha was not only a great religious teacher of the past, and a "thus-gone one" (*tathagata*) but somehow, in this temple, there was still something of his presence to be felt. Here was a temple complex blended into a royal palace and a relic that was undisputedly regarded as the palladium of the Sinhalese people. If the Buddha was not actually present, then his legacy certainly was.

I studied the spatial symbolism of the city of Kandy and found that it reinforced hierarchical conceptions of power within the Sinhala Buddhist traditional sociocosmic worldview. The Buddha and the king, in parallel fashion, had been placed at the apex of this hierarchy. I came to know clearly, and could see this with my own eyes, that Buddhism was a religion intimately bound up with the political history of the island and had made its pact consistently with the country's Sinhala kings, who had become the religion's chief patrons of support over many long centuries.

I was also impressed with the devotional expressions of religious piety I observed at the Maligava, especially among villagers who had come to pay their homage in the company of friends and family. I attributed to these people the social virtue of "communitas," a term coined by the anthropologist Victor Turner to describe a type of spiritual camaraderie that can be generated among collegial pilgrims, a social mysticism of sorts.

Thus, my image of the Buddha began to change. I began to see him not only in relation to lofty philosophical ideals articulated in venerable religious treatises, but also in relation to the sociopolitical history of the island, on the one hand, and as an object of personal veneration among the village laity, on the other. I began to suspect that, regardless of class, background, or station in life, the Buddha represented a valorization of the sacred for people of all walks of life in Sri Lanka. He was a bona fide "culture hero" in this country.

When I returned to Kandy three years later in 1982, however, there had been an explosion of the tourist industry in the meantime, not only in Kandy but throughout Sri Lanka. Almost at every *handiya* (intersection), there was a plethora of colorful home-made signs advertising the comforts of new guest houses with names like "Paradise Garden," "Shanti Rest," "Golden Horizon," and so on. Hawkers were in overabundant supply on the streets of Kandy. I myself felt like I was consistently among the most hunted. The Cultural Triangle people, with some loose affiliation of UNESCO, had gained control of some of the premises of the Kandy sacred area (I was unhappy that I had to pay in order to gain access to sacred shrines), and the ambience of Senkadagala had shifted inexorably, I thought, from the sacred to the profane. Though I realized that there is always an interesting connection between pilgrimage and tourism at most sacred places throughout the world, and that sometimes the lines between these two forms of social behavior are easily blurred, I was disappointed with what had happened in Kandy, and even more so in Anuradhapura and Polonnaruva, where exorbitant entrance fees had been introduced for foreigners. I am not arguing here, that Kandy had lost its sanctity for the village pilgrims who continued to visit, nor that the Diyawadana Nilame (lay custodian) should have been faulted for permitting the Maligava to become such a tourist attraction, but now religious culture had to share the place with another subculture, a subculture with an entirely different clientele, whose presence was more akin to leering voyeurs than devout worshippers. At the evening pujas, there were likely to be almost as many tourists in attendance as Sri Lankans. It began to dawn on me that to a certain extent, the marketing of Sri Lanka's new open economy included the marketing of the Buddha, and that this marketing was but part of the image of the "exotic East" sold through the media of the European tourist industry, an industry that some Sri Lankan government ministries and businessmen had so obviously and so eagerly begun to encourage. I recognized that the development of tourism was a useful strategy to help boost the fledgling Sri Lankan economy, to provide more jobs and to raise the general standard of living. But I also lamented the cultural costs. Unlike my experience in 1979, I also became much more aware of myself as a foreigner within the context of my visits to the Maligava. I was assumed by both temple officials and tourist hawkers to be a mark, a potential cash cow. Scholars and students loathe being regarded as tourists. I felt insulted. But being scholars and students doesn't make the nontourist Westerner any less foreign, in spite of a desire to understand culture empathetically.

In 1979, because there were so few Europeans visiting the temple, I think I must have forgotten what I, myself, had looked like on those occasions, or how I probably stood out in the temple crowd without even being aware of it. Then, I had had the sense that I was just blending in and that my presence was unobtrusive, precisely because there were no other foreigners around to remind me of my own "otherness." But at the Maligava in 1982, I could not help but feel that the place changed; certainly the social experience had changed and not only for me, but certainly for Sri Lankans as well. Sri Lankans now had to share the presence of the Buddha with others, others for whom the presence of the Buddha was but one more stop on a fun-filled holiday. I somehow found this incongruous and lamented the passing of an era. I was pretty naive in this regard too.

A few years later, a Sinhalese friend of mine took a photo of me and my son standing in a queue waiting, along with a small crowd of Sri Lankans, for the Katugastota bus in downtown Kandy. In the photo, our dress and facial expressions correspond exactly to those of the Sri Lankans. At that moment, we (the Sri Lankans, my son and I) were gawking in semi-amazement at two female German tourists dressed in very short shorts with skimpy tank tops. As they sauntered down the street we stared, and our friend's camera caught us all in an attitude reflecting how profoundly amazed we were at these tourists' "otherness." Yet at the same time, we were also oblivious to what we looked like too. We had become "indigenized" to some extent, wearing the same type of dress and sharing the same facial expressions indicating our similar reaction to that of the Kandyans; but for all of our acculturation, we also remained unmistakenly different, despite our own desires to be differentiated not so much from the Kandyan Sinhalese as from the German tourists.

I can only guess what goes on in the minds of Sinhalese villagers on pilgrimage to the Dalada Maligava when they encounter tourists with foreign tongues, foreign skins, foreign dress, foreign body postures, and the like. In a place that to them is a central symbol of their traditional culture and social identity, what they may encounter and what may be most memorable to them is their encounter with what is so distinctively foreign! While there is much irony here, it is also the case that the encounter with such foreign "otherness" only furthers, by contrast, the sense of one's own identity. That is, identity with the Dalada (Tooth Relic) and simultaneously in juxtaposition to the strange presence of foreigners at the Maligava both function in ways to sharpen an awareness of one's own distinctive identity.

In any case, my initial 1979 visit to Kandy, in contrast to my stay in 1982, had a far more profound impact on my understanding of the Buddha for Buddhists in Sri Lanka. It was then that I first began to come to terms with the complexity of ways in which the Buddha was understood in Sri Lanka. The Buddha was not just a profound teacher, but an object of veneration, and his symbolic remains were an emblem of religioethnic, or even, as I was about to see, of sociopolitical identity. I began to understand just how complex a role the Buddha had played in the unfolding of civilization on this island.

I would call the Buddha I met at the Dalada Maligava in 1979 a "royal Buddha." His presence, or more precisely his legacy, lived on in that hill country palace, was feasted every day, enjoyed musical orchestrations, and gave audiences to his reverently devoted, some of whom had come from quite far. Once a year, during the July/August Esala Perahara, his relic was mounted on the royal animal par excellence, the elephant, and paraded around his city attended by a vast retinue of officials and an array of entertainers including enthusiastic Kandyan dancers, in the process symbolizing his spiritual and temporal lordship over the kingdom. I later learned, from reading ethnographies, that the relic was thought to have the power to bring rain and, in the process, to safeguard the material well-being of this predominantly agricultural society. I also learned that the perahara was a ritual about ordering society, an annual collective statement of the community's identity, the parts of it in relation to the whole.

Indeed, from this first royal impression, I later came to a more thorough awareness of the conflation of royal imagery with the figure of the Buddha, a conflation that probably goes back to the very beginnings of the Buddhist tradition in India some two and a half millennia ago: after all, the Buddha had been born as Siddhartha, prince of the Sakyan clan; and, at his birth it had been prophesied that he would become either a buddha or a *cakravartin* (a dharma-minded universal conqueror). That mythic association doesn't mean that the Buddha was inherently political. Indeed, he is thought to have rejected the kingship that was his rightful dharmic inheritance. But it does mean that the association was present from the beginning, if we take his mythic biography seriously. Or, if we keep in mind other indigenous frames of reference, the royal conflation actually antedates the beginnings of Buddhist tradition in the *Jataka* stories (about the Buddha's previous incarnations). By this, I refer to the most well-known of all these 547 tales of the Buddha's previous rebirths, the *Vessantara Jataka*. Here the Buddha, in his last rebirth [as Vessantara], a royal one, before being reborn royally again as Siddhartha, gives away everything in his princely kingdom, including his wealth, wife, and children, in order to epitomize the radical extreme to which he quested: the realization of selflessness and detachment. The story of Vessantara remains extremely popular and well known even today. It has also been adapted dramatically for the stage by the renowned playwright Saratchandra. Again, it can be pointed out that Vessantara was giving away his princely domain and royal prerogatives. But he was a prince, nonetheless. I also became aware, in my further studies of Sri Lankan cultural history, of how many Sinhala Buddhist kings had aspired to become buddhas themselves, often stylizing their methods of rule in comparison to the selfless and compassionate bodhisattva. These more traditional associations of the Buddha with royalty, along with royal aspirations to become buddhas, were but preliminary insights into a growing awareness about the centrality of the Buddha figure for Sinhala culture in general.

One night in Tangalle, a day after Poson poya (full moon day in June) in 1982, when I had spent the day among lay religious observers who had taken vows in a local *pansala* (temple), I spent the greater part of an evening on the green adjacent to the major handiya in town amidst a partisan political crowd of Sri Lankan Freedom Party (SLFP) supporters listening to antigovernment speeches delivered from a blue-and-white draped platform. At the time, my Sinhala was not yet good enough to follow the substance of these speeches in any great detail. But by the angry denunciatory tone of the speeches, sprinkled with "UNP," "J. R. Jayewardene," "Premadasa," "Bandaranaike," and so on, I understood the drift of what was going on, especially because I had been reading about Sri Lankan politics fairly regularly since my original 1979 visit. What struck me, however, was not the style and tone of these ferocious oratories, but the unforgettable image of many monks seated on both sides of the platform facing the gathered crowd of supporters, a brilliant saffron line embroidering the presence of important lay politicos. Herein I realized that the legacy of the "royal Buddha" in a more traditional context was the realization of a "political Buddha" in the contemporary context.

It seemed to me, as I pondered what to me was such an extraordinary sight—those monks, or "sons of the Buddha," sitting on the platform for the political rally as if they constituted a chapter of militant cadres—that politics amongst the Sinhalese, perhaps since the 1956 election campaign of S. W. R. D. Bandaranaike, had become a matter of who could represent themselves as being the most Buddhist. That is, political discourse, either explicitly articulated or implicitly symbolized by the ritualistic actions of politicians or leaders in government, was thoroughly entwined with socio-religious discourses of a particular type and a public contest or vying of sorts was continuously being played out through the media. I shouldn't have been so surprised. By this time, I knew that Buddhism wasn't just a religion of elite, select religious virtuosos who had renounced the world and lived in relative solitude in their concerted quests for a spiritually otherworldly realization of nibbana. In retrospect, I shouldn't have been so non-plused at what I was witnessing at the time. I had previously studied Gandhi's religio-political worldview while pursuing a master's degree and I had been a sympathetic supporter of the Rev. Martin Luther King Jr. during my college days in the 1960s. Moreover, I had participated in a number of marches protesting American involvement in Vietnam and had marched side by side with many clergy of a variety of Christian persuasions. So, I knew religion and politics could be thoroughly related. In fact, I had thought that they should be. Indeed, in writing my master's thesis I had noted that Gandhi had said explicitly that the person who did not recognize that religion and politics were indelibly linked really didn't understand the meaning of religion. Still, I can remember how stunned I was to see all those monks up there on the political stage sanctifying the presence of those SLFP officials. This was the legacy of the royal Buddha I had not known before I had come to Lanka.

Perhaps seeing contemporary politically active SLFP monks as a legacy of the royal Buddha is a bit overly simplistic. Since those early days in Sri Lanka, I have read a number of Buddhistic political tracks. In addition to works on Buddhist socialism formulated in Burma by enthusiastic Buddhist Marxists in the 1930s, works that stressed affinities between Marxist positions on the individual, community, state, and private property and Buddhist positions staked out in the Pali Nikayas, a number of writers, the Indian scholar G. De among them, have tried to show how democracy has been part and parcel of the proceedings of the early Buddhist monastic sangha since almost its very inception. Variants on the theme of the royal Buddha could be the "Marxist Buddha" and the "Democratic Buddha" respectively. My point here is that being Buddhist does not really imply any particular political mindset. The Buddha's legacy could be appropriated by people of any given political persuasion. The same is quite obvious in America, where the spectrum of political persuasions of Christians runs the gamut from Jerry Falwell's "Moral Majority" on the right to Daniel and Phillip Berrigan on the left. What is interesting to me, however, is the fact that any politician or political ideology in need of legitimacy in Sri Lanka must somehow come to terms with the Buddha or Buddhist thought, which function as a kind of pole star, a fundamental directional force, for Sinhala culture as a whole. That is, whatever the ideology being proselytized or contested among the Sinhalese, it needs to become congruent with a vision, image or understanding of the Buddha or what he taught. I would argue that in postcolonial Ceylon/Sri Lanka, this situation is perhaps even more compelling than before.

What I have observed about politics in Sri Lanka is not exclusive to that domain of human endeavor. I think that the same might be said about many other arenas of human life and discourse in Sri Lanka. I have come to learn, for instance, that there are particularly Buddhistic ways of understanding health or medicine (ancient or modern), that there are Buddhistic approaches to science, economic activity, to the environment, to social roles among family members, to education, to art and music, and Buddhist dispositions toward war and peace. In saying this, I want to underscore that these approaches are not monolithic in nature, nor are they always consistent with one another. There is not just one Buddhistic approach to war or peace, for example, but a plethora of positions staked out that in one way or another, however, make an appeal to the example of the Buddha, the Buddha's "canonized" teachings or to various Buddhist cultural traditions that have been in place for centuries.

Here, I do not aim to make the case that Sri Lanka has always been and will continue to be only a Buddhist society and culture. History and demography are too variegated to make that naive claim. Moreover, Sri Lanka has been the venue of a fantastic degree of cross-fertilization among its various religious and ethnic communities who have found its shores congenial. Its Sinhala inhabitants have absorbed much from Tamils, Muslims, Portuguese, Dutch, British, Americans, and Japanese. The current pace of modernization in general is also quite furious. What I have observed, however, is an historical pattern of inclusivity among the Sinhalese in which the Buddha or Buddhism functions as an elastic legitimating or rationalizing factor in determining what makes for inclusion. The converse of this may be true also; that which is excluded or rejected is often done so on Buddhistic grounds.

Since the 1950s, copious quantities of articles in scholarly journals and numerous books have been published in social science academic circles about the twin processes of modernization and secularization in South Asia. Nehru's post-Gandhian vision of a secular independent India, together with various plans for economic transformations in South Asian countries, seemed to be proclamations of a fundamental transition that many assumed would alter the ethoses of South Asian societies. There is no doubt that economic development under the stewardship of both the United National Party, and the various alliances with the Sri Lanka Freedom Party at their core, have contributed to sea changes in the basic social experiences of Sri Lankans over the past forty years. Ultimately, these changes may be judged, in time, as just as significant as those wrought by the British colonial experience. My reference above to what had happened in Kandy at the Dalada Maligava between 1979 and 1982 is but an anecdotal confirmation of just one sort of change that has occurred. But what is even more interesting to me is that economic development has not been necessarily the bedfellow of secularization in Sri Lankan society on the whole. While this may seem to be the case among certain sections of the Colombo populace, the diffused presence of a Buddhistic ethos remains in place throughout most sectors of Sri Lankan Sinhala society. My comments about a royal and "political Buddha" represent my attempt to make this clear.

Too often, social change, when measured by Euro-American social scientists, is done so with the assumption that types of changes that have already occurred in European and American contexts represent a kind of inevitable future for Asian societies to negotiate. The anthropologist Clifford Geertz once labeled this tendency critically as the "world acculturative approach," an approach which assumes that the standards and goals of Western societies comprise a type of norm to be emulated by the non-Western. Insofar as Europe and America have become increasingly secularized societies in which the sacred has been increasingly relegated (and with diminishing intensity) to specified and limited time frames (Sunday mornings and Friday evenings) and to specific places (churches and synagogues) among decreasing numbers of religieux, it is assumed that capitalistic economic and democratic social transformations afoot in non-Western societies will lead to a similarly enervated condition of religion in Asia.

Perhaps it is simply a by-product of my own humanistic inclinations and an unwarranted projection of my personal experiences and observations onto the general trajectories of social experience in Sri Lanka as a whole, but

I suspect that these assumptions, especially the tendency to think that Sinhala Buddhist culture is headed in the uniform direction of secularization, may prove to be overly problematic. Yes, the experience of visiting the Dalada Maligava between 1979 and 1982 changed dramatically with the infusion of tourism into the local economy. But the same rites continued to be observed at the temple, and there remains no question that they will continue to be observed deep into any foreseeable future. There is not only an overt and explicitly Buddhist cultic community of religious practice thriving in Sri Lanka, but there also remains the function of the Buddha and his teachings as a kind of pole star. This, I think, is the nature of the implicit presence of the Buddha in Sri Lanka, and this presence, I would argue, may actually be far more profound than the explicit one.

This presence is a kind of diffused ethos that has been woven into the cadences of growing rice, getting healed, attending to the dying or dead, and so on, on one level, and deciding, for instance, on what moral bases that the government needs to predicate its various initiatives on behalf of the people on another. "Ethos" is a difficult word to define and its presence even more difficult to locate or reify specifically. I hesitate to use it here because I cannot think of an exactly precise equivalent term in Sinhala, but I know there are terms that come very close to its meaning. I would attempt to describe it as the character of a people that is shown by the manner in which various ideals have been suffused into social and cultural constructs. In Buddhist Sri Lanka, that ethos has been conditioned by the countless ways in which the Buddha has been appropriated.

Images of the Buddha in Sinhala culture are not fixed and assured, but rather shifting and transforming, continuously refracted anew in relation to the changing contours of the historical dynamic. My observation is congruent with what the Buddha taught about human experience in general: "Whatever is subject to uprising is also subject to cessation." Even images of the Buddha are not exceptions to the verity of this observation. Yet, having assented to that truest of maxims, pole stars exist over vast spans of time, and I have a feeling that the Buddha's star will not set on the Sri Lankan horizon for many eons yet. That is, I expect to see *pandals* being erected and lanterns lit for many Vesak celebrations still to come. And I expect the Buddha to figure prominently in defining the nature, inclusion, or exclusion of any social and cultural transformations in the making.

Losing the Way Home

Ramya Chamalie Jirasinghe

Language and religion are the major constituents of ethnic identity in Sri Lanka. In this moving poem, the poet expresses her distress at the ambivalent or perhaps even schizoid regard for language that her daughter must endure in a conflicted contemporary Sri Lanka.

The Principal's lips purse when
my daughter says, "Gedera yanna one."[1]
She tells us,
"We don't scold them for talking like that, but
some parents want us to talk to them in English."
We have come looking for the right school.

I feel like finding out what those parents spoke,
Queen's English; Singlish; Not-pot?
But I stop myself and watch the army of inverse snobbery
march up my Singlish bones:
an invading bacteria that turns around to accuse me of harbouring it.
After all, I almost voiced the question; almost rifled through the
    criteria; almost poked between the layers that define us "here."
"Here" where those who love to hear a piper piping
his songs of innocence on a hollow reed,
or listen to the child-monk's ditty to a king,
are no longer relevant.

There is only the din from
those who
shout their throats hoarse on public stages, who
batter our heads with moral righteousness
as they thump the heritage card.
But, behind their raucous is their own soft murmur
telling the Principal something else when they

drop their sons off at Kensington International School in
the morning.

Against this mad new gasp to learn a language,
overtly reviled and covertly hankered after,
we fill children's veins with hot air.
With daffodils and snow.
A Barney baby—a Dora daughter:
how will they grow,
what love, what spirit, what beauty will sustain them if their
inner world crumples and the self flails for its centre?

———

Is there a way to tell a child
that somewhere,
a dappled river laughing flows
on the bed of quiet existence?
Can I take her first to
that bank where the water stills:
and then let the
gate open,
bringing in myriad other lives, letting her know of their spirit,
and in some way give her a life that will let her offer them room,
beckon them with an open heart?

———

She asked to go home,
but I can not find it to take her there.
The river flows carrying broken selves.
This house has changed so horribly, so horribly,

so horribly.

Note

1. "I want to go home" (Sinhala).

MUSLIM IDENTITIES: AN INTRODUCTION

There has been a Muslim community in Sri Lanka for more than a millennium. Like those who belong to other emergent communal identities, the Muslims do not form a single homogenous social group. Rather, they are quite varied in their lineages and varied according to the specific region of Sri Lanka under consideration. However, they are the only "ethnic" group in Sri Lanka defined completely by their religion, since most of them speak Tamil but do not identify extensively with Tamil culture, despite various and overt Tamil attempts to encompass them for political reasons. Politically, Muslims predominate in sections of the east coast of the country, especially south of Batticaloa, and they often constitute an important swing vote in other regions of the country (on the west coast around Beruwala, about fifty kilometers (thirty miles) south of Colombo; around Puttalam, one hundred kilometers (sixty miles) north of Colombo; and also in the Kandyan district).[1]

In 1990, Muslims were driven out of the Jaffna peninsula by the Liberation Tigers of Tamil Eelam and settled in a refugee camp of approximately 100,000 people in Puttalam. A generation has now passed since this forced exodus. On the whole, the Muslim community has resisted the sorts of political radicalism now evident in other Asian Muslim communities, but some signs of tension are beginning to emerge between those advocating, on the one hand, the fundamentalist Wahabi form of Islam that looks to Saudi Arabia and, on the other, the more relaxed or inclusive Sufi-inclined traditions. The latter have often absorbed local elements of religious culture.

Note

1. This section of the *Reader* was compiled, edited, and introduced (in the next chapter) by Dennis McGilvray, with the exception the short story "Purdah's Lament" and this brief introductory section.

Origins of the Sri Lankan Muslims and Varieties of the Muslim Identity

Dennis McGilvray and Mirak Raheem

The Muslims are Sri Lanka's "other" minority, less often discussed despite their important role in the island's economy and their sought-after votes in key electoral districts. They have played a conspicuous economic role in Sri Lanka for more than a thousand years as traders, both internationally and internally. They were especially well-integrated into the Kandyan kingdom and have since come to flourish in coastal regions as well. The following general overview provides a brief introduction to the history and evolving identity of this community from the colonial period to the present.

Compared to Sinhala and Tamil prehistory, which extends back at least to the first millennium BCE, the origins of the Muslim community are more recent, which has meant that their presence on the island for "merely" a thousand years has been discounted in ethnonationalist debates. Although the earliest evidence from the Islamic period is limited to fragmentary travelers' accounts, early Islamic coinage, and some lithic inscriptions, the history of Sri Lanka's Muslims is plainly connected with the pre-Islamic seaborne trade between South and Southeast Asia and the Middle East. Not only Arabs but Persians too were frequent early visitors to the island. With the advent of Islam on the Arabian Peninsula in the first half of the seventh century and the subsequent conquest of Persia, trade across the Indian Ocean was increasingly dominated from the eighth century onward by Arab Muslim merchants from ports on the Red Sea and the Persian Gulf. Unlike the Persian and Turkic invasions of North India that established major states and empires, the Muslim impact on the coasts of South India and Sri Lanka was predominantly Arabic in culture and mercantile in motivation, part of the same historical stream that resulted in the Islamization of insular Southeast Asia.

The medieval Hindu and Buddhist kingdoms of Kerala and Sri Lanka,

eager for revenues from overseas commerce, allowed Arab merchants—
many of whom acquired local wives by whom they fathered Indo-Muslim
progeny—to establish a dominant economic position in port settlements
such as Calicut and Colombo. Thus, not long after Vasco da Gama's 1498 naval crusade against the well-established "Moors" of Calicut, the Portuguese
encountered Muslim traders in Sri Lanka who spoke Tamil, who had ongoing links with the Muslims of the Malabar and Coromandel coasts of South
India, and who had been given royal permission to collect customs duties
and regulate shipping in the major southwestern port settlements under the
suzerainty of the local Sinhalese kings of Kotte. Commercial, cultural, and
even migrational links between Muslim towns in southern India and Sri
Lankan Moorish settlements are confirmed in the historical traditions of
Beruwala, Kalpitiya, Jaffna, and other coastal settlements where Sri Lankan
Muslims have lived for centuries. Like the coastal Muslims of south India
and the Muslims of Southeast Asia, the Sri Lankan "Moors" are Sunni Muslims of the Shafi'i legal school, a shared legacy of their earliest south Arabian forefathers. To varying degrees, the Sri Lankan Muslims also preserve
matrilineal and matrilocal family patterns, the legacy of a "Kerala connection" that has shaped Tamil social structure in Sri Lanka as well.

Although the period of Portuguese and Dutch colonial rule was oner-
ous to all Sri Lankans, it was especially harsh for the Muslims, who were
subjected to special penalties and restrictions because of their Islamic faith
and the threat they posed to the European monopoly of overseas trade. One
of the effects of Portuguese policies was to encourage (and by an official
edict of 1626, to require) migration of many coastal Muslims inland to the
Kandyan kingdom, where they engaged in *tavalam* bullock transport and a
diverse range of other occupations. Ultimately, Muslims settled throughout all of the Sinhala regions of the island, where two-thirds of the Muslim
population currently reside. In 1626, King Senerat of Kandy is also said to
have resettled 4,000 Muslims in the Tamil-speaking Batticaloa region of the
east coast to protect his eastern flank from the Portuguese. Probably as early
as the fifteenth century, and certainly by the seventeenth, large numbers
of Muslim farmers were well established on the east coast—in the contemporary Batticaloa and Ampara Districts, and possibly also in the southern
areas of Trincomalee District—where they intermarried with local Tamils
and shared a common matrilineal social structure. The east coast has the
highest concentration of Muslims in the local population, and also is a region of vital importance to the ethnic conflict today. In addition, smaller
groups practicing Islam include the Malays, who are Sunni Muslims descended from Javanese soldiers and princes brought to the island during the

period of Dutch colonial rule in the seventeenth and eighteenth centuries and are now concentrated in the Slave Island area of Colombo and in Hambantota. Additionally, some exclusive groups of Bombay and Gujarati Muslim traders—Bohras, Khojas, and Memons—have professional and business interests in Colombo.

In terms of their historic position in the polity, the Sri Lankan Muslims—unlike the Mappilas, Marakkayars, and Deccani Muslims of south India—never played a dominant military or political role in the kingdoms of the island, and as a result they did not become identified with the state or develop their own political or military traditions of sovereignty. Because no Muslim dynasty existed in Sri Lanka, no distinctive genres of Muslim courtly high culture (poetry, music, art, cuisine) arose or were patronized on the island. Moreover, because the Muslim population is relatively small and geographically dispersed, the critical conditions for large-scale peasant uprisings or jihadist campaigns—such as occurred during the Mappila Rebellions in Kerala in the nineteenth and early twentieth centuries—have never existed here. Because the two main protagonists in the Sri Lankan ethnic conflict—the Sinhalas and the Tamils—justify their political claims in terms of ancient conquests and medieval control of territory, the Muslims find themselves at a "historical" disadvantage.

The Diversity of Muslim Communities in Sri Lanka

On every part of the island where they live, the Muslims are highly visible because of their distinctive dress, food, religious practices, and prominence in retail trade. In terms of ascriptive status, the Sri Lankan Muslim community as a whole is more egalitarian and homogenous than its south Indian counterparts. Although the wealth and class structure descends steeply from elite gem-trading millionaires to urban entrepreneurs to rural farmers and boutique keepers, the sorts of hereditary, endogamous, caste-like divisions that have been documented among the Muslims of India do not exist among the Sri Lankan Muslims.

However, in order to appreciate the complexity of the Muslim position in Sri Lanka's ethnic conflict, it is essential to note the distinctive features of Sri Lankan Muslim regional demography and local Muslim subcultures. The most obvious cleavage in the political geography of Sri Lanka is between the mainly Sinhalese southwest and largely Tamil northeast. Roughly two-thirds of all Sri Lankan Muslims reside in the southwest, with especially large concentrations in metropolitan Colombo, where at least one-fifth of the entire Muslim population lives, and in the highland region around Kandy and Gampola. Muslims are also historically associated with southern coastal towns such as Kalutara, Beruwala, Galle, and Weligama, where they dominate particular industries such as the gem trade. Elsewhere in the central interior of the island, in virtually every Sinhala town and village, Muslims form a widely dispersed community of agricultural small landholders and shopkeepers ranging from textile and hardware merchants to restaurant owners and tea shop proprietors.

In the Northern Province, Muslims constituted 5 percent of the overall population until their forcible expulsion by the LTTE in 1990. Historically, the largest concentration was in Mannar District, where they formed the majority in one rural Assistant Government Agent division, but they were also concentrated in Mannar town and Erukalampitty. Other northern Muslim population centers included Jaffna town and its environs, Mullaittivu town in Kilinochchi District, and smaller populations in coastal and agrarian villages. Since 1990, many of these displaced northern Muslims have been living in camps in Kalpitiya and in nearby Puttalam town, where they have increased the local Muslim population significantly.

The Eastern Province, however, is the region where dense Muslim settlements constitute the most critical feature of the ethnic landscape, and where a stable solution to Sri Lanka's conflict will require the greatest degree of Muslim participation. The Eastern Province consists of three districts—Trincomalee, Batticaloa, and Ampara—that are home to one-third of all Muslims in Sri Lanka. Muslims here live in interspersed Tamil and Muslim towns and villages along a lagoon-laced shoreline. The east coast Muslims, especially those of Batticaloa and Ampara Districts, also share a distinctive matrilineal kinship and matrilocal household system with their Tamil neighbors. Although some eastern Muslims are businessmen, weavers, and fishermen, the majority are paddy farmers and landed proprietors. In Trincomalee District, where Muslims constitute 24 percent of the population, the largest concentration is along the southern shore of Koddiyar Bay in the paddy-farming towns of Kinniya and Mutur. In Batticaloa District, which is 28 percent Muslim, the main Muslim towns are Eravur and Kattankudy. In Ampara District as a whole, Muslims constitute the largest ethnic community (42 percent) in comparison with Sinhalas (38 percent) and Tamils (20 percent). However, in the narrow Tamil-speaking coastal corridor of Ampara District, in a string of densely populated towns stretching from Kalmunai to Pottuvil, one-half to three-quarters of the population are Muslims.

The Construction of a "Moorish" Identity

After 300 years of Portuguese and Dutch colonial repression, the Muslims took advantage of gradually liberalized British policies in the nineteenth century that permitted freedom of commerce, urban property rights, purchase of Crown land, and the appointment of local Muslim headmen. However, they remained absorbed in their customary modes of livelihood and mosque-based institutions, influenced by Sufi disciples and pious Indian Muslim trader-missionaries from Kayalpattinam and Kilakarai, and strongly averse to mass literacy, the printing press, and English-language education, which was then available only through Christian missionary schools. The British-imposed exile to Sri Lanka in 1883 of a charismatic Egyptian revolutionary, Orabi Pasha, finally served to catalyze an Islamic revival and a movement to establish Muslim schools offering a secular, Western-style curriculum, but this still placed Muslims far behind the Sinhalese and even farther behind the Tamils, who had begun to enroll in Christian mission schools in Jaffna sixty years earlier.

From the beginning of the colonial period in the early sixteenth century, members of the predominant Tamil-speaking Muslim community in Sri Lanka were routinely designated by the colonial term "Moor" (*Mouro,* "Moroccan"), which the Portuguese applied to Muslims throughout their African and Asian empire, as well as by such familiar European terms as "Mohammedan" or "Mussalman." By the end of the nineteenth century, however, the west coast urban Muslim elite had begun to self-consciously promote their unique racial identity as "Ceylon Moors" (or *Sonahar* in Tamil) in order to establish a legitimate claim for seats in the colonial system of communal (i.e., "racial") representation that the British instituted and maintained for one hundred years. In this environment of rival "racial" claims, a prominent Tamil leader, Sir Ponnambalam Ramanathan, in a strategically calculated speech to the Legislative Council in 1885, marshaled linguistic and ethnographic evidence to argue that, apart from religion, the Moors and Tamils shared a great many cultural and linguistic traits resulting from conversion and intermarriage over the centuries. When he published it three years later as an essay on "The Ethnology of the 'Moors' of Ceylon" in the *Journal of the Royal Asiatic Society, Ceylon Branch* [see an abridged version in the next chapter], Ramanathan's views appeared to gain more academic legitimacy. Muslim leaders immediately perceived his well-argued but politically motivated conclusion, that the Moors were simply Muslim members of the Tamil "race," as an academic excuse for the continued political domination of the Muslim community by the Tamil leadership. Although Ramanathan's strategy failed when the British governor appointed a Moor to the Legislative Council a year later, his essay seemed to embody the patronizing Tamil outlook found on some parts of the island, where even today some high-caste Tamils look down on the Muslims as their inferior and uneducated neighbors. Muslim/Tamil acrimony over Ramanathan's "ethnological" thesis has been festering for well over a century, evoking feelings of ethnic betrayal on the part of Tamil chauvinists, and the LTTE in particular, over the Muslims' alleged disloyalty to the Tamil nationalist cause.

In the narrow rhetorical space of "ethnicized" colonial identities, the political implications of Ramanathan's aggrandizing thesis motivated the Moorish leadership to embrace the label of "Ceylon Moor" with great tenacity, repudiating their Tamil-ness and asserting their identity as "an entirely different race of Arab origin." In 1944 they founded the Moors' Islamic Cultural Home in Colombo as a center for the dissemination of Moorish history and genealogical information, just as the Dutch Burgher Union had been campaigning for Sri Lanka's Eurasian "race" since 1908. As Qadri Ismail has noted, this Moorish racial identity for the Sri Lankan Muslims was constructed to emphasize the idea that Muslims were peaceful Arab traders who valued the sanctity of the island (called *Sarandib* in Arabic sources) because legend says Adam and Eve fell to earth near Adam's Peak [see Jeganathan and Ismail under "History" in the "Further Reading" section]. Emphasizing their patrilineal Arab ancestry allowed Moorish spokesmen to conveniently ignore their maternal connections to Tamil wives and mothers, while the Moors' Tamil linguistic heritage could be characterized simply as a "borrowed" trade language.

Because language is the key marker for Tamil ethnicity, the Sri Lankan Muslims have had to find different ways of explaining their widespread use of Tamil—which in earlier generations was sometimes phonetically written in Arabic script—without surrendering their distinct identity. A few historians and spokesmen for the Muslim community have asserted that "Muslims have no commitment to any particular language," citing the willingness of Moors living in Sinhala-majority districts to enroll their children in Sinhalese-language schools . . . [thus] becoming "a linguistically divided community," and it is true that sermons at some mosques in Colombo are now delivered on certain days in English or Sinhalese instead of in Tamil. At the same time, however, some northern and eastern Muslims still use— or at least do not object to—the unifying phrase "Tamil-speaking peoples," despite its political implications in the context of the LTTE's campaign for a linguistically defined Tamil Eelam. Thus, the debate about whether Tamil and Muslim identities are linguistically divorced is not entirely resolved.

Muslim community leaders today understand that any kind of "Tamil" identity would be especially risky for Muslims living in Sinhala-majority parts of the country. They have not forgotten the most terrifying episode of their pre-independence history, the widespread 1915 Sinhala-Muslim Riots, which forced the Muslim community to seek the protection of the British colonial authorities. Since then, no Sinhala violence against Muslims has erupted on such a massive scale, but a number of small-scale anti-Muslim disturbances and confrontations have continued to occur in majority Sinhala areas. A recent example is the Mawanella riots of 2001, in which three Muslims reportedly died and 127 Muslim shops were burned along the Colombo-Kandy road. Every such incident, of course, has its own specific origins and provocations, but the Sri Lankan Muslims are always aware that they are vulnerable to such mob violence and that they need the state's protection. The 1915 violence also embittered the Muslims against the Tamil elite, who sought to retain Ponnambalam Ramanathan's prominence in the Ceylonese nationalist movement by rising to defend the Sinhala rioters against harsh British justice. In Muslim eyes, Ramanathan's stance revealed the hypocrisy of "Tamil-speaking" ethnic solidarity, and this betrayal was later recalled bitterly by Moorish politicians at crucial moments even in the 1950s and 1960s.

Adopting a Contemporary "Muslim" Identity

Despite the Muslims' racially complex and culturally plural origins, a simplistic dichotomous debate over "Arab" versus "Tamil" was sustained for many years, with more or less the same political subtext of ethnic estrangement and rivalry. However, by the middle of the twentieth century, a longstanding argument had intensified within the community itself as to whether the term "Moor" or "Muslim" was preferable as a group designation. Nativistic "Moor" partisans incorrectly asserted that the Portuguese applied this term only to racially pure Arabs and that "Muslim" adherents emphasized a broader pan-Islamic religious identity that would ignore race and language and, incidentally, make room for the Malays and Coast Moors.

By the 1970s "Muslim" had become the most common term used when speaking English or Tamil. The popular term *Sonahar*, an older Tamil and Malayalam word which originally denoted West Asians, especially Arabs or Greeks, has largely fallen out of fashion, although "Lanka Yonaka" was still used as an ethnonym for the Sri Lankan Moors in the 1971 census. In common English parlance, both "Moor" and "Muslim" can be used interchangeably today to refer to indigenous Tamil-speaking Muslim Sri Lankans, but

"Muslim" has now become the predominant usage. This makes the Muslims the only ethnic group in Sri Lanka to proclaim their identity under a solely religious label.

The mainstream Sri Lankan Muslim community shares a strong feeling of identity as orthodox Sunni Muslims who follow the Shafi'i school of Islamic law and jurisprudence. The Sunni/Shia division does not exist in Sri Lanka, except for some very small Gujarati trading communities, such as the Bohras, who belong to the Ismaili sect of Shi'ism. Likewise, a Muslim version of the Hindu caste system, common in many parts of India and Pakistan, has never arisen in Sri Lanka, despite the existence of some hereditary *Maulana* (Seyyid) religious elites and a low-status endogamous Barber-Circumciser community (*Osta*). Although there is clearly more to Sri Lankan Muslim identity than simply their shared Islamic faith, the religion is definitely a significant unifying and motivating factor. This is reinforced by the existence of a body of Muslim personal law that is recognized by courts in Sri Lanka, by a statutorily established Wakfs board that oversees Muslim religious properties and trusts, by an island-wide network of separate government Muslim schools, and—until quite recently—by a government Ministry of Muslim Cultural and Religious Affairs.

Internally, the Muslim religious landscape in Sri Lanka has been affected by the same sorts of global Islamic currents that are apparent elsewhere in the Muslim world. Reformist and revitalizing movements such as the Tabliqi Jamaat and the Jamaat-i-Islami are quite active in Sri Lanka, seeking to boost daily observance—and understanding—of the five pillars of the faith (creed, prayer, fasting, pilgrimage, and alms). Many in the Muslim community also share the view that various forms of Wahhabi and Salafist influence are entering Sri Lanka directly or indirectly from Saudi Arabia by concealed channels of money and proselytization. The influence of such strict interpretations of Islam is now being seen in a growing intolerance, exemplified in the mob violence and property destruction in Kattankudy in 2004–6, of mystical Sufi traditions of Muslim devotional piety celebrated at saintly tomb-shrines and under the guidance of Sufi religious teachers. Sri Lankan mosques, like those in most parts of South Asia, commonly house the tombs (*ziyarams*) of local saints to whom vows are made and for whom annual death anniversary festivals (*kandooris*) are performed. In recent decades, some of these saintly shrines have been condemned as idolatrous (*shirk*) and have been demolished in the name of Islamic purification. Most of the major Sufi saints' festivals, such as at Daftar Jailani near Balangoda, and at the Beach Mosque Shrine near Kalmunai on the east coast, are still popularly celebrated, but everyone is aware of strong fundamentalist opposition

to them. Several individual Muslim sheikhs (Sufi teachers) with strong supporters on the east coast of the island—Rauf Maulavi and Abdullah Payilvan
in particular—have been openly accused of blasphemy by reformist clergy
who take a dim view of what they regard as the "pantheistic" tendencies in
Sufi doctrine. As in other countries experiencing Islamic fundamentalism
and reform, women's dress has recently become a public indicator of religi-
osity, with Sri Lankan Muslim women increasingly adopting the *hijab* head
covering and *abaya* gown—and in some cases even the *niqab* face mask—in
place of the traditional sari that was worn by women of a previous generation in a distinctly Muslim way.

Overall, Sri Lankan Muslims in recent decades have felt the polarizing
power of a more narrow, literalist, and legalistic current in contemporary
Islam, which paradoxically seems to have also stimulated a renewed interest
in mystical, non-literalist Sufi traditions as well, especially among educated
middle-class Muslims. One sign of the direction this Islamic debate is taking is seen in the growing resistance to simplistic and doctrinaire brands
of Islam, a position represented by the informal label *"sunnattu jamaat,"*
the mainstream faction that honors customary Sri Lankan forms of Muslim worship. It is widely observed that, like Sri Lankan political leaders of
other faiths, some Muslim politicians continue to have their personal religious mentors, often Sufi sheikhs or Maulanas (Seyyids, descendants of the
Prophet) with whom they have a *murshid/murid* discipleship relationship of
some kind.

The essential point is that current Sri Lankan Muslim politics is not infused with religious ideology or sectarian jihadism. Humanitarian solidarity with fellow-Muslims who are endangered or oppressed is strongly felt,
as when the 2004 tsunami tragedy struck the east coast, inflicting roughly a
third of Sri Lanka's tsunami deaths on a community that is 8 percent of the
total population. The same sympathies have been felt toward those Muslims
who were expelled by the LTTE from the north and displaced from Mutur.
However, no major Sri Lankan Muslim religious political parties per se operate, such as one finds in Pakistan and Bangladesh, and while there may be
some vociferous preachers, no conclusive evidence of militant or violent Is-
lamist movements has been found. Although the founding manifesto of the
main Muslim party, the Sri Lanka Muslim Congress, states that it would be
guided by "Islamic principles," it did not constitute a theological platform.
Instead, the manifesto was intended to be read as a coded promise of honesty and integrity, as a Muslim anticorruption pledge. Broadly recognized
Islamic terms and concepts may be invoked during election campaigns,
but Muslim politicians tend to avoid sectarian intracommunity religious

quarrels. Muslims in Sri Lanka, like Muslims everywhere in the world, are taught to value the solidarity of the Umma, the universal community of believers, and many of the key elements of Islamic worship are group-based experiences such as Friday prayers and the pilgrimage to Mecca. Global issues affecting Muslims in other parts of the world in the first decade of the twenty-first century (for example, Afghanistan, Iraq, even blasphemous Danish cartoons) may arouse as much indignation as do threats to Muslims living in Sri Lanka. In this sense, the religious identity of Sri Lankan Muslims contributes to a political consciousness that links together Muslims from all corners of the island.

The Ethnology of the "Moors" of Ceylon

P. Ramanathan

The collective identity of the Sri Lankan Muslims has been a topic of contentious debate since the late nineteenth century, when a prominent Tamil leader, Ponnambalam Ramanathan, argued that the Moors of Ceylon were simply Tamils whose religion was Islam.

That section of our community which passes principally among our European settlers by the name of "Moors" number, according to the last Census, about 185,000 souls. They are all Muhammadans. In the Sinhalese districts they occupy themselves with petty trade of all kinds, as pedlars and boutique (small shop) keepers. The poorer classes are mostly boatmen, fishermen, and coolies. In the Tamil provinces they pursue agriculture and fishing. In physique and features they closely resemble the Tamils, and as to the language they speak, it is Tamil, even in purely Sinhalese districts. I propose in this Paper to consider the nationality of this community. . . .

Webster defines nationality to be "a race or people determined by common language and character and not by political bias or divisions." Professor Max Müller narrows this definition as follows:—" . . . Language alone binds people together and keeps them distinct from others who speak different tongues. In ancient times particularly 'language and nations' meant the same thing; and even with us our real ancestors are those whose language we speak, the fathers of our thoughts, the mothers of our hopes and fears. Blood, bones, hair, and colour are mere accidents, utterly unfit to serve as principles of scientific classification for that great family of living beings, the essential characteristics of which are thought and speech, not fibrine, serum, or colouring matter, or whatever else enters into the composition of blood." . . .

If therefore we take language as the test of nationality, the Moors of Ceylon, who speak as their vernacular Tamil, must be adjudged Tamils. But as some ethnologists, like Dr. Tylor, maintain that language of itself affords only partial evidence of race, I shall dive a little deeper and prove that the conclusion I have arrived at is supported as much by the history of the Moors (so far as it may be ascertained) as by their social customs and physical features. . . .

It appears to me that Kayal [Kayalpattanam on the southern Tamilnadu coast] contains the keystone of the history of the Tamil Muhammadans, just as Quilon and Calicut contain that of the Malaiyalam Muhammadans. The tradition in Kayal is, that a few missionaries or teachers from Cairo landed there and made it their headquarters in the early part of the ninth century. In fact, it is said that Kayal, or Cail, is only another form of Cairo, properly Kahira. . . .

[We may safely conclude] that, though Arabs, Egyptians, Abysinnians, and other Africans may have constantly come to and gone from Ceylon, as merchants, soldiers, and tourists, long before the fourteenth century, comparatively few of them domiciled themselves in the Island; and that the settlement at Beruwala, which the Ceylon Muhammadans generally admit to be the first of all their settlements, took place not earlier than the fourteenth century, say A.C. 1350. We may also safely conclude that this colony was an offshoot of Kayal-paddanam, and that the emigrants consisted largely of a rough and ready set of bold Tamil converts, determined to make themselves comfortable by the methods usual among unscrupulous adventurers. Having clean shaven heads and straggling beards; wearing a costume which was not wholly Tamil, nor yet Arabic or African even in part; speaking a low Tamil interlarded with Arabic expressions; slaughtering cattle with their own hands and eating them; given to predatory habits, and practising after their own fashion the rights [*sic*] of the Muhammadan faith;—they must indeed have struck the Sinhalese at first as a strange people deserving of the epithet "barbarians." It is only natural that other colonies should have gone forth from Kayal-paddanam, and not only added to the population of Beruwala, but settled at other places, such as Batticaloa, Puttalam, etc. With the advent of the Europeans, communication with "the fatherland of the Chonahar" (as Kayal is known) and Ceylon grew feeble, and during the time of the Dutch must have practically ceased, because the Muhammadan settlers, from their obstinate refusal to become Christians, became objects of persecution to the Hollanders, who imposed all manner of taxes and disqualifications on them. The distinction which the "Ceylon Moor" draws between himself and the "Coast Moor" (*Chammankaran*) is evidently the result of the cessation of intercourse thus produced and continued for several decades between the mother-country and her colonies.

Having thus shown that the history of the Moors of Ceylon, no less than the language they speak, proves them to be Tamils, it remains to consider their social customs and physical features. . . . I [previously] pointed out what the requirements of a marriage were according to the law of the Prophet, but how different were the rites and customs practised by the Moors, and how many of those customs, such as the *stridhanam* (independent of the *mohr*), the *alatti* ceremony, the bridegroom wearing jewels though prohibited by the law, the tying of the *tali,* the bride wearing the *kurai* offered by the bridegroom, and the eating of the *patchoru,* were all borrowed from the Tamils. . . .

I shall therefore pass on to their physical features. Of these, the best marked race-characters, according to Dr. Tylor, are the colour of the skin, structure and arrangement of the hair, contour of the face, stature, and conformation of the skull. On all these points there is, in my opinion, no appreciable difference between the average Tamil and the average Moor. If he were dressed up like a Tamil he would pass easily for a Tamil, and *vice versa.* . . .

To sum up. It has been shown that the 185,000 Moors in the Island fall under two classes, "Coast Moors" and "Ceylon Moors," in almost equal numbers; that the "Coast Moors" are those Muhammadans who, having arrived from the Coromandel coast or inner districts of South India as traders or labourers, continue steadily to maintain relations of amity and intermarriage with their friends in South India; and that such "Coast Moors" are Tamils.

As regards the nationality of the "Ceylon Moors," numbering about 92,500 out of the 185,000, we have ample reasons for concluding that they too are Tamils,—I mean the masses of them; for, of course, we meet with a few families here and there—say, five per cent of the community, or about 5,000 out of the 92,500—who bear the impress of an Arab or other foreign descent. Even the small *coterie* of the Ceylon Moors, who claim for themselves and their co-religionists an Arab descent, candidly admit that on the mother's side the Ceylon Moors are exclusively Tamil. All that remains to be proved, therefore, is, that their early male ancestors were mainly Tamils. For this purpose I have sketched the history of the Ceylon Moors. I have shown the utter worthlessness of a tradition among them that a great colony of Arabs of the house of Hashim made settlements at Beruwala and other parts of the Island, and have adduced reasons for accepting as far more probable the tradition reported by Mr. Casie Chetty, that the original ancestors of the Ceylon Moors formed their first settlement at Kayal-paddanam, and that many years afterwards a colony from that town—"the fatherland of the Chonagar"—migrated and settled at Beruwala. I have further shown how similar the history of the Ceylon Moors is to that of the Coast Moors; how intimately connected they were with each other till the Dutch began to persecute them in Ceylon; how the intercourse between the mother-country in South India and Ceylon was arrested about 150 years ago; and how the distinction arose thereafter between the Ceylon Moors and the Coast Moors. By tracing in this manner their history, that is, their descent, I arrive at the conclusion that the early ancestors of the "Moors," Ceylon and Coast, were mainly Tamils on the father's side, as admittedly they are exclusively on the mother's side. . . .

Language in Oriental countries is considered the most important part of nationality, outweighing differences of religion, institutions, and physical characteristics. Otherwise each caste would pass for a race. Dr. Freeman's contention, that "community of language is not only presumptive evidence of the community of blood, but is also proof of something which for *practical purposes is the same as* community of blood," ought to apply to the case of the Ceylon Moors. But, of course, in their case it is not language only that stamps them as Tamils. Taking (1) the language they speak at home in connection with (2) their history, (3) their customs and (4) physical features, the proof cumulatively leads to no other conclusion than that the Moors of Ceylon are ethnologically Tamils.

A Criticism of Mr. Ramanathan's
"Ethnology of the Moors of Ceylon"

I. L. M. Abdul Azeez

The wealthy, educated, urban-based Muslim leaders in Sri Lanka read Ramana-than's 1888 ethnological thesis as an attempt to preserve Tamil political hegemony over their community, and they were offended by his depiction of them as petty trad-ers, fishermen, and coolies. This reply by a prominent Muslim editor argues for their ultimate non-Tamil origins as descendants of early Arab seafarers.

The object of this pamphlet is to dispel the mistaken ideas entertained by some persons as to the origin and history of that section of the Moham-medan population of Ceylon which is called by the name of Ceylon Moors. While it is apparent to all that these people are not indigenous to Ceylon, the absence of an authentic history of their race has led some to form wrong opinions as to their origin and the period of their settlement in this Island. It is very annoying to see some irresponsible writers, who have not taken any trouble to investigate the matter they so glibly speak of, stating without the slightest justification that the ancestors of the Ceylon Moors were Tamils who had embraced the religion of Islam. . . .

It was in 1885 that Mr. Ramanathan first announced his great discovery that the Moors of Ceylon were Tamils in nationality and Mohammedans in religion, in the Legislative Council, while speaking on the Mohammedan Marriage Registration Ordinance. . . . When what he said in Council ap-peared in the English newspapers, the late Mr. Siddi Lebbe, who was then editing the "Muslim Friend," a Tamil newspaper founded by himself, criti-cised in that organ Mr. Ramanathan's statement, and wrote a series of ar-ticles producing historical and traditional evidences to prove the fallacy of his contention, and to establish that the Ceylon Moors were mainly the de-scendants of those Arabian colonists, who settled in Ceylon many centuries ago. Moreover, it was thought, nay believed, that his object in calling the Moors Tamils in race was to dissuade the Government from appointing a

Moorish member in Council, it having leaked out then that the Government were contemplating to appoint such a one, and to make them understand that there was no necessity for taking such a step, as the Moors did not form a distinct race. . . .

What I have stated above ought to show the readers that Mr. Ramanathan approached the subject of his Paper with prejudiced mind; but if that were not the case and my supposition be incorrect, it would be very difficult to account for the partiality evinced by the writer of "the Ethnology of the 'Moors' of Ceylon," all through the Paper, in ignoring studiously the numerous facts, which abound in the history of Ceylon, and which prove that the ancestors of the Moors were Arabs; and in endeavouring, with great forensic ability, to make capital out of some weak evidences and arguments which seem to support his contention. . . .

Mr. Ramanathan has thought it sufficient to refer to the Moors as petty traders, pedlars, boutique keepers, boatmen, fishermen, agriculturists, and coolies, but, I think, had he been a little more candid, he would have said that they included wholesale merchants, large shopkeepers, planters, and wealthy landed proprietors, and, in point of wealth, they were next only to the Sinhalese among the native races of the Island. In the matter of their influence and position Mr. Ramanathan has not done justice to the Moors. . . .

Mr. Ramanathan was wrong when he stated that the Portuguese gave the name, Moor, to the *Mohammedans* whom they met along the western coast of India and Ceylon. The fact is that they applied the term only to Arabs and their descendants. . . . When he said that Moor was not the name my community went by in its own circle or among its neighbours when the Portuguese came he did not speak the whole truth, for that community was known then, as now, in its own circle as *Sonahar,* and among its neighbours, the Tamils and Sinhalese, as *Sonahar* and *Yon,* both terms being the equivalents of the term Moor (Arab). . . . Arabia is in Pali *Yonna* and in Tamil *Sonaham,* as I shall show later on; hence to the Arab settlers, who were our ancestors, the Sinhalese and Tamils applied the names given in their respective languages for those people. . . .

I see the force of his argument that the language spoken by the Moors is an exponent of their nationality, because though diversities of creed, custom, and facial features prevail among the low-country and Kandyan Sinhalese, and among the Tamils of high caste and low caste, yet they pass respectively as Sinhalese and Tamils, for the reason that they speak as their mother tongue those languages. But what he has to consider, in the case of the Moors, is whether they speak Tamil as their own national language, as Tamils and Sinhalese do their respective languages, or as a borrowed one;

and whether there is a possibility of one race borrowing the language of another, and continuing to use it forgetting its own. . . . Their ancestors came from Arabia pursuing commerce and settled on the coasts of Ceylon. This Island had many attractions for them. It is the place where their primitive father, Adam, was when he obtained forgiveness of God for the sin of disobedience committed by him, and where the mountain, which bears his footprint, and which for that reason is visited by Muslims from time immemorial, stands. Its seaports were the centres of trade visited by not only the Arabian merchants, but the Persian, Chinese and other traders as well. It produced the aromatic drugs, gems, pearls, shells, cinnamon, etc., articles for which much demand existed in Egypt, in the lands washed by the Persian Gulf, and the other Western countries, between which and Ceylon the trade was largely in the hands of the Arabs. . . . Most of the ancestors of the Ceylon Moors were, according to tradition, members of the family of Hashim. Some of the Hashimites, and probably, a few of other tribes, who were less war-like and given more to the peaceful pursuit of trade naturally thought to hold themselves aloof from the amphitheatre of constantly changing political dramas in their own country, where lives and properties were not secure, and sought refuge in foreign lands. Some were actually driven by the tyranny of the contending rulers. At such a critical moment what other country could have been more attractive to them, as a place of refuge, than Ceylon, which had been their commercial resort for a considerable period? When they settled here they did so among the Tamils and not Sinhalese. This may appear strange to some for Ceylon was the country of the latter race, but history explains the matter. Those Arabs were traders, and, hence, it was natural that they should come in contact with the traders of this country. Our Sinhalese friends were not traders, they hated commerce and gave themselves up to agricultural and other pursuits. . . . Therefore, we can safely conclude that the Arabs had not the opportunity of having intercourse with the Sinhalese. Then it may be asked who were the people who received the strangers in the Southern districts and had intercourse with them. They were the Tamils, as I have said before, who were then called Malabars. They invaded Ceylon from Southern India on many occasions, and were found, in large numbers, in the seaports as well as the interior of the Island. . . .

Is there then any difficulty in believing that the Arabs, likewise, learned the language of the Malabars with whom they had business relation, and after settling among them, and ceasing intercourse with their own country, continued to speak it, with the result that their descendants have entirely forgotten the national language of their fathers, and stick to that which was borrowed by their fathers from their Malabar friends, and Malabar wives? Thus came the Moors of Ceylon to speak the Tamil language.

[The] most essential evidence required to decide the origin of a race is that of the blood and not that of the language or history. . . . But there are only about 114,000 Ceylon Moors, and the only conclusion we are led to arrive at, under the circumstances, is that they are mainly the descendants of those Arabs who settled in the Island about twelve centuries ago, and whose number was not necessarily large in view of the present number of their descendants; and considering [these] . . . it may be safely concluded that the number of the original settlers was not much more than 100. . . .

All the energies put forth by Mr. Ramanathan to find out what resemblance some of the social customs of the Ceylon Moors bore to those of the Tamils have been misspent, for there was no necessity whatever for him to be at pains to find them out, inasmuch as the Moors themselves have admitted all along that among their ancestors there were many who had married Tamil wives, whose language, habits, customs, and manners their descendants adopted in the long run. What the Parsees did in India the Moors have done in Ceylon, and it ought to be apparent to the readers how much more natural it is for the children to cherish and adopt the thoughts and habits of their mothers than of their fathers. It is true that the Ceylon Moors have the customs of *Stridhanam, alati,* the tying of the *tali,* and my explanation is that these have been borrowed by them from the Tamils, to whose race their mothers, in most cases, belonged, and among whom their fathers settled. . . .

In conclusion, I have to state that I agree with Mr. Ramanathan when he says that the 185,000 Moors found in the Island in 1881 were divisible equally between Ceylon Moors and "Coast Moors," but I have shown above that he has failed to prove his theory that the Ceylon Moors came from Kayal-paddanam, and have not a history different from that of the "Coast Moors." I have shown further that Kayal-paddanam was not in a position to send a colony of Mohammedans—Tamil or Arab—to Ceylon before the fourteenth century, which was the period when, according to him, the first colony of the Moors migrated from Kayal, and settled at Beruwala; that the Moors first appeared in the Island in the first century of the Christian era, and, by the early part of the thirteenth century, had completely established themselves at Beruwala; that at that period their services to the state were recognised by the Sinhalese King, who granted them privileges and immunities, which have been in later days fully or partly confirmed by the European conquerors of the Island; that the Mohammedans who had settled in the Island before the fourteenth century could not have been the descendants of the Moors who came from Kayal-paddanam, and that the emigrants from Kayal were either Arabs or Tamils in descent, and it is only a supposition of Mr. Ramanathan and not an established fact that they were the latter. I have pointed out the utter worthlessness of the arguments adduced by him to discredit the tradition recorded by Sir Alexander Johnston, to the effect that a colony of Arabs of the house of Hashim made settlements at different stations in the Island in the early part of the eighth century. With reference to the tradition reported by Mr. Casie Chetty I have shown that the Hashimite Arabs, mentioned in that tradition to have emigrated from Arabia in the life time (seventh century) of the blessed Prophet Mohammed (on whom be eternal peace), could not have formed settlement at Kayal-paddanam, because that town did not come into existence before the tenth century. I have also pointed out, with reason, that the conclusion arrived at by Mr. Ramanathan that the Ceylon Moors are Tamils because some of their social customs have been borrowed from the Tamils and because some Moors and Tamils resemble each other in physical features is erroneous. The inference drawn by him from the language spoken by the Moors is equally erroneous. I have shown that it is not unnatural nor unusual for a people to drop the language of their ancestors, and adopt that of the inhabitants of the country where they have settled; and I have explained how the Moors came to drop the Arabic and adopt the Tamil. It has also been proved that some districts in Ceylon, which are considered as purely Sinhalese, were, at the period when the Moors settled there under the control and influence of the Malabars, who over-ran them, and with whom the Moors associated with the result that the Tamil became their adopted language in those districts. In short, I have shown conclusively that neither the language, spoken by the Ceylon Moors, nor their history, social customs and physical features have singly or cumulatively proved that they are ethnologically Tamils.

Who Are the Moors of Ceylon?

S. L. Mohamed

A mid-twentieth century split developed between those attached to the older "Moorish" designation and those who favored adopting a purely religious identity as "Muslims." This popular pamphlet makes the case for preserving the unique racial and ethnic identity of the Sri Lankan Sonahars or Moors, and also preserving their control over Moorish mosques.

The Ceylon Moors find themselves in a curious position today. For the first time in their existence in this Island they are given the choice of either calling themselves Muslims or Ceylon Moors. They cannot be both.

The "law-makers" are none other than the Ceylon Muslim League, notorious for its anti-Moor activities, and its by-product, the Ceylonese Muslim Union. For reasons of political and personal rivalry the leaders of these bodies have ventured to deny the largest Muslim Community in this Island—the Ceylon Moors—who are also the third largest community in the Island, their race-name. A person is without self-respect if he has no pride of race. Neither can a man be called an intellectual if, while being conversant even with all the knowledge in the world, he is still ignorant of the history and traditions of his own race and religion. . . .

The Arabs were merchants. They sailed in European waters, gathered their merchandise and carried them over Arabia, from the European coast to the Eastern countries. There was no Suez Canal then. Some of the Arabs settled in the countries of their business, such as India and Ceylon. Their descendants in India are the Moplas, Memons and the Pattanis. In Ceylon the progenies of the Arab settlers are called Marakkala by the Sinhalese, Sonahars by the Tamils, and Moors by the Europeans. The Moors found an honourable place in Ceylon, so much that a Sinhalese King married a Moor lady. The rulers bestowed gifts of land on individuals as well as on institutions such as Mosques and cemeteries. The Moors served the Government and joined in the defence of the Island. To the Sinhalese they were one of the caste communities of theirs. They would have passed as Sinhalese of the

Islamic Faith like the Sinhalese Christians, but for the advent of the Portuguese in the Island. The Portuguese who had Moors of Spain and Morocco as their neighbours called them Moors, [and] that became the western name for the Marakkala or Sonahar during the last five hundred years. Their history of origin, the account of their services to the Island are well known to the indigenous population. The amicable relations subsisting between the Sinhalese and the Moors is obvious throughout the course of Ceylon's social life. The Marakkala are Muslims and their religion is Islam. There are large numbers of Muslims who sojourn in this country; they are Moplas, Memons, Hambayas, Borahs, Pathans, etc. They have their Mosques, Institutions, Associations and Clubs. They have their racial differences. The Hambayas Mosque in 2nd Cross Street, the Borah Mosque at 4th Cross Street, the Memon Mosque at 3rd Cross Street, the Moplah Mosque at Wolfendhal, Ahmedi Mosque at Negombo, and the Hanafi Mosques at Kandy and Gampola bear testimony to their distinct identity, like the local Malay Mosque at Slave Island and the Moorish Mosques all over the Island.

Of all the followers of Islam in Ceylon only the Moors and Malays claim Ceylon as their Home. The Moors are not Indians and no Indian or Pakistani is called a Moor in his country or anywhere else. By adhering persistently to the word Moor, the Marakkala or Yonakka wishes to be classed as a member of the indigenous population and not of the floating stock. The suggestion of the Aga Khan that the Moors should call themselves Sinhalese by race and Muslim by faith was welcome, but when the Moors found the Sinhalese tolerant and they held the Marakkala as a part of the Ceylonese permanent population they did not desire a change. The Marakkala are Moors by race and Muslims by religion. This distinct name "Moor" is to emphasize the fact that they are the pioneer Muslims in Ceylon, in contrast to those Muslims about whom the Hon'ble Sir P. Ramanathan, K.C., C.M.G., M.L.C. says:

> The Hambayas are Muhammadan immigrants from the east coast of South India. They are not permanently settled in Ceylon. They do not as a rule bring their wives and families to the Island. Sojourning in it for a year or two at a time for purposes of trade, they return periodically with their savings to South India. They do not intermarry with any of the other Muhammadan communities of Ceylon, the largest of which consists of those who have been settled in the Island for several centuries, and who from the days of the Portuguese Government have been known to the Europeans as the "Moors." They number about 235,000 souls. But the Hambayas do not count more than 33,000, and of this number it is well to bear in mind that those who opposed the issue of licenses to conduct

the Buddhist processions in Gampola and Kandy [prior to the 1915 Sinhala-Muslim riots] were principally the trustees of the Mosques and their immediate supporters. If other Hambayas were drawn into the affray, it was only through party spirit, or the desire to make common cause with those who appeared to be the leaders of that community. In Gampola and Kandy many of these Muhammadans have prospered in trade, and have generously met the religious requirements of their brethren by enlarging and rebuilding the mosques in those places. But, unlike the Moors, who had learnt in the course of centuries the necessity of living in peace with their Sinhalese fellow-subjects and being tolerant to their religious observances, the Hambayas sought for their mosques in the Kandyan territory greater respect from the Kandyan Buddhists than the Moors have been in the habit of claiming for their own mosques. These foreign Muslims sojourning in Ceylon for business were the cause which misled the Sinhalese to class the Moors as those allied to them and brought the Moors into conflict in 1915 by their running the laps of the Moors.

In all countries the different races of Muslims exist, [while] in religious matters brotherhood remains solidly. The Arab League is conducted on racial lines; no Muslim kingdom other than Arab can join it. In 1924 [the] Akbar Committee condemned the word "Mahomedan" and adopted the name Muslim for the followers of Mohammed and Islam for the religion of Mohammed. These designations are in use officially. When a follower of Mohammed is to be referred to by his religion he is called a Muslim. The Committee did not suppress the racial designation of Moor and Malay for the Muslims of Ceylon.

The Moors in Ceylon do not identify themselves with the Moors in Spain, Morocco or Moor of Philippine, nor do they identify themselves with any Muslims in India. They love the names Marakkala, Sonahar and Moor. According to the Ceylonese "citizenship" all Moors are Ceylonese, as the Moors of Ceylon have been born from generation to generation in Ceylon. The other non-Ceylonese Muslims need to be made so by application. The late lamented Moor Leaders maintained these distinctions. The late Mr. I. L. M. Abdul Azeez, President of the Moors Union, urged the Government to differentiate the Moors from the rest of the Muslims in Ceylon, and his suggestion was carried out at the 1911 Census, and through various means he established their separate identity. In his monumental work the "Ethnology of the Ceylon Moors" he had done a great service to his community, and in the Maradana Mosque rules and regulations he clearly laid down, as the Trustee, that no one other than a Moor (Sonahar) is to be a member of the congregation. In the debate in the Legislative Council [in 1924] over the incorporation of the Maradana Mosque Trustees, the late Mr. N. H. M. Abdul Cader, M.M.C., M.L.C., uncle of Mr. Falil A. Cafoor, said:

"It has been said by one Hon'ble Member that this Mosque is a Muslim mosque. I deny that it is so. I am prepared to prove that this mosque belongs to the Moors of Colombo, not the Muhammadans at large. I have brought with me the title deeds, which any Hon'ble Member who cares to do so can examine and satisfy himself whether this mosque does not belong to a section of the Moorish community of this city. I have with me a survey and plan dated 1847. In that survey the mosque is depicted as well as the surrounding ground of sixteen acres. The survey says that it is a survey of the Moorish burial ground called Marakkalapalliawatta and the surrounding ground Marakkalapallialanga; the name of the land is Kahatagahawatta, and it is situated at Maradana, within the gravets of Colombo in the Western Province. Again, it says that the site is said to belong partly by purchase and partly by Government grant to the Moorish inhabitants of the locality—not to the Mohammadans. If the Honourable the European Urban Member cares to look at this survey I will pass it on to him. The survey gives the lie to the statements made in this Council by the two Hon'ble Members that the mosque belongs to the Muhammadan community and not to the Moors. . . ."

"There are no members who are not Moors. The committee will bear witness to that. They examined several witnesses and they found that the members of the congregation of this mosque are only Moors. . . . Suppose the words 'Ceylon Moors' are deleted, does not Your Excellency think that we are leaving room for non-Moors to come in and argue that they are members of the congregation? I certainly think that if we remove the words 'Ceylon Moors' we are leaving a loophole for others to come in and claim the right of Management of this mosque." . . .

HON. MR. C. W. W. KANNANGARA: "In Select Committee, Sir, I suggested the deletion of the words 'Ceylon Moors (Sonagar)' and the substitution in their stead of the words 'those professing the Muhammadan religion who are permanent residents of Colombo' and so on. But the Hon. the Muhammadan Member was strongly against that suggestion, with the result that we had to call a volume of evidence. We found overwhelming evidence to show that the Ceylon Moors (Sonagar) were entitled to the control and management of the mosque. In these circumstances it was impossible for us to oppose the Honourable Member in his desire to retain the words 'Ceylon Moors (Sonagar).'" . . .

THE HON. SIR P. RAMANATHAN: "The name is a very valuable one, Sir, for this reason. Those who style themselves Moors were originally and are still called Sonagars. The Portuguese came here, and they were the first Europeans to arrive in the Island. They knew the importance of the Moors who had flocked into Spain and Portugal from Morocco and met Charlemagne on the plains of France. They came here and wanted to know who these people were. They were told that they were Sonagars. Well, they tried to learn and understand their habits and customs, and they applied to the Sonagar the name with which they were familiar, namely, Moors. For more than four centuries the Sonagars have got used to that name, and they like that name. Why should we deprive them of the pleasure and the honour of that name? It is no doubt sentimental; but everyone is full of sentiment on certain points at least, and it does not seem to me right that a body of gentlemen who are interested in the Maradana Mosque, who have had the management of that mosque from the beginning, and who have come to the Legislative Council asking for the incorporation of themselves, should be flung out violently by objection being taken to the name which they deeply love. I say that the name Ceylon Moors is valuable to the Ceylon Sonagar. Let us not deprive them of the pleasure and honour of that name." . . .

THE HON. MR. S. D. KRISHNARATNE: "Rule No. 1 in this Bill was taken from the old rules of the trustees of this mosque, and we as members of the Select Committee did not see sufficient reason why we should eliminate from it the word 'Sonagar.' . . . The Committee also pointed out to the Honourable the mover of the Bill that the Muhammadan religion was a very liberal religion, and that he ought not to take part in an act which limits their powers. We were told in reply that we could bring in Sub-section (c), which reads: 'It shall be competent for the congregation of the said Maradana mosque to admit by special resolution any Muhammadan though not a Ceylon Moor as a member of the congregation of the Maradana mosque at a duly convened meeting of the congregation.' That point was conceded to the Malays as a concession as a result of the unanimous opinion of the members of the Committee. I submit that the retention of this 'Sonagar' would do no harm. The Sonagars have had the management of the mosque for the past fifty years or sixty years. A plan of 1847 which was produced before us speaks of this land as 'Marakka-lapalyawatte.' From that time it has been in the hands of the Marakalayas or Sonagars and there is no reason why that name should be altered."

(Extracted from the Debates in the Legislative Council—1924.)

Muslims are Muslims religiously. When a Muslim's distinct feature is to be shown as a follower of one of the four schools of jurisprudence he is called a Shafi, a Hanafi, a Hambali, and Maliki. When he interprets Islamic theology according to orthodoxy he is a Sunnathi; otherwise he is a Shia, Khariji, a Koja, Ahmedi etc. When he performs intonations (Zikr) he is a Khadiri, a Shathuli, an Alavi etc. When he wants to show his race he is an Arabi, an Ajami, a Pathan, a Moplah, a Memon, a Pushti, a Huihui (Chinese Muslims), a Moros (Philippine Muslim), Kirkis (Russian Muslim), Riff (Tunisian Muslims), Kahkahs (Burmese Muslims), Pomak (Bulgarian Muslims), Tatars (Polish Muslims), Magyars (Hungarian Muslims), Moors (Morocco Muslims), Slamos (Madagascar Muslims), Moplas (Malabar Muslims), Pattanis (Madras Muslims), Sanmankarar (South Indian Muslims), Pathans (North Indian Muslims).

Why should not the Ceylon Muslims be continued to be called Moors, is what every genuine Ceylon Moor asks today.

The Bawas of Ceylon

R. L. Spittel

The vast majority of Sri Lankan Muslims are content to observe the five orthodox Sunni pillars of worship (creed, prayer, alms, fasting, and pilgrimage), but a distinctive group of religious mendicants—the Bawas, ecstatic faqirs belonging to the Rifa'i order of Sufism—still maintains traditions of ecstatic zikr performance much as they were described in the 1930s. See the illustration accompanying this chapter for their ritual implements.

We were seated close to the Valliamma temple. Gradually I became aware of a persistent drumming that proceeded from the Mohammedan shrine adjoining it. Going up to investigate, I found a number of long-robed dervishes seated in a circle on the ground, surrounded by a group of spectators. At the head of the circle sat the elders with evil-looking implements set before them, mainly long steel spikes, and what looked like knobberries—hollow metal globes, studded with short lengths of chain, mounted on stout six-inch spikes; these were called *daboos*.

A devotee picked up one of these and began to dance. Twirling the implement between his palms, he stepped to the rhythm of the drums. His movements, quiet at first, soon quickened with the music. He leapt, twisting his body and tossing wildly his unkempt head. Alternately he spun the daboos, and held it on high. Now he was leaping about like a maniac, stamping in perfect accord with the drum-beats. That there was more to it than a fanatical dance was evident from the insistence of the music and the expectant faces of the onlookers, in contrast to the stern, indifferent aspects of the fakirs themselves, and the complacence of the plump, bejewelled woman of their camp.

Suddenly the dancing figure swept down his head and drove in the spike. Then he straightened himself, supporting the instrument with his hand, and continued his dance. When he had done, he plucked it out, replaced it among the others, and resuming his place in the circle, picked up a drum and was soon contributing to the music.

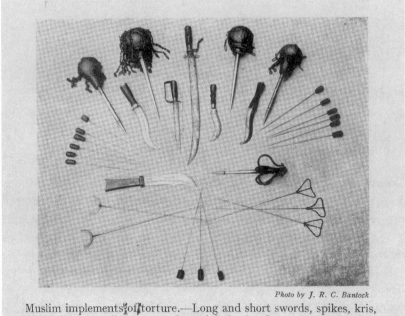

Muslim implements of torture.—Long and short swords, spikes, kris, and *daboos*—spikes mounted on globular heads (pp. 312 and 316).

Ritual implements of Muslim asceticism, 1933. Photo by J. R. C. Bantock. Caption within image reads: "Muslim implements of torture.—Long and short swords, kris, and *daboos*—spikes mounted on globular heads (pp. 312 and 316)."

A young bare-bodied Muslim now entered the space. A fakir took a long, pointed iron rod (*marathiya*) and transfixed his cheeks. He faced around exhibiting himself. Another moved in and held out his arms. Each of his biceps was gripped in turn and pierced, the steel protruding six inches on either side. He stood thus a full ten minutes. That his immobile face belied his feelings was evidenced by the barely perceptible nod with which he indicated which skewer he wished removed first.

A short, well-set man, with cropped hair, and face more of a villain than saint, took the floor, daboos in hand. For a little while he pranced to the drums; then jerking his head askew, thrust the point of the daboos into the outer angle of his orbit. He raised his head with the weapon in place, and displayed an eyeball that stood most horribly out of its socket. Many a face was turned away in pained disgust; but I imagine the protrusion was caused more by pressure than penetration, though it could not have been the less painful for that.

And now there stepped into the circle a tall, frowzy-headed dervish of commanding look, carrying a pair of daboos. He cast a glance round the row of drummers, and in obedience to it the music quickened. Still he stood surveying them, turning his head from one performer to the other. Then he snatched up a drum with a gesture of contempt, and smote it hard, loudening the din, speeding its pace, and alternately varying it from double to triple time—dum-dum, dum-dum-dum, dum-dum, and so on. He played till he was satisfied with the performance, handed back the drum to its owner, and stood listening to assure himself that the pitch was sustained.

Contented at last, he began to dance much after the manner of the first actor, but with a finer swagger, a fiercer abandon, a surer step. All eyes were focused on the tossing figure, treading in perfect time; all hearts throbbed to the accelerating drum-taps. Would the fulfillment justify the promise?

As he landed from a high leap, he buried the daboos in his head; supporting it with one hand, he knocked it in with the knob of the other daboos, using it like a hammer. Then he removed his hands, and there, sticking out of his crown, like the crest of a peacock, was the awful implement! He resumed his capers with unabated vehemence, while the top-heavy adornment swayed and its short chains clinked. To judge by its obliquity, it must have been driven in between the scalp and cranium. How fine a feat of endurance this was, may be imagined, when one remembers how exquisitely sensitive a structure the periosteum is, as every one knows who has had a kick on the shin, or a pebble on the head. What wonder the man made certain at the outset that the drums should not let him down!

These fakirs are religious mendicants. Between their acts of self-torture, the begging tray goes round; but the meagre pittance they glean from the poor that watch them is out of all proportion to their display. Such then are the deeds of both Hindus and Muslims at Kataragama, and a long way they come to have the privilege of doing them. If penance be a passport to paradise, then is Kataragama but a stepping stone to it.

Some months after I witnessed the scenes I have described, I was sauntering one evening along a jungle road at Kalkudah, when I met a man carrying a daboos and marathiya (spike). He responded to my scrutiny with a salaam. I asked him who he was and what he did with those implements. He answered that he was a Muslim fakir, and could drive the spike through his abdomen or neck from before backwards. I dared him to do the latter for a rupee, knowing quite well the feat was impossible, for his windpipe, vertebral column and spinal cord would have to be transfixed. He accepted the challenge.

Laying aside the bundle he carried, he took his two-foot skewer, and offered a short prayer to his saint. Then kneeling on the street, he gripped the instrument with both hands, and placing its point just above the Adam's apple, thrust his neck down on it, with the other end against ground. He jerked and wriggled his neck violently emitting the most frightful gasps and death rattles. I began to wonder whether I was going to be the end of him, but consoled myself with the thought that he would not have arrived at his age had he not known how to look after himself.

Soon, the point of the spike began slowly to protrude through the shaggy hair that covered the back of his neck, and now it stood out a good four inches. He seemed in such great distress that I had not the heart to part his hair and examine his skin. With a savage jerk and a final gasp he plucked out the weapon, fingered the marks it had made, and stood up before us, panting, but none the worse for his experience. I asked him to demonstrate to me the points of entrance and exit of the spike, but he said there were none to show, as his saint had seen to that! The artful trickster had no doubt cunningly, but most realistically I will admit, contrived to slip the implement by the side of his neck.

On another occasion, through the courtesy of Messrs. R. H. Bassett and J. R. C. Bantock, I had the opportunity of witnessing to what further lengths these people could go. About 10 o'clock one night a small crowd had gathered outside the gates of a Moorish house in Messenger Street, Colombo. From the well-lit garden within came the noise of drums. Moplahs (a Muslim sect) were partaking in a religious ceremony—the *Raffiyah* [Rifa'i] *Rathib*—in honour of their patron saint, Sultanul Arifin Seyid Ahamad Kabir Raffiyah [Rifa'i].

We were invited to enter, and took seats on the verandah. Before us, in the garden, under a white cloth awning, two rows of men with tambourine-like drums (except for the absence of the loose metal disks), sat facing each other, a space of some six feet between them. At the head of the lines, with their backs to us, sat two priests (*moulanas*), one the *seyid* or high priest. Open on a pillow before them was the *rathib*, an Arabic hymnal, from which they intoned a plaintive chant, the choral refrain of which the others repeated after them to the accompaniment of their drums. An old man, a sort of master of ceremonies, sang, beating time.

On either side of the priests burned candles and oil-lamps, and aromatic incense smoked in a brazier which was replenished from time to time. In front of them was a collection of weapons—a sword, wavy-bladed daggers called kris, skewers (*katirai*), and, perhaps most formidable of all, the daboos already familiar to us. Half kneeling, half squatting on his heels, and facing the priests, was a bare-bodied young man with a red kerchief knotted tightly round his head—a silent, impassive figure, whose part in the drama about to begin was only indicated by his prominent position.

He picked up two sinuous-bladed knives and gave them to the seyid, who tested their keenness by shaving the hairs on the back of his own hand. Then blessing the daggers, he handed them back to the man who presented them for benediction in turn to three or four of the moulanas. He rose, a kris in each fist, and strode slowly up and down between the lines of drummers. Suddenly he halted and gazed intently towards the cloth awning, as if he saw something beyond. Holding up the knives he shouted "Ya Sheik!" (My Master!). He commenced springing backwards and stamping in accord with the drum-beats, shouting "Ya Sheik!" from time to time. Quicker and quicker he leapt; the drumming changed from double to triple time, but for all that, could not outpace his agility. Now he bent his body down, bringing the daggers to the ground, then jerked up like a jack-knife, arching himself backward, and looking up with the gleaming blades on high. He kept repeating this body action, but varied that of his arms, crossing and uncrossing them over his abdomen with lightning rapidity in slashing movements, each time he arched back. He did this with a violence of gesture that suggested evisceration, when one remembered the razor edges with which he so recklessly played. After a succession of such passes, he walked up and down, taking a breath, and surveying his abdomen. Then he resumed his antics again. Watching him closely we saw no trace of blood, and surmised that here was only knife play falling short of injury. Even so, the manly grace and careless truculence of his performance was a reward in itself. But now as he moved towards us, we became aware of a messiness on the dark skin as the blood trickled down from a score of horizontal cuts, so deftly inflicted as to leave the muscles unscathed. Gory splotches stained his white cloth. Then "Ya Sheik!" and the mad passes again, the slashes and the bounds, with unabated vigour. He has had enough. Unfolding his red waist band, he spreads it over his bleeding belly, and returns the dripping knives to the priest, who places his healing hands on the wounds, uttering a short prayer. He smokes his abdomen over the burning incense, has a drink of water from a handy vessel, and quietly joins the crowd. . . .

All the acts here described I actually witnessed. There is no fake whatever about them. I closely examined the injuries afterwards. I must confess I would never have believed some of them possible had I not seen them myself. . . . They attribute their immunity from haemorrhage and infection, and their professed freedom from pain, to their implicit faith in their saint and the healing touch of the seyid. All the preparation they make for the

Rathib is to have a bath and wear clean clothes. They certainly do not dope themselves with alcohol or drugs, which are prohibited by their religion. The clean-living men of former times are said to have been capable of chopping chunks of flesh off themselves, cutting their tongues in two and handing the severed piece round for inspection, or even dividing themselves into halves, and in all instances reassembling the severed parts. These may be fairy tales, but they cannot discredit those acts our eyes actually witnessed.

The Fight for the Fez

M. M. Thawfeeq

Despite the many schisms of twentieth-century Muslim politics, there was a memorable moment when Sri Lankan Muslims united to assert their civil rights as an ethnic and religious community. Ironically, they were fighting for a sartorial symbol of Ottoman Turkish colonial culture. See the illustration that accompanies this chapter.

At this distance of time it looks incongruous that a mass meeting of Muslims of Ceylon should be held to protest against an order which prohibited a Muslim advocate from appearing in a fez in Court. But it must be remembered that it was not the headgear alone that aroused so much enthusiasm and unity but the fact that the community feared that this restriction was the first of a series of clamps-down that might affect its people. It was the show of Muslim unity and strength of purpose that is significant. Never again was such a spectacle witnessed nor such unity and determination shown. It should serve as a valuable lesson to Muslims of the present day who wrangle and divide themselves on matters pertaining to the community. The victory gained by the mass meeting of "The Mohammedans of Ceylon" held at the Maradana Mosque grounds Colombo on December 31, 1905 should also serve as a lesson to the present day Muslims of what could be achieved by unity.

A decade before the turn of the last century, the Muslims of Ceylon (then called by the misnomer Mohammedans) changed over from their calico caps and other types of headgear to the fez. They were inspired by the presence in Ceylon of the Egyptian exiles led by Arabi Pasha. They all wore fez caps. Some bright spark among the ingenious Muslim merchants thought it an excellent idea to import these Egyptian fezes. They were an immediate hit. The Muslims of Ceylon, with whom the Egyptian exiles—Arabi Pasha, Ali Fehmi, Mahmoud Fehmi, Toulba Pasha, Mohamed Sami, Abdul Aal (who died in Ceylon) and Yacoub, rebels against the British government in Egypt—identified themselves educationally, religiously and socially, idolised these Egyptian visitors. So the fez became their "national" headgear—

The Fez, 1970. Photo by Dennis McGilvray.

being worn to mosques, shops, weddings and other functions, in fact on every occasion when the Muslim had need to leave his home.

The fez, being brimless, was suitable for prostration on the prayer-mat— the Muslim praying at early dawn, mid-noon, late noon, sunset, and late night. So the fez became part of his apparel which he would not discard until he reached home. It soon attained a religious significance and the Muslim (especially the Ceylon Moor) seen without a fez appeared the odd man out. Before the Ramazan and Hajj Festivals or before his circumcision or wedding, the Muslim would purchase a new fez (they came in all shades of red—from deep crimson to scarlet). And Middle Eastern establishments in the Pettah, Colombo, like the Subys and the Dakkaks, made a roaring trade. And the older folk usually "retreaded" their old fezes on the copper blocks in these establishments.

At this distance of time when the fez has been discarded in the main, it sounds queer that in 1905 the fez caused a crisis in the Muslim community. It stirred a whole community to united action and brought all its leaders on to one platform. Never before, or never after, did the Muslim community show such strength and unity on any cause affecting it.

At the Appeal Court on May 2, 1905 Chief Justice C. P. Layard was hearing

Court of Request appeals. Mr. Muhammad Careem Abdul Cader, with his fez on his head, rose to address the Court, when the Chief Justice observed: "You are showing disrespect to the Court by appearing with your fez on. I disapprove of this practice and decline to hear you as counsel unless you conform to the rule hitherto followed."

Mr. Cader was taken aback. He tried to explain.

"I assure Your Lordship that I did not mean any disrespect by appearing with the fez; it is a practice followed in accordance with my religion. I beg to urge in this connection that the proper way a Ceylon Moor should show respect to any person is by putting on the headgear and wearing as a Ceylon Moor would in entering a mosque." But Justice Layard was adamant. "I decline to hear you," he said. "In this case you have adopted an European dress and have your shoes on. One end of your body must be bare."

Mr. Cader refused to doff his fez—and walked out.

This raised a big furor in Hulftsdorf [the neighborhood in Colombo where the courts are located]. The Jaffna Tamil lawyers asked: "Will the next blow fall on us? Will we be asked to remove our turbans?" The then Solicitor General Mr. (later Sir) Ponnambalam Ramanathan appeared before Chief Justice Sir Bruce Burnside with his turban on . . . [this being the first occasion] he gave up after 15 years the hat for the turban. His Lordship is said to have spoken to him in his chambers after his day's work was over and desired him to appear with his head uncovered as he had previously done before the Court. But His Lordship laid down no rule governing the case of those who had been, from the time of their admission to the Bar, wearing the turban when addressing the Court. A Jaffna newspaper argued: "We ask whether the Muslim nabobs who attended the coronation of His Majesty doffed their gorgeous turbans during the function. What is the practice in the Legislative Council of Ceylon? Does the Muslim member put off his hat?"

Then came the infamous minute of the Supreme Court, dated September 19, 1905 which prohibited the wearing of the fez in Court. This was in reply to two petitions submitted by Mr. Abdul Cader on June 30, 1905 and July 29, 1905. The first petition, besides other facts, submitted [that] "The late Mr. Siddi Lebbe, who was a proctor of the Supreme Court, when appearing in Court did not uncover his head, although he wore boots, nor does Mr. Sheriff, proctor of the District Court of Batticaloa, and formerly a member of the Ceylon Legislative Council, uncover his head or feet in Court." This petition had copies of letters from Messrs. A. Kanagasabai, Advocate and leader of the Jaffna Bar, M. C. Changarapillai, J. P. Proctor, Badrudin Tyabji, Judge of the High Court of Bombay, C. H. Setalward, M. L. C. Bombay, Nasrulla Khan, Barrister-at-Law Bombay, and P. S. Siva Swamy Iyer, High Court Vakil and M. L. C. Madras, that they and their colleagues in India and Ceylon wore boots and trousers with their fez, turban, or native headgear, as the case may be.

In the second petition Mr. Abdul Cader said that he was "prepared to adopt and wear in Court a long coat buttoned up to the neck which is not an entirely European costume." But in that minute the applications were not entertained, the minute concluding: "If Mr. Abdul Cader's prayer was granted in its entirety and he was allowed to appear with red fez and gown and bands, this Court could not prevent other advocates claiming to appear with their heads covered with turbans of various colours which are quite incongruous to the gown and bands, without which they have no right of audience in the Supreme Court. Further, the rule now prevailing as to advocates appearing in black coats could not be enforced, and Advocates [would] have to be allowed to appear in native dress of any colour they might select."

The leading Muslims met at "Muirburn House," Colombo, on October 27, 1905 and appointed a Fez Committee to convene a mass meeting "of the Mohammedans of Ceylon to consider the Fez question." . . . Leading Muslims of the Outstations were also appointed to help organise the mass meeting on December 31, 1905 at the Maradana Mosque grounds, Colombo.

The Fez Committee in a statement said: "A grievance of far-reaching consequences has been caused to the Mohammedans of Ceylon by the recent minute of the Supreme Court of the island, which, contrary to the practice of the Mohammedan Advocates wearing Muslim head-dress in India and other parts of His Majesty's dominion, prohibits the first Mohammedan Advocate in Ceylon from covering his head in the said Court with his usual Mohammedan headgear, the fez, and which orders him to conform, contrary to his own custom, to the usage of the non-Mohammedan Advocates and uncover his head in Court according to their custom. In Ceylon that right of a Mohammedan to cover his head in Court was never questioned before the said order was made. Here, the Mohammedans, who alone invariably cover their heads as a mark of respect, are now enjoying the privilege of wearing their headgear in the Legislative Council, the Supreme Court (as jurors and witnesses) and other Courts of Justice, the Government Departments, at the Levees held by His Excellency the Governor and other State functions. Therefore the said order of the Supreme Court against the wearing in Court of the national headgear by the first Mohammedan Advocate is regarded with fear as the thin edge of the wedge and, if confirmed, may be the first of a series of orders depriving the Mohammedans of their right of covering their head at public places and functions." . . .

Through Mr. Carimjee Jafferjee, a brilliant Muslim lawyer, Moulavi Rafi-

Uddin Ahmed Barrister-at-Law of Bombay, known as "The Lion of the Bar," was brought down to address the mass meeting. The Hon. Mr. W. M. Abdul Raheman M. L. C. presided. Mr. Rafi-Uddin Ahmed . . . [claimed] that he had worn the fez in the presence of the King and in the presence of the late Queen Victoria and that he had remained covered in Her Majesty's very chapel, where everybody uncovered except Muslims. If the fez offered no disrespect to the sovereign how could it show disrespect to a judge? British judges and statesmen paid so much deference to that particular custom of Muslims that English judges in Egypt actually wore the fez on the Bench. . . .

The Ceylon press was highly impressed by the united action of the Muslims. . . . [Quoting from] *The Times of Ceylon* (January 1, 1906): "The esprit de corps of the community is an object of admiration and inspiration to men of other persuasions. . . ." *The Times of Ceylon* (January 4, 1906): "The Mohammedan community have been awakening a great deal of late and comparatively theirs has been the fastest march onward. . . ." *Ceylon Independent* (January 3, 1906): "The Mohammedans of Ceylon have again distinguished themselves by their spirit of confraternity, common sense and determination to proceed in securing redress for their grievances on sound constitutional lines." *Ceylon Standard* (January 6, 1906): "We must record our appreciation of the perfectly legitimate and constitutional methods the members of this community have adopted in ventilating their alleged grievances. . . . Even for Government officials it is never too late to learn." The *Ceylon Independent* supported the Muslims' cause with two leaders—on January 4, 1906 and another on January 5. In both it judged the Chief Justice's ruling as "not merely vexatious" but "savouring of intolerance and persecution" and also as "plainly an invasion of the rights and liberties enjoyed by all communities under British rule."

The mass meeting appealed to the King (a.) to order the withdrawal of the minute, (b.) to grant Mr. Abdul Cader permission to appear before the Supreme Court covering his head with the usual Muslim headgear, the fez, and (c.) "to issue such orders as may be necessary to conserve the rights of His Majesty's Muslim subjects, hitherto uninterruptedly enjoyed, of covering their heads with their national headgear in Court and other places in conformity with the requirements of their religion and custom." Over 30,000 Muslims voted with one voice their approval of these submissions to the King.

Chief Justice Layard's ruling was reversed. The Ceylon Moor Lawyers were allowed the use of the fez in Court. Mr. Abdul Cader, the central figure of the crisis, died in June 1946.

The Purdah's Lament

M. L. M. Mansoor

In this wonderfully crafted short story translated from Tamil (its original title is ("Mukkaadukal Miiddum Mukaari Rakankal"), a woman's voice finds expression in the sequestered world of Muslim purdah.

"Behold another new day has dawned. It did not exist before. It will nor recur. In history this day appears only once."

My memory recalls these lines from a book lent me by Faiz naana.[1] As far as I am concerned, this statement has no significance whatsoever. I am unable to distinguish today from tomorrow and appreciate the difference as all my days dawn the same way, traverse the same beaten track and expire in the night without leaving a trace.

"Raheela, soak Vaapa's shirt and sarong in washing blue and wash them. He has to go to a wedding tonight."

Umma doesn't know how to talk softly . . . she has got used to speaking so loud that people living four doors away can hear her.

"Umma, please talk softly." One has only to utter these words for her to fly into a rage. "How dare you try to control me? Can you succeed?" She would start bawling. What would people think? I would feel thoroughly ashamed.

Vaapa too is thoroughly scared of Umma. I'm not that fond of Umma but when I think of Vaapa I feel somewhat worried. Vaapa too is very fond of me. He is more worried than Umma that I am not yet married.

Occasionally at night I have overheard him telling Umma as they go to bed, "We must do something about Raheela." Umma would raise her voice and say, "You'll go on repeating this and smoking beedis[2] till she turns into a hag."

When I hear this, tears come to my eyes. After that he would not speak a word. I would toss about sleeplessly for a long time. Nightmares would haunt my sleep. How many nights a gigantic elephant would charge and chase me and I'd open my mouth to shout but no sound comes. How I have suffered from these nightmares! How many times fear curdled my blood.

Eight o'clock. The Gampola bus comes, halts near the co-op shop and then drives away. I go to the backyard, take the broom and begin sweeping the compound. My mind is not on my work. My eyes rove seeking diversion, entertainment. I've now got used to staying put in one place and finding the world entertaining.

I can see the hamuduru from the pansala[3] near the water-spout coming along the lengthy ridge stretching from the pansala along the bank of the brook, umbrella in hand. Raising aloft the umbrella, he shoos away the cow grazing on the ridge and walks fast.

My younger brother and the hamuduru are good friends. He spends the better part of the day in the pansala; thereby, he benefits in many ways too.

When the coffee plants belonging to the pansala are leased out, he acts as the middleman. When coconuts are plucked in the pansala, our house too gets coconuts. When the brook dries up, we bathe in the water flowing from the spout. The hamuduru would tell my younger brother to ask us to bathe there.

Vaapa would say, "Swamy is a good man."

My eyes follow the hamuduru from the time he stepped onto the ridge till he disappears from view on the road. The green fields once again transfix my eyes.

These fields that spread out like a mat before the house, the brook that flows like the parting of the hair, through the fields, the winding Gampola road that disappears from view at the co-op store . . . the cattle, scattered here and there, grazing in the fields, Punchi Banda who is ploughing his field, making queer noises as if he is complaining to someone, the boys playing cricket in the evenings in the harvested fields. . . . how many years can you continue to gaze at them? I am bored. But when I think that one day I'll be parted from all these sights I feel sad too.

The fields which look like a green carpet; this brook which flows as if it were echoing the music of life itself; the mountains and the hills steeped in the silence of ages. How beautiful nature is!

"But you can't eat Beauty!" Faiz naana said. True, no doubt. He would speak only after thinking seriously about something. From him I have learned so many things about the world. The children who studied under him were very fortunate, I used to think. It is with the help of books lent by Faiz naana that I am able to pass my time these days.

It's more than ten years since I stopped going to school. My schooldays are only a dim memory now, like the half-forgotten dreams of the early part of the night.

I can see school children going up and down the path. It's the season when sports competitions are being held in the Sinhala school . . . happy days these. My schooldays come back to mind. How enthusiastically we threw ourselves into the annual Inter-House Sports Competitions. How many victories and honours I had won for the House I belonged to.

"In which House is Raheela this time?" was the question on everyone's lips; my reputation stood so high! When it came to the term examinations, there was no one to compete with me for the first place.

I can never forget the arts festival for schools in the district held at Kandy. Though thirteen years have passed, it has impressed itself on my mind's eye like an event that happened yesterday. Our school presented a song accompanied by gestures: Aneesa, Fatima, Hamsiya, Jezima and I all sang and gestured in unison. Viewed from the stage the hall, bathed in the soft light of multi-colored bulbs, seemed to me like a dream land overflowing with people full of life! All five of us wore identical red-and-white garments. I felt as if I were flying thousands of feet above the earth.

In the dim night, to the accompaniment of background music we sang:

Tomorrow dawns for us
To convey good tidings we've come.
To convey good tidings we've come.
The poor shall no more be seen on earth.
That's the tidings we've come to convey.
To conquer this world we've come.

How loud the clapping sounded! The praises showered on us! Oh, how sweet life is, I thought in my joy and delight.

Ultimately everything had turned out to be a lie, an old wives' tale. . . . only the rubble of memories remains!

The days I went to school along the bank of the brook, my head filled with dreams . . . the moments my friends and I savoured the veralu fruits seated in the shade of the mango tree in front of the lab, during the school intervals . . . , the occasions when Farook Master embarrassed me by playfully declaring, "Raheela, it's you whom I'm going to marry." . . . Those dreams, sweetnesses, sounds, enjoyments . . . all had vanished into thin air. I felt as if I were on a speeding rocking train that had suddenly braked to a screeching halt.

When I was in the 9th standard, Umma fell ill and was warded at the Kandy Hospital for a month. During that time I didn't attend school. I had to cook food for Umma. Even after she returned from the hospital, Umma was not in a fit condition to get about and do active work. I didn't have the time even to think about going to school.

"What you have studied is enough for a kumar.[4] What's the use of studying further? You're not going to become a Government Agent. You can stay at home in the future," Vaapa said.

Inwardly, I longed to go to school. But Vaapa had spoken and I couldn't brush his words aside. Even if I was ready to go to school, Umma would have definitely said: "She's not going to study but to catch a husband."

"I don't want any problems," I told myself and kept quiet.

I can see Yasavathy coming to the bank of the brook, with a bundle of cloths. The sun will be directly overhead by the time she finishes washing them. How energetically she carried out even the work of washing the dirty clothes of the villagers! While talking to Yasavathy one doesn't notice the time passing. It was only through talking with her that I learned to speak passable Sinhala. She is now an intimate friend of mine. She says I'm very beautiful. That's what everyone said when I used to go to school.

The friends of Faiz naana who had visited his house that day had fallen for me attracted by my beauty: Faiz naana told me this, after the visitors had left.

As for me whenever I hear this I feel like both laughing and crying at the same time. Nowadays I don't look at my face in the mirror. Besides, the mirror in our house had cracked so badly, there's only one piece left: that piece doesn't reflect the entire face at any one time. If it's held above, the nose and the eyes can be seen. If it's lowered a bit and turned, the lips and the neck can be seen, reddish in colour.

Vaapa's shirt and sarong have to be washed. Today there's a wedding ceremony at Matthisam house. For one week Umma has been working at the wedding house. Vaapa too will come from Matale before nightfall: Vaapa is the watchman of the pepper plantation in Matale bought by Matthisam maama.[5]

When I was in the eighth standard at school, Sinnona, Matthisam maama's daughter wearing only knickers, would stand in the compound sucking her thumb and ask lispingly as I passed whether I was going to school. Even in my imagination I can't picture her as the coy bride she's going to be today.

Umma said she is not old enough for marriage. But keeping a virgin in the house is like tying fire to one's stomach. "They have the money too." I could detect unfulfilled longing and the sense of helplessness in her voice.

While beginning a conversation with Yasavathy, I began soaking the clothes I had brought to wash. Talking to her is a pleasurable experience. How many things which I am ignorant of she knows! She tells me she was born in 1958. It's unbelievable! She is eight years younger than I.

"Why do you make friends with a dhoby-caste girl and bring her inside the house?" my Umma scolded me at the start. But within a few days she had won over Umma by affectionately addressing her as "Achchi."[6]

Yasavathy used to make frequent trips. Going all the way to Kandy all alone was nothing to her. Wearing a gown which exposed her throat and carrying a ladies' umbrella she would go to the hospital, to the perahara[7] and the cinema hall. When I saw her going attired in a gown and carrying the ladies' umbrella, I would feel envious. How many years have passed since I went to Kandy! The last time I went there was when Umma was warded in the Kandy hospital. It must be over ten years since then. How I long to see Colombo city and the sea before I die!

"I have yet to see the sea." When I said this Faiz naana's wife was astonished. I felt thoroughly ashamed.

Yasavathy had some entertaining experiences at the perahara.

She recounted how the boys used to pinch her waist and step on her feet, how she was pressed against people. She described all these as if they were normal. Her tone seemed to imply that these were normal occurrences to be expected; this used to give me goose flesh. Umma would have killed me if she had come to know that I was talking about such things with Yasavathy.

"Boys and girls don't come just to see the perahara," Yasavathy used to say. She may be right but why should I worry about that?

Though I didn't witness the Kandy perahara, every year I too watched a perahara. The temple in the adjoining village celebrated a perahara for seven days every year. On the eighth day the final perahara procession for the water-cutting ceremony went along the road in front of our house.

When I was a small girl how we looked forward to those Sundays when the final perahara procession passed by! Those who sold balloons, sugar-coated gram, sugar cane, and Bombay sweetmeats would come ahead hawking their wares. I was fond of sugar-coated gram.

Now when I watch this perahara, I sigh, thinking another year has passed away unnoticed.

As I watched the elephants stepping along majestically, wearing colourful regalia, I am surprised that these gentle elephants should chase me furiously in my dreams.

When I think of the perahara, I remember my vaapumma who has passed away. She would never watch a perahara. When she heard the beating of the drums in the distance, she would withdraw into the kitchen.

She would say that the Muslims who watched the perahara would be denied the privilege of witnessing the Prophet's divine marriage.

Five years have passed since she died but it seems to me she passed away only yesterday.

On holidays, at five in the evening, there would be a crowd seated on the railings of the bridge, smoking cigarettes and gossiping. Those in their group were friends who were educated and employed. Throwing pebbles into the brook, they would loudly debate something or other. Sometimes they would silently gaze at the mountains in the distance. They would joke with passers-by and laugh. Sometimes if I stood in the compound, some of them look in the direction of our house. Once in a way, one of them would come to our house, asking for a box of matches to light a cigarette.

None of them were married. Perhaps if they were, they might not come to the bridge in the evenings. Who knows?

"Whatever they say about passing their time, this is a disease that the unmarried suffer from," said Faiz naana.

I too felt a bit ashamed. Has this disease affected me too, I wonder.

Next month Yasavathy too will depart. She's getting married. She says it's a love marriage; she is very independent-minded. I can't even think of this. When I think of Yasavathy, I feel a bit jealous. My mind finds it difficult to accept that I am going to lose a friend very close to me. Let her find happiness! I too will have to go one day, leaving these fields, this brook, this bridge, the different types of people, this pleasant environment and go behind a previously unknown man, drawing tight my purdah. I'll have to bear his child. I'll have to tolerate the lacks and deficiencies, to bury my griefs and sufferings in my bosom and live like a submissive wife and a dutiful mother.

It's only through marriage that a woman's life blossoms, it is said. After seeing Aneesa, I have lost faith in this so-called blossoming.

Four years ago Aneesa got married. Bearing how many thousands of dreams in her head, she went to her husband's house! Within four years her dreams were in tatters. She came back to her mother's house, her body marked by poverty; she had grown thinner and darker too, with two children. The husband had sent her back to ask for the dowry.

I found it difficult to recognise Aneesa at first. She had become pathetically thin. How beautiful she was earlier! Now her front teeth had fallen and her face was disfigured. Oh, Aneesa, are you frightening me too? She must have been subjected to severe cruelties at her husband's house. She had learnt to be very reticent. She spoke only one or two words.

Can you remember, Aneesa, when we stood like little angels on the stage bathed in soft red light, and proudly raising our hands sang in unison: "To conquer the world we've come!" Can you remember that day? No, you've forgotten it. Where do you have the time to remember this in a world filled with pettiness? But Aneesa, I can remember that day when all of us held hands and thought: "Tomorrow dawns for us." Whom have we betrayed? Whose property have we stolen that we should all be dying like this?

I felt a desire surging within me to embrace Aneesa and cry my heart out!

Yasavathy comes to bid me farewell. For the first time I see her today in a saree. How beautiful she looks in a saree! She is going to Teldeniya in the evening with her husband.

"Raheela, you must write to me about your wedding. I will definitely come."

Holding her youthful hands and gently stroking them silently I lower my head. Is silence the outlet for grief? "I will never forget you, Raheela," she says in a broken voice in Sinhala, bends down and kissed me; the tears welling up in her eyes, wet my cheeks and splash to the ground.

A vast empty desert, void of sound, stretches before my eyes. In the hot sands of that cruel desert, I can see buried my grief-stricken tomorrows.

This year, the next year and the years after, the peraharas will come like wave after wave.

Feast days, fasting days the mosque Kandoori, the perahara. Yes, as a small girl, these annual festivals brought me limitless happiness and delight; now I'll have to face these annual events conscious that time is flying; and with a full heart I embrace my dear friend, sobs racking my body.

Translated by A. J. Canagaratna

Editor's Notes

1. *Naana*: an older female relative, often a grandmother.
2. *Beedis*: hand-rolled cigarettes.
3. *Hamuduru*: a Buddhist monk; *pansala*: a Buddhist temple.
4. *Kumar*: a prince.
5. *Maama*: uncle.
6. *Achchi*: grandmother.
7. *Perahara*: Buddhist procession.

Sri Lankan Malays

M. M. M. Mahroof

Introduced during the Dutch colonial era, the island's small Malay community has played a significant role in the formation of modern Muslim identity, especially through its traditions of government service and civic leadership.

The Malay community in Sri Lanka consists of less than fifty thousand individuals [according to the 1981 census]. They form one-twentieth of the total Muslim population and one-three-hundredth of the entire population of Sri Lanka. Nonetheless, they form a vibrant and forward-looking ethnic group in the island, with a distinct identity of their own. However, not much has been published about them.

The modern history of the Malays of Sri Lanka begins with the Dutch conquest of Ceylon in the mid-sixteenth century. Historically, the Malay community of Sri Lanka is composed of the descendants of the settlers from what is present day Indonesia and those from the landmass of present day Malaysia. There were earlier Malay settlers in Sri Lanka as well, remnants of the invasions of Ceylon launched by Malay states in their pre-Islamic period, most notably a putative Javanese chieftain named Chandrabhanu, who invaded Sri Lanka twice in the mid-12th century c.e.[1]

The Dutch introduced the Malays to Ceylon either as exiles or as serving soldiers. The former were from the Dutch Indonesian possessions. These exiles, being of the Shafi'i school of Islam, helped revive the Quranic madrasas among Ceylonese Muslims who were also Shafi'i. The other source of Malay influx [was, according to Codrington] comprised of "the Malays imported by the Dutch from the (Indonesian) Archipelago who were bound to military service." These Malay soldiers helped in the capture of Colombo and Mannar (in north-west Ceylon) from the Portuguese. At the end of their service they were granted lands. But they identified themselves more closely with the larger Muslim community in Ceylon. The Dutch perception of Ceylonese Muslims (the Moors) and Malays (Indonesian) was strikingly different. They looked upon the Moors as their trade rivals, "worthy" to be suppressed. As regards the Malays their steadfast loyalty and unflinching, almost reckless bravery, endeared them to the Dutch as it was later to do the British.

When the Dutch surrendered Colombo and their other Ceylonese possessions to the British in 1796 they numbered 1617 men, of which 845 were European and 772 Malays. Understandably enough, the Malay soldiers formed an important part of the subject of surrender proceedings. However, this number did not represent the total population of Malays in Ceylon at that time. A considerable number of them, particularly those established in the central highlands of Ceylon, were in service with the king of Kandy in which they distinguished themselves equally well as with the Europeans.

The economic, political and social developments in the nineteenth century were to have deep impact on the Malays of Ceylon. In the first place it altered their military character. . . . The Ceylon Malay Rifles, a thousand-man regiment, Malay-officered and Malay-manned which had garrisoned in Ceylon was disbanded due to financial reasons. However since the Malays had not hesitated even under the Dutch in performing public service, they saw no reason in shying away from service under the British. When opportunities in the army were closed on them they enthusiastically enrolled in the police force. With the result that, [according to M. Murad Jayah] "Every Police station became a Malay kampong. The Malays constituted over 75% of the entire Police Force. In nearly every prison, there was a Malay kampong, because Malays formed more than 90% of the staff of the Prison Service. The Colombo Fire Brigade quarters formed one large kampong as 100% of the staff were Ceylon Malays." . . .

In contrast [to the Moors], the Malay social organization was entirely different. In the first place, the Malays were small in numbers. In the second place, their sense of history was different from that of the Moors. The Malay historical sense was steeped in the feudal traditions of Jogjakarta together with the monarchical traditions of Malaysia. The panoply of sultan, tenku and santir (theologian) did not flower in Ceylon. . . . The Malays of Ceylon were too small in number and too "professionalized" to have any organic affinity with the indigenous political structures.

The Western, Central and Southern Provinces had the largest number of Malays, in that order. These three provinces had characteristics of their own. The Western Province was the seat of the administration of the colonial powers, the Portuguese, the Dutch and the British, and so it was natural that a substantial number of Malays were located there. The Central Province was the seat of government of the former kingdom of Kandy and so had a large number of former Malay soldiers and their descendants. The

Southern Province had the only Malay fishing community in Ceylon, and the existence of Malay-named towns (e.g., Hambantota) show a longstanding connection of this area with perhaps the Malay-Indonesians of South-East Asia.

In 1901, as much as one-third of the entire population of the Malays in Ceylon lived in the precincts of the Colombo Municipal Council. There were in that area some 4351 Malays. Of these most lived (and their descendants continue to live) in the area south-west of Colombo harbor known as "Kompanii Veediya," meaning "Company Street," the Company being the VOC (the Dutch East Indies Company), which then housed the storage facilities of the Company. It was popularly called "Slave Island" because presumably it had at one time housed Malay and other bonded servants of the VOC. The reasons for Malay concentration in this area were many. It was the seat of the Ceylon Malay Rifles till its demobilization in 1873. Afterwards, the ex-soldiers were settled in civilian jobs in the locality (till recently one road here was called "Rifle Street"). The historical connection of Malays with this area is still denoted by road names such as "Java Lane" and "Malay Street," . . .

Hambantota district, on the southern tip of Sri Lanka, had been traditionally known for its salt production. The British occupation of Ceylon gave a great boost to production. A Salt Department was organized and the duties of the Assistant Government Agent (generally an Englishman and member of the Ceylon Civil Service) included the organization of salt collection and its distribution. In course of time, a mini-bureaucracy of salt officials and care-takers from the Salt Superintendents emerged. Expectedly, they were all Malays. The affluence and efficiency of the government-service Malays gave them great influence with the British administration in this sparsely inhabited (at that time) district. That in turn created a professional class of legal executives, court interpreters, police officials and Kachcheri (district administrative office) staff.

The Kirinde fishing community [located east of Hambantota] was a traditional, older [Malay village], . . . They [were] ensconced among non-Malay and non-Muslim communities. They were the only Malays who practiced fishing as a group. Since fishing is a seasonal but exhausting occupation, with expectations of "windfall" gains, there is a job-satisfaction and a disinclination to attempt other activities. In consequence, there was some variation in the attitudes, linguistic and cultural structures of the [Kirinde settlement] as compared with other Malay [settlements]. . . .

Another factor in the weakening of the Malay . . . social organization was the progressive weakening of the Malay language as used in Ceylon.

The Malay language in Ceylon has been described as "a Batavian dialect." But it has vocabulary in use in Banda, Sumatra and other outlying parts, as well as from the areas of present-day Malaysia. Classical Malay (which . . . includes the languages used in what is present-day Indonesia) was written in the Arabic script and was called *Gundul*. Gundul had a wide relevance in Ceylon up to the twenties of this century. The traditional literati of the Moors of Ceylon used Arabic-Tamil (i.e., Tamil language written in Arabic script). They could read Gundul because the script was practically the same and comprehension was aided by the profuse use of Arabic words (sometimes Perso-Arabic words) in both languages. The traditional Moor literati and the traditional Malay literati were thus united intellectually. . . .

The fragility of classical Malay (Gundul) was soon to be demonstrated, however. As English began to be used by more and more Malays, Gundul-based Malay became marginalized and confined to mosque functionaries and Malay preceptors of Islam. (Not unexpectedly, the last recorded use of Gundul in Ceylon was in the recording and registering of Malay bills of marriages, the *kavin*, in the late 1920s.) The presence temporarily in Ceylon of Malay and Javanese Hajj pilgrims did not arrest the decline. That at the same period of time, Arabic-Tamil fell into disuse, and Moors of Ceylon began to write Tamil in Tamil script entirely, did not help matters any. . . .

So, Malay continued to be just a spoken dialect in Ceylon. However, a large stock of English, Sinhala and Tamil . . . began to enter spoken Malay, replacing Arabic words. In the period subsequent to 1956 when English was displaced as the official language and later, when Sinhala and Tamil became the medium of instruction, the number of Sinhala and Tamil words entering spoken Malay increased. Malay is an almost flexionless language, depending on the locational use of words; hence foreign words were accepted without much modification. Sinhala (an Aryan language) and Tamil (a Dravidian one), both highly flexional and complicated languages, usually break the bones of foreign words before they accept them into their vocabularies. . . . Since all Malays are fluent in Sinhala and/or Tamil, the use of Malay is not necessary for face-to-face communication. So, Malay descends sometimes to the level of a "privy language" for conveying information when non-Malays are present. . . .

Educational attainments, administrative access, and the respect they received from the British—all these factors made the Malays excellent mediators between the Muslim community of Ceylon and the government, acting as the principal spokesmen for the Muslims. Some Malays chose this vocation with a great sense of responsibility. Two of them need special mention. One was Tuan Burhanudeen Jayah and the other Maas Thajon Akbar.

Jayah, born in 1890, achieved importance in many fields as an education-ist, educational administrator, legislator, cabinet minister, and High Com-missioner for Ceylon in Pakistan. Early in his career, he and his colleagues set up the Ceylon Muslim League. . . . Maas Thajon Akbar was another Malay who devoted himself to the cause of Muslim education in Ceylon. Ten years older than Jayah, Akbar completed his Mechanical Tripos at Em-manuel College, Cambridge, went on to take his Law Tripos and was also called to the Bar. Soon after he entered the Official Bar in Ceylon and rose to the position of Senior Puisne Justice of the Supreme Court of Ceylon in 1936. But his enduring vocation was, as mentioned above, education, particularly education of the poor Muslims of Colombo. By the 1920s he had become a key official of the Ceylon Muslim Educational Society, then the main Mus-lim organization running Muslim schools. Obtaining permission from the authorities, for he was a senior law officer, he took to the field, collected pub-lic subscriptions and set up several Muslim schools, popularly and naturally called "Akbar Schools." . . .

The Malays of Sri Lanka have been characterized by love of sports and have had a flair for sports organization. The Malay Cricket Club is gener-ally considered the first cricketing club to be established in Ceylon. Malay prowess in soccer is well-known, even when playing bare-foot with booted Englishmen.

The Malays of Sri Lanka are thus a sub-community, but one which has adjusted itself to the changing times with finesse.

Editor's Note

1. Chandrabhanu's invasions occurred during the time of Parakramabahu II, which would date them to the second half of the thirteenth century, not the twelfth century.

TAMIL IDENTITIES: AN INTRODUCTION

The question of an emergent Tamil identity is every bit as complicated, if not more so, as the question of Sinhala and Muslim identities. Its substance is not merely one of language (Tamil) and religion (Hindu) because there also remains a distinctive sense of Tamil identity in the Jaffna peninsula, in the Vanni, along the east coast, in the plantation hill country, and in Colombo. Moreover, even more so than the Sinhalas in terms of percentage, many Tamils of Sri Lanka, historically, have converted to Roman Catholicism. And, while language has been a unifying factor, the social force of caste, like religion, has led to internal tensions. There has also been, to some extent, an "Indian factor" at play for the Tamil community, which makes it more likely that members will express an affinity for "Mother India." When this factor is coupled with the fact that many Tamils live in remote or peripheral regions of the island, at least in relation to the capital of Colombo, a greater sense of difference can be appreciated.

In the essays that follow, one can trace the evolution of an emergent identity that finally demands a separate political space. The elements that are appealed to, ultimately, are the frustrations experienced by a minority population in relation to its linguistic, religious, cultural, social, and economic aspirations. Like their Sinhala counterparts, Tamil politicians since the 1930s have not embraced a political perspective that transcends the ethnically self-interested. Their grievances have, indeed, often been compelling and their requests largely unmet, but some of their demands have, at times, transcended the abilities of a unitary state.

Language, Poetry, Culture, and Tamil Nationalism

A. Jeyaratnam Wilson

In this wide-ranging chapter from his book on Sri Lankan Tamil national-ism, A. J. Wilson describes how the religious awakening in the northern Jaffna peninsula—characterized by the Saiva Siddhanta thought of Arumuka Navalar in the late nineteenth century—was a catalyst for subsequent Tamil literary and linguistic movements that commanded political awareness in the twentieth. That is, while not politically motivated per se, the political ramifications of this Tamil cultural reawakening cannot be denied.

Professor Sinnappah Arasaratnam wrote in 1979 . . . [of] "conflicting loyal-ties to a language-culture unit." . . .

> In the past two and a half decades of the history of these Independent states, this has emerged as the single most cohesive factor in human group relationship. Language, poetry, culture and ethnicity are the ve-hicles that convey these "conflicting loyalties."

The Sri Lankan Tamils are no exception.

The nineteenth century threw up a powerful Ceylon Tamil literary fig-ure in Arumuka Navalar (1822–79), whose closest counterpart in the other community was Anagarika Dharmapala, the progenitor of a nationalist-oriented Sinhalese literary revival. Navalar's work uplifted Tamil ethnicity and pointed the way to a yet-to-be articulated Tamil national consciousness. He was not a dominant figure like Anagarika [Dharmapala], but there were certain important changes which he sponsored or introduced himself, and which can be connected to later developments in Tamil nationalism.

Navalar (the word means a man prolific in the use of his tongue—the title was bestowed on him by the Jaffna Tamils) undertook a large-scale revision and purification of Saiva Siddhanta (the "wisdom of Siva"), a special contri-bution made by Sri Lankan Tamil Hindus to Saivism. He was a pioneer in developing a Tamil prose style, where formerly the prevailing form of expression had been in verse. He wrote textbooks for Hindu children, was a literary textual critic and innovative in the manipulation of Tamil grammar. He also launched and organised a Tamil Hindu school system so that Tamil children would not become subject to conversion while attending Christian schools. Jaffna Hindu College is an enduring monument to his untiring efforts; it had started modestly as Jaffna Hindu High School in 1890, and did not at first receive the state of a college because of opposition from the Wesleyan missionaries. Navalar was an accomplished polemicist. He was critical of Christian proselytisation and tried to win those who had been converted back to Hinduism. Here he was countering Christian attempts to undermine the Hindu religion. He betrayed no bitterness about this; rather, he adopted a logical, defensive posture. His lack of rancour may be partly explained by the fact that his own education had been encouraged by the Rev. Peter Percival, who arrived in Jaffna in 1826. Navalar even assisted Percival in translating the Bible into the Tamil language. But, despite this, he engaged in polemics against the Christians and he was in this role without a rival. He had a school of distinguished disciples as well as many followers. In 1880, a year after his death, Navalar's activities resulted in the founding of the Saiva Paripalana Sabhai (Society for the Preservation of Hindu Saivism).

K. Kailasapathy remarked in 1982: "It is generally accepted that in many Asian countries political nationalism was preceded by religious awakening that arose in response to Christian missionary activities." This was certainly true in the case of Navalar. Not only did he provide the impetus for the revival of Hinduism in Jaffna, but he also had a social outlook that went beyond that of any other Tamil religious reformer of his time. He was critical of the Government Agent of Jaffna, W. C. Twynam, whose activities had made him unpopular. During the severe famine of 1876, Navalar undertook relief measures to help the hungry. He was instrumental in establishing the Jaffna and Batticaloa Commercial and Agricultural Company, with the immediate objective of developing agriculture in the Trincomalee district. He also played an active role in promoting P. Ramanathan's candidature for the Legislative Council.

Navalar's position as a revivalist of commanding stature won him great influence and a host of followers among his countrymen. There were such disciples as C. W. Tamotheram Pillai (1832–1901), a Christian who, according to A. V. Subramaniam Ayyar (1900–76), was the most eminent Tamil scholar in the last quarter of the nineteenth century; he belonged to the band of Jaffna Tamil scholars and was next in importance only to Arumuka Navalar, who exercised considerable influence over him and his literary work.

Tamotheram Pillai and the dedicated band of scholars known as the "Jaffna School" were influenced by Navalar during his lifetime and for some three decades afterwards spent most of their working lives in various employment in Madras. After a first-class education at one of the two best missionary schools in Jaffna, the Jaffna Central School, Pillai went on to the University of Madras to become one of its first graduates. Under Navalar's supervision and advice, he published in 1868 an edition of the second book of Tolkapiyam. Kailasapathy has remarked that Pillai was the pioneer in "the history of the periodization of Tamil literature," while in textual criticism "he was a pathfinder"; he asserted in 1982 that this scholar was "perhaps the best example of the advent of the modern intellectual in the Tamil literary scene."

More important, Pillai became a leading light in two Tamil linguistic associations which were ushering in an age of Tamil linguistic nationalism in Madras: the South Indian Tamil Association and the Dravidian Languages Association, founded in 1890 and 1879 respectively. In the preface to his edition of a pioneering work of exposition, *Kalikotai* (1887), Pillai referred to *thesabimanam* (love of country), *natabimanam* (love of the classical dance form) and *bashabimanam* (love of language). These were the later basic ingredients of a nationalism which had its roots not only in South India but in the native place of Tamotheram Pillai himself—namely Jaffna, the heartland of the Tamils of Sri Lanka. Country, language and religion (inclusive of classical dance) became inextricably a part of the Sri Lankan Tamil worldview wherever the people went, whether to the Sinhalese south, the Malayan peninsula or other parts of the British empire.

Two other aspects of the awakening of Tamil Saiva and linguistic consciousness should be noted. On the one hand Dagmar Hellmann-Rajanayagam emphasises the relationship between the Tamil language and Saivaite interpretations, which she asserts is connected with the Saiva Siddhanta teachings taken up by Arumuka Navalar and the late nineteenth-century sage Marai Malai Atikal:

> Language revival followed or accompanied religious revival and this language revival consciously tried to disconnect language from religion while upholding the social system both entailed. It is this strand which the Christians can also take up as a life line for their Tamil nationalism.

Secondly, an event of as much significance to the Tamil world, irrespective of place and time, was the publication in 1891 of a verse-play, *Manonmaniyani*, by P. Sundaram Pillai (1855–97), Professor of Philosophy at Travancore University in South India. Tamil in this celebrated play was termed "goddess," "divine" and "sacrosanct," and although it had its beginnings in South India, it received enthusiastic approbation from the Sri Lankan Tamils. Two journals, *Siddhanta Deepika* (1897–1913)—meaning "The Light of Saivaite Hindu Truth"—and *The Tamilian Antiquary* (1907–14), enjoyed the active involvement of eminent Sri Lankan Tamils such as (Sir) P. Ramanathan and (Sir) P. Arunachalam (who signed his article with his initials "P.A." to disguise his identity as a senior civil servant in the British administration).

In his Punitham Tiruchelvam memorial lecture of 1982 in Colombo, the leading Tamil literary intellectual K. Kailasapathy affirmed that although the cultural awakening began as a Hindu movement and was predominantly led by Saiva scholars, its character changed over the years. The prestige accorded to it by Christian missionary scholars such as Caldwell, Percival, Bower, Pope and Ellis "had the salutary effect of bringing the Christians into the mainstream." Kailasapathy also drew attention to the "accusation" made by some sectarian Hindus that Christians had infiltrated the movement through such learned men as Father S. Gnanaprakasar (1875–1947) and the internationally renowned Rev. Dr Xavier Stanislaus Thani Nayagam (1913–80); this, he argued, did not need to be taken seriously. Thus the movement for Tamil cultural awakening did not become segmented or sectarian. There was no conflict between Tamil Hindus, Tamil Christians and Saivaite Hindus. The Tamil language, with all its literary formulations, had a universal appeal which consequently made it a binding force of considerable strength in later promoting Tamil nationalism.

As important, if not more so, was the boost that Navalar gave to the Tamil language in making it a vehicle for the spread of Saivaism among the Tamil people. Again, paradoxically, instrumental in this were the writings of Christian missionaries such as the lexicographers, the Rev. Peter Percival (who arrived in Jaffna in 1826) and the Rev. Miron Winslow (1789–1864), as well as the pioneering works of the novelist Mrs. Isaac Thambyah. They did not anticipate the social consequences of their work. As mentioned above, Navalar had acted as consultant to Percival in his translation of the Bible, which was largely rendered in prose. Those scholars who engaged in Tamil studies at the time did so in the medium of verse. Winslow compiled a Tamil–English dictionary and in so doing observed: "Its [Tamil] prose-style is yet in a forming state, and will well repay the labour of accurate scholars in moulding it properly," adding that "many natives who write poetry readily cannot write a page of prose."

Navalar established a Tamil prose style, a popular medium adapted from the earlier abstract verse form. He well understood the implications of making the Saivaite scriptures available to everyone, and a grateful Tamil public remembered him and perpetuated his memory as the "father of modern Tamil prose." It was natural that Kailasapathy should conclude his piece on "Arumuka Navalar: The Central Years (1834–1848)" with the significant observation: "When Navalar came on the scene, he found a community in search of an identity. By the time he departed, not only he but his society had established their distinct personalities."

Navalar had no occasion, except when extolling the virtues of Saivism, to make references to Sinhala Buddhism or other faiths. He confined his mission to Jaffna, and was not concerned with the rest of Ceylon; Dagmar Hellman-Rajanayagam remarks that he "never seems to have set foot into Colombo." She adds: "the astonishing fact . . . for a writer from Ceylon is that the Sinhalese hardly figure at all in his books except in passing. His writings on Ceylon history casually make mention of a people called 'the Sinhalese' living to the south of Jaffna. Navalar never identified himself as a Ceylonese, but as a Tamil from Yalpanam [the Tamil name for Jaffna]."

The literary significance of the period after Navalar's death in 1879 is open to debate. Kailasapathy and to some extent the emigre poet R. Cheran contend that Tamil literary scholarship was either in a state of semi-dormancy or affected by the consequences of the political rupture between Sir P. Arunachalam and the Ceylon National Congress. Neither critic was able to come to a firm conclusion on this. At best they asserted that the literary output of the 1920s depicted the strained relations between the Sinhalese and Tamil anglicised elites. Neither Kailasapathy nor Cheran refers to any versification or prose-writing in response to the Sinhalese communalism of the Buddhist intellectuals and writers Piyadasa Sirisena, Anagarika Dharmapala and those of their genre. It is possible that the Tamil literati of this time were unaware of the chauvinism of this group because they felt secure under the benign rule of Britain and there appeared no likelihood of the imperial power relinquishing control.

So the Tamil writers of this period, voluntarily living in a separate world, misled themselves. Cheran states:

> Important signs of "rupture" between the Sinhalese and Tamil elites who had been articulating the interests of their communities became evident during 1920–1930. . . . The formation of the Thamilar Maha Jana Sabhai [Council of the Tamil People] (1921) had been an important landmark in the evolution of Tamil nationalism.

He adds that the prominent leaders of the late 19th and early 20th centuries were in the forefront of the movement to create a *Ceylonese Nationalism* with a multi-ethnic character and a secular outlook" (emphasis added). These leaders were emulating the Indian National Congress, all the time unaware of the vibrant national consciousness of their Sinhala-speaking counterparts that was emerging separately.

Kailasapathy too, in much the same way as Cheran but without advancing similar reasons, regards as a void the period between Navalar's death in 1879 and the emergence of what might be termed an ephemeral Tamil literature from the 1920s to the 1940s. Politically the Tamils were rudderless. They hoped that Britain would stay in the country to protect their interests. Naturally works were produced during this phase, but these were of little or no consequence.

The other key figures in Jaffna during this period were writers who put their faith in a single island entity. These included Periyatamby Pillai (1899–1978), Somasunthara Pulavar (1878–1953), Nallathamby Pulavar (1896–1951), and Thuraiappah Pillai (1872–1929). They thought in terms of a united Ceylon/Sri Lanka in their time—a consequence of the trust they felt in the presence of an impartial imperial ruler. For instance, Periyatamby wrote romantically about "Glorious Mother Lanka": "Ceylon a glorious pearl / is our country / I walked / it was a summer night." There was no reference to such concepts as separation, federalism or an independent Tamil state. While Somasunthara Pulavar, in his poem "The Bounty of Lanka," envisioned a united "Mother Lanka," the most outstanding of these writers, Thuraiappah Pillai, used ordinary language to convey his ideas on the need for social reform in the context of conservative Jaffna. More important, he sought to reach out to the general mass of people with his own patriotic vision of literature and the arts. This was all salutary, since he was advocating social reform in a tradition-bound society. But he was off the mark when he dwelt on a secular type of Sri Lankan nationalism, for it was at this very time that militant Buddhism was making its presence felt. Apparently Pillai was not affected by the communalist statements of Sinhalese Buddhist leaders during this phase.

Alongside these literary developments in favour of "a united Mother Lanka" there emerged a parallel political grouping, the Jaffna Youth Congress, whose idealism was embodied in a demand for full self-government—*purana swaraj* in Tamil. The leaders of the Congress, in particular the charismatic Handy Perinpanayagam, called for a boycott of elections to the legislature, the State Council, recommended by the Donoughmore Commission. The Congress was successful in its appeal. There were demonstrations in Jaffna against the Donoughmore constitution; however, it is debatable whether the mass support for the Congress was due to forces opposed to the Commission's recommendation to abolish communal representation or merely to sentiment opposed to the absence of independence.

Undoubtedly sections of Jaffna opinion would have been influenced by the contemporary agitation of the Indian National Congress for *purana swaraj*. In contrast with Jaffna, the more pragmatic Sinhalese leadership preferred gradualistic change and welcomed the abolition of communal representation and its replacement with territorial constituencies. They realised that this would mean an end to communal ratios between majorities and minorities; instead, the Sinhalese and the Ceylon Tamils would be granted representation in proportion to their numbers.

From the mid-1920s to the mid-1930s the Youth Congress inaugurated a literary revival too. Conferences on the Tamil language, and especially the introduction of the mother tongue as the medium of instruction, provided further points of agitation. The first Congress in 1924 conferred on "The Need for the Revival of Tamil Literature," and later Congresses continued the practice of devoting a day to the discussion of Tamil literature and culture. Little of any political importance came of these cultural endeavours, but Kailasapathy was of the view that "the activities of the Congress gave a positive fillip to creativity in literature."

The events of 1920–48 were followed by the emergence of a vibrant Tamil cultural movement, of which the leading light in the period 1948–70 was a scholar-patriot, the Rev. Dr Xavier Stanislaus Thani Nayagam, who received an appointment in the Faculty of Education, University of Ceylon, now the University of Peradeniya in Kandy. He fired up young Tamil academics at the University about the plight of the Tamils and the cultural oppression being inflicted on them. (For example, there was a ban on Tamil literature being imported from Madras.) The journal he published in Madras, *Tamil Culture* (1952–66), reflected the new thinking. It contained contributions from Ceylon Tamil academics on the discrimination being practised which compelled Tamils to pay serious attention to their parlous political situation. Thani Nayagam moved to Kuala Lumpur as Professor of Indian Studies at the University of Malaysia in the mid-1960s. There he did much to promote Tamil studies, launching the celebrated International Conferences on Tamil Research, and the International Association (IATR) that continued to be active mainly through his efforts. The conferences gained much publicity in the world of learning and were a positive encouragement to Tamil studies. Other distinguished Tamils included K. Kanapathipillai, whose play *Sankili* (1956) won much admiration, and S. Vithianathan, who devoted unflagging energy to the promotion of his key interest, Tamil village drama, or *koothu*. Two key works were C. S. Navaratnam's *Tamils and Ceylon* (1958) and K. Navaratnam's *Tamil Element in Ceylon Culture* (1959). H. W. Tambiah's pathbreaking *The Laws and Customs of the Tamils of Ceylon* (1954) was timely. Two academics, K. Indrapala and S. Pathmanathan, produced notable doctoral dissertations; Indrapala's "Dravidian Settlements in Ceylon and the Beginning of the Kingdom of Jaffna" (1965) and S. Pathmanathan's "The Kingdom of Jaffna" (1969, later published as a monograph, struck a note of great contemporary relevance when they appeared.

The dynamic literature of 1948–70 soon gave way to the literature of Tamil militancy. K. Kailasapathy expressed the transition thus:

> With this [i.e., up to ca. 1970] the linguistic consciousness would appear to have had its full run. Emanating from the upper classes it had touched the entire society in different ways. Although a general consciousness of language and culture was probably common to the entire community, its significance and importance was relative and felt differently by different social groups and classes. Furthermore what were at the beginning purely sentimental and symbolic issues evolved into concrete problems vitally affecting the social, economic and political life of the people.

To underscore this, he concluded: "the cultural nationalism of the Tamils is today at the crossroads. It is no more a mere question of linguistic and cultural identities. It is the basic question of nationality."

As we have seen, however, Kailasapathy said little about what happened in the years between Arumuka Navalar's death in 1879 and independence in 1948. In fact this was an unproductive period in Tamil politics and hence he was correct in his observation that these were halcyon days for the Tamil middle and upper middle classes. The classical Tamil dance form, the Bharata Natyam, and the Carnatic music of those times became the reigning orthodoxy and were proclaimed the divine arts. The language, dance and music became "deified," and stagnated in the absence of "experimentation and innovation." No interest meanwhile was shown in other art forms. Thus Kailasapathy deplored the absence of "any significant movement . . . for studying and cherishing the popular arts or what is often described as folk art"; and this was "the nature of the linguistic and cultural consciousness of the Tamils till the 1950s." Hence this phase can best be described as the celebration of Tamil ethnicity at its zenith; it occupied its own separate sphere, outside politics. But the increased levels of consciousness that resulted from this made it easier for a Tamil nationalist leadership to evoke Tamil national consciousness later.

The nationalist ethic was nevertheless kept alive, but only just. Mudaliyar C. Rasanayagam (1870–1940) published his celebrated Tamils of Ceylon in 1920. Despite inaccuracies, it was important as a much-needed boost for Tamil studies. So were the historical works of Father Gnanaprakasar, A. Muthuthamby and K. Velupillai (1860–1944). But their writing, in Kailasapathy's words, "were basically academic and amateurish in character."

There were others who viewed the island as a unity and "conceived Sinhala and Tamil as two eyes or two sisters or two companions and invoked the image of a united and happy home," but they could not have been more than dimly aware of developments on the political scene. On the other hand, there were minor poets who were influenced by India's national past, such as Subramaniam Bharathiar (1882–1921), described by Kailasapathy as "in more than one sense one of the progenitors of Tamil nationalism." From the 1930s onwards the influence of Bharatiar's works percolated through to Ceylon Tamil writers and even to politicians.

The movement was middle class in character, but this was the class that mattered at this time. Its leadership created a religious awakening that extended to the literary and linguistic spheres; as Kailasapathy observed, "it was a cultural self-assertion in the face of colonial domination." This included the typical Jaffna zeal, unlike that of south India, for Sen-Thamil "pure Tamil" language. Interests that had become more or less fossilised were revived by Sir P. Ramanathan and later his erudite son-in-law, S. Natesan, an educationist and a politician. Societies and conferences were convened to popularise the "pure" Tamil language education unique to the Tamils or . . . Jaffna, quite unlike that of Tamil Nadu, where it had been adulterated with Hindi and English.

Of greater significance was the adoption of the classical Indian dance (Bharata Natyam) and Carnatic music by the middle and upper-income segments of Colombo's Tamil society and later by their less privileged country cousins. Accomplishment in these two classical forms of Jaffna Tamil expression was considered essential for a young Tamil woman making her *arangetram* (debut) into the cultural world. They were held up as exemplars of Tamil arts and achievements; facility in these became the vogue among the Ceylon Tamil bourgeoisie, and they were eulogised as "Tamilian arts and achievements." Bharata Iyer and Rukmani Devi Arundale were two of those behind the founding of the Kalakshetra, the dance academy in Madras, which became the Mecca to which all parents who could afford it would send their daughters. In the early 1920s, under G. Venkatchalam's guidance, the Natyam came to be revered, in contrast to its parlous condition in the eighteenth and nineteenth centuries when it had become associated with nautch girls [or] temple dancers—who performed before the gods. Even before this development, the respected author Ananda Coormaraswamy had given great inspiration to this particular dance form in his writings *The Mina of Gesture* (1917) and *The Dance of Shiva* (1918). Carnatic music was extolled too by scholars. Kailasapathy appropriately observes that these forms were "carefully cushioned against any political intrusion especially of any ideas tinged with social reform or change . . . they were kept hermetically sealed by the upper middle class purely as status symbols and ethnic identities." It was not till the 1950s that forms of linguistic and cultural consciousness enjoyed a widespread renaissance among the Tamils.

The success of the Sinhala Buddhist movement in 1956 gave rise to two schools of thought. The first centred on the Progressive Writers' Association (PWA) led by K. Kailasapathy and K. Sivathamby, who expected their liberal preferences with regard to Tamil literature to flourish under the influence of the Sinhala Buddhists' revolution after 1956. This did not happen and they were to be sadly disillusioned, although they persisted in their thinking and writings till the full tide of Sinhala Buddhist chauvinism overtook the "progressivism" they had hoped to achieve. Members of this school expected that their left-wing approach would benefit from the fall-out of what they had hopefully interpreted as the progressive aspects of the Sinhala people's 1956 revolution. It is possible that if S. W. R. D. Bandaranaike had not been assassinated in 1959, the PWA's hopes might have been realised, and this would have been even more likely if the Marxist United Front government of 1970–7 had not backtracked on their Marxism . . . and gone the way of Sinhala Buddhist chauvinism instead. Thus the Kailasapathy–Sivathamby approach ceased to be viable.

At the other end of the spectrum was the literary school of Tamil purists exemplified in the writings of S. Sivanayagam, editor of the Federal Party's newspaper *Suthanthiran* (Freedom). Sivanayagam was influenced by the South Indian nationalist Dravidian Progressive Front (DMK) school of C. N. Annadurai and his followers, who called for an unadulterated Tamil language free from the influence of Hindi and Sanskrit. Sivanayagam had great skill and was a talented polemicist. His predecessors at *Suthanthiran*, A. N. Kandasamy and the trade unionist S. Natesa Iyer, had also been involved in the "pure Tamil" movement, with the difference that theirs was a mix of communism and the DMK. One of Sivanayagam's latter-day successors as editor of *Suthanthiran*, Kovai Mahesan, expressed ideas in the DMK way but in a more macho style. The FP/ITAK school condemned the PWA as collaborating with the Sinhalese hegemony, while the PWA in turn stigmatised its adversaries as Tamil chauvinists.

The beginnings of a culture of resistance first became apparent in 1965–70, when the FP joined the United National Party (UNP) in a coalition to enable the latter to give teeth to the Tamil Regulations which had been promised by S. W. R. D. Bandaranaike under the Tamil Language (Special Provisions)

Act of 1958 and the implementation of a scheme of District Development Councils (DDCS). The approach of Kovai Mahesan, now reinforced by the, much more belligerent Kasi Anandan, did not approve of the FP having anything to do with the UNP. Mahesan and Kasi Anandan were active leaders in the Thami Thai Manram ("the house of the Tamil mother"). During the early years of the 1965–70 FP–UNP coalition government, they laid the foundations for the literature that was to follow during the period of civil war in the 1970s and subsequently. This was influenced by the repression of the Sinhalese-dominated state and by DMK literature in neighbouring Tamil Nadu. The DMK had led a successful anti-Hindi agitation, among other things causing the state of Madras to be renamed Tamil Nadu in 1968, and in due course Tamil Nadu writers and actors who were also politicians, such as C. N. Annadurai, Karunanidhi and M. G. Ramachandran, and were in the forefront in the fight against north Indian and Hindi domination, became chief ministers of the state. All these activities left their mark on the ITAK/FP school which, however, had a more difficult task to accomplish.

The penultimate phase, in which the poetry of resistance would become a potent phenomenon, was from 1970 onwards. It was still believed that victory would be won by "the forces of righteousness." K. Sivathamby captured the change in a single statement: "the accent here in Jaffna, unlike in India, is on a Tamil togetherness and unity for ending a system that threatens the continued existence of the Tamil ethos in Sri Lanka." The movement, whose members belonged to the post-1960s generation came to full flower in the 1980s.

This new school of resistance focused on the oppressor state and looked upon it and its army as aliens. Its writings expressed great bitterness against the state's "barbarism." Two Tamil-speaking Muslims, M. A. Nuhman and Solaikili . . . , are examples of the new culture: unbending and expressing both complete alienation and the determination of a people not to surrender to the will of the "Sinhala terror state." The sufferings of a community on the run were also given voice in expatriate literature. The writing and theatre of this period speak of defiance and a determination to resist and die rather than be abject victims of the military superiority of the terror state. Kailasapathy, in winding up his Punitham Tiruchelvam Memorial Lecture of 1982, placed this all in perspective when he observed:

> Problems related to language, religion, literature etc. have become subordinated to the primary issue. To put it another way, the whole thing has become integrated. In that sense the linguistic and cultural consciousness . . . has reached new heights or reached its logical conclusion. Only

a proper solution to the main contradiction can create the appropriate conditions so necessary for the further development of this consciousness in a positive and productive manner.

Kailasapathy's final sentence contains a glimmer of hope that resolution of the conflict may come about within the confines of "the Sinhala-dominated state." If he had lived it seems likely that his optimistic vision would have faded. The Tamil language and literature await arrival of a democratic ethos in order that its flowers may bloom. The alternative is a literature of pain and despair.

Thus by the end of the nineteenth century, a vibrant Tamil nationalism had still to make itself articulate. There were signs of this on the distant horizon, but the ingredients had still to acquire form and substance. The Tamil elites still did not feel threatened: there was always the imperial arbiter who, they felt assured, would hold the scales evenly. So only the weakest sign was visible which was a felt desire to preserve identity as well as safeguard interests. Most affected was the field of literary endeavour, an area in which the savant Aramukha Navalar helped fill the gap. Till then this still-to-be-expressed nationalism required catalytic agents which were set in motion by an awakening Sinhalese nationalism whose torch-bearers increasingly realised that the interests of the Sinhalese and Buddhists had to be conserved and advanced if the Sinhalese Buddhists were to protect their "race" and culture in the years to come. That role was left to the Sinhalese literati and political elite. . . . When these catalytic roles were activated, Tamil elites reacted with their own brand of defensive nationalism. The resulting bi-ethnic conflict came to a climax in a war of secession from the 1970s onwards. For a peaceful Buddhist island this is a supreme tragedy.

The Dance of the Turkey Cock—
The Jaffna Boycott of 1931

Jane Russell

1931 was a pivotal year in Ceylon, with the establishment of the Donoughmore Constitution and universal enfranchisement—an experiment within the British colonial world. As such, it also marks the beginnings of the transfer of power to the majority Sinhalese community. In the following essay, Jane Russell details the far-reaching significance of the 1931 Jaffna election boycott, led by the Jaffna Youth Congress. The Congress challenged the dominance of traditional Vellala caste-based power and allied itself with the Indian independence movement but, ironically, thereby disenfranchised the Tamils of Jaffna; by refusing to participate in Ceylon governance, Tamil Jaffna was isolated from the rest of the country, Tamil and Sinhala. This account serves as an excellent background to the political dynamics that later gave rise to the Tamil separatist movement.

In April 1931, the Tamils of the Jaffna peninsula surprised the entire island by suddenly announcing a boycott of the first general election held under universal franchise. There were few south of Elephant Pass who either understood or sympathised with this defiant gesture. Most of the Sinhalese politicians, seeing in it yet another piece of Tamilian trickery, imagined it to be some devious manoeuvre to stop the island from reaping the newly-won benefits of the Donoughmore Constitution.

Relations between the Sinhalese and Tamil communities in Sri Lanka have been bedevilled in the last fifty years or more by a lack of mutual understanding and trust. For the main part, the Sinhalese had "fallen into the habit of considering Jaffna as a thing apart, a thing not distinctly related" to the rest of the island. This ignorance and indifference of Jaffnese affairs mattered little as long as the British remained in administrative control of the island but once power began to be transferred to the majority community, as happened from 1931 onwards, the gulf in understanding spelt disaster for intercommunal harmony and ultimately threatened the integrity of the unitary state itself.

Before going on to analyse the specific issues of the boycott, some preliminary observations should be made on the prickly and frequently misrepresented subject of caste. Caste is the characteristic of Jaffnese society least understood by those outside the peninsula. This is not to suggest that the Sinhalese politicians were unaware of the political influence of their own caste system. The more deft of Sinhalese political leaders were past masters of caste manipulation in their own constituencies, and at a national level. But even the most percipient were quite unable to grasp the caste system as it prevailed in Jaffna. Its subtleties evaded them.

In the 1930's, caste was the most pronounced feature of Jaffnese society. Its principles, as defined by Dravidian Saivite Hinduism were sufficiently differentiated from those which regulated caste among the Sinhalese, as to render its mechanism within the political process of Jaffna quite enigmatic to outsiders. It was this element of obscurity or political mystification in Jaffna politics which led to the generalised feeling of "unrelatedness" between the Sinhalese and the Jaffna Tamils. In the face of this alienation, which was accompanied as such feelings often are by an undefined sense of apprehension, the Sinhalese leaders adopted a "let sleeping dogs lie" approach to Jaffna's affairs. They gave up any attempt to integrate the peninsula into the central polity. For example, it can be argued that caste was the central issue of the boycott; the Sinhalese politicians were so mesmerised by their stereo-typed ideas of politics in Jaffna, that they failed to realise this, or even to sense the very radical nature of the political forces which had been unleashed in the peninsula. In driving the Jaffna Tamils into the political wilderness, the Sinhalese were not entirely innocent of the charge of having fostered the Hindu-Tamil chauvinist reaction which they purported to be against.

Caste, like other forms of racism, derives its logic and the moral basis of its authority from the assumption that certain groups of people are inherently different in biological as well as moral terms. In the small introverted society of Jaffna, caste differences were mythologically compounded to the point where they were endowed with mystical justification. The ordering of castes and the placing of individuals within the caste hierarchy assumed semi-divine importance.

Much of the homeostatic nature of Jaffnese society can be laid at the feet of the colonial powers. The Portuguese invasion in the 16th century effectively fossilised Jaffnese Hinduism, as it severed the connection between the peninsula and the roots of its culture in the South Indian mainland. The first victim was the Tamil language, which crystalised at that point. It retained its medieval structure until the reforms initiated by Navalar and the American missionaries. Secondly, the caste structure simply hardened into an ossified version of the 15th century. Thus while the caste structure in South India underwent considerable transformation in response to both internal and external pressures, the Jaffna caste system remained virtually static for three hundred years.

On top of this, the peculiar caste structure in Jaffna, with its top heavy layer of *vellala*, preponderant in numbers and wealth, tends to favour conservatism to a greater degree than other structures. The *brahmins* are so few in number that they have been relegated to the role of salaried servants to the *vellala*. Despite a modicum of inter-marriage with *brahmin* and *vaishya* clans, from South India, the *vellala* of Jaffna retained the characteristics of their *kshatriya* origins. They were particularly concerned therefore to maintain their privileges vis à vis all other castes, both in terms of feudal obligation and temple entry for the simple reason that they did not enjoy the ritual honours of the *brahmins*. As a community, the *vellala* were excessively caste conscious, which may explain why the dowry system has persisted as an effective caste sanction to this very day, despite one of the highest literacy rates in the world.

The peculiarities of a Hindu society in a *kshatriya*-dominated ambience are far beyond the scope of this paper, but it can be suggested that the ethos would tend to be more militantly conservative than that of a *brahmin*-controlled society.

Social cultures with a long history have a more pronounced sense of justification than those recently instituted. Not surprisingly therefore, the maintenance of the social and economic structure of Jaffna had become an article of faith among the *vellala* by the 19th and 20th centuries. Navalar, for example, although heralded as a reformer and Ceylon Tamil nationalist, was a strong opponent of any attempt to emancipate the non-*vellala* castes. In this context, the boycott, which was the most important event in the general rebellion of Jaffnese youth in the early thirties, takes on deep significance.

In 1930, there were two organisations representing political opinion in Jaffna. One was the All-Ceylon Tamil League, which was an island-wide umbrella organisation representing the conservative viewpoint. The other was the Jaffna Youth Congress.

The All-Ceylon Tamil League was a body organised and led mainly by the Colombo Tamils, although it loosely incorporated the Jaffna Association as one of its constituent organisations. Ponnambalam Ramanathan, who was the leader of the Ceylon Tamil conservatives for forty years, was a kind of ex-officio president until his death in 1930.

The ACTL's reactionary attitude was reflected in its unashamed opposition to any significant degree of social, economic or constitutional reform. The leaders of the League both inside and outside the Legislative Council had fought the acceptance of the Donoughmore Constitution tooth and nail in the late twenties. Universal franchise had been their particular bugbear. Ramanathan, who entered a pietistic stage at the latter end of his life had likened it to "throwing pearls before swine." From the conservative viewpoint universal franchise was unacceptable. First, it invoked the spectre of socioeconomic changes which threatened to upset the rigid caste structure which had underpinned Ceylon Tamil society for centuries. As *vellala*-caste Hindus, the leaders of the ACTL were perturbed that the system of feudal obligation, which [undergirded] their superiority in terms of economic advantage, educational opportunity and social status . . . , would be endangered. Secondly, the giving of votes to women undermined the dowry system, the key to the continuance of caste. Thirdly, universal franchise ushered in majority rule. Majority rule was [equal to] Sinhalese rule, which to sensitive Dravidians conjured up the prospect of an even less sympathetic administration than that of the British.

The Jaffna Youth Congress, the other body of political opinion in the peninsula, held an almost contrary viewpoint. Like the Colombo Youth League, the Jaffna Youth Congress was much influenced by Gandhi, Nehru, and Bose, and other leaders of the Indian independence movement. They sought to give a mass basis to the Ceylon movement for independence in the same way that Gandhi had done in India. However, whereas the Colombo Youth League remained a mere "radical gadfly" in comparison to other Sinhalese political associations, for six years the Jaffna Youth Congress became a popular vehicle of the aspirations not only for the Ceylon Tamil youth, but the entire peasant population of the Jaffna peninsula.

The leaders of the Jaffna Youth Congress were drawn from the ranks of the large body of middle-class young men turned out by the English medium collegiate school system in the peninsula. One of the distinguishing characteristics of Jaffna is that it had so many first-class collegiate, English schools. In 1930, the Northern Province had the highest literacy rate in English outside Colombo district, as well as one of the highest vernacular literacy rates, with five out of six children of school-going age attending some kind of school. Up to the late twenties, most of this output of English-educated young men had been absorbed by the civil and clerical services of the Federated States

of Malaysia. However, with the policy of Malayanisation and a general re-
trenchment in government services in all parts of the empire, following the
world depression, the possibilities of professional employment outside Jaffna
diminished considerably. The educated young Jaffnese were therefore faced
with a problem of unemployment. Although many of them became teachers
in the collegiate schools, it is important to realise that there were a number
of young educated Tamils with plenty of time on their hands to develop
the natural propensity towards political radicalism, which unemployment
among educated youth tends to create.

The leaders of the Jaffna Youth Congress were much affected by the ideas
put forward by Ramanathan's more brilliant and radical brother Ponnambalam Arunachalam from 1917 to 1921 in his famous series of speeches to the
Ceylon National Congress. In particular, his lecture on "Spiritualising Public Life" set alight a whole generation of young Tamils and Sinhalese with a
burning patriotic fervour. These young Tamils were recruited into politics
through the Tamil Maha Jana Sabhai in the early twenties. Among their ranks
they included S. H. Perinpanayagam, C. Balasingham, M. S. Balasunde, Ram
P. Kandiah, T. N. Subbiah, J. Muttusamy, T. C. Rajaratnam, M. S. Eliatamby
and P. Nagalingam. Dissatisfied with the communalist thinking of the Sabhai, they had formed the Jaffna Youth Congress in 1924.

The hub of the Youth Congress's activities was Jaffna College. The hard
core of its cadres was drawn from there, and J. V. Chelliah, the Vice Principal, was made the first President. A series of resolutions passed at its annual
sessions in 1925 indicates the Jaffna Youth Congress' radical programme:
they called for the abolition of the dowry system; advocated open temple
entry for the *harijans*; an end to [in]equalities based on caste; denounced
communal thinking and advocated full cooperation with the Sinhalese to
bring about early self government; advocated the adoption of national dress
and the use of the vernacular in place of English, and stressed the need for
young men to involve themselves in social service. To this end a Youth Service League was formed to perform social services in the villages.

Most of the ideas of the Jaffna Youth Congress were borrowed from Gandhi and Nehru. This is not surprising in view of the conservatism and communalism of the Tamil leaders after Arunachalam's death. Such a dearth of
imagination and boldness was bound to contrast unfavourably with the Indian independence movement in the eyes of idealistic young men. However,
it was not so much the policies of the Jaffna Youth Congress, as its remarkable, and immediate popularity which was the most surprising factor.

One of the major reasons for this lay in the emotional appeal of the *harijan* movement started by Gandhi in the late 1920's. It must be remembered

that Ramanathan and the "conservatives" took a very reactionary stance over the equal seating issue, and the sight of the *vellala* burning down schools in Jaffna must have made the idealistic young Ceylon Tamil Hindu ashamed of the backward nature of his people vis à vis the Indians. The geographic proximity of the peninsula to India facilitated easy communication between Jaffna and South India. Indian newspapers were widely read in Jaffna, and quite a few students went from the peninsula to study in Madras. They returned fired with enthusiasm by the exploits of the Indian National Congress.

Then, several young notable proponents of *swaraj*, among them Nehru, Satyamurti, Sarojini Naidu and Mrs. Kamaladevi, came to speak at vast concourses organised by the Jaffna Youth Congress between 1926 and 1931, and with their emotional rhetoric and idealistic appeal, they became cult figures for the Jaffnese youth. The Ceylon Tamils had always felt more integrally a part of "Mother India" than the Sinhalese, due to the strength of the race, language, and religion; the identification of the young Ceylon Tamils with their Indian counterparts is therefore understandable, especially at a time of increased political tension and activity.

Another reason for the success of the Jaffna Youth Congress was its superior organisation at grass-roots level. Unlike the Jaffna Association which restricted its membership to the professional and propertied elite in the peninsula, and the Tamil Maha Jana Sabhai, whose leaders were often resident in Colombo or else unwilling to communicate with the Jaffna peasant because of caste or social snobbery, or unable to do so because they lacked knowledge of Tamil, the Jaffna Youth Congress held its meetings in the villages, in the vernacular. The Jaffna Youth Congress leaders dressed in the peasant costume . . . , talked freely with all, regardless of caste or social status, and were willing to enroll any person who wished to join. The Youth Congress members performed social services in the villages, and their continual residence in the peninsula combined with boldness, enthusiasm and almost quixotic idealism, made the Jaffna Youth Congress a very potent force in the Northern Province from 1927 onwards, as signified by the very large numbers that they could mobilise. Over ten thousand attended the Nehru meeting.

Whilst the Tamil leaders in Colombo had been fighting the acceptance of the Donoughmore Constitution, and bickering amongst themselves about causeways, the young men in Jaffna had preempted their mass political basis in the peninsula. When the conservatives finally came round to accepting universal franchise and territorial representation in 1930 and began to prepare to fight elections in the Northern constituencies, they found themselves at the mercy of the Jaffna Youth Congress for the votes of the villagers.

This sudden access of power went to their young heads like old wine. Their attitude and actions became increasingly iconoclastic. In June, 1930, they publicly burned the Union Jack at the King's Birthday celebrations; they ran up a Ceylon flag at the funeral obsequies of Ramanathan in November, 1930; they heckled candidates ferociously at public meetings, and behaved with an "outrageous impropriety and disrespect." Formerly this would have brought down the wrath of the conservative leadership upon their heads. However, in 1930 and 1931, the conservatives had perforce to curry favour with the Youth Congress if they were to win a seat in the State Council. The discomfiture of the "conservative" candidates can be imagined.

The culmination of this heady rise to power was the "Jaffna Boycott." On the 25th April, 1931, just over a week before the election date (May 4), spurred on by the example of the Indian National Congress's recent boycott of the Indian elections, the Jaffna Youth Congress adopted this resolution at a public meeting:

> "This conference holds 'swaraj' to be the inalienable birthright of every people and calls upon the youth of the land to consecrate their lives to the achievement of their country's freedom. Whereas the Donoughmore Constitution militates itself against the attainment of 'Swaraj,' this Congress further pledges itself to boycott the scheme."

It was carried unanimously by the few thousands in attendance. Perhaps no action would have come of this, had not Mrs. Kamaladevi and Sarjojini Naidu been visiting Jaffna at the end of April to publicise the Indian National Congress boycott. The speeches by these two extremely passionate and powerful speakers, especially Mrs. Naidu, whose poetic rhetoric had caused her to be named "the songbird of India," seemed to turn the head of the Jaffna Youth Congress members completely. After the speeches they ran through the streets of Jaffna tearing down Union Jacks and shouting "Swaraj," "Boycott," and so on. Nehru's visit to Jaffna on May 8 further strengthened the resolve of the Youth Congress to show the Indian leader that Jaffna was also capable of direct action.

On May 1st, a significant date, the Youth Congress decided to force the candidates to boycott the elections by seeking a mandate from the villages. The conservatives were thrown into panicky confusion. Two days later, on the eve of polling, led by Duraiswamy and Balasingham, whom the Youth Congress leaders most respected among the "conservatives," they agreed to withdraw their candidatures. The *Ceylon Daily News* noted:

"It was not without some misgiving on the part of one or two of the less adventuresome candidates that this decision to boycott was finally given unanimous ratification."

Youth Congress members hurried to Mannar to ask G. G. Ponnambalam to withdraw from the elections and support the boycott. Characteristically he refused. He records that he thought the whole thing "a whim."

The *Ceylon Daily News* was resounding in its acclaim. "Jaffna, home of virile politics, had exhilarated" an otherwise "soporific performance by candidates in the general election" by "their display of crusading spirit." However, the plaudits of the Lake House Press could not make up for the fact that the boycott left Jaffna in complete political isolation. Not one Sinhalese candidate either joined or sympathized with the boycott, not surprising in view of its suddenness. D. B. Jayatilaka thought the boycott "frivolous" and others were merely confused as to what had taken place and why.

The "peninsularity of mind" which characterises so much of Ceylon Tamil political history was the nemesis of the Jaffna Youth Congress. The boycott which had seemed in the first flush the *pièce de resistance* of the Youth Congress's activities, within a week appeared to be a gross error of judgement. Within two years it had proved to be the *coup de grace* of the hopes of the "progressives" in reforming Ceylon Tamil politics.

The Youth Congress immediately appealed to the Colombo Youth League for support. This was rendered in the form of a resolution by that organisation calling on the Sinhalese to support the Jaffna boycott. However, the Colombo Youth League had a very limited influence in Sinhalese politics. Beyond this gesture there was little they could do. On May 8, at an enormous public meeting organised by the Jaffna Youth Congress addressed by the ex-candidates, a resolution was passed "calling on the people of Ceylon to boycott the State Council and to work for the immediate attainment of Swaraj."

The attitude of the Sinhalese political leadership to the boycott was on the whole one of disappointment and annoyance. The Ceylon National Congress leaders felt particularly piqued as they had made an eloquent plea to the Delimitation Commission early in 1930 to give extra seats to the Northern Tamils. G. E. de Silva and S. W. R. D. Bandaranaike, representing the Ceylon National Congress had said they "were anxious to conserve the present representation in the North and Eastern provinces" and asked for two extra seats for these areas. Even A. E. Goonesinha, by the latter 1930's an avowed Sinhalese communalist, had pointed out "the heart burning of the Tamils owing to their losing a great deal of representation and also their 2:1

proportion. In the interests of the country as a whole they should give more representation to the Northern Province than was necessary in order that there might be a contented people."

Weightage, normally in favour of the rural as opposed to urban population, is a widely-accepted principle in democratic systems generally, but among the Sinhalese, except for the Ceylon National Congress leaders, the suggestion of any kind of electoral concession was immediately thought to be a return to the communal principle of elections. Communal representation, or any diluted electoral mechanism associated with it, was as much a "bogey" to the Sinhalese, as "territorial representation" was to the Tamils. In a booklet published in 1939 the Youth Congress accredited the failure of the Sinhalese to join the boycott to this fear:

> "The Sinhalese were afraid to join the boycott and let slip the opportunity of once and for all abolishing communal representation. They thought if they boycotted, communal representation would not be abolished."

The conservative Tamils had uniformly asked for an allotment of seven seats for the Northern Province, three more than their numbers warranted. In requesting these extra seats H. A. P. Sandrasegera had drawn attention to the "over-representation of the Kandyans" due to the disenfranchisement of the Indian Tamils, as justification for the Tamils' special pleading. He argued:

> "The Tamils as a race were different from the Sinhalese, their habits and customs were entirely different. The Tamils did not want to be submerged."

If they were to be so, "they would prefer to separate from the rest of the island." S. Rajaratnam, part of the deputation from the Jaffna Association led by Duraiswamy, and editor of the influential *Hindu Organ*, maintained that it "was essential that there should be at least one Tamil in each of the seven State Council committees in order that Tamil interest could be safeguarded."

The Jaffna Youth Congress disapproved of this "communalist thinking"; they suspected that much of the agitation for seats stemmed from "self-interested politicians" who were trying to carve out electorates for themselves. One Youth Leaguer wrote to the *Morning Star* about the evidence of the Jaffna leaders to the Delimitation Commission, complaining that the "Jaffna Association was in a moribund state," with a membership composed only of "the turbanned heads who represent only the aristocracy of Jaffna, who go about echoing and re-echoing with redoubled force the sentiments of the uneducated populace concerning communalism in the constitution."

Despite the strong case put forward by the Ceylon National Congress and the Tamils, the Delimitation Commission refused to agree to any requests for special concessions, but carried out its terms strictly according to the letter. The constituencies were carved out on a uniform basis of 100,000 population. G. G. Ponnambalam cited the "artificial uniformity" of this delimitation in 1939 as one of the main grievances of the Tamil community. He claimed that this uniformity, based on population figures rather than the number of electors lacked "sufficient flexibility, quite apart from the communal considerations of the question." He spoke from personal experience. In 1931 he fought the Mannar-Mullaitivu electorate which was then the largest in the island, covering hundreds of square miles. Although some justification can be claimed for the Commissioners' rigidity in fixing the electoral boundaries, as they had to face many conflicting claims for partiality to this or that interest, when they were finding it difficult merely to ascertain the correct population figures, there is no doubt that it caused unnecessary grievances. Unfortunately, the number of seats in the State Council was reduced from sixty-five to fifty by the Colonial Office, which necessarily made the fixing of boundaries and the awarding of seats more restrictive. G. E. de Silva, for one, blamed much of the communal tension of the 1930's on this reduction from the original suggestion of the Donoughmore Commission.

The call on 8th May, 1931, from the Jaffna leaders to the "people of Ceylon to boycott the State Council and to work for the immediate attainment of Swaraj" went for the most part unheeded. The Colombo Youth League responded with a resolution of support for the boycott, proposed by T. B. Jayah and Valentino and Aelian Perera. Later a written request asking for support was sent to some of the Sinhalese leaders recently elected to the State Council, including D. B. Jayatilaka, D. S. Senanayake, S. W. R. D. Bandaranaike, Francis de Zoysa and E. W. Perera. Some of these

> "telegraphed to W. Duraiswamy that there was a strong feeling that a signed statement from the Jaffna leaders should be submitted supporting the demand for a Constitution granting Responsible Government based on adult suffrage without any form of communal representation."

This was deemed necessary in view of the fact that "allegations had been persistently made that Jaffna was still devising means of getting the question of representation re-opened." A number of the Ceylon Tamil leaders did actually sign such a document, (though the good faith of some of those who did so was questionable) and this statement was circularised in the south of Ceylon.

However, by the June of 1931 it was obvious that the boycott was a lost cause as far as the elected members were concerned. The Jaffna Tamils were, in the words of S. W. R. D. Bandaranaike "in the cold bleak desert of boycott." The Sinhalese leaders were unwilling to jeopardise the, as yet untried, Donoughmore Constitution and forfeit the opportunity for internal self-government merely to save the faces of the Ceylon Tamil leaders. Moreover even the three Ceylon Tamil members not involved in the boycott, Dr. R. Saravanamuttu returned for Colombo North, M. M. Subramaniam for Trincomalee-Batticaloa, and S. M. Ananthan for Mannar, and the two Indian Tamil members, Peri Sunderam for Hatton and S. P. Vytilingam for Talawakelle, disclaimed support for the Jaffna Tamils' boycott. Thus the First State Council opened on July 7, 1931 with much pomp and ceremony, but without any of the established Ceylon Tamil political leaders. As the Governor said at the opening of parliament:

> "I greatly regret that the Northern peninsula is unrepresented. I fear it is mainly due to hot-headed misrepresentations of the scope and spirit of the new constitution by those who should have known better. It is a loss to this Council that this important section of the island should remain entirely without representation. As soon as I am fully convinced of a genuine desire on the part of the majority of the people in the peninsula for representation in Council, I shall fix a nomination day."

In later years the Youth Congress leaders were to admit that they had acted precipitantly in 1931: "The country ought to have been more politically educated and organised on a mass basis before such direct action was attempted," but up to 1934 they continued to maintain that, the boycott had been fully justified "as a means of protest and creating public sentiment against the Donoughmore Constitution." However, the Jaffna middle class reacted with extreme indignation after the initial shock of finding themselves politically isolated. In an editorial published in 1932 the *Morning Star* bemoaned that "what was built up in a century has been destroyed in a year." The *Hindu Organ* later commented: "The Youth Congress are not the men to save the Tamils. The plain truth is that the great majority of Tamils feel sore over what has happened. They tried to emulate the boycott of the Indian National Congress. It was a sudden rush of blood, a misplaced sense of pride. Like the old proverb—'Because the peacock danced, the turkey cock tried too!'"

PART TWO—Aftermath

"This country is full of self-sacrificing people who are ready to render self-sacrificing services within the walls of this Chamber so that those who are in the cold, bleak desert of boycott feel themselves very helpless. A boycott was even tried in India by that enormously powerful body, the Indian National Congress. I venture to think that that boycott was not successful."—S. W. R. D. Bandaranaike

After the excitement of the "dance of the turkey cock," the Jaffna Youth Congress found that the desert of boycott was cold and bleak indeed. In an attempt to provide themselves with a more national and less youth-oriented image they formed the Northern Province National Association in March 1931, whose aim was "to replace the Ceylon National Congress as a national Ceylon body." This organisation failed to materialise into anything more than its founder members and late in 1932 the Youth Congress leaders decided to cooperate with the Liberal League, itself a valetudinarian body. This proved to be only a brief flirtation as the income tax issue soon separated the Founder-President, Francis de Zoysa, a free trader, from the other members. By the end of 1933 this attempt to forge a progressive Sinhalese-Tamil political party had foundered.

The revivification of the Liberal League was significant, however, for two reasons: first, because for a short time in 1932 it numbered both G. G. Ponnambalam and S. W. R. D. Bandaranaike among its members, and secondly, for the conference which was organised under its auspices in April 1933 in Jaffna.

The conference held in Jaffna on April 27, 1933, attracted a large number of the Jaffnese youth. The president of the Youth Congress, C. Balasingham, was carried on a *pandal* in procession to the meeting and he made a fiery speech attacking communal safeguards and calling upon youth "to identify itself with the independence movement." The Sinhalese were represented by Francis de Zoysa, S. W. Dassanaike and S. W. R. D. Bandaranaike, and the Tamils by the ever mercurial H. A. P. Sandrasegera, and V. Coomaraswamy, the first Ceylon Tamil Government Agent.

In January 1933, a "Conference of Tamils" was formed to oust the Youth Congress dominance and the anti-boycott campaign was formally initiated. Kanagasabhai, Mahadeva, and Sri Pathmanathan joined Ponnambalam and the anti-boycotters then to set about trying to secure a nomination day for a re-election in the Northern constituencies.

Throughout 1933, the peninsula was the scene of incidents of violence, as boycotters and anti-boycotters clashed in demonstrations and at public meetings. At the Liberal League-Jaffna Youth Congress conference in April, Balasingham's *pandal* was set on fire by anti-boycotters who tried to break up the meeting. The bitterness engendered in this year makes it a "time of troubles" in Ceylon Tamil political history. In the process, the ideals and policies of the Jaffna Youth Congress were so discredited as to be finally extirpated from the mainstream of Ceylon Tamil politics. By mid-1934, the Youth Congress "had ceased to command any influence" in the peninsula. The progressives had been successfully ousted by the conservatives. The idea of Lankan nationalism was almost completely effaced by Tamil communalism within a few months, and with it the attempt to reform Saivism. The *harijan* movement was relegated to occasional platitudes uttered from election platforms. Even the North Ceylon National League, a Catholic, non-*vellala* political organisation, which had fully supported the Youth Congress in 1931, said in 1936: "The Tamils in Jaffna have already had cause to regret the boycotting of the Council and trying to create a Ceylonese nation."

By the beginning of 1934, the Youth Congress leaders were disillusioned and on the defensive. Balasingham expressed this disillusionment when he noted the undermining of "the whole spirit of the boycott" by the "communal tinge" which certain people had sought to give to it. In justification for the boycott, which they now had to admit was a failure, they argued that it had "brought a political consciousness to the people" and asked, "Is not the change of attitude of our people towards one of the greatest evils of Tamil society, the caste system, due to the influence of Congress?"

In fact, there had been no such radical "change of attitude" among the Ceylon Tamils. Temple entry for *harijans* was attempted at only one temple and then abandoned in the face of rigid *vellala* hostility. "The bigoted mentality of the Jaffna man," as one Colombo Tamil correspondent to the *Ceylon Daily News* described it, had proved stronger than the whiff of Gandhian idealism propounded by the ardent but politically jejune young Tamils. As Governor Stanley had noted: "It is not easy to persuade the Tamils of Jaffna to adopt new methods. They liked the methods of their ancestors." In the splendid isolation of the peninsula, the *vellala* felt secure in their numerical predominance, and without their active cooperation any effective social transformation proved impossible.

The claim of the Youth Congress to have raised the political consciousness of the people seems, in retrospect, to have been grossly exaggerated. First, the turn-out in the 1934 and 1936 elections in the Northern Province was less than 50%, 10% lower than the national average in the 1931 elections. Only the Catholic segment of the non-*vellala* appears to have been sufficiently organised to have had any electoral influence. Moreover, the Youth

Congress and relevant Youth Congress candidates who fought in the 1936 and 1947 elections lost their deposits.

It is true that a number of non-*vellala* caste organisations were founded in the 1930's, the most significant being the Depressed Tamil Service League started by N. Selvadurai, Dr. Paul Crossett, and J. Hensman in 1929 with the active cooperation of the Youth Congress. This body performed useful work in encouraging education of the non-*vellala*, providing funds for schools, libraries, and so on. In 1930 and 1934 two labour organisations were begun: the North Ceylon Workmen's Union and the North Ceylon Vehicleman's Union. However, the most efficiently organised and consequently most influential body was the Jaffna Diocesan Union, a political association of the Catholic non-*vellala* in Jaffna town. Together with the North Ceylon National League, a larger Catholic political body, the Catholic minority in the peninsula was able to exert considerable electoral influence, and they performed the role of a small but highly mobilised pressure group. Other than this, the Central Free Library Association, begun by a Catholic, but aided by all sections of Jaffna society including the Youth Congress, organised the Jaffna Municipal Library in the early 1930's and encouraged the founding of libraries in the villages.

Oddly enough, the one major improvement for the poorer classes came with the eclipse of the temperance movement in the late 1920's in the Northern Province. The concomitant reorganisation of the toddy-tapping industry via the tree-tax system helped the lower castes economically and in other ways. Toddy, a rich dietary source of Vitamin B, was the "food of the poorer section of the people"; the prevalence of the toddy drinking habit in the Northern Province and Eastern Province was ascribed to be a major reason for the fact that those areas escaped the human devastation caused by the severe outbreak of malaria in Ceylon in 1934. To what extent the Youth Congress was responsible for the latter, and the extent to which they contributed to the non-*vellala* organisations remains unclear in the absence of documentation. Generally, it would seem that the Congress claim was overrated. With the advent of universal franchise and the governmental pressure regarding equal seating, there was certain to be some kind of interest taken in the politicisation of the Ceylon Tamil masses. Moreover, some diffusion of Gandhian ideas, considering the proximity of the Indian subcontinent, could hardly have been prevented.

The major significance of the Youth Congress lies in the fact that at its zenith in 1931 it was able to mobilise such huge numbers of people, a feat which remained unequalled in the succeeding two decades. Whether this is a sufficient justification for the boycott is a disputable point, but because of this, the Jaffna Youth Congress occupies an important place in Ceylon Tamil political history, and makes it worthy of further inquiry.

The Jaffna boycott is a unique political event in the history of 20th-century Ceylon. As a tactic, it was without precedent, and never repeated. It has therefore remained a largely unexplained, and often discounted, phenomenon which protrudes uncomfortably into the history of the last phase of colonial rule. This is not to say that the boycott was an "aberration" from the norm. Rather, it appears to be an extreme manifestation of the Indophilia which was prevalent among young Ceylonese, both Sinhalese and Tamils, from the first decade of the 20th century.

In 1915, A. E. Goonesinha, later leader of the Labour Party, founded the Young Lanka League. This organisation was the precursor of the Jaffna Youth Congress, the Colombo Youth League and other youth leagues. Largely, although not wholly, Sinhalese in composition, (there were a number of Colombo-based Tamil and Muslim members) it "proclaimed as its model the more radical aspects of the Indian nationalist movement" and the members "lost no opportunity of contrasting against these the overwhelming conservatism of the 'constitutionalist' leadership and their lack of idealism."

In 1918, Ponnambalam Arunachalam tentatively mooted the federation of Ceylon and India in order to facilitate the independence movement in Ceylon, and in 1920 he called for a boycott of the Constitution. The Sinhalese "constitutionalist" leaders regarded both these propositions with severe disapprobation and promptly disassociated themselves from what they regarded as the "disloyal" and revolutionary policies and tactics of the Indian National Congress.

It was Arunachalam, however, rather than his "conservative" brother Ramanathan or the Sinhalese elder statesmen H. J. C. Pereira or James Pieris, who inspired the rising generation of young Ceylonese, and particularly the Jaffna Youth Congress. Professor C. Suntheralingam, who returned to Ceylon to enter the Ceylon Civil Service and then became a teacher at Ananda College in 1922, says of this period:

> "At that time in Ceylon, there was not a single Secondary School worthy of its name which had a Ceylonese Principal. Even large estates which belonged to Ceylonese were being administered by European Agency Houses; and yet Ceylonese leaders, who were agitating for the return of the legislature and Executive Council, were pressing for more Representative Government for Ceylon. A senior English Civil Servant wag had contemptuously said: 'Give the Ceylonese the self Government they want and they will hand it over to Carson and Company.'"

The disillusionment of young Ceylonese, both Sinhalese and Tamils, with the Ceylon reform movement and its leaders was widespread.

In the 1920's and early 1930's, many Sinhalese students studying abroad were much influenced by the Indian movement. In London, for example, through Palme Dutt, an Indian who was a senior member of the British Communist Party, and Krishna Menon, an Indian socialist who was teaching in London, Leslie Goonewardene, Philip Gunewardene, and Dr. S. A. Wickremasinghe among others, came into contact with the Indian movement. Many of them became involved with the India League in London. Dr. Wickremasinghe, for example, joined Gandhi on one of his "salt marches." Bernard Aluwihare, leaving Oxford in 1930, went to India to join the Nationalist movement there and was imprisoned for his activities in 1931. S. W. R. D. Bandaranaike borrowed freely from Gandhi's ideas for his book *Spinning Wheel and Paddy Field*.

> "The eyes of the whole world are turned today on Mahatma Gandhi, and a new hope is springing up in the hearts of jaded men that perhaps this naked fakir has a message for this sick and weary world. . . . It seems worthwhile at a time when an ever increasing number in our own country are beginning to turn eyes of hope on this wooden wheel (Charka) and all that it is supposed to represent, to consider from our own point of view all the far-reaching implications that this movement does and may involve."

Bandaranaike was one of the several Sinhalese political leaders, G. E. de Silva being another, who attended some of the annual conferences of the Indian National Congress. E. A. P. Wijeyaratne drew attention to this in the State Council in 1933:

> "There is a feeling of restlessness among the younger minds. They naturally turn to the struggle going on in India in the hope and belief that by joining forces with those undaunted millions, we may be able to get back the political and economic independence which India is struggling to gain."

In view of the proximity of Ceylon to the sub-continent, it is hardly surprising if the Ceylon youth identified with the Indian independence movement, because the political future of Ceylon depended so much upon the result of that struggle. In 1918 Ponnambalam Arunachalam had bemoaned the fact that Ceylon should be administered by the Colonial Office, and not the India Office, as the latter had shown, by the Montagu-Chelmsford reforms, a far greater willingness to grant reform concessions. The Indian reforms became the "sheet anchor of political aspirations in Ceylon."

By 1931, however, the situation was reversed, and it was India which lagged behind Ceylon in terms of constitutional reform. The Donoughmore Constitution, with its provisions for universal franchise and "7/10ths swaraj" or internal self-government, was one of the most progressive of all the colonial constitutions, and out-stripped the Indian constitution considerably. The English and European newspapers acknowledged that in some ways the Donoughmore Constitution was a "test-case," the outcome of which would seriously affect the future of India and other parts of the Empire. In 1930, *The Spectator* said: "The working of this constitution will be followed with intense interest by every student of democratic method." The *Echo de Paris* pointed out that "Universal suffrage is an innovation without precedent in the Empire and will have consequences far beyond the Island."

The die-hard imperialists in Britain: Rothermere, Churchill, Page-Croft, Lloyd, et al., seeing in the Donoughmore Constitution a dangerous precedent for the granting of independence or quasi-independence to India, began a vitriolic smear campaign against the Ceylonese, and the Donoughmore Constitution. *The Patriot,* an extreme right-wing newspaper, called the constitution "a disastrous blunder, based on a bi-sexual [sic] mob electorate." It is interesting to note that Ramanathan expressed identical sentiments, though far less crudely phrased. It was no wonder, therefore, that the young Jaffnese should turn away from leaders whose views coincided with those of the most jingoistic imperialists in Britain, to seek inspiration from the Indian leaders.

The campaign carried on by Churchill in Parliament, and by Rothermere through his press and publishing houses, made the younger Ceylonese highly conscious of the fact that the eyes of Britain were scrutinising the political activities in the island. It also underlined the fact that the fates of Ceylon and India were indissolubly linked. In 1933, S. W. R. D. Bandaranaike made a scathing indictment of two Rothermere publications, *Britain's Folly* by J. G. Wall, and *Ceylon—A Mistake,* by B. Muirhead:

> "If the Donoughmore Constitution has done nothing else, it has at least succeeded in helping a few unknown British scribblers to emerge painfully and laboriously into the limelight. Scarcely had we time to forget the extraordinary literary efforts of Mr. Muirhead than we are afflicted with a no less remarkable effusion by a gentleman called J. G. Wall. This is a book of which I can say that only the cover is more illuminating than the contents. Sprawling insolently across the cover is The Rt. Hon. the Viscount Rothemere who we are told says in a foreword, 'Self government has been going on for two years in Ceylon. It is a complete and manifest failure. Let those who are pressing for a grant of Dominion Status to

India read this and then ask themselves, is it worth the risk?' The purpose of this book is quite plain. This is another discreditable effort to make use of the Ceylon Constitution as a stick with which to beat India."

There is, however, a striking contrast between the political attitudes and subsequent careers of the Sinhalese activists who were influenced by the Indian national movement and those of the Jaffna Youth Congress. The Sinhalese youth, unlike the young Tamils, never seemed to lose sight of the fact that at root the political situation in India, and the temperament of the Indian people, were radically different from the Ceylon situation and the Ceylonese temperament. The whole political ethos was dissimilar in the two countries. A. M. Nathaniel, a Ceylon Tamil journalist and teacher at Jaffna College, and a strong anti-boycotter, delineated this dissimilarity in striking if exaggerated terms:

> "Ceylon was constituted as a Crown Colony, and treated like an adopted child: coddled, cozened and coaxed, whereas India, was treated as a troublesome giant: calumnied, cribbed and confined. A child mentality was willingly produced in one; a slave mentality unwillingly forced on the other."

Compared to the Indian movement, the Ceylon Independence movement in the 1920's and 1930's appears staid and dull, even phlegmatic. But the aims and methods pertinent to India were quite inconsonant in Ceylon. The Sinhalese thoroughly appreciated this fact, and however much they were influenced by the Indian movement, even the most radical of them did not try to apply successful Indian tactics in Ceylon. It is true that Bandaranaike tried to set up a charka-cloth spinning factory in Veyangoda, but the project was soon abandoned. When he called for "non-cooperation" with the British in March 1932, he knew it to be an idle threat; it was neither possible nor necessary to implement that tactic in Ceylon. Dr. Wickremasinghe managed to work fairly happily within the framework of the Donoughmore Constitution in the First State Council, and N. M. Perera and Philip Gunawardene adapted their socialist ideas to fit the prevailing ethos of the Second State Council. The Independence Movement in Ceylon was firmly rooted in realpolitik, and the Sinhalese young men who returned fired with enthusiasm for the Indian movement quickly adjusted their views to suit the pragmatic nature of politics in the island.

The Jaffna Youth Congress leaders, on the other hand, tended to equate, if not confuse, the Indian Independence Movement with that in Ceylon. Obviously as Hindus they found the *harijan* movement especially pertinent to the Jaffna situation at that time. Moreover, their linguistic and cultural fellowship with South India reinforced their sense of identification with India and Indians. Thus the boycotters referred frequently to "Mother India," expressing a feeling of affiliation and apparentation which no Sinhalese Buddhist would have been willing to acknowledge so overtly.

It so happened that when the Jaffnese youth began to search for their cultural roots in order to articulate a growing sense of nationalism, which was in itself the same natural reaction felt by young Sinhalese towards a discredited colonial regime, they were led away from the "Ceylonese" or "Lankan" nationalism for which they had originally been questing and instead were drawn towards India as the source of Tamil culture. However, they themselves did not realise the significance of this. Enamoured as they were with the nationalist movement in India, in their blindness they misunderstood the nature of the political movement south of the peninsula. So dazzled were they by an unbounded enthusiasm for India, they did not realise that this enthusiasm was not shared to the same extent by the Sinhalese or even by the other Ceylon Tamils. It is significant, for example, that G. G. Ponnambalam should have likened himself to Jinnah in the late 1930's and identified the problem of the Ceylon Tamil community with that of the Muslims, not the Hindus, in India.

The relative geographical isolation of the peninsula reinforced this Indomania insofar as it hindered communication between the youth movements of the Sinhalese and the Jaffna Youth Congress in Jaffna. The peninsula thus acted as a kind of incubator which enabled exotic political ideas to grow to fruition. The fruit was the Jaffna boycott.

The greatest mistake committed by the Jaffna Youth Congress leaders was not the boycott itself as such, as their inability to learn from its failure. Instead of modifying their views to fit the political realities in Ceylon, the Jaffna Youth Congress leaders continued with the same policies, long after the boycott had failed to evoke material support, or even understanding, from any quarter. Even Nehru's stern condemnation in his speech in Jaffna the day after the boycott had no effect upon the leaders. Moreover, their continual harassment of the anti-boycott movement prevented the granting of an early date for re-elections by the colonial government. They used their considerable influence among the villagers in the peninsula, who were ill-informed about events outside the Northern Province, to urge a continuance of the boycott long after it had come to be thoroughly discredited among almost all the educated, and politically observant, Ceylon Tamils. By doing so the Jaffna Youth Congress leaders perpetrated the "Himalayan folly" of keeping the Ceylon Tamil leaders out of the first half of the State Council.

Secondly, by refusing to compromise in any way upon their demand for "immediate *swaraj* only" they denied the possibility of forming a viable political organisation with people of a progressive outlook among the Sinhalese and other communities. Instead they insisted on remaining "loyal to the principles of the boycott" and maintaining an attitude of pristine rectitude and moral superiority towards politics in Jaffna and Ceylon as a whole. In 1934, for example they held completely aloof from the elections except for interjections to the newspapers and at meetings concerning "the corruption of the villagers by the turpitude of the candidates." Such sentiments are very noble but the practice of politics demands something more than the mere condemnation of its processes from idealists who are frightened of "dirtying their hands." Ultimately it meant the demise of the Jaffna Youth Congress and with it the collapse of the organised forces for much needed social reform in the peninsula. It also denied the ordinary voter in the North the right to some form of organised opposition to G. G. Ponnambalam and his supporters. By the time the Jaffna Youth Congress leaders deigned to fight elections in their own right, they had completely forfeited their former avenues of support, and both Balasingham and Peripanayagam lost their deposits in 1947.

As the Jaffna Youth Congress became more and more disillusioned with what they viewed as the opportunism in Ceylon politics, they leant increasingly towards the Indian movement, which they felt to be the fount of purity and idealism in politics. In February, 1933, they called for "puma swaraj," which included the adoption of the vernaculars as the only medium of instruction, and they advocated the federation of Ceylon and "the mother country." The proceedings of the so-called "Tamil Nadu" conference of the Jaffna Youth Congress in October, 1933, the last large gathering of young Jaffnese, represented the culmination of this Indomania. Leading South Indian politicians came to speak at the conference and several portraits of Indian National Congress leaders were unveiled. Except for an homage to the Bo tree, and a plea for the colonisation of the Wanni by Ceylon Tamils, the conference might just as well have been conducted in South India.

In fact by this time, the Jaffna Youth Congress had lost touch with political reality in Ceylon. It was now anticipating the Ceylon Tamil separatist movement, which was to crystalise two decades later. By adopting an "Indian view" about politics, the Jaffna Youth Congress necessarily abdicated from any responsibility for the political future of the Jaffna peninsula and the Ceylon Tamils as a community.

Language and the Rise of Tamil Separatism in Sri Lanka

Robert N. Kearney

Perhaps no other issue has angered and alienated the Tamil minority more than the establishment of Sinhala as the official language of Sri Lanka and the concomitant restricted use of Tamil in official government transactions. At a minimum, the issue has been a catalyst for the aspiration of an independent Tamil homeland. The history of this grievance parallels the history of Tamil grievances in general, though the exclusive status of Sinhala is no longer Sri Lankan law.[1]

Language has served as a focus for political conflict between the major ethnic groups of Sri Lanka for a quarter of a century. At stake are advantages in securing employment (particularly much desired government employment), convenience in dealing with public agencies, and symbolic and status satisfactions. The conflict over language is a part of a more deep-seated clash of ethnic identifications based not only on language but on religion, ancestral territory, memories of a unique collective history, and a wide range of cultural attributes. Ethnic identifications are very strong in Sri Lanka. Every permanent inhabitant belongs to one and only one of the ethnic compartments into which the population is divided. The ethnic communities are referred to in official documents such as census reports as "races," which is technically inaccurate but suggests the depth of the differentiation and the sharpness of the perceived distinction between communities (a point we will return to later).

The Ethnic Groups and the Nature of Ethnic Identity. . . . The Sinhala population is divisible into Kandyan and Low-Country branches, a distinction originating in the differential impact of modernization and westernization in the low-country coastal areas and in the Kandyan hill country of the interior. The differentiation, however, is of rapidly declining significance. . . . Members of the Sinhala community are principally Buddhists and speak the Sinhala language, an Indo-European language brought to the island by migrants from North India about 2,500 years ago. [According to the Department of Census and Statistics in 1971, 72% of the population was Sinhala.]

The principal contestant in socio-political conflict with the Sinhala majority (and the group on which the latter part of this paper focuses) is the Ceylon Tamil minority [11.2% of the population]. The Ceylon Tamils, descendants of settlers who arrived from South India a thousand or more years ago, are predominantly Hindus and speak the Tamil language, one of the principal Dravidian languages of South India. The Ceylon Tamil community is concentrated at the far north of the island, on and near the Jaffna Peninsula, and along the east coast.

A second Tamil-speaking Hindu community, the Indian Tamils [9.3% of the population], are migrants or the descendants of migrants who have been coming from South India since the mid-nineteenth century, principally for employment as laborers on the tea and rubber estates. Most Indian Tamils live in the estate areas of the interior hill country. A majority of them are not citizens of Sri Lanka. Under agreements between India and Sri Lanka in 1964 and 1974, about three-fifths of the community [were] scheduled to depart the island for India by 1979, while the remainder are to receive Lankan citizenship.

Another minority community is composed of Ceylon Moors [6.5% of the population], a name given to the island's Muslims by the Portuguese in the sixteenth century. The Moors, of Arabic and Indian Muslim descent, live on the east coast interspersed among Ceylon Tamils, in small pockets on the west coast and around Kandy, and are also scattered across the island.

For most Ceylon Moors, the language of the home has been Tamil, although there is a marked tendency today for Moors living in the Sinhala-speaking areas to adopt Sinhala as their declared first language and to educate their children in that language (this is one example of a tendency toward a shift to Sinhala by linguistically marginal groups). Other ethnic communities consist of Indian Moors [0.2%], Malays [0.3%], and Burghers [0.4%], the latter being of Portuguese, Dutch or, more commonly, of mixed European and Lankan ancestry. In modern times, English has been the language of the home for most Burghers.

. . . Despite the existence of bilingualism and trilingualism, four-fifths of the population [speak] only one language. Among monolinguals, the ratio of Sinhala-to-Tamil speakers [is] slightly under three to one. Unfortunately, recent censuses have not reported comparable data on language.

Paul Brass, in a study of North India, has argued that, in a particular historical and social context, one ethnic trait or symbol may be identified as dominant and others as secondary. In North India, religion became the dominant symbol, while the language spoken and the script in which the language was written became secondary symbols. Political pressures developed to bring the secondary ethnic symbols into congruence with the dominant symbol. Thus, in North India, Hindus have increasingly adopted Hindi and the Devanagari script; Muslims, Urdu and the Persian script; and Sikhs, Punjabi and the Gurumukhi script.[2] It may be possible to describe a similar phenomenon in Sri Lanka, with language as the dominant symbol and other ethnic traits, including religion, as secondary symbols, which have tended toward congruence with the dominant one. Sinhala families that had been Christian for several generations have returned to Buddhism. European personal names, which had become popular even in the villages and among the working class, have been dropped in favor of Sinhala names. Even in the cosmopolitan urban upper classes, children are increasingly given indigenous rather than European names.

It might be more accurate in the case of Lanka, however, to postulate an ethnic identity based on a sense of "race" or "species" existing independently of any of the specific ethnic traits by which the identity is presumably defined. Ethnic groups in Lanka appear to be separated by such a sense of quasi-racial or quasi-species cleavage, overarching even the language cleavage. Sixty-five years ago, E. B. Denham observed in reporting on the 1911 census:

> "In spite of the closest political connection, the two races [Sinhala and Tamil] are as distinct to-day in Ceylon as the limits of their settlements are clearly defined. Though Tamils described themselves in the Census schedule as Buddhists, and Sinhalese entered Tamil as the only language they could read and write, it is inconceivable that any Sinhalese would enter himself as a Tamil, or a Tamil as a Sinhalese."[3]

The ethnographer's insistence that the differences between communities are essentially cultural rather than physical or racial does not seem to dampen the popular belief in totally separate ancestry and genetic makeup. In Sinhala, the word *jatiya* (an obvious cognate of the North Indian word *jati*), which carries connotations of a physical type or species, is often employed to refer to the type of group we are calling an ethnic community, as is the word *vargaya*, which also suggests kind, type, or species.[4]

In suggesting a tendency toward congruence of ethnic traits with a dominant quasi-racial, quasi-species identification, I have in mind not only the small cluster of traditionally Tamil-speaking Sinhala fishermen north of Colombo, who are educating their children in Sinhala and apparently abandoning Tamil, but also the members of the higher social strata who in the pre-independence generation did not bother to learn to read and write Sinhala (or Tamil), who regularly if not exclusively spoke in English with members of the family, and who employed spoken Sinhala (or Tamil) only in dealing with menials, servants, and others of lowly social status. Persons in these strata today, although English remains their first language, can read and write Sinhala or Tamil, increasingly speak to their children in one of those languages, and generally are educating their children in the Sinhala or Tamil medium.[5]

The ethnic situation in Lanka historically has been much less complex and ambiguous than in North India. The two principal indigenous communities, the Sinhala and Ceylon Tamil, have traditionally been differentiated by language and script, religion, social organization, territorial concentration, and sense of collective history. Aside from a few unusual instances of marginality or ambiguity (such as the Tamil-speaking Sinhala fishermen or usage of the Tamil language in the pre-nineteenth-century court of the Sinhala Kandyan Kingdom), seldom were the wide range of ethnic attributes not congruent within each of the two communities until the coming of Western colonial rule. The disruption of ethnic symmetry came from the introduction of the Christian religion and the English language, which were adopted by persons of both communities, but not necessarily by the same individuals. That is, a Christian might speak only Sinhala or Tamil, while one literate only in English might be a Buddhist or a Hindu.

Because of the exogenous nature of Christianity and the English language, adoption of one or both presumably did not necessitate abandonment (at least not totally) of the Sinhala or Tamil identity, and certainly did not confuse those two identities. With the growing force of nationalist sentiment, following on rapid social mobilization and accelerated by the demise of colonial rule, persons who had adopted English, Christianity, or a host of other European ethnic traits could easily retreat into the still remembered Sinhala or Tamil identity, despite the absence of any or perhaps all the specific symbols by which those identities were supposedly defined. Recent ethnic conflict has not infrequently pitted English-speaking, sometimes Christian or formerly Christian Sinhala politicians against English-speaking, often Christian Tamil politicians. Furthermore, when pressure for congruity developed, there was no ambiguity about the direction in which the congruity should be sought. The model for the Sinhala community was the Sinhala-speaking Buddhist. Although less sharply focused, the model for the Ceylon Tamil community tended to be the Tamil-speaking Hindu.

The Official Language Conflict. The stage was set for a communal confrontation over language by the combination of two circumstances—the unique position held by the English language, which provided those educated in that language with a tremendous occupational advantage and high social status, and the existence in Lanka of more than one indigenous language. Under British colonial rule, extending from the end of the eighteenth century until 1948, English had become the language of government, the professions, modern commerce, higher education, and, until well into the 1930s, even of politics. In 1953, an astounding 9.4% of the population five years of age and over (12.5% of males and 6.1% of females) were literate in English.[6] However, modernization and social mobilization had kindled aspirations for nontraditional employment, political participation, and improved mobility opportunities for the vast majority of the island's population that did not have access to English-language education. In the same census year, 68.1% of the Sinhala population were literate in Sinhala, 54.9% of the Ceylon and Indian Tamil populations were literate in Tamil (unfortunately, the two communities were not differentiated; the literacy rate is considerably higher among the Ceylon Tamils than among the Indian Tamils), and 52.2% of the Ceylon and Indian Moor populations were literate in Tamil.[7]

A "swabhasha" (or "own language") movement prior to independence had led to a decision that English was gradually to be displaced as the official language of the nation by both Sinhala and Tamil. Shortly after independence, however, a national resurgence among the Sinhala people, with roots extending back to the late nineteenth century, burst into the political arena. The demand among the majority community turned from "swabhasha" to "Sinhala only" as the official language. The official language controversy shifted from an attack on the privileged position of the English-educated multi-communal elite to a clash between ethnic communities. In 1956, following an election which for the first time since independence saw an incumbent government defeated at the polls and replaced in power by a group of opposition politicians, Sinhala was declared to be the sole official language.

Political conflict surrounding the official language issue tended to become the most intense of several intertwining lines of contention between majority and minority communities. The issue contained both material and symbolic dimensions. If Sinhala were the language of governmental administration, the courts, and, for the most part, higher education, persons whose mother tongue was Sinhala would have an advantage in entering and advancing in the most desired careers. One Sinhala complaint was that under colonial rule disproportionate numbers of Tamils had entered the government service, particularly in the administrative and professional grades, assisted by the early availability of education in the English language in the Tamil-speaking North. The Sinhala-only demand was propelled, in part, by the desire to correct and compensate for the (often grossly exaggerated) communal inbalance in government employment during the colonial eras.[8]

Following the transition from English to Sinhala as the language of government, Tamils complained bitterly not only of discrimination in public employment, but of inconveniences and difficulties created by receiving forms and correspondence from government agencies in Sinhala, which they could not read. Consequently, they were forced to go to other persons for assistance in deciphering the message, often concerning matters of a personal nature such as income taxes or inheritances. Tamil citizens . . . argued that, due to the Sinhala-only policy, they [were] treated as aliens in their own land.

Beyond the practical considerations of employment and communication with government agencies, the question of the official language vibrated with emotional and symbolic overtones. Language was central to the self-identification of both Sinhala and Tamil communities. In the entire world, Sinhala [was] spoken only by some nine million persons in Lanka. It was argued that, if not bolstered by becoming the sole official language, Sinhala would be in danger of atrophying and eventually disappearing as a living language. For the Sinhala people, the Sinhala-only demand reflected their aspirations to retrieve their cultural heritage, which they felt was endangered by the incursions of the West, and to reassert their position and prerogatives as the majority of the island's population. To the Tamils, the language dispute epitomized the dangers of political domination by the Sinhala majority, which could lead to the undermining of Tamil language and culture in Lanka and the eventual extermination of the Ceylon Tamil community as a distinctive and unique ethnic entity. As one Tamil member of parliament explained: "We speak often and repeatedly about language because that is so fundamental to us. Language today is the basis of our culture and our nationality."[9]

Another issue that enflamed relations between communities involved the government-sponsored movement of persons from the densely populated Southwest to the sparsely populated north-central and eastern "dry zone." The migrants were mostly Sinhala, whereas much of the territory to which they migrated had been inhabited by Tamils and was viewed by members of the Tamil community as their ancestral lands. The movement of Sinhala migrants into these areas was seen by Tamil political leaders as another effort by a Sinhala-dominated government to undermine the Tamil community by reducing its traditional lands.

The Crystallization of Separatist Sentiment. Although the official language controversy in the 1950s drove a deep wedge between communities and an occasional Tamil politician threatened to call for the political bifurcation of the island into separate Sinhala and Tamil states, no major political leader or group had proposed a total separation prior to the 1970s. After 1972, Tamil political leaders began moving steadily and rapidly toward advocacy of separation, culminating in May 1976 in an unequivocal public demand for a separate Tamil state.

The shift toward separation followed nearly two decades of frustration and disappointment for the Tamil political leaders. With the 1956 election, the Federal Party (or, in Tamil, the Ilankai Tamil Arasu Kadchi) had replaced the Tamil Congress as the dominant political party in the Ceylon Tamil regions. The Federal Party was dedicated to "the attainment of freedom for the Tamil-speaking people of Ceylon by the establishment of an autonomous Tamil state on the linguistic basis within the framework of a Federal Union of Ceylon."[10] For almost a decade, the Tamil politicians sought to wrench some concessions on the language and other communally charged issues from a succession of governments brought to power by Sinhala votes. In 1965, both the Federal Party and the Tamil Congress supported a self-styled "national government" in the expectation of scoring some gains on the questions of concern to the Tamil community. The following year, regulations were promulgated defining certain use of the Tamil language for public purposes, but the anticipated gains were allegedly eroded away in implementation. In 1968, after the government had abandoned a planned evolution of authority in certain fields to regional bodies, the Federal Party withdrew from the government. In 1972, the Federal party, the Tamil Congress, and other organizations and individuals banded together in a Tamil United Front (TUF), intended to demonstrate the cohesion and determination of the Tamil-speaking people in pursuing their demands and protecting their ethnic identity. Included in the TUF, although somewhat tenuously, was the Ceylon Workers Congress, an organization of Indian Tamil estate workers which serves as political spokesman for the Indian Tamil population.

The swift growth of sentiment for separation was fueled by the adoption of a new constitution in 1972 and pressed forward by mounting pressures from increasingly militant and impatient Tamil youths. The new constitution, in addition to reaffirming the position of Sinhala as the sole official language, conferred a special status on Buddhism and declared that "it shall be the duty of the State to protect and foster Buddhism."[11] The latter provision led TUF leaders to fear that government funds and powers would be used to promote conversions to Buddhism among Tamils belonging to the "untouchable" castes. A few Buddhist schools had been established in the North to instruct untouchable children in Buddhism—and in the Sinhala language. The TUF fear was that government-aided Buddhist educational activities would be used to encourage the assimilation of untouchables into Sinhala society, thus severing from Tamil society a significant number of its members and, hence, reducing its political power in the island.

Apparently an even more potent factor in propelling the TUF toward separatism was the appearance of rapidly increasing impatience and militancy among the youth of the North, including those associated with the TUF Youth Organization. As impassioned demands for swift and drastic action grew among youths, the older generation of TUF leaders reportedly felt impelled to move quickly toward the drastic solution of a separate Tamil state in order to retain any influence over the youths. One veteran political leader, in presenting an argument for a separate state, warned of "a new militancy among the Tamil youth who say that the program of their elders has not brought the desired results. This youth believe in confrontation which will inevitably become an international problem in the future." Particularly alarming to the veteran politicians were indications of increasing resort to violence, believed to be the work of an underground movement of Tamil youths with links to South India. Several bombings, shootings, and robberies occurred in the early 1970s. In 1975, the mayor of Jaffna, Alfred Durayappah, was assassinated following several unsuccessful attempts on his life. Durayappah had joined the Sri Lanka Freedom Party (SLFP) after the 1970 election, in which a United Front including the SLFP had come to power. Because of his association with the predominantly Sinhala SLFP and the central government in Colombo, Durayappah had been labeled a "quisling" by the young militants of the separatist movement.[12]

In early 1974, an international conference of Tamil studies was convened in Jaffna. Its proceedings were generally limited to scholars until the conclusion when a public session was held. At this session a clash occurred with police, resulting in eight deaths and a number of injuries. A short time later, a 23-year-old youth named Sivakumaran attempted to kill the superintendent of police, whom he presumably held responsible for the incident. When trapped by police following the assassination attempt, Sivakumaran committed suicide. A year later, a statue of the youth, depicting him bursting chains shackling his wrists, was erected a few miles outside Jaffna. In July 1976, two years after Sivakumaran's suicide, a service station operator and SLFP organizer named Nadarajah was killed by a bomb in front of his station a dozen yards from Sivakumaran's statue. Nadarajah was rumored to have assisted the police in apprehending Sivakumaran.

From 1972 to 1975, between forty and fifty Tamil youths, many of whom were active in the TUF Youth Organization, were held in detention by the authorities without charges being brought against them. A number of them were again taken into custody following the Durayappah assassination, and others after two audacious bank robberies in 1976. In 1977, five persons were arrested and charged with the Durayappah killing.

Several circumstances contributed to the growing restiveness and militancy of Tamil youths in the early 1970s. Youths of all communities were confronted by appalling levels of unemployment, which were particularly high among educated youths. A survey in 1969/1970, for example, found that among persons aged 15–19 years who had passed the General Certificate of Education (Ordinary Level) examination, taken after the tenth year of school, the rate of unemployment was 80.2%. Among those in the same age group who had passed the General Certificate of Education (Advanced Level) examination, taken after the twelfth year of schooling, or had reached a higher level of educational attainment, the unemployment rate climbed to 96.3%.[13] In addition to the general paucity of employment opportunities, the Sinhala-only policy and more indirect forms of discrimination seemed to make the problem of finding suitable employment particularly difficult for Tamil youths. Education in neither English nor Tamil promised reasonable employment opportunities.

A development regarding university admissions in the early 1970s triggered a particularly intense reaction among Tamil youths. The government instituted a so-called standardization of examination scores between language media, with the result that persons taking the examination in the Tamil language were required to achieve a higher score than those taking the examination in Sinhala in order to gain admission to the university. The proportion of Tamil students in many fields of study at the university dropped dramatically.[14] Standardization was justified on the ground that scores in the Tamil medium were consistently higher than those in the Sinhala medium, which could be the result of bias by examiners, or could be a product of greater determination and better preparation by Tamil students. Great emphasis has long been placed on education in Jaffna, at least within the middle and upper social strata. The densely populated and arid Jaffna Peninsula offered few career opportunities and for many decades Jaffna youths had sought higher education (then in English) as a passport to rewarding employment, often in the government service in the South. Although the adoption of Sinhala as the official language had severely constricted this much-traveled path, the added obstacle to obtaining advanced education was a particularly severe blow to the life chances of youths of or approaching college age. The immediate threat to their opportunities for education may help to explain the passionate urgency of the youths' demand for separation, since a solution a decade or more hence could not restore their hopes for their personal lives.

The objective of complete political separation was formally announced at a conference called by the TUF, at which the organization's name was changed to the Tamil United Liberation Front (TULF), in May 1976, twenty years after Sinhala was installed as the sole official language of Sri Lanka. A resolution adopted by the conference set forth a lengthy list of Tamil grievances against the government, including that of "making Sinhala the only official language throughout Ceylon thereby placing a stamp of inferiority on the Tamils and the Tamil language." Charging that the "Republican Constitution of 1972 had made the Tamils a slave nation ruled by the new colonial master, the Sinhalese who are using the power they have wrongly usurped to deprive the Tamil nation of its territory, language, citizenship, economic life, opportunities of employment and education thereby destroying all the attributes of nationhood of the Tamil people," the resolution concluded that "the restoration and reconstitution of the Free, Sovereign, Secular Socialist State of TAMIL EELAM . . . has become inevitable in order to safeguard the very existence of the Tamil Nation in this Country."[15]

The Ceylon Workers Congress dissociated itself from the resolution and effectively withdrew from the Front. As the Indian Tamils did not live in areas contiguous to the proposed Tamil state and were either seeking Lankan citizenship or preparing to leave for India, the idea of a Tamil state on the island had little attraction for them. Furthermore, their problems and circumstances differed significantly from those of the Ceylon Tamils. Largely estate workers and generally lagging behind the rest of the nation in education, the Indian Tamils have been more concerned with questions of labor relations and citizenship than with education and white-collar employment.

A parliamentary election in July 1977 provided the first major test of support for the TULF and its separatist cause among the Tamil-speaking voters of the North and East. The TULF entered the contest seeking a mandate from the "Tamil Nation" to establish a separate state which would include "all the geographically contiguous areas that have been the traditional homeland of the Tamil speaking people in the country."[16] The organization's election manifesto pledged "that a constitution would be drafted by representatives elected to the national parliament from the Tamil areas and an independent state would be created "either by peaceful means or by direct action."[17]

In the election, TULF candidates swept all fourteen seats and captured

68.5% of the total vote in the Northern Province. In the province's peninsular Jaffna district, where nearly half of the island's Ceylon Tamil population lives, eleven TULF candidates won a staggering 78.7% of the total vote despite the presence of 47 other candidates. The TULF's mandate was less clear in the Eastern Province, where Ceylon Tamils live interspersed with Tamil-speaking Muslims (ethnically classified as Ceylon Moors). The TULF won three of four seats from areas with Tamil majorities, but by narrower margins than in the North. No TULF candidate was successful in a constituency with a Muslim majority. Hence, the TULF could claim massive popular backing in the North and somewhat less emphatic support from the Tamil population on the east coast, but little evidence appeared of significant support from the east-coast Muslims. The stage appeared to be set for a confrontation between the TULF and the central government in Colombo.

Thus, two decades after adoption of the first legislation specifying an official language for the nation, the relations between the Sinhala majority and Ceylon Tamil minority appeared to have entered a new, and ominous, phase. Following the 1977 elections, communal violence flashed across the island, leaving an estimated 100 persons dead and thousands in flight from their homes. The violence was ignited by an incident in Jaffna in which Tamils were said to have attacked Sinhala policemen. Hostility and resentment toward the largely Sinhala police had been smoldering in Jaffna since the 1974 Tamil studies conference. As rumors of the Jaffna incident spread through the South, retaliatory attacks were made on the Tamils living in the Sinhala-majority areas. The newly installed United National Party government imposed a curfew, deployed police and military units to the troubled areas, and appealed to both communities for calm. The Statement of Government Policy opening the new session of parliament in August acknowledged that "there are numerous problems confronting the Tamil-speaking people. The lack of a solution to their problems has made the Tamil-speaking people support even a movement for the creation of a separate State." A conference of representatives of all political parties would be called to find solutions to these problems, the Statement promised.[18] . . . The post-election communal violence served as a stark reminder of the tenaciousness and explosiveness of communal stresses on the island.

Notes

1. [Due to space issues, this article has been heavily edited. Many of the tables and sources in the original are not shown—*Ed.*]
2. Paul R. Brass, *Language, Religion and Politics in North India* (New York: Cambridge University Press, 1971).

3. E. B. Dunham, *Ceylon at the Census of 1911* (Colombo: Government Printer, 1912), 196.

4. The 1971 census report used *jatiya* to refer to nationality (country in which citizenship is held) and *manava vargaya* (that is, the kind, type, or species of mankind) to refer to ethnic groups. (See the district reports, issued as parts of Department of Census and Statistics, *Census of Population, 1971*, vol. 1 [Colombo: Department of Census and Statistics, 1974–].) G. P. Malalasekera's *English-Sinhalese Dictionary*, 2nd ed. (Colombo: M. D. Gunasena, 1958) listed *vargaya* among the meanings for race, species, and kind, and *jatiya* among the meanings for all of those terms plus nationality. . . .

5. The government requirement that children classified as belonging to the Sinhala "race" (not the Sinhala-speaking population) be educated in the Sinhala medium whatever they claim as the language at home, of course, reduces the persuasiveness of the last cited development as an indication of a voluntary tendency. The proportion of students being instructed in the English medium hovered around 19% during the 1950s, then climbed steeply in the early 1960s, reaching 31% in 1963. However, by 1972, only 26,097 of 2,549,807 students, about 1%, were studying in the English medium. Of these, 21,918 were in the single educational district of Colombo South. Data for the 1950s and 1960s are from Department of Census and Statistics, *Statistical Abstract of Ceylon* for the years 1960–64 (Colombo: Government Press, 1961–65). The 1972 data are from *Statistical Profile of Children and Youth, Sri Lanka, 1975* (Colombo: Department of Census and Statistics, 1975), 54.

6. Department of Census and Statistics, *Census of Ceylon, 1953*, vol. 1 (Colombo: Government Press, 1957), 192–93, 196.

7. Ibid., vol. 3, pt. 2 (Colombo: Government Press, 1960), 5–20.

8. The origins and course of the language controversy through the mid-1960s are portrayed in more detail in the author's *Communalism and Language in the Politics of Ceylon* (Durham: Duke University Press, 1967).

9. House of Representatives, *Parliamentary Debates*, vol. 39, col. 409 (August 25, 1960).

10. *The Case for a Federal Constitution: Resolutions Passed at the First National Convention of the llankai Tamil Arasu Kadchi*, pamphlet (Colombo: Ilankai Tamil Arasu Kadchi, 1951), 19.

11. *The Constitution of Sri Lanka (Ceylon)* (Colombo: Department of Government Printing, 1972), 4.

12. The assassination of Durayappah is attributed to Velupillai Prabhakaran, the leader of the Liberation Tigers of Tamil Eelam (LTTE).

13. Department of Census and Statistics, *Socio-Economic Survey of Sri Lanka, 1969–70, Rounds 1–4*, vol. 1: *Population, Labour Force, and Housing* (Colombo: Department of Census and Statistics, 1973), 36, 39.

14. C. R. de Silva, "Weightage in University Admissions: Standardization and District Quotas in Sri Lanka, 1970–1975," *Modern Ceylon Studies* 5 (July 1974): 151–78.

15. "Political Resolution Unanimously Adopted at the 1st National Convention of the Tamil Liberation Front Held at Pannakam (Vaddukoddai Constituency) on 14.5.1976, Presided over by Mr. S. J. V. Chelvanayakam, Q.C., M.P."

16. "Tamil United Liberation Front Manifesto, General Elections, 1977."

17. Ibid.

18. National State Assembly Debates, *Official Report*, vol. 23, cols. 111–12 (August 4, 1977).

The Militarisation of Tamil Youth

A. Jeyaratnam Wilson

How and why Tamil youth have engaged in a separatist political and military strug-
gle is the subject of the following essay. A. J. Wilson traces the major trajectories of
Tamil politics from the period preceding independence to the brink of the contem-
porary period, when the LTTE (Liberation Tigers of Tamil Eelam) gained absolute
power through its violent methods of dispensing with rivals.

Paradoxically, Tamil electors have tended to close ranks behind a single party in the face of common danger. From 1944 to 1952 the All-Ceylon Tamil Congress, led by its man of iron G. G. Ponnambalam, was almost blindly followed. The years 1952–6 produced a hiatus; then Chelvanayakam provided leadership during the mounting crisis of 1956 and continued at the helm till his death in 1977.

From 1977 to 1983 Appapillai Amirthalingam took on Chelvanayakam's mantle. He was a popular civilian political leader, skilled as a public speaker and a debater in Parliament. He was in fact leader of the Opposition in the 1977 Parliament. Although he received a mandate from the majority of Tamil electors to launch the struggle for a separate sovereign Tamil state, Amirthalingam did not plunge the Tamil people into armed conflict. He was a gradualist and an incrementalist, preferring to proceed step by step, and carefully straddled the civilian and militant wings of the Tamil movement. During his time as leader of the Opposition he was vilified by the extremist Sinhalese fringes of the governing UNP [United National Party], but enjoyed the confidence of both Sinhalese and Tamil members of the Opposition.

Then in 1983 came the major outbreak of Sinhalese violence against the Tamil in all parts of the island. This Kristallnacht-like pogrom was in immediate reaction to an ambush by the Tamil Liberation Tigers of an army truck in which thirteen Sinhalese soldiers died. It has been suggested that the pogrom had been pre-planned, and that some of the communal-minded ministers in J. R. Jayewardene's cabinet were involved in launching the assault on innocent Tamils throughout the island.

President Jayewardene was unequal to the task. At first he seemed numbed and unable to confront the crisis, but he then proceeded from blunder to blunder. He appeared on television on 26 July 1983 with the purpose of assuaging the fears and hysteria of the Sinhalese people, but he did not utter a word of regret to the large number of Tamils who had suffered from Sinhalese thuggery masked by nationalist zeal. Jayewardene's ultimate blunder was when he had Parliament enact the Sixth Amendment in August 1983. This required Tamil Members of Parliament and others in public office to take an oath of allegiance "to the unitary state of Sri Lanka." Naturally Amirthalingam and his TULF [Tamil United Liberation Front] MPs refused to do so and quit Parliament. The consequence was that leadership of the Tamil movement fell to Veluppillai Prabhakaran and his Tamil Liberation Tigers, and he seized the opportunity to establish his leadership in the Tamil areas. He had exceptional military talent. His forces took on the Sinhalese army, won victories and inflicted sizeable casualties on them. The Liberation Tigers proved themselves daring fighters. They claimed to be the direct inheritors of Chelvanayakam's legacy.

All this was yet to come in 1976–83, watershed years for the Tamil movement with the shift to calls for independent statehood. On 19 November 1976, shortly before his death, Chelvanayakam said in Parliament:

"We have abandoned the demand for a federal constitution. Our movement will be all non-violent. . . . We know . . . we will be able to establish a state separate from the rest of the island."

In the general election soon after Chelvanayakam's death, the manifesto of the Tamil United Liberation Front explained the reasons for the decision to opt for a separate sovereign state. It declared that "it views the forthcoming general election as an opportunity to obtain the mandate of the Tamil Nation," on the basis of which it would proceed "to claim the right to self-determination, to re-establish the state of Tamil Eelam, and the expression of the sovereignty of the Tamil Nation." The manifesto stated how this would be achieved:

The Tamil-speaking representatives . . . while being members of the National State Assembly of Ceylon, will also form themselves into the "NATIONAL ASSEMBLY OF TAMIL EELAM" which will draft a constitution for the state of Tamil Eelam and thereby establish the independence of Tamil Eelam by bringing that constitution into operation either by peaceful means or by direct action or struggle.

Clearly this meant that the Tamil representatives would remain for as long as possible in Parliament (that is, the National State Assembly), which would be the forum for TULF MPs to air Tamil grievances, while at the same time the proposed National Assembly of Tamil Eelam would carry on its work of drafting a constitution for a separate sovereign state. Whether it would have been permitted to do this by the Sinhalese-dominated state is another question. Probably the Assembly would have been banned under a state of emergency, and if it had refused to give up its activity, the TULF would in all likelihood have been proscribed. Thus a vacuum would have been created, which would have been filled by the Tamil militants. So whether or not the TULF persisted in pursuing the path of secession, the time had come for the Sinhalese-dominated government in Colombo to reassess the situation.

The next stage in the break-up of the Sinhalese-controlled state was soon reached. Tamil parliamentary politics ceased and Tamil civilian political parties became irrelevant, giving way to the militants. If the Sinhalese state had acted differently by offering compromises, this outcome might have been averted; as it was, no alternative was possible. Even the framework contained in the District Development Councils' legislation of 1981 would have provided a breathing space, but President Jayewardene dragged his feet over its implementation.

Without Sinhalese aggrandisement, Tamil social and national awareness would not have transformed itself into a defensive nationalism. But driven to the wall by evictions, plunder and subjection to all kinds of humiliation in the Sinhala and even Tamil-speaking provinces, many Tamils retreated to their traditional homelands as their last bastion. Chelvanayakam's concept of a traditional Tamil homeland was now a reality. A new dimension was added as hundreds of thousands of Tamils fled to other countries, mainly India but also to Western Europe and North America. The Tamil question consequently became internationalised, because the expatriates in Western Europe and North America, many of them professionals and intellectuals, formed powerful lobbies.

The shift from Tamil national consciousness to a defensive nationalism had thus come about in several stages. When the Tamil Federal Party [FP] was launched in 1949, the principal issue was that the Tamil homelands should be a component of a federated Ceylon. The federal movement had a pervasive effect on the Tamil national identity: the leadership emphasised the twin aspects of Tamil language and Tamil territory, and provided that these could be assured; no question of separation or secession arose. There was nevertheless a fringe of Tamil nationalists within the FP keen on promoting the idea of a separate Tamil state, but they were kept on a tight leash by Chelvanayakam's desire to maintain an integrated island entity.

These dissident nationalist elements came into their own after Chelvanayakam's death. They were encouraged by the actions of the Sinhalese state and the new leadership was not strong enough to control them. Chel-vanayakam had not been successful in his summit diplomacy with three Sinhalese prime ministers (S. W. R. D. Bandaranaike, Mrs Sirimavo Bandaranaike and Dudley Senanayake), all of whom reneged on their promises. The Tamils were being subjected to increasing discrimination from the Sinhalese state over employment, admission to the universities (the last straw) and discrimination in the allocation of lands in the Tamil homelands of the Eastern Province in particular. There was increasing evidence of such policies amounting to deliberate hegemonism. One way out was to make common cause with the progressive Sinhalese forces in the south. But these (the progressive Marxists), tiring of opposition, had joined with the pro-Sinhalese Buddhist Sri Lanka Freedom Party in a coalition government in the last six months of 1965 and again in 1970–5, the worst phase of the Sinhalese state's "anti-Tamilism." The option for the Tamils of working within the framework of "Sinhalese first" and reconciling themselves to second-class status was never seriously considered; they found it objectionable and overwhelmingly rejected it.

In effect Tamil national consciousness, especially in the period of the All-Ceylon Tamil Congress, the Federal Party and the Tamil United Liberation Front, had the substance of a defensive nationalism which could manifest itself if Sinhalese-Tamil relations were to go awry. The suspicion between the two communities was mutual: the Sinhalese felt that in the centuries of foreign rule they had been deprived of their proper share of the national pie. This was especially true of the British rulers, whose supposed preference for Tamils in the public services, the Sinhalese regarded as part of their "divide and rule" policy. This was a useful stance for Sinhalese communal politicians, but Britain had not in fact pursued such a policy: selections to the public service were based on merit and the Tamils had fared well because they had attended superior Christian secondary schools.

The central argument is whether a single state can accommodate two mutually hostile nationalisms. In 1848 Lord Durham saw in Canada "two nations warring within the bosom of one," but he was optimistic then and believed that the two nationalisms could be accommodated within one state, a belief rejected by Quebecois nationalists in the twentieth century with their demands for a separate state. Our view is that within a single state there is space for only one nationalism, that of the majority community. The nationalism of the other will at best be tolerated. When Sinhalese politicians talk of Sri Lanka being a multi-ethnic state, they are (it is alleged by the Tamil political elite) concealing their rhetoric behind the façade of an island entity, with the minorities dispersed, and where the will of no community but that of the majority will prevail when it conflicts with the interests of the majority. In such a scenario there would be no contiguous Tamil territory to be claimed as a traditional homeland, because state-aided Sinhalese colonisation of the Tamil homelands would then have made the Tamils a minority in these areas.

In 1978 the present writer described Tamil national consciousness as a "sub-nationalism" and other writers on the subject have used this term in other contexts, but we now find this phraseology flawed. There cannot be a sub-nationalism; either it is nationalism, a quasi-nationalism, or national awareness or national consciousness. The last mentioned could ultimately transform itself into nationalism if not properly channeled, as through consociational arrangements, and could result in an agitation for separate statehood.

Then there are the descriptive phrases "ethnicity" and "ethnonationalisms." Again we have, as far as possible, avoided using the prefix "ethno" or the term "ethnicity" because in our view these are merely a rephrasing in new terminology of the old phenomenon of "nationalism." Ethno-nationalism is in fact nationalism, not retribalisation. Western writers on the subject take as a given the artificial geographical expressions left behind by the decolonisers. In fact these were pieces of real estate given names, with different tribes and ethnic groups forced into territory behind barbed wire. After independence, democracy, the rule of the majority, came to be misinterpreted as the rule of an ethnic majority, not a majority based on socio-economic issues. In such a context, the deprived ethnic minorities sought to assert themselves. Having failed to persuade the ethnic majority of the need for a fair distribution of the limited economic assets, these minority ethnic groups tried their weapon of last resort, wars of independence. Most such conflicts have been savagely suppressed, although there have been significant exceptions.

Thus an assertion of ethnicity with a surge towards statehood is neither ethnicity, nor ethno-nationalism, nor a primaeval reversion to tribalism. It is nationalism. We return to the question of whether two or three nations and nationalisms can flourish within a single state. We reiterate: the answer seems to be no. Communist terminology tried to explain away the phenomenon by referring to these minority groups as nationalities when in fact they were nations struggling to be born. The problem of nationalities or "the national question," according to communist ideology, could be resolved by structural adjustments and economic regeneration. The Marxist solution was a chamber of nationalities, federalism, a union of republics as well as economic development so that in material terms there would be enough for all. Communism believed that national assertion was the consequence of economic deprivation, and that if the economic problem could be resolved, the ethnic factor would wither away. This has frequently been disproved. Ethnic ties cut across frontiers and classes in the same way as national emergencies cause class divisions to be ignored. Therefore, when ethnicity is prevalent in geographically contiguous areas (as for example among the Tamils of Sri Lanka, the Sikhs of the Indian Punjab and the Quebecois) it becomes a fully fledged nationalism if all other attempts at accommodation have failed. Ethnicity also has relevance to dispersed nationalities which do not occupy geographically contiguous territories but are nevertheless conscious of their national character—e.g., the Chinese of Malaysia, the Muslims of India and most of the Muslims of Sri Lanka.

Where do the Tamils of Ceylon stand in all of these definitional arrangements? They have realised that they are a nation with a right to self-determination. Up to 1976, there existed a heightened Tamil national consciousness, a quasi-nationalism which desired to coexist within the federal framework of one state. The Sinhalese majority were unwilling to accept the compromise of federalism, arguing that the Ceylon Tamil component in such a federated state would at some point join up with Tamil Nadu in India. But not only would the Republic of India not permit such a union in the interests of its world standing, but it would fear that such a union might engender Tamil separatism in India within its own borders and, in the words of Rajiv Gandhi, "a hundred Eelams." Besides, Tamil Nadu has no sovereign powers to encourage such an enosis. Furthermore, the Ceylon Tamils themselves would avoid a link-up, out of a wish to preserve economic and employment opportunities for themselves within the island state. They would not want "Tamilians" from Tamil Nadu (as they are commonly referred to by Sri Lanka Tamils) to compete with them in the job market.

Equally unsustainable is the other Sinhalese fear that because in the distant past the island had been subject to South Indian Tamil invasions, this phenomenon could be repeated. But the Chola, Chera and Pandyan empires are all now distant memories of a vanished era. India is no longer divided into Chola, Chera and Pandyan provinces. The boundaries have been altered. There cannot be separate invasions of Sri Lanka from sections of the Union Republic as long as the centre holds. There has been no evidence that a break-up of India is possible; indeed the trend there is towards a greater concentration of powers at the centre in New Delhi.

With the state apparatus controlled by the Sinhalese majority, the Ceylon Tamils made herculean efforts to seek redress for their grievances. Under neutral British rule, there could be little complaint that one community was favoured above another. Speeches by the English-speaking Sinhalese middle class during that period, even when partial self-government was bestowed under the Donoughmore Constitution of 1931, showed little or no evidence of Sinhalese resentment against Britain favouring the Ceylon Tamils above themselves. However, with a universal franchise (1931) Sinhalese communalism provided a ready vehicle for use by aspiring Sinhalese politicians to appeal to the Sinhalese constituency. Whether this was "racism" or a lurch towards preserving the support of the ethnic majority in a democratic set-up is a matter for conjecture. Perhaps it was a mixture of the two.

However, this trend towards Sinhalese communalism produced a reaction in the Tamil demand for balanced representation: the call for 50 per cent of the seats in the legislature and executive to be reserved for the ethnic minorities. The "fifty-fifty" demand failed when pressed before the British-appointed Soulbury Commission of 1944, although the Commissioners' objections were not convincing. This demand was more an expression of Tamil solidarity—of Tamil quasi-nationalism (short of independence) rather than Tamil nationalism per se. When the demand failed, the All-Ceylon Tamil Congress, which had been in the vanguard of the movement, campaigned against the Soulbury Constitution at the general election of 1947. The Congress won the support of the entire Tamil heartland of the Jaffna peninsula, but failed to carry its message to the Eastern Province Tamils, winning only one of the seats it contested there.

The Congress requested a vague mandate from the electors for responsive cooperation with progressive Sinhalese political parties. D. S. Senanayake's UNP won more seats than any other single party and then did exactly what the Soulbury Commissioners had not expected to happen: it gained the support of one or more of the minority groups and in time established itself with a comfortable majority. After sitting in opposition for some eighteen months, the Tamil Congress leader, G. G. Ponnambalam, and a majority of Congress parliamentarians realised that the conflicting and rival opposition parties would never coalesce to form an alternative government. Ponnambalam therefore decided to accept a portfolio in Senanayake's cabinet. He attached no pre-conditions, such as the establishment of two official languages (Sinhala and Tamil), an end to state-aided colonisation of the Tamil homelands, the re-enfranchisement of the disfranchised Indian Tamil plantation workers, or addressing the question of a national flag. His failure to resolve these issues before joining the cabinet caused a split in his party. A group led by S. J. V. Chelvanayakam broke away and formed the Ilankai Thamil Arasu Kadchi (ITAK, the party for the formation of a Tamil government), which referred to itself in English as the Federal Freedom Party of the Ceylon Tamils. Its spokesmen made it clear that they were demanding a federal constitution in which the rights of the Tamils would be regained and preserved more or less within the four points referred to above.

In five general elections—those of 1956, March 1960, July 1960, 1965 and 1970—the FP received a mandate from the Tamil people on their four-point demand. They failed in the 1952 election, but in the other five the support they obtained was unchallengeable. The party's leader, S. J. V. Chelvanayakam, concluded agreements and an understanding with three prime ministers in 1957, 1960 and 1965, but all three reneged on their obligations, mainly because of the threat of back-bench revolts in Parliament and obstruction from the Buddhist clergy. In protest, the FP mobilised Tamil national consciousness, raising it to such a level that it became a quasi-nationalism, but it stopped short of a demand for statehood.

That there was a gradual and creeping awareness of the inevitability of statehood was not understood by the Sinhalese politicised class. Anton (A. S.) Balasingham, the theoretician of the Liberation Tigers of Tamil Eelam (LTTE), was correct when he wrote in 1983:

> Tamil nationalism arose as a historical consequence of Sinhala chauvinistic oppression. As the collective sentiment of the oppressed people, Tamil nationalism constituted progressive and revolutionary elements. . . . Tamil national sentiment found organisational expression in the Federal Party which emerged as a powerful political force in 1956 to spearhead the Tamil national movement.

Balasingham added that the FP was dominated by "bourgeois and petty bourgeois class elements" and was "a nationalist party founded on a conservative ideology." However, "as a national movement" it "was able to organise and mobilise various strata of classes and castes into a huge mass movement." It should be noted that neither Balasingham nor other Tamils had yet begun to use words such as "nation" and "the right to self-determination," which had still not been introduced into the vocabulary of Tamil politics. More time had to pass and further repression before they developed into common currency.

The Tamils were therefore still on the threshold of calling themselves a nation and evolving their own nationalism. A nationalist party need not necessarily opt for statehood. The key factor is its awareness of its ability to protect the national interest of its people. When it realises that there is no other hope of doing so, then national awareness transforms itself into a claim for recognition as a nation with the right to self-determination and statehood.

Such a demand became vocal during the crucial period when the United Front government of Mrs Sirimavo Bandaranaike (1970–7) enacted a constitutional revolution by promulgation of a constitution in 1972 with a bias that was markedly pro-Buddhist, and in favour of the Sinhala language. The Ceylon Tamils spearheaded by the FP, agreed then to join with all other Tamil political parties under the banner of the Tamil United Liberation Front. The TULF adopted the historic Vaddukoddai Resolution of 1976 claiming the right to self-determination and independent sovereign statehood. At the general election of 1976, it asked for and received a mandate to constitute the Tamil homelands into a separate state. Thus Tamil national consciousness had reached the stage where the Ceylon Tamils decided to take their future into their own hands.

The passing of the Vaddukoddai Resolution had one serious implication for Tamil politics. Parliamentarism would soon be replaced by the gun in the freedom struggle. This meant that the moderates and constitutionalists would be displaced by a militant movement of Tamil youth, who had no faith in Parliament. But there was an interval before the militants emerged. It was up to the new TULF leadership under Appapillai Amirthalingam and M. Sivasithamparam to refashion itself as a political wing of the militarised youth. The TULF was not prepared for such a radical shift, but it bided its time.

The party now negotiated an agreement with the executive president of the country, J. R. Jayewardene. A stop-gap solution was successfully reached, embodied in the ill-fated District Development Councils' scheme of 1980–1. The TULF leadership hoped that this would be a stepping-stone to independent statehood, depending largely on how the scheme would be implemented. They did not, however, expect the Sinhalese leadership to play fair and to provide for Tamil national consciousness to be contained within the DDC framework. They were right in their thinking but wrong in their timing. Tamil youth, increasingly impatient of their virtual suffocation by the Sinhalese state, began to batter at the door. For a time they were kept at bay.

Then came the pogrom of 1983. Many politicised Sinhalese, ashamed of this display of barbarous behaviour, blamed Sinhalese hoodlums for the pogromisation of middle-class and other Ceylon Tamils. In fact, however, the 1983 pogrom was the last significant outbreak of Sinhalese nationalistic violence. Rohan Gunaratne confirms this view in his observation: "Mathew [President Jayewardene's Minister of Industries, Industrial Research and Fisheries], though outspoken, was not airing just his personal point of view. These were the grievances perceived by a majority of the Sinhalese too."

Gunaratne also says that Mathew adopted an "eye for an eye approach." He was the leading Tamil-baiter in the Jayewardene cabinet.

Thus this Sinhalese Buddhist nationalism had far-reaching implications. First, middle-class Tamils who fled the country formed themselves into influential lobbies in the Western countries where they sought asylum, so much so that the (by then) former President J. R. Jayewardene referred to these Tamils as "the world's most powerful minority." Secondly, the Sinhalese state increasingly found itself dragged down in a self-destructive war, with a large slice of its budget set aside for military expenditure at the expense of economic development. Thirdly, countries providing aid to Sri Lanka began pressing the government to come to a negotiated settlement with the Tamils. Additionally, and most important, a powerful Tamil military force under the leadership of Velupillai Prabhakaran was engaging the Sinhalese army in bitter battles, some of the more strategic of which were won by the Tamils through Prabhakaran's superior generalship. The Tamil independence struggle seized the world's attention, as did Prabhakaran's successes in the battlefield. What the Sinhalese Buddhist nationalists most feared came to pass—India's intervention—almost a self-fulfilling prophecy. Meanwhile, the pogromisation of Tamils and retaliation against Sinhalese by Tamil militants caused an unprecedented internal refugee problem which became a financial burden on the state.

In his pamphlet *Liberation Tigers and Tamil Eelam Freedom Struggle*, A. S. Balasingham draws pointed attention to the objectives of the only Tamil fighting force striving explicitly for independence. The other groups (on which we dwell later) were eliminated by the LTTE or fell prey to the machinations of India's Research and Analysis Wing (RAW), which set them off against each other. Balasingham emphasises that at the general election of 1977 the TULF had obtained an irrevocable mandate from the Tamil people to secede from Sinhala Ceylon and form an independent Tamil state on the basis of the right to self-determination. He accuses the TULF leadership thus:

> Jayewardene [the ruling President] in his Machiavellian shrewdness soon realised that TULF leaders were not serious in their secessionist demand but sought alternatives to deceive the Tamil masses. The real threat of secession, the government thought, arose from the militant Tamil youths who are unappeasable, irreconcilable and committed to the core to the goal of an independent socialist Tamil Eelam.

Balasingham states with precision why this situation had arisen. He writes:

Plunged into the despair of unemployed existence, frustrated without the possibility of higher education, angered by the imposition of an alien language, the Tamil youth realised that the redemption to their plight lay in revolutionary politics, a politics that should pave the way for a radical and fundamental transformation of their miserable conditions of existence. The only alternative left to the Tamils under the conditions of mounting national oppression, the youth rightly perceived, was none other than a revolutionary armed struggle for the total independence of their nation.

Among other methods, President Jayewardene's government sought to crush the youth movement by getting Parliament to enact the draconian Prevention of Terrorism Act on 29 July 1979. It had precisely the opposite effect to the one intended, and succeeded only in stiffening the Tamil resistance movement. Furthermore, age was affecting the President, who was in his seventies. His bureaucrats tended to deceive him. Those who framed the Prevention of Terrorism Act had informed him that they had incorporated all that was "good and humane" in anti-terrorist legislation the world over, particularly in Northern Ireland and South Africa. With the powers assumed by the state under this Act, the President hoped that he could crush the youth movement, but in this he betrayed a simplistic understanding of the Tamil mind shared by other Sinhalese leaders as well. Jayewardene, who did not understand the Tamils outside Colombo's narrow elite circles, thought that he could separate the militant youth from their seniors in the TULF. But Amirthalingam was determined to keep the military wing of the TULF and use it as a lever to extract concessions from the President.

However, Amirthalingam and his fellow TULF MPs were too slow for the impatient generation of young people, who had confidence only in S. Kathiravetpillai, the radical MP for Kopay. Kathiravetpillai continuously warned his colleagues and the old generation of Tamils that a catastrophe would soon overtake the entire Tamil community unless meaningful concessions were wrung from Jayewardene. The President for his part preferred to follow a policy of "wait and see." His attitude was "let it simmer"—meaning that the outbreak of violence in Tamil areas should remain on the boil for some time without boiling over.

The origins of the young people's armed struggle can be traced to the founding in 1970 of the Tamil Students' Federation (TSF), which produced its first martyr in Sivakumaran, a young public servant who killed himself by swallowing a cyanide capsule to avoid capture by the police. The TSF was later renamed the Tamil New Tigers and then, in 1975, the Liberation

Tigers of Tamil Eelam (LTTE). This guerrilla organisation in time acquired the reputation of being the world's deadliest, and since 1975 has been in the forefront of the Tamils' freedom struggle.

The TSF pursued an independent path. The TULF for its part had its own military wing, the Tamil Youth Front (TYF), under the leadership of Mavai Senathirajah, which expressed its belief "in violence as a method of self-defence." The militant youth groups were at first united by overlapping memberships. For example, one prominent youth leader, Uma Maheswaran, was at first both chairman of the LTTE and Colombo secretary of the TYF. These youth organisations advocated a *punitha yutham*, a "[pure] holy war," against the Sinhalese state which was fast acquiring characteristics of a terror state. Although by a quirk of fate (the result of the first-past-the-post electoral system) Appapillai Amirthalingam became the official leader of the Opposition, he denied having anything to do with youth violence. On 18 May 1978 he said in Parliament: "the TULF has nothing to do with violence." The connections may have been tenuous, but the TULF was manipulating militant Tamil youth as a lever to obtain concessions from an incompetent President.

Two incidents during this phase inflamed youth violence. The first was the unprovoked police assault on some 100,000 Tamils who had gathered in Jaffna town on 10 January 1974 on the last day of the fourth International Conference of Tamil Research. As stated earlier, the police attacked the crowd with batons and tear gas. Eight or nine Tamils were electrocuted and many others were injured in the stampede. The second was the barbarous burning, by a security unit, of the Jaffna Library with its 97,000 books and unique manuscripts. Rohan Gunaratne writes that "at least one cabinet minister and a Deputy Inspector General of Police fuelled the sentiments of the angry policemen and participated in the burning of Jaffna that shameful night."

With "the holocaust and pogromisation" of Tamils in 1983, more than 100,000 Tamils fled to India and several thousand others sought refuge in the West. The violence of Sinhalese Buddhist nationalism took the Tamil militants by surprise. Kittu (Krishnakumar), the Jaffna commander of the LTTE, said in a private communication to a friend that the LTTE had not expected the repercussions that followed the killing of thirteen Sinhalese soldiers in a mine blast in Jaffna. They therefore had to place themselves on a war footing at very short notice when they were only prepared for guerrilla tactics. It was the same with the other groups. However, there was a multiplicity of mutually suspicious and hostile Tamil organisations, even in the hour of their gravest crisis. All the hard work done by S. J. V. Chelvanayakam and his FP to unite the Tamils under one umbrella leadership during the period 1956–83 was allowed to fritter away.

Rohan Gunaratne records the existence of no less than thirty-seven groups, many of whose members fled to India and received military training under the auspices of India's RAW. It is not clear what India's reasons for this were, but certain inferences can be drawn. The Indian government was under much pressure from the state government of Tamil Nadu, which was a strong support base for Mrs Gandhi in national elections. India also feared that Sri Lanka's Trincomalee harbour in the Eastern Province would become available to the US government as an excellent naval base; and the UNP government could be sure of its control there. Thirdly, there was personal animosity between Mrs Gandhi and President J. R. Jayewardene, who had become known for his diplomatic gaffes. In a state visit to New Delhi at the time when Morarji Desai was Prime Minister he had made derogatory references to Mrs Gandhi. After that Mrs Gandhi never failed to refer to the two men as "the two old foxes." Similarly on a visit to Pakistan, Jayewardene applauded Islamabad's stand on the disputed territory of Kashmir.

Of the thirty-seven Tamil militant groups, only five were of significance: the LTTE under the leadership of Velupillai Prabhakaran; the People's Liberation Organisation of Thamil Eelam (PLOTE), headed by Uma Maheswaran; the Thamil Eelam Liberation Organisation (TELO), controlled by Sri Sabaratnam; the Eelam People's Revolutionary Liberation Front (EPRLF), led by K. S. Padmanabha; and the Eelam Revolutionary Organisation of Students (EROS), commanded by Velupillai Balakumar. RAW committed the crucial blunder of manipulating one militant group against the other, with the objective of establishing an Indian-controlled force in Sri Lanka. The result was internecine warfare between the groups, the leaking of information about each other to the Sri Lankan intelligence authorities, and the ultimate emergence as leaders of the group India disliked most—the independence-minded LTTE. The latter proved ruthless in the destruction of its rivals PLOTE, TELO and EPRLF. With EROS it came to a working arrangement.

PLOTE was essentially a high-caste Vellalar-oriented organisation led by Uma Maheswaran (also known as Mukunthan), a surveyor who knew the jungles of Vavuniya and was in charge of the group from the beginning. Maheswaran had at first worked with the LTTE and was chairman of its Central Committee. In 1981 there was a split and he broke away from the LTTE to form PLOTE. It had then obtained adequate finance and was second in strength to the LTTE among the Tamil militant groups.

According to Dagmar Hellman-Rajanayagam, PLOTE "follows a hard Marxist-Leninist line advocating a social revolution of the workers and peasants, though its members mainly come from the highest caste, the Vellalar." PLOTE may have started with Marxist-Leninist ideology but it later resorted to kidnappings and robberies, especially of banks, to supplement its meagre financial resources. Apparently Maheswaran was a leader who could not get on with his party. He and his followers were divided over the group's political programme, strategy and terrorism; he had committed thirty-eight murders and was criticised for his "headless and useless strategy." At a PLOTE Congress in July 1985 an influential group of dissidents withdrew from the party and Maheswaran was left with a rump. He lost his base in India and Jaffna and was finally murdered in 1989 by unidentified assassins.

TELO—the Thamil Eelam Liberation Organisation—was another powerful group until its decimation by the LTTE. It claimed seniority in the militant movement on the grounds that it was founded in 1967–9 by Tangaturai, one of the prime organisers of the robbery at the People's Bank, Neerveli (12 miles from Point Pedro in the Jaffna Peninsula) when Rs. 7.5 million were stolen. Tangaturai was one of several prominent resistance leaders killed by Sinhalese prisoners in the notorious Welikada prison massacre in July 1983. He was then succeeded by Sri Sabaratnam.

TELO was distinctly Vellala-oriented and was acknowledged by all, including Tamil expatriates, as being "high-caste." One of the motives behind its elimination by the LTTE was jealousy and suspicion that most of the expatriates' funding reached TELO hands. The LTTE felt that despite its great performances in the battlefield, it was not receiving its due recognition. Moreover, the LTTE accused TELO of becoming India's little soldiers and acting on instructions from India. In April–May 1986 TELO's cadres, comprising between 150 and 300 members and including Sri Sabaratnam, were ruthlessly gunned down by the LTTE. TELO's military wing was the Thamil Eelam Liberation Army, whose leader too was allegedly killed by LTTE men in 1984. The LTTE thus destroyed TELO, supposedly in the Tamil national interest.

The EPRLF was founded during 1981–4. Before its emergence as a fully fledged organisation, it claimed that it had held organisers' conferences in 1981 and 1983 and met together in a party Congress in 1984. It had two distinguishing features. The first was that during the occupation of the Northern and Eastern provinces by the 70,000 soldiers of the Indian Peace-Keeping Force (IPKF) the group became India's puppet government in the area. Secondly, the organisation had a considerable Marxist component, represented by the general secretary K. S. Padmanabha and his supporters. Although the EPRLF did not engage in day-to-day warfare, it was involved in a number of daring feats. It was responsible for the Batticaloa jailbreak of September 1983 when political prisoners were rescued, including a number of EPRLF cadres.

The kidnapping of Penelope Willis, a BBC reporter alleged to be a friend of President Jayewardene, and the missionary couple, the Allens, who were accused without any foundation of being CIA spies, was another of its publicity stunts; they were released, supposedly after pressure from M. G. Ramachandran, the Chief Minister of Tamil Nadu.

Dagmar Hellmann-Rajanayagam observes that "among all the groups, the EPRLF propagandists appear to be among the cleverest, most intelligent, most logical and absolutely ruthless ones." She adds: "The EPRLF would probably stop at very little if it thought it would advance its power."

Some of Padmanabha's Marxist ideas are clearly spelled out in the EPRLF's programme. For instance, in its manifesto for the 1989 provincial council elections the emphasis was on equal rights for all ethnic (caste) groups and opposition to religious (Saivaite) bigotry. The EPRLF's objective was to fight a people's war in which not only students but the lower classes (castes), workers and peasants would be involved. Party spokesmen talked in Marxist terms when referring to "centralised democracy" and "intra-party democratic structures." Their main support base was in Batticaloa in contrast to the LTTE's stronghold in Jaffna.

The EPRLF's most egregious blunder was in cooperating with India and Colombo in implementing the provincial councils scheme. Both sides let it down. Colombo's Sinhalese communal bureaucracy failed to provide either finance or devolution. India provided the Chief Minister with money for rehousing projects, but threw the EPRLF into a panic when talk of the IPKF's withdrawal became serious. The organisation's close ties with India discredited it in the eyes of the local population, who were subjected to frequent harassment by the IPKF.

The last of the less powerful groups was EROS—the Eelam Revolutionary Organisation of Students—which in the course of time allied itself with the Liberation Tigers. First launched in London in 1975 under the organisational leadership of Eliathamby Ratnasabapathy, EROS derived its strength originally from a student group in Madras, the General Union of Eelam Students (CUES). Its strongholds were mainly in the Batticaloa and Amparai districts. EROS was the best organised of the lesser groups and had a highly intelligent idealogue in Velupillai Balakumar, who is now also its chief. It was the only group which sought an understanding of the Muslim position. An engineering graduate of Lumumba Friendship University in Moscow, A. R. Arudpragasam, also known as Arular, was a second strong Marxist theoretician in the EROS ranks. The group concentrated on economic warfare and carried out a number of successful attacks on government buildings in Colombo and the Eastern Province. In time EROS splintered into several factions, losing CUES and Ratnasabapathy in the process. At the time of writing it continues to profess Marxist objectives but how these can be reconciled with its present pro-LTTE stance (the Balakumar faction) is difficult to understand unless this is a deliberate Marxist tactic. The other important EROS faction is led by the military expert Shankar Raj, and has support in Colombo, Madras and London. It is pro-Indian and maintains ties with RAW. It formed a political wing, the Eelavar Democratic Front (EDF) and put forward candidates as independents at elections in the north-east. Thirteen EROS MPs were elected to Parliament at the general election in 1989.

In the middle of 1991, the LTTE placed Balakumar under house arrest, and shortly afterwards his EROS faction joined the Liberation Tigers. Prabhakaran, the LTTE leader, appointed senior members of EROS to important portfolios in his administration. Balakumar was placed in charge of food, co-operatives and rehabilitation while another MP, Ravi Murugada, was made head of the important LTTE Research Organisation of Tamils (ROOT).

There were many other Tamil military formations which need not occupy us. The only explanation for their multiplicity is the tendency towards individuality, competitiveness and private enterprise among the Jaffna Tamils. This may be a general stereotyping but there is much to be said for it. These other little groups also enriched themselves, by criminal methods for which they claimed patriotic justification, by cooperating with the Sri Lankan forces, but there is no hard evidence that they supplied valuable information. The public's explanation is that these groups were paying off old scores against their adversaries and, in so doing, giving false leads to the Sri Lankan security personnel who had no proficiency in the Tamil language and lacked even the barest knowledge of Tamil culture.

One such group involved in this gamesmanship was the Eelam People's Democratic Party (EPDP) led by Douglas Devananda, the adopted son of K. C. Nythiananda, a renowned trade union organiser who was highly regarded among the Tamils because he had made considerable personal sacrifices for the Tamil cause in the early post-independence phase. (He led a number of strikes of government clerks against the state. From being included with the Moscow Communist Party, he switched to the FP in his sympathies, which cost him promotion and led to his being transferred to insalubrious locations.) Devananda had a serious grievance against the LTTE, which had murdered his close relatives. He wished to be avenged on them, but was not unaware that his primary loyalty was to the Tamil people. He had undergone high-grade guerrilla training abroad, particularly in Lebanon, and offered his services to the Sri Lankan Defence Minister and the President, both of whom were simpletons in granting him time, interviews and financial assistance. Thus Devananda supposedly provided information to security personnel, collected a fortune from the coffers of a credulous government, and remains engaged in political manoeuvring. With such an outcome unpredictable, it cannot be ruled out that he will return to the resistance fold.

The other thirty-odd little groups also supposedly provided assistance and collected a good deal of money. Be this as it may, these were all resistance groups primarily fighting the repression of the Sinhalese state. They had no properly formulated ideology of national regeneration and could not really be regarded as manifestations of Tamil nationalism. They had no destination or goals of which they were aware. They were essentially a nuisance to the Sinhalese state, but beyond this they could not be counted as political forces. Above all, except for the LTTE and Balakumar's EROS, the other groups professed pseudo-Marxist goals, and these had little meaning to the Tamil people in their hour of crisis.

Thus we come to the last, most ruthless and solidly nationalistic of the Tamil resistance organisations—the much dreaded Liberation Tigers of Tamil Eelam. On the whole they have the support of the Tamil people in general, as well as sections of the hard core of elite Tamils—professionals, wealthy business people and others both in the island and outside. Those in the island are naturally reluctant to make their opinions public, but in private conversation among themselves they do not conceal their sympathies. Sinhalese of the politicised class are often misled because these Tamils deplore the activities of the Tigers when talking with their Sinhalese acquaintances. Hence the latter gain the false impression that the majority of Tamils are with them, that they are awaiting a peaceful solution, that they want to remain at peace with their magnanimous Sinhalese brethren, and so on. This has gone on since the days of G. G. Ponnambalam and the Tamil Congress, but the Sinhalese have still not got wise to this kind of double-speak. Such conversations take place between members of majority and minority groups not only in Sri Lanka but the world over. It could be said that majorities believe what they want to believe, just as imperial rulers did until they were confronted by non-violent resistance or armed insurrection.

The Liberation Tigers have the support and sympathy of major sections of the Tamil community. This is not only because they have taken on the Sinhalese forces and won spectacular victories. It is also because they, alone among the Tamil resistance groups, have a formulated policy and a constructive nationalist ideology. In Velupillai Prabhakaran they had much to boast about. He is a remarkable tactician who has beaten off the Sinhalese army and the Indian peacekeepers. He has won unswerving loyalty from his men and from his large following of young Tamil men and women. Whether these see him simply as a crisis leader for whom they would not find much use in a free and fair election is yet to be tested.

Of the groups, only the Tigers (except for the civilian TULF) have declared themselves the heirs to Chelvanayakam:

> The gun in their hands, the fire of freedom in their hearts, arises the third generation: . . . S. J. V. Chelvanayakam's heroic policies cannot be bartered away; in strength his heirs rise LTTE members have come into his heritage in the battlefield!

The LTTE has a well-thought-out plan of action, quite unlike the other groups which have concentrated only on resistance and fighting the centralised Sinhalese state. Their plea for national self-determination is that society in Tamil Eelam is prevented from not being able to determine its fate itself. On the other hand, the Tigers operate a de facto government and have declared that "the Sinhalese constitution does not apply to Tamil Eelam, as the Liberation Tigers demonstrate."

Prabhakaran has made no secret about the form he thinks the future state should take. In an interview in 1986, he said:

> The government of independent Eelam will be a socialist government; there will be only one party supported by the people; I do not want a multi-party democracy. Under a one-party government Tamil Eelam can develop and change much faster. In a socialist constitution the needs of the people will have priority.

The Tigers' methods of struggle are clearly outlined. Every soldier must swear an oath of loyalty to Prabhakaran. And then comes the deadly suicide capsule:

> The thought of certain death is a great trial. But to whom? Certainly not to us. Because we are married to our cyanide. Yes, our death lives with us. It sleeps with us. We carry it in our shirt pockets and around our necks. That makes us clear-headed and purposeful!

What drives them to such acts of desperation?

> Our houses became our graves . . . our villages became cremation grounds. The Sinhalese racist demons slowly take over our ancient land. On our own soil, where we were born and have lived since time immemorial, our people are turned into refugees, into slaves; they are being destroyed!

The Tigers insist that it is useless to negotiate or come to a compromise settlement with the Sinhalese. "Every Sinhalese," they insist, "is fed hatred for the Tamil race with mother's milk." Therefore, "whoever accepts or supports the Sri Lanka unitary constitution, the Sinhala anthem, the Sinhala national flag is a definite traitor to the Eelam Tamils."

Since 1992, however, the LTTE has stated that it will consider an alternative to a sovereign independent state of Tamil Eelam should the Sri Lankan government present a compromise settlement. The alternatives they had in mind include two virtually sovereign states joined together under a confederal arrangement. They are also willing to consider a special relationship with Colombo like that between Delhi and Kashmir. In essence the Tigers claim that the Tamils want to be left on their own and not participate in the language and religious politics of the south. These positions do not appear to be irreconcilable assuming Sinhalese recognition of a "Tamil territory."

The LTTE has not hitherto outlined the essentials of a formula for peace. The UNP government for its part, while professing to the world that it was seeking a peaceful resolution—an obvious attempt to obtain assistance from the Aid Ceylon Consortium (a group of foreign powers, most notably the United States and Japan, which have pledged development aid to Sri Lanka)—was in reality seeking a military solution by every method at its disposal. It imposed a food embargo to prevent the vast majority of the 800,000 civilian population in the Jaffna peninsula from obtaining supplies; permitted atrocities such as gang rape and wholesale plunder by Sinhalese soldiers; and bombed churches, temples, hospitals and innocent civilians in the peninsula, as well as military targets. Observers have commented that victory is not obtainable by either side. Various foreign powers have offered to mediate, but the Sri Lanka government has rejected these offers. At the same time around US $2 million a day (provided for civil projects and general purposes by the Aid Ceylon Consortium consisting of Britain, Canada, France, Germany and Japan) is being spent on a war that is ultimately unwinnable.

The question arises as to whether the LTTE's position is representative of Tamil nationalism or, since the Tigers are willing to consider alternatives such as a loose federation, they are merely seeking autonomy for the Tamils and a rigid border for their traditional homeland. There is truth in both these propositions. A representative section of Tamil opinion believes that only independence can put the Tamils beyond the reach of deception by the Sinhalese state. As the historian Professor S. Arasaratnam stated in 1979:

> The Tamil community in Sri Lanka . . . has embryonic elements for the whipping up of nationalist opinions. It had an authentic memory of shared

historical experience. Even from the evidence of the Sinhalese chronicles Tamil connections were almost as old as the early Sinhalese settlement.

Thus like any historic people, the Tamils carry with them the burden of memory. The tragedy is that the Sinhalese have not allowed the Tamils to coexist peacefully with them. If they had done so, there would have been two nationally conscious peoples living within the confines of a single state. An all-island Sri Lankan nationalism could have evolved.

Whether Sri Lanka remains a unitary, quasi-federal or loose federal state is now a superfluous question. As Professor Arasaratnam has stated:

> The Tamils possess many of the characteristics that contribute to modern nationhood. They have a shared historical experience, a continuous linguistic and cultural tradition, a common way of life, the result of a traditional system of beliefs and values dominated by Saivism and, most important of all, a defined territory as homeland.

The tragedy of all this is that:

> The prominent Tamil leaders of the late nineteenth and early twentieth centuries were in the forefront of the movement to create a Ceylonese nation-consciousness and to use this consciousness to wrest constitutional concessions from a reluctant colonial administration.

A remarkable case of the revolving door of history.[1]

Editor's Note

1. In February 2003, the LTTE and the Sri Lankan government agreed to a cease-fire and talks facilitated by the Norwegian government. A series of talks were convened with no substantial understandings reached, and in January 2008 the Sri Lankan government under President Rajapakse rescinded its commitment to the cease-fire and launched a military offensive. The offensive culminated in the resounding defeat of the LTTE in mid-May 2009 and the forced encampment of nearly 300,000 Tamil civilians near Vavuniya, at the southern edge of the Vanni. By November, most of the civilians had been released. By mid-2010, no government initiatives to address the grievances of the Tamil people had been discussed. The general secretary of the United Nations, Ban-Ki Moon, had appointed an advisory committee to look into the question of possible war crimes committed by both sides in the closing months of the war. For continuous updates on the evolving political situation, see www.theacademic.org.

Womanhood and the Tamil Refugee

Joke Schrijvers

The plight of the Tamil refugee, particularly the women and children among them, remain aspects of Sri Lanka's ethnic conflict that are severely underplayed. In the following essay, the Dutch scholar Joke Schrijvers explores the confluence of womanhood, Tamilness, and refugee status as these appeared to her during the late 1990s.

At the time in which this book went to press, between 265,000 and 300,000 internally displaced Tamil refugees were huddled into "Manik Farm" and other smaller camps in the vicinity of Vavuniya as a consequence of the government's final push to defeat the LTTE just north of Mullaitivu. The secretary general of the United Nations had just visited the camps and had called on the Sri Lankan government to open up access to them in order that the plight of refugees could be more adequately addressed. That request had been denied initially while reports coming from these camps suggested that conditions were especially difficult in terms of food, personal security, and sanitation. Surely the situation of these refugees will be documented in the future. For now, we can rely only on analyses of the sort offered by Schrijvers, based on conditions endured by Tamil refugees a decade earlier.

Introduction. The civil war in Sri Lanka between the government and the Liberation Tigers for Tamil Eelam (LTTE) . . . has created two extreme images of Tamil women: aggressive women soldiers and suicide bombers in the LTTE [and] pathetic, poverty-stricken, dependent war victims in refugee camps. In between these extremes many variations have developed and women themselves actively try to influence the creation of these images. However, the various new identities have not replaced the earlier "traditional" image of Tamil womanhood which is still at the back of everyone's mind in the Tamil community. . . .

Constructions of gender, of "feminised" and masculinised practices and ideologies in the imagined community of the nation are central elements in nationalist movements. Gender discourses are tied up with nationalist projects, and in war-torn societies differences between men and women are exaggerated. Nationalist projects use gender notions to the extreme: . . . men are represented as the creators and defenders of the (new) nation and women as the core symbols of the nation's identity. The Tamil struggle in present-day Sri Lanka is not mainly over territory but over Tamilness as well. Representations of "womanhood" are strategic symbols in this struggle.

In this article I will focus on the identity constructions of Tamil women in Sri Lanka and in particular, of women whom I met in refugee camps (so called "welfare-centres") in the capital of Colombo and in Vavuniya in the north. Internal refugees in Sri Lanka are the subjects of cultural and political control, severely restricted in their physical and social mobility, restricted by discourses and practices that homogenize and degrade them and transform them into vulnerable, dependent, low-status social categories. Yet many internal refugees in Sri Lanka . . . have impressed me precisely by the opposite qualities: by their resilience, their capacity for . . . survival, and their potential to rebuild their lives. How have they maintained . . . [a] sense of self? How are they maneuvering within the politics of space and control . . . ? My answers . . . are based on the study of literature and on anthropological research. . . .

When I speak of Tamil people in Sri Lanka, I refer to . . . many [who] have been forced to move from home, sometimes temporarily but mostly for a period of years without any security of ever being able to return home. This . . . condition of homelessness and the continuous feeling of threat and violence that at any moment may force them to flee, has become the reality of everyday life for Tamils in Sri Lanka. During a conversation in January, 1998, an academic colleague in Colombo told me: "Every Tamil is displaced." She missed "her own soil," she said, not being able to return to the north where she had been brought up. . . .

Although people from other communities in Sri Lanka have been forced to leave their homes as well, the Tamil internal refugees constitute by far the majority. According to estimates, they make up around 80% of the internal refugees in the country, whereas 13% are Muslims and 7% Sinhalese. The total number of internal refugees has fluctuated between half a million and 1.2 million, i.e. between one-tenth and one-fifth of Sri Lanka's total population.

Tamilness and Tamil Womanhood. The Tamils comprise very different communities: the "Sri Lanka" Tamils (69%) who consist of both the "Jaffna" and "Batticaloa" Tamils who have lived in Sri Lanka since times unknown, and the "Indian" or "plantation" Tamils who are the descendants of a plantation work-force imported by the British from Tamil Nadu in South India, in the nineteenth century. The majority of the Sri Lanka Tamils live in the northern and eastern parts of the island. There are important socio-cultural differences between Tamils from the north and the east, as well as class and caste differences within all Tamil communities. . . .

The prolonged civil war in Sri Lanka has not only exaggerated the social identities available to Tamil women; it has enabled the construction of a whole range of different practices and discourses on family values and women. At the one extreme there is the LTTE propaganda of "Tamil liberation" by the representation and actual practice of young women as militant fighters. At the other extreme, a most conservative discourse has emerged about the complete collapse of "family values"—not only in the refugee camps but in Tamil society as a whole; and about the breakdown of relations between adults and children and between men and women. At the core of this discourse about the collapse of the earlier "family values" is the concern about the reputation of women and gender power relations—discourses in which ideas on women's freedom of movement and the control of their bodies and sexuality form a crucial element. This new conservatism is a reaction to real changes. For instance, a Tamil woman in Colombo, who lives on her own, recently told me that she has much more freedom of movement and behavior now than before the war. Most of her relatives have gone abroad and this has substantially decreased the social control.

Although constructions of masculinity—e.g., men as the creators and defenders of the "nation" and the "community"—are part and parcel of these discourses, the images of men as a rule are taken for granted and so far I have not met any men in Sri Lanka who openly confessed to feeling confined or distorted by gender representations. . . .

I do not view any of these constructs as the outcome of a passive victimization of the people involved. Neither Tamils, nor women, nor refugees, should be seen as passive victims of mechanisms of control from above. They bring into play their own agency, their actions and initiatives and they create spaces even in situations that from the outside do not seem to provide any scope for exerting influence at all. People have, and use, different options and different means of power, however small, and use these even under extremely restrictive circumstances. A telling example is the way in which Tamil women in Sri Lanka at present are dealing with the prescribed pottu, the decorative mark worn on the forehead.

The Pottu as Ethnic Gender Marker. Woman's appearance and dress in many cultures are seen as symbolizing the community or nation she belongs to. Hindu girls and women are expected to wear the pottu as a symbol of auspiciousness, a custom which has been adopted also by many Protestant and Roman Catholic Tamil women. Married women wear a red pottu, which connotes active sexuality and which should be ritually removed when they become a widow. In Sri Lanka, however, Sinhalese and Muslim women do not wear the point. Therefore, in this country in which one's ethnic background has become a primary means of identification, the pottu has become an ethnic marker par excellence. Tamil women in present-day Sri Lanka face a dilemma: should they stress their Tamilness by applying the pottu, or should they hide their ethnicity for security reasons? Or, to put it more bluntly: should they renounce their sense of self, their deepest identity as a woman of good reputation and adapt to the habits of the "other" who is experienced as the oppressor? For some Tamil women . . . , this is a fundamental and emotional issue; for others it is one of those questions that can be solved in a pragmatic manner.

Banu, a married woman of 25, helped me as a research assistant in Batticaloa. When we visited Tamil communities she applied her pottu, but when we were about to go to a Muslim community she used to wipe it off as she was afraid that by labeling herself as a Tamil she might unnecessarily antagonize the Muslim people. Her husband once commented: "Now see, like this you look like a widow." Banu is now living in Colombo with her husband and two little children. Their house is in a Sinhala neighbourhood and for security reasons and following her husband's advice, she has stopped altogether applying the pottu.

Shyantala, a woman of international repute, in her early forties, started wearing the pottu at the age of 30, although she was and remained, unmarried. This, as she says, to be given the respect she needs. She dresses "traditionally" but highly fashionably, using her pottu not only to be given respect, but as a symbol of fashion, too.

Rajini, a lecturer at one of the universities, married, about forty, . . . would rather die than remove her pottu. "Not to wear it would be like going out undressed," she said, . . . [with] a long explanation about the positive functions of the pottu, stressing that besides symbolising the essence of a married woman, it protected from the evil eye and that it was good for health as the act of applying it every day stimulated the underlying chakra, having meditational value as well.

Cowry, middle-aged and with a good position in the higher management of a bank, explains that she stopped wearing the pottu altogether during the most difficult years in the 1980s and early 90s. She did not want to draw more attention to her "Tamilness," feeling that the pottu might antagonise her colleagues. Now, she applies it only when she wears a saree and leaves it off when she dresses in western clothes. At times, however, when she likes to challenge people, even when wearing western dress she applies the pottu very consciously as an act of defiance.

Sitha, an unmarried girl in her mid-twenties, has been trying hard not to be recognised as a Tamil at all. She never wears a pottu, she has practised her Sinhalese to get rid of her accent and says she feels satisfied that she even "looks like a Sinhalese." . . .

Devi, a well-to-do middle-aged woman who drives her own car, removes her pottu each time she approaches a check point, pastes it onto the dashboard and puts it back only after she has passed the area.

Many more women told me how they manoeuvred the pottu during the past years, having become aware of the different meanings attributed to it. Again, I was struck by the extremes: women who consciously chose to apply the pottu as an act of defiance on the one hand, and on the other those who altogether stopped wearing the pottu and tried to erase all other outward signs of Tamilness—with all the options in between. Even widows have started to use the new space created by the war: increasingly they are wearing the pottu as a public sign of rejecting the inauspicious, out-cast status traditionally attributed to Hindu widows. I heard about a group of war-widows in one of the refugee camps in the east who collectively decided to continue wearing the pottu. The "personal" in this context is extremely political.

Discourses on Tamil "Womanhood." The various ways in which Tamil women in Sri Lanka manoeuvre the pottu do not reflect merely individual attitudes. The various choices are informed—consciously or not—by a mixture of discourses that represent collective tendencies. Images of "womanhood" in all their variations are part and parcel of this. For instance, in conversations with Tamil people about the present-day political situation, I encountered mixtures of extremely different constructs of womanhood that can be classified into four categories. For analytical reasons I have labeled these as gendered discourses. . . .

I. *"Traditional" Tamil discourse:* Women in their behaviour and appearance represent and symbolise the ethnic community, they are ethnic markers. . . . The pottu has become essential for (Hindu) Tamilness and Tamil womanhood. The red pottu on women connotes active sexuality controlled by stable marital relations which are the very base of one's community and personhood; family values centre around these stable marital relations. The "good" woman and "good" morals are set against the imagined "loose morals" in refugee camps where "some women establish relationships with men without being married, in exchange for protection, gifts, or even money." These women are stereotyped as devadasi's, i.e., promiscuous women and prostitutes.

II. *Nationalist, "ethnicised" discourse:* Tamils belong to the north and east, it is "their own soil." There is increasing fear that the Tamil community and culture will gradually disappear and ultimately be wiped out altogether. The Tamil diaspora is scattered around the globe, and Tamil culture is under severe attack. Women should wear the pottu as a symbol of their nation. Women are the mothers and caretakers of the nation, and their responsibility as the guardians of Tamil culture is more crucial than ever before. Not only that, their role as biological procreators is crucial as well: they should counteract the present population decline by producing Tamil children without any restriction of modern contraception. This discourse is produced in its most extreme form by the LTTE, but it can be encountered less pronounced in other Tamil circles as well.

III. *Leftist Tamil critique:* "Traditional Tamilness" has to be combated; it is seen as a positive development that inter-caste marriages have significantly increased as a result of the war and the influence of leftist nationalist Tamil movements. This development should be encouraged so that the caste system will finally break down. Women, whether or not they wear the pottu, have to be emancipated as co-revolutionaries, but within the limits set by the leftist male political agenda. Women should not have an agenda of their own, their role has to he limited to defending the new Tamilness.

IV. *Feminist critique:* Feminist values have inspired a critique of the discourses of both "traditional" and leftist Tamilness. Women members of the nationalist movements of the 1980s have made use of the new political space to assert themselves as defenders of their own women's rights. The dependence of women on men and inequality between marriage partners is seen as a negative situation that should be changed. However, the use of ideas of women's liberation solely or mainly, for military purposes (the woman Tiger with gun) is rejected. The pottu can be worn as a symbol, an identification with "Tamilness," or a fashion, or it can be dropped—what matters is that women can make their own choices.

. . . I was struck by the ease and flexibility with which various elements of these gendered discourses could be mixed within one conversation. For example, an academic colleague told me, within a half hour, how she missed her own soil (discourse 1), that, luckily, the number of inter-caste marriages in the north was increasing fast which showed that caste barriers were eroding (discourse 3), that Tamil women in general and Tamil widows in particular were rather conservative (discourse 1, 2 and, because of the implicit criticism, 4), that she was very worried about Tamil fertility going down (discourse 2) and that she was also concerned about the loose morals in the refugee camps (discourse 1). Finally, she was quite emotional about the fact that according to traditional Jaffna Tamil family law a married woman (she herself included) cannot do any transaction without her husband's permission (discourse 4). Gender and ethnicity, although circumscribed by what is considered to be "culture" and "tradition," are flexible and dynamic constructs, interlinked with each other and prone to fundamental or subtle changes, depending on the dynamics of the political discourses and practices by which people are informed.

The "Traditional" Discourse on "Tamil Womanhood." According to the "traditional" discourse in all communities in Sri Lanka, women are conceptualised on the basis of their relations with men: they are daughters, sisters, wives and mothers, not persons in their own right. Although the Sri Lankan women's movement in all its diversity as well as some of the by-products of globalisation have created counter-discourses, the "traditional" discourse is still very influential. . . . This ideology is characteristic of Sri Lanka but also of (South) Asia as a whole: the duties of the good wife or daughter of a political leader, for instance, encompass the willingness to look after the whole nation in case of the decease of the husband or father—as shown for instance by Indira Gandhi, Benazir Butto, Sirima Bandaranaike and Chandrika Kumaratunge.

According to the old ideal of Tamil "Womanhood," girls were expected to be obedient daughters to their parents, wives had to obey their husbands and widows their brothers and adult sons. Women should be chaste, caring and self-sacrificing . . . symbolically expressed in their body language and way of dress. They should move around in a chaste manner, keep their legs together and cover their bodies decently. They should reserve their sexuality only for their legal husband and bestow on him respect and procreation. If possible, they should display their husbands' affluence by the wearing of rich sarees, brilliant jewellery. . . . But they should also be brave: in times of conflict, mothers should be willing to send their husbands and sons to the battlefield for the well-being of their nation. . . .

These images, used by the militant Tamil nationalist movements that emerged in the 1980s, were moulded into a miraculous combination of motherhood and violent battle imagery: the woman who holds an automatic rifle in one hand and a child in another. Military men are represented as the heroes and their mothers as heroic women who sacrifice their children for the nation. However heroic, women according to this representation still have to be obedient, chaste and "pure." There have been struggles in Jaffna, between the local women's movement and the militant groups, about newly prescribed restrictions on women's dress and behaviour. Coomaraswamy (1996: 10) comments: " . . . the LTTE ideal of the armed guerilla woman puts forward an image of purity and virginity. . . . The women are described as pure, virtuous. Their chastity, their unity of purpose and their sacrifice of social life supposedly gives them strength. They are denied sexual or sensual experiences. . . . The armed virginal woman cadre ensures that this notion of purity, based on denial, is a part of the social construction of what it means to be a woman according to the world view of the LTTE."

Militant Nationalist Discourse on "Tamil Womanhood." Such Tamil nationalist representations of "woman" rest on images of firm family relations: stable families with chaste, obedient women and a strict hierarchy between men and women, parents and children, brothers and sisters. In discourse as well as in practice, this ideal was undermined by the civil war between the Sri Lankan government—in the late 1980s assisted by the "Indian Peace Keeping Force"—and the LTTE. The war has resulted in vast and continuous movements of people, forced and voluntary migration, a growing diaspora of Tamils all over the world, the disruption of the earlier generational, age, class and caste hierarchies and an increasing demographic imbalance due to the shortage of men, young men in particular. All this has had deep effects on the ideal and practice of "stable family relations" in the north. This, in its turn, has fed a strikingly conservative discourse when it comes to the so-called private sphere. The LTTE is clever in playing on people's deep-felt emotions about their family values and culture. . . .

In the context of a prolonged civil war, the geo-politics of a "Tamil homeland," the ethnic cleansing that took place when in 1990 the LTTE by force expelled all Muslims from the north, the reduction of the population by the war, the large-scale people's movements, all this instigated the LTTE— besides stressing woman's responsibility to participate in the military—to emphasise the crucial importance of woman's reproductive role.

The LTTE therefore banned all family planning services from the health departments and urged women not only to sacrifice their sons and daughters for the nation, but to produce as many children as possible to expand the nation that was threatened by decline and extinction. Now unmarried mothers were no longer regarded as the ultimate stigma of their community, but they were encouraged to have their babies and then hand them over to the LTTE to be brought up as heroes for the nation. The state's family planning policy was depicted as a conspiracy to control the demographic size of the Tamil population (Maunaguru 1995: 164). Although this conspiracy theory does not rest on official government policy, in fact during my own research quite a few Sinhalese civil servants expressed ideas to me that came close to eugenics. For example, in 1993, a matron in a public maternity clinic where a woman of one of the refugee camps in Colombo had just given birth, referred to "these Tamils reproducing themselves like rats, they should all be sterilised." Seeing the expression on my face she explained: "When her son (pointing at the new-born baby) gets 14, he will take a gun and kill us all." Only later I heard that this nurse had lost her own son when he was fighting in the army.

According to Maunaguru (1995: 163–164), until the late 1980s women in the militant Tamil movements were only involved in propaganda, medical care and fund raising. But after the number of males available for fighting significantly decreased (due to the IPKF occupation and the number of Tamils who left the country), women in the movements were trained as fighters as well and the LTTE was in the forefront of providing military training to women. This resulted in a categorical shift in the construction of "woman" from "brave mother" to that of "woman warrior." . . .

Feminist Critique. The acceptance of the militant Tamil groups, however narrow, of women's liberation as one of the ultimate goals provided an important space for feminist activism in the north (Maunaguru 1995: 164). Although in the 1980s the women there saw women's oppression mainly as stemming from economic relations, they also raised other issues such as rape in connection with the general violence against women. Another act of protest was that women organised themselves as groups of mothers, such as "The Mothers' Front" in the north, protesting against the gruesome human rights violations. Thus, by using the traditional, accepted identity of the mother, they went beyond the limitations of their gender, openly protesting against the violent repression of the state. "While the nationalist ideology perceived women as objects that were to be controlled for their interests, women formulated constructions that expressed gender interests that attempted to empower women" (Maunaguru 1995: 168).

The phenomenon of the armed women fighters of the LTTE, too, is "against the current" of mainstream thinking about women (Coomaraswamy 1996: 8). Is this a "welcome step in the liberation of women" as Adele Balasingham (1993, quoted in Coomaraswamy 1996: 9) suggests? Sri Lankan feminist writers think otherwise: Kumari Jayawardena's (1986) analysis of the limitations of nationalist movements for women's space to develop their own aspirations would equally apply to the gender imagery in the LTTE nationalism. Radhika Coomaraswamy (1996: 10) summarises her feminist criticism of the LTTE-propagated identity of women as follows: The earlier Tamil notion of the ideal woman, however negative, was a celebration of life. Prosperity, sexuality, love of music and the arts were all important aspects of the married woman's paradigm. The LTTE, in contrast, puts forward as ideals self-sacrifice, austerity and androgyny, and death, not life, is celebrated.

The LTTE ideal of androgyny celebrates only the "masculine" qualities, negating and eradicating constructions of "femininity." . . . In the LTTE discourse there is no notion of woman as an independent person, empowered by her own agency, who makes decisions for her own self-realisation. . . . "Her liberation is only accepted in so far as it fits the contours of the nationalist project" (Coomaraswamy 1996: 10). And, I add, these contours are defined by the male leaders of the movement. The LTTE ideal of the armed guerilla woman puts forward an image of purity and virginity. Their chastity and sacrifice of social life give them strength. To take this further, it comes close to the ideal of complete disembodiment, the ultimate release from the body. According to this discourse, cleverly manipulated by the LTTE, women, who are believed to suffer from bodily disadvantages and impurities more than men, have a congenital handicap, but they can be released from this by becoming martyrs; traditionally, as widows, by sati—self-immolation; and today, as suicide bombers, by dying for the nation (Trawick 1996). Coomaraswamy (1996: 10) concludes that "unless feminism is linked to humanism, to non-violence and to a celebration of life over death, it will not provide society with the alternatives that we so desperately seek."

"Womanhood" and "The Refugee." The above discussion makes clear that neither "Tamilness" nor "Tamil womanhood" are static qualities, although these notions are informed and circumscribed by "culture" and "tradition." They are socio-cultural and historical constructs; dynamic, multidimensional and multi-layered and the outcome of both mechanisms of control and struggles for liberation. Women have been making use of the new spaces created by the political movements and the war, with their resulting mixture of gendered discourses, to reconstruct their identities and to put their own issues on the agenda. So far, however, the voices and agency of Tamil refugee women have remained in the dark; the different discourses I refer to mainly spring from urban, middle-class circles and have not been informed by the experiences and views of internal refugees in Sri Lanka— a group which, although extremely marginalised, should be taken into account, if only because of their sheer numbers and political importance. How do they come into the picture?

During my work with refugees and particularly women refugees, one of the recurrent questions that came to my mind was how these women, living under radically new, however miserable circumstances, reconstructed their identities (cf. Schrijvers 1997). Did they, too, like the Tamil women in the north who participated in the movements, make use of the new space for changing their gender identities? Tamil refugee women are living under and manoeuvring within, two "systems of control": patriarchy and extreme political repression. Both systems are severely oppressive and strengthen each other: both Tamil women and refugees in Sri Lanka's present political situation are the subjects of cultural and political control, restricted in their physical and social mobility, restricted by representations and practices that tend to homogenize and degrade them, that can transform them into non-autonomous, vulnerable, dependent, low-status social categories. This double—patriarchal and political—system of control not only restricts their free movement, it can make them dependent on patronizing and de-powering "protection" in the private as well as the public sphere, and it can exclude them from participation in decision-making at all levels, including decision-making about their own private lives. Patriarchal control, thought to be "natural," tends to degrade them into second-class citizens, not allowing them full space for self-determination and self-definition, whereas the political control of refugees has turned them into third-class citizens who have been living as outcasts and prisoners of the state. The most extreme situation I encountered during my research was in Vavuniya, in January 1998, where twelve and a half thousand Tamil refugees—driven from home by the on-going war in the north of the country—were forced to live in (semi) closed detention camps.

This sounds miserable, and it is. At the same time, however, the representation of victimised outcasts does not correspond with the overall impression women in refugee camps in Sri Lanka gave me. Many refugees in Sri Lanka, women in particular, have impressed me precisely by very different qualities: by their resilience, their capacity for physical and mental survival, their flexibility, their potential to reconstruct their lives—each and every time after each new flight. In spite of the "traditional family values" with their strong patriarchal aspects, in spite of the control and terror from the side of the Sri Lanka Army, the LTTE and other movements and in spite of all the restrictions in their freedom of movement, many women refugees have created spaces within these two systems of control; they have enabled themselves to a certain extent to see to their family interests and to survive as human beings. I will try to illustrate these observations.

To start with, I found women refugees in camps in Sri Lanka to be very different from the image created in governmental and non-governmental documents. Although of course they were in need of the most basic things in life, they were neither extremely vulnerable nor predominantly miserable. On the contrary, in all the camps I visited (altogether around 15 in Colombo, Puttalam, Batticaloa and Vavuniya), many women impressed me precisely by their activity and their pragmatic approach to coping with all difficulties. Of course, the camps sheltered many types of people and it would be unrealistic and degrading to describe them as one homogeneous category. People were differentiated according to class, caste, age, regional background, past experiences and personality. There were very miserable and very tough refugees. In terms of socio-economic background, the refugees staying in the camps in the main belonged to the poorer, lower-class and lower-caste sectors.

The internal refugees in Sri Lanka form an under-class among all people (Schrijvers 1997). Both in the Tamil camps in Colombo and in Vavuniya the majority of the people most probably came from the plantation sector— being so-called "Plantation" or "Indian Tamils" who had been affected by the anti-Tamil riots in 1977, 1983 and thereafter. They were not even the Tamils for whose cause the LTTE was at war with the government! They were a group severely discriminated against in Sri Lanka already before the riots against Tamils increased during the 1970s and 80s and also looked down upon by the Sri Lanka Tamils. Now, they had become the most downtrodden outcast Tamils of all. So, most probably, although it is bitter to say, the previous experiences of these women of having to cope with a very insecure life world in which socio-economic discrimination and difficulties of daily survival were the "normal" state of affairs, had helped them to carry on. When evaluating women's agency in the camps, then, it is necessary to keep in mind that the majority of the internal refugees are not from an (upper) middle-class/caste background—whereas this probably, although implicitly, is the primary reference group of the feminist writers quoted above.

There were five gendered elements of people's lives in the refugee camps in Sri Lanka that particularly struck me:

1. *Gender differences in coping with refugee life.* On the whole, it was my impression that women more than men had been able to make the best of their new identity of "The Refugee." There was an alarming degree of male alcoholism coupled with violence against women and children (cf. Schrijvers 1997). . . . According to this group of women, the problem had increased tremendously after they had started living in camps. For the men, taking to drinking provided an escape from the reality of having lost everything— their work, their status, their network of relations, their property—in short, the core of their male identity. I was struck by the apparent ease with which women, uprooted from their homes and everybody and everything known to them, managed to cope with the facts of life. Widows and women with young children found it most difficult to cope. Many women whom I met in the camps, whenever they were allowed to leave the camps, had taken up work in factories and companies, they worked as housemaids, made food items and sold them in or outside the camps, they sewed, made flowers and knitwear, or were sweeping roads. For the majority, and in particular

for the women belonging to the community of the plantation Tamils, this was in a way a continuation of their earlier work experiences as poor, low-caste women who had been used to a tough life as second-class citizens in the class, caste and gender-hierarchy. However, I met women belonging to more affluent families of protected, middle-class backgrounds, who had for the first time in their lives taken up work outside, now transgressing the strict boundaries of their gendered, caste and class determined identities.

According to my analysis this capacity of women to adapt to the role of "The Refugee" is linked, on the one hand, to the continuity in their gender roles—they continued their primary tasks as mothers, housewives, and second-class citizens, although under extremely miserable circumstances. Paradoxically, women adapted more easily to this new fate precisely because they were used already to living dependent, restricted and in many cases oppressed lives. For them, there was no rupture with the past such as most men had experienced (cf. Schrijvers 1997). But, on the other hand, the fact that even middle-class housewives, who had not seen much of the world outside their homes, took up paid work outside the camps and in a way enjoyed their new independence, shows that they made use of the situation to transgress the strict confines of their gender identity. As social agents they contributed to the changing images of womanhood. . . .

2. *Gender differences regarding the identification with ethnic politics.* The women whom I met in the camps generally had a strong distaste [for] discussing ethnic politics and sometimes plainly refused to occupy themselves with what they experienced as a most depressive and destructive subject. "We don't like politics, we hate all the groups," women in Sithamparapuram told me in January 1998, when I commented that generally when I talked with a group of men they immediately started discussing political affairs. Of course this does not mean that women were a-political, or not involved in a political sense. Taking a stand for peace is at least as political as taking part in war. However, in contrast to many men, women were involved predominantly with the down-to-earth responsibility of day-to-day survival of their family group—a gender-prescribed responsibility which did not tally with what they experienced as life-threatening and destructive politics. When the political situation was touched upon, many women in the camps referred to the danger that the LTTE and other movements formed for their sons and daughters. Very often they preferred to stay in the camps hoping to prevent their children from joining the LTTE. "We don't bring up our children to have them shot by the army," they explained. Men were worried about their children as well, but expressed this much less directly. Their communications with me were shaped more by the dominant, ethnicised discourse.

It was as if most of the men tried to reconstruct their identities by stressing their ethnic community and the characteristics that symbolized this. Women's behaviour and the "family values," resting on clear patriarchal principles, formed the core of this ethnic discourse (Schrijvers 1997). . . .

3. *The gendered expression of the need for human dignity.* Most refugees experienced the camps as giving at least a basic sort of protection and security, which they had lost completely in the outside world. Increasingly I learned that this need for security should not be understood merely in its physical, material sense. It equally involved the regaining of (self) respect and human dignity—and this involved the emphasis on certain cultural, religious and family values. For example, one day a refugee woman asked me to visit her "house" in Sithamparapuram camp in Vavuniya, consisting of one 6m × 6m room, in which she lived with her husband and two grown-up children. Compared to other rooms I had seen, this one was extremely well-kept. A decorated hand-woven mat covered the well-swept floor and the room was tidy with the few belongings stored away behind a mat-curtain that separated off almost one third of the room. The woman gestured me to have a look behind the curtain: this was their prayer room, with a small Hindu altar constructed in the corner! It was obvious that all this was essential for her to live not as an animal in a shed, but as a cultural and spiritual human being.

Regaining a feeling of dignity was closely connected to the right of getting the space and freedom of movement to achieve at least a minimum of self-sustainability and self-determination. Again and again, in all the camps, people during our conversations stressed that they did not want to be refugees, they just wanted to have the space, however little, to live and work in freedom. For instance, in January 1998 I asked women in Sithamparapuram camp, in Vavuniya, whom I had also met in Saraswathie Hall in Colombo, in 1993, which camp was better. Without any hesitation they chose Saraswathie Hall: "There we did not need a pass to go out!" This in spite of the fact that they had lived there collectively with a few hundred people in one big hall and in Vavuniya their children had a better education. They mentioned this several times during our talk. It was precisely this freedom of movement and therefore the opportunity to earn which the government had taken away from them. When in 1993 and 1994 in Colombo all Tamil refugee camps were closed, the people who wanted to stay in the capital and continue their work in the informal sector were not allowed to. They were all transported to "transit camps" in the east and the north, to be subjected to a much more severe and oppressive "pass system" that forced them to get permission to leave the camp, to identify themselves at each and every checkpoint, and to report back in the camp on the same day after a varying number of hours.

This third element, I found, did not differ greatly regarding women's and men's approaches. Regaining a sense of dignity was equally important for both sexes. For both women and men, reconstructing their identity and their sense of human dignity was a priority, but they expressed and shaped this need in very different ways. The expression of the need for human dignity was therefore gendered. This is not surprising when keeping in mind that the male and female gender identities are constructed in different ways. For the men, who primarily identified themselves with their public roles and interests outside the home, it was taken for granted and considered to be "natural" that they talked politics and reconstructed their selves through contrasts, oppositions and antagonisms with other ethnic groups. In this process, stressing the "family values" and "women's behaviour"—as opposed to the "customs" of other communities—were central elements (cf. Schrijvers 1997). For the women, however, regaining a sense of self and self-respect first of all seemed to emerge from the ability to continue their prescribed gender responsibilities in the private sphere, by providing the necessary motherly, wifely and household care. Paradoxically, and this was crucial, those women who transgressed gender boundaries by contributing to the family income, gained self-respect and confidence in themselves.

4. *The gendered processes contributing to the refugees' feelings of dependence.* There are many ways in which the deep-felt need for regaining dignity and self-respect described above can be taken more seriously. For instance, the encouragement of male and female refugees to form self-organizations and participate in structures of decision-making which directly affect their life-worlds in the camps, could be an important step forward. Unfortunately, the actual situation is the opposite. Both the discourse on "The Refugee" as well as the practice regarding refugees, have increased their dependency. Only recently representations of "The Refugee" in NGO-reports in Sri Lanka have started to include statements like: "While most expressed a gratitude for the assistance received, there is a general feeling that the dependency on relief is humiliating and that personal liberty is somewhat (sic!) restricted in the camp" (Sperber 1996). Yet, the dominant representation of refugees in these reports is still transforming them into miserable victims who should receive (not co-determine) aid and support—of a material kind only. Certain types of refugee women are represented as particularly in need of support: widows, female heads of household, young mothers, single women—as a rule to be mentioned together with other pitiful categories such as "the elderly," the "handicapped," the "physically weak" (Sperber 1996). Although widows

and single mothers do constitute the most vulnerable group in conflict situations, I feel that reproducing discourses and practices that merely stress their misery and falsely suggest that they are passive victims, does not really help them. Widows, and particularly Hindu widows, feel degraded when they are unidimensionally identified and lumped together according to this inauspicious status.

The dominant practice of creating more dependency instead of less has had a tremendous impact on the overall attitude the refugees have developed towards the outside world. Many have started acting according to the miserable imagery of "The Refugee." In my encounters it was evident for instance that people first of all hoped to get some concrete, material help from me—for them, I was a potential new resource to be tried out. . . .

Sometimes people who had already been in the camps since 1983 could no longer imagine an independent, secure life outside the camp. But in general, when given a choice, men and women would always opt for conditions enabling them to sustain themselves again. When, for example, I asked a group of six women in Sithamparapuram camp, where they thought I could meet them in five years time—where would they be by then?—they said without any hesitation: "We hope to be abroad, in India!" Four of them for a few years had stayed in India in refugee camps and had been forced to return. They preferred to go back to India immediately, because they liked it over there: "We had work, food was cheap, there was enough to eat and we did not have passes there. The biggest problem here is the pass system." In other words, the best situation they could think of at the moment was a working life that would give them security, freedom and autonomy—even if this would be abroad. They could not return to the "uncleared" areas they came from, in Kilinochchi and Mullaitivu in the north, and were not entitled to benefit from the government resettlement programme in Vavuniya, because this was only for people who had lived there since at least 1990.

5. *The gendered discourse on the "collapse of family values."* Outside the camps, when talking with different people—governmental and non-governmental officers, policy-makers, academics, journalists, human rights activists—many of them reproduced the conservative discourse about collapsing family values, moral deterioration, et cetera, particularly in reference to the situation in refugee camps. In this discourse gender and age relations had a central place. For example, a concerned journalist in Vavuniya told me about the camps: "You know, all social values have gone, and family bonds are not there. There are not only broken families, but the people are kept inside the camps as if in a prison, women cannot attend to their natural problems during their sick days, they are living in the common hall so they cannot

change clothes. If they keep on living like this for another few years, what will be their mentality? The families are split, women are without their men and children without parents and the values are gradually decreasing.". . . Other people stressed the dangers of what they imagined to be the crux of life in a camp: promiscuity and prostitution. In their representations, too, gender and age were important dimensions, in that the imagined evils were projected onto women and youngsters. These representations and family values have been formed by the Brahmanical values of patriarchy, which are still very influential. . . .

In fact, within the camps I did not get the impression that there was more "promiscuity" or prostitution than in the other situations of poverty with which I am familiar in Sri Lanka and elsewhere. Women, as far as they could, managed to keep their broken families together, they earned an income if they could and some women engaged in different sorts of (sexual) relations in exchange for protection, affection and maintenance (which exchange is fundamentally not very different from the exchange in a bourgeois marital setup) and some women prostituted themselves if there was no other way to keep their families going—just like in "ordinary" situations of poverty. . . .

In Conclusion: Manoeuvring Within the Politics of Space and Control. In spite of the lack of gender-sensitive, let alone emancipatory support structures, many Tamil women in refugee camps in Sri Lanka . . . have increased their space for manoeuvring vis-à-vis their men and vis-à-vis people visiting their camps. As far as I know, they have not started any women's self-organizations in order to see to their rights as refugees and as women. Their experiences and views so far have not informed the different gendered discourses that are influencing mainly the lives of urban, middle-class people. Interestingly, however, without having had any support from a women's movement or women's organization within the camps, these refugee women voiced ideals that came very close to a feminist discourse, according to which women can assert themselves as defenders of their own women's rights. Many of these refugee women are actually representing and even practising the ideal of women's liberation as formulated by Radhika Coomaraswamy (1996: 10): " . . . an independent woman, empowered by her own agency, who makes decisions for her own self-realization . . . (with) autonomy or empowerment as an end in themselves."

It was precisely this element however that provoked concerned people of Tamil background, when it came to women and gender relations, to fall back on a most conservative, patriarchal discourse of "Tamilness," stressing the danger of "the collapse of family values," and the "breaking down of the family structure." These dangers were being projected onto the imagined life in the refugee camps, where women in particular were thought to represent the imagined promiscuous chaos. However, according to my own observations, refugee life in the camps was not representative of "an overall breakdown of family values." It mostly reminded me of other situations of extreme poverty I am familiar with, aggravated by the humiliating state control and complete lack of freedom of movement. The situation was worst in the camps in Vavuniya, where all Tamil refugees were treated like dangerous criminals instead of war victims—a war for which the Sri Lankan state in the first place has to be held responsible.

Although living for years in a refugee camp is probably one of the worst possible situations to be in, the changes in "family values" that have occurred in the camps and, more generally, as a result of the war, need not be interpreted as a process with only negative aspects. The new spaces created by chaos and change have been used by Tamil women refugees themselves to increase their autonomy and self-esteem. They have taken on whatever work they could get, evaluating this not as a collapse of family values, but as an opportunity to gain more control over their lives and to survive at least somewhat better as human beings. Tamil women refugees have to endure what I have called "two systems of control": severe political repression and patriarchy. As Tamils and as women, they are forced to live a grim life affected by ethnic violence and double discrimination. However, many of them, by working and earning inside or outside the camps, have managed to loosen the grip of the state and of patriarchal control, finding spaces for transgressing earlier restrictive gender boundaries. In summary, by connecting the constructs of "Tamilness," "Womanhood," and "The Refugee," I have tried to make clear how Tamil women in Sri Lanka and Tamil women refugees in particular, are continuously manoeuvring between these identities, negotiating new spaces and transformations. The outcomes are shaped by ethnic, gender, caste, class and age relations, by collective and personal identifications in which politics and power dynamics play a crucial and complicated role. There will never be a static "Tamil identity," "Woman identity," or "Refugee identity." Although informed and circumscribed by notions about "traditional culture," such representations and practices are mouldable social constructs that, especially in the context of conflict and war, are not without danger. They can be, and are all the time, misused by those in positions of power, who stigmatize, humiliate and endanger particular categories of people, such as Tamils and particularly also Tamil internal refugees, in Sri Lanka. It is not Tamils, refugees, or women that are the problem, however. It is the violent discourses about them and the resulting practices that are dangerous. The support to the peace-process, however modest, that academics can give is mostly non-material, but nonetheless substantial: by trying to deconstruct and reconstruct these discourses we can help to dissolve dangerously uni-dimensional constructs and to support processes of "multi-identifications" that support people to identify themselves with different dimensions of social life. I feel that listening to Tamil women refugees themselves and taking seriously their own analyses that point to the need of transformed and multiple identities, is the most constructive contribution I, as an outsider, can make at this moment.

Works Cited

Coomaraswamy, Radhika. 1996. "Tiger Women and the Question of Women's Emancipation," *Pravada* 4, no. 9: 8–10.

Jayawardena, Kumari. 1986. *Feminism and Nationalism in the Third World*. London: Zed Books.

Maunaguru, Sitralega. 1995. "Gendering Tamil Nationalism: The Construction of 'Woman' in Projects of Protest and Control." In Pradeep Jeganathan and Qadri Ismail, eds., *Unmaking the Nation: The Politics of Identity and History in Modern Sri Lanka*. Colombo: Social Scientists Association. 158–75.

Schrijvers, Joke. 1997. "Internal Refugees in Sri Lanka: The Interplay of Ethnicity and Gender," *European Journal of Development Research* 9, no. 2: 62–81.

Sperber, Ulla Glavind. 1996. "Return Home? Social Survey of IDP's and Indian Returnees in Vavuniya District (cleared area)." Report for UNHCR (unpublished).

Trawick, Margaret. 1996. "Gendered Aspects of International LTTE Image- Formation." Paper for the Conference on Violence against Women in South Asia, ICES, Colombo, 27–31 March 1996 (unpublished).

Translating Remembering

Benjamin Schonthal

Part of the LTTE's appeal as "the boys" rested on its ability to present itself as the legitimate defenders of the Tamil nation. Its fallen cadres were understood as national heroes or martyrs to the cause. How the LTTE made use of religious imagery to promote their cause has been recently debated by some scholars. Benjamin Schonthal discusses how some of the language used by the LTTE seemed to be intentionally "ambivocal." His essay is particularly salient given the spectacular events of May 2009, when the LTTE was defeated in terms of conventional warfare and its leadership, including Vellupillai Prabhakaran and his senior followers, almost entirely wiped out. How will they be remembered?

Remembering

On May 18, 2009, regular broadcasting on Sri Lanka's public TV stations was interrupted to cover breaking news. The Sri Lankan army had found the body of the leader of the Liberation Tigers of Tamil Eelam (LTTE). After weeks of speculation about his whereabouts (some saying he had escaped to India or Malaysia, others saying he had retreated to more secure bunkers in the North), a corpse appeared on TV that seemed to confirm what many had considered impossible: Velupillai Prabhakaran was dead. In the hours and days that followed the announcement, this image of Prabhakaran came to dominate the Sri Lankan media, a corpse, in crumpled fatigues, eyes open, wilted torso raised slightly off the ground by soldiers' hands, another set of hands fixing a small piece of cloth around his head, covering the spot where a bullet had entered.

Around Sri Lanka, in homes, in train stations, peering in the windows of electronics stores, people watched these broadcasts, stunned. Prabhakaran had been a media recluse, virtually never giving interviews or appearing publically, especially in the later years. When he did appear, LTTE photographers and videographers carefully choreographed the shots, transmitting images of a stout, erect man, seated or standing next to a red-and-yellow

LTTE flag, uniform ironed, revolver holstered to one side of his belt. This was the vision that was fixed in people's minds, and the vision that they struggled to reconcile with the footage of the mustachioed corpse which was recycling over and over on the special report. It was not only the fact of Prabhakaran's death that shocked people, all over the island there had been rumors suggesting it. What stunned many was the way in which this death was presented—not in the usual wide-angle view of a soldier's coffin or bodies scattered on a battlefield, but in a wandering, close-angle zoom on the pallid flesh and vacant eyes of an individual dead body.

This visual rendering of Prabhakaran as a lifeless human body, a corpse among others on a battlefield, was the emphatic opposite of how the LTTE had managed its own images of its leader and of its war dead. From the late 1980s onwards, by which time the group had established its dominance in the North through killing and intimidating all rivals, the LTTE spent considerable energy and resources to ensure that its war dead were not remembered as ordinary casualties of war, corpses drawn from a battlefield, but were memorialized in more solemn and lofty ways. To do this, the LTTE developed and administered a comprehensive campaign of commemoration for its dead soldiers, beginning with memorial ceremonies for those killed in battle and evolving into an elaborate collection of roadside monuments, posters, military grave sites, songs, videos, speeches and regular, annual celebrations. The object of these commemoration practices was to transform the memory and meaning of soldiers' deaths from something tragic into something inspiring;[1] rather than signs of loss, the bodies of soldiers who died in battle were eulogized as seeds out of which would grow a future Tamil homeland.[2] This symbolic transformation of the meaning of soldiers' deaths was especially important in the case of the LTTE's suicide cadres, called Black Tigers.[3] Through commemoration, the LTTE recollected Black Tigers' deaths not as a negative or common act of suicide (Tamil: *taRkolai*) but as a positive and extraordinary act of giving oneself (Tamil: *taRkoTai*) for a greater cause. These commemoration practices were essential to the LTTE, both as a way to maintain public support for the war and as a way to motivate its soldiers in battle.

The LTTE spent enormous amounts of time and resources commemorating its dead. By 2005, the group had erected, in concrete and stone, dozens of roadside monuments in the North and East and had undertaken regular campaigns of postering and graffiti on the walls surrounding the main streets of towns and villages. On the Jaffna peninsula and in the Vanni, where water and fuel were in extremely short supply, the LTTE landscaped its military cemeteries with lush, irrigated gardens and installed rows of generator-powered lights to make sure soldiers' graves stayed illuminated throughout the night. . . . The LTTE maintained a special department to oversee these sites and projects. An "Office of Great Heroes," staffed by soldiers who were injured on the battlefield was responsible for the maintenance and upkeep of 21 military cemeteries, as well as the periodic burials and rites that took place there.

Perhaps the centerpiece of the LTTE's practice of commemorating its dead was an annual "Heroes Day" speech delivered by Velupillai Prabhakaran on November 27 that eulogized the LTTE soldiers who died in battle. From the early 1990s until 2008, this speech was given yearly and it articulated the LTTE's vision for the future, its reasons for fighting and its admiration for soldiers. These speeches were broadcast by local radio, satellite and internet, to parts of Sri Lanka and around the world. For journalists, these speeches provided glimpses of the LTTE's military and political objectives, a lengthy, coherent enumeration of its rationales and reactions to current events. For scholars, these speeches offered a further glimpse into the grammar of LTTE commemoration, the language used to describe and remember soldiers.

Central to scholarly analyses of these speeches, and to analyses of LTTE memorial practices more generally, has been a consideration of what role religion plays in the imagery and terminology of commemoration. On one hand, there are those who underscored the importance of religion and who argued that LTTE memorial practices drew much of their symbolism from Christian and Hindu religious traditions and, as a consequence of that borrowing, linked images of military discipline with images of religious devotion, such as Christian martyrdom or Hindu asceticism.[4] On the other hand, there are those who downplayed the significance of religion in LTTE commemoration and who argued that, although the LTTE invoked (unintentionally or intentionally) certain terms and symbols derived from Hinduism and Christianity in its memorial practices, the group neither understood itself in religious terms nor motivated its fighters with promises of martyrdom or mokśa.[5] These observers also pointed out that the LTTE described itself as a secular organization and portrayed the state of Eelam, for which it was fighting, as a secular, socialist state.

Conflicting opinions on the role of religion in LTTE speeches and commemorations have had more than hermeneutic significance; there have been political implications as well. Studies that amplified the importance of religious rationales and imagery in LTTE commemoration practices have had the indirect effects of linking the LTTE with expressly religious militant groups who also undertake suicide attacks, such as Al Qaeda and Hezbollah.[6] These analyses have also undercut the LTTE's own narrative about it-self as a resolutely secular force which is fighting against a zealous Buddhist chauvinist Sri Lankan state. Similarly, analyses that downplayed the motivational significance of religious tropes in LTTE commemoration have been read by some as reproducing the LTTE's own insistence on secularism and, therefore, as affirming uncritically the organization's official self-presentation.[7] Thus, academic investigations of the role of religion in LTTE discourse have overlapped, often unwittingly, with political arguments about the group's underlying motives, its commensurability with other internationally censured militant groups and the legitimacy of its own self-depictions.

With these political implications in mind, this essay argues that the significance of religious imagery in LTTE Heroes Day practices of commemoration cannot be determined definitively—and, thus, the above debate cannot be adjudicated definitively—because the language which the LTTE used to describe its war dead is dually connotative. LTTE descriptions of commemoration can be read both as speaking in religious and non-religious idioms because many Tamil words used in these descriptions have two valences of connotation. This is particularly true in LTTE Heroes Day speeches, which employ dozens of, what I will call, *ambivocal* terms: these are words that, on one hand, have a lexical value in Hindu worship, concepts and terms which are used in the context of temple (*kōvil*)-based deity devotion or which are associated with certain, authorized (*śruti* and *smṛti*) Sanskrit or Tamil texts (*sutras, śastras, purāṇas* and *āgamas*); and, on the other hand, they are also words that, in other contexts, do not directly refer to Hindu worship or texts, connotations of heroism, resolve, dedication, etc. (There are Christian connotations as well, but for the sake of focus, I will only concern myself with Hindu connotations in this essay.) To illustrate this point, I will undertake a close analysis of one section of one LTTE Heroes Day speech from 1997 and examine how the opposing connotative possibilities of ambivocal terms used in that speech create alternate narratives of commemoration which can be read as both religious and as non-religious in tone.

Heroes Day

Before beginning an analysis of the text, I want to give some context as to the occasion for which the text was prepared. The speech, which the transcript transcribes, was given during an LTTE commemorative event on November 27, 1997 called *māvīrar nāḷ*, literally translated "Great Heroes Day," but rendered by some as "Martyrs Day." Great Heroes Day is the largest event in a calendar of nine different *vizā,* or festivals, which the LTTE celebrated annually to commemorate its soldiers. The general outlines of

"Graves" from set of *LTTE Cemetery*. Photo, May 20, 2004, by Ananthan Sinnadurai.

1997 Heroes Day celebrations in the North and East of the island are important for understanding the speech. Heroes Day ceremonies were held at LTTE military cemeteries called *māvīrar tuyilum illam*, literally translated "the home of sleeping great heroes." . . . Ceremonies began at 5:45 pm with a speech delivered by Prabhakaran, most likely from headquarters in Killinocchi, and broadcast to other parts of the island by an LTTE radio station called "Voice of the Tigers." At 6:05 pm, a large torch standing in the middle of LTTE military cemeteries was lit to mark the time of death of the first *māvīrar*, Lt. Cankar, a close confidant of Prabhakaran who died on the same day (November 27) in 1982.[8] At the same moment as the torch lighting, festival organizers rang a bell cuing friends and relatives of deceased soldiers to light smaller oil lamps in front of other graves. The ceremony ended with participants singing songs, specially composed for the event, which mourn deceased LTTE soldiers and express resolve to continue fighting.[9]

Translating a Heroes Day Speech

The Heroes Day speech discussed below was composed in Tamil. The transcript used was taken from a pro-LTTE internet website, and would have been intended, most likely, for LTTE supporters observing Heroes Day in the diaspora, in places like Australia, America, Canada, the UK, Germany, Switzerland and New Zealand. The written version of the speech was distributed to international news agencies, websites and other media outlets by the media department of the "LTTE secretariat" in two versions, a Tamil-language transcript and an English-language translation. Both versions from 1997, Tamil and English, are represented below. The Tamil transcript serves as the basis for three translations, two which are my own and one which is from the LTTE: In Translation 1, I translate the Tamil transcript giving *maximal stress* to the religious connotations of Tamil words used in the speech. That is, I try to make the Hindu-centric connotations of Tamil terms legible to an English reader by deliberately choosing English terms which, typically, implicate the category of religion for Anglophone readers.[10] In Translation 2, I translate the same Tamil words giving *minimal stress* to words' religious connotations, choosing English terms that do *not* directly or conspicuously suggest the category of religion. Translation 3 is an unaltered reproduction of the LTTE's official English translation of the speech, arranged spatially to correspond with my own translations.

These three translations of the Heroes Day speech are juxtaposed . . . in order to cast light on two features of the rhetoric of LTTE commemoration. First, this arrangement foregrounds and magnifies the *ambivocality* of certain words used to describe soldiers who have died in battle and the act of remembering them.[11] Second, [it] illuminates how the LTTE have translated these ambivocal Tamil terms in their own English translations. Examining the three translations side by side, each amplifying different connotative possibilities of the Tamil original, gives the reader an insight into contrasting religious/non-religious tones that make up the language of commemoration used by the LTTE to remember its dead soldiers.

TRANSLATION I (MY RELIGION-MAXIMAL RENDERING OF TAMIL SPEECH)
My beloved and esteemed people of Tamil Eelam,

[1] Today is Heroes' Day. It is a *sacred* day for us to remember and honor our beloved *martyrs*, who *sacrificed* their precious lives for the freedom of our nation, and who continue to fill all our hearts. These *martyrs*, who committed themselves to the one great ideal of freedom for [our] people, lived for that ideal, struggled unwaveringly to achieve that ideal, and *sacrificed* their very life in a war for that ideal, they are magnificent human beings.

[2] I honor these *martyrs* as *sacred individuals*. They, who are pulled by a common feeling of *devotion*, being the freedom of their mother country, fully *renounce the* solitary *bonds of their worldly desires* and *material attachments*. They gave up *the worldly pleasures* of their individual life and are em-

bracing the lofty values of a public life. They dare to *sacrifice* their very-own lives for that common ideal. I regard this as an act of *holy asceticism!* We should *worship* these *martyrs* who shine as *exemplars of this sacred asceticism,* as nothing other than *sacred individuals.*

[3] Our liberation organization awards great prestige and respect to its *martyrs* because they are supreme *martyrs* who, selflessly destroy even themselves, in the service of freedom, without expecting any benefit for themselves. We *worship* our *martyrs* as national heroes, as historic leaders in the war for our beloved freedom. We observe these *memorial ceremonies* for them, so that they should remain firmly in our hearts, where their memories do not fade with time. We honor them, raising memorials for them. Sowing the seed-bodies of the *martyrs* with *rituals to worship* the hero, planting memorial stones, *worshipping* their graves *as sacred symbols,* and *worshipping* their final sleeping homes as *sacred sites of pilgrimage,* [all these practices] have become beloved customs for our people.

TRANSLATION 2 (MY RELIGION-MINIMAL RENDERING)
My beloved and esteemed people of Tamil Eelam,

[1] Today is Heroes' Day. It is a *special day* for us to remember and honor those beloved *persons who dedicated themselves,* who *gave* their precious lives for the freedom of our nation, and who continue to fill all our hearts. These *great heroes,* who committed themselves to the one great ideal of freedom for [our] people, lived for that ideal, struggled unwaveringly to achieve that ideal, and *dedicated* their very life in a war for that ideal, they are magnificent human beings.

[2] I honor these *great heroes* as *pure individuals.* They, who are pulled by a common sense of *commitment,* being the freedom of their mother country, completely *give up* their own solitary *interests and close relations.* They gave up *creature comforts* of their individual life and are embracing the lofty values of a public life. They dare to *dedicate* their very-own lives for that common ideal. I regard this as an act of *pure commitment!* We should *honor* these *great heroes* who shine as *exemplars of this pure commitment,* as nothing other than our *pure individuals.*

[3] Our liberation organization awards great prestige and respect to its *great heroes* because they are supremely *dedicated persons,* who, selflessly destroy even themselves, in the service of freedom, without expecting any benefit for themselves. *We acclaim* our *great heroes* as national heroes, as historic leaders in the war for our beloved freedom. We hold these *memorial festivals* for them, so that they should remain firmly in our hearts, where their memories do not fade with time. We honor them, raising monuments

for them. Sowing the seed-bodies of the *great heroes* with *observances* to *honor the hero*, planting memorial stones, *honoring* their graves as *symbols of purity* and *honoring* their final sleeping homes as *places of purity*, [all these practices] have become beloved customs for our people.

TRANSLATION 3 (PUBLISHED LTTE TRANSLATION)

My beloved people of Tamil Eelam,

[1] Today is Heroes' Day, a *sacred* day in which we honour and remember our beloved *martyrs* who have *sacrificed* their lives for the cause of freedom of our nation. Our *martyrs* were *extra-ordinary human beings*. They chose the noble cause of liberating our people. Having lived and struggled for such a cause they finally *sacrificed* their precious lives for that higher ideal.

[2] I *venerate* our heroes since they *renounced their personal desires and transcended their egoic existence* for a common cause of higher virtue. Such a *noble act of renunciation* deserves our veneration.

[3] Our liberation movement pays highest respect and reverence to our *martyrs* for their *supreme sacrifice*. We honour our *martyrs* as national heroes, as creators of the history of our national struggle. We *commemorate our heroes* and erect them *memorials* so that their memories should remain forever in our hearts. It has become a popular norm to bury our *martyrs* with honour, erect stone monuments for them and *venerate* these war cemeteries as *holy places of tranquility*. The practice of *venerating heroic martyrdom* has become an established tradition in our society.

These three translations of the Heroes Day speech render ambivocal terms in the Tamil original in divergent ways and, as a consequence, produce texts of different lengths and with different visions of commemoration. Differences in length are evident between the LTTE's translation (Translation 3) and my translations (Translations 1 and 2) and are owed, in large part, to translation-style: Translations 1 and 2 take a perhaps less fluid, word-by-word approach, whereas Translation 3 ostensibly takes a more impressionistic tack, preferring idiomatic expression over one-to-one transcription from Tamil to English. Yet, the brevity of the LTTE's official translation also derives from the fact that Translation 3 omits phrases, collapses two or three sentences into one, and summarily treats ideas that are more elaborately described in the Tamil, a subject which will be addressed below.

Aside from length, different translation choices express contrasting descriptions of the memorializing process and different understandings of what it means to fight and die for the LTTE. Translations 1 and 2 produce quite different narratives as a result of choosing between the English terms "sacrifice" and "give" (in the case of the Tamil word *īkamceytu*) and choosing between "sacrifice" or "dedicate" (in the case of the Tamil word *arppaṇittu*). By choosing to render the Tamil words as "sacrifice," Translation 1 selectively highlights the religious valence of a word that has connotations extending in the direction of both Hindu devotion and non-religious commitment. As a consequence, Translation 1 valorizes soldiers' deaths in battle as an act of self-offering, giving oneself to the "ideal of freedom for [our] people" as one would give one's life to the divine. The two Tamil words which Translation 1 rendered as sacrifice, *īkamceytu* and *arppaṇittu,* may be applied both to narrative about religious vows or in a narrative concerning disciplined self-denial and political struggle. Translation 1's choice of "sacrifice" skews the semantic range of the Tamil word (perhaps slightly, but definitively) towards the religious pole of interpretation, a pole which equates soldiers' deaths in battles with acts of Hindu piety.

Contrasting images of death and commemoration may not be plainly evident when comparing the translations of single words—after all, "sacrifice" in English shares some of the Tamil term's ambivocality. However, different understandings of soldiers' deaths, and the religious significance therein, take shape when one begins to consider the larger imagery of an entire paragraph. Consider, for example, the possible connotations of paragraph three. For a reader unfamiliar with Tamil, the passage gives a significantly different picture depending upon whether a translation chooses to describe Heroes Day as a "memorial ceremony,"[12] consisting of worship,[13] rituals[14] and pilgrimage sites[15] (Translation 1) or as "memorial festivals" consisting of honoring, observances and places of purity (Translation 2). In the first case, deceased soldiers' graves are cast as holy places, similar to Saivite pilgrimage places (*s/talam*), and are to be treated in a manner usually reserved for sacred Hindu sites. In the second case, soldiers' graves may be regarded as monuments, places for solemn reflection, but not specifically objects of ritual action.

The degree of religious significance which people attribute to LTTE Heroes Day speeches often hinges on how readers/listeners interpret key terms that the LTTE use to describe their soldiers. Often great emphasis is placed on the etymologies of these words and their potential links to terms contained in important Sanskrit or Tamil religious texts. However, as a consequence of words' shifting semantics and usage in modern language, even terms that trace to ancient religious texts take on ambivocal connotations in modern usage. This is seen particularly in one word which many scholars and, in some cases, the LTTE themselves translate as "martyr," the word *tiyāki.*[16] Many observers argue that *tiyāki,* as used by the LTTE, is a specifically Hindu term with linguistic roots (as Sanskrit *tyāgin*) that go back to Patanjali's *Yoga Sutras, Bhagavadgītā* and other Sanskrit *sutras, śastras* and *purāṇas.* Although *tiyāki* has these etymological moorings, the modern Tamil term *tiyāki* is used rather differently than is *tyāgin* in ancient Sanskrit texts. In the *Bhagavadgītā, tyāgin* refers to one who acts without consideration for the results, goals or "fruits" of that action.[17] However, in the above Heroes Day speech, *tiyāki* refers to a rather different actor: for the LTTE, *tiyāki* does not refer to one who renounced concern with the goals of action, but someone who renounced his/her life *for* a political goal. In each case, one acts selflessly, but, in its usage by the LTTE, *tiyāki* describes a focused, goal-oriented, goal-motivated actor, not someone aloof from worldly calculations. This use of *tiyāki* in the 1997 speech shows affinities with the writings of Dravidian nationalists in India, who used the term to describe, for example, activists who died while protesting against legislation that would make Hindi the state's official language (*mozi tiyāki*).[18] *Tiyāki* like so many terms in LTTE speeches suggests both a religious agent (a *bhaktin*) and a political agent (a Dravidian nationalist), depending on which linguistic genealogy one refers to.

The LTTE's English translation of the Tamil Heroes speech renders the Tamil ambivocality in ways that, at times, enhances and, at times, effaces their religion-related connotations. This oscillation between foregrounding religious connotations and muffling them can be seen, in particular, by tracking how the LTTE translated the Tamil word *puṇita,* a term that contemporary Tamil writers often use to translate the English words "holy" or "sacred"[19] and a word that Translation 2 renders in a slightly less idiomatic way as "pure."[20] In the above Tamil speech, *puṇita* is used to describe Heroes Day,[21] the dead soldiers,[22] soldiers' acts of dedication[23] and graves.[24] In the English translation, the LTTE renders *puṇita,* as I have in Translation 1, as "sacred" or "holy," when it refers to Heroes Day (a "sacred day") or soldiers' graves ("holy places"). In other cases, such as the second paragraph of Translation 3, LTTE translators ignore the word completely—in this case, omitting the phrase which I translated "sacred individuals" in Translation 1. In yet other places, the LTTE translates the term using an English term which does not implicate the category of religion in obvious ways, such as in paragraph two of Translation 3 where the LTTE rendered *puṇita* as "noble." In the case of *puṇita,* the LTTE translation does not resolve the ambivocality of the Tamil word into one valence of meaning in its English translations. The LTTE translation renders the word in both religion-maximal and religion-minimal ways, using different English terms in different contexts. Rather

than isolating one connotation of *puṇita* to the exclusion of others, or finding a perfect English surrogate which would capture both senses of the term,
the LTTE English translation (3) reproduces the ambivocality of the Tamil
text by alternating between English terms that are marked and unmarked
for religion.

In its description of soldiers' deaths and LTTE memorials, the 1997 Heroes Day speech does not always oscillate between religion-maximal and
religion-minimal translations of ambivocal words. In some cases, the LTTE's
translation (Translation 3) uses English words that reflect one pole of connotation over another and, in other cases, Translation 3 ignores ambivocal
words and phrases altogether. In paragraphs one and three, for example,
the LTTE's English translation uses English terms that suggest martyrdom,
sacrifice, holiness and veneration (closer to my religion-maximal Translation 1) rather than English terms that communicate dedication, giving and
commendation. In paragraph two, the LTTE's English translation favors the
opposite pole of interpretation, muffling dramatically the religious connotations of two sentences and omitting most of the substance of the paragraph.
In this paragraph, the shortened phrase "renounced their personal desires
and transcended their egoic existence" seems to stand in for a longer section
of Tamil text that describes (in the religion-maximal sense in Translation
1) how martyrs are to be venerated as ascetics,[25] who piously renounced[26]
the tethers of worldly desire[27] and the bondage of sensual pleasures.[28] The
terms are strung together in the Tamil original in phrases that can be read
as referring to a fundamental theme in *Saiva Siddhanta* religious philosophy that describes the process through which Saivite devotees eliminate
mundane concerns (Tamil: *pācam,* Skt: *pāśa*) in order to prepare their souls
(Tamil: *pacu,* Skt: *paśu*) for union with Siva (Tamil and Skt: *pati*). However,
the LTTE English translation hints very slightly at, if not altogether ignoring,
those Saivite connotations.

The above analysis of one part of one Heroes Day speech and its use
of ambivocal Tamil terms illustrates, on a small scale, the complex role of
religion in LTTE commemoration practices. In the Tamil original, if one
focuses on religious connotations, this speech can be read (or heard) as a
being studded with religious overtones, images which equate soldiers'
deaths with asceticism, sacrifice and even union with the divine. If one focuses on themes of militant heroism in the Tamil original, the language
of the speech seems to describe soldiers' deaths in a different light, one
characterized by ideals of bravery, valor, dedication, loyalty and commitment to a political cause. Finally, if one reads the LTTE's English translation, the text strikes a more intermediate tone which oscillates between

religion-maximal and religion-minimal registers. The above presentation illustrates a general point: depending on which section of which text one reads, with which interpretive tendencies, in which language, LTTE commemoration can be regarded as a project which eulogizes dead soldiers in religious terms, or as a project which honors soldiers as exemplary (but not holy), persons, or as a project which combines elements of both.

Translating Remembering

Some have pointed to the coincident religious/non-religious interpretative possibilities of LTTE grave sites and commemoration practices as a characteristic genius of LTTE memorialization. The interpretative coincidence of the LTTE's death symbolism (as simultaneously religious/non-religious) may have helped the group speak to two audiences at once, in language that would appeal to and comfort both.[29] On one hand, Tamil Hindu families and friends of killed LTTE soldiers might hear/read and interpret Heroes Day speeches in a more religion-maximal way, thus interpreting death through familiar, and thus consoling, concepts of renunciation or sacrifice. On the other hand, other readers (particularly those who are non-local, non-Tamil and non-Hindu) might read these speeches and their translations in a more religion-minimal way—or, at least, a less Hindu-centric way—and thus not encounter any conceptual contradictions between the language of commemoration and the LTTE's secular creed. Thus, in this perspective, the ambivocal language of Heroes Day speeches appears to be one component of a deliberate discursive strategy employed by the LTTE to address separate (in-group and out-group) audiences and to mobilize religious concepts and imageries in a way that does not directly compromise its stated, official "secular" position.

However, from another perspective, the religious/non-religious diglossia of LTTE Heroes Day speeches could be understood, not as a linguistic strategy, but as a rhetorical style that is endemic to military commemorations more generally. The ambivocal language of the above speech may be regarded as analogous to memorializing practices employed by other armies and militias (and the states or organizations that sponsor them). From this viewpoint, the LTTE, like other militaries, uses ambivocal terms because terms that are drawn from the lexicons of religions often provide a convincing and concise language for articulating absolute and monopolistic claims on loyalty, morality and legitimacy. (One might imagine a similarly religion-maximal reading of the US State of the Union speech of the commemorations at Arlington National Cemetery.) Equally, ambivocal language may suit military commemorations because of the functional symmetry between memorializing dead soldiers and religious practices in general (as understood by thinkers like Clifford Geertz):[30] memorial rites, sites, monuments, speeches, songs and other practices function as symbolic and enacted systems that order and orient human experience according to shared, enduring, absolute goals and, in the process, recode even traumatic experiences (including the trauma of a loved one's death) as something explainable, significant, consonant with structural logic of the system. In this perspective, LTTE commemoration, as an instance of military memorializing, uses religiously-resonant language because it shares some of the functions of religion; it aims to make human death intelligible, meaningful, and (at some level) justifiable.

In concluding, it must be stressed that the LTTE not only engaged in a constructive process of producing new memories of soldiers' deaths, they also engaged in a project of muting or muffling memory—occluding the regular violence of war, the routine suffering of soldiers and civilians, the temporary, fragile nature of human life. For soldiers and civilians who lived through 30 years of civil war, the death of soldiers and civilians became a tragically regular occurrence. This situation was especially true for people living in the North and East of the country, in the areas where the LTTE operated. LTTE commemoration practices, in large part, worked to camouflage this regularity of death with language and symbols which cast human loss as extraordinary, special, something more unusual and exemplary. It was this camouflaging which was exposed that day in May when Prabhakaran's body was shown, undisguised, on the TV.

Immediately after the special report announcing Prabhakaran's death, new, competing processes of memory-making and memory-camouflaging began. Certain LTTE supporters denied that the corpse was Prabhakaran, producing a specious portrait of the man holding a newspaper and watching a TV program which post-dated his death—"proof" that Prabhakaran had not died, that he was living safely in hiding. In response, the Sri Lankan army insisted that the body on TV was indeed that of the LTTE leader and combat officers promptly took to the task of forensically verifying and then cremating the body in Mullaitivu without much publicity, "as they would any other terrorist" the spokesman said. These competing accounts of the veracity of Prabhakaran's death marked the first salvo in a new confrontation. Within 24 hours of the government declaring an end to its 30-year-old civil war, another conflict has begun, a contestation over the memory of what had happened.

Notes

1. Peter Schalk, a senior scholar of religion at the University of Upsala, Sweden, brought these practices to academic attention in the 1990s, and has written extensively on the topic. He first suggested that LTTE commemoration transformed understandings of death. His studies should be consulted for further reading.

2. Dagmar Hellmann-Rajanayagam, "'And heroes die': Poetry of the Tamil Liberation Movement in Northern Sri Lanka," *South Asia: Journal of South Asian Studies*, 28, no. 1 (2005): 112–53, passim.

3. Between 1980 and 2003, the LTTE carried out the most suicide attacks of any group in the world, a full 25% of all attacks. Robert Pape, *Dying to Win: The Strategic Logic of Suicide Terrorism*, 1st ed. (New York: Random House, 2005), 16.

4. See, e.g., Michael Roberts, "Saivite Symbols, Sacrifice, and Tamil Tiger Rites," *Social Analysis* 49, no. 1 (2005): 67–93.

5. See, e.g., Peter Schalk, "Beyond Hindu Festivals," in *Tempel und Tamilen in Zweiter Heimat*, ed. Martin Baumann et al. (Berlin: Ergon Verlag, 2003), 395.

6. For a rejection of this comparison, see ibid., 393–5.

7. Roberts, "Saivite Symbols," 67–69.

8. Peter Schalk, "The Revival of Martyr Cults among Ilavar," *Temenos* 33 (1997): 173–76.

9. Field notes, informal interviews, Jaffna, September 2005.

10. Cautious readers will point out that "the category of religion" is a problematic assumption and one cannot assume all English readers interpret these terms similarly. I do agree. Considerations of space and audience have led me to avoid a longer theoretical discussion. For the assumptions that follow, I beg some theoretical leeway.

11. In this section, I evaluate these valences primarily using the standard dictionary for modern Tamil: *KriyA Tamil Dictionary* (Chennai: Cre-A Publisher, 2008). I recognize that dictionaries cannot be considered natural, comprehensive or authoritative codifications of meaning, especially for living languages with evolving and disappearing vocabularies and argots. Moreover Cre-A is based mainly on Tamil Nadu Tamil, not Jaffna Tamil. These caveats aside, I hope to use Cre-A as a guide, however incomplete, for unpacking some of the semantic range of LTTE rhetoric.

12. *nin_aivu vizA*

13. *vazipaTuvatum*

14. *caṭagku*

15. *puṇita talagkaḷ*

16. The LTTE is not the only Sri Lankan Tamil organization who uses the term *tiyāki*. In September 2005, I observed a poster near the center of Jaffna advertising an event hosted by a former-militant Tamil nationalist group, the EPRLF (Eelam Peoples Revolutionary Liberation Front). The flier mentioned an EPRLF memorial day on June 19, 2005, which was called *"tiyāki's* day" *(tiyākikaL tin_am)* and it commemorated the killing of one EPRLF leader, K. Patmanāpa, on June 19, 1990.

17. See *Bhagavadgītā* 6 (63).40.18.11.

18. Sumathi Ramaswamy, *Passions of the Tongue* (Berkeley: University of California Press, 1997), 229.

19. *Puṇita* is used for the modern Tamil transformation of the Christian concepts Good Friday and Holy Ghost—*puṇita veḷḷi, puṇitāvi.*

20. *puṇita* derives from the Sanskrit past participle *punīta* meaning purified.

21. *puṇita nāḷ*

22. *puṇitarkaḷ*

23. *puṇita tuṟavaram*

24. *puṇita ciṉṉagkaḷ, puṇita talagkaḷ*

25. *tuṟavaram*

26. *turantuviṭukiṟārkaḷ*

27. *pācavuṟavuakaḷaiyum*

28. *cukapōkagkaḷai paṟṟukkaḷaiyum*

29. Cristiana Natali, "Building Cemeteries, Constructing Identities: Funerary Practices and Nationalist Discourse among the Tamil Tigers of Sri Lanka," *Contemporary South Asia* 16 (2008): 287–301.

30. Peter Schalk has noted this in "The Revival of Martyr Cults among Ilavar," *Temenos* 33 (1997): 151–90, at 156–57.

Nallur

Jean Arasanayagam

Few poets have captured the pathos of the ethnic conflict in the manner of Jean Ara-
sanayagam, one of Sri Lanka's most prolific and widely read poets, whose work is
extraordinarily politically sensitive. "Nallur" refers to one of the most celebrated
Hindu temples on the Jaffna peninsula, a site of terrible violence and death during
the 1990s.

It's there,
　　　　　　　beneath the fallen fronds, dry crackling
piles of broken twigs abandoned wells of brackish
water lonely dunes
　　　　　　it's there
the shadows of long bodies shrunk in death
the leeching sun has drunk their blood and
bloated swells among the piling clouds
　　　　　　it's there,
　　　　　　　　　death,
　　　　　　　　　　　　smell it in the air
its odour rank with sun and thickening blood
mingling with fragrance from the frothy toddy
pots mingling like lolling heads from
blackened gibbets,
　　　　　　it's there
　　　　　　　　amid the clangour of
the temple bells, the clapping hands, the
brassy clash of cymbals,
　　　　　　　　the zing of bullets
　　　　　　　　cries of death
　　　　　　　　drowned in the roar
　　　　　　　　of voices calling Skanda
　　　　　　　　by his thousand names

Murugan, Kartikkeya

Arumugam . . . . . .

"We pray, we cry, we clamour
oh Sri Kumaran, be not like the god
who does not hear, deaf Sandesveran."
Thirtham now no longer nectar of the gods
brims over but is bitter, bitter,
and at the entrance to Nallur
the silent guns are trained
upon a faceless terror
Outside,
        the landscape changes
the temples by the shore are smoking
ruins charred stone blackened,
on empty roads are strewn
the debris of warfare,
stained discarded dressings
burnt out abandoned vehicles
 a trail of blood
soon mopped up by the thirsty sun

Turned away, from bloody skirmishes
of humankind, the gods are blinded
by the rain of bullets,
six faced Arumugam
all twelve eyes
close in darkness

The land is empty now
the pitted limestone
invaded by the sea
drowns, vanishes,
waves of rust swell and billow
beating into hollow caves and burial urns
filled with the ash of bodies
cremated by the fire of bullets.

CHRISTIANS AND BURGHERS:

AN INTRODUCTION

This brief section is not meant to encapsulate the full extent of Christian significance in the history of Sri Lanka. The sections on the Portuguese, Dutch, and British contain much that is quite relevant to the Christian question per se. The question of the Christian community in Sri Lanka has always been linked intimately to the politics and culture of Westerners and Westernization, a factor that accounts for the cultural uniqueness of the Christian community. Here, both language (English) and religion (Christianity) do not necessarily equate to ethnic identity, but certainly do define a separate social identity. To a large extent, the issue of Christian affinity to Westernization remains so today and helps to explain how and why it was the case that many Christians of Sri Lanka (Sinhala, Tamil, and Burgher [Eurasian]) overwhelmingly opposed "free education" (the national takeover of schools) and *swabasha* (that the standard educational medium in the schools should be in the vernacular languages of Sinhala and Tamil). One of the consequences of these crucial reforms in education was the emigration from the island of a significant number of Christians, especially Burghers, in the years following independence, a social phenomenon that accounts for the decline in the Christian percentage of the population from roughly 10 percent at independence to less than 7 percent today.

Christians in a Buddhist Majority

Paul Caspersz, S.J.

What has been the nature of the Christian identity in Sri Lanka? Paul Caspersz, an academically inclined and socially activist Roman Catholic priest, notes what has separated Christians historically from the other major religious traditions in Sri Lanka: their Westernizing cultural influence, their support for the political status quo during the colonial era, a tendency not to initiate social change, and in the years leading to independence, the foundation of educational institutions that promoted an English curriculum.

It would seem rash and presumptuous to explain the role of a group so heterogeneous as the Christians in Sri Lanka—in denominational affiliation, in social status or class, language, caste, direction and degree of politicalization. For there would be as many roles as there have been, are, and will be, Christians. Indeed, to the extent that each Christian acts out his Christian status vis-à-vis a whole array of other social actors, there are as many role-sets as there are Christians. The brief analysis here attempted, therefore, is only a generalization.

The generalization may be stated in the form of two clear hypotheses: first, that the role of Christians until about a decade ago [the early 1960s] was to achieve, preserve and confirm the specific identity and distinctness of the minority Christian group not only in regard to all other religious groups but also in regard to the nation (however difficult the former, and even illogical the latter, enterprise); second, that in very recent years the role is being increasingly viewed as an outward and adaptive one in terms of the achievement of a national socio-cultural equilibrium by means of the fostering of creative inter-action, on the one hand, of the four main religious groups in a situation of accepted religious pluralism and, on the other, with the ideologies of secularism and Marxist socialism.

. . . The status of the Christian group is that of a minority in a social system in which the Buddhists are the majority. In the system the percentage of Catholics is 6.9, other Christians 0.8, Buddhists 67.4, Hindus 17.6, Muslims

7.1, and all others 0.1. It is significant—though the fact does not appear to have been noticed by, still less perturbed, the Christian group—that the percentage of Christians has steadily decreased since the census of 1946 when it was 9.1. In 1953 it was 9.0, in 1963 it recorded 8.3, while in the 1971 census it showed a further decrease of 0.6, registering only 7.7 percent.

One explanation of the decrease is probably the emigration of Christians. The present writer has not been able to secure the religious distribution of postwar emigrants, but it is his impression that the Christians, especially the Burghers, are more than proportionately represented in it (for the reason that they have been more than proportionately dissatisfied with the ongoing changes in the social system since dominion status): in the census of 1971 the Burghers, who are nearly 100 percent Christian, were only 44,250 or 0.3 percent of the population.

A second explanation of the decrease is that more than a third of the Christians are urban and their literacy and level of education proportionately to their numbers are higher than in other religious groups: the pressures of urban living, literacy and education seem to have outweighed the classic Catholic resistance to limitation of births, though, in the absence of figures, it is not possible to say whether the limiting factor has been the use of contraceptive devices (in opposition to official ecclesiastical directives) or abstention resulting from the rationalization of procreative processes (itself a result of the greater influence of western culture on the Christian than on other religious groups).

It was earlier suggested that the role of Christians until the 60s was conceived in terms of its minority identity. In the sociological studies of minority groups it has often been found that they manifest a fierce desire to protect the cohesiveness of the group in the face of threats, real or imaginary, of being taken over by the majority. Within the Christian group in Sri Lanka this minority consciousness was strengthened by the presence within it of a large percentage of Tamils, who are themselves a linguistic minority in the social system. The Tamil Christians, therefore, had a double reason to pressurize for a "hands off the Christians" attitude: one, because they were Christians, the other, because they were Tamils. This sheds light, incidentally, both on the efficiency of the Christian schools in Tamil areas and on the loyalty of the Tamils to them.

In the first decade and a half after Dominion status the role of Christians was essentially a continuance of the role as it was played since the establishment of the Christian Church in Portuguese times. It is all too facile to criticize this role in the light of the perceptions of a later period. When the first converts were made—by means fair, dubious or foul—the predominant concern of the pastors, who were Europeans, was to protect their faith from the influence of other faiths. At a time when religion was so deeply imbedded in secular culture as to be wholly indistinguishable from it, the Church set about the establishment of an alternative culture for the Ceylonese who adopted the Christian faith. The search for separate identity from other religious groups and from the rest of the nation had begun.

The dream of the formalization of culture through widespread schools for the people was still far-off in all parts of the world and therefore the first attempts at the building of a specific Christian culture in Lanka were through the medium of stone. Don Peter cites a letter of 1622 about the Jesuit Church in Colombo:

"It is built in Corinthian style, and is well proportioned and handsome. The facade is magnificent, and if it is not the best, it will certainly be the second best in the whole of India."

The style of all these early stone instruments of culturalization was, so far as we know, western, and was in sharp contrast to the Buddhist, Hindu and Muslim styles of architecture. Added to the influence of architecture was the gradual introduction—fostered by the early and the later schools—of western languages, western names and surnames, western music, western dress and habits of eating. It may of course be contended that similar cultural specificity had already made the three existing religious groups inter-distinguishable, and hence that there was nothing strange about the quest for the specificity and distinctness of a fourth group. What was unique, however, was that this fourth group by its western character soon began to distinguish itself not merely from each of the three existing groups taken separately but from the three of them taken together. The other three were eastern, Ceylonese: this one western, Portuguese, and later Dutch or British.

Brought into the country as a new way of life for all takers by the white foreigners, led for four centuries by foreigners sometimes of the same nationality as the foreign rulers or, in later days, by local clergy trained by the foreigners, the Christian Church succeeded in establishing not just a cultural uniqueness for the Christians but a western cultural uniqueness. The westernized and westernizing culture was a social advantage to the Christians when the country was under the western imperial power. As late as 6 January 1887 at a ceremony in Colombo constituting the Catholic hierarchy of Ceylon, Archbishop Bonjean pronounced "an eloquent allocution ending with acclamations to the Pope, to the Cardinal Prefect of Propaganda, to Mgr. Agliardi (Apostolic Delegate to the East Indies) and to Queen Victoria, in which the clergy and people joined." The imperial government could not but take note of such a show of loyalty. In 1948 it was no longer possible to acclaim the foreign overlord. Instead, a directive from the Archbishop exhorted Catholics "to decorate their houses, churches and schools during the Independence Week, prominence being given to the Papal Flag and the National Flag." Even in independent Ceylon the Church leaders sought to maintain the old cultural specificity.

It could be objected that the westernization of the Christians affected only a minority among them—those in the upper social and income brackets, who lived in Colombo and a few other towns and spoke English—and that the majority of Christians continued to live according to the culture of their forefathers even after they received the water of baptism. Even as late as 1970 the Houtart Survey estimated that the social distribution of Catholics was as follows: upper classes 4 percent, intermediate classes 28 percent, lower classes 68 percent. Numbers, however, did not call the tune during the long period of the search for Christian identity. In both State and Church, society was hierarchically constituted and thus the dominant pressures of the Christian upper classes were felt all down the line of the social stratification of Christians. Indeed, when numbers began to tell after universal franchise was introduced in 1931, it did not take very long for the role to be questioned and a new role to be sought.

If the western character of the specific cultural identity of the Christians caused tensions between them and other religious groups and between them and the nation as a whole, the pro–status quo character of the group (certainly of its leaders who exercised an autocratic control over the rank and file) made the Christians liable to a charge of dubious loyalty in the minds of all those who challenged the status quo. The challenge came first from the nationalists, then from the socialists.

There is probably in all religious institutions an inbuilt conservatism, an inherent fear of disturbing the existing order. The order may not be the ideal one, but at least the religious institution has learnt to live with it and hence fears its change. When the institution is old, highly organized, well financed, centralized—as in the case of the Christian institution—the pressures to conserve are enhanced. On the eve of independence, the editorial in *The Ceylon Catholic Messenger* could hardly have been more unequivocal:

"Let our Independence then be marked by conformity with the established order which it is beyond the right of mere mortals to alter or disturb; let our new Government stand the supreme test—that of fidelity to the moral law which it can violate only at its own peril. And let the chief contribution of the Catholics to the political progress of the country be the realization of this great desideratum."

According to the accepted interpretations of its phenomenological reality, religion is concerned with the ordering of human life in society in accordance with some ultimate right order. During the colonial and post-independence periods, the Christian Church defended order, but made insufficient assessment of the rightness of the order. The concept of order is more static than dynamic, and the Church defended it. The concept of the rightness of order is more dynamic than static, and the Church was uncritical about it.

The concern of the Church over its specific identity vis-à-vis the other religious groups and the nation was so over-riding that the Church made no significant attempt at a courageous solution of the contradictions within the Christian group itself. These contradictions were present first for detection and then for resolution in the fields of the integration of social classes and castes within the group, of the rural with the urban Christians. Christian parish priests and vicars in rural areas did not see their role as a socially catalytic one, nor did the chaplains on the estates do anything significant to secure conditions of elementary humanity for the estate labor. An exception in the Christian record of non-initiation of social change would probably be the Social Justice Movement started in Colombo in the late 30s by the Peter Pillai group but "this was a group that was basically reformist within the framework of capitalism and foreign exploitation." Peter Pillai in his later years showed himself to be increasingly uncomfortable with the social and educational policies of the more people-oriented political groups: it was also a period during which he was the chief theoretician of the Christian group.

The concept of the role in terms of an identity search explains the position taken by the Church in the field of education in the contemporary period. Free education was opposed because it would break the bonds that bound the better schools to the Christian managements and thus expose Christian children to the influence of Buddhist and secularist cultures. Swabasha was opposed because more English, better taught, was a characteristic of the urban Christian schools and constituted their chief advantage to the children of the affluent non-Christian patrons. The takeover of schools was violently opposed because it was felt that with the schools would go the last bulwarks of the identity of Christians in the nation. In the Christian school structure Houtart sees the validation of a socio-political order by an educational system resting on religion. The present writer would consider this the latent function or the unintended consequence of the Christian school system.

Its manifest function or its intended consequence was the achievement and consolidation of identity. By fulfilling it the Church certainly opened avenues of upward social mobility to many urban working-class and lower middle-class Christian families. That the three major educational reforms mentioned were a similar move towards a leveling of educational opportunity, but over a wider range, the majority of Christian leaders did not or was unwilling to see—until the middle of the last decade.

The change in the perception of the role of Christians was stimulated by several factors. The exogenous factors were first those inducing change in secular society all over the world. Vastly improved conditions of travel and transport, the growth of the mass communication media, the spread of conflicting ideologies, rising educational standards for increasing numbers of people, higher levels of consumption, the emergence of youth culture, the appearance of a third world: all these factors make it impossible for Lanka not to be a society in transition. Within the Church the greatest single factor promoting change was the Vatican Council, 1963–1965.

The endogenous factors were chiefly the growth of popular participation in government after 1931, the expansion of education through schools and the electoral progress, the dissemination of Marxist ideas and the evolution of a strategy for the socialist development of the country. In the earlier period the Christians did not see their role as being that of initiators of change. Now they were forced to follow the changes in secular society.

The Houtart Survey, seeking a generalized picture as to how Catholics situate themselves in their national social context, from its valid interviews of 1361 persons (responding out of a sample of 1500 persons) selected from 50 parishes situated in the six Catholic dioceses, concluded to two tendencies in the Catholic population. The first, accounting for more than half the Catholic population, was a dynamic and forward one, "characterized by a hope in the future and by an acceptation of the social changes." The second, accounting for about a quarter of the population, was a static and conservative one. The remaining quarter had no convictions in either direction.

In Christian circles much is sometimes made of the fact that the Christian schools nurtured a generation of the elite which led the country to independence from the colonial regime. That the British were largely able to talk to a group of upper and middle-class leaders together—regardless of the fact that the group contained individuals divided according to religion, root language and caste—was, it is alleged, the result of the Christian schools where these leaders were educated together. However, even apart from the fact that some elitist leaders experienced their Christian educational background to be rather an embarrassment, the charge is sometimes heard that it was precisely this background that served to distance the elite from the masses. The Church played its part in the formation of the elite. Its role now is to form them again—without the aid of the schools which have now almost completely been removed from Church control—to work alongside and with the people. A reformed Christian elite will still have a useful role to play in the present phase of the country's development. Part of this role is to understand what the country now requires. The conditions for the successful fulfillment of the role have been well expressed by Farina Bhatty:

> "Contributions that a minority community will make would therefore depend on how well it can redefine its distinctiveness and mould it into forms which are in harmony with the changing environment and have a creative context."

The greater contact which the Christian group had and still has with the culture of the west, and its greater assimilation of that culture—once a source of suspicion of the group—can now lead it, if it is joined to the sympathetic perception of social change, to contribute vitally to the rationalization and modernization of the country's socio-economic structure. If Sri Lanka, like the rest of the world, is moving into a new technological era, Christians will perhaps be better placed than other religious groups both to understand and to adjust to the demands of the new era.

Will Herberg's thesis that the three main religious groups in America—Protestants, Catholics, Jews—are equi-legitimate expressions of American religion, indeed of American society, is well known. Christians in Sri Lanka have been here long enough to seek to be an equi-legitimate expression of the country's life and character. With the Buddhists, Hindus and Muslims and all who are concerned about society, Christians should seek to hammer out a national equilibrium of culture without which it will not be possible to achieve the type of nation which most of the inhabitants of the country probably desire.

On the Meaning of "Parangi" and "Burgher": Symbolic Discourse of Subordination

Michael Roberts, Ismeth Raheem, and Percy Colin-Thomé

Burghers are those Sri Lankans who trace their lineage to a liaison between a European (usually a male) and an indigene (usually a female). Burghers tended to be raised as Christians and historically occupied a vocational and economic class between the European and the Sinhala and Tamil. They were often "middle management" types. In the following extract, various terms from Sinhala and Tamil are understood "analogically" to determine the manner in which Burghers have been regarded through the eyes of the indigenous.

The multiple meanings attached to the word *parangi* . . . have provided the Sinhalese (and other Sri Lankans) with a condensed understanding of the period of Portuguese rule. This evocative symbol has regularly entered the didactic and polemical expressions of Sinhala cultural producers in the twentieth century, be they poets, novelists, pamphleteers, film-makers or politicians. It is arguable that in popular and populist historiography the impact of Portuguese rule has always been etched into Sinhala perceptions at a deeper level, so to speak, in sharper, more traumatic ways, than the Sinhala reading of Dutch and British rule.

Analogic Extensions. In his initial draft of this chapter in late 1984, Michael Roberts ventured upon two speculations: firstly, that *parangi* could be extended to encompass all whites (*suddo*), that is, extended to the Dutch (*midas*) and English (*ingrisi*) as well; and secondly, that *parangi* could be extended to all those descended from European rulers, i.e. to the Burghers.

These speculations have since gained partial confirmation. Sinhala speakers have since confirmed that it is possible to use *parangiya* in the sense of a "foreign intruder." This is entirely in line with the meaning which had been attached to *"Firangi"* in British India by the nineteenth century, so that a dictionary noted in 1885 that it was "now used to denote any European." In Sri Lanka the extension of the label *parangi* in this manner undermined the respect which could be attached to the word *"sudda"* by rendering the two terms more or less synonymous. It is probable that this process was accelerated by the vociferous rhetoric of Anagärika Dharmapala (1864–1933), who was wont to speak of the "increasing misdeeds of the Tamils, Moors and Europeans," with the latter being characterized significantly, as "infidels of degraded race." These themes were incorporated into the speeches and journalese of the trade union leader A. E. Goonesinha, and his followers during the 1920s and 1930s: Goonesinha often made disparaging references to the *suddo* and condemned them for eating meat and drinking brandy. From the 1930s the "whites" also became the target for a different sort of polemic marshaled by the Leftist parties in their campaign against imperialist domination and institutionalized privilege.

The more significant extension of the term *parangi* is its usage to encompass Burghers. In Sri Lanka this has been encouraged by the influence of the Tamil language. The standard word for a Burgher among Tamil-speakers is *parangiyär*, or in shorter form, *"parangi."* Around 1953 the Tamil translation of an official publication used the term as a synonym for Burgher and elicited a letter of protest from Dr R. L. Brohier in his capacity as the President of the Dutch Burgher Union. Dr Brohier granted that the reference was not intended as an insult, but contended that the term had "a derogatory significance in common speech" and had therefore "given great offence to members of the Burgher community." Our researches indicate that the denotation of Burghers as *parangi* is especially prevalent among Muslims, most of whom use Tamil as a mother tongue. When an old Moorish gentleman was asked whether he knew the origins of the Ceylonese-English epithet, "War" (poor Burgher . . . or *säpattu lansi*: see below), he responded with some embarrassment and profuse apologies before indicating that in Galle in the past they used to speak of the *lafai parangi* (i.e. poor Burghers). A Burgher friend in Melbourne also recalled an incident at a leading school in Kandy during his teenage days in the early 1950s. On this occasion he was the object of a homosexual advance by a non-Burgher boy who proceeded to stroke his thighs and, as he did so, salaciously purred: *"parangi, parangi."* This incident is particularly revealing because the non-Burgher was a Malay youth, and thus not a native speaker of Tamil. Because Tamil-speaking Muslims are interspersed among the Sinhala population, their use of *parangi* as a standard term for those whom the Sinhala knew as *lansi* could only encourage the latter to equate the two terms, especially in such polyglot localities as Slave Island in Colombo.

The expansion (on select occasions) of the label *parangi* to encompass all the European nationalities who ruled Sri Lanka as well as European descendants was the working out of a logical possibility. It was an analogic extension. This type of analogic transference has been called the *atidesa* function by Ranajit Guha with specific reference to the response of the underclasses or victims of oppression. His illustrations are drawn not only from instances of Indian peasant revolts, but also from the agitation of rural proletarians in early nineteenth-century England, where a movement which initially sought to destroy the new threshing machines that endangered their livelihood moved on to attack all machines.

Guha's approach is informed by Gramscian perspectives. He regards the *atidesa* function to be a product of the "negative consciousness" of subordinated elements or classes in a social formation. In Sri Lanka the "negative consciousness" of the Sinhalese of all classes, as we have indicated, was the outcome of several waves of European intrusion. Such a consciousness penetrated the outlook of most indigenes who had resided in the Sinhala areas for some time: Moors, Malays and Colombo Tamils also employed the pejorative phrases which this chapter is concerned with.

In these analogic ways, therefore, one can move from "eaters of stone and drinkers of blood," "*parangi*" and "*lafai*" to "*lansi*." The Sinhala word *lansi* is a contracted derivation from the phonetic rendering of the Dutch word *Hollandsche*. In Dutch Ceylon *Hollandsche* referred to the respectable strata of the European population, those who were loosely regarded as "Dutch," that is, to those of European extraction on the paternal side, including thereby those of mixed blood (the *Mixties*). The term was employed to differentiate these people from the Portuguese descendants of mixed origin known as the *Topaz* or *Tupass* and from the emancipated slaves known as "*Libertines*." The picture was never as clear as all that . . . , but for the moment let it be noted that the distinction between *Hollandsche* and the *Tupass* was carried through into the period of British rule in the nineteenth century, with the "Burghers" (by which the *Hollandsche* eventually came to be designated) being distinguished in the English language from those who were variously described as "Portuguese Burghers," "*Tupass*," "*Tupasses*," "*Topazes*," "*Mestizos*" and "*Mechanics*"; while in Sinhala the *lansi* were distinguished from the *tuppahi, parangi* and *sinno*. In Sinhala usage at this point of time *lansi* appears to have been a term of respect.

By the twentieth century the situation had begun to change. The terms "Burgher" and "*lansi*" appear to have been increasingly employed by non-Burghers in a generalized sense to describe (i) those whose pedigree went back to both the *Hollandsche* and the *Tupass* of the late eighteenth century as well as (ii) those known as the "Eurasians," the local label for the descendants of liaisons between British or European males and indigenous women during the period of British rule. In such circumstances the word *lansi* appears to have developed new possibilities. While it could be used as a term of respect, or in a neutral, descriptive sense, it could also, as signaled to listeners by the intonation, the context and the sequential order of face-to-face interaction, be employed disparagingly, contemptuously. In the latter form it became a weapon which in effect cast the *lansi* as aliens in comparison with those whom the speaker deemed to be true sons of the soil or *bhumiputrayo*.

This form of boundary definition, this act of outcasting, applied not only to those Burghers whose pigmentation marked them out as European descendants. It even worked against the dark-skinned Burghers, by virtue of the surnames they bore and their self-identity. The Burghers were (are) sufficiently versed in the Sinhala language to grasp the implications of such verbal weaponry: "the word Ransil has now acquired such an odour as to have lost its original meaning," lamented R. G. Anthonisz in 1928.

The partial transformation of *lansi* into an offensive term was assisted by the process which converted *lansi* and *tuppahi*, Burgher and *Tupass*, into synonyms for each other in colloquial usage. Party to this process was another epithet, *karapotta* (cockroach) or, in its plural form, *karapottas* or *karapotu lansi* (both in English and Sinhala) which came to be widely applied to Burghers by the 1910s, if not earlier. Both in its origin and in certain contexts of twentieth-century usage this disparaging term was reserved for the so-called Portuguese Burghers, or *Tupass*. Thus several Sinhala speakers took great care to inform us that the term was not applied to the Dutch Burghers. But the fact remains that in the twentieth century the distinction between a "Dutch Burgher" and a "Portuguese Burgher" has not always been self-evident, especially in the interactions between strangers. And in moments of anger all such restraints are thrown overboard. In the late 1910s, for instance, Miss ZYX's father referred to a young Burgher soldier as a *karapotta* when telling his daughter that he strongly disapproved of the interest which he was showing in the young lass. When Mrs Rutnam was headmistress of the primary school at Ladies College, an irate Muslim parent stormed in one day and told her that he was removing his daughter from the school because they had been taught the song: "When Five Little Pigs went to Market"; and his parting shot was "We don't want our daughter to learn your damn *karapotu* songs." Ohnimesz noted in 1934 that the derogatory epithet was "betrayed [i.e. before Burghers] . . . only in moments of wrath or provocation," while E. F. C. Ludowyk recalled that the "favourite term of abuse and contempt thrown at Burghers was *karapotta*." It takes little imagination for one to conclude that it was more widely used in circumstances when no Burghers were present.

There are several interpretations in circulation in the folklore today which purport to explain how and why the Burghers came to be burdened with this epithet. These post facto speculations are of considerable significance from an anthropological point of view, but this is not the occasion to dissect these stories. The startling fact is that this epithet goes way back to the eighteenth century and originated among the *Hollandsche* themselves. Hobson Jobson has this revealing statement under the head "Cockroach":

> This objectionable insect (*Batta orientalis*) is called by the Portuguese *cacalacca*; a name adopted by the Dutch as *kakkerlak* and by the French as *cancrelat*. The Dutch also apply their term as a slang name to half castes. But our word seems to have come from the Spanish *cucaracha*.

In other words, the superior layer of Europeans or European descendants in the eastern colonies used *kakkerlak* or *cacalacca* as a contemptuous reference for the half castes (the *Tupass* or Portuguese Burghers in Dutch Ceylon). This label was clearly informed by colour prejudice—a prejudice which was carried through into British times and which led some segments of the ex-*Hollandsche* population to look down with distaste upon the growing population of "half-castes" generated by liaisons between the British and the "native women."

While directed by racial prejudice and social airs, the choice of the epithet *cacalacca* may have been influenced by the *Tupass* habit of wearing a *topi* or hat known as the *carapuca*. Alternatively, one can argue that it arose from one of the outstanding features of the *Tupass* life style: their love of music, song and dance—a tendency that has (ironically) passed down the centuries and been extended to Burghers in general, for in the typical Sinhala view in recent times, the Burghers are *natumkäravo*—(dancing types—"*kana bona minissu*," and "eating drinking people, making merry not thinking about tomorrow . . ."). One of the songs favoured by the *Tupass*, it seems, was the "La Cucaracha." This typical song is said to have become the superior "Dutchman's" typification of the "half-caste" *Tupass*.

As a derogatory label, *cacalacca*, *kakkerlak* and *karapottä* had other, germane implications which may not have been lost upon the speakers, the victims, or the bystanders. Cockroaches who have dwelt in obscure recesses where they have not been exposed to sunlight undergo a moulting process which renders them an off-white colour, albino-like. The albino cockroach has a shade of white which a Sinhalese would call *sudu*. On exposure to the light these specimens of cockroach (and they are specimens not species) get progressively darker, browner. The history of some European descendants was not altogether dissimilar. As those of mixed parentage married each other, or established connections with indigenous residents, their progeny grew progressively darker. Whether such an observation was the raison d'etre for the choice of such an epithet by the *Hollandsche* in Dutch times, or whether the Sinhalese of subsequent periods read such implications into the label, we can never know for certain. However, it is significant that one of the contemporary explanations for the linkage between Burgher and *karapottä* holds that the albino cockroach is a suitable representation of the pigmentation of the Burghers as well as Europeans. Yet another explanation holds that the eruption which develops on one's (that is, an Asian's) skin when a cockroach deposits its droppings on an exposed part of the body has a colour that is not dissimilar to that of a Burgher.

What is striking in this body of ethnographic data is the colour coding that was associated with the Sinhala people's response to the European powers. The descendants of Europeans were also brought within the ambit of this coding activity. The intermingled history of the epithet *karapottä* and the analogic extensions in colour coding are attested by the following illustrations. There is a young Burgher lad in Kandy who is disparaged as "*sudu karapottä*" by the children of his neighbourhood. And recently, when a friend of ours had visited World's End in the Horton Plains and was returning along the rough track she was mistaken for a non-Sinhalese because of her fair complexion and her wearing of trousers by a party of men and women whom she encountered, and whom she discovered subsequently to be school teachers from an interior town, [who] indulged in a series of rude comments during the course of which they disparagingly referred to her first as "*suddi*" and then as "*karapotti*."

In brief, *karapottä* and *sudda* can be linked, or deployed interchangeably. It is also possible to speak of *karapotu sudu* or cockroach white. This describes a whiteness like that of a typical Burgher. Indeed, the albino cockroach is sometimes described as a *länsi karapottek*. Likewise there is a *lansi-yakada* (steel), a *länsi bitala* (sweet potato), a *länsi-yatura* (key) et cetera. There is also an uncommon pinkish-white fruit in the hill country which is popularly described as a *länsi-gediya* and on one occasion a Moorish trader displayed great reluctance and embarrassment when a lady whom he mistook for a Burgher insisted on knowing what it was. Such descriptive usage is relatively neutral. This is rarely so in the use of the epithet *karapottä*.

The insidious power of such epithets has been such that some Burghers have attempted to deflect its effects by incorporating it into their vocabulary as a form of self-description. For instance, Bevis Bawa informed us that Dr. Garvin Mack used the phrase "we *karapottäs*" quite frequently. Again, in late July 1985 Bruce Kapferer was witness to a revealing exchange when he was enjoying a drink at a swimming club in Colombo with X, a Tamil friend. X was approached by a well-inebriated gentleman, Y, an acquaintance of Portuguese Burgher descent (from Batticaloa), who proceeded to hail him thus: "Well, what do you make of these buggers?"—the latter being a reference to the Sinhalese in the light of current news headlines. X's cautious response led Y to press his point: "You know I am just a cockroach. But I cry for you a lot. We are getting beaten too. I have never been political. What to do?" This self-derogatory comment and subsequent reference to "we *karapottäs*" encouraged X to open up. When Y left, X even spoke affectionately of him. What had been communicated by Y, then, was their common membership in a field of discrimination, outside the Sinhala order. Here, then, was an instance of what Gramsci would perceive as hegemonic practice, when those in a subordinate position adopt the symbols of their subordination.

Emergent Perspectives in Modern Art: The '43 Group—Formation of a Sri Lankan Avant-Garde

Larry D. Lutchmansingh

Emergent Lankan identities, whether understood as fusions of European and local sensibilities in form and content, of the modern and traditional, or as a consequence of a newly acquired freedom of aesthetics, became apparent in the transformations of Sri Lankan painting reflected in the so-called Group of '43. Probably no other artist reflected this transformation more than George Keyt in his paintings. In the essay below, Larry D. Lutchmansingh discusses many previously unexamined issues, including the genesis of the Group of '43 as a response to the conservative Ceylon Society of Art, the variegated styles of the different members of the group, the influence of Ananda Coomaraswamy, and the effect of colonialism on its expressions of modernism. In this art, the effects of political history are not difficult to perceive.

Sri Lanka experienced one of the longest periods of European occupation in the annals of colonialism, which rendered the condition of its non-modern arts particularly dire. But the record of one artistic movement, the '43 Group, founded on the eve of independence, marked an illustrious albeit brief achievement in an otherwise lackluster record of the country's visual art since its independence. The interpretive literature relating to the group is sparse, yet replete with such judgments of their achievement as "the most important milestone in the history of modern art in Sri Lanka," "the avant-garde of Ceylonese painting," and "the *invention* of a modern and yet distinctively local tradition."[1] However, that literature tends to trace the Group's achievement as a relatively untroubled narrative from difficult beginning to the triumph of a body of work claimed to have achieved a synthesis of modernity and tradition, the international and the local, and individual and group artistic ends. Largely unexamined are such issues as the degrees of differentiation, discordance, and ambivalence that marked their works, be-

Women Pounding Rice by George Keyt. Oil on canvas, 1952. Sapumal Foundation, Colombo.

Woman with Flower by George Keyt. Oil on canvas, 1964. Sapumal Foundation, Colombo.

Kacha and Devayani by George Keyt. Oil on canvas. Sapumal Foundation, Colombo.

liefs, values, and career trajectories; the premature curtailment of artistic careers, psychological unease, visionary experience, in-group conflict, emigration and perhaps self-exile; and the ways in which the group was conditioned by the colonialist enterprise, its modernization project, and its ramified confrontation of non-modern "traditions."[2] The limited scope of this paper will permit only a brief view of a few of those concerns.

Certain seemingly innocent terms in the evaluative phrases cited (randomly) above pinpoint the kinds of interpretive problems that lurk in the historiography of Sri Lankan visual art in the early-to-mid-twentieth century period. For example, the concept of an "important milestone" arose out of the 18th c. Euro-American Enlightenment discourse of a future-oriented development towards an incremental social progress, which was projected by the colonizing powers and their indigenous confederates as an alternative to a stagnating conformity to canonical and pre-established precedent. The concept of an "avant-garde" was first publicly mooted in 1825 in France to enlist progressive artists in the project of transforming and redirecting

The '43 Group by Aubrey Collette. *Clockwise from lower left:* Geoffrey Beling, Harry Pieris, Richard Gabriel, Ivan Peries, George Keyt, Lionel Wendt (seated), George Claessen, Aubrey Collette, Justin Daraniyagala, Manjusri Thero. Water color on paper (61 × 70 cm.), 1943. Sapumal Foundation, Colombo.

the popular consciousness towards social reform.[3] And the kind of discursive contradiction thrown up by the confrontation of colonizer-modernizer and colonized-traditionalist is seen in the illogical formulation—"the *invention* of a modern and yet distinctively local *tradition*."

The '43 Group was founded on August 29, 1943 by a core membership of nine remarkably different men, with whom another group, including women artists, were affiliated. The diversity demonstrated by their works was paralleled by the ethnicities involved (Sinhalese, Burgher, Indian), the languages (Sinhalese, Sanskrit, Pali, English, Dutch, perhaps Marathi), the religions (Buddhism, Roman Catholicism, Hinduism), the education (in local atelier and British, French and Indian higher institutions), their social class, and character and personality types. If there is some justification for defining them in the imported term, "avant-garde," they did not, like European avant-gardes, subscribe to a group style, canvas their ideas in joint manifestos, or present themselves as an artistically and intellectually concerted group (notwithstanding their group exhibitions).

The immediate forces that led to the foundation of the group included rejection of the work of some members for exhibition by the entrenched and "conservative" Ceylon Society of Arts (founded 1891), whose academic style represented "the artistic tastes of the middle class expatriates in the Colonial Administration and the elite among the Ceylonese."[4] The Society's hegemonic position had come under increasing challenge by the foreign and modernist influences that shaped the careers of younger artists, increasing exposure to Western art through foreign visitors, travel, books and magazines, and the general ferment of ideas and culture among an enthusiastic younger generation in a period of worldwide uncertainty and war, national political agitation, and concern with such issues as individual and national identity, and the nature and place of art itself on a rapidly changing international and local stage.

In the youth or early careers of these younger artists, public awareness of some of the issues raised above had been largely informed by Ananda K. Coomaraswamy's *Mediaeval Sinhalese Art* (1908), with its scathing references to the deterioration of the visual arts and their productive institutions under the impact of modernization, an ascendant capitalist and industrial order, and colonial administrative policies. The interpretive problems raised by Coomaraswamy's work partly stem from a largely uncritical use of Western-derived terms of analysis—showing the impress of his major source of influence, William Morris—in the different setting of colonial Sri Lanka.[5] Coomaraswamy argued that the decay of Sri Lankan art during "a century of foreign government" should be understood in light of the proposition of the *Mahavamsa* that the ancient kings were "one with the religion and the people," an ideal "hopeless of attainment by a foreign ruler."[6] As an example of the idealist turn in Coomaraswamy's theory, consider the following:

> Seeing that God alone is truly beautiful, and all other beauty is by participation, it is only a work of art that has been wrought, in its kind . . . and its significance, after an eternal model, that can be called beautiful. And since the eternal and intelligible models are supersensual and invisible, it is evidently "not by observation" but in contemplation that they must be known.[7]

The earnest authority of Coomaraswamy's argument, with its unyielding dualities (e.g., intellection vs. feeling, rhetoric vs. aesthetic, convention vs. innovation), shaped a widespread view of the relationship of Asian/Sri Lankan tradition and Western modernity. This partly explains the mixed responses of the '43 Group artists to such issues as the relationship of a Western-inspired artistic modernity to traditional or non-modern social, religious, and cultural values, and the calibration of individual autonomy against the demands of group, audience, community, and nation. A consistent principle of the traditionalist position, much canvassed before and during the period of the Group's formation, was that the historical conjunction of modernity—capitalism—industrialization, having weakened the hold of onto-theological principles, had rendered modern people unsure of "what kind of life it is that we ought for our own good and happiness to imitate, and are for the most part convinced that no one knows or can know the final truth of anything: we only know what we 'approve' of, i.e., what we *like* to do or think."[8] The local artistic tradition having fallen into decay and the foreign example been poisoned by irreligion and commercialism, Coomaraswamy proposed that there was only one choice for Sri Lankan artists, namely to seek the resources of cultural renewal in the ancient parent tradition of India.[9]

Some of the '43 Group artists took Coomaraswamy's injunction more earnestly than others. The extremism of his position seemed to present a false choice to artists of a later generation and a different mode of consciousness. For it saw no prospect of modernity being critiqued or reformed from within—a principle which was, after all, constitutive of artistic modernism (predisposing it, for example, to continual technical and stylistic experimentation, self-reconstruction, and the foundation of successive "avant-gardes"). This explains the inability of traditionalist arguments about the arts to move more flexibly and critically between such counterposed terms as "alien" and "local," "Eastern" and "Western," etc.

To artists engaged in European-derived practices and conventions, i.e., portable oil-on-canvas painting, secular portraiture, landscape, public exhibition, open critique, etc., in the colonial, traditional/modernizing, mixed cultural heritage of mid-20th c. Sri Lanka, such dichotomies necessarily came with the practice, and the main problem lay rather in how cultural confrontations between the opposed terms were to be negotiated in specific instances. Some had traveled to and studied in England, Europe and India, and increasing access to print media kept them informed about developments in Europe and America. They would then have been aware of the influence of non-Western (e.g., Japanese, African, Meso-American) artistic values and practices on the formation of European modernism. Notwithstanding the claim of stylistic purification, appropriation and hybridization were perceived to be central to the formation of modern Western art, so the formation of a "modern" art in Sri Lanka did not necessarily entail a rejection of any geographically or temporally removed resource.

In engaging on a modernizing project, '43 Group artists, like their Western exemplars, would have been but dimly aware of the complex terms and evolving possibilities of the enterprise to which they were contracting. The resulting blessings were mixed: freed of royal and ecclesiastical authority, but also bereft of reliable sources of patronage and the sustenance of craft solidarity; free to experiment with new materials, techniques and technologies of representation and to give "expression" to subjective experience, but with results which might be opaque to compatriot audiences; cultivating a transformative vision, but at the mercy of cold market forces. Negotiating the diverse demands of an artistic career in the social-economic-psychological minefield of a society in the throes of colonization, modernization, secularization, and capitalist economic transformation required—in addition to individual courage and inventiveness—substitutes for declining traditional institutions and practices, the structuring of new social and professional protocols, and, in the absence of religious and metaphysical sources of legitimation, the consolidation of new value systems and principles of their application—in sum, the formulation of a new "artistic contract," as invoked by the Group's willingness "to test itself within the severely critical frame of European practice."[10]

Certain facts of the Group's formation give evidence of their determination to steer their art into a new, post- (not anti-)traditional, professional order. As noted, they opposed the restrictive exhibition policy of the Ceylon Society of Arts and the "Victorian naturalism and artistic sterility" of its exhibits.[11] In a spirit of openness and democracy, the fledgling '43 Group offered membership to artists as well as interested members of the public. Even more radically, they proposed that "contributing artists will select their own work" for exhibition, that all works submitted would indeed be exhibited, and that even non-members might on occasion be invited to submit exhibits.[12] With these seemingly simple measures, the groundwork of art in Sri Lanka was being significantly changed—that is, "modernized." The defining style of the Ceylon Society of Arts was directed to a specific social class formation, patronage, and public relation structure, based upon the favor and financial support of a restricted social elite (of colonizer expatriates and local Western-acculturated groups).[13] By their adoption of modernist styles and professional procedures the '43 Group signaled a culturally and politically significant reorientation—towards the Sri Lankan public at large, in the interest of broadening the common culture and enlisting in an international enterprise. As it turned out, those purposes were in part subsequently frustrated by factors of which they perhaps did not take sufficient account.

Of course, the radical exhibition policy of the '43 Group courted the risk of inviting "unworthy" works. But unlike a temple fresco or church vestment, such works were not subject to the question, "Is it ritually correct?" That is, they now had only to address endogenous criteria, such as the force of the artist's vision and the aptness of material, form, and mode of representation. Further, the very nature of the artist, artwork, and the understanding and critical assessment of art, were being substantially redefined. The earlier rise of Western artistic modernism had entailed many such changes. For example, when the French National Assembly abolished the restrictive Royal Academies in 1792, it decreed the annual Salon exhibition be open to "all artists, French or foreign, members or not of the Academy," and in 1795 declared that the resulting "feeble and discordant voices" to be heard (i.e., *seen*), in the open "public exhibitions" would have the salutary effect of improving the artistic knowledge and powers of discernment of both artists and public.[14]

Secession from Ceylon Society of Arts ideas and practices brought to light other problems of that organization's "high bourgeois" fixation. Their retrograde policies had the effect of sequestering their art within the narrow social space of a privileged minority ethos. In the West, similar situations had driven dissident artists "to work at a moment when the culture is marked by a prevalent style of perception and feeling; and their modernity consists in a revolt against this prevalent style, an unyielding rage against the official order."[15]

Since the European Renaissance and Protestant Reformation period, and for various reasons, such antagonism had resulted in the separation of the arts from mainstream society, and the pattern recurred in Sri Lanka.[16] It was compounded by the market structure in which the production, dissemination and reception of artworks took place: the novelty of portable framed canvases to be hung on walls, a secularizing representational and sometimes unintelligible content, produced by single and sometimes eccentric artists sequestered from the public eye, and submitted to the mercy of anonymous market forces. Peter Bürger explains the result in terms of a structural disjunction between the *institutional frame* or *form* of art (e.g., the formation of artists and audiences, exhibition policy, and evaluation—all exogenous factors) and its *content* (e.g., religious inspiration, artistic experimentation—endogenous factors). By the late 18th c. modernizing European art had already become autonomous *in form,* but the autonomy of *content* only came about in the late 19th c. At that point, curiously,

> The apartness from the praxis of life that had always constituted the institutional status of art in bourgeois society now becomes the *content* of works. *Institutional frame* and *content* coincide. . . . In Aestheticism [late

19th c. art and literary movement] . . . [there is an] ever-increasing concentration [which] the makers of art bring to the *medium itself.* . . . At the moment it has shed all that is alien to it, art necessarily becomes *problematic for itself.* As institution and content coincide, social ineffectuality stands revealed as the essence of art in bourgeois society, and thus provokes the self-criticism of art. It is to the credit of the historical avant-garde movements that they supplied this self-criticism.[17]

The '43 Group artists also made some tentative steps in the direction of autonomy and self-criticism, as witnessed by their rejection of the vested class-interest of the Ceylon Society of Arts and, again, willingness to submit to international standards of criticism. The terms "autonomy," "apartness," "purification," "disinterestedness," "self-criticism," and "aestheticism" came to be used as rough synonyms to define the autonomization of modernist art's *form* and *content.* It helps to think of the autonomy which European music attained when it gave up vocalization for pure instrumentation, whose significance relied not on "external" linguistic reference (e.g., to biblical or mythological texts) but to purely internal relations (note, pitch, interval, harmony, etc.). This quest for autonomy sometimes took both the artist's consciousness and its representational means into strange and uncharted territories:

> The quality of life defined in [those] . . . Modernist purification rites involves a spiritual crisis that can be ameliorated only by negation of past history and exploration of new temporal sequences having little relationship to daily or routine activities. This sense of time is connected, instead, to what we find in a shaman's or hypnotists' duration: it forces first a displacement, then a renewal. When Freud moved from hypnosis and cocaine to self-analysis and analysis, from disorderings to reorderings, from displacement of time and even space to a renewal of self, he followed, in brief, the same path as the avant-garde.[18]

Even by '43 Group standards, the 1949 painting by Justin Daraniyagala (1903–67), *The Fish* was radical in its mapping of the representational strategies of artistic autonomy. Daraniyagala pitched the imagery of his painting somewhere between realism and abstraction, so that, for example, it is difficult to tell whether the adult is man or woman, or the child boy or girl. What strikes the viewer instead is the vigorous and heavy application of the pigment, the intermixing of colors, some of which are "unnatural," e.g., the reds, blues and yellows on the body surfaces, and the lateral spread of the figures across the full extent of the canvas, which confuses the spatial

The Fish by Justin Daraniyagala. Oil on canvas (90 × 119 cm.), 1949.
Dr. and Mrs. Ralph Daraniyagala Collection, Colombo.

effect. Rather than demanding the viewer's matching of image and "external" reality, the painting forces us to submit to the forceful effects of the handling of brush, pigment, color and light to evoke responses quite unlike what we might encounter in "real life."

'43 Group modernism was conditioned by one significant factor not applicable in the West, namely colonization, whose influence included the foregrounding and problematization of issues of identity. Colonial administration required that the prime imperatives of economic extraction and political domination be underwritten by policies that would induce mimicry, dissimulation, obeisance, and self-denial. This was notoriously instanced by Lord Thomas B. Macaulay's formula for reconstituting native Indian "interpreters" between the state and the masses into a "class of persons, Indian in blood and colour, but English in taste, opinions, in morals, and in intellect."[19] Homi Bhabha proposes that in this equation, "to be Anglicized is *emphatically* not to be English."[20] For the colonizer envisioned his "intermediary" as improbably hybridized of a truncated Indian and a counterfeit Englishman, therefore inhabiting elusive and spectral identities, to be summoned only by what Bhabha terms "metonymies of presence."[21] Hence the frequent figuration of mimicry and simulation in writings about the colonial condition, e.g., in Kumari Jayawardene's observation that the British produced a Sri Lankan bourgeois class of "black Englishmen" who "spoke, dressed, ate, drank, lived and thought like themselves," but were mocked in Sinhala plays of the late 19th century for their "aping of Western manners"; Michael Roberts on H. Jeronis Pieris (grandfather of '43 Group artist, Harry Pieris), who "modeled himself on his own conception of the proper Victorian gentleman—and perhaps fancied himself as one," and who railed, "Look how barbarous the Kandyans are still! I wish all of them would soon turn Christians and leave off their old nasty customs"; and Susantha Goonathilake, who noted the prevalence of "mimicry" in an area where creativity is essential—the arts.[22]

The motif of uncertain identity and induced mimicry was evident in the careers and works of '43 Group artists, complicating their increasing social apartness and search for aesthetic autonomy. Consider Harry Pieris poignantly regretting being more English than Sinhalese, and the irony of his admission that "it was in Europe that I became acquainted with the art of the east";[23] the variable measures of eroticism and melancholy with which George Keyt invested his subjects taken from village society or ancient Indian myth; or Ivan Peries, long settled in England but obsessively producing over several decades there a steady stream of visionary views of the same suburban south-Colombo littoral.

Typically in those paintings, Peries renders land, sea and, where included, human figures, in the mode of *tableux vivants*, tranquil, contemplative, and relatively motionless, as in *The Return* (1956). The generally neutral colors, verging on monochrome, heighten the effect of distance in time and place, and the figures, minimally modeled and with generalized bodily and facial features, echo the spatial order of certain traditional temple frescoes. Significantly too, there are few signs of physical work, indeed of any exertion of physical effort. Instead, the figures invoke a time when the putative harmony of Nature and humanity had not yet been shattered or submitted to the law of instrumental rationality and economic extraction. There is already in these paintings a prescient use of artistic modernism to engage in critique of social and economic modernity. It's as if the painted scene stages a fantasy of return to a lost paradise, which the artist knew to be impossible in reality; but then, in reality, he longed to escape England for the cherished environs of south Colombo, in vain, as it turned out.

The Return by Ivan Peries. Oil on canvas (56 × 86 cm.), 1956.
Heritage Collection, Colombo.

A different register of the issue of identity is raised by Geoffrey Beling's
still-life, painted in Colombo in 1930, probably after study of a printed reproduction, in what would then have become the dated formula of Parisian late
Cubism, a style conditioned by the urban, media-and-technology driven,
imperial capital that was Paris on the eve of World War I.[24] From one point
of view, the painting stages a historical-cultural impasse, for it cannot be
what it ostensibly claims to be—a representation of a historical mode of
being and consciousness of an earlier time and a foreign place. This work

Still-Life by Geoffrey Beling. Oil on canvas (55 × 55 cm.) , 1930. Sapumal Foundation, Colombo.

would have been an extraordinary novelty in 1930, with its painter seeming to bear the eyes and wield the brush of a Picasso (Franco-Spanish pioneer of Cubism) who himself had since moved into several very different artistic directions.

A discerning interpreter of the '43 Group notes that in the post-independence period, "the situation for the '43 Group had changed unfavourably," and "by the mid-1960s, the Group had lost momentum as an entity."[25] Since the serious work of charting its history and interpreting its artistic achievement seems to have hardly begun, it may be too early to assess the attempted "synthesis" of the Western modern and the local non-modern, the complicating effect of the collusion between modernism and colonialism, and the effort to forge an aesthetic for a newly-independent democracy. But theirs remains one of the few Sri Lankan achievements of their time to shine on the international stage.

Notes

1. S. Wanigaratne, *George Claessen: Artist, Sculptor and Poet* (London: Paradise Isle Publications, 2000), 13; S. Bandaranayake, "Ivan Peiris [Peries]: [Paintings 1939–1969]: The Predicament of the Bourgeois Artist in the Societies of the Third World," *Third Text* 2 (Winter 1987): 78 (emphases added); and S. Kirinde, cited in S. Tammita-Delgoda, *The World of Stanley Kirinde* (Pannipitya, 2005), 110.

2. The notable exception is the contribution of Senake Bandaranayake, "Ivan Peiris [Peries]."

3. Olinde Rodrigues, "L'Artiste, le savant et l'industriel," in Henri de Saint-Simon, *Opinions littéraires, philosophiques et industrielle* (Paris: Galérie de Bossange Père, 1825), 331.

4. Wanigaratne, *George Claessen*, 13.

5. See L. D. Lutchmansingh, "Ananda Coomaraswamy and William Morris," *Journal of the William Morris Society* 9, no. 1 (Autumn 1990): 35–42; S. Bandaranayake, "Ananda Coomaraswamy and Approaches to the Study of Traditional Sri Lankan Art and Society," in *P. E. P. Deraniyagala: Commemoration Volume*, ed. T. T. P. Gunawardena, L. Prematilleka, and R. Silva (Colombo: Lake House, 1980), 68–84; and K. Oldmeadow, "Ananda Coomaraswamy," *Traditionalism: Religion in the Light of the Perennial Philosophy* (Colombo: Sri Lankan Institute of Traditional Studies, 2000), 26–35.

6. A. K. Coomaraswamy, *Mediaeval Sinhalese Art* (1908; New York: Pantheon, 1956), v. Recently Coomaraswamy's son, Dr. Rama P. Coomaraswamy, recalled that "the devastating effects of western education and the withering blight of Occidental industrialism pained him greatly" and redirected his attention from a professional career as geologist to an "in-depth study of the indigenous arts and crafts." R. P. Coomaraswamy, "Introduction," *The Essential Coomaraswamy*, ed. R. P. Coomaraswamy (Bloomington, Ind.: World Wisdom, 2004), 3.

7. A. K. Coomaraswamy [1946], in *The Essential Ananda K. Coomaraswamy*, 29.

8. Ibid., 28–29.

9. Coomaraswamy, *Mediaeval Sinhalese Art*, ix.

10. Neville Weeraratne, *The 43 Group* (Victoria, Australia: Lantana Publishing, 1993), 4.

11. The Ceylon Society of Arts was founded in 1891 on the initiative of the colonial administration. Weeraratne (12–13), associates its foundation in accordance with the stipulation, rather in the spirit of Macaulay's Indian directive, that Sri Lankan civil servants should "become acquainted with all the extra-mural activities of those they were to serve," so that "the creature to emerge from this was the totally incongruous westernized oriental."

12. Appendix A, "Minutes of the Inaugural Meeting 29 August 1943," in Weeraratne, 146.

13. Kumari Jayawardena notes the vast sums spent by this "colonial bourgeoisie" on their conspicuous consumption, including "palatial residences . . . with mock-Italian décor, large gardens and wedding-cake architecture," one example of which, quaintly named "Elscourt," was owned by the grandfather of one of the prominent artists of the '43 Group. The style of painting termed "Victorian naturalism" would have been destined precisely for such homes. See K. Jayawardena, *Nobodies to Somebodies: The Rise of the Colonial Bourgeoisie in Sri Lanka* (Colombo: Social Scientists' Association and Sanjiva Books, 2000), 258.

14. Cited in E. G. Holt, "Paris: The Official Exhibition of the State" and "Official Catalogue: Salon of the Year IV (1795)," in *The Triumph of Art for the Public: The Emerging Role of Exhibitions and Critics*, ed. E. G. Holt (Garden City, N.Y.: Anchor/Doubleday, 1979), 41, 49.

15. Irving Howe, *Decline of the New* (New York: Harcourt, Brace and World, 1970), 3.

16. P. Bürger, *Theory of the Avant-Garde*, trans. M. Shaw (1974; Minneapolis: University of Minnesota Press, 1984), 26.

17. Ibid., 48 (italics added). An influential formula of this development was Clement Greenberg's: "The essence of Modernism lies . . . in the use of the characteristic methods of a discipline to criticize the discipline itself." C. Greenberg, "Modernist Painting," [1961] in *Art in Theory, 1900–1990*, ed. C. Harrison and P. Wood (Oxford: Blackwell, 1993), 755.

18. Frederick R. Karl, "Purifications," in *Modern and Modernism: The Sovereignty of the Artist, 1885–1925* (New York: Athenaeum, 1988), 166–67.

19. T. B. Macaulay [1835], cited in J. McLeod, "Introduction," *The Routledge Companion to Postcolonial Studies*, ed. J. McLeod (London: Routledge, 2007), 3.

20. H. Bhabha, "Of Mimicry and Man: The Ambivalence of Colonial Discourse," [1984] in *OCTOBER: The First Decade, 1976–1986*, ed. A. Michelson, R. Krauss, D. Crimp, and J. Copjec (Cambridge: MIT Press, 1987), 322. N. Wickramasinghe writes that, in the Sri Lankan context, "the dual system of education that became entrenched was founded on the Macaulayan notion of a privileged few educated in English and the masses educated in the vernacular. . . . There were also Anglo-vernacular schools that attempted to straddle both cultures, but were not very successful." N. Wickramasinghe, *Sri Lanka in the Modern Age* (Colombo: Vijitha Yapa Publications, 2006), 75.

21. Bhabha, "Of Mimicry and Man," 320.

22. Jayawardena, *Nobodies to Somebodies*, 247; M. Roberts, *Facets of Modern Ceylon History through the Letters of Jeronis Pieris* (Colombo: Hansa Publishers, 1975), 27; S. Goonathilake, *Crippled Minds* (Colombo: Lake House Bookshop, 1982), 103.

23. H. Pieris, quoted in Weeraratne, 51.

24. In A. Dharmasiri, *Modern Art in Sri Lanka: The Anton Wickremasinghe Collection* (Colombo: Lake House, 1988).

25. S. Bandaranayake and M. Fonseka (1996), 39. [This citation is incomplete in the original and untraceable—*Ed.*]

IV

Independence, Insurrections, and Social Change

Our extended discussion of the emergence of various communal identities is one way of accounting for the substance of Sri Lanka's collective experience of modernity, but the establishment and shaping of the country's political culture by its dominant prime ministers and presidents (D. S. Senanayake, S. W. R. D. Bandaranaike, his wife Sirimavo Bandaranaike, their daughter Chandrika Kumaratunga, and J. R. Jayewardene), the subsequent crises brought about by the JVP (Janata Vimukti Peramuna, or People's Liberation Front) in the insurrections of 1971 and 1988–89, and the terrible ethnic riots of 1983, are also important to the trajectory of recent Sri Lankan history. The JVP insurrections and the ethnic riots against Tamil people were watershed moments resulting in major political paradigm shifts. The "open economy" ushered in by the newly installed UNP (United National Party) government in 1977 is also another such moment. In this fourth section of *The Sri Lanka Reader*, the contours of Sri Lanka's postindependence political culture are explored, first, by three eminent academic expert observers; then, the class-induced insurrections of 1971 and 1988–89 and ethnic riot of 1983 are described in detail. Two essays follow that focus on the novel social and economic experiences of women who have entered the open economy work force as housemaids employed in the Middle East or as garment factory workers in the new free trade zones established in the late 1970s; the social ramifications of these gender-based economic developments are explored in depth. This section also includes a personal essay on cultural relations between India and Sri Lanka and an account of the tsunami of December 26, 2004, which took the lives of approximately forty thousand Sri Lankans.

Sri Lanka in 1948

K. M. de Silva

At the dawn of Sri Lanka's independence, the country was "an oasis of peace, stabil-ity and order." But "beneath the surface . . . , religious, cultural and linguistic issues were gathering momentum and developing into a force too powerful for the existing social and political set-up to accommodate or absorb. They were to tear the country apart within a decade." So begins and so ends K. M. de Silva's insightful resume of the condition of Ceylon in 1948 as it made the transition from British colony to political independence. His essay is perhaps the most cogent assessment yet of D. S. Senanayake, the country's first prime minister.

A perceptive observer watching the collapse of European empires in Asia af-ter the Second World War would have been struck by the contrast between the situation in Sri Lanka and in the rest of South Asia including Burma. It could hardly be expected that the transfer of power in the Indian subcon-tinent would be free of turmoil, but the violence that raged over British India on the eve of independence was on a scale which few but the most pessimistic could have anticipated. The dawn of Indian independence was marred by massacres and migrations in the Punjab on a scale unparalleled in world history in time of peace. There was a similar extension of mas-sacres and migrations in Eastern India. The sub-continent seemed to be on the verge of calamitous civil war. In Burma too the situation was equally fraught with turmoil and conflict. Aung San, the youthful leader of Burma's independence struggle, did not live to see the signing of the treaty (which he had negotiated) between Britain and Burma on 17 October 1947 which granted Burma her independence; he was assassinated along with a group of his closest associates on 19 June 1947. If the civil war which at one stage seemed India's inevitable fate was avoided through the drastic device of par-tition, Burma was not so fortunate. There, civil war erupted almost from the very first week of the existence of the new Burmese republic.

Sri Lanka in 1948 was, in contrast, an oasis of stability, peace and order. Set against the contemporary catastrophes in the rest of the former British possessions in South Asia, the industrial disputes and the general strike of the years 1945–47 paled into utter insignificance in the scale of violence involved. The transfer of power in Sri Lanka was smooth and peaceful. More importantly one saw very little of the divisions and bitterness which were tearing at the recent independence of the countries in South Asia. Within a few months of independence in 1948 one of the most intractable political issues in the country—the Tamil problem—which had absorbed the energies of its politicians and the British themselves to an inordinate degree since the early nineteen-twenties seemed on the way to amicable settlement. G. G. Ponnambalam, who had led the Tamils in their political campaigns since his entry into the State Council in 1934, became a member of the Cabinet, bringing with him into the government the bulk of the leadership and members of the Tamil Congress. In so doing he helped convert the government into very much a consensus of moderate political opinion in the country.

The final phase in the transfer of power had begun under the leadership of D. S. Senanayake. There are two noteworthy points of interest in his negotiations with Britain on this issue. Firstly, he was guided by a strong belief in ordered constitutional evolution to Dominion Status on the analogy of constitutional development in the White Dominions. In insisting that Dominion Status should remain the prime object of policy, and that this should be attained in association with rather than in opposition to the British, he placed himself in direct opposition to the views adopted by the Ceylon National Congress in 1942 (in response to the younger policy makers who were becoming increasingly influential within it) that independence rather than Dominion Status should be the goal of Sri Lanka's development. Secondly, he feared that with the British withdrawal the British empire in Asia in the familiar form in which it had existed would have ended, and that the political prospects in Asia would be hardly encouraging. A profound suspicion of India was the dominant strand in his external policy. Accordingly it was as a policy of re-insurance for the country during the early years of independence, when it was not impossible that there might be a political vacuum in South Asia, that he viewed the agreements on Defence and External Affairs negotiated by Whitehall as a prelude to the grant of Dominion Status to Sri Lanka.

It was in his internal policy that he left the impress of his dominant personality and his moderate views. The guiding principles were: the conception of Sri Lanka as a multi-racial democracy and his commitment to the maintenance of the Liberal ideal of a secular state in which the lines between state power and religion were scrupulously demarcated. Here again he placed himself in opposition to an increasingly influential current of opinion which viewed the Sri Lanka polity as being essentially Sinhalese and Buddhist in character, and which urged that government policies should be fashioned to accommodate a far-reaching transformation of the island's politics to build a new Sri Lanka on traditional, ideal, Sinhala-Buddhist lines. Implicit in this was a rejection of the concept of a multi-racial polity, as well as the concept of a secular state.

D. S. Senanayake, in contrast, was sensitive to minority anxieties. This was not merely a matter of political realism but also sprang from a deep conviction of the need for generous concessions to the minorities, ethnic, communal and religious, to ensure political stability in a plural society such as Sri Lanka in the vital last phase in the transfer of power. An analysis of his response to the political implications of minority anxieties on Sri Lanka's development as an independent state needs much more space than is available in a very brief introductory chapter such as this. One needs to draw attention, briefly, to at least three points of interest.

Firstly, there were the guarantees against legislation discriminating against minorities, incorporated in the Soulbury Constitution. These guarantees had been borrowed from provisions in the Ministers' Draft Constitution of 1944 which had been introduced on D. S. Senanayake's initiative as a gesture of generosity and re-assurance to the minorities. In retrospect it would seem that the rights of minorities had not received adequate protection in the Soulbury Constitution, but in 1946–7 the constitutional guarantees against discriminatory legislation seemed sufficiently reassuring to them largely because of the trust and confidence they had in D. S. Senanayake.

Secondly, there was the initiative he took in forming the United National Party. This was designed to make a fresh start in politics in the direction of a consensus of moderate opinion in national politics; it was to be a political party necessarily representative of the majority community but at the same time acceptable to the minorities. His own standing in the country was sufficient guarantee of its being acceptable to the majority, but there is no doubt that its position among the Sinhalese was strengthened by S. W. R. D. Bandaranaike's decision to bring in his Sinhala Maha Sabha. From the beginning it had the enthusiastic approval of the small but influential Christian minority, and the Muslims who had in the past given substantial support to the Tamils in their political campaigns at last broke away and sought association with the new party. When the Tamil Congress crossed over to the government in 1948 the equilibrium of political forces which D. S. Senanayake had sought to establish was stabilised at a level which he found acceptable, even though the Tamil Congress did not lose its separate identity and despite the fact that a section broke away from it into a stubborn but, at that time, seemingly futile opposition. Only the Indian community, consisting in the main of plantation workers, was left out. But there were special reasons for that, for they were regarded as an unassimilated group without roots in the country. The decision to leave them out was deliberately taken on that account. To the extent that he shared the attitudes and prejudices of the great majority of Sinhalese politicians with regard to the Indian question, the status of Indian plantation workers in the Sri Lanka polity, and more specifically to deny them unrestricted rights to the franchise—his conception of a multi-racial polity was flawed.

Thirdly, D. S. Senanayake thwarted all efforts to abandon the concept of a secular state, and the principle of the religious neutrality of the state. He succeeded in this to the extent that in 1948, despite some Buddhist displeasure over the continued prestigious and influential position enjoyed by the Christians, there seemed little or no evidence of the religious turmoil and linguistic conflicts that were to burst to the surface in 1956.

If the political leadership in Sri Lanka took pride in the smoothness of the transfer of power, they seemed oblivious to the political perils involved in making the process so bland as to be virtually imperceptible to those not directly involved. The last British governor of the island became the island's first Governor-General after independence. Next there was the notable difference between the constitutional and legal instruments which conferred independence on Sri Lanka, and the cognate process in other parts of South Asia—for India and Pakistan, Acts of Parliament; for Burma, a specially negotiated treaty; for Sri Lanka, a mere Order-in-Council. All this seemed to suggest a qualitative difference in the nature of the independence that was being achieved when no meaningful difference in status was either intended by Britain or accepted by Sri Lanka's leaders, in the Board of Ministers first of all, and later, in the Cabinet. There was also the fact that the constitution under which the new Dominion began its political existence was of British origin in contrast to the autochthonous constitution drafted for the Indian Republic by a Constituent Assembly. Once again there was an element of exaggeration in the criticism, for the new constitution of Sri Lanka was basically the one drafted for D. S. Senanayake by his advisers in 1944—and approved subsequently by the State Council—modified to suit the needs of the changed circumstances of 1946–7. And these modifications were few and not very substantial or significant. Above all the Agreements on Defence and External Affairs negotiated prior to the transfer of power helped to give an air of credibility to the argument that the independence conferred on Sri Lanka was flawed. The Agreements themselves were regarded as badges of inferiority, and checks on full sovereignty in external affairs; moreover fears were expressed about secret clauses not divulged or a secret treaty even more detrimental to the island's status as an independent nation. Events were to prove that these fears and suspicions were without foundation in fact, and certainly that no secret undertakings had been given by Sri Lanka in 1947–8, but until 1956–7 suspicion persisted and could be used by critics of the UNP and the constitution.

Thus the real worth of D. S. Senanayake's achievement came to be denied because the means adopted for the attainment of independence under his leadership were not as robust and as dramatic as they might have been. By laying so much stress on the decorous and peaceful processes of constitutional agitation the Board of Ministers had deprived themselves, perhaps consciously, of the opportunities of exploring the numerous chances they had of making a more emotional and vigorous commitment to nationalism. Left-wing critics of the government were able to argue that the independence achieved in 1947–8 was "spurious." The gibe of "fake" independence which they kept hurling at the government evoked a positive response from a wider circle of the political nation than merely the left wing alone, largely because the Indian experience seemed to provide a more emotionally satisfying example than the process by which power had been transferred in Sri Lanka—independence granted from above (as Sri Lanka) was regarded as being much less satisfying to the spirit of nationalism than if it has been won after prolonged strife and untiring sacrifice.

As regards the economy, much more so than with the political structure, the mood of the day was singularly sober and realistic though not unduly pessimistic. There were, on the contrary, high hopes for economic achievement. For the country's assets were not unimpressive: though the population was increasing rapidly, it was, compared with that in other countries in South Asia, well fed and literate; the government of Sri Lanka was the largest landholder in the country, controlling no less than 3.25 million acres of land (the bulk of this land was waste forest and required the provision of roads and electricity to be rendered productive); the administration was competent, and the island was well equipped with social and economic overheads; above all, there were the large sterling balances accumulated during the war.

Nevertheless the economic legacy left behind by the British was just as ambiguous, and perhaps even more so, than the political. The crux of the problem was that foreign income which directly or indirectly constituted the bulk of the national income began to fall rapidly while there was a rise in the cost of imports. This was reflected in the country's balance of payment, which fell consistently from a handsome surplus in 1945 to a heavy deficit in

1947. For a country which practically lives by foreign trade, an authoritative contemporary economic survey pointed out, "no economic indices could be more significant. It represented a fall in national income and a march towards greater poverty and insecurity."

D. S. Senanayake's government inherited an undiversified export economy dependent principally on three crops, tea (which in terms of export earnings was the most important), rubber and coconut. The weakness of the economy lay in the fact that the revenue from these exports was subject to wide fluctuations, a reflex of world economic conditions. This was quite apart from the fact that foreign commercial firms—largely British—had a dominant controlling position in the plantations, especially tea and rubber, and in the export of plantation products.

One of the most striking features of this economic structure was the absence of an industrial sector independent of the processing of tea, rubber and coconut for export, and the engineering and mechanical requirements of these processes. Nevertheless there had been since 1931 and more particularly since the outbreak of the Second World War, some state-sponsored industrial ventures. None of these proved to be of more than marginal significance, and on the whole little progress had been made. Private enterprise was reluctant to embark on industrial ventures in the absence of firm support from the government. Though the new government declared that the country cannot "depend on agriculture alone to provide the minimum standard we are aiming at for our rapidly increasing people," this was merely lip-service to the almost religious faith among the intelligentsia in industrialization as the panacea for Sri Lanka's economic problems.

Traditional agriculture—subsistence farming—lagged far behind the efficient plantation sector in productivity due to the long-term impact of a multiplicity of factors. Sri Lanka could not produce rice needed to feed a growing population: the bulk of the country's requirements in rice and subsidiary foodstuffs was imported and accounted for more than half the imports.

Looking ahead in the years after independence the Senanayake regime placed its hopes on the achievement of self-sufficiency in rice and subsidiary food-stuffs; " . . . increased production particularly in the matter of home-grown food," it declared, "will be given a place of supreme importance in the policy of the Government. . . ." The principal means of achieving this objective was the rapid development of the dry zone, the heartland of the ancient irrigation civilization of Sri Lanka. Thus in this enterprise one discerned too the search for inspiration from the past and the traditional sources of legitimacy of Sri Lanka's rulers.

All in all, there was no great emphasis on far-reaching changes in the economic structure inherited from the British. This latter had taken firm root in the period of British rule, and the process of introducing changes in it was more difficult than it seemed, while any hope of dismantling it was beyond the realms of practical politics. For the export of estate products enabled the people of Sri Lanka, or a large part of them, to be fed and clothed. Besides the system itself was still viable and its potential for expansion was, if not undiminished, at least reasonably good. And it was also true that the political leadership of the day was reluctant to make changes in an economic system with which their own interests were identified. The result was that in the economic structure, as in the political, there was an emphasis on the maintenance of the status quo.

There were other problems as well, and of these much the most important was the rapidity with which population was expanding. A knowledgeable commentator on the country's affairs warned the country in 1949 of the economic implication of the fact that the island's rate of natural increase of population had reached "the astonishing rate of about 3.3 percent per annum. There can be no doubt," he added, "that this is the fundamental problem of the economy of [Sri Lanka]. . . ."

In the general elections of 1947 left-wing parties made substantial if not spectacular gains, and held between themselves and their fellow-travelers about a fourth of the elected seats. Earlier they had organised a series of major strikes culminating in the general strike of 1947. These strikes had been the most noteworthy demonstrations of solidarity of the working class and white collar workers up to that time. The strikes were as much political demonstrations as they were trades disputes—one of the main demands was the rejection of the Soulbury Constitution. The strife generated by these strikes served the purpose of underlining the difference in approach between two concepts of nationalism. The "moderates" had come into their inheritance, and the "radicals"—in the sense of the left wing—had demonstrated their determination to deprive them of it. They had taken a stand against the Soulbury Constitution, and they dismissed the grant of independence in February 1948 as a cynical deal between the imperial power and their pliant agents in Sri Lanka to preserve the old order in the guise of independence.

Though the Board of Ministers had been constrained to treat the strikes of 1945–7, and in particular, the general strike of 1947 as a serious bid for political power by Marxists, they soon realized that the challenge from the left wing had been needlessly exaggerated, and that they were by no means a threat to the country's political stability. While the social order was under increasing pressure from a politicized urban working class and white collar workers, the peasantry was a stable element and D. S. Senanayake sought to meet the left-wing challenge by the operation of a socio-economic policy which assumed if not an identity of interests between the governing elite and the peasantry, at least a potentially harmonious working relationship between two conservative social groups. In the early years of independence this policy was proving to be increasingly successful. Secondly, the social welfare schemes of the Donoughmore era were continued beyond 1947 as a means of blunting the challenge of the Marxist left. Sri Lanka, poor though she was, enjoyed a much higher standard of living than India, Pakistan and Burma and the national finances seemed adequate to maintain the welfare measures to which the country had grown accustomed in the last years of British rule. In 1947 the total expenditure on welfare absorbed 56.1% of the government's resources; the corresponding figure for the late nineteen twenties has been a mere 16.4%. It was not yet evident that the burgeoning costs of these welfare measures were an unsupportable burden for a developing country and one which "added a dimension of weakness to an economy whose principal feature was its dependence on the vagaries of a world market."

Ironically, however, neither of the protagonists—the government led by D. S. Senanayake, nor its left-wing critics—showed much understanding of the sense of outrage and indignation of the Buddhists at what they regarded as the historic injustices suffered by their religion under western rule. The affront was to culture no less than to religion, and the resentment was felt even more strongly by the ayurvedic physician, the Sinhala school master and the notary than by the *bhikkhus*. And as regards religion it was the withdrawal of the traditional patronage and consequent precedence and prestige that was resented. Beneath the surface these religious, cultural and linguistic issues were gathering momentum and developing into a force too powerful for the existing social and political set-up to accommodate or absorb. They were to tear the country apart within a decade of 1948 and accomplish the discomfiture of both the UNP and its left-wing critics.

The Bandaranaike Legend

James Manor

While D. S. Senanayake's United National Party (UNP) dominated the first years of the country's political independence, the Bandaranaike "dynasty" (husband, wife, and daughter) that intermittently controlled Sri Lankan politics over the next fifty years, came to power in 1956. In the conclusion to his authoritative study, James Manor measures the political realities of S. W. R. D. Bandaranaike's government following his watershed and populist 1956 election victory—a campaign that was based on a platform of "Sinhala-only" and Buddhism's favored status within the state—against the Bandaranaike legend, which was occasioned, championed, and politically exploited chiefly by his widow following his assassination in 1959 by a leading Buddhist monk.

Bandaranaike's murder traumatized the nation. People reacted with astonishment and with genuine grief. Nearly half a million waited patiently, day and night, five deep in two six-mile-long queues for an average of seven hours to file past the body at the late premier's home and then at Parliament. Colombo—from the business district to the shanty towns—was a city draped in white, the traditional colour of mourning. Provincial towns were at a standstill.

The island's politics, which have often been marked by callousness and viciousness, can at times produce immense outpourings of warmth and generosity. This was such a moment. Bandaranaike's shortcomings as Prime Minister were forgotten by many and became unmentionable by the rest. The air was thick with adulation that he could never have hoped for had he lived to face the dilemmas which his misjudgments and the ill-considered doings of his erstwhile allies had created. His assassination was likened to those of Lincoln and Gandhi. It was said that he had become "a Bodhisattva" (a Buddha-to-be) and that he was "now in the Devyaloka" (a Buddhist heaven) "silently inspiring and guiding us from the other world." A great deal of this was the sort of short-lived hyperbole that attends such occasions everywhere. But Bandaranaike has remained—thanks in no small part to the promotional efforts of his widow—a legend who led a life of sacrifice and struggle for the common man and for a new national identity.

It was as much the manner of his death, in which the theme of sacrifice acquired compelling authenticity, as his achievements in life that accounts for this. It is no accident, for example, that Bandaranaike Day, until recently a public holiday, falls on the day of his death rather than his birth.

The film biography which the government later made begins and ends with the massive funeral and his interment in a monumental tomb on the family estate at Horagolla. This burial place, which is adjacent to the main Colombo-Kandy road, is still visited by large numbers of people. Some have even used it as a shrine, lighting lamps or candles—which to many Sinhalese denote a presence—and offering prayers or swearing vows to Bandaranaike.

His story, with its ghastly end, has often been seen as a tragedy at both the personal and the political levels, although many Ceylonese conditioned by the personalized politics that result from elite dominance of parties—perceive no distinction between the two. There can be no doubt that at a personal level—for Bandaranaike, his family and close associates—this was a tragic end. A man in his prime, with great gifts and a zest for life, was brutally cut down before his time. But was it a political tragedy?

His murder can only be seen as a tragic episode in political terms if it deprived him of an opportunity to achieve something significant. By mid-1959, he had lost so much power and credibility that he no longer had such an opportunity. The riots of the previous year, the polarization of society along linguistic lines and the chaos within his Cabinet virtually guaranteed that his bold move to the left would have led nowhere. In other words, Bandaranaike's failures had rendered him something of a tragic figure even before his death. Indeed, although it is a harsh thing to say, the assassination has obscured the wasted opportunities of his premiership by distracting attention from the disintegration of the political experiment that he had undertaken as Prime Minister. His murder and the legend which grew up around him thereafter did more to revive the fortunes of that experiment than could anything that he might have done had he survived.

Legends are, necessarily, uncomplicated. Legacies and assessments of leaders' achievements are more ambiguous. Bandaranaike can be credited with the creation of a party and an electoral coalition that in 1956 offered voters a realistic alternative to a dubious incumbent government. The ruling UNP was led by a man who sometimes exhibited a brutish contempt for basic human rights and the representative process, who sought to prevent participation by disadvantaged Sinhalese castes, and who was dangerously insensitive even to the concerns of village-level elites. Bandaranaike enabled both the disadvantaged and the village elites to express their alienation from Sir John [Kotelawa] and the UNP within the existing political structures, and thereby contributed mightily to the credibility and survival of representative institutions.

By creating a centre-left alternative and by then embodying his intention to seek greater social justice in new government initiatives and in popular symbols and slogans, Bandaranaike firmly institutionalized social welfare programmes that had enabled Ceylon to achieve such remarkable results in infant mortality, life expectancy and literacy. UNP leaders from the 1940s onward share in the credit for this, but the presence of a rival party on their left flank ensured that there would be no retreat from these programmes for nearly two decades.

Nor, by 1959, was this any longer the result of uncoordinated ad hoc-ism. In that year, Bandaranaike's government produced a cogent ten-year economic plan which Michael Lipton has described as "a fundamental departure in development thinking" in that "its emphasis upon and analysis of the need to relieve poverty and unemployment (even at the cost of 'growth') was far ahead of western models of its time." That achievement is not nullified by the subsequent implementation of the plan under Mrs Bandaranaike in a manner that was far too heedless of the need to consider economic growth. Some of those later problems were inherent in Bandaranaike's excessive optimism about the capacity of poorer folk to use new opportunities: to create wealth, but in the late 1950s such hopes were widely—and, at that time, understandably—shared in most of the emerging nations of Africa and Asia.

In 1956, Bandaranaike had attracted the votes of disadvantaged castes that had seldom participated in earlier elections. They supported him not because large numbers of his candidates were of less exalted status than those of the UNP in general, they were not—but because he and they were seen to care more for the needs of ordinary people. Once in power, he moved to ensure that even if the UNP tried energetically to prevent such groups from voting—as, in their complacency, they had largely failed to do in 1956—this would be impossible. He ordered a marked increase in the number of polling stations so that such groups could vote close to home without the threat of the road blocks and intimidation of old, and by nationalizing the bus companies, he removed the main means of intimidation. His government also provided the poor with imaginative, meaningful legal reforms including a legal aid programme and tribunals to resolve disputes before they reached overburdened courts—thanks to an altruistic and creative Law Minister. Wider use was also made of the vernacular in government offices. Though some labour unions abused the government's generosity, urban workers in several sectors gained improved wages, conditions and negotiating leverage. State-aided insurance, sickness benefit and retirement funds for many manual and clerical workers were created or bolstered.

Bandaranaike's adroit use of symbols and slogans to stress to ordinary people that this was a caring, responsive government both reinforced these reforms and compensated somewhat for omissions on other fronts. His adaptation of the Buddhist ideal of "the Middle way" to describe his party's position between the Marxist left and the UNP right was particularly ingenious. His constant references to their era as "the age of the common man" and as an "age of transition" to a new, more fully democratic future were widely known and appreciated. He also had an acute instinct for the telling gesture, as when he picked a poor man from the crowd at the opening of a new bridge and had him cut the ribbon. Such incidents crystallized in the minds of many a belief in the intentions of the regime to back its promises with action, even if its delivery of tangible resources lagged badly, as it did in many spheres between 1956 and 1959.

Many of these changes—both concrete and symbolic—dismayed elites that had prospered under previous governments, but since one of their own stood at the helm of the new regime, their dismay was tempered by a certain reassurance that the Prime Minister was a gradualist who understood them. On certain important occasions—most notably the struggle over the Paddy Lands Bill—prosperous groups and their representatives within the government became alarmed and combined to thwart change. But numerous other reforms came quietly into being without public outcry, thanks in part to the Prime Minister's patrician status.

The government suffered far more from the truculence of Sinhalese Buddhist extremists and from Bandaranaike's staggering miscalculations in handling them. But we must not forget that he had inherited a well nigh impossible situation from his predecessors. By 1955–56, Sir John and the UNP had allowed so much resentment to build up that inflated demands from extremists were inevitable, and major concessions to Buddhism and Sinhalese language and culture were essential. Many of the steps that were taken in response—the "Sinhala Only" Act and the conversion of Buddhist *pirivenas* or centres of higher study into universities and much else—were unavoidable and in large measure creative. Changes in foreign and defence policies—establishing diplomatic ties to Communist nations, the adoption of a non-aligned posture and the closure of British bases in Ceylon—also began to instill in people a new identity and sense of direction. As his most perceptive Tamil critic said after the assassination, "under his rule the Ceylonese began to understand that they were first-class Asians, not third-class synthetic Europeans."

After the assassination, Bandaranaike's party—amid confusion and internecine strife—was forced to an election in March 1960, under the leadership of C. P. de Silva, much recovered from the previous August. The result was inconclusive and there followed another election, in July 1960, which was won by an SLFP-led alliance with Mrs Sirimavo Bandaranaike as its leader. (She held power until 1965 and again—after a spell of UNP rule—from 1970 to 1977, when the UNP again displaced her.) In what was a very tearful campaign, much was made in mid-1960 of her personal loss and of her husband's thwarted dreams. These themes proved highly effective and, in the years thereafter, she mounted a systematic effort to sustain and enlarge upon the Bandaranaike legend. It was in her interest to do so. The more the legendary Bandaranaike towered over the political landscape, the more important his widow became, since she had the closest tie to him. It is a trifle ironic that Mrs Bandaranaike should have had such a major impact on the island's politics after her husband's death because she had had only marginal influence during his lifetime. As one close relative put it, "In Solla's [Bandaranaike's] time Sirima presided over nothing fiercer than the kitchen fire."

Nevertheless, she proved herself a forceful, perhaps too forceful, leader and her custody of his legend needs to be carefully assessed. Three of the changes which some people expected during his premiership have never fully materialized. The first was a departure from the traditional dominance which supreme leaders had always exercised over Ceylon's major parties. Bandaranaike himself had done nothing to dilute it. His eagerness for mass participation in elections did not imply a similar interest in turning decision-making within his party over to subordinates or the rank and file. This owed something to his suspicion of extremists in the SLFP [Sri Lankan Freedom Party], but the basic reason was his lifelong predilection to dominate any organization that he led. Mrs Bandaranaike did likewise after him, as did the UNP's leaders until the mid-1970s, when J. R. Jayewardene took only some modest steps in that direction. The conflicts and extremism that resulted, after 1977, from that change within the UNP may suggest that elite dominance in the island's major parties was a good thing. But in ways too complex to explain here, an earlier and more carefully planned decentralization might have helped to curtail Sinhalese chauvinism and the unrealistic political expectations that have always attended it.

The other two changes, unlike the first, had been actively sought by Bandaranaike. The first—the creation of elected councils at the provincial or district level—would also have diminished the power of those at the apex of the political system. But he welcomed this sort of decentralization since he felt that it would give ordinary people the chance to choose representatives to councils that were close to home and thus more accessible and observable than was Parliament in Colombo. He also knew that if regional councils had meaningful powers, they would go some way towards easing the alienation of Tamils and promoting accommodation between the two main linguistic groups, which was the other major change that he sought once he became Prime Minister. It was of course for that very reason—because regional councils were seen by Sinhalese chauvinists as a concession to Tamils—that no progress occurred on that front under governments led by either of the Bandaranaikes. A UNP government created District Development Councils in 1981, but Sinhalese extremists again ensured that their powers were inadequate. At this writing, Provincial Councils are being created, but it remains to be seen how much power they will be given. Mrs Bandaranaike was less committed than her husband to a liberal, cosmopolitan vision, and she was acutely aware of the political utility of Sinhalese chauvinism. So the accommodation between Sinhalese and Tamils which he had sought was not adequately pursued in her time.

After his death, most of the changes which SLFP-led governments did introduce were presented as tributes to his memory and as fulfilments of his grand design. Many of these would clearly have pleased him. The final abandonment of the old headman system, the changeover to the use of Sinhala in lower courts, the provision of banking facilities and credit to ordinary villagers, and the land reform of the early 1970s—these and other programmes to assist the common man would have won his hearty approval.

Certain other things done in his name would probably have distressed him, however. The promises of far-reaching nationalization of private firms that appeared in his 1956 election manifesto were mainly concessions to his leftist allies. He welcomed the state takeovers of the buses, since it meant an end to a major source of thuggery, and of the Colombo port. He would also have supported some further extensions of state ownership, but it is unlikely that he would have wished it to embrace the tea plantations, and he would probably have opposed the complex array of state controls on the economy which his widow's governments imposed. He would certainly have resisted the nationalization of the major newspaper chains and the conversion of the print and broadcasting media into mouthpieces for the ruling party. And his refusal during his premiership to yield to Buddhist pressure to take over

Christian schools—which in his view would have intruded too much upon minority rights—suggests that he would also have opposed his widow's initiatives on that front. Many features of the republican Constitution of 1972 would have pleased him, but not its illiberal manipulation to put off an election by an extra two years. It would not have surprised him that, after that episode, the rival UNP indulged in similar abuses once it regained power in 1977.

Mrs Bandaranaike understood that her husband's overgenerous ways as Prime Minister had created major problems and she was determined to be radically different. But there can be no doubt that he would have recoiled from many of the abrasive and often vindictive acts that occurred under her regimes, especially after the abortive 1971 insurgency by leftist Sinhalese youth. Ministers' extravagant insecurities in that period led to rampant nepotism—which Bandaranaike had scrupulously avoided—and to spiteful, brutish treatment of both the opposition parties and the Tamils of the Northern Province. The needless imposition in the north of an ill-disciplined and frequently abusive army that was overwhelmingly Sinhalese instilled much of the bitterness which later generated armed resistance there. So did that government's patent discrimination against Tamils in areas such as higher education. His bouts of chauvinistic rhetoric notwithstanding, Bandaranaike had viewed the "state" as an arena within which all social groups ought to be able to compete on equal terms, and as an agency from which all ought to receive evenhanded treatment and protection, and he had believed that the "nation" should embrace all of the island's people. In the years since his death, these notions have been largely overtaken, with the "state" being seen as the partisan instrument of the ruling party, and the "nation" being equated with the so-called Sinhalese "race."

Bandaranaike's story is a tangle of ironies and incongruities. He was born at the pinnacle of the old Ceylonese social order, and yet he did more than any other leader to draw rural dwellers into a sense of involvement with democratic institutions. His overweening elitism led him to an abhorrence of caste prejudice and to vague but genuine egalitarian views. He was steeped in western learning which he mastered and loved, and he had great difficulty reading Sinhala, but it was he who first made Sinhala and Sinhalese Buddhist culture central concerns of the state. He gave Sinhalese Buddhists greater confidence in themselves and their culture, even as he failed to prevent their insecurities from producing excesses, and from becoming a firmly institutionalized element in the island's politics. He was both a utopian idealist and an avid opportunist, relentlessly pursuing short-term political gains. But after thirty years of seeking supreme power in that manner, when he achieved it, he let it slip heedlessly away. Given all of this, it is hardly surprising that he failed to resolve the dissonance between the two themes that dominated his career: Sinhalese parochialism and cosmopolitan reform. The incongruity between them stands at the core of his life, legend and legacy.

He had hoped to use chauvinism as a means to achieve power, believing that he could disarm it by making modest, long-overdue concessions to Sinhalese Buddhist interests, and then by concentrating on reform to remove social injustice and soothe the anxieties of would-be communalists. He did not succeed, partly because the problems that he had inherited were so severe, partly because his ruling coalition contained too many contradictions, partly because his government functioned so sluggishly, but very substantially because of the way Bandaranaike himself thought and acted.

Had he not squandered his power in reckless generosity to groups frivolous and nefarious, had he asserted his authority in the country and the Cabinet, there was a reasonable chance that tangible reforms, promptly and effectively delivered, could have captured the popular imagination and served as a potent and lasting distraction from anti-Tamil bigotry. There is no reason to suppose that his efforts had to fail. But fail they did, and they were never adequately revived by those who later acted in his name. As a result, the two themes remained as antagonistic after his death as before.

The Bandaranaike legend served to sustain and enlarge the already unrealistic expectations that had developed during his premiership both among those who sought greater social justice and among Sinhalese communalists. The legend, and the expectations that attended it, were so over-inflated that they eventually became destabilizing liabilities that bred cynicism among both reformers and chauvinists. When excessive state controls caused the economy to stagnate, that cynicism turned to anger—first among those who had hoped for reform, in the insurrection of 1971, and later in the communalist upsurge that followed the election of a UNP government in 1977. The first produced a harsh response from Mrs Bandaranaike that so undermined liberal practices that they could not be revived under the UNP regime that came after her. The second has led to ghastly civil war and has contributed to the maiming of democratic institutions. Behind all of this—the memory of a lively democracy, the dream of a fairer society, and the vile reality of chauvinism that has blighted them both—stands the complex, inconstant visionary, Bandaranaike.

After Forty-Five Years

Howard Wriggins

Before Howard Wriggins was appointed United States ambassador to Sri Lanka by President Jimmy Carter, he was already regarded as one of two Americans (Robert Kearney being the other) at the forefront of analytical expertise on the politics of Sri Lanka. In this brief but wide-ranging memoir, Wriggins recounts his encounters and impressions of three of the major prime ministers or presidents of Sri Lanka and their policies from the 1950s through the 1990s: S. W. R. D. Bandaranaike, J. R. Jayewardene, and Chandrika Kumaratunga (Bandaranaike's daughter).

I write with some hesitation, for it has been seven years since I was last in Sri Lanka and twenty years since we lived there. The country has experienced such dramatic changes, even well before the awful events of 1983, that some of what I write will inevitably seem outdated. But then to be reminded once again of whence we have come may not be entirely amiss.

Early Perspectives

In the 1950s, when teaching comparative politics at Vassar College, I began to look seriously at Ceylon. From a distance, its peaceful transition to independence appeared to be a remarkable achievement. The late 1940s and the 1950s were the decades of independence movements in Asia and Africa, a tumultuous change from the Euro-centric colonial system to independent statehood. By living in Ceylon and studying closely the efforts its leaders were making to shape a peaceful and prosperous future I hoped to learn something of the challenges and creative efforts necessary for coping with this great transition.

Ceylon seemed very promising. Here was a newly independent country that by negotiating its independence had avoided the turmoil and human cost of the independence struggle of its neighbor India or colonies of France and Holland. A succession of constitutional reforms since the turn of the century had permitted a step-by-step transition from a colonial system of command to one of considerable democracy. It had been given universal franchise in 1931, seventeen years before independence, only three years after women in Great Britain had received the vote. There had been a number of orderly elections with little apparent intimidation.

Nearly Inclusive Multi-ethnic Polity

To me it seemed a model in other ways. Like many other Asian colonial states, it was a pluralist, mosaic society, containing a number of distinctive peoples. The Sinhalese majority of 72% and a longstanding Tamil minority of over 10% had shared the island for much of the last thousand years. Another 10% were recently dis-enfranchised Tamil-speaking labourers brought from South India in the late 19th and early 20th century to man the tea and rubber estates, the principal earners of indispensable foreign exchange. Another 7% were Moors, many of them Tamil-speakers and all of them Muslim. Burghers, Eur-Asians, added to the mix. Three languages were spoken—Sinhalese, Tamil, and English. Followers of four faiths practiced their religions; 69% were Buddhists, 15% Hindus, 9% Christians and perhaps 8% Muslims. In this notably diverse society, there was relatively little overt conflict between them. Unlike in India, there had been few ethnic or religious riots except one in 1915; and that over 30 years before our first visit. Moreover, compared to any of its neighbors and the emerging states further to the east, a much higher proportion of its young people went to school; its population was far more literate and health services were far more widespread. In these and other ways, Ceylon seemed blessed compared to its neighbors.

I was already somewhat familiar with the similar problems we faced in New York City, with its incredible mix of nationalities and religions. How carefully leaders had to proceed so as not to unwittingly trigger race or religious riots. I had also read enough about other new states to know that governing multi-ethnic states requires special political ingenuity and care. Newspaper cuttings accumulated in the library of the Royal Institute of International Affairs gave me some advance familiarity with energetic and sometimes bitter debates in the Ceylon Parliament. These debates were about the carefully balanced negotiated independence constitution, the national flag, the disenfranchisement of the Indian Tamil estate workers, educational and language policy, etc. There were also complaints that the English-speaking elite dominated the country by occupying most of the country's positions of influence and wealth. So all was not roses. I had many unanswered questions. Nevertheless, the future then seemed promising. . . .

After 45 years of association with Ceylon, my strongest sense now is one of sadness and disappointment. Sri Lanka, my second home, is riven by a seemingly interminable ethnic/secessionist war. An estimated 60,000 people have been killed, and many more maimed by conflict. Many hundreds have been tortured by police or by zealous separatist militants seeking information about other citizens; the separatists have dramatized their cause by selective assassinations, bombing government buildings or public transport. Hundreds have disappeared. Many thousands have fled the country; many more thousands have been driven from their homes.

So many unforgivable acts perpetrated by each group against the other; so many opportunities at best postponed or perhaps permanently lost. . . .

At a large garden party in Colombo 7 in the fall of 1955 I was first introduced to S. W. R. D. Bandaranaike, then the leader of the Opposition. My friend explained to him that I was a visiting professor of politics from the States who hoped to write a book about Ceylon's first years of Independence. Already the issues of Sinhala language and the condition of Buddhism on the island were much talked of, and everyone I had earlier met urged me to be sure to meet him.

He cheerfully welcomed me to Ceylon, and urged me to drop by at his Rosmead Place office whenever his secretary could arrange a time. He struck me as a man of considerable energy, perhaps a bit high strung but at the same time casual, taking pleasure in conversation like so many of his compatriots. After some small talk, including his appreciation for Tom Sawyer and Huckleberry Finn, I asked him how his campaign was going? He thought it was going well; he was working closely with others to forge a broad opposition coalition. The *bhikkhus* were actively behind his effort as were those who believed the Sinhalese language should have its proper place. It was high time for a political change.

Whether it was in that first conversation or some time later at his spacious home, as we explored the rising *swabasha* movement demanding a change in official language policy, I was startled to hear him say: "you know, Professor Wriggins, I have never found an issue as good as the language issue for exciting the people." I thought this a remarkable statement, and have always thought so since. My mind immediately ran back to the kind of passionate religious and ethnic violence that was all too familiar in India. He said it in a way that suggested he was confident the excitement could be managed. I worried that out of such optimistic political judgements, troubles might lie ahead. Of course, he knew his country better than I, a relatively new visitor; perhaps his and others' enthusiasm for such a change would not cause major difficulties.

He continued, saying that there were thousands of people in this wonderful country who felt no identity with their government because its official business was still conducted mainly in English. Like many others, he urged me to go to the countryside, where the bulk of the island's people lived. Go see yourself.

For three months before the 1956 election, with an insightful Oxford-trained anthropologist as consultant and interpreter, I visited many rural districts. We sought out the village school teachers, ayurvedic physicians and local *bhikkhus* in their temples. What a world away that was from the westernized capital!

Sitting under the coconut palms, hearing the birds, seeing the lush greenery and noting the austerity of these middle-class people's lives, I felt I was on another planet. And yet, as we talked, it was clear we were not subjectively that far away. The island was too small for that. With the help of political activities, the palpable sense of invidious grievance appeared to grow. The teachers compared their positions with those of the staffs of the English-language institutions in the major towns and cities. They had professional grievances—second-class status compared to the English teachers, low salaries, victimization by the Ministry of Education. Ayurvedic physicians also felt aggrieved, believing they had virtually no recognition from the government, and little real support from the Ministry of Health compared to all the care lavished on western medicine. The *bhikkhus* were bitter that Buddhism did not have state support as in the ancient golden days. Those few who cited the *Mahavamsa* reminded me of the special mission reportedly assigned to their country by the Buddha. How could the English language be on an equal footing with the language of the people chosen by the Buddha? At least in conversation with me at this early stage, little of this was explicitly turned against the Tamils.

On these issues Mr Bandaranaike and his party in 1956 romped home in Ceylon's first dramatic electoral transformation. He had correctly sensed the resentment against the English-educated and their privileges and stimulated the hopes of Buddhist activists.

Giving in haste highest status to the vernacular language of the majority and lowering the status and contracting the opportunities for a language spoken mainly by an educated elite is a difficult business under the best of circumstances. By making language and Buddhism the focus of his campaigning, he raised the level of Sinhalese cultural and religious nationalism to an intensity that had never before been projected into the political arena.

To be sure, political rivalry within the Tamil community had already led their competing spokesmen to establish contending Tamil parties, each seeking to outbid the other as the staunchest defender of the Tamil people. In his famous 50/50 proposal, G. G. Ponnambalam argued that half the seats in the legislature should be reserved for the minorities, while the majority should be content with the other half. To many, this became a symbol of the unreasonable ambition of that energetic minority.

In one sense, Bandaranaike's efforts materially broadened political participation among the hitherto politically more passive Sinhalese. He drew them into closer identity with the elected government, a move many thought a good thing.

I well recall the excitement of the days immediately after that election as the people swarmed into the Parliament building, dramatizing their presence in a new way. It seemed to this American a bit like a Ceylonese Jacksonian revolution. But in the excitement and impatience of electoral politics, the drive to replace English virtually overnight and to ensure the proper place for Buddhism ignored the concerns of the Tamil-speaking peoples. Nearly 25% of the population seemed to have been suddenly forgotten. Moreover, the original negotiated bargain on which independence had been peacefully achieved had been unilaterally abrogated. As we now see, the gains to the polity from increased participation of the majority were more than balanced by the terrible future costs that followed.

It would be wrong to assign all the blame (or credit) for this to Mr Bandaranaike alone. Others, far more passionately committed to Sinhalization of Sri Lanka than he, seized the opportunity and pushed all the harder. They found ready acolytes, and no leaders of principal parties dared stand against the tide. When the leaders of the UNP called the 1956 election, they had controlled 76 seats in Parliament. Afterwards they held only 8. They never forgot that political debacle. Its shadow persisted to inhabit even the strongest future political victor following 1977.

I must own that in the late 1950's it never occurred to me that the language zealots and the Buddhist enthusiasts, who had been so successful in demanding Sinhalese Only, would go so far as to reject the very idea of a plural polity, which seemed to me such a fundamental part of Ceylon's life. Nor did I at the time imagine that the *Mahavamsa* would eventually come to provide the dramatic text for so many, casting the contemporary Tamils living in Jaffna, Colombo and elsewhere in the east and the south as the virtual equivalents of the invading Tamils of nearly a thousand years ago!

These exclusivist ideas combined with a near stagnant economy became a highly dangerous mix.

The Marginalization of the Tamils, 1970–1977

During the period of the United Front, between 1970 and 1977, the Tamil minority increasingly saw themselves becoming second-class citizens. Already a number of the most talented had emigrated, finding responsible jobs at the United Nations, in western universities and international businesses abroad.

The new Bandaranaike government that came to power in 1970 sharply changed the terms of entry into the university system. Formerly Tamil youths entered the university each year in numbers that aroused resentments among the Sinhalese. New regional distribution requirements and the "standardization" of examination grades now worked to the relative disadvantage of the Tamils. Entry to the university system became substantially more difficult for them; Tamil recruitment to the army and police virtually ceased as all new positions went almost entirely to Sinhalese Buddhists. Since mastery of Sinhalese was now mandatory for entry into the public service, that range of opportunity was also foreclosed.

Had the economy been even moderately buoyant, alternative jobs, though of lower status, might have been more widely available to soften the growing resentment among the unemployed Sinhalese and Tamil young men. Unfortunately, as K. M. de Silva vividly shows in his *Reaping the Whirlwind*, economic activity contracted as a result of the oil crisis of 1973–74, a series of poor monsoons and the accumulation of stifling government regulations and nationalizations that flowed from a number of influential Marxists in the cabinet. I recall during the 1970's on a visit to friends at the University of Peradeniya, my surprise at seeing bread lines in district towns along the way. Resentment naturally followed protracted unemployment. The more extreme among the Tamil youths demanded independence; some even robbed banks to help finance their movement and indulged in selective assassinations. By the time of the 1977 election, the demand for a separate Tamil state held first place in Tamil political rhetoric and in the rivalry between contending Tamil candidates in Jaffna. . . .

In August 1977, when I returned as United States Ambassador, my wife and I arrived at Katunayaka airport in the midst of the curfew following the post-election anti-Tamil riots. Several hundreds were killed, thousands were rendered homeless, and a number of Tamil businesses burned. These attacks could hardly have reassured the Tamils about their future. Not surprisingly, the zealous among the Tamil youth cared little that their campaign of violence and their demands for an independent Tamil state that claimed nearly a third of the land area had greatly exacerbated Sinhalese bitterness against them. Indeed, some of the more imaginative observers saw these riots as organized by Sinhalese zealots precisely to warn Jayewardene not to try any compromise with this obstreperous minority.

I was struck by how much more separate the two communities had become. Some of my friends showed a kind of wariness if not actual distrust toward members of the other community, when before I had understood them to have been close friends. Ancient history now had a remarkable presence in public rhetoric.

What would we not have given at that time to have had already in hand mutually agreed understandings between leaders of the majority and minority communities! We all know about the Bandaranaike-Chelvanayakam pact of 1957, and how that was opposed by activists among the Buddhists, the language enthusiasts and the leaders of the then Opposition, the UNP, including Mr Jayewardene. In an almost exact replay with roles reversed, in 1965, 8 years later, the Senanayake-Chelvanayakam agreement was similarly opposed by the Opposition, the SLFP [Sri Lankan Freedom Party] this time, and as would be expected, by assertive elements of the Buddhist clergy. Moreover, to be fair, both the SLFP and UNP Governments faced opposition within their own cabinets, and without support from at least some elements of the Opposition, no formulation could find a Parliamentary majority. Each opponent found different reasons for agitating against the other party's proposal. However, as we now look back, the refined differences were not so far from what many would now welcome with relief.

The First Years of the Jayewardene Government

In all that has happened since the terrible eruption of 1983 and its puzzling immediate aftermath, it may be easy to forget what a sense of new energy and fresh possibility came with the Jayewardene government. With him came a number of able younger men, including Ranasinghe Premadasa, Lalith Athulathmudali, Gamini Dissanayake; too many already assassinated. Unfortunately, the 1977 riots were so severe that Jayewardene's efforts to correct the most egregious forms of constitutional and educational discrimination against the minorities were largely discounted by the minority they were designed to reassure.

It may also be forgotten how vigorous were the economic reforms during those first years. Used to the usual slow pace of the Government, I was astonished to watch the speed with which old regulations and cumbersome administrative practices were swept aside. Surprisingly quickly, hitherto latent entrepreneurial energies were released. I watched with admiration—

and some anxiety—the way the President and his team obtained more support per capita from abroad for a number of ambitious economic programs than any other aid-receiving country at the time. Foreign donors even competed against each other to build dams! I worried about the inflationary side-effects of this sudden spurt of activity. I was less confident than the Government that the food stamp scheme would adequately replace the most necessary subsidies. I would have built fewer dams and put more resources into upgrading infrastructure and communications. But the changes were startling and very quickly a new energy coursed through the country's economic life.

Under more normal circumstances, one might have expected Jayewardene's smashing victory would have induced the government to make a more energetic effort to respond to the moderate Tamils' desire for devolution of certain powers. After all, the government had quickly dealt at least temporarily with a major grievance, university entry. And constitutional changes provided some constitutional restitutions. But the riots provided dramatic evidence of just how volatile the majority was at the time. Any visible steps toward devolution might have been seen by the anxious Sinhalese as the first steps onto the slippery slope toward Tamil Eelam. Political prudence cautioned Jayewardene not to grasp promptly the nettle of negotiating with the TULF [Tamil United Liberation Front] on devolution. There were others at the time, however, who argued that it was already almost too late. By then, extremist Tamil leaders were energetically inspiring acts of violence and direct action against officials. The longer the government postponed responding directly and visibly to longstanding Tamil grievances, the more radical and violent the Tamil youth would become. As a result, less and less room for manoeuvre would remain to their parliamentary leader, Appapillai Amirthalingham.

Perhaps had the Tamil leader been more restrained in his public utterances, or publicly appreciative of the improvements already undertaken, less intimidated by the radical youths, or as a person, been more like S. J. V. Chelvanayakam or M. Tiruchelvam, Jayewardene would have been readier to run the obvious political risks of at least opening negotiations earlier. At the same time, however, economic policies and large construction programs demanded presidential attention. The effort to sideline Mrs Bandaranaike, which seemed to the watching diplomats hardly consistent with the talk of a *Dharmista* ("Righteous") Society, also took up time and presidential energy. In addition, the manoeuvre could not help but intensify antagonism between the major parties, making it still more difficult for the two parties to cooperate on any issue of truly national importance.

"Shelter for You Nirvana for Our Son" by Tilak Jayatilaka,
2008. Drawn especially for *The Sri Lanka Reader.*

Not until two whole years had passed since the election did the government establish a Presidential Commission, with the help of S. J. V. Chelvanayakam's son-in-law [Prof. A. J. Wilson] from Canada as mediator. It was
to address in detail how District Development Councils might be both a
useful and politically acceptable way to devolve some powers downward
from the admittedly overly centralized Colombo ministries. Despite a reluctant commission chairman, the President with a handful of trusted advisors,
pushed ahead. In 1981 legislation was eventually passed over the objections
of the SLFP members and a number of Government supporters. Before the
new District Development Councils could become channels for meaningful devolution, however, the events of 1983 swept away such constructive
measures. Of course, there is no guarantee that had the President moved
more rapidly on the devolution question, Mr Amirthalingam could have
delivered his increasingly radicalized following on something less than independence. But by the time the commission began its work, Tamil youths
were even more demanding.

Since 1994

I had hoped after the SLFP and its associates won the election of 1994 that
the new generation of Sinhalese political leaders might approach their par-

"Naya" (Serpent) by Vidiya Bandara. Drawn especially
for *The Sri Lanka Reader*.

"Handiya" (Intersection) by Tilak Jayatilaka. Drawn especially for
The Sri Lanka Reader.

tisan rivalry in a different way. Might they have learned from observing the many difficulties which their predecessors had encountered, and had in part generated for themselves? When the leader of the SLFP [Chandrika Kumaratunga, the daughter of S. W. R. D. Bandaranaike] bravely ran on a ticket seeking peace with the secessionists and won office by a large margin, it looked as if the old mould had been broken. The government's proposals for devolution looked promising, even though remaining incomplete. However, once again, as in the previous generation, the Opposition almost automatically attacked it.

It is almost as if a deeply ingrained character of Sri Lanka's political culture forbids any collaboration between the two principal Sinhalese parties, even when the country faces its gravest crisis. The temptation to play the ethnic card seems just too promising, or longstanding family rivalries override all other considerations.

To this observer it appears that unless the two principal Sinhalese parties shape together a serious proposal to offer to the minority communities, or at the least, one of the two mainstream parties fully supports their opponents' initiative, no proposal can carry the weight of plausibility in the eyes of the minorities. All will remember the too brief existence of earlier agreements. That is why the quality of relations between the Government and its mainstream Opposition is of critical importance in finding a resolution.

Equally important, there will be no resolution unless V. Prabhakaran and the LTTE [Liberation Tigers of Tamil Eelam] revise their position of independence or nothing. His determination to physically eliminate all his Tamil rivals, his authoritarian rule and its brutality toward his own people as well as to Sinhalese and Muslims who stand in his way, together are sorry recommendations for any regime he and the LTTE might create. His unilateral breaking of cease-fires at LTTE convenience does not encourage future experiments at negotiation. All these impediments notwithstanding, without a fresh approach to relations between the two mainstream parties on the crucial issue of devolution, no offer by the Government stands a chance of being taken seriously by politically active Tamils.

The fate of this island it not foreordained by events as described in ancient manuscripts, but lies in the hands of Sri Lanka's leaders and peoples today. The difficulties now facing the country are indeed intractable. But history in Sri Lanka has taken many unexpected turns in the past 50 years. We may hope that similarly unforeseeable developments may yet bring an end to these miserable events.

The Ceylon Insurrection of 1971

Robert N. Kearney and Janice Jiggins

In April 1971 the island was rocked by a violent insurrection led by the Janata Vi-
mukti Peramuna (JVP), a nascent ultra-leftist rural Sinhala movement intent on
overthrowing the elected United Front government. The account given by Kearney
and Jiggins of causes for the insurrection provides an effective overview of the po-
litical, social, and economic issues that dominated Sinhala politics from the 1950s
through 1971. Though the movement was completely put down within a few weeks,
the JVP leaders and their movement would resurface again in spectacular fashion
and lead another siege of the government between 1988 and 1990. Many of the same
causes cited by Kearney and Jiggins were also responsible for the later uprising. In-
deed, few of them have been seriously addressed to this day.[1]

In April 1971 an insurrection erupted in Ceylon, producing a convulsion of political violence on a scale previously unknown to the nation. A number of distinctive features marked the uprising. Probably the most striking was the almost exclusively youth character of the revolt. Furthermore, the upris-ing sought the armed overthrow of a popularly elected government which less than a year earlier had scored a resounding election victory, and the attack was staged by a self-professed Marxist-Leninist organisation against a United Front government that included Ceylon's two largest Marxist par-ties. The insurrection was planned and launched by a semi-clandestine organisation called the Janatha Vimukthi Peramuna (People's Liberation Front, or JVP). The JVP had covertly carried on propaganda and recruitment campaigns, conducted indoctrination and training sessions for recruits, col-lected weapons and explosives, and manufactured hand bombs in a number of secret locations. The organisation had first appeared in public during a parliamentary election campaign in May 1970, when JVP members worked for a United Front consisting of the Sri Lanka Freedom Party (SLFP), the Lanka Sama Samaja Party (LSSP), and the "pro-Moscow" Communist Party (CP), which won a stunning victory. The movement that became the JVP had been under police surveillance for a number of years, and its leader, Rohana

Wijeweera, had been taken into custody shortly before the 1970 election, but was released the following July. Commencing in August, the JVP began to stage public rallies, at which the grievances of unemployed youths were articulated and the United Front government was subjected to sharp criticism. In March 1971 accidental detonations of stockpiled explosives and police discovery of other caches of arms and explosives alerted the government to the likelihood of imminent violence. A fire-bomb raid, in which a police officer was killed, was made on the American embassy in Colombo on 6 March by a group reportedly calling itself the "Mao Youth Front." This attack may have been executed by another clandestine revolutionary group, an offshoot and rival of the JVP. On 16 March, in the face of mounting evidence of pending violence, the government imposed an emergency and placed armed forces and police on an alert footing.

A rural police station and its small police party were attacked in the early morning hours of 5 April. That night simultaneous attacks were made on at least 74 police stations at widely scattered points across the island. The insurgents, outfitted in home-made dark blue uniforms, were armed primarily with shotguns, home-made hand bombs, and petrol-filled bottles. The strategy of the insurgents was to seize power by a single bold stroke of violence, a "one-day revolution," which by its audacity and surprise, would disrupt the government, throw the island into confusion, and allow the rebels to seize strategic objectives and capture government officials before the police and military were able to mount an effective response. In a subsequent statement to the police one insurgent leader described Wijeweera's alleged instructions to a meeting of JVP leaders in December 1970: "He told us that we must capture power at once in all parts of the Island. He wanted to take control of all Police Stations and the Forces. . . . At the same time as the Police are attacked, all the high ranking Government officials like Govt. Agents [public servants in charge of administrative districts], Superintendents of Police, Ministers and M.PP [sic] too should be taken into custody. . . . The attack of Police Stations should be done by attacking smaller stations first and there after [sic] with those arms to surround the bigger stations."

The Prime Minister and the leaders of the LSSP and the CP, the other two parties in the governing coalition, were to be kidnapped and forced to record speeches to the nation, presumably urging public acquiescence in the coup. Another JVP leader reportedly explained to police: "The plan of attack was to cut off power supply, communication, obstruct roads by cutting trees, to take explosives from strong rooms, to blow bridges, surround Police Stations and attack and seize firearms and collect guns from licence holders [persons with licences to own firearms]. After the attack to take the admin-

istration [in]to our hands and to wait." Regional J V P leaders were designated
to assume the titles and functions of government agents, judges, and other
officials. Government security forces in 1971 were ill-prepared to meet a major armed challenge. The police forces in 1970 had numbered 10,605. They
were assigned to 266 police stations, of which 172 were staffed by 20 or less
policemen, and 41 small offices. Police stations were supplied with fifty-year-
old bolt-action rifles and very small quantities of ammunition. The military
services had remained small, generally poorly armed and equipped, and
without experience in military campaigning. The suppression of communal
riots in 1958 constituted virtually their only experience with violence. In
1970 the authorised other-ranks cadre of the army was 6,578; of the navy,
1,718; and of the air force, 1,397. In their initial attack, the insurgents overran
a few small police stations and forced the abandonment of others, seized or
destroyed a number of public buildings, and cut major roads and railroads,
virtually isolating Kandy and severing communications between Colombo
and the commander. In several major towns police and public servants were
besieged in public buildings, while the insurgents moved freely through the
remainder of the town. In the Kegalle district, hard-hit by the uprising, an
army officer reported that on 10 April "only about three acres of land on
which Kachcheri [district office], Police Station and the Courts of Law stood
under the control of Government security forces." The Inspector General of
Police explained: "As police stations were withdrawn and civil administration collapsed in these areas, the insurgents took over. They distributed food
from Co-operative Stores, sold stamps at the Post Office and even held their
own Courts of Justice."

However, the "one-day revolution" failed. The earlier emergency proclamation, the transmission on 5 April of news of the early morning attack,
and the last-minute revelation by an informant that attacks were planned
for the night of 5–6 April resulted in most police stations being alerted for
an assault. Although many police and military detachments ran precari-
ously low on ammunition in the first days of the uprising, the insurgents
suffered heavy casualties in frontal attacks on police and troops. Gradually
the insurgent attacks were broken off and, with the deployment of troops to
augment the police and the arrival of arms and ammunition from abroad,
the government forces began to assume the initiative. Particularly severe
fighting continued along the Colombo-Kandy road around Kegalle and in a
few areas in the far south, where the small towns of Elpitiya and Deniyaya
were held for some weeks by insurgents. About five weeks after the uprising
the Prime Minister issued a call to the insurgents to surrender to prevent
further loss of life. By July about 14,000 persons were held in custody in

connection with the rebellion, and the Prime Minister estimated the death toll at 1,200, including 60 fatalities among the armed forces and police. Unofficial estimates generally put the death toll much higher. Although a few deaths occurred among the civilian population, the overwhelming proportion of the casualties were unquestionably suffered by insurgents or suspected insurgents.

The possibility of foreign instigation or involvement was the subject of much speculation, heightened by the fact that on 13 April, the North Korean embassy was closed and the entire staff was ordered from the country. Suspicion of Chinese involvement followed the allegedly mysterious departure from Colombo harbour of a Chinese ship, said to be carrying a cargo of arms bound for Tanzania, after the outbreak of the insurrection. The Ceylon government, however, steadfastly denied any foreign involvement. According to Prime Minister Sirimavo Bandaranaike, "the insurgent leaders had led their supporters to believe that arms, supplies and moral support would be forthcoming from certain foreign powers, and their supporters seem to have believed this. I am satisfied that these terrorist leaders made these false claims to rally support to their cause and there seems to have been no basis for any such claim." The North Koreans, Mrs. Bandaranaike related, had been told that the effect of certain activities carried on by them was giving strength and support to these terrorists, and they were ordered from the country when they failed to comply with her request that those activities cease. Diplomatic relations had been established between North Korea and Ceylon only after the United Front had come to power less than a year earlier. The activities that led to their expulsion were not described, but the North Korean embassy staff had been energetically engaged in disseminating revolutionary propaganda, including the placing of full-page newspaper advertisements quoting from the works of Kim Il Sung on revolutionary techniques. The North Koreans had also sponsored more than forty "friendship societies" across the island. A statement to police attributed to one JVP leader contained a reference to JVP contact with personnel of the embassy of the People's Republic of China. From the left parties came arguments that the JVP was sponsored and the insurrection instigated by the American Central Intelligence Agency as a provocation to justify a right-wing coup. The question of possible external incitement or encouragement seems unlikely to be completely resolved in the near future, if ever. No evidence has appeared of arms or training supplied from abroad.

The Ceylon government obtained arms, ammunition, and equipment from India, Pakistan, Egypt, Yugoslavia, Britain, the United States, and the Soviet Union. India and Pakistan provided Ceylon with helicopters, which in the early days of the insurrection were vital to the supplying of hard-pressed military and police units. At Ceylon's request, Indian naval vessels patrolled the island's coastline. A detachment of 150 Indian troops was stationed at Bandaranaike International Airport near Colombo. Government sources denied that any foreign personnel were involved in combat against the insurgents.

The Insurgents. Some compelling and dramatic conclusions can be drawn regarding the composition of the movement that launched the insurrection. The insurgents, the JVP supporters, and the persons held in custody as suspected insurgents are not necessarily identical. Many insurgents were killed and others presumably escaped arrest. Some persons involved with the JVP may not have participated in the preparations for the uprising and many, including most of the leaders, did not take part in the armed attacks. Furthermore, the detained suspected insurgents almost certainly included persons with marginal or perhaps no connections with the JVP or the revolt. Nonetheless, these three groups unquestionably overlapped to a major degree, and there is no evident reason to believe that they differed significantly in social background.

Data is available regarding the persons who were arrested or surrendered and were held in detention as suspected insurgents. The data starkly confirms that the insurrectionary movement was one of youths in their late teens and early twenties, a major proportion of whom had received at least secondary education, and almost all of whom belonged to the island's Sinhalese Buddhist majority. The age distribution of the respected insurgents is as follows: nearly 90 per cent were under 30 years of age. Furthermore, almost three-quarters were between 17–25 years of age. Thirty-eight per cent had passed the General Certificate of Education (Ordinary Level) examinations or had attained a higher level of education, while under 20 per cent had only primary or no higher education.

Despite rumours that significant numbers of girls were involved in the uprising, only 2 per cent of the detainees were female. About 18 per cent of those in custody were totally unemployed. However, 13 per cent were students and most of the others seem to have held irregular, poorly paid, or low-status jobs. Most apparently were from rural families of low or modest socio-economic status. The Inspector-General of Police noted that investigations prior to the insurrection indicated that the JVP was composed of "unemployed educated youth generally from poor families." Data on the ethnic community of the detainees is not available but can be inferred from their religion. The virtual exclusion of the ethnic and religious minorities is striking. Of the detainees 94 per cent were Buddhists and almost certainly belonged to the Sinhalese ethnic majority. Christians, who accounted for under 4 per cent of the detainees, certainly included some Sinhalese and may have been mostly Sinhalese. Less than 1 per cent were Hindu and presumably Tamil, and 0.5 per cent were Muslims and ethnically Moors or Malays. Non-Sinhalese may have accounted for less than 2 per cent. The JVP was accused by critics of being communally chauvinistic and hostile towards minorities. Its supporters appear to have been largely from Sinhalese village backgrounds and to have been educated in the medium of the Sinhalese language, possibly producing a parochialism that encouraged communal exclusiveness. In his testimony before the Criminal Justice Commission, JVP leader Rohana Wijeweera noted, "The many efforts we made to build cadres among comrades of the national minorities were fruitless."

Many of the insurgents are believed to have belonged to the Batgam and Vahumpura castes, both castes of low traditional status which also tend to be economically depressed, while the JVP leadership was disproportionately drawn from the Karava caste, a small but economically influential caste concentrated on the southwest coast. The most intense and prolonged fighting of the insurrection occurred in areas containing heavy local concentrations of Batgam and Vahumpura and in the southwestern coastal region. Of 41 alleged insurgent leaders on trial before the Criminal Justice Commission, 14 were Karava, four were Vahumpura, and one was Batgam. In comparison, 11 belonged to the Goyigama caste, the largest and highest in status of the Sinhalese castes, which is frequently assumed to include about half the Sinhalese population. Members of the Karava caste had long been exposed to Marxist campaigning and agitational activities and the areas populated by the Karava are also longstanding strongholds of LSSP and CP electoral support. The role of caste in the revolt remains ambiguous, however.

Among the insurgents were said to be many former members of a "land army" that was formed in 1967 to provide employment in conservation and reclamation activities for unemployed youths, but disbanded in 1970. Although the founders and leaders of the JVP largely came from the pro-Peking Communist Party, as is discussed later, the insurgents included members or former members of the youth leagues of all major political parties, including the SLFP, LSSP, and pro-Moscow CP then in power. Prime Minister Sirimavo Bandaranaike described the insurgents as "a group of disgruntled and designing persons drawn from the rejects and the unwanted of practically every recognized political party, motivated by overweening personal ambitions, personal frustrations, and disappointments and ready for instant solutions to all ills of the world."

The Demographic and Socio-Economic Environment. The striking concentration of suspected insurgents in the ages 17–25 suggests the influence of demographic factors in the social uprising. The island's population had been growing very rapidly, particularly since the late 1940s, when an abrupt drop in the death rate followed the near-eradication of malaria and the implementation of other public health measures. Deaths per 1,000 population plummeted from 21.9 in 1945 to 14.3 in 1947 and thereafter steadily declined, reaching 7.5 in 1970. In the 45 years between 1901 and 1946 the island's population grew by about 3 million, while in the 25 years between 1946 and 1971, about 6 million persons were added to the population. . . . It has been suggested that swift population growth and the accompanying rapid increase in the numbers of young persons within a society [are] likely to heighten the potential for social unrest and political turbulence. Youths under 25 constitute a very large and gradually rising proportion of the Ceylonese population. In the 24 years between 1946 and 1969–70, the number of persons aged 15–24 almost doubled. In economic terms the population explosion resulted in sharp increases in the number of youths entering the labour force annually, at the same time that heightened longevity resulted in the retention of more older workers in the labour force for longer periods. The soaring numbers of youth cohorts presumably produced for the youths growing up in the 1960s are significantly different society, particularly susceptible to millennial ideologies and movements that promise immediate solutions to problems and discontents, and are more inclined than older people to take risks and engage in dangerous actions. When large numbers of youths are unemployed and consequently lack socially accepted and economically productive outlets for their energies, as was the case in Ceylon, the political volatility of the youthful population may be expected to be particularly great.

A second major change in Ceylonese society in the years before the insurrection was a rapid expansion of education. The levels of education and literacy had advanced steadily in Ceylon since the late nineteenth century. In the decade before 1971, however, a veritable educational explosion occurred. Rapidly widening educational opportunities stimulated rising aspirations and expectations among youths, but lagging economic growth led to massive unemployment and thwarted expectations, presumably producing a steep rise in alienation, disillusionment, and a sense of deprivation among educated youths.

The number of students enrolled in primary and secondary schools rose from 867,000 in 1945 to 2,244,000 in 1960, and in 1970 the figure climbed past 2,700,000. The swift growth in education was accompanied by a steady extension of education in the Sinhalese and Tamil languages through progressively higher levels. Striking advances occurred not only in the diffusion of basic education but also in the levels of education attained. By 1969–70 65 per cent of youths aged 15–19 and 61 per cent of those aged 20–24 had completed a middle school (10th grade) or higher education.

Before 1959 university instruction had been conducted in English, effectively limiting admission to those able to attend English-medium secondary schools, which were considerably more accessible to the affluent and to urban residents. From 1959 university admissions were opened in the Sinhalese and Tamil languages in order to provide broader and more egalitarian opportunities for higher education and the careers to which it led. The language change was followed by a tremendous growth in enrolment. The number of university students rose from 3,177 in 1959 to a peak of 15,046 in 1966, and thereafter slumped to slightly under 12,000 in 1970. The number of university graduates produced annually shot up from 533 in 1959 to 4,317 in 1970, an eight-fold increase in eleven years.

Employment opportunities for educated youths, however, markedly failed to keep pace with the spiraling output of the island's secondary schools and universities. In the decade between 1959–60 and 1969–70, unemployment climbed from about 340,000, or 10.5 per cent of the labour force, to 546,000, or 13.9 per cent of the labour force. In 1960–70, youths aged 15–24 accounted for 82 per cent of all unemployed persons. Unemployment was particularly severe among youths who had completed a secondary or higher education. . . . In the 15–24 year age group, the unemployment rate for males completing GCE "O" Level was double that for males with no schooling or with only primary schooling. Among females in the same age group the incidence of unemployment rose steeply with education to reach a staggering 90 per cent at "A" Level and above. The extent to which unemployment was concentrated among the young is indicated by the dramatic differences in unemployment rates between age groups at each educational level. At GCE "O" Level, 51 per cent of males and 79 per cent of females aged 15–24 but only 7 and 31 per cent, respectively, of those aged 25–34 were unemployed. For educated youths the period of idleness before finding employment was frequently very long. . . . Education, which had long been an important avenue of social mobility, became a prelude to unemployment.

Despite the dismal employment prospects confronting youths, government spokesmen denied the central importance of unemployment in the 1971 revolt. Finance Minister N. M. Perera in late 1971 argued that "the frustration of unemployment was not the specific driving force [behind the uprising] though it was used as a propaganda motivation." The official interpretation was based on the fact that, as indicated earlier, only about 18 per cent of those in custody as suspected insurgents were totally unemployed.

However, nearly 13 per cent were students, contemplating the grim employment situation they would soon face, and many of the others were employed only intermittently or in very poorly paid occupations. About one-tenth were classified as casual labourers and more than a quarter as cultivators. Also it is likely that many of those with jobs had experienced a long and frustrating wait before they were able to find employment. Indeed, given the magnitude of unemployment among the 15–24 age group and the average period of time before employment was found, it seems unlikely that any sizeable body of youths would have been spared employment-related frustrations and disappointments.

The educational explosion not only produced soaring aspirations and expectations among youths, which outran the ability of the labour market to absorb the educated youths, but also opened a wide generational cleavage in the villages. Many youths who obtained intermediate, secondary, or even higher educations by 1971 were the first members of their families ever to receive an education beyond the most rudimentary. Free education and the proliferation of schools put additional years of schooling within the reach of the sons and daughters of the small cultivators, petty traders, and even agricultural labourers in the villages, producing the confrontation of an educated younger generation with an often barely literate older generation. Although the education provided in the rural schools was often poor in quality and inappropriate in content, the differential in education between generations probably contributed to the undermining of parental authority and traditional values and norms of behaviour, and possibly spread among youths disillusionment with the existing social and political order associated with the older generations.

The Political Background. In the decades preceding 1971 political change had been rapid and pervasive in Ceylon. The political process that had emerged after the termination of colonial rule in 1948 was characterised by the presence of a multiplicity of political parties, vigorously competitive election contests from the national to the local levels, and repeated transfers of power between rival parties. In each of the five parliamentary elections after 1952 the governing party or coalition was defeated and replaced by an opposition group. After the introduction of universal suffrage in 1931, and particularly since the mid-1950s, mass political awareness spread rapidly throughout Ceylonese society. Popular participation in recent elections has been remarkably high. More than 80 per cent of the electorate voted in the parliamentary elections of 1965 and 1970. The voting age was reduced from 21 to 18 years in 1959. Although the politics of the island often seemed turbulent, representative institutions based on universal suffrage had functioned without interruption for forty years, and civilian government headed by popularly elected officials had never been overthrown.

The generally conservative United National Party (UNP) governed the country from 1947 until its election defeat in 1956 at the hands of a coalition led by the Sri Lanka Freedom Party. An election in March 1960 briefly returned the UNP to power but in the second election the following July the SLFP won control of Parliament by a narrow margin. Faced with declining parliamentary strength, the SLFP in June 1964 formed a coalition with the Lanka Sama Samaja Party. The following December the coalition government fell on an adverse parliamentary vote when the conservative wing of the SLFP abandoned the party. The SLFP-LSSP coalition was defeated in the resulting 1965 election, which brought to power a self-styled "National Government" formed by the UNP and several smaller parties. The pro-Moscow Communist Party fought the election in alliance with the SLFP-LSSP coalition and soon after the election the three parties combined to form a United Front. In May 1970 the United Front scored an overwhelming election victory.

The rise of controversy over the official language in the first decade after independence galvanised communal solidarity and played a major role in the political mobilisation of the rural population. The official language issue initially arose as an attack on the advantages of a small class of Ceylonese who were educated in the English language and virtually monopolised the more rewarding and prestigious posts in government, education, commerce, and the professions, The language controversy, however, eventually led to conflict between the island's Sinhalese-speaking majority and Tamil-speaking minority. Appeals to Sinhalese Buddhist sentiments, combined with promises of material and symbolic gains for the underprivileged classes, allowed the SLFP-led alliance of 1956 to defeat the seemingly solidly entrenched UNP. The political turnover in 1956 is thought to have had far-reaching political repercussions, demonstrating to the public the efficacy of election contests and stimulating mass political awareness. From the 1950s have come two major political tendencies of considerable continuing force: the drive for recognition and recompense by the Sinhalese Buddhist majority, and the egalitarian demands of the economically underprivileged strata of society.

Developments within the Marxist movement over the decade preceding the insurrection played a significant role in the creation and character of the JVP. By 1971 a vigorous and vocal Marxist movement had existed in Ceylon for thirty-six years. The oldest and most influential of several Marxist parties was the LSSP, followed by the pro-Moscow CP. In the early years of independence, the Marxist parties constituted the principal organised opposition to the governing UNP. It was the non-Marxist, populist, and vaguely socialist SLFP, however, that succeeded in displacing the UNP in power in 1956. In the fifteen years before 1971 the major Marxist parties were drawn into increasingly close association with the SLFP. An electoral agreement had linked the LSSP and the CP with the SLFP in the election of 1956, and this cooperation was repeated in the July 1960 election contest. In late 1963 the LSSP, the CP, and a third self-professed Marxist party, the Mahajana Eksath Peramuna, joined in forming a United Left Front, the strongest expression of Left unity in more than two decades. The front collapsed in the following year, however, when the LSSP abruptly accepted an SLFP invitation to join in a coalition government without its United Left Front partners. In 1965 the SLFP-LSSP alliance was broadened to include the pro-Moscow CP and consolidated into the United Front that came to power five years later. With their growing association with the SLFP, the LSSP and the CP gradually abandoned thoughts of violent revolution and became increasingly committed to seeking power through elections and the control of Parliament. A few months before the 1971 uprising, Leslie Goonewardene, long the LSSP general secretary, wrote of the party's adaptation to parliamentary and electoral politics: "It was our belief at the time of the formation of the Lanka Sama Samaja Party that Imperialism and Capitalism [could] be destroyed and a Socialist Society created only through the smashing of the power of the Imperialists and Capitalists and the seizure of power by a mass uprising. We believed that the uprising may even have to be an armed uprising." However, following the 1956 election, which produced the defeat of the LSSP's old arch enemy, the UNP, the LSSP came to the conclusion that a Parliament elected by Universal Franchise is an instrument that can be used for the movement towards Socialism. As the established Marxist parties became absorbed in the problems of election contests and the activities of elective bodies, their romantic appeal to radical and idealistic youths as parties of heroic revolutionaries presumably waned. Subsiding revolutionary fervour was accompanied by growing identification with the existing political and social institutions and established elites. Although the LSSP and the CP were swept into power by the 1970 United Front election victory, the influence of the Marxists within the governing alliance was limited. The SLFP, despite its increasingly intimate association with the Left and a steady attrition of its right wing, remained a heterogeneous party containing a variety of sentiments, perspectives, and interests, some of which were clearly opposed to the radical social reconstruction sought by the party's Marxist allies. In the 1970 election the SLFP won 90, the LSSP 19, and the CP 6 seats in Parliament. The Marxists were required to make many compromises and concessions in the United Front's common programme, as well as in the actions of the post-1970 government. The slow pace of implementation of the United Front programme and the reappearance of old practices of disseminating patronage and favours after the election were thought to have contributed to the impatience and exasperation of youth and thus to have enhanced the following of the JVP. While the major parties of the Left were cementing their association with the SLFP and adjusting to the established political order, the Left was shaken by a series of schisms. Reverberations of Sino-Soviet ideological rivalry produced a split in the CP in 1963, when a group of pro-Peking dissidents were expelled from the party for challenging the stoutly pro-Moscow stance of the party leaders. The pro-Peking Communists promptly formed a rival Communist Party, which in turn experienced a number of schisms, expulsions, and resignations. The LSSP's entrance into the 1964 coalition with the SLFP caused the LSSP to be expelled from the Fourth International, to which it had been affiliated for nearly a quarter of a century, and led to a party split when the more doctrinaire Trotskyists withdrew from the party to form the Lanka Sama Samaja Party (Revolutionary), or LSSP(R). In 1968 a wing of the small LSSP(R) split away to form a minute separate Trotskyist group.

The Revolutionary New Left of Youth. A serious and costly insurrection became possible when, by the beginning of the 1970s, the frustrations and grievances of youths had created an explosive situation that could be ignited by a spark of leadership, organisation, and ideology. It was a small, clandestine band of disillusioned young Marxists who channeled the discontent of youths into conspiratorial revolutionary political activity, culminating in the 1971 uprising.

The declining revolutionary fervour of the major Left parties and the simultaneous schisms, ideological confusion, and internecine conflict within the Left of the 1960s provided the environment within which the JVP movement was founded. A handful of impatient young radicals resolved to abandon the existing parties of the Left and seek to create a New Left oriented towards youth and committed to the revolutionary seizure of power. JVP leader Rohana Wijeweera contended "it was because the old Left Movement had no capacity to take the path of socialism, had gone bankrupt and deteriorated to the position of propping up the capitalist class and had no capacity to protect the rights and needs of the proletariat any longer, that we realized the necessity of the New Left Movement."

The schisms of 1963–64 had produced two small "ultra-Left" parties—the pro-Peking CP and the LSSP(R)—that, at least in rhetoric, maintained their devotion to the old ideas on violent revolution and class collaboration. Even these parties, however, did not appear to be promising vehicles for the impatient youths who formed the JVP. The idea for the movement that became the JVP was formulated by a small group of disenchanted young men associated with the pro-Peking CP shortly after that party had undergone an internal crisis and split in late 1964. Wijeweera describing a growing "feeling of disagreement, distrust and dejection" within the party, explained, "We saw that both the Chinese Wing [i.e., pro-Peking CP] and the other leftist political parties had a common origin and a common programme of action, with the only difference that the Shanmugathasan [pro-Peking CP leader N. Shanmugathasan] clique was paying homage to China in a most degenerate manner." Initially, Wijeweera and his associates apparently hoped to reconstruct the party from within. By mid-1966, however, they had been expelled from or had abandoned the party. Shanmugathasan, who was taken into custody during the insurrection but was released after ten months' confinement, later claimed that the pro-Peking CP was the first political party "to expose the counter-revolutionary nature of the JVP long before the insurrection."

LSSP(R) leader Bala Tampoe had served as a lawyer for some of the JVP leaders prior to the insurrection and he later defended several of those charged with organising the uprising in the Criminal Justice Commission proceedings. During the insurrection, he addressed a series of letters to the Prime Minister objecting to the latter's labeling the insurgents as "terrorists" and protesting against infringements of public liberties in the suppression of the revolt. There is, nonetheless, no indication that any significant links existed between the minute, urban-based, trade union-oriented LSSP(R) and the JVP. Wijeweera explained that after the abandonment of revolutionary principles by the major Left parties, the few Marxists of the older generation who continued to be revolutionary "remained engrossed in the concepts and politics that were part and parcel of the old Left Movement and to which they were most accustomed. . . . Therefore the new Movement that was being formed had to follow a methodical plan of development peculiar to it."

The origin of the JVP movement may be traced to a May 1965 meeting of a handful of youths from the pro-Peking CP, prompted by their mutual dissatisfaction with the state of the party. After their break with the pro-Peking CP about a year later, the members of this small group launched a campaign of agitation and propaganda intended to win individuals to their point of view on political questions facing the Left parties at the time. Until the end of 1969 no formal organisational structure existed and the "movement" consisted of the small clique of friends from the pro-Peking CP, joined by a few other activists, most of whom came from one of the Left parties, and followed by a slowly expanding band of sympathisers. The coterie of founders initially sought to win support from within the youth leagues, student associations, and trade unions of the existing Marxist parties. As one of the JVP founders was employed by the Land Development Department of the Ceylon government, the JVP founders focused for a time on the department's worksites and the trade union of departmental employees. In 1966 a decision was made to emphasise efforts among the peasantry, and the members of the movement began to explore problems of the rural population. In 1968 they began to concentrate efforts on the universities. Later, Mahinda Wijesekera, a member of the pro-Moscow CP and a student leader at Vidyodaya University, after brief passage through the pro-Peking CP, shifted to the JVP, bringing with him a large portion of the pro-Moscow CP's student organisation. The movement also began to establish training camps lasting several days, according to Wijeweera for intensive political education and discussion, but said by Wijeweera's rival for JVP leadership, Nimalasiri Jayasinghe, known as Loku Athula, to include quasi-military exercises and instruction in the use of weapons.

In late 1969 the leaders of the movement decided to build a more formal and coherent organisation intended as "a school for the training of Marxist Revolutionaries; an embryonic Marxist Party." At the base of the structure were cells of at least five members; each cell was to be isolated from any contact with the others. Above the cells ranged a hierarchy of local, regional, and district committees, each headed by a secretary. Disagreement exists on the character of the JVP's structure above the district level. One JVP leader described a central committee of eleven members, each with functional and territorial responsibilities, and referred to Wijeweera as the organisation's general secretary. Loku Athula claimed that a twelve-member politbureau was formed in August 1970 and identified twenty-five central committee members. He described Wijeweera as the JVP's "self-appointed General Secretary." Wijeweera, however, denied that the JVP had either a central committee or a politbureau and, while acknowledging he was the organisation's "leader," did not claim to hold any specific title.

Whatever the formal structure, the JVP seems to have retained the informal leadership patterns of its "movement" days. In a statement to the Criminal Justice Commission, one evidently disillusioned JVP activist bitterly criticised four leaders who, he claimed, had dominated the organisation and had named their "close and trustworthy buddies" as district JVP leaders. He charged: "The Janatha Vimukthi Peramuna, on principle, refused to disclose in full the nature of its party organisation even to its members. It was only after I came to prison, that I myself came to know that the Janatha Vimukthi Peramuna had a politbureau. There was a Central Committee secretly set up in the Party. The four who were the Party's leaders for life were the first to decide on all issues. . . . [The JVP's] members were made to act as mere puppets of the four leaders."

Wijeweera conceded that "from the time we started this Movement, from the earliest days, a few of us used to get together and discuss matters." Regarding the domination of the four leaders, he explained: "All these four comrades were known in the Movement. They [the other members] knew that these persons had been working in the Movement from the very start. And for that reason they had got used to doing what these persons wanted them to do."

Shortly before the 1970 election the name Janatha Vimukthi Peramuna was adopted for the movement, and the JVP leaders resolved to support the United Front in the election. Wijeweera was arrested before the election but other JVP activists campaigned for United Front candidates. The following August, after Wijeweera's release, the JVP commenced overt political activities in its own name by staging a series of meetings, at which the United Front government was subjected to strident criticism.

The movement was permeated with factionalism and internal rivalries from an early date. Small groups often split from one of the established Left parties and moved into the JVP in a body, retaining within the fledgling movement a sense of mutual identity and continuing to act together as a factional group. One recruit from the pro-Moscow CP, called "Castro" Dharmasekera for his advocacy of Cuban-style revolution, brought some followers with him into the JVP and reportedly recruited supporters independently of the main movement. In 1970 he broke away with his faction and formed a separate group. As the JVP expanded in 1970, authority and control within the organisation became increasingly confused and incoherent, compounded by the appearance of bitter cleavages and rivalries among the leaders. Some JVP groups resorted to robberies to obtain funds and began gathering arms and manufacturing bombs, allegedly without the authorisation and even without the knowledge of the top leaders.

The JVP membership seems to have been characterised by an amorphousness similar to that of the movement's organisational structure. One leader claimed the JVP never had "members," only "sympathisers." Another recounted that at a December 1970 central committee meeting the preparation of two lists of members was ordered. The first list was to include the names of those members who were the most active and trustworthy. They were to be used in attacks on police stations and assigned all other important tasks. Members on the second list were to engage in propaganda activities. Wijeweera denied the existence of the two lists, contending that the only division of the membership was into candidate and full members. The size of the JVP remains subject to conjecture. The JVP membership—or body of supporters—had apparently remained very small until 1970, but expanded considerably throughout 1970–71. Wijeweera claimed that when the movement was given an organisational structure at the beginning of 1970 it contained 500 to 600 members. Around a core of dedicated activists there are probably considerable numbers of sympathisers or momentarily interested members of uncertain commitment. The number of persons who were associated with the JVP is frequently estimated at 10,000 or higher. A considerably larger number of persons probably attended JVP or had some other superficial contact with the movement. During the uprising one cabinet minister estimated the number of insurgents at between 5,000 and 7,500. An army officer reported that about 1,000 insurgents had occupied the southern town of Elpitiya.

An axial role in the JVP efforts to mobilise support was played by a series of five lectures that were given to small groups of potential recruits, commencing in early 1968. The lectures (or classes), as explained by Wijeweera, were intended as a teaching device for the politically unsophisticated and were designed to deal in simple terms with easily grasped ideas. They were not viewed as constituting a JVP manifesto or policy statement. Wijeweera asserted: "Nobody becomes a Marxist by following these five basic classes. These classes were only used as a bridge to draw people from the bank of capitalist thinking to our bank of Marxist thinking." He described the five lectures as follows: the first, "The Economic Crisis," dealt with "the crisis of the colonial and neocolonial capitalist system, which . . . is in the process of being transformed into a political crisis"; the second, "Independence—a Neo-Colonial Strategy," argued that "the so-called Independence [obtained in 1948] was a neo-colonialist trick and an imperialist fraud"; the third, "Indian Expansionism," developed from Chinese arguments at the time of the 1962 Sino-Indian border conflict, claimed that the nature of Indian capitalism led that nation to seek domination over its smaller neighbours, and linked this characteristic to the Indian merchants and plantation labourers in Ceylon (other reports described it as virulently hostile to the Indian minority in Ceylon); the fourth, "The Left Movement in Ceylon," vigorously denounced "the policies and programmes of the Old Left Movement . . . from its inception to the present day"; the fifth lecture, "The Path the Ceylonese Revolution Should Take" (also known by two other slightly different names), was described as an attempt to counter proponents of the Cuban, Russian, and Chinese paths to revolution for Ceylon and to argue that the particular circumstances of Ceylon dictated the path suitable for the nation.

According to Loku Athula the fifth lecture, given only to trusted members of the movement, advocated a seizure of power by a simultaneous uprising throughout the country in a single day, rather than by protracted guerilla warfare or by commencing in the cities and spreading to the rural areas or commencing in the rural areas and surrounding the cities.

The JVP leaders seem to have been action-oriented, more concerned with immediate organisational and agitational questions than with theoretical issues or policies to be pursued after attaining power. Some tendency was evident for the peasantry to be substituted for the urban proletariat as the centre of JVP concern. Wijeweera explained: "The entire Working Class falls into three categories namely the Rural, the Urban and the Plantation Sectors. . . . We could not establish ourselves in the Urban Sector because of the influence of the old traditional leftist movement. Likewise we could not establish in the Plantation sector because of the racial divisions and the lack of Caders [sic]." Hence, for a mass base the JVP could look only to the rural, non-plantation population. JVP pronouncements reiterated that the principal enemies to be fought were American and British imperialism and Indian expansionism, vigorously condemned unemployment among youths, and called for a diversification of agriculture and the introduction of collective farming. The attention of the JVP, however, was riveted on the seizure of power. The movement's principal theoretical contribution was Wijeweera's idea for gaining power by a sudden uprising throughout the nation. Loku Athula appears to have been completely preoccupied with staging the revolution. He declared, "Until socialism is built the problems of the masses will not be solved, therefore socialism should be built. That could be done only by a violent revolution." The JVP continued to prepare for an armed uprising after the 1970 election, he claimed, because "the government in power, whether it be the U.N.P. or the S.L.F.P. did not matter. When we were *ready* we wanted to launch the attack." In explaining the overwhelmingly youthful character of the JVP movement and its rapid growth after 1969, Wijeweera referred to the world-wide restiveness and radicalism of youth in the 1960s, the loss of revolutionary fervour by Marxist parties throughout the world, and the ideological ferment generated by the Sino-Soviet dispute in international communism. In Ceylon, he argued, "Because of the traditional reformist, leftist influence, the members of the older generation who were sunk in reformism and were disillusioned and dispirited were drawn into the tide of the new radicalisation only in comparably [comparatively] small numbers. It was in such a socio-political situation where . . . under the U.N.P. Government [of 1965–70] the youth and student frustrations had increased and a general bitterness was being felt at the plight of the new generation, that the youth of this country including young workers, and students who had been caught in the wave of radicalisation and had been showing signs of militancy were brought to the position of demonstrating their hostility toward the existing conditions. While, under the U.N.P. Government, unemployment was spreading more and more and the cost of living . . . was spiraling higher and higher, radicalism began to take hold of the young generation."

The Plunge into Rebellion. The appearance of the JVP can be linked to the shifts in tactics and policies and the schisms and internal discord of the Left parties during the 1960s. The movement's ability to mobilise support among youths can be explained in terms of the educational explosion and the staggering levels of unemployment among educated youths, together with the more subtle social, political, and attitudinal changes that had been occurring in the Sinhalese villages in the decades preceding the insurrection. What remains unanswered is how this movement came to launch the costly and disastrously unsuccessful uprising of 1971.

The members of the JVP movement had always held the conviction that the new socialist society could be ushered in only through violent revolution. The JVP's most strident criticism of the old Left parties was for their retreat from the belief that only through armed revolution could they obtain political power to achieve their goals of social reconstruction. Within the movement, hence, the expectation was ever present that armed seizure of power would be inevitable at some time, and the principal mission of the movement was to lay the groundwork so that when the "revolutionary situation" described by Lenin arrived, it could be ignited into a successful proletarian revolution. The veteran JVP activists had presumably steeled themselves to the prospect of violence.

In early 1970 a new consideration intervened. The UNP, considered by the Marxists to be the political embodiment of the implacable class enemy, was in office. JVP leaders professed to have believed that the UNP would not hold the parliamentary election due in 1970, or would relinquish power if defeated by the United Front, but would resort to a dictatorship in association with the military. Consequently the JVP began to make preparations for armed resistance to the anticipated dictatorship. As explained by one JVP activist, "The members of the Janatha Vimukthi Peramuna had a strong belief that a counter-revolution might take place in 1970. On this belief, it was stated that the Party [JVP] was prepared to launch a general armed rebellion." In such an endeavour they could anticipate cooperation from the United Front parties and their supporters could expect wide popular sympathy. This was not conceived as the coming of the great proletarian revolution, the time for which was not ripe, but simply as resistance to a repressive and illegal regime. It was at this time that rumours began to circulate of revolutionary groups of youths, dubbed "Che Guevarists" by the press, assembling weapons and laying plans for disruption and violence.

When the election was held the United Front scored a resounding victory, the UNP relinquished power, and the JVP's plans and preparations were therefore rendered obsolete. The drama and sense of adventure generated by the plans for insurrection, however, may have continued to captivate some, at least, of the JVP leaders and members. Within a few months the JVP and the United Front began to clash. The JVP commenced holding public rallies at which the government was criticised for inaction and delay. The parties of the old Left now in power, responded by accusing the JVP of being a tool of the American CIA, composed of "petit-bourgeois" adventurers. A statement issued by the United Front parties in August 1970 charged that the JVP, "despite its ultra-revolutionary slogans and its use of the names and ideas of certain leaders of the International Revolutionary Movement, is in fact nothing more than an agency of reactionary forces." The recriminations between the United Front and the JVP steadily mounted in bitterness and intensity.

Despite its commencement of overt activities in 1970, the JVP retained its clandestine and conspiratorial character. It is difficult to say whether the preparations for rebellion begun before May 1970 were completely dismantled after the election or not. In any case, police files bulged with reports of secret meetings at which plans for violence were discussed. As the organisation, which had a short time earlier been planning armed revolt, became increasingly critical of the government, it seemed to the authorities to represent a threat to security and order. In August 1970 the Inspector-General of Police described the objective of the JVP as armed rebellion. Police began to take measures against the movement, including the arrest of its activists. Most of the leaders went into hiding.

Faced with mounting police repression, some JVP units began to collect weapons and engage in robberies to obtain funds. Simultaneously, the JVP was beset by particularly severe quarrels and struggles for power among its leaders, allegedly disrupting centralised control and leading to independent action by factions and units within the organisation. Pressures were reportedly building up within the rank and file and some elements of the leadership for dramatic and audacious action. Wijeweera related that comrades of certain districts had become obstinate and adventurous. These people said that the leadership of the movement had become revisionist, trying to kneel before the Parliament, not launching a revolution but had betrayed the revolution and they were the revolutionists who would launch the revolution. Thus a situation had arisen where certain comrades and certain groups of a number of districts were trying to launch different causes of action by the end of 1970.

In February 1971 Wijeweera made what he conceded to have been a fateful decision. In view of the increasing police repression, which he saw as threatening to destroy the movement (perhaps also concerned that he might lose control of the organisation), he concluded that "the masses should be armed," and he "acted accordingly." An intensification of preparations for insurrection was noted by the police in early 1971.

There seems to have been sharp disagreement within the top leadership circle on the advisability of armed revolt in early 1971. The leaders on trial before the Criminal Justice Commission, not unnaturally, sought to blame each other for the course of events leading to the April uprising. One version was that Wijeweera gave instructions for a seizure of power at a central committee meeting in December 1970. The picture drawn by Wijeweera was that his rival, Loku Athula, was independently preparing for an uprising, using the appeal of militant action to win support away from Wijeweera among the rank and file. Wijeweera later claimed: "While the State was openly repressing us outside there was Loku Athula and his followers brandishing their swords inside saying that only they were ready to face the repression." On 6 March the attack on the US embassy occurred. The following day the Prime Minister announced a deployment of the armed services "for the maintenance of public order." Wijeweera was found by the police and arrested on 13 March. A few days later, after further discoveries of hidden arms and explosives, an emergency was declared. It was in this setting, with the JVP leadership in disarray and growing numbers of JVP members in custody, that a small group of leaders allegedly met on 2 April and resolved to execute pre-existing plans for an uprising at 11.30 p.m. on 5 April. Reportedly, many leaders and units believed the time was not right (the "revolutionary situation" had not developed), but when the uprising exploded, they felt compelled to join their comrades. Thus the JVP seems to have stumbled into a disaster for itself and a fearful trauma for the nation.

Rank-and-file impatience, leadership rivalries, and fear of suppression of some movements all seem to have played a role in the JVP's plunge into insurrection. An eventual armed revolt had long been anticipated within the movement. The idea of a "one-day revolution" had been in existence for some time before 1971, and detailed plans were presumably formulated before the May 1970 election. The preparations for an uprising and seizure of power in 1970 may have created dreams of power and destiny among the youthful jvp members and leaders (at the time of the insurrection, Wije-weera was 28 and Loku Athula 26; nearly all the other jvp leaders were also under 30) that were not easily abandoned. They also left a legacy of sus-picion and disapprobation among government authorities, contributing to efforts to suppress the jvp, which in turn pushed the jvp towards armed revolt. As the movement was confronted with mounting police repression and was torn by factionalism by late 1970, the impatient and rash among the jvp activists began to refurbish their plans for revolt. It could have been easy for youths, caught up in the drama and excitement of an armed rebellion, to have ignored the very different circumstances in which they were now proposing to act, and to have shifted easily from the objective of resisting an unconstitutional usurpation of power to that of overthrowing a popularly elected government. Hence the elaboration of plans for revolt prior to the 1970 election may have set in motion a train of events that carried the jvp into the grim tragedy of April 1971.

The Aftermath. Although the government's response to the insurrection was generally stern, from an early date a tendency appeared to distinguish between the leaders of the revolt and the rank-and-file recruits, who were viewed as "misguided youths." In the first week of the insurrection Prime Minister Sirimavo Bandaranaike contended that those behind the uprising were "operating through young men and women who they have success-fully led astray," and spoke with regret of "these misguided youth[s] who are laying down their lives through youthful folly." At the end of April she issued a call to surrender to "the young people who were misled by their evil and designing leaders." The distinction between culpable leaders and "misguided" rank and file opened the way for a programme of "rehabilita-tion" for the latter, with their early return to society planned. By mid-1973 more than 10,000 had been released. A special Criminal Justice Commission, operating with broad powers and under altered rules of evidence, was cre-ated to try the accused insurgents. The trial of 41 alleged leaders (including two who were believed dead and three who had not been captured) com-menced in June 1972 and was still in progress more than two years later. Of those who pleaded guilty to charges stemming from the insurrection, 2,100 received suspended sentences and 120 were sentenced to between one and eight years' imprisonment. About 600 others still awaited trial.

The economic costs of the insurrection were immediate and severe. As described by Minister of Finance N. M. Perera: "Not only the Governmen-tal machine, but the whole economy came to a grinding halt. Departments ceased to function; industrial establishments closed down; factories were damaged; paddy crops remained unreaped and where reaped, the harvest could not be gathered. . . . Police Stations, Co-operative Stores and Post Offices were demolished and ransacked. Motor vehicles, including buses and lorries, were destroyed and many houses were gutted. This is the dreary path of counter-revolution that ravaged the country for 3 to 4 months."

During 1971 per capita gross national product at constant (1959) prices fell by 1.1 per cent, the first decline in a decade. The economic shock of the insurrection was followed in quick succession by poor harvests due to inadequate rainfall, the world food shortage, and the world economy plunging Ceylon into desperate economic circumstances.

The insurrection was an agonising experience for the veteran Marxists of the LSSP and the CP, who found themselves participating in a government that was forced to rely on the police and military to crush a revolt by a professed radical movement. The JVP's failure to establish a broad popular base, its highly personal style of leadership, communal exclusiveness, and strategy of seizing power by a sudden putsch-like uprising were subjected to scathing criticism by the older Left parties. A resolution of the CP central committee described the revolt as "essentially a reactionary and potentially counter-revolutionary one." LSSP leader N. M. Perera called it "a misguided adventure carried out at the behest of scheming individuals who hoped to profit from the political confusion that ensued." He later claimed that "the stamping out of insurgents could well have overflowed into an onslaught on leftism but for the fact that the leaders of these parties were Ministers of the Government." Leslie Goonewardene, who took a somewhat more dispassionate view of the insurgents than other Left leaders, linked the JVP movement with the world-wide revolt of youth of the 1960s, taking the particular form it did on the island because of "Ceylon's long tradition of Leftism and Marxism." He conceded that the United Front's slow pace of implementation of radical reforms may have heightened disillusionment among youths and thus contributed to the rapid growth of the JVP after the 1970 election. The uprising, he argued, was nonetheless doomed to defeat because the JVP had relied on a secret organisation and conspiratorial tactics and had failed to seek mass popular support, resulting on the outbreak of the revolt in the "awful isolation of the insurrectionists."

. . . One immediate result of the uprising was an expansion in the size of the armed forces and an increase in expenditures for the modernisation of their arms and equipment. The significance of the military in politics, which had previously been small, seemed likely to increase. In 1973–74, the pro-Moscow CP experienced an internal upheaval and momentary schism, at least in part reflecting stresses traceable to the insurrection. Parliamentary by-elections in 1972–73 suggested a slump in support for the governing

United Front, but no startling realignment of politics. The major beneficiary of sagging United Front fortunes was the long-established and scarcely revolutionary UNP. A by-election in July 1973, necessitated by the death of former UNP Prime Minister Dudley Senanayake, was significant for the absence of evident repercussions of the insurrection. The area had been a centre of insurrectionary activity, believed concentrated among youths from the Vahumpura and Batgam castes. These castes had provided an important bloc of support for the United Front parties in the past and, as the United Front government had put down the insurrection, with considerable force in this area, it was thought that support for the United Front might fall precipitously. However, although the United Front (SLFP) candidate won a smaller proportion of votes than in 1970, the drop was not severe and indicated that no wholesale shift of political loyalties had occurred. The United Front candidate and the UNP candidate together obtained 99 per cent of the votes. One of the two independent candidates was rumoured to have had some links with the JVP and to be seeking votes sympathetic to the insurgents. He won scarcely a handful of votes, receiving only slightly more than 200 out of the 42,500 cast.

For the youths who had been caught up in the insurrection, the fear of arrest and prosecution or the period of incarceration after 1971 seemed initially to have had a sobering and inhibiting effect. . . . Despite enhanced governmental concern with educational reform and alleviation of the unemployment problems of youths, the underlying socio-economic circumstances that presumably facilitated the growth of the JVP have changed little. The youthful naiveté and impetuousness that seem to have contributed to the 1971 uprising, however, may have vanished. Whether mounting economic problems will galvanise the youths into renewed political action—peaceful or violent—remains to be determined.

Editor's Note

1. Due to space limitations, I have been forced to cut the copious notes originally appended to this article. Those interested may find them in the original source of publication, listed in the Acknowledgment of Copyrights and Sources section of this volume. The major sources used included *Criminal Justice Proceedings*, *Parliamentary Proceedings*, police station interviews, the *Final Report of the Police Commission*, the *Report of the Armed Services Pay Committee*, government census figures, and the *Ceylon Daily News*.

The Colombo Riots of 1983

S. J. Tambiah

The JVP insurrections of 1971 and 1988–89 were class-based rural Sinhala challenges to the entrenched interests of the English-speaking upper-middle class and urban elite; the events of July 1983, by contrast, were a Sinhala pogrom against Tamil people living throughout southern Sinhala-dominated parts of the island, and were the shock that galvanized Tamil aspirations for a separate state. Though it was preceded by previous hostilities between ethnic communities, journalists and scholars often point to the riot of 1983 as the beginning of Sri Lanka's "ethnic conflict" or civil war, because of its extreme nature and its comprehensive scope. For five days in the Sinhala regions of the island in the south and central highlands, Tamil people, their homes, and businesses were unmercifully attacked by squads of Sinhala thugs, many organized by sections of the UNP-led government of J. R. Jayewardene. Cyril Mathew, a prominent cabinet minister in the UNP government, was reported to have played an important role in organizing this perpetration of violence. Relations between the ethnic communities of Sri Lanka have never been the same since.

The course of the Sinhalese riots against the Tamil minority in Sri Lanka in 1983 has been documented by me elsewhere. Here let me summarize what we know of the locations at which the arson and violence took place and the kinds of participants—"the faces in the crowd."

The 1983 riots began in Colombo on July 24. . . . They spread to other parts of the country from this point of origin, especially to the towns of Gampaha and Kalutara in the southwest; Kandy, Kegalle, Matale, Badulla, and Nuwara Eliya in the central tea plantation districts; and Trincomalee in the Eastern Province. Although the official death toll was about 470, it has been estimated that about 2,000–3,000 people were murdered, many of them in a brutal manner. Thousands were displaced from their homes, most of them ending up in about a dozen makeshift refugee camps. Within the city of Colombo almost a hundred thousand people, more than half the city's Tamil population, were displaced from their homes, and many never returned to their neighborhoods or to their workplaces. Outside the country, it was estimated that there were about 175 thousand refugees and displaced persons. In this account I shall limit myself to happenings in Colombo.

One feature of these riots that I want to underscore is their actual beginning, which bears some resemblance to the inception of the Delhi riots of 1984, in that an incident of violent death had traumatic and emotionally heightening effects on a crowd and worked as a triggering event for acts of crowd violence, which escalated rapidly into large-scale, spreading ethnic riots.

The conventional story is that the most proximate triggering event was the ambush of an army truck and the killing and mutilation of thirteen soldiers at Tirunelveli, a place in the heart of Sri Lankan Tamil territory in North Sri Lanka, which had been under the occupation of a Sinhalese army for some time. The ambush was the work of Tamil insurgents belonging to the Liberation Tigers of Tamil Eelam (LTTE). This was certainly a moment of escalation in the ethnic conflict. India had begun to supply the Tigers with the Claymore land mine as a way of enabling them better to withstand the Sri Lankan Army (overwhelmingly Sinhalese in composition). Although skirmishes had taken place before, never before had so many Sinhala soldiers been killed at once. On July 23, certain elements in the army decided to bring the corpses in their mangled state to Colombo at the central Kanatte cemetery in Borella before giving them a military burial.

The preparations for the burial were complicated and plagued by adventitious and uncontrollable factors. One of the soldiers killed was a young second lieutenant, who had apparently been a popular student at Ananda College, a premier Buddhist school, located in Maradana. Many pupils of this school, together with their parents and teachers, gathered at the cemetery and awaited the arrival of the bodies.

In the meantime, the plane transporting the bodies to Colombo from Jaffna was delayed, and the waiting crowd, increasing in size, also became increasingly restless. After arrival, the bodies were to be taken to a funerary home next to the cemetery for preparation, but the delay also caused the police and army troops who had gathered in numbers at Borella to become emotionally agitated. And, as might be expected, the Sinhala media added further fuel to the mounting grief and rage. (There are separate Sinhalese and Tamil newspapers, radio, and television channels in Sri Lanka.)

In the end, the long delay in the arrival of the bodies at Ratmalana airport, the unruliness of the packed crowd at the cemetery, and the demand of the grief-stricken relatives of the dead that the bodies be handed to them so that they could conduct their own rites forced the authorities to cancel the official burial at Kanatte. The bodies were taken to army headquarters. The crowd then erupted in spontaneous violence and surged into the streets.

Reviewing the trajectory of the riots, it seems plausible to suggest that they went through two phases. The first phase began in the vicinity of the cemetery in Borella, more or less as an overflow of heightened emotions on the part of the crowd gathered there—the schoolboys, friends, and relatives of the dead, some of the security forces, plus some of the local populace in Borella.

Soon after the mortuary rites, street thuggery, stopping of traffic, and physical attacks broke out in Borella, Thimbirigasyaya, Nugegoda, Wella-watte, and Bambalapitiya, and almost a whole day passed before the army and police were called upon to intervene. This first phase of violence lasted one day; it was only after a short lull that crowd violence resumed in a form that was decidedly more destructive and homicidal, showing firm evidence of planning and direction, the participation of certain politicians (especially from the ruling party) and government employees (minor staff, laborers, technicians), and the use of government vehicles and buses.

A conspicuous feature of the 1983 riots was that the mob violence, espe-cially in its second phase, was organized and for the most part purposive. The crowds came armed with weapons such as metal rods and knives and carrying gasoline, which was frequently confiscated from passing motor vehicles. Evidence of the rioters' prior intent and planning was the fact that they carried voter lists and the addresses of Tamil owners and occupants of houses, shops, industries, and other property. Moreover, the gangs fre-quently had access to transportation; they arrived mostly in government-owned trucks and buses or were dropped off at successive locations by the Colombo coastline trains.

Affirmation of these incidents comes from a senior official in the Sri Lankan Ministry of Foreign Affairs, Ambassador T. D. S. A. Dissanayaka, who has written a detailed and graphic account of the rioting in Colombo and elsewhere. He writes: "In the afternoon [of July 25] the violence took a different turn. There was organized violence by gangs which were obvi-ously trained and who operated with military precision. Their targets were the economic bases of the Tamils in Colombo and their homes."

This kind of organized violence first occurred in Ratmalana, on the southern periphery of Colombo, which had the largest concentration of fac-tories in Sri Lanka, and then it moved northwards into the city. It coincided with another organized operation: a train traveling from Galle was made to make unscheduled stops in Ratmalana, and then at each stop into the city, at Dehiwela, Wellawatte, and other places, "squads were discharged. . . .

They demonstrated remarkable skill in destroying homes. . . . Tamil homes were identified with pinpoint accuracy using electoral lists. In attacking shops, the trained squads responded to three commands in Sinhala: 'kada [break], adha [haul],' and 'gini [set fire].'" At this phase of the violence, there was little looting of property, only systematic destruction of Tamil property and the eradication of the alleged affluence.

A well-informed friend of mine has pointed out to me that the "liberalized economy" introduced from 1977 onwards had opened up new commercial and business opportunities. Many shops selling imported and local goods had opened. New business premises and houses had been constructed in Colombo, and higher rents had become possible. At the same time, this had aggravated competition, and the riots gave some Sinhala businessmen an opportunity to wipe out their competitors, enabled some landlords to get rid of unwanted tenants, and so on. It has also been suggested that Cyril Mathew, the chauvinist minister of industries, was vociferous that Tamil businessmen in Colombo were working both sides of the street—collaborating with the government in Colombo and with the Tamil insurgents in Jaffna—and that they therefore deserved to be "taught a lesson." Mathew's ministry was a repository of knowledge about businesses, including details of their locations and owners. Its employees also provided the manpower for the government union called the Jatika Sevaka Sangamaya, which was involved in punitive actions and thuggery. It was also the source for vehicles that were used for political purposes.

In a retrospective look at the manner in which events unfolded, it is plausible to suggest that there was a deadly confluence of two separate but complementary streams. Certain segments of the government, particularly Minister Mathew and his agents and client cohorts, had gathered information and made plans for punitive action against the Tamils in Colombo, and the ambush and killing of the thirteen Sinhalese soldiers in the north and the subsequent events at the Kanatte cemetery afforded the occasion for the prepared pogrom. That the army authorities and the minister of defence handled the deaths of the soldiers and their mangled corpses in polythene bags in a manner that would, whether intended or not, inevitably excite the emotions of the Sinhalese public at large is made even more problematic by the fact that news of the army's retaliatory violence on July 24 in Tirunelveli and Kantharmadu (in Jaffna), which resulted in an estimated 50 to 70 Tamils being killed, was suppressed from the media, both newspapers and radio, which in the meantime transmitted the inflammatory news of the dead Sinhalese soldiers and the conveyance of their dismembered remains to Colombo.

Ambassador Dissanayaka, who, I presume, had access to official records by virtue of his high position, reports that by Monday, August 1, when the riots had virtually subsided, the following number of incidents had taken place in Sri Lanka overall: 471 deaths, 8,077 cases of arson, and 3,835 cases of looting. Colombo district topped the list with 227 deaths, 2,720 cases of arson, and 1,712 of looting; Kandy district suffered 31 deaths, 1,065 acts of arson, and 132 of looting. Other districts where much violence occurred were Badulla (52 deaths, 838 cases of arson, and 630 lootings), Matale (3 deaths, 1,131 acts of arson, and 838 lootings), Kegalle (24 deaths, 390 cases of arson, and 195 lootings). Leaving aside Colombo district, one may reasonably conclude from the location and demographic profile of the other districts, which are mostly located "up-country," where tea plantations and the towns servicing them are located, that not only Sri Lankan Tamil but also Indian Tamil business establishments, and the Indian Tamil labor working in the plantation sector were targeted.

It may also be noted that Trincomalee district in the Eastern Province, in which there has been tension between the Sri Lankan Tamil residents and the allegedly newly arriving Sinhalese settlers, experienced 634 incidents of arson, and Jaffna district suffered 70 deaths, the second-largest number, primarily owing to the security forces taking punitive action against Tamil civilians as a sequel to the killing of 13 soldiers of the Sri Lankan Army in the north on July 23, 1983.

The following is a list of the locations and the kinds of property methodically burned, destroyed, and looted in Colombo:

1. Tamil houses in Colombo's middle-and lower-class residential wards of Ratmalana, Wellawatte, Dehiwela, Bambalapitiya, and Kirillapone.

2. Tamil shops—groceries, textile shops, tea boutiques—lining Colombo's principal waterfront thoroughfare, especially in Bambalapitiya, and also in well-established residential and business zones such as Borella and Kotahena. In the densest shopping district, Pettah, Tamil shops and the shops of Indian merchants, principally selling cloth and wholesale foodstuffs, were targeted. Moreover, shops located in the city's newer and expanding residential areas such as Timbirigasyaya and Nugegoda were also affected.

3. Textile mills, garment factories, rubber-goods factories, and coconut-oil processing plants at Ratmalana, Grandpass, Ja-ela, and Peliyagoda, at the edges of the city, owned and managed by Tamil entrepreneurs and large businessmen.

4. The Indian Overseas Bank, the principal bank for Sri Lankans of Indian origin and Indian citizens in Sri Lanka.

The victims in Colombo were Tamil shopkeepers, Tamil homeowners, especially of the middle class and administrative/clerical/professional categories, Tamil large business capitalists and entrepreneurs, and Indian merchants, both Tamil and non-Tamil.

These facts clearly indicate that the locations affected were central market and business zones, sites of new industrial development stimulated by the economic liberalization initiated by the new government of J. R. Jayewardene in 1977, and middle-class residential areas. There was practically no arson in slums and working-class residential zones.

At the most general level, the rioters on the Sinhalese side were all male and virtually all drawn from the urban population of Colombo and its suburbs. Those who actually committed murders, inflicted bodily harm, and engaged in arson, property destruction, and looting were typically drawn from the urban working class. A more detailed enumeration would include the following categories: wage workers in government and private factories and mills; transport workers, such as bus drivers and conductors, and workers in railroad yards and electrical installations; petty traders and market workers, including fish sellers and porters; small shopkeepers and salesmen in government corporations; hospital workers; high school students and the students of technical and tutorial institutes, including recent school leavers. The literacy explosion and the poor employment prospects of school graduates and leavers were potent factors in motivating the last category. Finally, there was the urban underclass of unemployed and underemployed shanty-town dwellers.

It would be a mistake to exclude from the list of participants those whose involvement was less visible but nonetheless crucial to the hatching, organization, and direction of the riots. Certain Sinhala politicians and their local agents, organized crime figures and smugglers, and small businessmen seeking to eliminate rivals were all involved in directing and manipulating the violence. Some of these might be described as "riot captains" who were experts at "raising a mob" (to use expressions current in England in the nineteenth century). In addition, some militant Buddhist monks played a role in inciting crowd action, sometimes as supportive witnesses and orators. Finally, it has been well attested that many members of the police force and security forces stood by during the 1983 riots—unwilling to restrain the rioters, showing sympathy for their actions, and in a few instances actively participating in the work of destruction.

An intriguing question that some interpreters have grappled with is why, after a hiatus of some nineteen years since the last Sinhala-Tamil riots of 1958, a crop of riots of mounting violence should have occurred at short intervals in 1977, 1981, and 1983. Since the last three upheavals took place on the watch of the United National Party, it has been asked to what extent the "liberalized open economy" and capitalist, market-oriented policies introduced by President Jayewardene created economic dislocations injurious to segments of the Sinhalese population, who might have sponsored, supported, and even participated in varying degrees in the spate of riots against the Tamils.

The Tamils were targeted for a combination of reasons: they were perceived as privileged and a suitable object of redressive action on behalf of the majority Sinhalese population, especially its poorer segments; because they were convenient victims, against whom aggression that could not be directed at the state could be displaced; and because Tamil business interests could be dispossessed or eliminated to the advantage of Sinhalese small-scale entrepreneurs and traders, who suffered most in the changeover from the state-regulated welfare and protectionist policy of the previously ruling Sri Lanka Freedom Party to the capitalist, market-oriented, free-trade policy heralded by the UNP in 1977.

In sum, the 1983 riots were a kind of pogrom, which was motivated, purposive, systematic, and organized. Politically and economically, they were a punitive action against Tamils. Those who stood to gain most were, firstly, middle-level Sinhala entrepreneurs, businessmen, and white-collar workers, and, secondly, the urban poor, mainly through looting. Many of the latter were recent migrants from rural areas, whose living conditions had deteriorated as the open economy created and widened disparities of wealth and income distribution. Despite rising wages, their real incomes had declined as a result of inflation, urban housing scarcities, and the issuing of food stamps in place of the former subsidized rice program. Moreover, the measures taken to create an open-market economy caused short-term internal dislocations and imbalances, which were aggravated by pressure from the World Bank, the International Monetary Fund, and other international organizations.

"In the Month of July" and "Voyagers"

Jean Arasanayagam

"In the Month of July" and "Voyagers," by the celebrated Sri Lankan poet Jean Ara-sanayagam, are graphic reflections on the significance of the tragedy of "Black July" (1983), when mobs of Sinhala goons attacked innocent Tamil people in their midst. The poet, a Burgher married to a Tamil schoolteacher and writer, was chased from her home with her two children by a Sinhala mob. She knows firsthand the fear, violence, and hatred marking that July.

In the Month of July

Childhood is far away
beneath a tree
playing with pebbles
skillfully tossing them
from back of hand
to palm
requiring a certain skill and
magical ritualistic incantations.

As one grows older
the pebbles grow too
into great stones and
rocks hurled with violence
smashed skulls spilled brains
splattering the pavements.

In the month of July
a man fled from his pursuers
he climbed a tree
the mob aimed stones at him
until they got him down

probably fell off, his grasp loosened
slippery with blood, his body already battered
and then they trampled him to death.

Voyagers

We have to rediscover new myths and legends
To describe our journey, the old false maps
Don't, oh no, they don't, help us any more
To chart our voyages.

The one-time conquerors are dust,
Their bones, the weather vanes of Time
Twisted in the storms that once
Raged over the palms to bend
And then uprooted, fall upon the strand.

Then the nuts burst and shattered,
Their milk, bitter, irrigate the wounded
Earth.

The routes we now retrace,
The boundaries and frontiers
Of our own making efface the ancient
Markings of out-dated maps,
Guiding once the archaic traveler
And now, our own journeys.

Patriotic TV

K. Jayatilake

K. Jayatilake captures something of the pathos of the Friday afternoon of that last riotous week of "Black July" 1983, his wry humor touching on aspects of fear not easily explained by other means. His short story also records for posterity the police corruption that enabled the extensive damage to personal property that occurred during these riots, the most anarchical disturbances the country may ever have experienced.

It was a very bad day for business. Except for Sirisena, other salesmen had not reported to work. Sirisena kept watching the pedestrians, standing at the entrance of the shop. On a normal day of business the Mudalali-shopkeeper would not let Sirisena stay like that without doing some work. The Mudalali would ask Sirisena from time to time, "What is the situation now? Is there anyone to be seen at Rajadurai's shop? Is it still burning?" Mudalali did not expect an answer to such questions. His real interest was on another thing. Men and women of all races had been coming to the shop during the past two or three days, bringing all kinds of items to sell. Such transactions always ended, after much bargaining, for the profit of the Mudalali. Where did they get all those loads of goods? They had been all looted from Tamil shops. The mobs, after breaking into shops, pulled out everything and dumped them into the streets. Not only the looters, but anyone passing by on the road could take them. Things were sold at very low prices. Even TV sets worth a few thousand rupees were sold for a few hundred rupees.

Dharmadasa Mudalali was not scared to buy such booty. He could sell them later for a big margin of profit. Having bought something from a looter, Mudalali walked with him to the front door and peeped into the road. Sirisena moved away and went in. For a moment, the road looked deserted, although there were some people still walking hurriedly. They looked agitated and violent. Rajadurai's shop was almost burned down. Sirisena could see smoke and flames through the front door. Suddenly a rowdy gang appeared round the bend led by a Buddhist monk. Immediately behind him some young men carried lion flags. The mob, brandishing swords, sticks, iron bars and knives marched behind. They were shouting and mulling along the road blocking the traffic. Sirisena saw the mob stopping in front of a two storied-building, which had not been attacked by those who had come before. The mob first started throwing stones at the windows, then tried to break in. But as the iron-gate didn't give in, they used a tractor to break the front gate, looted the store and set fire to it. Within seconds the building was engulfed in flames. The mob moved on shouting menacing slogans.

"Alas, what a waste," Mudalali uttered, but Sirisena kept quiet as this was not directly addressed to him.

An army truck came from the direction of Maradana. There were soldiers bearing guns and rifles in it. The mob shouted *"jaya vewa"* cheering the troops as the truck went past. An old man walked by the shop, obviously moved by what was happening. Mudalali called out to him: "How is it over there? Are there troubles there too?"

"What do you say Mudalali? Maradana and Borella are full of smoke and flames." "What a sinful thing," Mudalali sighed. "Yes, Mudalali, it is one thing if they stop loot and burn. But why do they kill? And it is not just an immediate death. They lock them in cars, pour petrol and set them on fire. I can't understand how our people can be as cruel as this."

"But don't you know how these Tamils are?"

"I think there are reasons for that too. A Tamil man can be much more cunning than a Sinhala man. But you see, can we buy something from a Sinhala shop today? They treat the customers as if they go in to beg things for free. But if we go to a Tamil shop, they talk to us kindly, answer our questions well, attend to us carefully and never charge us more than the correct price."

"O.K., O.K., we will discuss this some other time," so saying Mudalali, he went back into his shop. Sirisena saw people carrying away all kinds of electrical goods on the road. He looked with special interest at those who were carrying TV sets. He remembered how his son and daughter had been pestering him for a TV. His son and daughter had gotten crazy about TV after his neighbor had bought one. First the neighbor's children would call them to watch TV at their place. But little by little, they began passing hints. "Please, Dad, bring us also a TV." They did not know how poor he was and how he was just meeting the most important expenses at home. When he remembered how his children were humiliated by the neighbor's children, he then began considering buying one. When he saw the looters carrying TV sets and selling them cheap, he was wondering whether he could buy one. As if sensing what was going on in Sirisena's mind, a man stopped in front of him. The man put down a large box with the picture of a TV printed outside.

"Buy this one, Sir. You will never again have a chance like this," he said.

Sirisena was tempted. He looked around. Then he saw a policeman walking a few yards away. He was carrying a gun but looked tired. The officer looked at the man and then at Sirisena and said. "Just take it and pack off."

This was something that Sirisena had never expected from a policeman. During the past few days he had seen a number of soldiers and policemen just looking on, without doing anything to stop the rampage. Are they also not human beings? They must still be concerned about the thirteen soldiers who were assassinated in the north.

"How much do you want?" Sirisena asked.

"Three hundred," the man said.

"No, I don't have that much money," Sirisena said feeling for money in his pocket. "How much can you give, Sir?" the man asked again. "One hundred."

"Give me two hundred."

"No, only one hundred."

That was the deal and Sirisena was about to take what he had bought when, as he turned around, a crowd came running from the Maradana side. Sirisena saw both fear and fatigue in their faces.

"Why are you running like this?" Mudalali asked them. *"Koti, koti!"* [tigers, tigers!] a man shouted. "There are Tigers attacking the Fort. Close down your shop and run for your life!" someone else shouted.

"Seven Tigers!" another man yelled.

"What! Only seven Tigers? What can they do?" More and more people came running from the direction of the Fort. *"Koti, koti!* Fort is finished. Devastated!" "Fifteen Tigers have gone into a building. Now they are shooting from the roof tops."

In the meantime a row of police and army vehicles came from Maradana with soldiers waving guns. Two of the army trucks stopped on the way and told something to the crowd. People started running in all directions jumping over the fence dividing the road. The situation was getting dangerous, Sirisena thought. "Sirisena, close the shop at once," Mudalali ordered. After doing so, Sirisena stood with his package, alone in front of the shop. He was scared, but happy at the same time. There was no sign of a bus, especially the bus he was waiting for. He had to go home to Navala, even if he had to walk it. Carrying his package, he walked as fast as he could towards Maradana. There was an even bigger crowd at that junction. Some young men, stopping vehicles passing by, forced men and women into them. "Come, Come, get in, Aturigiriya, Rajagiriya." Even before Sirisena could reach one, the two buses started off. "Come on," said one young man to a driver. "Come on now, this is the time we must save our Sinhala brothers." As Sirisena was waiting impatiently, the patriotic youths stopped several vehicles and shoved in people into them by force. Presently a white Lancer car came by and the youths stopped it and pushed Sirisena into its boot with his box containing the TV. As the car began moving, Sirisena heard someone saying, "Twenty-five Tigers have come to the Fort. They are now engaged in a shoot out with the army. Already seven of our soldiers have died."

When the car arrived at the Ayurveda junction, they saw three half-burned bodies of Tamil victims at the round about. Suddenly a mob brandishing weapons stopped the car. They were so violent that they reminded one of the forces of Mara! Most of them were drunk and shouting slogans with words such as "kill, burn, cut, chop," etc. Some of the rowdies peeped into the car and asked, "Are there any Tamils here?"

"No, we are all Sinhala."

"Fine, but to prove it. Recite the *gatha* for offering flowers."

One of the passengers uttered, "Itipiso Bhagava. . . ."

Another one started, "vanna gandha . . . ." Sirisena couldn't remember the correct *gatha*, but he began, following others, "poojemi buddham . . . ."

"Alright, looks like you are all Sinhala, but remember, and don't forget, we have a duty by our nation, so give us some petrol and go."

One of the thugs tried to grab the car key from the driver. Then something unexpected happened. A bus came at break-neck speed from the direction of Colombo, packed with passengers and when it slowed down, some of them shouted, "About three hundred Tigers are coming this way after capturing Fort!" When the mob heard those words, they began to flee in fear. The car with Sirisena jammed into started out on its journey again.

They arrived without any further interruptions. Finally, Sirisena got off near his home and walked down the mud-road carrying his new prey and reached home. The children noticed that their father had brought a TV. "It is a TV, it is a TV!" they danced around the box. But Sirisena's wife looked on with a worried look unable to understand how her husband could afford to buy a new TV.

"It seems that Tigers have invaded Colombo. I was so worried about you," she said.

"Yes, there's such a rumor, but I didn't see any Tigers," Sirisena answered with a victorious look on his face.

"But people were running in fear all over here too," she said.

"What! Here too? Which way did they run?"

"I don't know where to. But I kept our children in, without letting them go out." Sirisena's son pleaded, "Dad, please, turn on the TV."

"No programs at this time son. Wait a little."

"Oh! This is much bigger than Varuna's!" The little boy hopped around the box.

"But theirs is a color TV," joined in his sister.

"Why, ours too is a color TV," the boy protested.

"Yes, son, this is a color TV."

Everyone waited impatiently till the TV was fixed up and switched on. When it was finally turned on and worked without any problem, Udayana, the little boy, began complaining, "What is this Dad, this one has no antenna, that's why we don't get programs with dancing, singing, shooting and fighting. I want to watch those kinds of programs!"

"Son, this one doesn't need an antenna. You'll see your favorite programs later." The little boy ran out and came back after a few minutes. Sirisena asked where he had been. "I ran to Varuna's to tell them that we too have a TV now."

"What did they say?" asked Sirisena's wife.

"Oh, uncle said that ours is not a SONY, but a 'Jaatyaala' [Patriotic] TV instead. Why is that, Dad?" the little boy questioned.

"Oh, *Puta*, why did you go there? Now just wait here and watch TV."

Sirisena could not sleep well that night. What he heard and saw during the day reappeared in his mind over and over again. The TV he brought home was troubling him. He had worked under Dharmadasa Mudalali for such a low salary, as he could not find a better job after graduation. Being an arts graduate, it was very difficult to find a job with his qualifications. When talking about the riots, Mudalali was telling that all Tamil people must be driven back to India. Sirisena could never agree with Mudalali. He argued with him saying that Tamils in Sri Lanka should be given more opportunities and power. But it would be bad for the future of Sinhala people to give everything the Tamils were asking for. Whatever it is, "I too got involved in this unpleasant thing today by buying this TV," Sirisena regretted. Then a loud announcement was heard coming from the road. "Please listen. This is a special Police announcement. Those who are keeping stolen or looted items at home must bring them to the roadside before morning. For such people, there will be no punishment. But those who do not obey this order will be punished severely."

"Did you hear that?" Sirisena asked his wife.

"Yes, I did, what shall we do now?"

"Let's take the damn thing and leave it on the road before the children wake up. When I can afford it, I'll buy another one."

"That's better, I think. To keep this is a disgrace," Anoma said.

The children woke up in the morning to find their new TV missing and began crying. Anoma told them that the TV had been stolen during the night. Sirisena got ready to go to work earlier than usual. "Mom, where did father go so early today?"

"I think he went to the police station to complain about the theft."

"Will father bring back our TV when he comes home in the evening?"

"Probably not today. It will take a few days before they catch the thief."

After about a week, the little boy came home running leaving his friends with whom he had been playing. "Dad, Dad, Police uncle too has bought a TV. It is exactly like the one you bought for us. When are you bringing back ours, Dad?"

"Tomorrow or day after," Sirisena answered.

"Hooray! Tishoon, Tishoon." The little boy ran out again imitating a fight he had seen on TV.

Translated from Sinhala by Udaya P. Meddegama

Search My Mind

Jean Arasanayagam

The JVP insurrection of 1988–89 was perhaps as harrowing a social and political experience as the Sinhalas have experienced in their collective history. At the time, the country was gripped by what was popularly referred to as "the fear psychosis." Especially in the rural and upcountry regions of Sri Lanka, one could not be exactly sure where the loyalty of one's neighbor would lie: with the insurgents of the JVP (Janatha Vimukthi Peramuna, or People's Liberation Front)—"the unofficial government"—or with the government of President Ranasinghe Premadasa, who brutally put down the insurrection following twelve months of increasing anarchy, murder, and intimidation. The causes of the JVP insurrection were probably not much different from those outlined by Robert Kearney and Janice Jiggins in their analysis of the aborted 1971 revolution, but the sheer length and psychological depth of the 1988–89 crisis proved far more profound. Not until the incarceration and death of the JVP leader, Rohana Wijeweera, in November 1989, did a sense of normalcy begin to return to the country. During the months of insurrection, fear reigned on both sides: fear of JVP cadres and fear of government reprisals. Some 40,000 youth disappeared during the uprising and its repression and remain unaccounted for still today. No formal and sustained investigations into the causes of either the insurrection or the government's unprecedented crackdown were undertaken by the authorities; the investigations that did take place were perfunctory and led nowhere. Jean Arasanayagam's short story "Search My Mind" captures the pathos of those tragic months when the country was paralyzed, caught between forces bent on change by violence and forces bent on preservation by even more violence.

I was returning home from the teachers' training college where I teach when a young soldier stopped the van we were travelling in. He was standing guard near the gate of the Peradeniya Botanical Gardens. Behind him, the branches of the ahela trees were a mass of golden yellow flowers. But he seemed oblivious of them, intent only upon his duty and the T-56 rifle in his hands. The youth today carry burdens we never had to.

"Get off," he commanded all the passengers peremptorily. "You, stop there!" He indicated to the driver the spot a little way ahead of us, where he wanted the van parked.

"Line up! Show me your bags! Open your parcels!"

We lined up obediently before him. One does not question a man with a gun. We were all tense and silent. It was 1988. The radicals were trying to topple the government, to destabilize the capitalist state. They believed that capitalism was immoral and alien to our land. Everyday life was disrupted by lightning strikes and protest campaigns. Overnight the walls were covered by posters bearing their slogans. Identity cards had to be surrendered to them. The transport systems in the cities were paralysed, checkpoints sprang up everywhere, and tea factories were set ablaze. There were many tales of sporadic violence, and rumours of arrests, disappearances, detention camps and deaths. Indoctrination cells and safe houses were being increasingly mentioned.

I stood before this young soldier and showed him the contents of my shabby, well-worn leather bag. Text books: *The Merchant of Venice* and *The Village in the Jungle*. Some fifty-cent and one-rupee coins for the van. The conductors grumble if you didn't have the correct change. A few exercise books containing lecture notes, with half-finished poems written on the last pages, poems which nobody read.

The soldier peered in dispassionately. I wondered what he expected to find in the bag of a middle-aged teacher of English literature. A time bomb? Firearms?

Finally all the bags were inspected and we were told we could move on. We walked past him in silence, climbed into the van and were driven off. No one uttered a word.

In times before the troubles began, one saw young men and women from the university, which lay just beyond the crossing, sitting in pairs, lost in their private world beneath the shady trees of the gardens. Beside the gardens, there is an intersection where many roads meet. There is a small grassy plot there, which used to be filled with brilliantly-coloured beds of canna lillies and colias, interspersed with small trees with feathery leaves. There also used to be a signboard there, saying "Welcome to Kandy." Now there was a small encampment of soldiers on that plot, and it was covered by canvas tents. The young soldiers gazed with indifference at the roads around them. I wondered about the journeys which these soldiers observe. Many journeys from the nearby university now, I was sure, were those with no return. After all, this was where many of these radicals belonged, from where young men were taken away in locked vans. Through the barred windows, you could see only the backs of their heads.

The van passed the spot where I had taken a walk earlier today with Soma, who works in the kitchens of the teachers' training college. This used to be the royal gardens of the Kandyan kings, a beautiful place filled with kitul palms, breadfruit and mango trees. She told me disturbing rumours of what was happening in the various colleges. The young clerk of the training college had been arrested. One of the assistant superintendents of the hostel had been killed. It was whispered that he was an informer. His body was found abandoned one morning with gunshot wounds, beneath the spreading branches of a mango tree. A senior registrar of the university had also been killed by insurgents. There were retaliatory killings soon after. Fifteen insurgents had been decapitated, their heads arranged around the ornamental pond at the centre of the university campus. No one could go anywhere in the university without passing this spot and seeing these bizarre new additions to the landscaped garden.

"We are sinners," Soma said. "That is why we have to see such sights. Yesterday there was one body burning on the road, with tyres placed on it. Today it is still burning. Yesterday, the face was recognizable. Today, it's a charred mass. My daughter was with me today. She wanted to go closer and look at it. I told her, 'Mala, I'll thrash you if you speak about it to anyone.' Just burning, burning. Must have been a young man—his hair was thick and black."

Every day, the world changes around us, especially among the young. On my way to work, I saw schoolboys with handkerchiefs tied across their faces like masks to ward off the fumes of burning tyres set up as roadblocks. A crowd of schoolboys from one of the government schools crowded around the gates of a leading private college, urging these students to join their protest march.

Another day, on the way from work in a private bus, I saw some schoolchildren standing on the grounds of their deserted school, hurling stones at passing buses. Our bus slowed down to a crawl, and I held up my bag to ward off the stones. A schoolgirl came up to the bus to reassure us. "The stones are only thrown at the state buses," she announced calmly. Many buses now have slogans in thick black paint scrawled across their metal bodies. Posters are pasted on every available bit of space—walls, lamp posts—criticizing the government and its leaders.

Children stop the van I usually travel on, board it, and hold out empty tins for collections. They buy firecrackers with the money. You can hear the intermittent bursts as they explode. Students are shot while they demonstrate. Buses are burnt. Bus drivers are shot for disregarding the orders of the insurgents. White flags are hung across on ropes and barriers of old rubber tyres are placed on the road. Processions of students, carrying white banners proclaiming their protests, march on the streets. The police jeeps crawl beside them. They dare not do anything to the protesters. The arrests come later.

Nowadays as the troubles draw close again, I began to question my own role in teaching English literature to students who left the classroom to tear down the edifices of the past. On the ruined walls, they scrawled their own burning messages. I had to find parallels and relevance to this reality in my lectures. I had been out of the country for many years and the new faces of our youth were revelatory.

In the staff room, colleagues discussed their experiences of the day. Clement said, "We heard the sound of gunshots last night near our home in Bowala. I went early in the morning to investigate. I had a good look at the corpses. Blindfolded. Hands tied behind back and shot. The milkman passed by at that moment. No one came to claim the bodies."

"Life goes on as usual?" I queried.

"Of course," replied Clement. "How else are we to live?"

The images permeated the assignments that my students handed in to me. Shantha, one of the quietest students in my class, wrote, "A body is swung in a hammock over a fire, roasting. The men sit around. They dip their bloody fingers into tins of savoury biscuits. The smell of the burnt flesh pervades the cool night air." What images are our children growing up with?

Our nights are filled with the sound of gunshots and surreal dreams. Daylight astounds us as we wake. We feel ourselves spectres and phantoms, spirits emerging from the grave.

The attendance in my classes starts diminishing, especially the older students, the veterans of the 1971 insurgency who had returned to college. These were the students who I felt were more dedicated to their work. They had experienced so much that they were incapable of the youthful frivolity of some of my other younger students. Especially two of them, to whom I was very close. Perhaps they felt more able to relate to an older woman than their fresh-faced young classmates.

Sumedha had led a prison riot at Bogambara jail for better conditions for the political prisoners when he was imprisoned there after the 1971 insurgency. He showed me the bullet scars on his neck and told me stories of his prison experiences. "I got shot but escaped with my life. I was helped later on to get back to life after my release, with the help of a Roman Catholic priest . . . He said I should be a teacher, which is why I am here. . . ."

Sumedha was always irregular in attendance. Now, after the troubles started again, he began to disappear more regularly, sometimes for weeks. His home is in the village of Mahawa, in Wanni, the north central province of the island. I know the area well. My family has coconut plantations there. The 1971 insurgency had been deeply entrenched in that region. I think that he probably goes back to organize lectures for new recruits from his village. But I know he feels it is important for him to get his teacher's qualifications. So he suddenly came back to lectures, just before the examinations. "Madam, let's get on with the text. I've got to catch up with what I've missed."

I asked him once about how he felt about the failure of the insurgency, what it was that drove the young to sacrifice all. He was passionate in his explanation. "Madam, at least we have taken one step forward, for the revolution."

My other pupil who was in the 1971 insurgency is Saman. He told me that he was inculcated into the insurrection when he was very young. "I was in school. My teacher indoctrinated me. I was in one of the attacks on a police post. Was arrested. Spent six years in prison. Tortured. Strung up from the roof beams." He told me the story of how he was arrested. The boys had planned an attack on a police station. But the policemen had been forewarned and they were prepared for them. When the busload of students arrived the policemen were all in position, perched on the branches of trees around the station, camouflaged behind the leaves. They had shot a stream of bullets into the bus. By the end, the floor and seats were awash with blood. All the boys were killed or arrested. Saman also told me of his six-year ordeal in prison, and showed me some roughly-written pages about his experiences. I had sent the manuscript to an English literary journal, but it had not been accepted. As the troubles started again, Saman too became more and more irregular in attending classes.

Meanwhile, we tried to carry on classes as normal, tried to have our usual writers' workshops and seminars. But this resulted in a brutal reminder that all was not well as many academics and writers from Colombo and further away now refused to come to Kandy. They thought it was too dangerous. In the end, we were able to organize just one seminar. Ricardo, a young poet, actor and theatre director, came one day to talk about his favourite play, *The Merchant of Venice*. Ricardo was something of a cult figure—his poems and plays have provided a new and exciting cultural forum for many. For once, the lecture theatre was crowded in a way it had not been for months. In the corner, I saw both Saman and Sumedha.

Ricardo was riveting that night. With his richly resonant voice and charismatic personality, he presented the play to us in terms of the reality of our own lives and times. For us, he said, as for the Venetians, life was so frag-mented. For us, there was the revolution in the south as well as the ethnic conflict between the majority Sinhala community and the militant Tamil guerilla forces fighting for a separate homeland in the north and north-east of the island. But we should not let our vision be blinkered by where a per-son came from, he argued passionately. "Look at this room," he declaimed. "There are students from all the communities—Sinhalese, Tamils, Mus-lims. This is the kind of unity we need to aim for." The Christians of Venice were racist, he explained. They persecuted Shylock because he belonged to the minority Jewish community. I could see my students getting wide-eyed as they listened to him, the play taking on a new meaning in their eyes. Who could have known then that Ricardo would be abducted from his home one night, tortured and murdered? His bullet-ridden body would be dropped into the sea from a helicopter, and later washed ashore to be discovered by a fisherman.

Every evening, the lights went off in our housing colony. The roads too were dark. All doors were firmly locked and all windows shut in each house. Each householder had put up new protective barriers around his property. Some had built walls; others, like us, had propped up the sagging old iron gates and straightened the barbed wire fence to demarcate the boundary between ourselves and the world of threatening darkness outside. Those barriers would turn out to be too fragile. Nothing could withstand the radi-cal forces of the changing times. All traffic ceased after nightfall. The sound of each lone motorbike on the road brought a cold chilling sense of fear to the heart. But it always passed on, and we breathed a sigh of relief, yet felt compassion for the people of whichever house it had stopped in front of.

One evening, the motorbike stopped at our gate. The gate creaked open, dragging against the pebbles and sand with a rasping sound. Each of us, in our own rooms, raised our heads to follow the sounds. Footsteps, treading lightly, came towards the front door. Then there were light staccato taps on the wood, which sounded as if they were made by a clenched fist.

My husband emerged from the study where he was reading *An Historical Relation of Ceylon* by Robert Knox, who had been a prisoner in the Kandyan kingdom from 1659 to 1667.

"Who is this at such an ungodly hour?" I turned to him to ask softly.

"We shouldn't open the door to anyone," Raj was insistent.

Rima, my elder daughter, had not heard the sounds for she had been in the kitchen. Hearing our voices, she called out to us. "I've heated the food. It's on the table. Let's finish our meal early so that we can turn off the lights. We shouldn't attract attention to the house." She was a student at the University. When she received no response, she came out into the hall and saw us standing huddled there, staring at the silent door.

"Did someone knock on the door?" she asked us. We stood there, still silent.

"It must be one of them," she said. "They come at this hour generally."

There was a second knock on the door, more insistent this time.

"Open the door. We have to find out who it is," I told Raj.

"Don't open it! That would be folly!" Rima said. It was uncharacteristic for this calm daughter of mine to get agitated, but maybe she knew much more than we do about what was happening.

But Raj, murmuring "just investigate . . . ," had already turned the key in the lock, half-opened the door and was peering out into the darkness.

There are two figures on the threshold, two young men in leather jackets and crash helmets. The one in front was held up by the second one, who had one arm around his waist and the other behind his sagging shoulders.

I peered into their faces through the helmets. I recognized the one in front, it was Saman. The other, whose face was in the shadows, I did not know.

"It's Saman. One of my students. I know him," I told Raj.

Saman and his friend stood on the step at the door, and it was as if this was a scene from the past which I had read about and heard about, and which was now being enacted in front of me. It was not something I had ever imagined I would actually see. Saman slowly unzipped his jacket and removed his crash helmet with great effort. Blood had seeped from his wounds, his hair was caked with blood and mud.

His first words were tentative. "Madam, I need your help. I trust only you."

"Saman, where have you been all these weeks? You appear suddenly like this . . ." I said. I felt the futility of my question—where would he have been but with others from the movement? But I had no reaction adequate to the situation.

"Madam," he stammered, "madam, so many of us arrested . . . holding classes for the new recruits . . . others who were putting up posters . . . we were all taken to a detention centre, in a Roman Catholic college, opposite an army camp . . . Last night, ten of us were taken out of the city in a truck, far out into the countryside . . . We were all blindfolded, hands tied behind our backs . . . lined up . . . shot . . . several shots . . . I fell . . . felt bodies, limbs, twitching, writhing in the throes of death . . . So I lay there, pretending to be dead too . . . After a long time, they left. I waited even longer. Then I crawled into the undergrowth . . . huge leaves cool against my body . . . pain, blood, mine and that of those dead. Finally I got up. There was not a soul in sight. I staggered like a blind man along the stream, and reached Rohitha's place. He lives close by . . . Madam . . ."

Rohitha spoke out of the pool of darkness by the door. His words were clipped, but his voice was firm and authoritative. "Shelter for the night. Till we attend to the injuries. Shift him to a safe house tomorrow."

We were still all at the door, but we couldn't remain there forever. The blood splotch was growing larger on Saman's white shirt, a student's shirt. His face was ashen. "Madam," he pleads. "Madam, you taught us, remember? *The Merchant of Venice.* There is that bit in it: 'The quality of mercy . . . is not strained . . .'" In his exhaustion, the words come out slowly.

Rima had been standing quietly at the back, her stiff posture indicating her reluctance to have anything to do with Saman. Now suddenly she came forward to continue the lines Saman seemed to be too weak to quote:

"It droppeth as the gentle dew from heaven
Upon the place beneath. It is twice blessed. . . . "

Raj opened the door wider. We stretched out our hands to help Saman in. In this time of darkness, we need all the blessings which we can get.

Saman staggered into the drawing room. Rohitha turned away and vanished into the darkness. We closed the door and locked it. Outside, the motorbike revved up and departed. Silence enveloped our road again. We switched off all lights. I lit a candle and we led Saman into an inner room.

Tomorrow I will read the trial scene, act iv, scene i, of *The Merchant of Venice* with my students. I will refresh their memories of all that has gone before. And what will happen again and yet again.

The Great Divide

Antoinette Ferdinand

It is not uncommon to hear older generations of people in Sri Lanka talk about the kinds of social relations that existed between members of the various ethnic communities before the ethnic conflict became so politicized and violent. Antoinette Ferdinand captures their sentiments poignantly in this short story, but she also signals how those interactions are by now a lost artifact in Sri Lanka. This short story is especially affecting because of its setting in a refugee camp. In 2009, some half million Sri Lankans found themselves in refugee camps, nearly 5 percent of the country's total population.

"Here! Use this. You can keep it. I've another piece somewhere," said old Sathiyadevi, stretching out her hand towards Sumithra. In her palm lay a half-used stump of yellowish washing soap. Sumithra looked at the old lady, huddled in a corner of the large hall. In spite of the rags she wore, in spite of the dust and squalor around her, it was obvious there was refinement and character in her. The stamp of a grand old lady showed even through the ragged attire.

They were all refugees, living together in the large school hall which was their home for the time being. Sumithra had been about to take her two none-too-clean grandchildren—her daughter's little ones, to the common tap outside, to give them a wash. She'd been rummaging among her own bundled belongings, looking for the one piece of soap she had. It was not there now—probably filched by some other occupant. It was then that Sathiyadevi had uttered those words, offering her the soap.

Sumithra looked hesitantly at Sathiyadevi. Slowly, very slowly, she took the piece of offered soap. She made as if to move off. Then, instead of moving away at once, she turned to look at Sathiyadevi. A reluctant, gentle smile touched her lips. She was acknowledging at last, that she too, like Sathiyadevi remembered—remembered those days, long ago now, more than 30 years ago, when they had been in the same Convent school in Colombo together, in the same class, enjoying the fun of school life, as only those of the peaceful, pre-communal days knew how to; sharing together whatever they had, like sisters of one large happy family, sharing their books, their notes, their stationery, sharing everything, sometimes even their snacks and drinks.

And the words, "Here! Use this. You can have it!" had released a flood of hard-to-forget memories for them both. How many times had they said to one another, "Here! Use mine!" There had been no barriers then, nothing to divide them; there had been no hostilities then; nothing of this wretched suspicion or hatred they had now, when they looked at one another. Only gay camaraderie.

Sumithra walked slowly towards the tap outside, the two little ones, a boy and a girl, scantily dressed, hanging on to her. Back in the hall, Sathi-yadevi huddled closer into her corner, drawing the ragged bundle of her belongings towards her. In the minds of both women, both nearing fifty years of age now, the same memories persisted—the memories which those simple words had evoked.

What a cosmopolitan crowd of youngsters they had been! Sathiyadevi, of Jaffna-Tamil parents, staunch Hindus. Shyalini, also Jaffna-Tamil but Christian by faith. Sumithra, a Sinhala Buddhist. Doreen and Camille, the vivacious, fun-loving Burgher girls, Clarice, Laila, Reihana; so many of them— Tamil, Sinhala, Muslim, Burgher, Buddhist, Christian—but they had hardly thought of those divisions then. Those labels had hardly existed for them. It had not mattered at all. In class, they had all been one big happy group. Pretty, doe-eyed, quiet Laila had once been Virgin Mary at the Christmas tableau—and it was Sathiya's blue saree she had draped over her head. Sumithra and Chamari had sung a duet in the Chapel, and they had all been there to hear the lovely, lilting voices rise in praise of a God the two did not worship. At the social they had all borrowed clothes from Sathiya, Shyalini and Thiogini and come attired in traditional Tamil garb. The end-of-term concert, when Sathiya herself had acted a blushing Kandyan bride, dressed in Renu's sister's bridal attire. Prankster Doreen, always getting into hot water with the Irish nuns, Geraldine, who had wanted to fly a plane one day. What fun it had all been! How free, gay and happy-go-lucky, the lives they had led! No one had ever said, "You did this to our people," for they had all been one people then. No "Year this Tamil" or "Year that Sinhala." It had simply been standard this or that.

The halcyon days had passed gently. They had all been close to wom-anhood. The parting came and they had each gone their separate ways. Clever Laila to medical college, Thiogini to university, Doreen and Clarice to Australia with their families, Sathiyadevi had been the first of the clique to marry. Following the fortunes of the man chosen for her by her parents, she'd been to almost every corner of the island, and finally settled down in Vavuniya. Her memories from then on were bitter. Her son, her only child, much against his parents' wishes, had followed the rebellious dictates of his heart, had been a leader of a militant group, fighting for the freedom he believed in, until he had been relentlessly done away with by his enemies. Her husband, unable to bear the shock of seeing the battered, bullet-riddled body of his son, had succumbed to his grief soon after. But Sathiya had carried on, refusing all offers of help, all offers of friendship, shutting herself in, in her bitterness.

She remembered recognising Sumithra, when Sumithra first came to Vavuniya, with her daughter's family. Sumithra's son-in-law was a doctor in the forces. They had quarters close to the camp. She had seen Sumithra several times, driving along in an army jeep or car, with her daughter or grandchildren. But she had not wanted to renew that comradeship of long ago.

Then it had happened all so suddenly one weekend. Sumithra's daughter and son-in-law had both been away in Colombo. No one knew how, why or when it started. All they knew was utter pandemonium. They were fleeing from burning buildings, exploding gun fire—seeking shelter anywhere. They were all herded into this school hall, weeping children, wailing women, helpless men. Sumithra had been forced in there too, with the two bewildered children. Sathiya, alone, bitter, a hardened grudge against all humanity contracting her heart, clutched her bundled belongings as if clinging to all that was now family to her.

Sumithra, at the tap outside, washing the two children as best as she could, kept remembering the same events. She felt sorry for Sathiya, and she felt guilt too at having refused to recognise her. But she had had to be careful. She had not wanted to jeopardise her son-in-law's position in any way. There was so much suspicion and prejudice around. So, even after she had quietly found out Sathiya's sad story she had been careful not to communicate her sympathy in any way.

"I'll talk to her when I go in now," thought Sumithra. "Poor soul! How it must all have been for her! How lonely she must be now!"

Word had come to her that she and the two children were to be flown to safety anytime now. So she did not worry overmuch. She returned to the hall, and slowly, hesitantly, walked towards the corner where Sathiya sat. But the old woman had withdrawn into herself again. She lay huddled in her corner, her head buried in her arms, the fingers of her right hand clutching tightly at the bundle beside her. She looked up, just once, fleetingly, as Sumithra came up, but turned her face abruptly away again. "No!" she thought fiercely, "No, I won't talk to her again. Let her go away. I don't want her pity, her sympathy. Let her go away to safety, to her people!" And she buried her head deeper into her bundle. . . .

A Land Divided

Jean Arasanayagam

The prolonged ethnic conflict has alienated many from their ancestral lands in the war-wracked north. In this wistful, melancholy poem, Jean Arasanayagam reflects on her husband's childhood home, now separated from its centuries of familial tradition and in the hands of newly arrived others. That home had always been somewhat distant to her because she is Burgher by origin and her in-laws are high-caste Tamils. And yet the home somehow endures, through the rituals that the family once participated in and that continue to be performed there, without them. The poet captures for her readers how war transforms but cannot completely defeat culture.

Blueprint for a House

How can you rebuild an edifice that no longer
exists, that blueprint misplaced except in the
mind and imagination which searches for
those old historical maps of a family's beginnings?

But were those maps ever there, preserved with care,
and if they were, where are they now
with their carefully marked demarcations,
family names inscribed on that parchment
the land handed down from generation to generation
fruitful and yielding plentiful harvests with its
well of brimming water gushing from springs that
never went dry, each plot with the name of bygone ancestors.

Even if a new blueprint is created
is there space left to put up a new abode
on the vestigial remains of the old foundations?

Strangers now exist cheek by jowl with each other,
they have erected homes from their own memories

their own needs for shelter, for a roof over their
heads, for protection, escaping from the shambles
and debacles of wars where now a transit
point becomes permanent in their perpetual
migrations. (and their search for safe havens)

Moreover those hundreds and hundreds of
palmyrah trees have been razed to the ground.
When will the gouged out wounds heal?

The roots of the family tree struggle to survive,
roots wrenched out screaming with the pain of dismemberment
wrapped in the muddied blood of displacement and division.

The architecture of that structure from the past
changed with time, the vagaries of the climate,
the seasons, with their monsoon rains and parching
droughts, only the vague outlines appear mirage-like
in that denuded landscape.

Colours, textures, shape and form altered beyond
recognition, botched with age, discoloured plaster
peeling off in swaths before brick by brick
the ageing walls disintegrate.

The unblemished faces of youth peer from
behind those cracked glass frames, the photographs
blistered with the passage of the years are
things of the past, the living visages wrinkled
and lined, the once smooth brow furrowed and
grooved emerging from the sarcophagi of the past.

Pata's horoscope, his lifespan, his history
etched with sharp and pointed stylus in
an ancient script on dried and yellowing
leaf of palm is all that remains, his atman
dwelling far from this earthly plain.

In your mind perhaps you will place
those coconut wood pillars speckled and
grained, standing tall and straight and firm
in those imagined formations holding up the

heavy raftered roof closely set with earthen
tiles mossed with a green patina on red and
yellow ochre sun-dried and wood-fired.

Where is that structure that once upheld
a noble house, sheltered an un-warring people?

I recollect those pillars on an earlier visit
yet I cannot now with exactitude count
their numbers in my mindscape.

I had not gone to that village to wind
festive garlands round the pillars but
entered that house with an invisible guide-
book in my hands as if I had come to
view a world freshly discovered.

I had to know where their roots belonged,
roots of a family whose fortunes for better
for worse, I now shared, invited albeit
with reluctance to take my pick from those
over-brimming coffers filled with myth and legends,
lending a pliant ear to those perpetual monologues
laced with pithy asides and dramatic soliloquies
from my husband's recollections of those temple
presangams enacted on the stage during the
temple festivals night after night till early dawn,
epics from the Ramayana and the Mahabaratha,
the heroic deeds from the Puranas setting the blood
afire while from time to time the holy men and
swamis tramping from village to village entered
the grove sharing their homespun philosophies
with the family they parleyed with as they
prepared for the next lap of their journey,
without worldly possessions, travelling light.

The game is over now, the chequerboard swept
clean, a hand, that of a victor or of the defeated
sweeps off the battling chessmen, leaving that
microscopic world away.

The Pillars

They once stood in that open atrium
looking out upon the inner courtyard
with its pomegranate tree studded with
ripening fruit, half-hidden jewels in a
cusp of leaves, a golden slant of fish
dazzling a ripple in a breeze-starred
pond, the jasmine bush starred with
clustering white blossoms spreading their
fragrance through the pillared hall.

Who thought then that all would pass,
the bricks, the pillars, the tiles vanish bit by bit
leaving an empty abode exposed to inclement
weather, gaps in the disintegrating roof through
which sere leaves and withering blossoms fell
onto the cracked marble floors on which no
echoes of football or twinkling anklets could
ever be heard again.

Those inhabitants?
Did they for a moment think that their
lives would take migratory routes,
reach new destinations or wander homeless
through the waste of no-mans-land pock-marked
and weltered by the wounds of war?

Did they ever envisage a return to that
grove to gather the fruits of the land,
laving their bodies with margosa oil and sunning
their supple limbs, lathering themselves with ground
ciakka nut and cleanse themselves with sparkling
water from the well, their bodies tender and smooth
as young tamarind pods, a velvety sheen on the skins?

Only their dreams remain
Others perhaps who have wandered so far
Away, have lost their desire, the wish, to stir
those dying embers with the fire heart consumed
so that no flame flares up again, of remembrance.

Mirrors

Images rubbed off like water pictures leaving
a fleeting impression on the glass.
Reality. Fantasy.
A trickle of light reveals half-effaced
fragments, dream-like of those faces that gaze
at me then vanish, smudged lineaments are
all I see in the corroded glass.

Mirrors, cloudy, blurred with a fine overlay of dust.
My finger traces my imagined impressions
for a memory-book.

The womenfolk must have stood before those mirrors
combing out the oiled strands of hair for braiding
or knotting up, coils resting on the nape of the
neck, blue-back with silvery glints.

My mother-in-law placing the kumkumum on the
straight parting of her hair with its shimmer
of vermilion, the third-eye pottu placed coin-
shaped on her forehead, the ever-dutiful matriarch
of that family, maintaining the rituals and traditions
preserver of a sacred trust, dispensing the customary
offerings to all the deities, interpreting her dreams,
praying and making her poojas, the hereditary trustee
of an inheritance which I, the outsider was to rifle through,
never yet myself becoming an incumbent of that temple.

The Rooms

Those bedrooms choc-o-bloc with furniture
bedsteads ranged against the walls, bedheads
profuse with carvings, birds, tendrilling vines,
grape clusters, old stuffed, cotton mattresses covered
with blue and white ticking faded and dusty
with tufts of cotton fluff and coir strands peeping
out through the fraying cloth.

Through the open windows while the womenfolk
slept and dreamed, fragrance crept in from the

jasmine bushes and margosa trees and at night
curtains were drawn to cover mirrors to screen
off fantasies and apparitions in sudden wakening from
startled dreams, the huge teak almirah locked,
the dressing table with innumerable drawers once,
filled with everyday garments and linen, empty now.

And the next room filled with pettagams
in which brass, silver, copper vessels, chembus
trays, kuthuvillaku were preserved with care.
Whether they were used or not, inventorized possessions.

How much polishing they must have needed,
first, a thin layer of ash and lime applied
on the surfaces again and again, rubbed off
with wads of soft old cloth until the gleam and
shine appeared to reflect a glittering face,

iron safes with heavy keys containing wealth,
gold sovereigns, English banknotes, heirloom jewellery,
Deeds of land and property ownerships, Wills,
family documents, maps of territory owned,
genealogies, all the paraphernalia of lineage.

Everything's vanished.
Possessions vanished.
How long will that lineage be preserved?

Routes

Can they ever be retraced, those routes?
Journeys taken in the past, arrivals, departures,
returns assured. Nothing, nothing is certain now.
No one who belonged to that family can go there,
Embark on the new hazards such travels would entail.

Inner courtyards are a thing of the past, a place
for malingering, sitting on the thinnai and listening
to the recital of epics and spreading a mat to lie on,
feeling the cool breezes, all this belongs
to the narratives of lost generations,
the land is crowded now with strangers

to whom family names, inheritance, lineage
mean nothing.

the creation of those personal epics matter
not a whit to those who've stated new claims
where Deeds and Wills do not exist, fit only for
archival memories lost in the pillage of wars.

Who cares now about caste,
who cares about those ancient royal names,
power has slipped off their grasp never to be
reclaimed, the gold-edged shawls, the elephants,
the palanquins, where are they now,
the naked sole of the wanderer tramps on the
burning land, the sandal thongs long given way.

Temple Rituals

I make no claims that I belong to their hierarchy.
I can name myself. Interloper, but I'm no imposter,
no importunate pleader, all I am is that unofficial
scribe who receives no emolument for my labour,
the documentor of an history no one wants to recall,
however for me, it's all grist to the mill and the
terrain, certainly harsh and uneven tenanted by
inhospitable inhabitants yielded much scope for the
intrepid explorer.

I pitched my tent joining the caravanserai of
Nomadic wanderers, made my expeditions
travelling into a mapless land where I came upon
hidden, secret knowledge known only to the mystics
and visionaries of the past, those ancient prophets
of the wilderness interpreting the portents of Yahweh.

I shifted the rocks and stones that impeded my
path, compelled by a superhuman strength I never knew
never had possessed before in that past,
deciphered with the new powers that entered
my imagination, a script of a people whose
history stemmed form the Agni-worshippers
in those pre-Vedic times.

But why do all these thoughts come into my mind?
This time it's because a snapshot comes in an envelope
sent from that village in the North, a picture of the
hoisting of the temple flag initiating the traditional
ceremonies for Pillaiyar held by that family generation
after generation never forgotten, never abandoned
in all these years.

It was Pata, my beloved father-in-law, the only one
I loved in that imperious family who, year in,
year out, who for well over half a century, hoisted
that flag, now I see many of the temple priests
unfurling those heavy white folds of cloth, suspend
it from the Kodimaram surrounded by devotees
with hands folded in reverance and supplication,
pleading hands beseeching Pillaiyar for protection
to preserve their lives and those of their families
outstretched in worship those hands both young and old.

My husband looks hard at the snapshot
"Oh, how that simple temple has changed," he exclaims.
The walls were plain, whitewashed once, now it's
embellished with murals of the deities, the statue of Pillaiyar
bedecked with flower garlands freshly plucked
from gardens and groves, decorations suspended form vaulted ceilings.

I can never return in this lifetime
to perform these rites and rituals but they will always
continue for as long as the people not only of the village
but those who have found refuge here leaving
their war-ravaged villages, still have life and breath.

One can see it's a prosperous temple now,
the young pusari domiciled in Canada,
comes over for the annual flag-raising ceremonies,
performs the ritual with the older left-behind
priests and all of us send the expenses for the
festival, perhaps donations are also given by those
who have taken over the land, most of them have
relatives living abroad who send remittances
for their survival.

It's a truly ancient temple, goes back centuries
perhaps to those eras of the early South Indian
invasions. The Cholas? The Pandyans? The Cheras?
It has belonged to our family for generations.
The younger ones have all gone away
there are new names for their migrations and for
themselves, diasporic journeys, asylum seekers,
no one speaks of the pain of exile and homelessness
of the schizophrenia of migrants, of the trauma of
displacement, of murderous, destructive dreams
and transformations.

Who is there to recite the epics or is there silence?
Is it because there is no one left to remember
that past or is because the deeds of ordinary
people and their sagas of survival have taken
over, form the new epics?

My own entrance into family enclaves left me too
an outsider, I was a mere visitant entered
that temple as a visitant where my husband
worshipped, listened to all those stories, a wealth
of stories stored, in his memory from his childhood
in the village, from his mother, from the family
history so that for me knowledge of that other world
grew, a world which at first I knew nothing of.

I listened, the language in which the deities
Were addressed resonated in my ears.

I felt I had placed tentative footsteps in
Kailasa, found it a comfortable place
in which to retreat to even meditate in,
remembered Mt. Kailasa of my Indian journey
that rock cave filled with sculptured deities
from a long forgotten time, began to understand
the beliefs of the family, their faith, their veneration
which helped their pada yatra, their pilgrimages
through life and although the white pavadai would never
be spread for me to tread on my arrival never
heralded by thavil and nadhesweran

When my younger sister-in-law's marriage
procession trod on yard after yard of
white cloths I was not invited to join
that family entourage but lurked, half-
concealed, behind a pillar.

I wouldn't do that now
I've learned to do away with all impediments
circumvent the obstacles, kick them out of the way
iconoclastic of all the obstructions that would halt my journey.
No one bothered to explore my identity
to find out who I was so I could try out
countless nom-de-plumes, adopt different
personae, take on aliases, camouflage myself,
engage in subversion or espionage, it would
not have mattered to anyone really
never then, never now too humdrum
to be recorded in the family annals.

New Landscapes

Did I once come here to view great spectacles
of history?

Did my eyes create new landscapes loaded
with symbols, seeks through language the metaphors
to describe an inheritance totally alien to me?

So have I wandered through great houses
in the past in other countries, name them now
in memory, Chatsworth, Colquhoun, Edinburgh Castle, Reed Hall,
country houses, palaces, castles, gazed my fill of portrait
galleries, each portrait belonging to epochs and eras,
huge historical canvases bearing emblems of monarchs
and aristocracies, clothed in full royal regalia with elaborate
trappings, those epic narratives connected to my life
through imperial adventurers and expeditions.

Entering spacious salons and bed chambers
walking endless miles of carpeted corridors
I observed the artifacts of kings, queens, plenipotentiaries,

the cloisonné, ormolu, intricately carved chinoiserie,
priceless jewels, heirlooms, the Chippendale and Louis
Quatorze, cultures that entered those empires through
imperial acquisition of land and territory
indestructible unless you perceive that the ravages of
time have left their mark with the Fall of Empires
and the depredations of marauding invaders.

Still, even to this day, anxious ghosts hover reluctant
to leave their homing grounds, I feel their breath
touch my shoulders, in my ears a soft susurrus
of silken robes as their trains and hems sweep the floor.

Taken I was to view those towering edifices,
those thousand thousand acres, parks, forests
teeming with game, deer, wild boar, pheasants,
the fleeing fox pursued by slavering hounds
sport for brute hunters wearing the camouflage of
decadent civilizations, the primitive predator
instincts barely concealed as they dug their spurs
into the flanks of their horses, goading them on.
I walked beneath bowers, paused by rose gardens
flowerbeds ordained by a metaphysical hierarchy,

fountains spraying a rainbow iridescence over the lawns,
gazebos, hot houses, green houses, tropical gardens
proliferated, ponds replete with fish swans, mallard
ducks, nothing miniature in proportion, a world
that screened off the slaves toiling, perishing in the mines
prising out the precious ores of gold and silver.

What remembrances do I take back with me
jars of conserves, preserves, home-made cakes
and sweets from the well-stocked kitchens of
the Stately Homes on my grand tours of the
one-time empire builders, tasting the flavour
of afternoon tea, Darjeeling, Typhoo, Orange Pekoe
from the empire's tea gardens, silver and porcelain
laid out on occasional tables on the green lawns
where the colonials played croquet while
empires rose and fell.

Now far from those historical expeditions
I think of my husband's family and their
possessions, looking back on my non-punitive
excursions into territory I had no wish to acquire.

I did not ever desire to carry off booty
from their well-filled coffers nor did I
wish to share the bounty of the land
yet today my progeny question me
"Why was our birthright denied us,
Why were our names left out when the family
land was apportioned out among the heirs,
was our father too not one of the sons and heirs,
entitled to his inheritance?"

Is it because that family never forgave his
act of rebellion, thought it a transgression
against the sacred norms of their hierarchy
our hybridity unacceptable within its kinship?

With time that land became a lost horizon
yet those who went away on journeys of no return
thought that the maps would never change.

That dispossession was not by their own volition
but swept away by the great cataclysmic
cascades of war and those displaced by the
wars became the new invaders undeterred by
checkpoints, the barriers of caste and lineage
only remembered myths and symbols, that massive
iron gate that stood at the entrance to the grove
keeping all and sundry out so that no new claimants
could raise the clamour of their vociferous pleas
no longer stood as a barrier
no longer held back those who sought
refuge and haven there.

What if you were to return braving the landmines
and the heavy shelling?

What if you were to return
no one would care to even recognize
or even acknowledge you,

What if you were to say,
"All this belongs to me, our family, documented
for centuries in the Deeds, we are the heirs."

"Once," they may say, "once but not any longer.
It's we who draw the new design for the kolam
on our thresholds the symbols that your ancestor
drew those traditional designs have changed
but we still pick the jasmines off the bushes for
our poojas and weave the garlands for Pillaiyar our Protector,
gather in the harvest of honey-sweet mangoes,
drink of the water from the well that is ever
replenished from its source, pick the kindling
from the grove to light our hearths,

Even from far away my husband hears
the echoes of the clashing cymbals, the plangent
notes of ragas from the nadhesweran, the thud
of drums, the bhakti cries the haro hara to Pillaiyar
voices singing thevaram, the priests chanting slokas.

My husband recalls,
"An old Dutch road runs past that temple,
those seventeenth-century invaders carved out
their conquest routes even at that time."

Nothing really has changed.
Invasions. Conquests. Acquisition of territory
still part of history, the soldiers trod those
paths in their march to the next stage of their
journey.

Nothing really has changed.
One day will the new wars
become legends, epics?

And to those seeking refuge from the line
of battle, sheltering beneath sparse-leaved
trees, bellies hollow with hunger, thirsting
for fresh water, will traditions, rites and
rituals, genealogies and lineage matter
as they flee from the shelling and the crossfire
travelling light as the swamis did in the
past tramping from village to village?

Neither Sinhala nor Tamil—
On Being a South Asian in Sri Lanka

Sree Padma

The ethnic conflict has seriously tested political relations between India and Sri Lanka, especially following the 1987 Indo-Lanka Accord, when thousands of Indian troops were deployed to the north and northeast of the island to secure these regions, first from the Sri Lankan Army and then from Tamil militant groups, especially the LTTE (Liberation Tigers of Tamil Eelam). When, in the early 1990s, the rise of the JVP (Janatha Vimukthi Peramuna, or People's Liberation Front) in the Sinhala regions of the south was fueled by the presence of these troops, President Premadasa asked the Indian troops to leave the island. Political relations have since been somewhat strained (owing to the delicate position maintained by India's central government because of domestic politics in Tamilnadu), but cultural relations still run very deep between India and Sri Lanka. Since 1985, however, the limits imposed on travel between the countries have meant that many Sri Lankans, especially most Sinhalese, have little first-hand knowledge or experience of India or Indians. Moreover, the limited scope of historical education in Sri Lankan schools has restricted broader awareness of South Asia in general. In the memoir that follows, the author reflects on the ambivalence among the Sinhalese in Sri Lanka toward some aspects of Indian culture.

Born and raised in Andhra Pradesh, India, as a Telugu female, I have always been very secure about my own identity. That is, until the moment arrived for me to pass through a security checkpoint on my first visit to Sri Lanka. As we approached, our driver, staring at the mark on my forehead, suggested that I should remove my *bindi* (a red dot on the forehead, variously called *sindhur* and *tilak*, worn traditionally by Hindu females as a sign of auspiciousness) in order to not raise any suspicions among the military guards. I then realized that wearing the bindi in Sri Lanka among the Sinhalese means declaring one's identity as Tamil. I did not want to posture as a Tamil. Neither did I want it assumed that I was other than Hindu. In India, usually it is only Christian and Muslim women who do not wear the bindi. Nonetheless, I removed the bindi and, by doing so, unknowingly passed a threshold of uncertainty about who I was and how I was to be regarded in this country.

When I first came to Sri Lanka, I had not paid much attention to India's protectionist attitude towards Sri Lanka, this small island country in what India considers its own "backyard." I was also unaware of Sri Lanka's ambivalence towards India: its Sinhalese Buddhist majority treats the north of India as a sacred land, but at the same time sometimes seems suspicious of New Delhi's political motives. Culture and politics do not always mesh. Moreover, I was not altogether well-informed about the depth of contemporary Sri Lanka's ethnic problems either. Ancient history being my professional focus, I assumed that both Tamils and Sinhalese in Sri Lanka shared and celebrated their cultural roots with India. Most significantly, I had almost no notion of how many Sinhalese seem to have very little knowledge about India or how they might share in a larger south Asian culture. It was also not immediately apparent to me how four hundred years of European presence in Sri Lanka had put pressure on Sri Lankans to reinvent their own identities.

As I made more visits to Sri Lanka, again and again I faced the same question about who I was. I could hold many different possible identities in the eyes of the Sinhalese I met: sometimes they guessed Pakistani, other times north Indian, a few times I was referred to as an "Andhra Tamil!" or even, on occasion, of being an elite from Colombo 7. When I acquired some measure of Sinhala, I would sometimes answer the inevitable questions about where I came from with "Mama Sinhala wage." ("I am Sinhala-like.") But I could also then feel the unstated response: "Eya Sinhala wage nae!" ("She is not like a Sinhala.")

Buddhism Runs in Our Veins

My first visits to Sri Lanka were during anything but quiet times. Although Sri Lankan Tamil nationalism had made its deadly mark on Indian soil with the assassination of our prime minister, Rajiv Gandhi, just a few months before, and the Sri Lankan president Ranasinghe Premadasa was subsequently assassinated, I was always eager to return to Sri Lanka. This was due, no doubt, to my own background as a researcher studying ancient Buddhist sites in Andhra Pradesh and the knowledge I had gained over the years about Andhra's intense cultural interactions with Lankan Buddhists historically.

Amaravati, one of the early Buddhist sites in Andhra that thrived for six centuries from the third century BCE, is famous for being a genesis of the Mahasamghika school of monasticism, a sect that encouraged some of the earliest consecrated standing Buddha figures in preaching, teaching, and meditation poses. The style of these images came to be known as the Andhra, or better, the Amaravati school of art that influenced the art of many Buddhist communities in South and Southeast Asia, the prime example being third-century CE images of Anuradhapura. Inscriptions at Nagarjunakonda, another famous Buddhist site in Andhra, refer to a monastery dedicated exclusively to monks coming from Sri Lanka. Archaeological finds in Sri Lanka, on the other hand, prove that many sculptural representations carved in green-hued limestone specific to the Krishna River Valley of Andhra were imported into Sri Lanka for ritual use in Anuradhapura's famous Buddhist monasteries. They have also been found at Sigiriya, Kurunegala, Trincomalee, and Kuccaveli. Knowing these early Buddhist connections, I was excited when I actually saw saffron-robed monks and met lay people who sincerely venerate the Buddha. Although Buddhism had been a dominant religion in Andhra until at least the third century CE, it gradually gave way to Jainism, Saivism, and Vaishnavism, leaving almost no trace except in its archaeological ruins and in its abstract philosophical influence on Hindu thought. An average Hindu in contemporary Andhra may acknowledge the Buddha as an incarnation of Vishnu if the Buddha's image is placed in one of the avatar niches of temples dedicated to Vishnu. But that is the extent of his veneration. Also, it is a common understanding in India that Buddhism, like Vedic religion, is a kind of resplendent marker in the evolution of Indian cultural history that has contributed to contemporary Hindu religious understandings. Buddhism is regarded as an integral part of our own heritage. During my first visits to Sri Lanka, I was blissfully unaware of how the expression of this Indian sentiment could offend some Buddhists in Sri Lanka. Neither was I aware that although the Sinhalese have preserved many Pali Buddhist chronicles, including the *Dipavamsa*, *Mahavamsa*, and *Culavamsa*, and have cultivated a keen historical consciousness based on these texts, they do not necessarily share a wider south Asian historical consciousness, nor do they emphasize their own historical roots on the subcontinent. So, what I came to know was that while I considered Buddhism as part and parcel of my historical past, many Sinhalese had a penchant for defining themselves over and against Hindu India. Buddhism is not what links us, but instead what separates them from us. Coming from Andhra, I felt that Buddhism was an affinity that I share with the Sinhalese and so did not think of them as "other" to me. But I was definitely regarded as "other" to them. From their perspective, their Buddhism was the difference between us.

Love or Hate or Both?

Another apparent gaffe on my part was my tendency to report to friends how my experiences in Sri Lanka were similar to visiting neighboring Indian states, or to visiting Kerala, Gujarat, or Bengal. What I meant by this was that although people in different states in India speak different languages, eat different food items, and, at times, follow different ritual traditions, they share a bulk of culture that is common throughout India. While Hinduism, Buddhism, Sikhism, and Jainism may be different religions, they share much of the same religious vocabulary. Moreover, throughout South Asia, people also share somewhat similar appearances and mannerisms. They carry their body postures in certain recognizable ways. They shake their heads in similar fashion. They walk and eat in the same ways. Taking my first trips on Sri Lankan roads, the familiar sight of Bajaj three wheelers, old Tata buses, and lorries, clubbed with Sri Lankans strolling along the roads resembling their Indian counterparts in recognizable mannerisms and gestures made me feel anything but foreign.

In the early 1990s, some of the same Hindi "teledramas" ("soap operas") were being telecast in Sri Lanka just as they were throughout India. These were still early times for TV culture, before the production of soap operas in more local languages. So, in non-Hindi states where Hindi is taught in high schools (with the exception of Tamil Nadu, where it is not), the audience who glued themselves to TV sets had the opportunity to improve their Hindi skills. At least, this was the case in Andhra. In Sri Lanka, I noticed how some of my Sinhala friends had taken a liking to Hindi soap operas and watched them very intently. They often appeared spellbound by the action, the story, the dialogues, etc. I remember one instance in which, knowing the fascination of one of my Sinhala friends towards these Hindi serials, I wanted to humor her in Hindi. By doing so, I hoped to see her face light up in just the same way. To the contrary, she looked very puzzled. I repeated myself to be more audible. This time, in addition to her puzzled expression, she signaled with hand gestures that she did not understand what I was saying. So, it was my turn to be puzzled. There was a Sinhala attraction to things Indian, but not necessarily a deep understanding.

Sinhala, as an Indo-European language, shares a linguistic affinity with the north Indian group of languages from which it stems, although it also has some influence from Tamil. In this sense, Sinhala is probably unique: while speakers of non-Hindi languages in north India, for instance Marathi, Gujarati, Oriya, or Bengali, have some familiarity with Hindi, Sinhalese do not seem to have any familiarity. No doubt this is due to geographic and political realities. Nevertheless, I often have encountered Sinhala youth who, in thinking I was north Indian, were very friendly and told me how much they loved Hindi. They beg me to speak a few phrases, as if it is some melodious song that they would like to hear. I did, of course, gather that this fascination came from watching Hindi movies and soap operas. Nevertheless, I did have to wonder: if they knew me to be from south India and not north, would they have been as friendly and endearing?

While I have always lived with Sinhala people in Kandy, one of our Tamil neighbors used to bring us snacks in the form of idli, vada, dosai, etc. I asked our Sinhala cook whether she could prepare any of these food items. Not only did she not know how to make them, but also she was completely unfamiliar with their key ingredient: *urundu dal* (black gram). Neither she, nor any of my other Sinhala friends, seemed to know how to make curd either, which completely surprised me since curd is so commonly made throughout India. On the other hand, I would imagine that Sri Lankan Tamils might not be familiar with some quintessentially Sinhala food items either. In just the same way as many Tamil food items are similar to other south Indian cuisines, Sinhala food items are similar to Kerala cuisine. So, I was surprised to know how few of my Sinhala friends were aware that many Sinhala dishes, such as *appa* ("hoppers") and *indiappa* ("string hoppers") are also Keralite dishes. Neither are many aware that the traditional sarong and blouse they wear is also a traditional Kerala costume. This puzzled me because of Kerala's close proximity. It would be interesting to know whether these "disconnects" occurred during colonial times.

So Near and Yet So Far

By studying the history of cultural relations between India and Southeast Asian countries, I have been made aware of the popularity of Indian epic literature (the *Mahabharata* but especially the *Ramayana*) outside of the Indian sub-continent. The *Ramayana* lives in the popular consciousness of these Southeast Asian countries in such a way that even in a majority Muslim country like Indonesia, the story is treated as if it is a national epic. The *Ramayana* has thrived in Burma, Thailand, Laos and Cambodia, all sharing a nominally Theravada Buddhist religious culture with the Sinhalese. So, when I was traveling in Sri Lanka and came across place names such as Ravana Falls, my immediate assumption was that the Sinhalese, because of their proximity and cultural ties with India (not to mention the ubiquitous belief that Sri Lanka was Ravana's Lanka), would know these epics very well too. It was astonishing for me to find out how few Sinhalese are aware of these epics. My surprise was heightened further when I attended in Kandy a performance of Jayadeva's *Gita Govinda* by a troupe of Kathak dancers from India. The performance was attended by many people from the university community who were given a detailed explanation for each of the items performed. Performed by highly talented artists, it was an aesthetic feast to behold, but unfortunately I realized that it made very little impact upon my scholarly friends. As though to lift my spirits, a monk-scholar, with his knowledge of Sanskrit, came by to share with me his appreciation of the play. Over the years, I have sensed that those in Sri Lanka who know something about Indian Hindu literature are limited to those who have studied Sanskrit and Pali formally, or those who belonged to an older generation of well-read scholars.

However, there are some exceptions to this pattern. The quintessential south Indian dance, Bharata Natyam, which is accompanied by Sanskrit, Telugu, Tamil, and Kannada songs, is widely patronized by contemporary middle-class Sinhala families. Not as popular as Bharata Natyam dance, south Indian music, along with north Indian Hindustani classical music, is also patronized by the Sinhalese middle class to some extent. Whether Indian movies and television play a role in this popularity is an interesting question. But the reality is that classical Indian dance and music employ themes from the epics and *Puranas* almost exclusively, and by not knowing this literature, only a very partial appreciation of these arts is possible.

Sinhalese Historical Consciousness

In Sinhala (and even some English) medium schools, students are taught the island's history basically as it appears in the *Mahavamsa*. The *Mahavamsa* is a venerable text, but it is, at best, what the Theravada Buddhist monastic community has wanted to remember about what past kings on the island have been able to do for the religion. It certainly sinks a deep shaft into Sri Lankan history, but being a very clear example of history written with a specific motive, it is not wide-ranging by any standard. Consequently, there is very little in school textbooks about how the island has shared aspects of its culture with south India since pre-historic times. Very little is known to an average Sri Lankan about how various groups from Kerala, Tamil Nadu, and other parts of India have come to Sri Lanka and have been assimilated into the island's evolving communities. There is also very little discussion of how for more than three centuries, starting from the early thirteenth century, Jaffna and the Vanni were isolated from the rest of the island under the influence of rulers (*aryacakravartis*) who came from south Indian Tamil regions. It is also never emphasized that the Jaffna peninsula, because of its proximity to Tamil Nadu, was influenced by continuous waves of Saivism and Vaishnavism, while the east coast developed into yet another unique cultural zone with predominantly Keralite populations who brought elements of Vaishnavism. While it is emphasized how the rest of Sri Lanka retained the vitality of its strong Buddhist past and acted as a bastion for the Theravada Buddhist world, very little emphasis is given to the ethnic diversity of the Kandyan kingdom, the last of the indigenous dynasties, with its various migrant groups coming from Kerala, Tamil Nadu, and even at times from Andhra and Karnataka, people who arrived in different periods as mercenaries, merchants, and even as administrators and rulers. These populations mixed thoroughly with the majority Sinhalese eventually becoming Buddhists while enriching Kandyan culture by introducing the salience of so many new cultural traits whose origins are now forgotten. It seems as if only the Muslims retained their distinctiveness in that context. Perhaps the European colonial presence on the island changed historical consciousness dramatically. Especially when the British started administering the whole island from Colombo, more general group consciousness along the lines of language and religion, and culture was enhanced. It was in this context that Sinhalese and Tamils began to reach deep and exclusively into their perceived unique and isolated pasts to generate wholly distinctive national identities. Unfortunately some of them began forging fragmented historical consciousnesses that lay claim to an exclusive ownership of the unitary whole of the island.

I cannot blame Sinhala people for not including or embracing me in just the way I had expected or hoped that they would. And I realize that Sri Lanka is not simply derivative of India; it is, indeed, its own unique mix. But it is a mix that has been called home by many who have come, ultimately, from disparate regions of the subcontinent. So, it is indelibly linked to the Indian subcontinent, despite some of the recent strident claims that emphasize its separateness.

Female Labor Migration from Sri Lanka to the Middle East

Michele Ruth Gamburd

Because of limited economic opportunities (in spite of the "open" economy), and in part a consequence of the ongoing ethnic conflict, 20 percent of Sri Lanka's foreign earnings come from remittances from overseas workers. Two-thirds of those workers are women who toil in countries of the Middle East. The social and cultural consequences of this economic reality, as the long-time visitor and anthropologist Michele Gamburd writes, are prodigious and far-reaching.

Introduction. When discussing international migration of labor, several issues arise. The first is the common conception of "push and pull" factors: why are people willing to leave their own country, and why do they seek work in a particular destination? Another concerns the social structures (gender relations, household organization, class stratification) that facilitate migration, and the effects that migration has on these.

History. One cannot understand local dynamics without attention to global context. Understanding "the push and pull" factors involved with Sri Lankan migration to the Middle East requires a brief discussion of global economics.[1]

Why are people willing to leave Sri Lanka to work elsewhere? The answer lies in economic necessity. It is not easy to leave familiar places and beloved family and friends. Migrants usually say that they go abroad because they cannot make ends meet in Sri Lanka, or—even if they can make ends meet—that they are unable to get ahead. Families often see migration as a good strategy to procure money for one-time, large-scale purchases. Most migrant women state that they wish to buy land and build a house. They calculate that they can earn us$4,000–5,000 to accomplish this goal by working for four or five years in Saudi Arabia, Kuwait, or the UAE. In addition to housing, people often spend money on children's education, daughters' dowries, or business ventures.

Why do people feel that they need to go overseas to earn this money? This answer lies in Sri Lanka's position in the world economic system and how neoliberal capitalist dynamics affect both national and international economies. Like many other developing nations, Sri Lanka is deeply indebted. In the 1970s and 1980s, the country received loans for development. The expected development failed to happen, yet the loans remain. The International Monetary Fund stepped in to implement Structural Adjustment Programs (SAPS). SAPS are economic austerity policies designed to help a country repay its debt. These programs open the economy to international investment while simultaneously curtailing government spending on price subsidies, health care, education, and social security networks. Poor families, particularly women and children, feel the adverse effects of SAPS more than wealthier people do. As it becomes more difficult to make a living locally, poor people see labor migration as an increasingly viable and attractive option.

Another cause of Sri Lanka's difficult economic circumstances is the ongoing ethnic conflict, which has spoiled the atmosphere for international investment, dampened enthusiasm in the tourist market, and driven the government of Sri Lanka deeply into debt for the purchase of military equipment. But the war has created employment opportunities for poor young men. Increasingly, poor men enlist in the army; women work in garment factories or take jobs in the Middle East as "housemaids," as domestic servants are referred to in both English and Sinhala.

What exactly pulls people to the Gulf? The answer: oil, and the money made from its sale on the international market. The Organization of Petroleum Exporting Countries (OPEC) raised the price of oil in 1973, and money began to flow into West Asia. Foreign laborers soon followed the money. In 1976, laborers from Sri Lanka started to go to West Asia, with men working as heavy machinery drivers, masons, carpenters, and electricians, providing labor for a construction boom. Since then, ever-increasing numbers of guest workers have flooded into the Middle East from Sri Lanka and many other countries.

As part of a newly affluent and leisurely lifestyle, households in the Middle East soon began to employ domestic servants, and the early 1980s saw the beginning of female labor migration from Sri Lanka. Women go abroad predominantly as domestic servants, although some also work in garment factories. The numbers of Sri Lankan guest workers has increased steadily. In 2005, the Sri Lanka Bureau of Foreign Employment reported that over 1.2 million registered Sri Lankans were working abroad, 89 percent of them in the Gulf (SLBFE 2006: 57). Few registered migrants come from the country's north and east; most come from the heavily populated southwest (SLBFE 2006: 28). During the last twenty-five years, the majority of migrants have been women. In 2005, two-thirds (800,000) of the estimated stock of overseas contract workers were women (SLBFE 2006: 57). The high representation of women reflects demand for particular workers in the Middle East. There are also jobs for men (such as chauffeurs, gardeners, grocery stock boys, and air conditioner technicians), but these are scarcer, and therefore more expensive to procure.

Getting a job and working abroad. There are two ways for a Sri Lankan woman to get a job abroad. One is to work through a job agency; the other is to work through informal connections. Women procure "agency jobs" as follows. When a sponsoring family in the Gulf wants to hire a domestic servant, they go to a job agency. The agency in the Gulf is in touch with job agencies in labor-sending countries. The Philippines, Indonesia, and Sri Lanka are the main countries sending women to work in the Gulf. In Sri Lanka, women interested in working as housemaids get in touch with job agents, sometimes through a local subagent. A woman fills out an application for a job, and the Sri Lankan agency sends this information to its contact agencies abroad. When a sponsor in the Gulf selects the woman's application, the two job agencies arrange for the woman to get a passport and a visa, undergo preliminary job training, pass a medical test, and purchase an airline ticket. The woman flies to the host country, the agent delivers her to her employers, and the woman's two-year contract begins.

Sinhala-Buddhist women pay job agents US$300 to procure a job. Muslim women often go abroad without paying fees. This reflects demand in the Middle East, where sponsors may pay US$400 for a non-Muslim housemaid and US$800 for a Muslim housemaid. The fees paid by the sponsors are supposed to cover all the women's expenses, with a signing bonus for Muslim women, but extralegal charges whittle the Muslim women's bonus down to nothing and add extra charges to be paid out of pocket by the non-Muslim women. Most migrant women do not have enough cash on hand to pay the agent. Since the prospective migrants are poor and have no collateral to offer for a loan, banks refuse to lend to them. Women turn to informal moneylenders, who charge high rates of interest. Migrants often pay back twice what they borrow; having taken $300, women will often repay a moneylender $600. Since women make on average $100 a month, this means that they will work half a year to pay for their job placement.

Because of the expenses involved with "agency jobs," both domestic servants and sponsors prefer to arrange overseas employment through a second, less formal strategy: "ticket jobs." A sponsor interested in hiring a servant can talk with friends or relatives to find out if any of their house-maids know someone in Sri Lanka who is interested in working abroad. If a suitable person can be found, the sponsor will arrange a ticket and visa for the new housemaid, and she can fly to the Gulf without the aid of an agency. The recipient of a "ticket job" usually pays $200 to the housemaid who arranged the job. This fee comes out of the arriving housemaid's first two months' wages, so she does not need to borrow from a moneylender. The providing housemaid often waives the fee for close friends and family members. Ticket jobs are cheaper for the sponsors, too; they pay only the airfare and the charges for procuring a visa.

Abroad, a housemaid's work is often difficult and dull. Domestic servants prepare and cook food, do laundry, clean bathrooms, vacuum and sweep the house, dust and polish furniture, look after gardens, pets, livestock, and ve-hicles, and care for children and the elderly. Domestic servants live in their sponsors' homes, and are on call at all times of the day and night. They often report working for sixteen or more hours a day, and they rarely receive days off, despite the wording of the contracts (written in Arabic and English) that they sign when hired. Isolated in homes, far from friends and relatives, and speaking little Arabic when they first arrive, these women workers occupy a vulnerable position. Advocacy workers estimate that up to 20 percent of do-mestic servants face abusive situations. The most common complaints are nonpayment of the agreed wages, lack of contact with family, and physical and sexual harassment (SLBFE 2006: 61).

The system does contain some protections for migrant women. For those who go abroad on "agency jobs" and run into trouble, host-country agents will in theory find other sponsors for housemaids or send them home free of charge during the first three months. But the agencies lose money through failed placements. Job agents therefore often seek to keep women in unfa-vorable situations until the three-month period has passed, after which the woman has to pay her own airfare home. Women who go abroad on "ticket jobs" can appeal to the housemaid who arranged the employment, but she too is in a relatively powerless situation and cannot provide much help. Women feel, however, that going abroad on a "ticket job" is safer than trust-ing an agency, since the contact housemaid can learn something about the host family before deciding whether she thinks they would make good em-ployers. Women who run into untenable situations can call the agency, the police, or the Sri Lankan consular office for help, but cannot count on effec-tive support from any of these sources.

At the end of a two-year contract, the housemaid and sponsor may agree to continue the employment relationship. In this case, the sponsor will pay for the domestic servant to fly home for a month's vacation and then return to the Middle East. If either housemaid or sponsor wishes to terminate the relationship, the housemaid will return to Sri Lanka, and both migrant and sponsor are free to set up a relationship with other parties. Housemaids who return repeatedly to the same household are envied. They usually have safe work environments, they often get a raise when they return for repeat contracts, and they do not have to spend money (on job agencies and money-lenders) each time they go abroad. In addition, appreciative employers may reward loyal servants with gifts of goods and money. Housemaids who work repeat contracts abroad report that they have come to love their sponsors' families as much as their own.

Back in Sri Lanka. Migrants, both men and women, remit money to their families in Sri Lanka. In 2005, overseas guest workers made up 16.25 percent of Sri Lanka's labor force, and their remittances totaled US$1.9 billion (SLBFE 2006: 88). More than half of this money came from the Middle East. In many developing countries, migrants' remittances exceed both foreign direct investment and money coming into the country as grants and loans. The government of Sri Lanka is very pleased to have migrants' remittances, because these bring hard foreign currency into the country. Remittances help the balance of payments: foreign debts and military purchases must be repaid in hard currency, such as that from the Gulf countries, rather than in the Sri Lankan rupee, which is a soft currency prone to inflation and devaluation.

Migrants' remittances support a large number of people in Sri Lanka. Several studies suggest that each migrant woman supports an average of five members of her family. It follows that the 800,000 women working abroad support roughly 4 million people (over 20 percent of Sri Lanka's estimated population of 19.5 million) through their migration. Sri Lanka is deeply dependent on migrant labor and on the continued well-being of the Gulf nations. This dependence was graphically illustrated in 1990, when Iraq invaded Kuwait. One hundred thousand Sri Lankans and countless guest workers from other countries were employed in Kuwait at the time. The invasion caused international chaos. People fled to Jordan and Saudi Arabia, and thereafter returned home. Many arrived back in Sri Lanka with only the clothing on their back, and the country lost their remittances while also having to support the returnees.

Despite the uncertainties in the Gulf, the difficult and dirty work, and long absences from family and friends, migrants still eagerly pursue jobs abroad. They do this, they say, for the sake of their families. And as families adjust to migration, family structures and gender relations shift and change.

Effects on the people left at home. Family structures facilitate migration; reciprocally, migration has altered family structures. Most Sri Lankan female migrants come from the 20–45 year age range, have six to nine years of schooling, are married, have two or more children, and have not otherwise worked outside the home. They say that they go abroad for the sake of their family. When women and men leave for extended periods of time, households have to make alternative arrangements to cover the domestic duties these absent members used to perform. Women often entrust children to relatives—usually grandmothers and other female kin, but also fathers and grandfathers. The extended family plays an important role in enabling migrant mothers to leave their children.

In conditions of poverty, the extended family serves as an insurance policy, cushioning people from economic hardship. Poor women often share with kin the care of children and elders. The intensive, exclusive mothering found in middle-class nuclear families is not the norm in much of the world. Instead, different people take on the bundle of duties considered as "motherhood." This fragmentation of motherhood allows women to work outside the home or even outside the country while others take over necessary household tasks.

Although poor Sri Lankan women have always worked, a dominant ideal of motherhood suggests that women should be in the home with their children. Migrant mothers often run up against this image and face accusations that they have "abandoned" their children to work abroad. Women pragmatically counter this charge, saying that they have not gone abroad for personal satisfaction or pleasure. Instead, they have worked and suffered to improve conditions for their families, especially their children. Husbands and wives agree that providing food, shelter, and education for children is the primary parental duty. Which parent earns money and which one nurtures is less important; the job must get done by someone. When a mother can more easily find lucrative employment, nurturing may fall to the father.

As women move into the waged labor market, the value of domestic service changes. Duties women once did for free, at home, they now do abroad for money. This quantitative remuneration for domestic duties makes clear that housework, or women's work, is real work and holds a waged value. Domestic service also clearly demonstrates how absurd it is to try to split the domestic from the public sphere.

As women receive wages, their power within the household increases. Women who have missed their children's childhood want to have something concrete to show for their years away. They are therefore committed to achieving the goals they set for their migration, which in many cases means buying land and building a cement house with a tile roof. Women gain power in the village and the family by making decisions about how to spend their money.

As women work abroad and gain more say in consumption choices, men also experience a shift in their household duties and gender roles. In particular, women's work abroad challenges the ideal of the male breadwinner. Women have always worked, but their extended work outside the country can create a crisis of masculinity. In particular, men feel awkward taking over the domestic duties in their wives' absence. Men with steady jobs who provide for the family while the women earn money for a one-time large-scale purchase are not as threatened, particularly if a female relative has taken over household chores. But men who substitute for their absent wives can feel diminished. Pressure to conform to unattainable gender norms, combined with continued poverty, can drive men to turn to one readily available avenue to reinforce their masculinity: alcohol use. A common stereotype predicts that a migrant woman's husband will eat, drink, waste her money, and forget to repay the moneylender. But research reveals that most husbands deal much more responsibly with their duties on the home front. In the face of long-term female migration, local gender stereotypes are changing, though slowly. Women are gaining some power and authority, but not as much as a straightforward equation of wage-earning with empowerment would predict. And men are still uncomfortable with the "stay-at-home dad" role, despite pragmatic arguments in its favor.

Migration affects not only household structures and gender relations, but other village statuses including class and wealth. Formerly poor households use migrants' remittances to buy land, build new houses, start businesses, educate their children, and provide large dowries for their daughters. As new money rolls in, it puts older class hierarchies in flux.

What might the future hold? The government of Sri Lanka has a lot at stake in transnational labor migration. In the past few years, legislators have proposed several migration-related initiatives, ranging from an effort to ban the migration of women with children under the age of five to an effort to raise the minimum wages for migrant domestic workers from $100 to $200 a month. Neither initiative has been successful; the courts shot down the first as a violation of women's fundamental rights, and job agents protested the second, saying that host countries would turn to laborers from other countries if Sri Lanka implemented its proposal. Due to Sri Lanka's weak international position, the government has not been effective in providing for more than the minimal safety and well-being of migrant workers abroad. True changes in this respect will only flow from international labor organizations, multilateral efforts between labor-sending countries, and collaboration with labor-receiving countries.

Changes will also flow from the internal evolution of household structures. After thirty years of labor migration, Sri Lankan villages are now sending a second generation of migrants abroad. In part due to the hard work of migrant parents in providing childhood opportunities, the second generation has different aspirations and ideals. These youngsters are generally better educated than their mothers and fathers. And while the older generation sent mostly women abroad, the second generation is sending both men and women. These young migrants go abroad before they are married, or at least before they have children. The young women have higher aspirations than to work as housemaids. The young men are working as heavy machinery drivers or other semiskilled labor. This generation hopes to work not in the Gulf but in other developing or developed countries, such as Korea, Malaysia, Singapore, and Italy, with more opportunities for entrepreneurship and advancement. Migrants who go to Italy have few expectations to return permanently to Sri Lanka. This may prove difficult for the elder generation, the caretakers who looked after their grandchildren while the first generation of migrants was abroad. If the youngsters leave Sri Lanka for good, taking their nuclear families with them, who will look after the elders? The next ten years may bring interesting changes for family structures and larger national and regional economic dynamics.

References

SLBFE (Sri Lanka Bureau of Foreign Employment). 2006. *Annual Statistical Report of Foreign Employment—2005.* Battaramulla, Sri Lanka: Research Division, Sri Lanka Bureau of Foreign Employment.

Gamburd, Michele Ruth. 2000. *The Kitchen Spoon's Handle: Transnationalism and Sri Lanka's Migrant Housemaids.* Ithaca: Cornell University Press.

———. 2005. "Lentils There, Lentils Here: Sri Lankan Domestic Labour in the Middle East." In *Asian Women as Transnational Domestic Workers,* edited by Shirlena Huang, Brenda S. A. Yeoh, and Noor Abdul Rahman, 92–114. Singapore: Marshall Cavendish.

———. In press. "Milk Teeth and Jet Planes: Kin Relations in Families of Sri Lanka's Transnational Domestic Servants." *City and Society.*

Note

1. I use "the Middle East," "West Asia," and "the Gulf" interchangeably to refer to a varied and diverse region with many cultural traditions. This rich complexity gets lost in many Sri Lankan accounts of migration, where migrants are said to work in "Arabia," "the Middle East," or merely "abroad."

Juki Girls: Gender, Globalization, and the Stigma of Garment Factory Work

Caitrin Lynch

One of the byproducts of the "open economy," or liberalization of the economy that began in 1977, was the establishment of many garment factories located chiefly in and around the northern suburbs of Colombo, but also throughout many other Sinhala regions of the island, which provided young women with a new employment option. Working conditions and salaries in these factories, many of which produce lines of apparel famous in the West, are not often conducive to their workers' social or economic well-being. Caitrin Lynch examines how the epithet "Juki girl" and its associated stigma have arisen and the steps that have been initiated to counter it.

Introduction. Women's labor has been an important cornerstone of economic development in Sri Lanka's "open economy." The nation's largest source of foreign exchange is the export-oriented garment industry, which employs 83 percent women, most of whom are Sinhala Buddhists (Tilakaratne 2006, 2–5; Arai 2006, 35).[1] And yet, the women who work in this critical economic role are commonly known by derogatory and sexually connotative nicknames, such as "Juki girls," "Juki pieces," or "garment pieces." The word "Juki" in these nicknames is derived from a Japanese industrial sewing-machine brand commonly used in Sri Lankan factories.[2] The Sri Lankan economy was liberalized in 1977. By 1979, the Juki-girl stigma had emerged. As I write in 2008, this stigma still stands as a powerful critique leveled at the hundreds of thousands of women employed in the garment industry. A case study of the rise and persistence of the Juki-girl stigma provides critical insights into global processes that obtain in many postcolonial nations today. In these first thirty years of the liberalized economy, gender has been a key element of Sri Lankan responses to globalization. By understanding how this happened, we can begin to understand the centrality of cultural norms and expectations concerning gender to economic processes in Sri Lanka.

In this essay, I describe how and why gender has played out as a central focal point in Sri Lankan political and social debates about globalization. I then turn to analyze the ways in which the Katunayake Free Trade Zone has been the focus of societal concern about Juki girls, and the role the mass media has played in sustaining the Juki stigma. I conclude the essay with a discussion of recent attempts, albeit with different motivations, by industrialists and women's rights advocates to counter the stigma.

Nation's Modernity, Women's Morality. In Sri Lanka, postindependence political discourse, but especially post-liberalization discourse, has focused on how to reconcile modernity and morality, or economic gain and social obligation. In effect, Sri Lankans have been asking: "How can our country be economically strong and competitive but still follow its age-old traditions?" This common postcolonial question comes with a distinctly nationalistic edge for many contemporary Sinhala Buddhists in light of two perceived threats to the nation. A separatist movement by the LTTE [Liberation Tigers of Tamil Eelam] has threatened the integrity of the nation-state's borders since the early 1980s, and Westernization threatens the integrity of the nation's culture.

In the face of these twin threats, many Sinhala Buddhists consider women to be the agents who will hold the nation together. Women have been invested with such a responsibility because—as is the case in many societies throughout the world—they are imagined to be at the core of Sri Lanka's moral identity. Many Sinhala Buddhists are thus especially concerned about the social implications of women's central role in the liberalized economic arrangements. Garment workers have become a chief focus of societal concerns, as evidenced by the definite stigma that attends to garment factory employment.

The derogatory nicknames for female garment workers originated in reference to women who work in factories in and around Colombo. Today they also, though to a lesser extent, refer to women employed in the garment industry that has reached into rural areas since the early 1990s. Both the terms "Juki pieces" and "garment pieces" objectify the women in question by making them seem like nothing more than things or pieces of dry goods. As one Sri Lankan newspaper editorial notes, the term "Juki pieces" indicates that these women "are treated like some expendable commodity" (*Daily Mirror* 2005, n.p.; cf. Hewamanne 2002, 7–8). Like the English term, the Sinhala term for "pieces" also has powerful sexual connotations, and all these nicknames connote sexual promiscuity.

The stigma of being a garment worker is so damaging and widespread that Sinhala newspaper marriage proposals sometimes disqualify garment workers with the phrase "no garment girls" or "no Juki girls" (Tambiah

1997). In the face of globalized economic and cultural processes, concerns about how women should behave are central to how Sri Lankans understand the effects of economic liberalization on their society. In many times and places, women have become symbols of the nation; the situation is no different in postcolonial Sri Lanka. In association with the symbolic elevation of women, daily practices have emerged to monitor and control female modesty and respectability as a measure of national status and prestige. The Juki girl stigma must be understood in this national context.

Juki Girls and the Katunayake Free Trade Zone. The centerpiece of the government's 1977 economic liberalization package was the establishment in 1978 of the Katunayake Free Trade Zone on the outskirts of Colombo.[3] Situated near the international airport, the Katunayake FTZ is by far the largest of Sri Lanka's eight FTZs today. From its inception, the workforce consisted primarily of women migrants from villages, most of them unmarried and Sinhala Buddhist. Soon after its establishment, there emerged considerable societal concern about good village girls going bad in Katunayake. Given the concentration of women in the area, and given that the women in question had acquired a reputation for inappropriate sexual behavior, several nicknames emerged for the town and the FTZ, among them *istiripura*, which literally means "women's city," but it has the subtle undertone of a "city of easy women or easy virtue." Other Sinhala phrases, plays on words, were invented to connote Katunayake as being "the zone of prostitutes," "the zone of free trade," or the "zone of love."[4]

The moral campaign against FTZ women has focused on reports of the following issues: prostitution, premarital sex, rape, sexually transmitted disease, abortion, and sexual harassment. In the 1990s and 2000s, repeated newspaper features as well as popular "teledramas" and feature films focused on FTZ women. Between 2001 and 2003 alone, four popular Sinhala-language feature films focused on women garment workers—all in regard to their relationships with army men (Hewamanne 2008). With the intensification of the government's war against the LTTE since the mid-1990s, the parallel processes of militarization and globalization have increasingly become the foci for gendered debates about the nation's future. These visual media often focus on women's sexuality through a dichotomy of city and village represented by stark good versus bad conflicts. The clear message in these media is that the suitable role for women is as wives and mothers, that the village is a haven where women fulfill their expected roles, and that garment factories are contributing to the rapid erosion of national traditions.

The social category "Juki girls" is a key symbol of national anxieties about fading traditions. Colombo is perceived by many Sri Lankans to be a corrupt, morally degrading space, and this perception is symbolized by the position of Juki girls. Of the thousands of factory workers in Colombo, by far the most work in the garment industry. These women generally have migrated from their villages, and so they live in boarding houses away from their parents. They are frequently seen walking in the streets, going to movie theaters and shopping, and socializing with men.

The Juki nickname is part of common parlance today, and women and men of various backgrounds throughout the island use the term. When used by people other than urban factory workers, the term unequivocally connotes sexual promiscuity. In field research in rural garment factories, I often heard rural factory women use it to disparage urban garment workers. However, I have heard anecdotal evidence that, as of 2003 or so, urban garment workers had begun to construct a positive identity around the term, using the term "Juki" with pride, as a way of asserting their difference from other women.[5] Other types of women's employment do not present these extreme social problems for the workers (nursing, teaching, domestic service, and even work in a porcelain, biscuit, or match factory). Garment factory work has a special place as a particularly disrespectable job.

In terms of the social history of the Juki nickname, there are two interrelated issues to consider: Why did this nickname emerge so soon after the economy was opened to foreign investment? Why did it disparage working women in sexual terms? The UNP [United National Party] government was elected in 1977 and immediately liberalized the economy. Critics of the UNP—the SLFP [Sri Lankan Freedom Party] and the JVP [Janatha Vimukthi Peramuna, or National Heritage Party]—were quick to construct and draw attention to what they saw as certain alarming moral issues surrounding this new economic strategy. The behavior of FTZ women was one such issue, for soon after Katunayake opened, there were reports of inappropriate sexual behavior between area men and female workers. For instance, in the period just after the FTZ opened, rumors circulated about men being brought in by the vanload to attend industry-sponsored nighttime music shows at which there would be vast numbers of unaccompanied women in the audience.[6] The fact that these women were unaccompanied was significant, for it meant that they were away from those who normally monitor women's behavior: parents, brothers, husbands, boyfriends, relatives, or other villagers.

Clearly, identifying women with sewing machines, as the Juki nickname does, dehumanizes the women who feel that they are already treated like machines in the workplace (see Lynch 2007, 121–23). The Juki nickname seems to have emerged as part of a political strategy by critics of the government to draw attention to the dehumanization inherent in global capitalism. The Juki stigma thus seems to have emerged from political concern with issues regarding the nation, inequality, and global economic strategies. Yet, rather than focus directly on class inequality, this approach criticized women in sexual terms. Why sex? With women's respectability indexed to their sexual behavior, Sri Lankans want to ensure that women remain the guardians of traditions. Any suspected violations of these cultural norms are problematic.

Other researchers have argued that the attitudes of the people who live in the town of Katunayake have been largely responsible for perpetuating the negative Juki girl stereotype (*Voice of Women* 1983; Weerasinghe 1989). While I concede that the jealousy of unemployed men or the parents of local girls who are eclipsed for jobs by out-of-towners may play a role, the stereotype is not simply a local problem. The Juki girl stigma has held firm for three interrelated reasons. Underlying all three are concerns about the agency being exhibited by young women in their encounters with economic globalization.

First, critics seem to read the public visibility of these women as indicative of their lack of adherence to traditional roles for village women. These roles involve a seamless transition from daughter to wife and, soon thereafter, mother (Bandarage 1988). Within traditional expectations, someone must always control women: parents, husband; brothers can substitute for either. There is no stage of life considered appropriate for single, unmarried women to live away from parents and families.[7] Meanwhile, most of the Katunayake garment workers live in boarding houses away from their parents, so they enjoy more freedom in their social lives than other single women of their age. They walk home from work in groups or with boyfriends, and some go with men to films or to watch airplanes at the nearby airport. Criticisms of these women often articulate a concern that young women who are not controlled by parents will not be controllable at work: they will not behave correctly in their expected roles in a disciplined industrial labor force.

Second, there is an important class dimension to the Juki stigma, a point also noted by the sociologist S. T. Hettige (2000, 190–91). Class mobility exhibited by poor village women (as manifested in their new fashions, consumption patterns, and ways of speaking, and their participation in various forms of entertainment) is perceived as a threat to the status quo by middle- and upper-class Sri Lankans, in the cities as well as the villages. In this regard, during my extended field research in the mid-1990s, middle-class Sri Lankans in Kandy and Colombo sometimes told me that they could not distinguish between factory workers and office workers on their commute.

They also told me they could no longer find good domestic servants because garment factories now employed many people who would have previously become servants.

Third, there may also be present an element of male anxiety about female employment, especially given the fact of widespread male unemployment. Masculinity in Sri Lanka is measured in part by men's abilities to take care of women—their mothers, sisters, wives, and daughters. For this reason, men in all classes of Sri Lankan society are generally expected to tell their wives to quit their jobs as soon as they marry. Because the garment industry employs only a small percentage of men, many unemployed men have seen women receive jobs that they wish were open to them. Asoka Bandarage (1988, 69, 72) argues that these women, like Sri Lankan women who work as domestic servants in the Middle East, are condemned because they are away from the patriarchal control of husbands or fathers, and their economic and social independence threatens male authority.

Taken together, these three points reveal that urban women garment workers are violating social norms that hold urban poor and rural women "as the sole upholders of the manners, customs and traditions of a glorious Sinhala past" (de Alwis 1998, 193–94). Despite an expansion of women's involvement in paid work since the economy was liberalized in 1977, the Juki stigma has held on with remarkable tenacity and has even reached beyond the urban areas to women working in garment factories in their very own villages (Lynch 2007).

The Future of the Juki Stigma. Since early 2005, the Sri Lankan garment-manufacturing landscape has shifted in response to changes in global trade regulations. On 1 January 2005, the worldwide Multifibre Arrangement (MFA) for trade was discontinued, concluding a phaseout that began in 1994. The MFA was inaugurated in 1974 to regulate global trade balances, placing trade restrictions and allotments on exporting countries. Small countries such as Sri Lanka benefited greatly from this "quota system." Prior to the MFA's end, some analysts had predicted that without the benefit of guaranteed quotas, 60 percent of the Sri Lankan garment industry could be in danger of failing.[8] Garment industrialists, organized as the JAAF (Joint Apparel Association Forum), have responded to these shifts by promoting the nation as a producer of "premium" apparel (Tilakaratne 2006, 9–10).

JAAF has especially concentrated on building the Sri Lankan industry's reputation as a fair trade destination, with the mid-2006 launch of its "Garments without Guilt" program. The program's website boasts, "Ethical sourcing and sustainable development practices resulting in the empowerment of women, development of sustainable eco-friendly solutions to apparel manufacturing and poverty alleviation has made the 'Made in Sri Lanka' label synonymous with quality, reliability and social and environmental accountability" ("Welcome" n.d.). The notion is that certification under the program for qualifying factories will demonstrate to the primarily Western garment buyers, and ultimately consumers, that the garments were produced under fair labor conditions. The industry has received global recognition for compliance with international labor standards (Tilakaratne 2006, 10–11), and yet trade unions continually raise concerns. For instance, shortly after Garments without Guilt was launched, union organizer Palitha Atukorale contested JAAF's claims about the industry and cited problems such as long hours, wages that keep workers below the national poverty line, unrealistic production targets, and barriers to unionization (Lanka Newspapers 2006).

Atukorale's concerns bring into relief the program's focus on "women's empowerment." In a polished promotional video, for instance, the narrator notes the following, as the viewer watches images of contented women working at Juki machines: "Members of Sri Lanka Apparel follow a comprehensive social responsibility policy that protects children and supports women's empowerment. Because wherever women are empowered, you'll find better schools, healthcare, ecosystems, and economic prospects" ("The Way We Make Garments," n.d.). The video and website, which are aimed at attracting foreign investors to Sri Lanka, invoke modern institutions and concepts and employ categories and terms that would appeal to prospective investors.

Can we really speak about "women's empowerment" when this work brings so much stigma to the vast number of women garment workers—not to mention the concerns about labor standards and rights raised by trade unionist Atukorale? Garments without Guilt, and related programs, include job training and performance recognition for women workers. It is too early to measure the program's long-term effects on women's empowerment and the Juki stigma.[9] Although it is not simple to change prevailing social perceptions, in recent years, both industrialists and women's rights advocates have attempted to harness popular music as a medium to counter the Juki stigma. In late 2003, the JAAF sponsored a pop music CD about garment workers, which was intended to help raise their status (Uvais 2003). Themes to the songs included "breadwinner," "creator of neighborhoods," "working conditions," and the export of Sri Lankan–made garments all over the world. Three years later, in late 2006, the Women's Centre, an organization that campaigns for the rights of women workers in the Katunayake FTZ, launched a music CD about women garment workers that they hoped would "help change social attitudes toward garment sector workers." The coordinator of the Women's Centre, Padmini Weerasuriya, noted, "These girls are treated very badly by our society. They are called all kinds of derogatory names like juki *badu* [things], *keli* [pieces], and so many worse names. They are harassed on the roads and preyed upon by everyone. But they are the people earning money for this country. We want to tell people not to treat them badly" (qu. in Samaraweera 2006, n.p.). But can listening to lyrics really change attitudes? Can thirty years of stigma be erased? These remain open research questions.

Industrialists blame the Juki stigma for high levels of unfilled vacancies in the nation's garment industry. A 2006 editorial in the *Sunday Times,* a Sri Lankan English-language newspaper, noted that there were 30,000 vacancies in the industry (10 percent of the total workforce). This editorial quoted the JAAF's Ajith Dias's explanation for women not joining the workforce: "They are not joining because of the negative perception. Some of the reasons we have found is that for example in some of Sinhala tele-dramas, the bad person or the one who suffers is the garments girl. These girls are looked down upon society. They are called Juki girls. Because of these perceptions, they believe that if they go into the garments trade their marriage prospects would be affected" (qu. in *Sunday Times* 2006, n.p.).

Women's rights advocates have long focused on the poor working, living, and traveling conditions of workers in the Sri Lankan garment industry. While the JAAF focuses on the ways in which the stigma serves as a *barrier* to employment, according to journalist Dilshani Samaraweera, women's organizations cite problems facing women who *are* employed in the industry, such as "harsh living conditions like unhygienic boarding facilities, inadequate transport facilities, particularly after dark, and the increasing cost of living" (Samaraweera 2006, n.p.). Whether the aim is to fill more jobs or to eliminate daily and long-term physical and social problems facing working women, industrialists and women's rights advocates are joined in their efforts to erase the Juki stigma. But a careful analysis of the contours of and reasons for the Juki stigma reveals its deep roots in the Sri Lankan postcolonial response to globalization. With the Juki stigma, gender has become a critical arena for expressing anxieties about whether the country can be both modern and moral. It would be challenging to erase these concerns.

In sum, it is clear that the Juki girl stigma is important to understanding Sri Lanka's experiences with globalization since the advent of the Open Economy, the meanings of the "Made in Sri Lanka" label for the women behind it, and the future directions of the industry.

References

Arai, Etsuyo. 2006. "Readymade Garment workers in Sri Lanka: Strategy to Survive in Competition." In *Employment in Readymade Garment Industry in Post-MFA ERA: The Cases of India, Bangladesh and Sri Lanka*, edited by Mayumi Murayama. Institute of Developing Economies, Japan External Trade Organization, Joint Research Program Series, no. 140 (March 2006). At www.ide.go.jp/English/Publish/Jrp/; accessed January 9, 2008.

De Alwis, Malathi. 1998. "Maternalist Politics in Sri Lanka: A Historical Anthropology of Its Conditions of Possibility." Ph.D. dissertation, University of Chicago.

Fine, Janice, with Matthew Howard. 1995. "Women in the Free Trade Zones of Sri Lanka." *Dollars and Sense*, November/December, 26–27, 39–40.

Gunatilaka, Ramani. 2001. "Freedom of Association and Collective Bargaining in Sri Lanka: Progress and Prospects." Colombo: International Labor Office.

Hettiarachchy, T. 1991. "A Report on the Socio-Economic Problems of the Workforce at Katunayake Export Processing Zone." *Island* (Colombo), December 29, n.p.

Hewamanne, Sandya. 2002. "Stitching Identities: Work, Play, and Politics among Sri Lanka's Free Trade Zone Garment Factory Workers." Ph.D. dissertation, University of Texas at Austin.

———. 2003. "Performing 'Dis-respectability': New Tastes, Cultural Practices, and Identity Performances by Sri Lanka's Free Trade Zone Garment-Factory Workers." *Cultural Dynamics* 15: 71–101.

———. 2008. *Stitching Identities in a Free Trade Zone: Gender and Politics in Sri Lanka*. Philadelphia: University of Pennsylvania Press.

Joint Association of Workers Councils of Free Trade Zones. 2001. *Slaves of "Free" Trade: Camp Sri Lanka*. Videocassette. Seeduwa, Sri Lanka, Joint Association of Workers Councils of Free Trade Zones.

Karp, Jonathan. 1999. "Sri Lanka Keeps Victoria's Secret: Island Workers Produce Panties in Cool Comfort." *Wall Street Journal*, July 13, B1, B4.

Kelegama, Saman. 2005. "Ready-Made Garment Industry in Sri Lanka: Preparing to Face the Global Challenges." *Asia-Pacific Trade and Investment Review* 1, no. 1 (April): 51–67. At www.unescap.org/tid/publication/aptir2362_research3.pdf.

Labor Video Project. 1993. *Women of the Zone: Garment Workers of Sri Lanka*. Videocassette. San Francisco, Labor Video Project.

Lanka Newspapers. 2006. "Garments without Guilt to Come out in the Wash." Lankanewspapers.com, September 25. At www.lankanewspapers.com/news/2006/9/8665.html; accessed January 9, 2008

Lynch, Caitrin. 2007. *Juki Girls, Good Girls: Gender and Cultural Politics in Sri Lanka's Global Garment Industry*. Ithaca: Cornell University Press.

Perera, Vernon. 1998. "Juki President Impressed by Local Workforce." *Sunday Observer* (Colombo), October 11, Business, n.p.

Rosa, Kumudhini. 1991. "Strategies of Organisation and Resistance: Women Workers in Sri Lankan Free Trade Zones." *Capital and Class* 45: 27–34.

Samaraweera, Dilshani. 2006. "Garment Girls Say No to Harassment." *Sunday Times Online* (Colombo), November 26, n.p. At http://lakdiva.org/suntimes/061126/FinancialTimes/ft328.html; accessed 9 January 9, 2008.

Sunday Times. 2006. Editorial: "Garment industry campaign to counter stigma for working women." *Sunday Times Online* (Colombo), December 10, n.p. At www.sundaytimes.lk/061210/FinancialTimes/ft309.html; accessed January 9, 2008.

Tennekoon, Ranjith. 2000. "Labour Issues in the Textile and Clothing Industry: A Sri Lankan Perspective." International Labour Office, Geneva, Sectoral Activities Department (SECTOR), Workshop Background Paper. At www.ilo.org/public/english/dialogue/sector/papers/tclabor/index.htm.

"The Way We Make Garments." n.d. Video about Garments without Guilt website, www.garmentswithoutguilt.com/index_1.html; accessed January 9, 2008.

Tilakaratne, W. M. 2006. "Phasing Out of MFA and the Emerging Trends in the Ready Made Garment Industry in Sri Lanka." In *Employment in Readymade Garment Industry in Post-MFA ERA: The Cases of India, Bangladesh and Sri Lanka*, edited by Mayumi Murayama. Institute of Developing Economies, Japan External Trade Organization, Joint Research Program Series, no. 140 (March 2006). At www.ide.go.jp/English/Publish/Jrp/; accessed January 9, 2008.

Voice of Women. 1983. *Women Workers in the Free Trade Zone of Sri Lanka*. Colombo: Voice of Women.

Weerasinghe, Rohini. 1989. "Women Workers in the Katunayake Investment Promotion Zone (KIPZ) of Sri Lanka: Some Observations." In *Women in Development in South Asia*, edited by V. Kanesalingam. New Delhi: Macmillan India.

Weerasuriya, Padmini. 2000. "The Conditions of the Workers in the Free Trade Zones as a Result of Sri Lanka's Open Economy." Women's Group of ASEM 2000 People's Forum conference on Women's Strategies to Challenge Globalization. At www.women21.or.kr/data/women21/ENGPDS_X/asem2000.doc; accessed June 1, 2006.

"Welcome." n.d. Opening message on Garments without Guilt website, www.garmentswithoutguilt.com/index_1.html; accessed January 9, 2008.

Notes

1. According to Etsuyo Arai's 2006 study, the garment industry as a whole has roughly 1,000 factories (accurate figures are not available) and employs over 300,000 people. The majority are women between eighteen and twenty-five years of age, mostly unmarried. Arai's team found that women tend to work five years before leaving and that marriage is the most common reason to stop working (cited by 45 percent of respondents) (Arai 2006, 49). There is a gender division of labor inside factories, with men tending toward middle and senior management. Women are generally machine operators, checkers, ironers, helpers, and supervisors (Tilakaratne 2006, 3).

2. The Juki Corporation, a Japanese company, is the world's largest manufacturer of industrial sewing machines, and it has been selling sewing machines in Sri Lanka since 1976 (Perera 1998).

3. For studies of Sri Lankan FTZ workers see Fine 1995; Gunatilaka 2001; Hettiarachchy 1991; Hewamanne 2002, 2003, 2008; Joint Association of Workers Councils of Free Trade Zones 2001; Labor Video Project 1993; Rosa 1991; Tennekoon 2000; Voice of Women 1983; Weerasinghe 1989; Weerasuriya 2000.

4. The quote about *istiripura* is from Voice of Women 1983, 69.

5. I have yet to come across usages of the term that do not have these negative connotations, although one might imagine that garment workers who are referred to as Juki girls might make their own sense of it. The factory women I know used it negatively to describe other workers. Hewamanne (2003) argues that some urban garment workers who would be labeled as Juki girls actually celebrate the Juki identity.

6. Ajit Serasundara, personal communication (October 18, 2001).

7. One obvious exception would be university residence halls, but the "wardens" who run these single-sex halls act very much as parental figures.

8. United Nations Industrial Development Organization, "Trade Capacity Building: Case Studies: Sri Lanka," www.unido.org/doc/27889. Other analysts predicted that Sri Lanka would fare well because it produces quality garments that are in demand and cannot be produced just anywhere. See, for instance, Karp 1999. See also Kelegama 2005.

9. As I write in 2008, Fulbright scholar Rachel Weeks is researching "Garments without Guilt" and other socially responsible garment industry initiatives in Sri Lanka.

A Place with No Room

Ramya Chamalie Jirasinghe

Snake bites leading to death occur more frequently in Sri Lanka on a per capita basis than in any other country in the world, with the exception of Burma. Yet the serpent is both feared and admired in Sri Lanka. The naga (serpent) is a primordial presence in Sri Lanka's ancient culture and fills an important place in traditional South Asian lore. Indeed, one of the ancient peoples of the island were known as Nagas. (According to the Mahavamsa, the Buddha once came to the island to pacify a feud between two Naga kings.) The serpent is also at once a symbol of feminine fertility, often identified with the goddess in Tamil popular culture, and a symbol of protection in Sinhala Buddhist popular culture, a guardian figure. In the poem that follows, the poet laments that there is no room left for the serpent in today's Sri Lanka.

The serpent's
forked tongue
licks the air as
it tries to unwind
its form,
benumbed by others'
shaping.
The tongue flicks,
searching, stabbing for
water in the air,
sunlight in
a garden.
This room is full.
There is no crevice
for the length of a snake
that has been
winding slithering
poisonous-harmless

feared-trembling
venerated-
death defying
life sustaining
Buddha sheltering
this dancing Naga.
There is no room here,
in this sanitised house.
Here
where the serpent's skin,
speckled grey-green
rainbowed by light,
is
stripped,
burnt
and
hung.
Its
charred
scales
highlighted
against an
insidious
saffron:
A
Lesson
in
Darkness.

The Wave

Ramya Chamalie Jirasinghe

The vicissitudes of Sri Lanka's political history continue unabated as this volume goes to press, but they were complicated, and in some ways their causes and concerns were quite leveled, if not temporally contextualized, by the volatility of nature. On December 26, 2004, "the tsunami" struck the southeast, south, and southwest regions of the island; Ramya Chamalie Jirasinghe writes lyrically of that fateful day.

Most of the people who did see a wave rise from the sea around Sri Lanka on the 26th of December, 2004, never survived it. The few people who lived to speak about the moment when the sea lifted itself into a towering wave, a vertical sheet of water hunched and foaming at the edge that covered the horizon before it fell thundering onto the land, remember being engulfed by a terrible darkness. For others, the wave came as a sound. A blast so powerful, so deafening and yet hollow that they thought everything around them had been shattered by the wind. Many have no memory of what happened immediately before the wave. They remember only the horror of the water suddenly engulfing them and being swept by its force towards loss and survival. . . .

The tsunami of the 26th December was caused by an earthquake of 9.3 magnitude that took place in the northwestern coast off the Indonesian island of Sumatra. The earthquake was the second largest since the invention of the seismometer 100 years ago and was the largest earthquake in 40 years. It caused a complex slip on the fault where the oceanic portion of the Indian Plate slides under Sumatra, a part of the Eurasian Plate, and deformed the ocean floor, pushing the overlying water up into a tsunami wave.

The first wave arrived in Sumatra on the 26th morning at 6:58 local time. In about two hours the waves had reached Sri Lanka, when it was just past 9:00 in the Eastern and Southeastern coasts of the island. On the west coast, according to residents, clocks that stopped because of the seawater recorded 9:20 am. The point above the sea level of a tsunami when it rises from the sea, known as the run-up elevation, ranged from less than 3 meters to over

12 meters around the Sri Lankan coasts. The impact of the wave differed depending on the topography. Where the sea was shallowest, the run-up elevation was highest. . . .

Only animals escaped, not by chance, but by some instinctive sense that had been wired into their biological and sensorial systems which compelled them away from the disaster. According to the US Geological Survey: "Both domestic and wild animals were seen evacuating to higher ground long before the tsunami arrived on the south coast of Sri Lanka." Close to the Ruhunu National Park (Yala) in Hambantota, many people lost their lives. However, game keepers did not find many animal carcasses.

More than 230,000 people from around the world died or were reported missing from the tsunami; 1.2 million people were displaced. In December 2005, Sri Lanka confirmed 30,322 deaths and disappearances from the tsunami. Over 516,150 were displaced, and the estimated overall damage to Sri Lanka was US$1 billion.

For the people who were caught up in the tsunami and were devastated by the losses it wrought, the 26th of December 2004, will be the darkest moment in their lives. The sea transformed into a monster: murderous and unpredictable. Over time, however, the coastal communities' fear of going back to the very places that were devastated and razed to the ground has lessened. The entire coastline that was affected by the tsunami in Sri Lanka, which two years ago was a shamble of debris, is now beginning to return to what it looked like before December, 2004. Today, most of the people have gone back to the sea and the beach. They have returned to it for their livelihood, for the evening swim and for the family outing. Houses have come up where hundreds of lives were lost. But the signs of the tsunami are there. The look of normalcy that greets the visitor now is not the normalcy of the past but that of the present where changes wrought by the devastation have been embedded into places and lives. Like "before," children are going back to school. Yet, unlike before, many of these children do not live where they once did and some no longer have their own families. The faintest rumor of an earthquake in the ocean sends the coastal communities into disarray: people start running, families grab their belongings and leave their homes, everybody rushes away and the day turns into a nightmare.

While the survivors are teetering on the brink of moving on from the events of the tsunami, many of them are still struggling to define their new lives, they are trying to understand the future that has been offered to them. For survivors, this unknown future has taken the form of a house they never owned or the prospect of better living conditions, but their new life will always be one that was catalysed by a tremendous loss. . . . [15–18]

The disruption caused by the tsunami was unique. For the first time, although briefly, religious, ethnic and social differences ceased to matter, and people related to one another with an acute awareness that the only link that counted, once all else had been destroyed, was the common bond of being human. The very nature of the chaos the tsunami wrought and the complete isolation and inaccessibility that it caused also had the power to create a suspension of all the petty human agendas that manifest through the socio-political machinery. The lashing from nature destabilized and overturned all existing physical and administrative structures and systems that usually hold society together. The result of the immediate aftermath of the tsunami was therefore a space-in-between this lashing, and the human effort to bring back the order and systems that contain society and individual lives within a manageable and controllable setting. This was the space that allowed actions of selfless courage and human generosity. It was a space that suspended a person's ethnic or religious affiliations. But it was also a place where greatness was contrasted against human greed through actions such as looting, theft and murder. In essence, however, this was a space where on the human spirit could have tipped the balance, and during the first few weeks following the tsunami in Sri Lanka, the best of human nature came to the surface and triumphed. . . . [42–43]

There are hundreds of blogs and emails circulating on the internet for information on people missing from the tsunami. As late as November 2006, the occasional news clip appears in the papers when relatives send out a search for a lost family member. National authorities call for individuals of surviving families who are presumed to have been separated from their parents during the tsunami. Several children have been found after the tsunami with families that *"could not produce any documentary evidence to prove a child's parentage."* The newspapers carry photographs of wide-eyed children, some less than three years old. Some of the photos are the most recent image the family has of the child before he or she went missing in the tsunami. Even in those, which are badly reproduced in the newspaper, the image seems distant and out of date.

Coping with the loss of a loved one has been the most difficult for a survivor when no remains of the lost person were found. The sense of finality that comes with death has been prevented by the hope the person may be found, as some were, through luck and weird twists of fate. There are stories of the infant who was lifted off in a plastic pail by the waves to be later found lodged, unscathed, in the branches of a tree, or the man who regained his memory weeks later and wandered back searching for his family. Yet these

are outweighed by the heartrending tales of survivors who are still searching and waiting for the appearance of even one loved one. . . .

Also, the tsunami was not selective in its devastation. It lashed into people's lives with no regard for a person's educational background, ethnicity
or place on the social ladder. Society was leveled. One of the survivors in
Hambantota made a very pertinent comment: *"See, everybody lost something.
No one was alone in that sense, and there seemed to be always a person who had lost
more than us."* [43–47]

V

Political Epilogue

The spectacular events of May 2009 will likely prove to be yet another watershed in Sri Lanka's political history. So many critical questions await answers in the months and years ahead. Will the defeat of the Liberation Tigers of Tamil Eelam usher in an era of peace for Sri Lanka? Will the Sinhala-dominated government now respond genuinely to legitimate Tamil grievances? Will the LTTE transform itself into a different type of resistance movement, one more committed to a democratic process and less dependent upon weapons? Will a moderate Tamil opinion resurface within public political discourse? Will the militant Tamil diaspora moderate its demands for a separate country? With the LTTE defeated (at least in Sri Lanka), will legitimate Tamil grievances be viewed more sympathetically by the international community? Will India's stance toward Sri Lanka change? Will the Sinhala-dominated government soon eschew the provocative "triumphalism" displayed in the immediate aftermath of the Tigers' defeat? Will the Sri Lankan army become an army of occupation in the north? Will festering human rights issues be genuinely recognized and addressed by the government? Or will disappearances continue, along with harassment and threats to journalists who are not seen as sympathetic to government positions?

The essays that follow are drawn largely from the op-ed pages of significant publications in Sri Lanka, India, Canada, and the United States. They ask many of the questions raised above, and a few more as well. They also comprise a broad spectrum of responses to the military defeat of the LTTE and the decimation of its Sri Lankan leadership.

And Then They Came for Me

Lasantha Wickrematunga

It is difficult to say exactly when the erosion of human rights became such a serious issue in post-independence Sri Lanka, but the 1950s and then the 1980s seem to have ushered in a period when the perpetrators of public violence against individuals acted with a sense of impunity. There is little doubt in the historical record, for instance, that powerful individuals in the government participated in the anti-Tamil pogrom of July 1983. Moreover, it is general knowledge that during the insurrection led by the JVP (Janatha Vimukthi Peramuna, or People's Liberation Front), many innocent people were wrongly suspected by the government, detained without due process, and tortured; many disappeared. Some estimates place the number of missing at around forty thousand. While it is true that the Sri Lankan government has been placed under siege by Tamil militants and the JVP over the past thirty years, it is also true that a government under siege sometimes reacts by putting its own law-abiding citizens under siege. Fear of the "white van without license plates" continues in contemporary Sri Lanka. Paramilitary agents allegedly sponsored by the sections of the state continue to intimidate the opposition, both Sinhala and Tamil. One of the most intimidated sections of the public is the profession of journalism. Reporters Sans Frontiers in 2010 ranked Sri Lanka 165th out of 173 countries in terms of freedom of speech, and the 5th deadliest country for a reporter to work in. Direct coverage of the war was not possible in any manner after the Scandinavian monitors were asked by the government to leave the country in 2008. The editorial that follows is about human rights abuses. It was written by Lasantha Wickrematunga, founding editor of the opposition paper, the Sunday Leader, *with instructions for it to be published in the event of his murder. It is a powerful indictment, published in the* Sunday Leader *on January 11, 2009.*

No other profession calls on its practitioners to lay down their lives for their art save the armed forces and, in Sri Lanka, journalism. In the course of the past few years, the independent media have increasingly come under attack. Electronic and print-media institutions have been burnt, bombed, sealed and coerced. Countless journalists have been harassed, threatened and killed. It has been my honour to belong to all those categories and now especially the last.

I have been in the business of journalism a good long time. Indeed, 2009 will be *The Sunday Leader*'s 15th year. Many things have changed in Sri Lanka during that time, and it does not need me to tell you that the greater part of that change has been for the worse. We find ourselves in the midst of a civil war ruthlessly prosecuted by protagonists whose bloodlust knows no bounds. Terror, whether perpetrated by terrorists or the state, has become the order of the day. Indeed, murder has become the primary tool whereby the state seeks to control the organs of liberty. Today it is the journalists, tomorrow it will be the judges. For neither group have the risks ever been higher or the stakes lower.

Why then do we do it? I often wonder that. After all, I too am a husband, and the father of three wonderful children. I too have responsibilities and obligations that transcend my profession, be it the law or journalism. Is it worth the risk? Many people tell me it is not. Friends tell me to revert to the bar, and goodness knows it offers a better and safer livelihood. Others, including political leaders on both sides, have at various times sought to induce me to take to politics, going so far as to offer me ministries of my choice. Diplomats, recognising the risk journalists face in Sri Lanka, have offered me safe passage and the right of residence in their countries. Whatever else I may have been stuck for, I have not been stuck for choice.

But there is a calling that is yet above high office, fame, lucre and security. It is the call of conscience.

The Sunday Leader has been a controversial newspaper because we say it like we see it: whether it be a spade, a thief or a murderer, we call it by that name. We do not hide behind euphemism. The investigative articles we print are supported by documentary evidence thanks to the public-spiritedness of citizens who at great risk to themselves pass on this material to us. We have exposed scandal after scandal, and never once in these 15 years has anyone proved us wrong or successfully prosecuted us.

The free media serve as a mirror in which the public can see itself sans mascara and styling gel. From us you learn the state of your nation, and especially its management by the people you elected to give your children a better future. Sometimes the image you see in that mirror is not a pleasant one. But while you may grumble in the privacy of your armchair, the journalists who hold the mirror up to you do so publicly and at great risk to themselves. That is our calling, and we do not shirk it.

Every newspaper has its angle, and we do not hide the fact that we have ours. Our commitment is to see Sri Lanka as a transparent, secular, liberal democracy. Think about those words, for they each have profound meaning. Transparent because government must be openly accountable to the people and never abuse their trust. Secular because in a multi-ethnic and multi-cultural society such as ours, secularism offers the only common ground by which we might all be united. Liberal because we recognise that all human beings are created different, and we need to accept others for what they are and not what we would like them to be. And democratic . . . well, if you need me to explain why that is important, you'd best stop buying this paper.

The Sunday Leader has never sought safety by unquestioningly articulating the majority view. Let's face it, that is the way to sell newspapers. On the contrary, as our opinion pieces over the years amply demonstrate, we often voice ideas that many people find distasteful. For example, we have consistently espoused the view that while separatist terrorism must be eradicated, it is more important to address the root causes of terrorism, and urged government to view Sri Lanka's ethnic strife in the context of history and not through the telescope of terrorism. We have also agitated against state terrorism in the so-called war against terror, and made no secret of our horror that Sri Lanka is the only country in the world routinely to bomb its own citizens. For these views we have been labelled traitors, and if this be treachery, we wear that label proudly.

Many people suspect that *The Sunday Leader* has a political agenda: it does not. If we appear more critical of the government than of the opposition it is only because we believe that—pray excuse cricketing argot—there is no point in bowling to the fielding side. Remember that for the few years of our existence in which the UNP [United National Party] was in office, we proved to be the biggest thorn in its flesh, exposing excess and corruption wherever it occurred. Indeed, the steady stream of embarrassing exposés we published may well have served to precipitate the downfall of that government.

Neither should our distaste for the war be interpreted to mean that we support the Tigers. The LTTE are among the most ruthless and bloodthirsty organisations ever to have infested the planet. There is no gainsaying that it must be eradicated. But to do so by violating the rights of Tamil citizens, bombing and shooting them mercilessly, is not only wrong but shames the Sinhalese, whose claim to be custodians of the dhamma is forever called into question by this savagery, much of which is unknown to the public because of censorship.

What is more, a military occupation of the country's north and east will require the Tamil people of those regions to live eternally as second-class citizens, deprived of all self respect. Do not imagine that you can placate them by showering "development" and "reconstruction" on them in the post-war era. The wounds of war will scar them forever, and you will also have an even more bitter and hateful Diaspora to contend with. A problem amenable to a political solution will thus become a festering wound that will yield strife for all eternity. If I seem angry and frustrated, it is only because most of my countrymen—and all of the government—cannot see this writing so plainly on the wall.

It is well known that I was on two occasions brutally assaulted, while on another my house was sprayed with machine-gun fire. Despite the government's sanctimonious assurances, there was never a serious police inquiry into the perpetrators of these attacks, and the attackers were never apprehended. In all these cases, I have reason to believe the attacks were inspired by the government. When finally I am killed, it will be the government that kills me.

The irony in this is that, unknown to most of the public, Mahinda [president of Sri Lanka] and I have been friends for more than a quarter century. Indeed, I suspect that I am one of the few people remaining who routinely addresses him by his first name and uses the familiar Sinhala address *oya* when talking to him. Although I do not attend the meetings he periodically holds for newspaper editors, hardly a month passes when we do not meet, privately or with a few close friends present, late at night at President's House. There we swap yarns, discuss politics and joke about the good old days. A few remarks to him would therefore be in order here.

Mahinda, when you finally fought your way to the SLFP [Sri Lankan Freedom Party] presidential nomination in 2005, nowhere were you welcomed more warmly than in this column. Indeed, we broke with a decade of tradition by referring to you throughout by your first name. So well known were your commitments to human rights and liberal values that we ushered you in like a breath of fresh air. Then, through an act of folly, you got yourself involved in the Helping Hambantota scandal. It was after a lot of soul-searching that we broke the story, at the same time urging you to return the money [approximately US$900,000 that had been placed for "safekeeping" in his sister's bank account]. By the time you did so several weeks later, a great blow had been struck to your reputation. It is one you are still trying to live down.

You have told me yourself that you were not greedy for the presidency. You did not have to hanker after it: it fell into your lap. You have told me that your sons are your greatest joy, and that you love spending time with them, leaving your brothers to operate the machinery of state. Now, it is clear to all who will see that that machinery has operated so well that my sons and daughter do not themselves have a father.

In the wake of my death I know you will make all the usual sanctimonious noises and call upon the police to hold a swift and thorough inquiry. But like all the inquiries you have ordered in the past, nothing will come of this one, too. For truth be told, we both know who will be behind my death, but dare not call his name. Not just my life, but yours too, depends on it.

Sadly, for all the dreams you had for our country in your younger days, in just three years you have reduced it to rubble. In the name of patriotism you have trampled on human rights, nurtured unbridled corruption and squandered public money like no other President before you. Indeed, your conduct has been like a small child suddenly let loose in a toyshop. That analogy is perhaps inapt because no child could have caused so much blood to be spilled on this land as you have, or trampled on the rights of its citizens as you do. Although you are now so drunk with power that you cannot see it, you will come to regret your sons having so rich an inheritance of blood. It can only bring tragedy. As for me, it is with a clear conscience that I go to meet my Maker. I wish, when your time finally comes, you could do the same. I wish.

As for me, I have the satisfaction of knowing that I walked tall and bowed to no man. And I have not travelled this journey alone. Fellow journalists in other branches of the media walked with me: most of them are now dead, imprisoned without trial or exiled in far-off lands. Others walk in the shadow of death that your Presidency has cast on the freedoms for which you once fought so hard. You will never be allowed to forget that my death took place under your watch. As anguished as I know you will be, I also know that you will have no choice but to protect my killers: you will see to it that the guilty one is never convicted. You have no choice. I feel sorry for you, and Shiranthi will have a long time to spend on her knees when next she goes for Confession for it is not just her own sins which she must confess, but those of her extended family that keeps you in office.

As for the readers of The Sunday Leader, what can I say but Thank You for supporting our mission. We have espoused unpopular causes, stood up for those too feeble to stand up for themselves, locked horns with the high and mighty so swollen with power that they have forgotten their roots, exposed corruption and the waste of your hard-earned tax rupees, and made sure that whatever the propaganda of the day, you were allowed to hear a contrary view. For this I—and my family—have now paid the price that I have long known I will one day have to pay. I am—and have always been—ready for that. I have done nothing to prevent this outcome: no security, no precautions. I want my murderer to know that I am not a coward like he is, hiding behind human shields while condemning thousands of innocents to death. What am I among so many? It has long been written that my life would be taken, and by whom. All that remains to be written is when.

That *The Sunday Leader* will continue fighting the good fight, too, is written. For I did not fight this fight alone. Many more of us have to be—and will be—killed before *The Leader* is laid to rest. I hope my assassination will be seen not as a defeat of freedom but an inspiration for those who survive to step up their efforts. Indeed, I hope that it will help galvanise forces that will usher in a new era of human liberty in our beloved motherland. I also hope it will open the eyes of your President to the fact that however many are slaughtered in the name of patriotism, the human spirit will endure and flourish. Not all the Rajapakses combined can kill that.

People often ask me why I take such risks and tell me it is a matter of time before I am bumped off. Of course I know that: it is inevitable. But if we do not speak out now, there will be no one left to speak for those who cannot, whether they be ethnic minorities, the disadvantaged or the persecuted. An example that has inspired me throughout my career in journalism has been that of the German theologian, Martin Niemüller. In his youth he was an anti-Semite and an admirer of Hitler. As Nazism took hold in Germany, however, he saw Nazism for what it was: it was not just the Jews Hitler sought to extirpate, it was just about anyone with an alternate point of view. Niemüller spoke out, and for his trouble was incarcerated in the Sachsen-hausen and Dachau concentration camps from 1937 to 1945, and very nearly executed. While incarcerated, Niemüller wrote a poem that, from the first time I read it in my teenage years, stuck hauntingly in my mind:

> First they came for the Jews
> and I did not speak out because I was not a Jew.
> Then they came for the Communists
> and I did not speak out because I was not a Communist.
> Then they came for the trade unionists
> and I did not speak out because I was not a trade unionist.
> Then they came for me
> and there was no one left to speak out for me.

If you remember nothing else, remember this: The *Leader* is there for you, be you Sinhalese, Tamil, Muslim, low-caste, homosexual, dissident or disabled. Its staff will fight on, unbowed and unafraid, with the courage to which you have become accustomed. Do not take that commitment for granted. Let there be no doubt that whatever sacrifices we journalists make, they are not made for our own glory or enrichment: they are made for you. Whether you deserve their sacrifice is another matter. As for me, God knows I tried.

Checkmate!

The Island

Over the years, The Island newspaper has tended to represent mainstream Sinhala opinion in support of successive governments dominated by the Sri Lanka Freedom Party (SLFP). The editorial reprinted below appeared in the newspaper on May 16, 2009, on the eve of the Sri Lankan army's crushing defeat of the LTTE, and is representative of the Sinhala mindset that supported war as a solution to the ethnic conflict. It begins by restating the government's assertion that in the final days of the war, it sought to undertake "the biggest ever rescue operation in the world to save tens of thousands of civilians." Subsequently, those Tamil civilians, numbering almost 300,000, were placed in "welfare villages," a euphemism for hastily constructed refugee camps where all, even the very old and the very young, were interned without freedom of movement and in squalid sanitary conditions referred to by the secretary general of the United Nations as "appalling." The editorial concludes with criticism of those governments, including the United States, Britain, and France, that had urged a diplomatic approach to the end of the conflict.

The Sri Lankan army has done the civilised world proud by undertaking probably the biggest ever rescue operation in the world to save tens of thousands of civilians taken hostage by a terrorist outfit banned in many countries.

Yesterday, the troops smashed the LTTE defences in the "civilian safe zone" enabling over 35,000 men, women and children to move to safety in the government-held areas. Prabhakaran's death squads, true to form, used suicide bombers and fired heavy weapons killing as they did dozens of civilians in a desperate bid to prevent them from fleeing. But, civilians keep pouring out of the LTTE-held "safe zone." With the army breaching the LTTE's FDL [front defense lines] at several points and facilitating a mass exodus, Prabhakaran and his fellow criminals will soon be left without any more women's clotheslines and babies' cots to hide behind. They will now have to come out and face the army or bite their cyanide phials.

The influx of civilians into the government-controlled terrain has once again given the lie to the Tiger lobby's claim of genocide in the Vanni. If those hapless people had any fear of genocidal violence, would they ever seek protection from the military?

Yesterday's daring rescue operation also exposed the international community's impotence. Not even the powerful countries like the US could pressure the LTTE to let go of civilians. All their pleas were in vain and they had egg on their face. But, the Sri Lanka army spoke the language the LTTE understood and 35,000 people were able to escape within hours.

No one in his or her proper senses would expect the LTTE to release civilians on its own. Prabhakaran took them hostage for a purpose. His strategy was to create a humanitarian catastrophe and jolt the world into stepping in to stop the war so that he and his partners in crime could escape death. His plans went awry for three reasons. The government wisely added a humanitarian prong to its war effort; the military, to its credit, acted with restraint in spite of all provocations by the LTTE; and civilians trusted the army and began to flee the LTTE, braving reprisals.

But, Prabhakaran is still under the delusion that his backers abroad will manage to extricate him from the mess of his own making on the pretext of saving civilians and commit Sri Lanka to a protracted truce so that he could make a comeback.

There is hardly any difference between Prabhakaran and the Somali pirates who took a US national hostage the other day or the terrorists who attacked Mumbai last year. The US and India swung into action, eliminated terrorists and rescued their citizens. Any other powerful state would have acted in a similar manner in case of a hostage drama. Therefore, Sri Lanka's right to neutralise terrorists and rescue her citizens cannot be questioned on any grounds.

Now that the army has opened up the LTTE-held "civilian safe zone" for people to flee, as for his survival, Prabhakaran has the same chance as a cat in hell. Foreign governments and their diplomats here who are making a last-ditch attempt to throw a lifeline to Prabhakaran are only exposing themselves as bedfellows of terrorists.

The only way they can save their striped friends is to make them surrender without causing any more bloodletting. And fast!

Our Holocaust

The Tamil Guardian

The following editorial from a Tamil diaspora newspaper published in the United Kingdom was posted on the Internet site Tamilnet on May 16, 2009, the same day that the editorial from The Island *appeared (see preceding chapter). By comparing these two editorials, one can begin to appreciate how great the divide is between the two Sri Lankan ethnic communities. While* The Island *editorial seems to indicate that the end of a conflict is near, the* Tamil Guardian *warns ominously that the bloody events of the final days of conventional warfare "on the sands of Mullataivu" will inspire a continuing resistance so that "Sri Lanka shall never be able to live in peace."*

The relentless massacres of Tamil civilians by the Sri Lanka state over the past few months had resulted in almost 7,000 deaths and twice that many seriously wounded by May 1. But the slaughter over last weekend is unparalleled in the brutality unleashed by the Sinhalese since independence; over two thousand Tamil lives were snuffed out in a hail of artillery shells. The makeshift hospital—blood-splattered room in a shattered house in the Mullaitivu enclave—has been blasted time and again, the accuracy of the Sri Lankan shells guaranteed by the GPS coordinates passed on by the ICRC [International Committee of the Red Cross].

All this in plain sight of the international community. Even the Western states which have—along with China, Russia and India—stood solidly behind the Sinhala state for the past three years were shaken. As the edition goes to print, US President Barack Obama has also stated the oft-repeated urging of the Sinhala state to cease its "indiscriminate" shelling. We doubt Sri Lanka, secure that China and Russia will thwart any repercussions at the UN Security Council, will pay any heed this time either.

What the Western states, operating with theories of "internal conflict" and "terrorism," can't comprehend is why the Sinhala state insists on using heavy weapons on the civilians packed into a sliver of land. They also don't understand why Sri Lanka is blocking international assistance from reaching the 190,000 recently displaced people concentrated in militarized camps. The Tamil people, of course, understand: this is genocide.

For several years the Tamils have been appealing to the international community that there is a "slow" genocide underway in Sri Lanka since independence. These arguments were dismissed—laughed off, actually—as hysteria or propaganda. Yet, quite apart from the pogroms against Tamils up to 1983, in the period since, a hundred thousand Tamils have died in massacres, indiscriminate shelling and bombing, and by starvation due to government embargoes on the Tamil homeland. However, since January "genocide" has not been some abstract concept. The world has witnessed it every single day since as first dozens, then scores, then hundreds of Tamils were killed and wounded. Even by Sri Lanka's horrific standards, the rate at which our people have been slaughtered is stunning.

What has also become clear is that the international community has knowingly and deliberately allowed this slaughter to proceed. The ideological fixation with "fighting terrorism" and "ending armed conflict" has meant that in the interests of destroying the Liberation Tigers, any number of Tamil civilians are expendable. Notice that even though it is the Sinhala state that is pounding the civilians, blocking food and medicine and repeatedly blasting the hospital, it is the LTTE that has drawn the focus of the UN's condemnation?

Notice that even though the Sinhala state launched major offensive operations in April 2006 (displacing over 40,000 Tamil civilians in three days), ordered international NGOs and UN agencies out of Vanni in mid-2007, tore up the Norwegian-brokered Ceasefire Agreement in January 2008, and, even before this year's slaughter began, had killed several thousand people in LTTE-controlled areas while abducting, murdering or disappearing over 5,000 Tamils in its own controlled areas, it is the LTTE that international actors in all this time have cursed and blamed?

Notice that even though the LTTE called for ceasefire and peace talks in 2006, 2007 and 2008 and that all these calls were dismissed out of hand by Colombo, the international community continued to look to the Sinhala state for a solution? The paradox of asking a state [that has been] starving, bombing and disappearing . . . [the Tamil] people to put forward [a] political solution to meet the political aspirations of that people has completely escaped the international community.

There is only one solution for us now: the independent, sovereign state of Tamil Eelam. The rationale for that is etched out in the bloody sands of Mullaitivu. If the Tamils accept any thing short of independence, if we allow ourselves to be placed under Sinhala dominion as part of a "solution," they will simply wipe us out at some point in the future. It is self-evident that the close scrutiny of the international community, the pleas and pointed warnings by powerful states and the disgust of the world has not impressed a Sinhala state, polity and people drunk with racism. Not one Sinhala political actor—not even the UNP [United National Party], the darling of the liberal West—has condemned the slaughter. It is inescapable that whatever the international community does, the Sinhala state will continue to pose an existential threat to the Tamil people unless we are protected by our own borders and security forces.

The sixty-year-old struggle for Tamil liberation is entering a new phase. On the one hand the Tamil nation, going through a Holocaust of its own, is no longer under any illusions about the Sinhala state and people. The international community will never be able to reason with or restrain them. On the other hand, contrary to Sinhala expectations, Tamil militancy will remain central to Sri Lanka's future. As the LTTE, which has transformed itself—yet again—for a new kind of war, bluntly put it last month: as long as the Tamils are oppressed, "Sri Lanka will never be able to live in peace."

Moderation the Only Way

Lilani Jayatilaka

The editorials in most Sinhala and Tamil newspapers on the defeat of the LTTE *by the Sri Lankan army were as politically predictable as those generally found in the editorial pages of* The Island, *a Colombo newspaper, and the* Tamil Guardian, *as well as the slant provided by Sri Lankan television stations. A more moderate, humane, and nuanced perspective was reflected, however, in the following article, published in* The Island *on May 17, 2009. It is noteworthy not only for its exposé of the internment camps containing Tamil refugees but also for its insistence on the need for Sri Lankans not to be held hostage by Sinhala ultranationalists, on the one hand, or by Tamil separatists, on the other.*

Yesterday, I met up with a Catholic nun who shall remain nameless at a place in Colombo which too shall remain nameless. There were six of us present, of whom two were lay people. This nun was here on a short visit from the Wanni where she lives and works with the IDPs [internally displaced people]. Apart from this nun, I was the only Tamil present and hence she told her story in halting Sinhala as she didn't seem comfortable speaking in English. She was here on a mission, not to disseminate information as such, but to gather together such necessaries as were needed by the people to whom she was ministering. We had recently made a collection of clothing which she had taken back with her to the Internally Displaced People. She was now back to collect more clothes, as well as other items—rubber slippers, which could be worn into the makeshift toilets used by the IDPs, sanitary towels with loops to be used by women who had no underwear, rudimentary medicines like panadols and Siddhalepa, to be distributed amongst the families and even some exercise books and crayons to keep the little ones occupied.

We listened to her tale with fascination tinged with horror. There were heartwarming stories amidst the horror stories. She spoke about the various camps to which only two nuns at a time were given permission to visit. There were altogether 10 members of the clergy, belonging to various Catholic orders who took it in turns to visit and minister to these needy people.

The largest camp, the Menik farm was the show piece that was displayed to visiting dignitaries. However, the parts on show were only a small portion of the whole. Whether the parts which were not on show are as good, remains open to speculation.

The government provides the basic food items like rice and dhal and the people in the camp cook the food themselves. All other items have to be found. The kachcheri van is allowed into the camp with biscuits and water and the clergy trails along in its wake, carrying in other items like clothing, panadol, sugar etc. The nun who was recounting this tale said that recently, while they were distributing cups of sugar to some of the families, a little sugar spilt on the ground. Immediately all the children in the vicinity went down on all fours, swiping the floor with the palms of their hands and then licking them off their palms. This nun said that she could not hold back her tears as their mothers explained that the children had not seen sugar in more than two years.

Though in the Menik camp, the people cooked their own rice and dhal, the other camps were more dependent on the good offices of the clergy and other well wishers. The nun spoke of another nun, neither old nor young, who visits the camps on her scooter. She is the only one, trusted implicitly both by the army and the LTTE, and allowed to cross the mental and physical barriers dividing the two. Everyday, she personally cooks (I presume she must have help from one or two others) and delivers 2,500 packets of food to some of the smaller camps. The "two members of the clergy at a time" rule does not seem to apply to her as she is allowed to visit the camps and hospitals as often and whenever she wishes to. The others must abide by the rules. They do what they can, but two can do little to minister to the ills of the body, mind and soul of thousands. We asked this nun how the army viewed the activities of the clergy and about their attitude to the unfortunate people in the camps. Her answer was that the ordinary soldier was helpful and compassionate towards the people whom they were required to guard and protect. For instance she told us about the checkpoint at Omanthai. This is the entry point for the IDPs whose credentials are checked before they are sent to one of the camps. Because the checking process is necessarily slow and laborious, many thousands congregate there, without food or water, and without shelter from the scorching heat of the hot, noonday sun. The nuns bring them biscuits and soft drinks when there is insufficient water to go around. They even set up open fires, where they brew great quantities of hot sweet tea to refresh these weary people. The soldiers are usually helpful and compassionate towards the people and help these nuns to do what needs to be done. Once, they encountered a higher ranking official, who dismissed them brusquely saying, "No one can go there." The soldiers who heard him, muttered beneath their breath to the nuns saying, "Take no note of him. He is not right in his head."

The nun also spoke of the hospitals. Two members of the clergy are allowed to visit the main hospital in Vavuniya twice a day, for an hour at a time. Here are housed the latest casualties of war. It is not difficult to imagine the scenario that prevails here with critically injured men, women and children in their thousands needing treatment, with just three doctors to see to everyone. (One senior member of the clergy who was present on this occasion, reminded us that the numbers mentioned are unverifiable and that this nun could only be making an educated guess as to the statistics. I bear this in mind.) Most patients who are not critically ill, are treated by the nurses and even by some of the nuns themselves, who prescribe medicines to the sick. She also told us about the "chicken pox" hospital. Within the crowded conditions of the camps, any communicable disease reaches epidemic proportions within a short time. A makeshift structure was constructed to house about 900 chicken pox victims (the numbers have dwindled down to about 600 now)—men, women and children. This was a rudimentary building with some poles planted on the ground covered by a woven cadjan roof. The structure must certainly have been far cooler than the alternative—plastic tents sent from Western countries, which are murder in the Sri Lankan climate, where it is hot, hot and humid! However, when the rains started, they beat in on the hapless patients who had no choice but to endure this further onslaught.

In the hot and humid conditions in the Wanni, a bath becomes not a luxury but a necessity. When I asked the nun about this, she said that a bowser brings water to the camps and the people collect their share in plastic buckets. A daily bath is not possible, but most people manage to have a wash of sorts using the limited water available to them. Large areas of forest and scrub land were cleared to house the IDPs. As a result there are no trees to shelter the people from the blazing heat of the sun, and since the plastic tents would broil them during the day, as many people as could possibly fit into a small space, huddle beneath the shade of two trees which have been allowed to remain in one camp. The soldiers are helpful and run little errands for the people. Some of the people entrust their precious cash to the soldiers to purchase some much needed items. As I understand it, there have so far been no complaints by the IDPs of being cheated of their money by the soldiers.

Many of them left their homes clutching their precious worldly possessions to them. Since it is the Tamil custom to invest one's savings in gold jewellery, many have valuable items of jewellery with them which need to be safely deposited in a bank. As I understand it, arrangements are being made to meet this need. One old man, this nun tells me, was clutching a pillow to his chest. On closer examination at the checkpoint, it was found to contain 5 lakhs of rupees that he had saved over the years, with labour and privation. He was encouraged to deposit his money in a bank that had been set up to meet such requirements.

While doing what they could to alleviate the suffering of these people, the nuns would chat to them. During the course of these chats, it emerged that all these people were more than willing and able to work hard and support themselves if they were allowed to return to their lands and their occupations. No one there wanted to live off the charity of either the government or even other charitable organizations and people, but they had no choice but to do so. The work ethic is an intrinsic feature of the Tamil psyche and there was a good deal of frustration at the enforced idleness of their present condition.

The nun's task in speaking to us ended at this point. She had recounted her experiences and made her plea for help with procuring the essential goods needed for these displaced people. The rest of us were left to ponder on the imponderables. What would become of these people? What would be the fate of the people trapped between an armed force determined to prosecute the war to its bitter end and an intransigent, desperate and ruthless guerrilla force. This is a manifestation of that eternal conundrum—what happens when an irresistible force meets an immovable object? The correct answer to that is that both cannot exist at one and the same time. It is a semantic impossibility. In real life however things are not that simple.

The Sri Lankan army has proved that it has the power to destroy the immovable object. But if it uses its power to decimate that immovable object, it will unleash a force that would boomerang and destroy it as well. For, if the Sri Lankan army as the representative of a democratically elected government ignores its obligations to safeguard its Tamil civilian population, then the Tamil diaspora would find an outlet for its justifiable wrath in new and perhaps terrible ways.

"The radicalization of the Tamil Diaspora" is a phrase that is on everyone's lips these days. As a Tamil, with family residing in different parts of the world, I have some sense of what this radicalization means. As the margin of safety becomes narrower and narrower and time runs out for the men, women and children trapped between the LTTE and the armed forces, the diaspora is becoming increasingly agitated. For the many, who left after the excesses of 1983, the relentless prosecution of the war by the government regardless of the human cost, becomes a haunting reminder of the vulner-ability of the Tamil people; for many who have close relatives and friends trapped in the Wanni, the fear and pain of loss and separation becomes al-most unbearable; then there are the Tigers who manipulate the emotions of the vulnerable with information and misinformation.

But then there is information and misinformation disseminated by the government of Sri Lanka as well. The Sinhala supremacists and the radical-ized Tamils make an emotional choice as to whom and what they will be-lieve, fuelled by their ethnic loyalties. Each has access only to partial truths, which they believe are whole truths. In this lies their blindness. I write in favour of moderation—to see these partial truths for what they are and to recognize the fact that the whole truth will continue to elude us; to beware of the rhetoric of hate and to refuse to become a pawn in the diabolical vi-sion of either the nationalists or the separatists. For while the ultranation-alists and the separatists pursue their own ends, the people of this land of whatever ethnicity are being required to pay with their lives for the intoler-ance and intransigence of a bigoted few.

Kingship-in-the-Making

Doug Saunders

While many in the Tamil community were sorely aggrieved by the spectacular de-mise of the LTTE and the incarceration of some 300,000 Tamil civilians in May 2009, some Sinhalese in the south were euphoric. For them, the destruction of the LTTE heralded the beginning of a new era in which the politics of fear, honed to perfec-tion by attacks on the Sri Lankan public by the LTTE over more than two decades, could now be left behind. Many likened the atmosphere to November 1989, when the leader of the JVP (Janatha Vimukthi Peramuna, or People's Liberation Front), Rohana Wijeweera, was arrested and shortly thereafter killed while in custody. In the aftermath of Wijeweera's death, "the fear psychosis" abated with a gradual return to public normalcy. What is new in the present situation is that the country's leader is now receiving adulation in traditional categorical terms. Some are regard-ing his accomplishments in comparison to great Sri Lankan kings of the past, or in relation to the mythical exploits of national guardian deities. While a political cult of personality was a feature of the LTTE's Vellupillai Prabhakaran in the past, the following article written for Toronto's Globe and Mail *signals the beginnings of one for current President Mahinda Rajapakse.*

As the President's motorcade passed slowly through Colombo Monday, 20-year-old university student Chaturi Waidyasekera pressed her head to the ground, then rose and chanted, "Praise our king."

Dozens of others did the same, beneath billboards that pictured Sri Lankan President Mahinda Rajapaksa in the white robes of a Buddhist deity. Ms. Waidyasekera explained, calmly, that she believes the elected leader of Sri Lanka should remain in office for life because last week he ended a 26-year civil war with the violent defeat of the Tamil Tigers.

"For once in our history we have a leader who has made our island into one kingdom," she said. "Why do we need elections any more? He is the king we need." She was actually one of the more moderate voices along the route: For others, the President was nothing less than a living god.

After the Liberation Tigers of Tamil Eelam were defeated last week, it seemed like this was simply a victory celebration, a mass depressurizing of a people made tense by years of war. Members of Sri Lanka's majority, Sinhalese-speaking Buddhists, took to the streets in a celebration that lasted days.

But in the days since, it has evolved into something larger. Over the weekend, huge statues of the President began appearing along the pitted two-lane highways that cross the island. In the cities, large billboards and posters are placed on every block, showing the President in white robes, or in fatigues, hugging his brother, Gotabaya, the Defence Secretary. (His other brother, Chamal, is Ports and Aviation Minister.) At first, they carried slogans like "Mission Accomplished." But now new ones have begun to appear, reading "King Mahinda Rajapaksa: Our saviour." It is impossible to avoid them: They are on every street corner, every public building, every shop front.

On state television, an advertisement seems to run several times every hour in which a woman sings, over utopian scenes of loyal workers, that the President has saved the nation and deserves to be crowned king.

"The messaging has been singularly Buddhist in its nature and expression," says Sanjana Hattotuwa, a democracy activist with the Centre for Policy Alternatives in Colombo.

"The defeat of the LTTE is being portrayed as the establishment of one country along the lines of the Sinhala kingdoms of old times, with the deification of the President as a religious king, and the victory of the army as an event foretold in the Mahawansa, the Sinhala Buddhist historical chronicle."

All of this is deeply alarming for the Tamil-speaking, mainly Hindu minority, who represent 13 per cent of the population, or about two million people, and whose language, religion and mythologies have been notably absent from Mr. Rajapaksa's grandiose moment.

While he did deliver a few phrases of well-practised Tamil in a speech to parliament—probably the first time any Sri Lankan leader has done so since independence from British rule in 1948—he has subsequently delivered addresses in which he has said the country will be rebuilt in "Buddhist values," and declared that there will be "no more minorities," a phrase meant to promote universal values, his supporters say, but which Tamils see as another declaration of Buddhist superiority.

Never before has a leader of this traditionally mild-mannered democracy adopted such a regal stature, and never before have the people seemed so willing to deify a leader. This is a country, after all, whose founders, memorialized in statues in Colombo's Independence Square, are lawyers in business suits.

Larger-than-life figures have figured in this island's politics, but the stakes have always been partisan and the dramas have usually been of the operatic, and sometimes soap-operatic, variety, such as the long-running feud between President Chandrika Kumaratunga and Prime Minister Ranil Wickremesinghe, which paralyzed the legislature until Mr. Rajapaksa won the presidency in 2006.

Since his election, Mr. Rajapaksa has seen the opposition parties wither and fragment, leaving him with a hold on power that could last for years, even decades. At the same time, he has aligned Sri Lanka away from the United States, Britain and Europe—which initially supported his unyielding approach to defeating the Tigers but then backed away—and toward China, Russia, Japan and Iran, which have supported and armed his struggle.

In the years before his election, you had to travel to the island's LTTE-controlled north to see a full-scale cult of personality, with images of the leader, Velupillai Prabhakaran, on every wall and a population revering him as a godlike figure. Today, that has become the style of politics in the south. Along with it has come a quick and sometimes total condemnation of anyone who dares question the execution of the war.

"It seems to be true what they say, that you have to become something in order to defeat it," Mr. Hattotuwa says. "This deification is of an unprecedented degree, it is absolute. The commander-in-chief has unprecedented social and political support across the country. This is beyond politics, it is religion and mythology."

Acknowledgment of Copyrights and Sources

Part I: From Ancient to Early Modern

"Buddhist Visions of a Primordial Past," anonymous, compiled by Mahanama Thera, from *The Mahavamsa, or The Great Chronicle of Ceylon*, edited and translated by Wilhelm Geiger and Mabel Haynes Bode (London: Oxford University Press, 1912), Pali Text Society Translation Series no. 3, vol. 1: 1–5, 51–54, 55–61.

"A Tamil Hindu Vijaya: Yalpana Vaipava Malai," anonymous, from *Yalpana Vaipava Malai, or The History of the Kingdom of Jaffna*, translated by C. Brito (New Delhi: Asian Educational Services, 1999), 1–7. Reprinted by permission of Asian Educational Services.

"The Saga of Dutugemunu" by Devarakkhita Jayabahu Dharmakirti, from *Saddharmalankarya*, edited by Kalutara Sarananda Thero (Colombo: Ratnakara Press, 1953), 449–76. Translation © 2011 Udaya P. Meddegama.

"Sirisamghabodhi and the Ideals of Buddhist Kingship," anonymous, compiled by Mahanama Thera, from *The Mahavamsa, or The Great Chronicle of Ceylon*, edited and translated by Wilhelm Geiger and Mabel Haynes Bode (London: Oxford University Press, 1912), Pali Text Society Translation Series no. 3, vol. 1: 261–63.

"Anuradhapura: Fifth-Century Observations by a Chinese Buddhist Monk" by Fa-Hien, from *A Record of Buddhistic Kingdoms: Being an Account by the Chinese Monk Fa-Hien of His Travels in India and Ceylon (AD 399–414) in Search of the Buddhist Books of Discipline*, translated by James Legge (New Delhi: Asian Educational Services, 1933; originally published by the Clarendon Press at Oxford, 1886), 100–110. Reprinted by permission of Asian Educational Services. Please see the original text for complete footnote references.

"Path of Purification" by Bhadantacariya Buddhaghosa, from *The Path of Purification: Visuddhimagga*, by Bhadantacariya Buddhaghosa, translated from the Pali by Bhikkhu Nyanamoli (Berkeley and London: Shambhala, 1976), 1–3. Reprinted by permission of the Buddhist Publication Society.

"A Hydraulic Civilization" by Chandra Richard de Silva, from *Sri Lanka: A History*, by Chandra Richard de Silva (New Delhi: Vikas Publishing House, 1987), 45–49.

"Sigiri Graffiti," anonymous, from *An Anthology of Sinhalese Literature up to 1815*, edited by Christopher Reynolds, translated by S. Paranavitana and W. G. Archer (Battaramulla: Sri Lanka National Commission for UNESCO, 1995), 27–31.

"Set in Stone," first section, by Mahinda IV, from *Archeological Survey of Ceylon: Epigraphia Zeylonica: Being Lithic and Other Inscriptions of Ceylon*, edited by Senarat

Part II: The Colonial Encounter

THE PORTUGUESE

"An Early Observer" by Duarte Barbosa, from *The Book of Duarte Barbosa*, edited and translated by Mansel Longworth Dames (London: Hakluyt Society, 1921), vol. 2, chapter 95.

"Visions from the Mid-Sixteenth Century: The Economist, the Viceroy, and the Missionary," first section, by António Pessoa, from "Enformação das cousas de Ceilão" by António Pessoa, in *Livro que trata das cousas da Índia e do Japão* [1548], edited by Adelino A. Calado (Coimbra, 1957). English translation by Chandra R. de Silva in *Portuguese Encounters with Sri Lanka and the Maldives: Translated Texts from the Age of Discoveries* (Farnham, England, and Burlington, Vt.: Ashgate, 2009), 31–34. Reprinted by permission of the translator.

"Visions from the Mid-Sixteenth Century: The Economist, the Viceroy, and the Missionary," second section, by Dom Alfonso de Noronha, from *The Catholic Church in Sri Lanka: The Portuguese Period*, by V. Perniola (Dehiwala: Tisara Prakasayako, 1989), vol. 1, *(1505–1565)*, doc. 113: 290–94, 296, 298–99, 301, 308.

"Visions from the Mid-Sixteenth Century: The Economist, the Viceroy, and the Missionary," third section, by Manuel de Morais, from *The Catholic Church in Sri Lanka: The Portuguese Period*, by V. Perniola (Dehiwala: Tisara Prakasayako, 1989), vol. 1, *(1505–1565)*, doc. 121: 318, 323–25.

"The Spin Doctors at Work: The Island as 'New Portugal,'" first section, by Francisco Rodrigues de Silveira, from *Reformação da Milícia do Estado da Índia Oriental* [1599] by Francisco Rodrigues de Silveira, edited by Luís Filipe Barreto, George Davison Winius, and Benjamim N. Teensma (Lisbon: Fundação Oriente, 1996), book 3, chapter 11, 219–222. Translation © 2011 Robert Newcomb. Used by permission of Fundação Oriente.

"The Spin Doctors at Work: The Island as 'New Portugal,'" second section, by Jorge Pinto de Azevedo, from *Advertencias de muita importancia ha Magestosa Coroa del Rey Nosso Senhor Dom João o 4º* . . . [1646] in Artur Teodoro de Matos, "'Advertências' e 'queixumes' de Jorge Pinto de Azevedo a D. João IV em 1646, sobre a decadência do Estado da Índia e o 'proveito' de Macau na sua 'restauração,'" *Povos e Culturas* 5 (1996): 464, 497–99, 509–11. Translation © 2011 Robert Newcomb. Used by permission of Artur Teodoro de Matos.

"Kandy in the 1630s: Through the Eyes of a Soldier-Poet and a Soldier-Ethnographer," first section, anonymous, from *Jornada do Reino de Huva, por Constantino de Sá de Noronha* . . . [1635], Biblioteca da Ajuda (Lisbon, Portugal), cod. 52-vI-51, published in *The Expedition to Uva Made in 1630 by Constantine de Sa de Noronha, Captain-General of Ceylon, as Narrated by a Soldier Who Took Part in the Expedition* . . . , edited and translated by S. G. Perera (Colombo: A. C. Richards, 1930), 54–56.

"Kandy in the 1630s: Through the Eyes of a Soldier-Poet and a Soldier-Ethnographer," second section, by Constantino de Sá de Miranda, from *Formas de todas as fortalezas de Ceilão* [1638], Biblioteca Universitaria de Zaragoza (Spain), ms. 13, published in *Os olhos do Rei: Desenhos e descrições portuguesas da ilha de Ceilão (1624, 1638)*, edited by Jorge Flores (Lisbon: Comissão Nacional para as Comemorações dos Descobrimentos Portugueses, 2001), 152–53, 158–59, 171–72. Translation © 2011 Robert Newcomb.

"The Final Dreamers," first section, by João Ribeiro, from *The Historic Tragedy of the Island of Ceilão*, by João Ribeiro, edited and translated by P. E. Pieris (New Delhi: Asian Educational Services, 1999), book 1, chapter 24. Reprinted by permission of Asian Educational Services.

"The Final Dreamers," second section, by Fernão de Queiroz, from *The Temporal and Spiritual Conquest of Ceylon*, by Fernão de Queiroz, edited and translated by S. G. Perera (New Delhi: Asian Educational Services, 1992), vol. 1, book 1, chapter 15. Reprinted by permission of Asian Educational Services.

"The Catholics' Last Sigh: Oratorian Missionaries in Eighteenth-Century" by M. da Costa Nunes, from *Documentação para a história da Congregação do Oratório de Santa Cruz dos Milagres do clero natural de Goa* by M. da Costa Nunes (Lisbon: Centro de Estudos Históricos Ultramarinos, 1966), 115–17, 173–75, 509–11, 585–87. Translation © 2011 Robert Newcomb.

THE DUTCH

"A Dutch Prelude" by Sebald de Weert, from "Letter from Sebald de Weert at Achin to Wybrand van Warwijck at Bantam," in *The Earliest Dutch Visits to Ceylon*, edited by Donald Ferguson (New Delhi: Asian Educational Services, 1998), 57–74. Reprinted by permission of Asian Educational Services.

"Jaffna and Kandy through Eyes of a Dutch Reformed *Predikant*" by Philip Baldaeus, from *A Description of the Great and Most Famous Isle of Ceylon* by Philip Baldaeus, translated from the high Dutch at Amsterdam, 1672 (New Delhi: Asian Educational Services, 1996), 812–16, 820–22. Reprinted by permission of Asian Educational Services.

"The Price of Good Cinnamon" by Sinnappah Arasaratnam, from *Dutch Power in Ceylon: 1658–1687* by Sinnappah Arasaratnam (Amsterdam: Djambatan, 1958), 181–93.

"How the Dutch Ruled" by Ryckloff Van Goens, from *Selections from the Dutch Records of the Government of Sri Lanka*, edited and translated by Sinnappah Arasaratnam (Colombo: Department of National Archives, 1974), 39–45.

"Dutch Policy towards Buddhism in Sri Lanka" by K. W. Goonewardena, from *Asian Panorama: Essays in Asian History, Past and Present*, edited by K. M. de Silva, Sirima Kiribamune, and C. R. de Silva (New Delhi: Vikas Publishing House, 1990), 319–52.

THE BRITISH

"A British Description of Colombo, 1807" by James Cordiner, previously published as "Colombo circa 1807" in *A Description of Ceylon*, by James Cordiner (originally published 1807), reprinted in *The Ceylon Historical Journal Monograph Series* (Dehivala: Tisara Prakasakayo, 1983), vol. 4: 16–37.

"The Final Tragedy of the Kandyan Kingdom" by John Davy, from *An Account of the Interior of Ceylon*, by John Davy (originally published 1821; reprinted Dehiwala: Tisara Prakasakayo, 1969), 237–42.

"The Rebellion of 1818 and Consolidation of British Rule" by Jonathan Forbes, previously published as "The Rebellion of 1818" in *Eleven Years in Ceylon* by Maj. Jonathan Forbes (London: Richard Bentley, 1840), vol. 1: 47–55.

"The 1848 Rebellion," letter from Governor Torrington to Lord Grey, from *Letters on Ceylon, 1846–1850*, edited by K. M. de Silva (Kandy: K. V. G. de Silva and Sons, 1965), 92–102. Reprinted by permission of K. M. de Silva.

"Leonard Woolf's Ceylon" by Leonard Woolf, from *Diaries in Ceylon, 1908–1911, Records of a Colonial Administrator: Being the Official Diaries maintained by Leonard Woolf while Assistant Government Agent of the Hambantota District, Ceylon, during the period August 1908 to May 1911* (Dehiwala: Tisara Press, 1962), lxxvii–lxxviii, 117, 241–42, 287, 280–86. Reprinted with permission of the University of Sussex and the Society of Authors as the literary representative of the estate of Leonard Woolf.

"The Establishment of the Tea Industry in Ceylon" by L. A. Wickremaratne, previously published in *Ceylon Journal of Historical and Social Studies* 2 (1972): 131–53. Reprinted by permission of the author.

KANDYAN CULTURE IN THE COLONIAL ERA

"Vimaladharmasurya: The First Kandyan King," anonymous, from *The Culavamsa*, edited and translated by Wilhelm Geiger (Colombo: Ceylon Government Information Department, 1953), vol. 2: 227–30.

"Concerning Their Religions . . ." by Robert Knox, from *Historical Relation of the Island Ceylon* by Robert Knox (originally published London, 1681), reprinted with an introduction by H. A. I. Goonetileke (New Dehli: Navrang Publishers, 1984), 83–90.

"Poetry and Proclamations in the Kandyan Kingdom," first section, "Galakaeppu Sahalla," anonymous, translated by P. B. Meegaskumbura, previously published as "Galakaeppy Sahalla (a poem to Devata Bandara)" in *The Buddhist Visnu: Religious Transformation, Politics and Culture*, by John Clifford Holt (New York: Columbia University Press, 2004), 303–9. Copyright © 2004 Columbia University Press. Translated from the original Sinhala in Charles Dias, ed., *Galakaeppu Sahalla* (Colombo: Samayawardhana Press, 1926). Reprinted by permission of Columbia University Press.

"Poetry and Proclamations in the Kandyan Kingdom," second section, "The Ballad of Pitiye Devi," by anonymous, translated by P. B. Meegaskumbura, a portion of the celebrated poem *Dolaha Deviyange Kavi* ("Poem of the 12 Gods") from *Sinhala Kavya Sangrahava* (Colombo: Sri Lanka National Museum, 1964), 221–26. English translation by P. B. Meegaskumbura, previously published in *Buddha in the Crown: Avalokiteśvara in the Buddhist Traditions of Sri Lanka*, edited by John Holt (New York: Oxford University Press, 1991), 133–37.

"Poetry and Proclamations in the Kandyan Kingdom," third section, "Urulewatte Sannasa," by Kirti Sri Rajasimha, from *A Gazetteer of the Central Province of Ceylon (excluding Walapane)*, by Archibald C. Lawrie (Colombo: George J. A. Skeen, Government Printer, 1898), vol. 2: 887–88.

"An Open Letter to the Kandyan Chiefs" by Ananda Coomaraswamy, from the *Ceylon Observer*, February 17, 1905.

"Colonial Postscript: The Other Eden" by Richard de Zoysa, previously published as "This Other Eden" in *An Anthology of Contemporary Sri Lankan Poetry and Literature in English*, edited by Rajiva Wijesinha (Colombo: British Council, 1988), 58–59.

Part III: Emerging Identities

BUDDHIST IDENTITIES

"Old Diary Leaves" by Henry Steele Olcott, from *Images of Sri Lanka through American Eyes: Travellers in Ceylon in the 19th and 20th Centuries*, edited by H. A. I. Goonetileke (Colombo: United States Information Service, 1978). Reprinted from Henry Steele Olcott, *Old Diary Leaves*, Second Series: 1878–83 (2nd ed. 1928), 158–59, 162–65,170–75, 304–7, 314–20; Third Series: 1883–87 (2nd ed. 1929), 355–57; Sixth Series: 1896–98 (2nd ed. 1935), 180–85.

"The Western Invasion and the Decline of Buddhism" by the Anagarika Dharmapala, from *Return to Righteousness: A Collection on Speeches, Essays, and Letters of the Anagarika Dharmapala*, edited by Ananda Gurugé (Colombo: Ministry of Education and Cultural Affairs, Government Press, 1965), 494–500.

"Ape Gama (Our Village)," first section, "A Religious Festival," by Martin Wickramasinghe, from *Lay Bare the Roots* by Martin Wickramasinghe, translated from the Sinhala by Lakshmi de Silva (Nawala, Rajagiriya: Sarasa, 2007), 88–93. Reprinted by permission of the Martin Wickramasinghe Trust.

"Ape Gama (Our Village)," second section, "The Jungle Hunters," by Martin Wickramasinghe, from *Lay Bare the Roots* by Martin Wickramasinghe, translated from the Sinhala by Lakshmi de Silva (Nawala, Rajagiriya: Sarasa, 2007), 15–20. Reprinted by permission of the Martin Wickramasinghe Trust.

"Sarvodaya in a Buddhist Society" by A. T. Ariyaratne, previously published as "Uplifting All in a Buddhist Society" in *Collected Works*, by A. T. Ariyaratne (Moratuwa: Sarvodaya International), vol. 1: 131–135.

"Politically Engaged Militant Monks" by Walpola Rahula, previously published as "Bikkhus and Politics" in *The Heritage of the Bhikku: A Short History of the Bhikku in Educational, Cultural, Social, and Political Life*, by Walpola Rahula, translated by K. P. G. Wijayasurendra (New York: Grove Press, 1974), 131–33. Copyright © 1974 by Walpola Rahula. Used by permission of Grove/Atlantic, Inc.

"Politics of the Jathika Helu Urumaya: Buddhism and Ethnicity" by Mahinda Deegalle, previously published as "Politics of the *Jathika Hela Urumaya* Monks: Buddhism and Ethnicity in Contemporary Sri Lanka," by Mahinda Deegalle, in *Contemporary Buddhism* 5 (2004): 83–103. Reprinted by permission of the author.

"A Buddha Now and Then: Images of a Sri Lankan Culture Hero" by John Clifford Holt, from *Excursions and Explorations: Cultural Encounters between Sri Lanka and the United States*, edited by Tissa Jayatilaka (Colombo: US/Sri Lanka Bi-national Fulbright Commission, 2002), 33–43.

MUSLIM IDENTITIES

"Origins of the Sri Lankan Muslims and Varieties of the Muslim Identity" by Dennis McGilvray and Mirak Raheem, originally published as sections of the chapter "History, Culture, and Geography: The Sources of Muslim Identity" in *Muslim Perspectives on the Sri Lankan Conflict* (Washington: East-West Center, 2007), 3–14. Please see the original text for complete references. Reprinted by permission of the East-West Center.

"The Ethnology of the 'Moors' of Ceylon" by P. Ramanathan, from *Journal of the Royal Asiatic Society, Ceylon Branch* 10, no. 36 (1888): 234–62.

"A Criticism of Mr. Ramanathan's 'Ethnology of the Moors of Ceylon'" by I. L. M. Abdul Azeez, from *Muslim Guardian* (Colombo: Moors' Union, 1907).

"Who Are the Moors of Ceylon?" by S. L. Mohamed (Colombo: Moors Direct Action Committee, 1950).

"The Bawas of Ceylon" by R. L. Spittel, from *Far Off Things: Treating of the History, Aboriginies, Myths, and Jungle Mysteries of Ceylon*, by R. L. Spittel (Colombo: Colombo Apothecaries, 1933), 312–21.

"The Fight for the Fez" by M. M. Thawfeeq, from *Muslim Mosaics*, by M. M. Thawfeeq (Colombo: Al Eslam and Moors Islamic Cultural Home, 1972), 128–31.

"The Purdah's Lament" by M. L. M. Mansoor, translated by A. J. Canagaratna, from *A Lankan Mosaic: Translations of Sinhala and Tamil Stories*, edited by Ashley Halpe, M. A. Nuhman, and Ranjini Obeyesekere (Dehiwala: Three Wheeler Press, 2002), 293–304.

"Sri Lankan Malays" by M. M. M. Mahroof, previously published as "The Community of Sri Lankan Malays: Notes toward a Socio-Historical Analysis" in *Journal of the Institute of Muslim Minority Affairs* 14, nos. 1 and 2 (January and July, 1993): 143–55. Reprinted here with permission from the publisher.

TAMIL IDENTITIES

"Language, Poetry, Culture, and Tamil Nationalism" by A. Jeyaratnam Wilson, previously published as "Language, Poetry, Culture and Nationalism" in *Sri Lankan Tamil Nationalism: Its Origins and Development in the Nineteenth and Twentieth Centuries* by A. Jeyaratnam Wilson (London: Hurst, 2000), 27–40. Reprinted by permission of Hurst & Co.

"The Dance of the Turkey Cock—The Jaffna Boycott of 1931" by Jane Russell, from *Ceylon Journal of Historical and Social Studies* 8 (1978): 47–67.

"Language and the Rise of Tamil Separatism in Sri Lanka" by Robert N. Kearney, previously published as "Language and the Rise of Tamil Separatism" in *Asian Survey* 18, no. 5 (1978): 521–34. Reprinted with permission of University of California Press.

"The Militarisation of Tamil Youth" by A. Jeyaratnam Wilson, from *Sri Lankan Tamil Nationalism: Its Origins and Development in the Nineteenth and Twentieth Centuries*, by A. Jeyaratnam Wilson (London: Hurst, 2000), 113–35. Reprinted by permission of Hurst & Co.

"Womanhood and the Tamil Refugee" by Joke Schrijvers, from *Women, Narration and Nation*, edited by Selvy Thiruchandran (New Delhi: Vikas Publishing House, 1999), 169–99.

"Nallur" by Jean Arasanayagam, from *An Anthology of Contemporary Sri Lankan Poetry and Literature in English*, edited by Rajiva Wijesinha (Colombo: British Council, 1988), 1–2. Reprinted by permission of the author.

CHRISTIANS AND BURGHERS

"Christians in a Buddhist Majority" by Paul Caspersz, S.J., previously published as "The Role of Sri Lanka Christians in a Buddhist Majority System" in *Ceylon Journal*

Part IV: Independence, Insurrections, and Social Change

Suggestions for Further Reading

History

Abeyasinghe, Tikiri. *Portuguese Rule in Ceylon, 1594–1612*. Colombo: Lake House Investments, 1966.

Arasaratnam, Sinnapah. *Dutch Power in Ceylon*. Amsterdam: Dhambatam, 1958.

Ariyapala, M. B. *Society in Mediaeval Ceylon*. Colombo: Department of Cultural Affairs, 1956.

Bandarage, Asoka. *Colonialism in Sri Lanka: The Political Economy of the Kandyan Highlands, 1833–1886*. New York: Mouton Publishers, 1983.

Bell, H. C. P. *A Report on the Kegalle District of the Province of Sabaragamuwa*. Colombo: George Skeen, Government Printer, 1904.

Blackburn, Anne. *Locations of Buddhism: Colonialism and Modernity in Sri Lanka*. Chicago: University of Chicago Press, 2010.

De Silva, Chandra R. *The Portuguese in Ceylon, 1617–1638*. Colombo: H. W. Cave and Co., 1972.

———. *Sri Lanka: A History*. Delhi: Vikas Publishing House, 1987.

———. *Sri Lanka and the Maldives*, London: Ashgate, 2008.

De Silva, Colvin R. *Ceylon under the British Occupation, 1795–1833*. 2 vols. 1941; Delhi: Navrang, 1995.

De Silva, Kingsley. *A History of Sri Lanka*. 1981; Delhi: Penguin Books, 2005.

Dewaraja, Lorna. *The Kandyan Kingdom of Sri Lanka, 1707–1782*. 2nd ed. Colombo: Lake House, 1988.

Ellawalla, H. S. *Social History of Early Ceylon*. Colombo: Department of Cultural Affairs, 1969.

Ferguson, Donald. *The Earliest Dutch Visits to Ceylon*. 1927; Delhi: Asian Educational Services, 1998.

Flores, Jorge. *"Hum Curto Historia de Ceylan": Five Hundred Years of Relations between Portugal and Sri Lanka*. Lisbon: Fundação Oriente, 2001.

———, ed. *Re-exploring the Links: History and Constructed Histories between Portugal and Sri Lanka*. Wiesbaden: Harrassowitz Verlag and Calouste Gulbenkian Foundation, 2007.

Geiger, Wilhelm. *Culture of Ceylon in Mediaeval Times*. Wiesbaden: Otto Harrassowitz, 1960.

Goonewardena, K. W. *The Foundation of Dutch Power in Ceylon, 1638–1658*. Amsterdam: Djambatan, 1958.

Gunawardana, R. A. L. H., S. Pathamanathan, and M. Rohanadeera. *Reflections on a Heritage: Historical Scholarship on Premodern Sri Lanka*. Colombo: Central Cultural Fund, Ministry of Cultural Affairs, 2000.

Harris, Elizabeth. *Theravada Buddhism and the British Encounter: Religious Missionary and Colonial Experience in Nineteenth-Century Sri Lanka*. London: Routledge, 2006.

Jeganathan, Pradeep, and Ismail, Qadri, *Unmaking the Nation: The Politics of Identity and History in Modern Sri Lanka*. 2nd ed. Colombo: Social Science Association, 2009.

Lawrie, Archibald. *A Gazateer of the Central Province*. 2 vols. Colombo: George Skeen, 1898.

Liyanagamage, Amaradasa. *The Decline of Polonnaruwa and the Rise of Dambadeniya, circa 1180–1270 A.D.* Colombo: Department of Cultural Affairs, 1968.

Malalgoda, Kitsiri. *Buddhism in Sinhalese Society, 1750–1900*. Berkeley: University of California Press, 1976.

Mendis, G. C. *Ceylon under the British*. Colombo: Colombo Apothecaries, 1952.

Parker, Henry. *Ancient Ceylon*. 1907; Delhi: Asian Educational Services, 1981.

Peebles, Patrick. *Social Change in Nineteenth-Century Ceylon*. Delhi: Navrang, 1995.

Peiris, G. H. *Sri Lanka: Challenges of the New Millennium*. Kandy: Kandy Books, 2006.

Percival, Robert. *An Account of the Island of Ceylon*. 1803; Delhi: Asian Educational Services, 1990.

Perera, Lakshman. *The Institutions of Ancient Ceylon*. 3 vols. Kandy: International Centre for Ethnic Studies, 2005.

Perniola, V. *The Catholic Church in Sri Lanka: The Portuguese Period. Original Documents Translated into English*. 3 vols. Dewihala: Tisara Prakasayako, 1989–1991.

Pieris, P. E. *Ceylon: The Portuguese Era*. 2 vols. 1913; Dehiwala: Tisara Press, 1992.

———. *Ceylon and the Hollanders*. 1918; Delhi: Navrang, 1995.

Quéré, Martin. *Christianity in Sri Lanka under the Portuguese Padroado, 1597–1658*. Colombo: Colombo Catholic Press, 1995.

Queryroz, Fernao de. *The Temporal and Spiritual Conquest of Ceylon*. Translated by S. G. Perera. 3 vols. 1930; Delhi: Asia Educational Services, 1992.

Roberts, Michael. *Sinhala Consciousness in the Kandyan Period, 1590s to 1815*. Colombo: Vijitha Yapa, 2004.

Rogers, John. *Crime, Justice and Society in Colonial Sri Lanka*. London: Curzon Press, 1987.

Sirisena, W. I. *Sri Lanka and South-east Asia: Political, Religious and Cultural Relations from A.D. c. 1000 to c. 1500*. Leiden: E. J. Brill, 1978.

Skinner, Thomas. *Fifty Years in Ceylon*. Dehiwala: Tisara Prakasakayo, 1974.

Spencer, Jonathan, ed. *Sri Lanka: History and the Roots of Conflict*. London: Routledge, 1990.

Strathern, Alan. *Kingship and Conversion in Sixteenth-Century Sri Lanka: Portuguese Imperialism in a Buddhist Land*. Cambridge: Cambridge University Press, 2007.

Tennent, James Emerson. *Ceylon*. 2 vols. 1859; Dehiwala: Tisara Prakasakayo, 1977.

Wickramasinghe, Nira. *Sri Lanka in the Modern Age: A History of Contested Identities*. Honolulu: University of Hawaii Press, 2006.

Winius, George. *The Fatal History of Portuguese Ceylon*. Cambridge: Harvard University Press, 1971.

Politics

Alles, A. C. *The J.V.P., 1969–89*. Colombo: Lake House Investments, 1990.

De Silva, K. M. *Reaping the Whirlwind: Ethnic Conflict, Ethnic Politics in Sri Lanka*. New Delhi: Penguin Books, 1998.

———. *Sri Lanka: Problems of Governance*. Kandy: International Centre for Ethnic Studies, 1993.

———. *Sri Lanka's Troubled Inheritance*. Kandy: International Centre for Ethnic Studies, 2007.

De Silva, K. M., and Howard Wriggins. *J. R. Jayewardene of Sri Lanka*. 2 vols. Honolulu: University of Hawaii Press, 1988 and 1994.

Devotta, Neil. *Blowback: Linguistic Nationalism, Institutional Decay, and Ethnic Conflict in Sri Lanka*. Stanford: Stanford University Press, 2004.

Dharmadasa, K. N. O. *Language, Religion and Ethnic Assertiveness: The Growth of Sinhalese Nationalism in Sri Lanka*. Ann Arbor: University of Michigan Press, 1992.

Dixit, J. N. *Assignment Colombo*. Delhi: Konark Publishers, 1998.

Ghosh, Partha. *Ethnicity Versus Nationalism: The Devolution Discourse in Sri Lanka*. New Delhi: Sage Publications, 2003.

Gooneratne, Yasmin. *Relative Merits: A Personal Memoir of the Bandaranaike Family of Sri Lanka*. London: C. Hurst, 1986.

Gunasekara, Prins. *Sri Lanka in Crisis: A Lost Generation*. Colombo: Godage Bros., 1998.

Hewamanne, Sandya. *Stitching Identities in a Free Trade Zone: Gender and Politics in Sri Lanka*. Philadelphia: University of Pennsylvania Press, 2008.

Hoole, Rajan, et al. *The Broken Palmyra: The Tamil Crisis in Sri Lanka—An Inside Account*. Claremont, Calif.: Sri Lankan Studies Institute, 1990.

Horowitz, Donald L. *Coup Theories and Officers' Motives*. Princeton: Princeton University Press, 1980.

Jiggins, Janice. *Caste and Family in the Politics of the Sinhalese, 1947–1976*. Cambridge: Cambridge University Press, 1979.

Jupp, James. *Sri Lanka: Third World Democracy*. London: Frank Cass, 1978.

Kapferer, Bruce. *Legends of People, Myths of State: Violence, Intolerance and Political Culture in Sri Lanka and Australia*. Washington: Smithsonian Institution, 1988.

Kearney, Robert. *Communalism and Language in the Politics of Ceylon*. Durham: Duke University Press, 1967.

Kemper, Stephen. *The Presence of the Past: Chronicles, Politics and Culture in Sinhala Life*. Ithaca: Cornell University Press, 1992.

Kiribamune, Sirima. *Women and Politics in Sri Lanka: A Comparative Perspective*. Kandy: International Centre for Ethnic Studies, 1999.

Kodikara, Shelton. *Foreign Policy of Sri Lanka*. Delhi: Chanakya Publications, 1992.

Manor, James. *The Expedient Utopian: Bandaranaike and Ceylon*. Cambridge: Cambridge University Press, 1989.

Richardson, John. *Paradise Poisoned: Learning about Conflict, Terrorism and Development from Sri Lanka's Civil Wars*. Kandy: International Centre for Ethnic Studies, 2005.

Risseeuw, Carla. *Gender Transformation, Power and Resistance among Women in Sri Lanka*. Leiden: E. J. Brill, 1988.

Rotberg, Robert, ed. *Creating Peace in Sri Lanka: Civil War and Reconciliation*. Washington: Brookings Institution Press, 1999.

Rupesinghe, Kumar, ed. *Negotiating Peace in Sri Lanka: Efforts, Failures and Lessons*. 2 vols. London and Colombo: International Alert and Foundation for Co-existence, 1998 and 2006.

Seneviratne, H. L. *The Work of Kings: The New Buddhism of Sri Lanka*. Chicago: University of Chicago Press, 1999.

Silva, K. T. "Caste, Ethnicity and Problems of National Identity." In *Nation and National Identity in Sri Lanka*, edited by S. L. Sharma and T. K. Oommen, 201–15. Hyderabad: Orient Longman, 2000.

Smith, Bardwell, ed. *Religion and the Legitimation of Power in Sri Lanka*. Chambersburg, Pa.: Anima Books, 1978.

Spencer, Jonathan. *A Sinhala Village in a Time of Trouble*. Delhi: Oxford University Press, 1990.

Tambiah, S. J. *Buddhism Betrayed? Religion, Politics and Violence in Sri Lanka*. Chicago: University of Chicago Press, 1992.

———. *Leveling Crowds: Ethnonationalist Conflicts and Collective Violence in South Asia*. Berkeley: University of California Press, 1997.

———. *Sri Lanka: Ethnic Fratricide and the Dismantling of Democracy*. Chicago: University of Chicago Press, 1986.

Warnapala, Wiswa. *Ethnic Strife and Politics in Sri Lanka: An Investigation into Demands and Responses*. Delhi: Navrang, 1994.

Wickramasinghe, Nira. *Ethnic Politics in Colonial Sri Lanka*. Delhi: Vikas Publishing, 1995.

Wickremeratne, Ananda. *The Roots of Nationalism: Sri Lanka*. Colombo: Karunaratna and Sons, 1995.

Wilson, A. J. *The Break-up of Sri Lanka: The Sinhalese-Tamil Conflict*. Honolulu: University of Hawaii Press, 1988.

———. *Politics in Sri Lanka 1947–1979*. London: Macmillan Press, 1979.

———. *Sri Lanka Tamil Nationalism: Its Origins and Development in the 19th and 20th Centuries*. New Delhi: Penguin Books, 2000.

Winslow, Deborah, and Michael Woost. *Economy, Culture and Civil War in Sri Lanka*. Bloomington: Indiana University Press, 2004.

Wriggins, Howard. *Ceylon: Dilemmas of a New Nation*. Princeton: Princeton University Press, 1960.

Culture

Bandaranayake, Senake, and Gamini Jayasinghe. *The Rock and Wall Paintings of Sri Lanka*. Colombo: Lake House, 1986.

Bartholomeusz, Tessa. *Women under the Bo Tree*. Cambridge: Cambridge University Press, 1994.

Berkwitz, Stephen. *Buddhist History in the Vernacular*. Leiden: E. J. Brill, 2004.

Bond, George. *Buddhism at Work*. West Hartford: Kumarian Press, 2003.

———. *The Buddhist Revival in Sri Lanka: Religious Tradition, Reinterpretation and Response*. Columbia: University of South Carolina Press, 1988.

Carrithers, Michael. *The Forest Monks of Sri Lanka*. Delhi: Oxford University Press, 1983.

Collins, Steven. "What Is Literature in Pali?" In *Literary Cultures in History*, edited by Sheldon Pollock, 649–88. Berkeley: University of California Press, 2003.

Coomaraswamy, Ananda. *Mediaeval Sinhalese Art*. 2nd ed. New York: Pantheon Books, 1956.

Daniel, E. Valentine. *Charred Lullabies*. Princeton: Princeton University Press, 1996.

De Mel, Neloufer, and Minoli Samarakokody, eds. *Writing an Inheritance: Women's Writing in Sri Lanka 1860–1948*. Colombo: Women's Education and Research Centre, 2002.

Deegalle, Mahinda, ed. *Buddhism, Conflict and Violence in Modern Sri Lanka*. London: Routledge, 2006.

Dohanian, Derek. *Mahayana Buddhist Sculpture in Ceylon*. New York: Garland Publishing, 1977.

Duncan, James. *The City as Text: The Politics of Landscape Interpretation in the Kandyan Kingdom*. Cambridge: Cambridge University Press, 1990.

Evers, Hans-Dieter. *Monks, Priests and Peasants: A Study of Buddhism and Social Structure in Central Ceylon*. Leiden: E. J. Brill, 1972.

Gamburd, Michele. *Transnationalism and Sri Lanka's Migrant Housemaids: The Kitchen Spoon's Handle*. Ithaca: Cornell University Press, 2000.

Godakumbura, G. C. *Sinhalese Literature*. Colombo: Colombo Apothecaries, 1955.

Gombrich, Richard. *Precept and Practice: Traditional Buddhism in the Rural Highlands of Ceylon*. Oxford: Clarendon Press, 1971.

Gombrich, Richard, and Gananath Obeyesekere. *Buddhism Transformed: Religious Change in Sri Lanka*. Princeton: Princeton University Press, 1988.

Goonasekera, Sunil. *George Keyt: Interpretations*. Kandy: Institute of Fundamental Studies, 1991.

Gooneratne, Yasmin, ed. *Celebrating Sri Lankan Women's English Writing*. Vol. 2. Colombo: Women's Education and Research Centre, 2002.

Goonesekere, Savitri, and Camena Guneratne. *Women, Sexual Violence and the Legal Process in Sri Lanka: A Study of Rape*. Colombo: Center for Women's Research in Sri Lanka, 1998.

Goonetilleke, D. C. R. A., ed. *Modern Sri Lankan Drama*. Delhi: Sri Satguru Publications, 1991.

———, ed. *Sri Lankan Literature in English, 1948–1998*. Colombo: Department of Cultural Affairs, 1998.

Gunawardana, R. A. L. H. *Robe and Plough*. Tucson: University of Arizona Press, 1979.

Hallisey, Charles. "Works and Persons in Sinhala Literary Culture." In *Literary Cultures in History*, edited by Sheldon Pollock, 689–746. Berkeley: University of California Press, 2003.

Halpe, Ashley, M. A. Nuhman, and Ranjini Obeyeskere, eds. *A Lankan Mosaic: Translations of Sinhala and Tamil Short Stories*. Colombo: Three Wheeler Press, 2002.

Holt, John Clifford. *Buddha in the Crown: Avalokitesvara in the Buddhist Traditions of Sri Lanka*. New York: Oxford University Press, 1991.

———. *The Buddhist Visnu: Religious Transformation, Politics and Culture*. New York: Columbia University Press, 2004.

———. *The Religious World of Kirti Sri: Buddhism, Art and Politics in Late Medieval Sri Lanka*. New York: Oxford University Press, 1996.

Ilangasinha, H. B. M. *Buddhism in Medieval Sri Lanka*. Delhi: Indian Book Centre, 1992.

Jayaweera, Sawarna, ed. *Women in Post-Independence Sri Lanka*. Colombo: Vijitha Yapa Publications, 2002.

Kapferer, Bruce. *A Celebration of Demons*. 2nd ed. Oxford: Berg Publishers, 1983.

McGilvray, Dennis. *Crucible of Conflict: Tamil and Muslim Society on the East Coast of Sri Lanka*. Durham: Duke University Press, 2008.

Mirando, A. H. *Buddhism in Sri Lanka in the 17th and 18th Centuries*. Dehiwala: Tisara Prakasakayo, 1985.

Obeyesekere, Gananath. *The Cult of the Goddess Pattini*. Chicago: University of Chicago Press, 1983.

Obeyesekere, Ranjini. *Jewels of the Doctrine: Stories of the Saddharma Ratnavaliya*. Albany: State University of New York Press, 1991.

———. *Sri Lankan Theater in a Time of Terror: Political Satire in a Permitted Space*. Walnut Creek, Calif.: Altamira Press, 1999.

Parker, Henry. *Village Folk-Tales of Ceylon*. 3 vols. 1910; New Delhi: Asian Educational Services, 1997.

Percival, P. *Tamil Proverbs*. 1874; New Delhi: Asian Educational Services, 1996.

Prothero, Stephen. *The White Buddhist: The Asian Odyssey of Henry Steele Olcott*. Bloomington: Indiana University Press, 1996.

Rahula, Walpola. *History of Buddhism in Ceylon: The Anuradhapura Period*. Colombo: M. D. Gunasena, 1956.

Reynolds, Christopher, ed. *An Anthology of Sinhalese Literature of the Twentieth Century*. Battaramulla: Sri Lanka National Commission for UNESCO, 1994.

Seligman, G. C., and Brenda Seligman. *The Veddas*. Cambridge: Cambridge University Press, 1911.

Seneviratne, H. L. *Rituals of the Kandyan State*. Cambridge: Cambridge University Press, 1978.

Smith, Bardwell, ed. *The Two Wheels of Dhamma*. Chambersburg, Pa.: American Academy of Religion, 1972.

Southwold, Martin. *Buddhism in Life: The Anthropological Study of Religion and the Practice of Sinhalese Buddhism*. Manchester: University of Manchester Press, 1983.

Trainor, Kevin. *Relics, Ritual and Representation: Rematerializing the Sri Lanka Theravada Tradition*. Cambridge: Cambridge University Press, 1997.

Trawick, Margaret. *Enemy Lines: Warfare, Childhood and Play in Batticaloa*. Berkeley: University of California Press, 2007.

Von Schroeder, Ulrich. *Buddhist Sculptures of Sri Lanka*. Hong Kong: Visual Dharma Publications, 1990.

Wickramasinghe, Martin. *Landmarks of Sinhalese Literature*. 2nd ed. Colombo: M. D. Gunasena, 1963.

Wickremeratne, Ananda. *Buddhism and Ethnicity in Sri Lanka*. Delhi: Vikas Publishing House, 1995.

Woolf, Leonard. *Diaries in Ceylon, 1908–1911*. 2nd ed. Dehiwala: Tisara Prakasakayo, 1983.

Yalman, Nur. *Under the Bo Tree*. Berkeley: University of California Press, 1971.

Index

John Clifford Holt is William R. Kenan, Jr., Professor of Humanities in Religion and Asian Studies at Bowdoin College in Brunswick, Maine. He has written many books, including *Spirits of the Place: Buddhism and Lao Religious Culture* (2009), *The Buddhist Visnu: Religious Transformation, Politics and Culture* (2004), *The Religious World of Kirti Sri: Buddhism, Art and Politics in Late Medieval Sri Lanka* (1996), *Discipline: the Canonical Buddhism of the Vinayapitaka* (1981), and *Buddha in the Crown: Avalokitesvara in the Buddhist Traditions of Sri Lanka* (1991), for which he received an American Academy of Religion Book Award for Excellence. He has also been awarded an honorary Doctor of Letters from the University of Peradeniya in Sri Lanka and was selected by the University of Chicago Divinity School as its Alumnus of the Year in 2007.

Library of Congress Cataloging-in-Publication Data
The Sri Lanka reader : history, culture, politics / John Clifford Holt, ed.
p. cm.—(The world readers)
Includes bibliographical references and index.
ISBN 978-0-8223-4967-9 (cloth : alk. paper)—ISBN 978-0-8223-4982-2 (pbk. : alk. paper)
1. Sri Lanka—History. 2. Sri Lanka—Civilization.
3. Sri Lanka—Politics and government.
I. Holt, John, 1948– II. Series: World readers.
DS489.5.S728 2011
954.93—dc22
2010054505